AMERICAN DELINQUENCY
Its meaning and construction

The Dorsey Series in Sociology

Advisory Editor
Robin M. Williams, Jr.
Cornell University

Consulting Editor
Charles M. Bonjean
The University of Texas at Austin

AMERICAN DELINQUENCY

Its meaning and construction

LAMAR T. EMPEY
Department of Sociology
University of Southern California, Los Angeles

1982 Revised edition

 **THE DORSEY PRESS** Homewood, Illinois 60430

Cover photos: Richard Younker (boys); Ellis Herwig/Stock, Boston, Inc. (skyline)

© THE DORSEY PRESS, 1978 and 1982

ISBN 0-256-02677-7
Library of Congress Catalog Card No. 81–82916

Printed in the United States of America

1 2 3 4 5 6 7 8 9 0 H 9 8 7 6 5 4 3 2

PREFACE

This book was designed to tell a story, to describe the changing construction of American delinquency. Since its original publication, experience had indicated the need for modifications in the story that not only improve the form in which it is told, but which take better account of the unprecedented events of recent years. Hence, *American Delinquency* has been revised as follows:

Part I—*The Creation of Childhood and Delinquency*—has been shortened to provide a more concise introduction to the historical interdependence of our concepts of childhood, delinquency, and juvenile justice.

Part II attempts to improve our understanding of *The Extent and Nature of Delinquent Behavior* (1) by using census data to standardize official measures of illegal conduct, (2) by including the latest surveys of self-report and victim accounts of the same behavior, and (3) by using all three measures to seek out areas of agreement and disagreement in order to assess the trends and implications of the past 20 years.

Part III has been reorganized and now includes only *Positive Explanations for Delinquent Conduct*. In the first edition, by contrast, all types of theory—labeling and radical as well as positive—were included in this section. But for several reasons, this organization proved unwise.

Not only were students confronted with the task of learning and reconciling a host of disparate points of view, but they found it difficult to relate those points of view to the changing events of history. Because the earlier theories of the positive school were lumped together with those of the labeling and radical schools, students failed to realize that, while positive theories were instrumental in justifying and rationalizing our traditional concept of juvenile justice, the latter were instrumental in discrediting it. Consequently, four steps have been taken to rectify these problems: (1) the introduction to this section makes explicit the interdependence of positive criminology and the traditional juvenile court; (2) the section omits any discussion of labeling and radical theories and, along with neoclassical theory, presents them later in the book; (3) the section incorporates more recent research on female delinquency; and (4) it includes a new chapter which summarizes the principal findings of positive research and their implications for the prevention and control of delinquency.

Part IV presents and evaluates our *Traditional Concept of Juvenile Justice* and the way that concept affected the actions of the police, the juvenile court, and corrections until late in the 1960s. It shows how, in response to the implications of positive theories and the modern concept of childhood, the various elements of the system were supposed to operate, how they actually operated, and how, as a result of mounting criticism, faith in their efficacy and usefulness began to decline.

Part V now provides a more coherent and historically accurate description of the *Current Revolution in Juvenile Justice.* Conceptually, this account can be divided into three parts:

The first part is devoted to the intellectual foundations of the revolution. It describes the emergence of labeling, radical, and neoclassical theories and indicates how, in response to widespread despair and cynicism, they helped to provide the justification for a new concept of juvenile justice.

The second part, a chapter called the "Schizoid Revolution," indicates how labeling and neoclassical theories have been incorporated into two new models for juvenile justice—a family court model and a just deserts model. And while the family court model is the more traditional of the two, the limitations associated with such "reforms" as decriminalization, diversion, and deinstitutionalization suggest that the just deserts model is likely to be the one that dominates the conduct of juvenile justice in the future. Far more than in the past, the avowed goals of juvenile justice will be punishment and deterrence rather than rehabilitation.

Finally, the concluding chapter recapitulates that which has been learned throughout the book: the incipient development of a new concept of childhood amid unparalleled cultural and demographic changes, how little the nature and social location of serious delinquent behavior has changed over the years, the remarkable transformations that have occurred in the interests and policy recommendations of criminologists, and the implications of a more classical model of justice for juveniles. Without doubt, we have been witness to a stunning shift in our attitudes toward the young.

LaMar T. Empey

CONTENTS

AMERICAN DELINQUENCY
Its meaning and construction

Delinquency consists of many things: young people, illegal behavior, police action, courts, and places of confinement.

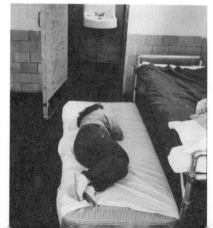

HOW DELINQUENCY IS CONSTRUCTED

This book is about smoking pot, stealing cars, skipping school, joining in a gang fight, mugging an old lady, making out, writing laws, getting busted, going to court, being put on probation, and getting locked up—all the many and different things we call "delinquency."

Today, people are preoccupied with delinquency: Why do so many young people misbehave? What can honest people do to protect themselves from young hoods? Why do kids insist on violating rules? Why don't they do the things that parents, teachers, ministers, legislators, police, and judges consider best for them?

These are important questions. They will occupy much of our attention in this book. But they are not only questions we need to ask. Indeed, if we limit ourselves to questions like these, we will be using tunnel vision. Few people even know, for example, that *delinquency* as we use it, is a new word. It was not employed much until the 19th century, and the juvenile court was not created until the turn of the 20th century. As an important element in the history of civilization, therefore, "juvenile delinquency" is a new phenomenon.

Does this mean, then, that youths did not drink, steal, and fight before the 19th or 20th centuries or that they have only just begun to break the law? Of course not. Young people have always engaged in acts of this type. Behavior that we now define as delinquent has been common among young people throughout history, but it has not always been illegal nor has it always been called delinquency.

As late as the 17th and 18th centuries, European children continued the medieval practice of wearing and using arms (Ariès, 1962:315–321). Boys as young as five years old wore swords and not just as ornaments. The schools of the 17th-century France were marked by so many duels, mutinies, brawls, and beatings of teachers that regulations were eventually written forbidding pupils to keep firearms, swords, or clubs in their rooms or to bring them to class. But, even then, these weapons were not taken from their youthful owners, just stored in a central place for use outside the school.

The use of arms has obviously declined over

time but at different rates in different settings. While student violence and rebellion decreased in France during the 18th century, they increased in England. English schools were often taken over by students, and in some cases, their rebellions had to be put down by troops armed with bayonets.

Medieval license with regard to wine and sex also carried over into later centuries. Public schoolboys, said Montaigne, "practiced more vices by the age of 16 than anyone else would have by 60" (Ariès, 1962:321–324). A hundred of them had caught the pox before they read their first lesson in Aristotle, and they read Aristotle young! "If I were a woman," wrote one author, "I would rather go with a student than with the most splendid courtiers in France. A student. Ah! He's the pearl of mankind" (Ariès, 1962:321–322.)

Similarly, the young were heavy drinkers. Schoolmen tried to control traditional drinking practices, first by setting up regulations designed to reduce them and then by forbidding them entirely. Students, as a result, simply retired to nearby taverns where drinking was not forbidden. French students apparently became somewhat more sober by the 18th century, but English students bravely carried on into the early 19th century.

Modern concern over drugs was also unknown until recently, even though the use of opium began 4,000 years before the birth of Christ (Ray, 1972:181–191). Although people did not fully understand its chemical properties, they certainly grasped its effects. As a consequence, they used it for recreational as well as medicinal purposes.

In 1805, a London youth bought some laudanum (an opium derivative) for a toothache, reported in ecstasy that he had discovered the secret to happiness, and continued to use and write about it throughout his life (Quincey, 1907:179). Opium was introduced into the United States in the second half of the 19th century. By the end of the

century, more Americans were probably addicted to it than there have been before or since. Until 1914, it could be purchased legally at the neighborhood drugstore, and it was viewed with little concern. But in contrast to the present, the addict was typically a middle-aged white female, not a young person. (Ray, 1972:189).

It was not until the 19th century that much of the behavior that had been entirely acceptable in the Middle Ages and only partially lamented in the 17th and 18th centuries became cause for great alarm. Writing on the evils of sex, an anonymous London author decried the extent to which novels pictured "the dissipated rake, who glories in his debaucheries . . . as humane, generous and benevolent; whilst the heedless female . . . forgets his want of principle, his diseased body, and his rotten heart" (Sanders, 1970:93). And, during an age of unparalleled optimism, 19th-century Americans exhibited fright and pessimism over the behavior of youths. No decent man could safely walk the streets of San Francisco (Bell, 1962:172); the term *hoodlum* was coined to describe the members of teenage gangs (Bruce, 1959:13); young girls, many of them under 12, were described as "brutalized . . . by premature vice, . . . with harsh laughter and foulness on their lips, . . . with thief written in their cunning eyes and whore on their depraved faces . . ." (Nevins and Thomas, 1952, Vol. 2:56); and it was said that the police could enter the central New York area near Broadway only if they went armed and in pairs (Bell, 1962:171). One author declared that "crime, especially its more violent forms, and among the young, is increasing steadily and is threatening to bankrupt the nation" (Wasserman, 1965:24).

How should all these past events and descriptions be interpreted? If delinquency in our terms, is a recent invention, what should we make of our current preoccupation with it? Two interpretations are possible. Either the behavior of young people has somehow grown worse over the centuries, or significant changes have occurred in the way we now define and react to it. History indicates that the latter interpretation is probably the more accurate. Delinquency is a social creation of relatively recent times. It is a concept designed to focus our attention upon forms of youthful behavior which, though they have been common throughout history, have become of increasing concern in recent centuries.

The significance of this conclusion is great. People born into a particular society at a particular time tend to take that society for granted, as though its beliefs were timeless and its ways universal. Modern Americans, for example, are inclined to believe that children have always been seen and treated as they are now. Most believe that children are born fragile and innocent. To insure their proper development, therefore, they must be stringently safeguarded by their parents, they must receive a long and carefully directed education, and only after many years of moral and physical quarantine can they be allowed to join the adults. It is only when this quarantine breaks down that juvenile delinquents are spawned: when parents, schools, and communities fail to do their jobs and when they permit poverty, ignorance, and vice to intrude upon their sacred duty to raise children properly. Thus, it would surprise those who unquestioningly accept such beliefs to find that they have not always prevailed, that children have not always been perceived as delicate and innocent, nor has their departure from innocence always been defined as legally delinquent.

The point is that while strongly held beliefs and customs are common to all societies, the forms they take may differ greatly. Hence, something like delinquency that is seen as a problem in one society, or at one point in time in several societies, may not be defined as such at other times or in other societies. One cannot understand delinquency, therefore, merely by looking at the illegal behavior of children or by an unthinking concern with the immediate present—whether working mothers ought to stay home with their kids, whether marijuana ought to be legalized, whether more police and judges are needed, or whether everything would be all right if there were more child guidance clinics. A broader perspective is needed, one that not only looks at the currently undesirable behavior of children, but that questions why that behavior is now of overriding concern. Without revealing the whole story, therefore, the remaining sections of this introductory chapter provide a sneak preview of what we will be studying in this book. They will help to spell out the meaning of delinquency in its broader terms.

CREATION OF CHILDHOOD AND DELINQUENCY

The modern juvenile court exists as a result of widespread beliefs that children are different from adults and therefore require special legal protections and special kinds of care. In the United States and in many countries throughout the world, the legal codes now specify that a child can be brought under the jurisdiction of court authorities for one of three major kinds of problems: (1) cases in which the child has been neglected, exploited, or cruelly treated by adults; (2) the type of criminal offenses for which adults can be punished, such as robbery, assault, or car theft; or (3) juvenile "status" offenses that apply only to children because of their age—drinking, truancy, or running away. For any one of these problems, children can be legally processed but are not treated the same as adults.

If they have been neglected or exploited, steps may be taken to insure that children have adequate food, clothing, and shelter; they may actually be removed from their own homes and placed in the care of others; or their parents may be required, under the threat of legal punishment, to change the way they treat their children.

If children are charged with criminal offenses, there are special procedures through which police, court, and correctional agencies must go in dealing with them. The laws stipulate that officials should treat children less formally than adults and should help to solve their problems rather than just punish them.

Finally, children's status offenses not only incorporate special treatment of alleged offenders but are unique in themselves. They include such things as "incorrigibility," "truancy," "waywardness," "idling," "being in danger of lewd and immoral conduct," or "being beyond reasonable control." Adults cannot be charged with such offenses, but children can. In many states, in fact, status offenses are so broadly defined and so subjective in character that almost any child could be referred to court if some parent or official believed court action was warranted. Why is this? Why are children singled out and treated differently from adults?

The answer is that childhood, like adulthood or old age, is a social status—a position in the social structure and a phase in the life cycle to which a special set of beliefs and expectations are attached. Most modern cultures imply that children are different from adults: more innocent, less guilty of criminal intent, and more in need of both protection and discipline than grown-ups. The term *status offense*, in fact, implies the acceptance of these many beliefs, indicating that children are to be treated in a special way because of their age. This means, therefore, that if we are to understand the social nature of delinquency, why special laws are written for children, and why the juvenile court was invented, we must first explore the meaning of childhood. We cannot understand why children are singled out for special treatment until we determine how and why their special status developed.

What is a child?

There has been enormous variation, historically and culturally, in the meaning of the term *child*. Some of this variation is apparent today. *Webster's Dictionary*, for example, defines a child as "a young person of either sex between infancy and youth." In advancing this definition, it implies that there are at least three periods in the life of a young person: (1) *infancy*—the first few years of life; (2) *childhood*—the period between infancy and youth (or adolescence); and (3) *youth*—the period between the onset of puberty and full adulthood. Yet, *Webster's Dictionary* also agrees with the law in most states by noting that a child is "a person not yet of age," that is, a person who has not reached the legal age of adulthood. In practical terms, this means that most young people under age 18 must be treated as delinquent rather than criminal for committing a crime, and that they cannot assume full responsibility as an adult until age 18 in some states or age 21 in other states.

Childhood, in short, is not a sharply defined status in our society. In one sense, it is defined as ending at puberty while in another it continues on until adulthood. Though such a definition is terribly ambiguous, we can make some sense out of it by considering the assumptions that are made about the development of children (Skolnick, 1973:316–321):

1. Children go through several stages of development which are qualitatively different from one another. These stages coincide generally with those described in *Webster's Dictionary* and postpone entrance into full adulthood until the 20s or even later (Coleman et al., 1974). The developmental process takes that long to complete.

2. Throughout the various stages of development, children are qualitatively different from adults: "Adults work and are responsible, children play and are

irresponsible; adults are controlled and rational, children are emotional and irrational; adults think abstractly, children think concretely; adults are sexual, children are asexual; and so on" (Skolnick, 1973:316).

3. Until their full emotional, moral, physical, and rational skills have been cultivated, the appropriate place for children is at home, in school with their peers, and in constructive places of recreation. Until they mature fully and until they are well educated, they should be quarantined from adult vices, activities, and responsibilities. Though this quarantine may be reduced gradually as children proceed through the developmental process, it should not be lifted entirely until adulthood has been achieved.

In a very real sense, then, we view young people from birth to adulthood as children in different stages of development. Though we certainly do not react to a six-foot, 200-pound adolescent in the same way we do to an 85-pound 10-year-old, we do not view either of them as fully responsible either. Instead, we see them at different places in the process of growing up. That is why our society is ambivalent about granting full rights to young people even of college age. Although we have recently lowered the age at which people can vote to 18, we are reluctant to grant them full recognition as adults until they have completed school and have found regular employment. And, even then, there is a tendency for parents, employers, coaches of professional sports teams, or politicians to call them *kids*—young people who are not quite mature or experienced enough to merit full acceptance as adults.

How old is this concept of childhood?

Recent historical works tend to suggest that our current concept of childhood is a product largely of the past few centuries. Prior to that time, much less attention was paid to the development of children. Perhaps because death rates were so distressingly high, infants were seen less as human beings than as strange formless little creatures somehow different from people who had survived for a few years and with whom strong emotional ties were to be avoided. Yet, even when they did survive, people we would call children today were regarded more as small or inadequate versions of their parents than as sacred beings in need of special protection. Consequently, many unwanted children, particularly girls, were put to death at birth, were deliberately abandoned, were sold into prostitution, or, at best, were left to be raised by others. Most parents, in short, simply were not greatly involved with their children except insofar as they could help to preserve the family line or could serve some economic purpose.

For those parents who could afford it, the preferred method for taking care of newborn babies was to send them out to be wet-nursed and raised by indifferent women who rented out their milk and services, often with deadly consequences for their own babies. If the wet-nursed baby survived the first few years of life, it was soon apprenticed to another family to be of service and to learn the skills of a trade appropriate to its station in life, whether noble or commoner. Children were not spared, as they are now, from full participation in hard work, lewd jokes, sexual acts, or adult greed and manipulation. At a very early age, all these became a routine part of their lives.

This is not to suggest that young people occupied a status equal to that of adults. They did not. As apprentices they were subject to the whims and demands of their masters and were expected to make a contribution. Further, it was through their apprenticeships and services to others that they gained their educations, not in a classroom organized according to some graded scheme of child development. The modern notion that growing up requires careful guidance through a series of physical, moral, and intellectual stages, in fact, has been totally alien to most people throughout Western history. It did not even occur to them.

It was not until Europe began to awaken from the intellectual hibernation and social stagnation of the Middle Ages that a handful of moral philosophers began to question the customary treatment of children. Over a period of the next two or three centuries, age-old tendencies either to ignore or to exploit them were replaced with an ardent concern for their moral welfare: parental care for children became a sacred duty; the school gradually replaced the apprenticeship system as the second most important child-raising institution; and childhood became a transitional period in which protection from, rather than indulgence in, adult activities became the rule.

Out of this process grew the modern concept of childhood—a concept stressing the idea that children have value in their own right and that because of their sweetness and simplicity they require a careful preparation for the harshness and sinfulness of an adult world. Furthermore, it was only after childhood became a special status in the life cycle that the concept of a special court for juveniles began to develop. Along with the changing image of childhood, there was an increasing tendency to be less harsh with children charged with crimes. Though they were subject to the same laws and courts as adults, officials were more and more inclined to refrain from holding them fully responsible for their acts and to pardon those who were actually found guilty of crimes. But, as mentioned, it was not until the very last year of 19th century that the first juvenile court was created and not until the first quarter of the 20th century—just yesterday—that every state had created one. The view of delinquency as something uniquely applicable to children had been gaining increased acceptance for many years, but it was not until society had prepared special machinery for dealing with it that its full impact as a unique social creation was actually felt.

Our first task in assessing the meaning of delinquency will be to review this fascinating history in greater detail. By so doing, we will seek to determine what factors led to the discovery of the modern concept of childhood, why juvenile delinquency was invented, and what social reformers sought to accomplish by creating it. Such a background is vitally important because the safeguarding of children is now assumed to be an absolute necessity and the special laws that were written to protect them were originally hailed as a Magna Charta for the young. But are these social creations living up to the great goals expected of them?

Many modern critics are not so sure. Though they may not want to return to the child-raising practices of the Middle Ages, they do not like our current treatment of children either. They suggest instituting new reforms.

RULES THAT DEFINE DELINQUENCY

Part of the process of discovering childhood and inventing delinquency involved the gradual evolution of an elaborate set of social rules or norms designed to govern the lives of children. First came a set of informal rules or customs which, before they were ever written into law, helped to create an ideal image of childhood toward which parents were expected to strive in raising their children. Though that image is now changing, the social rules that helped to give it its character are still thoroughly familiar to all of us: children should be obedient, hardworking, and diligent in their educational and other pursuits, submissive to the authorities who guide them in these pursuits, self-controlled, modest, and far from the evils of drinking, sex, and other adult vices. That they should avoid the dishonest acts and predatory crimes in which adults engage goes without saying.

Several characteristics of rules like these are central to the meaning of delinquency. The first is the fact that they define and set apart undesirable as well as desirable behavior. Not only do they indicate how the ideal child should behave, but they become the standard for indicating when he or she is out of line. Thus, where there are rules, there is not only conformity but rule breaking. For the young, rule breaking may be relatively innocuous, like talking back to one's parents or failing to do the dishes, or it may be serious, like getting kicked out of school or using heroin. Since rules are the standards by which behavior is judged as good or bad, attention must be paid to the nature and character of those rules. To be concerned solely with delinquent behavior, without looking at the rules that define it, is like trying to eat soup with a fork. It is not very productive.

Second, history reveals that as reformers sought to moralize the young, to protect them from exploitation, and to safeguard their premature induction into the corruption of an adult world, they looked at the age-old actions in which the young had customarily engaged and discovered immorality. In seeking to foster greater conformity to the ideal image of childhood, they discovered rampant immorality. In seeking to make children more virtuous, they defined more of their acts as deviant. And, in encouraging greater discipline and control, they narrowed the range of acceptable childhood conduct.

It was out of the long and evolutionary process of developing new rules to govern childhood that the invention of delinquency grew. There came a time when the informal controls of home, school, and neighborhood no longer seemed adequate for insuring conformity to the rules thought desirable for children. Thus, formal legal rules were written, and a juvenile justice system was created to enforce them. From vague and informal changes beginning in the 16th century, formal legal structures grew in the 19th and 20th centuries.

Third, history suggests that the ideal image of childhood from which these legal structures developed was a white middle-class image. While that image seemed to the emerging middle class to be particularly well suited to its interests and aspirations, it overlooked the fact that in Western societies in general and in American society in particular, all people are not cast in the same mold. American society, for example, is a pluralistic society in which a variety of different ethnic and class groups abound. All young people are not equally socialized or taught to conform to the social and legal standard by which delinquent as well as conformist behavior is now judged. Opportunities to conform and thereby to escape censure are not equitably distributed.

It is for all these reasons and many more that a review of the rules by which delinquent behavior is judged will constitute the second main segment of our analysis. On the one hand, organized human society implies the existence of social rules. Without them people cannot do business with one another. On the other hand, existing rules are not necessarily sacred and need not prevent us from asking some important questions: To what extent is there agreement upon or conflict over existing rules? Under what circumstances may rules, perhaps more than rule breakers, be at fault? To what degree do existing rules fail to realize the purpose for which they were created.

Rare is the circumstance where the worth of all existing rules is universally hailed and where everyone willingly adheres to them. Is this due to an innate human perversity, or does it signal the need for even greater attention to the rules by which conduct is governed and the worth of people called into question? Conversely, rule violation may become so extensive that human predators are spawned whose acts threaten both the physical and psychological well-being of the many. What should be done about this?

There was a time in more stable societies when rules seemed to take on an immutable quality since they were the product of a relatively unchanging world. That day has passed. Today change is rapid and ubiquitous. It is for this and many other reasons that we will be exploring the rules that determine what delinquent behavior is, to what degree they are violated, and how and upon whom they are enforced.

BEHAVIOR THAT VIOLATES RULES

San Francisco is often hailed as one of America's most elegant and civilized cities. But, on a sunny fall afternoon recently, six muggings occurred in stunning succession—all within 30 minutes: (*Los Angeles Times,* December 1, 1974).

> In that period, six passengers aboard separate Municipal Railway buses—including a 95-year-old woman—were assailed by groups of youths who clawed for their victims' wallets, tried to pull rings from their fingers, and, in one instance, cut a man's arm in an attempt to slash open his pants pocket.
> Authorities estimate that up to 85 percent of the violence and vandalism aboard city buses and streetcars is committed by juveniles.

Two months later, young vandals caused about $45,000 damage to a shiny, new, and unusually equipped high school in Los Angeles. A fire was set in the security office, school records were destroyed, closed-circuit television sets, expensive tape decks, and amplifiers were destroyed, walls were defaced, cafeteria tables were overturned, and food supplies were thrown about (*Los Angeles Times*, January 27, 1975).

Violence and destruction by the young are not confined to California cities. Asphalt-bound citizens of New York are warned not to enjoy the precious pastoral qualities of Central Park;

congressmen and senators as well as ordinary mortals are attacked and robbed in the nation's capital; and students are cautioned not to walk alone at night on or near the campus of the University of Chicago. If the rumors about delinquency and crime and media accounts of them are to be believed, the nation is under seige from an army of juvenile and adult felons gone berserk. But are popular accounts and rumors to be believed?

If our attempt to discover the meaning of delinquency is to be successful, we must go beyond rumor and sensational accounts. Lurid accounts not only fail to paint an accurate picture of actual crimes committed by children, but fail as well to acquaint us with the other kinds of behavior called delinquent—the status offenses with which adults cannot be charged, or the instances in which children are abused and neglected. In pursuit of a more accurate picture, therefore, we will be looking at delinquent behavior from three perspectives.

The first will utilize reports from official sources, primarily the police and courts. They provide a systematic method for determining whether official delinquency rates are climbing higher and whether more youth are becoming officially delinquent.

For a view from a second angle, we will turn to the self-reports of children. Instead of relying solely on official accounts, the results of scientific studies will be reported in which young people were asked how many, and in what kinds of, delinquent acts they have engaged. Social scientists began collecting this kind of information for two reasons: because they suspected that most children commit delinquent acts without ever being caught and because official records are often a better indicator of official behavior than of youth behavior—whom officials are lucky enough to catch, upon what segments of the youth population they concentrate their attention, with which kinds of illegal acts they are most concerned, and so on. As might be expected, therefore, official and self-reports differ markedly, sometimes in surprising ways. When young people report what they have done, their accounts do not always conform to many cherished beliefs about who is delinquent and why. Thus, they provide us with a picture of delinquent behavior from a different perspective.

Finally, we will turn to the victims of crime and delinquency for yet a third view. In 1967, the president of the United States appointed a special commission to study crime and delinquency and to make recommendations. As a part of that effort, the commission initiated the first national survey of crime victimization ever conducted (President's Commission on Law Enforcement and Administration of Justice, 1967). The study found that there were far more crime victims than there were crimes being reported by officials or being solved by them. The picture was not a happy one. Since that time, the U.S. Department of Justice, in collaboration with the Census Bureau, has begun to conduct annual surveys of this type. These more recent surveys indicate that the results of the first survey were no fluke. The large gap between official and victim accounts continues to appear. Indeed, when all three views—official, self-report, and victim—are joined together, they provide us with a picture of delinquent behavior that is often in sharp disagreement with the pictures that have been presented heretofore.

EXPLANATIONS FOR DELINQUENT BEHAVIOR

Explanations for delinquent behavior constitute the next major set of factors that must be reviewed in attempting to assess the meanings of delinquency. Some explanations emphasize such things as broken homes, irresponsible parents, and emotional disturbance; others stress poverty and the lack of opportunity; still others focus upon the way

delinquent habits might be acquired through associations with the wrong kinds of friends. In order to understand fully these theoretical explanations, we will look not only at their more obvious aspects—factors such as home conditions, class membership, or delinquent friends—but at the assumptions about human nature and social order upon which they are based.

Theories of delinquency have changed markedly in the past 200 or 300 years, not because they were always given a thorough test, but because of the changes in the way children (and adults) are viewed. As the basic beliefs of influential philosophers, religious leaders, and other reformers have changed, so have their theories. In fact, it is only in recent times that we have stressed the word *theory* and applied the methods of science in attempts to understand delinquency. In earlier times, few attempts were made to empirically test influential ideas. It is important, therefore, to pay attention to the many beliefs that predate science and to determine in what way they now affect our current thinking.

Thomas Hobbes (1957), a 17th-century English philosopher, assumed that the tendency to misbehave is natural in people. Humans are predatory by nature. If there were no enforcement of rules, they would be governed by their passions—the desire for power, self-preservation, and personal gain. If one were seeking to explain delinquent acts, therefore, one would have to look no further than the inborn tendencies of the young. Since they are naturally delinquent, there is nothing to be explained. Rather, the real task is that of finding ways to control their brutish tendencies and to train them to be law-abiding citizens.

By contrast, other philosophers, such as Cesare Beccaria, an Italian, and Jeremy Bentham, an Englishman, emphasized the doctrine of free will and believed that individuals are governed by reason, not passion

(Vold, 1958:14–26). In pursuit of their own interests, people seek to maximize pleasure and to minimize pain. Hence, according to this view, delinquency is inherent in the exercise of a rationally directed free will and the desire to maximize personal satisfaction. If a person believes one can gain more pleasure than pain by committing forbidden acts, one will do so. If not, one will refrain from delinquency. So influential were the beliefs of Beccaria and Bentham that long before they could be tested systematically they found their ways into the laws that govern crime and the methods of punishment. They became the foundation for what is now called the classical school of criminology. Since the causes for rule breaking were assumed to reside in the exercise of free choice, much less attention was paid to why people commit illegal acts than to how punishment could be used to convince them that crime does not pay.

Yet a third set of theories has been produced by the same forces that produced the modern concept of childhood and the idea that children must be carefully nurtured if they are to grow up correctly. These theories reject the notion that people are completely free to choose who they will be and how they will behave. Instead, they suggest that behavior is determined by forces over which the individual has little control. The way people perceive the world, the choices available to them, and ultimately their social conduct are products of the process of socialization—the process by which the individual acquires a sense of self and learns how one is expected to behave from those around him.

Theories of this type range from the common sense idea that children's family, friends, and neighbors will heavily influence their final character to highly sophisticated notions advanced by biologists, psychologists, and sociologists. Ultimately, however, all imply that human behavior is determined, not free. Whether people become thieves, famous athletes, or successful lawyers, their careers will be the result of the way they have been raised and with whom they have associated.

The implications of these kinds of theories are profoundly different from Hobbes' idea that people are inherently inclined to be evil at birth or Beccaria's idea that they are free to choose between good and evil. Such differences might be intellectually interesting but relatively unimportant were it not for the fact that elements of all three kinds of theory lie buried in our juvenile system today. Hence, it is important that we remain aware of this and seek to determine how much they and other traditional beliefs affect our current explanations for delinquent behavior.

Besides looking at the more apparent aspects of our modern theories, we will want to ask what kinds of hidden assumptions lie behind them. What presuppositions about human nature and social order do they make? Are young people thought to be inherently brutish, inherently rational, or are they thought to be dependent beings whose basic natures are simply the products of the kinds of groups in which they live? Depending upon the basic assumptions upon which modern theories rest, they will vary considerably. Furthermore, these assumptions will greatly affect the construction of social rules or the kinds of social controls that are thought necessary to govern behavior. In short, it is imperative that we ask ourselves how much our traditional beliefs about people tend to affect the explanations for delinquent behavior that are currently popular and the ways we react to those we call delinquents.

SOCIETY'S REACTIONS TO DELINQUENT BEHAVIOR

Society is now organized to react to delinquent behavior in certain ways. The way it does react, in fact, both reflects and influences our explanations for delinquency, how serious it is assumed to be, and whether children are treated differently from adults. As we have seen, there was no separate juvenile justice system in this country prior to the 20th century. Those who upheld the criminal law were officially supposed to react to, and to punish, youthful lawbreakers over age seven in the same way that they punished adults. After the discovery of childhood, however, pressures for change eventually culminated in the creation of a new system. That system today is comprised of police, prosecutors, defenders, courts, probation officers, correctional institutions and their personnel, and a host of other public and private agencies all charged with correcting the problems of difficult children. Most of these problems are technically legal, but the law is written in such a way that they might be of almost any conceivable type—emotional, educational, economic, or social. As originally conceived, the juvenile justice system was to become society's superparent.

Whenever there was a breakdown in any other social institution—the home, school, neighborhood, or world of work—the juvenile justice system was supposed to solve it. How did all this come about? The criminal justice system for adults is designed primarily to deal with crime. Why was the juvenile justice system expected to become a superparent?

The answer lies in the evolution of Western culture and its changing treatment of children. Consider an example. There was a time in American history when children helped to colonize this country and to extend the frontier. Later, they worked on farms and in factories, contributing important sources of inexpensive and much needed labor. The results, at least according to present standards, were both good and bad. On the one hand, youth were seen as economic assets, and their separation from the world of adult work was not so great as now. Dignity, as well as toil, was associated with their contribution to home and community.

On the other hand, children did not always realize much direct benefit from their labors. In our terms, they were exploited, largely because vestiges of the medieval apprenticeship system were present in the settling of America and because the economic system relied upon the use of cheap labor. In the early colonies, they were indentured to farmers and artisans and were required, with little choice on their parts, to serve the masters to whom they were apprenticed. Later, they were employed in sweatshops, mines, and factories. They were forced to work up to 12 hours a day for a pittance, sometimes under the most miserable of conditions. The children of the poor, in particular, were little more than slaves. Indeed, there were few legal protections for any children. They were expected to be obedient and to accept the subservient role assigned to them. Furthermore, if they got into trouble or disobeyed, the right to punish them was lodged with the persons who were their masters not in a court of law. Methods of control for children were stern and by no means entirely formal.

Today, by contrast, child labor laws, designed to prevent the exploitation of children, also prevent employment for many of those who would like to work. Several factors have contributed to this state of affairs—the belief that the tender and undeveloped natures of children are harmed by premature toil and responsibility, technological developments which have shrunk the demand for unskilled labor, and a high level of affluence which permits the country to support a large portion of its population, its children, without their having to contribute anything of an economic nature. As a result, participation in economic affairs by the young has dwindled to almost nothing. Apprenticeship, which until the 20th century was the main method by which children learned their future roles and thus gained their educations, is virtually nonexistent. In its stead, the family and particularly the school have assumed greatly increased importance. It is these institutions, rather than apprenticeship, to which society looks to have its newer generations trained.

In part, it is because these institutions often fail that the juvenile justice system was created. While it was clearly expected to get children out of adult jails, courts, and prisons, it was also designed to enforce society's modern view of children. With regard to education, for example, the delinquency laws stipulate that a child can be defined as delinquent for defying school authority, for being truant, or for dropping out—something that would have been unheard of in an earlier day. Likewise, instead of requiring that children obey their apprenticeship masters, laws require that they obey their parents. Any child can be brought to court if he or she is "incorrigible" or "beyond reasonable control." If other institutions fail, the legal superparent will step in.

After attempting to fulfill this kind of a function for three quarters of a century, the juvenile justice system is now undergoing changes—changes that are every bit as revolutionary in character as those which led to its initial creation. Modern-day reformers have grown disillusioned with the notion that it can serve effectively as a superparent and are seeking to reduce its power and influence. Whether these reforms will somehow lead to outcomes that are more desirable than those already being produced is difficult to predict. The desirability and acceptability of social change depends more upon the emergence of new values and beliefs than upon some immutable standard of goodness.

Consequently, the best we can do in preparing ourselves to determine whether we approve of current changes or whether we prefer that the juvenile justice system operate as it has in the past is to examine such issues as the following: how and why society has organized childhood the way it has; what special institutions, particularly legal ones, it has set up to govern children's lives; what kinds

of people, with what kinds of of values, seem to provide leadership in these institutions; what kinds of changes are now being introduced; and how will these changes likely affect the future. These, as well as illegal acts themselves, are factors which help to give delinquency its full meaning.

SUMMARY AND CONCLUSIONS

In summary, this introduction has suggested that delinquency is a social construction comprised not merely of the illegal acts of children but of many other social phenomena as well. Hence, the remainder of this book will be organized to take them into account:

Part I will be concerned with the creation of childhood and delinquency—the discovery of childhood, the invention of delinquency, and how these are defined according to American rules.

Part II will be concerned with the extent and nature of delinquent behavior as indicated by accounts from officials, from young people themselves, and from the victims of delinquent acts.

Part III will be concerned with the evolution of scientific explanations for delinquent behavior, the philosophical assumptions upon which they were based, and their implications for the way delinquents were viewed and treated during much of this century.

Part IV will be concerned with the legal institutions that society has created to enforce its beliefs about children, and how their formation and modes of conduct were governed by a rehabilitative concept of justice.

Part V will be devoted to the revolutionary changes of the past few years—the bodies of theory which defined the juvenile justice system as ineffective and repressive, the growing disillusionment with the concept of rehabilitation, the incipient emergence of a new concept of childhood, and the transformations these have wrought in the administration of juvenile justice and the treatment of children.

REFERENCES

Ariès, Philippe.
    1962   *Centuries of Childhood.* Translated by Robert Baldick. New York: Alfred A. Knopf.
Bell, Daniel
    1962   *The End of Ideology.* 2nd ed. New York: Collier Books.
Bruce, Robert V.
    1959   *1877: Year of Violence.* New York: Bobbs-Merrill.
Coleman, James S., et al.
    1974   *Youth: Transition to Adulthood.* Chicago: University of Chicago Press.
Hobbes, Thomas
    1957   *Leviathan.* London: Oxford University Press.
Nevins, Allan, and Thomas, Milton, H.
    1952   *The Diary of George Templeton Strong.* 4 vols. New York: Macmillan.
President's Commission on Law Enforcement and Administration of Justice
    1967   *Task Force Report: Crime and Its Impact—An Assessment.* Washington, D.C.: U.S. Government Printing Office.
Quincey, Thomas De
    1907   *Confessions of an English Opium Eater.* New York: E. P. Dutton.
Ray, Oakley
    1972   *Drugs, Society and Human Behavior.* St. Louis: C. V. Mosby.
Sanders, Wiley B., ed.
    1970   *Juvenile Offenders for a Thousand Years.* Chapel Hill: University of North Carolina Press.
Skolnick, Arlene
    1973   *The Intimate Environment: Exploring Marriage and the Family.* Boston: Little, Brown
Vold, George B.
    1958   *Theoretical Criminology.* New York: Oxford University Press.
Wasserman, Al
    1965   *NBC White Paper: Terror in the Streets.* Unpublished script for NBC television broadcast, April.

THE CREATION OF CHILDHOOD
AND DELINQUENCY

Introduction: Approaching history objectively

In a number of recent and fascinating historical works, several writers have come to the conclusion that the modern concept of childhood in Western civilization is a product largely of the past few centuries (Ariès, 1962; Bremner, 1970; Mause, 1974; Gillis, 1974; Hunt, 1970; Laslett, 1972; Stone, 1974). These writers are not in total agreement on all the important facts that relate to childhood nor on how those facts should be interpreted (Stone, 1974). These differences exist, surprisingly, because historians have just begun to inquire into the history of childhood. Yet, among the important conclusions upon which they all agree is that childhood has not always been a time in life to which much importance has been attached. Indeed, the opposite has often been true. For instance, Mause (1974:1) says that "the history of childhood [in Western civilization] is a nightmare from which we only recently began to awaken." And, while Stone (1974:29) is somewhat more cautious, he still concludes that the historical treatment of children is a "catalogue of atrocities." How, then, did our modern concern with children come about? Why, today, do we pay so much attention to it?

In order to answer these questions fully, it is necessary that we understand three basic concepts: *culture, childhood,* and *ethnocentrism.*

CULTURE

Anthropologists and sociologists have long been intrigued by the perseverance and continuity of society. If you or I should die tomorrow, society would continue. With scarcely a ripple, most people would rise at their usual times, eat their usual breakfasts, go to the usual places of employment or schooling, and return home at their customary times. Why is this? Why is life in any society broadly predictable?

Social scientists attribute this predictability to *culture:*

> The concept of "culture" is familiar enough to the modern layman. It refers to knowledge, beliefs, values, codes, tasks and prejudices that are traditional in social groups. Our American language, political habits, sex mores, taste for hamburger and cokes, and aversion to horse meat are parts of American culture. We take for granted that the contrasting ways of Hindus, Chinese, and Navahos are for the most part a matter of indoctrination into different culture (Cohen, 1955:12).

An awareness of cultural differences is important to our understanding of childhood because of the unique stamp that American culture with its strong ties to Western civilization has put upon it. We construct and organize childhood in a particular way because of our cultural traditions.

CHILDHOOD

In Chapter 1, it was pointed out that childhood in American and most Western societies has become a special phase in the life cycle, set apart from adulthood or old age. It is treated as a unique period in life because of prevailing beliefs that children are different from adults, more innocent, less capable of evil intent, and, therefore, more in need of protection, careful direction, and training. Only after many years of physical, moral, and intellectual quarantine in home and school should they be required to confront the harsh realities of adulthood.

Childhood, however, is not a product of nature, like a rock or a tree. Instead, childhood is a product of culture. To be sure, young *Homo sapiens,* like the offspring of other animals, are less well developed physically, sexually, and intellectually than are adult members of the species. But the notion that they should sleep in a bassinet rather than in a cradle board, that they should be fondled by loving parents rather than wrapped tightly in swaddling clothes, that they should be sent to school rather than farmed out to others as servants or apprentices, and that they require treatment rather than punishment for their misdeeds is man-made.

Childhood, in short, is a social construction. As such, it can be viewed and analyzed as something apart from the young people who are affected by it. Young persons exist in every society, but the values, beliefs, and social institutions that organize their lives vary greatly. Childhood, as we know it, has not been universal throughout history, nor is it universal among all people today. Instead, it is something that is peculiar to our time and place in history. That is why this and other chapters are concerned with the historical factors that have given rise to our particular construction of it. Because it determines the way we view and organize the lives of young people, it leads us to define certain acts as delinquent, to write laws to control those acts, and to organize a juvenile justice system to administer them. As a set of cultural patterns, therefore, childhood provides the context within which the young in our society can best be understood.

ETHNOCENTRISM

One reason that it is important for us to be aware of our particular construction of childhood is that most people tend to be *ethnocentric,* that is, to use their own way of life—in this case, their construction of childhood—as a standard for judging other peoples and ways of life. Having been raised according to the dictates of their own culture, they tend to assume that those dictates are, or should be, universal. Hence, any departure from them by another group or person is a sign of inferiority. Such beliefs, however, are a serious impediment to a full understanding of the range and potential of human existence.

In the first place, excessive ethnocentrism inhibits a full appreciation and comprehension of one's own culture. To the degree that we assume that our own way of life is eternal and immutable, we blind ourselves to reality. Our culture has been anything but eternal and unchanging. Hence, if we ignore its unique development and character, we will be unable to put it into some larger perspective—a perspective that might permit us to ask important questions, to seek out injustices, or to recognize that alternative ways of life are possible.

Excessive ethnocentrism also inhibits an understanding and appreciation of other peoples and cultures. An inclination to brand others as inferior because their way of life is different overlooks the fact that their behavior cannot be judged meaningfully outside the cultural context of which they are a part. Though we may choose eventually to disagree with them and to prefer our ways of doing things, it is important to recognize that behavior that they regard as truthful, right, and moral is dependent upon the particular values and beliefs of their culture. Just as our construction of reality tells us we are right, so their construction of it tells them that they are right.

The fact that we are ethnocentric will soon become apparent when we delve into the history of childhood. We will encounter beliefs and practices so different from our own that they will shock and displease us. The fact that historians have called that history a "nightmare" and a "catalogue of atrocities" is evidence of their application of our cultural standards to what they found. But while according to these standards, shock and disbelief may be merited, we will miss much that is important if that is all we experience. Childhood has been constructed differently in other times and places, not merely because other people were somehow less sensitive to the young than we are, but because of the unique circumstances to which their societies had to adapt. What we seek from our review, therefore, is some understanding of these circumstances in Western civilization so that we may place our own construction of childhood and delinquency into a larger context. Should we be successful in that endeavor, we may be better prepared to approach our own beliefs, as well as those of others, somewhat more rationally.

In order to determine how our own concept of childhood came about and how delinquency was invented this part of the book will be divided into three major chapters:

In *Chapter 2*, we will examine that period in Western history during which children were treated with indifference and even cruelty.

In *Chapter 3*, we will trace the gradual discovery of childhood and the development of the beliefs that make it what it is today.

Finally in *Chapter 4*, we will assess the transformation that the discovery of childhood brought to modern society, including the invention of delinquency and the creation of a juvenile court.

REFERENCES

Ariès, Phillippe
  1962   *Centuries of Childhood.* Translated by Robert Baldick. New York: Alfred A. Knopf.
Bremner, Robert H., et al., eds.
  1970   *Children and Youth in America: A Documentary History.* 2 vols. Cambridge: Harvard University Press.
Cohen, Albert K.
  1955   *Delinquent Boys: The Culture of the Gang.* New York: Free Press.
Gillis, John R.
  1974   *Youth and History.* New York: Academic Press.
Hunt, David
  1970   *Parents and Children in History: The Psychology of Family Life in Early Modern History.* New York: Basic Books.
Laslett, Peter
  1972   *Household and Family in Past Time.* Cambridge: Cambridge University Press.
Mause, Lloyd de, ed.
  1974   *The History of Childhood.* New York: Psychohistory Press.
Stone, Lawrence
  1974   *"The Massacre of the Innocents." The New York Review,* November, 14:25–31.

For most of recorded history, children have labored. Here they carry clay in an English brickyard.

We are shocked today by occasional reports of child battering and abuse, but if historians are correct, practices we now define as abusive have been a common feature of Western life for much of recorded history. To begin with, infanticide—the deliberate killing of infants—was a regular practice in ancient civilizations and not uncommon as late as the 18th century. Whether in the civilizations of the ancient Middle East, in Greece or Rome, or among the Gauls, the Celts, and Scandinavians in Europe, newborn infants were thrown into rivers, flung into dung heaps, left to be eaten by birds and animals of prey, or sacrificed to the gods in religious rites. The bones of child sacrifices are still being discovered in the walls of buildings constructed from 7000 B.C. to A.D. 1843.

INFANTICIDE

Mause (1974:25) maintains that the killing of legitimate children was only slowly reduced during the Middle Ages—the period roughly from A.D. 500 to A.D. 1400—and that the practice of killing illegitimate ones persisted even into the 19th century. In support of this conclusion, he cites historical references suggesting that infanticide may have been only sporadically punished prior to the 16th century and that during the Middle Ages children were still being deliberately suffocated by their mothers or left in the streets to die. He quotes a priest in 1527 who said that "the latrines resound with the cries of children who have been plunged into them" (Mause, 1974:29). Likewise Marvick (1974:282) notes that the criminal law of 17th-century France enumerated the conditions under which a father had the right to kill an adult son or daughter and indicates that the right to kill an infant may not even have needed official sanction. And, in England during the same period, midwives had to take the following oath (Illick, 1974:306):

> I will not destroy the child born of any woman, nor cut, nor pull off the head thereof, or otherwise dismember or hurt the same, or suffer it to be so hurt or dismembered.

The need to have such an oath for the persons who delivered most of England's babies is some indication that deliberate destruction was still occurring.

The practice of infanticide was apparently rooted in cultural values and beliefs that defined which children should, and should not, survive. In antiquity, any child who was not perfect or seemed to cry too much was generally killed. As the Roman statesman Seneca (1963:145) put it in Christ's time: "Mad dogs we knock on the head, the fierce ox we slay; sickly sheep we put to the knife to keep them from infecting the flock; unnatural progeny we destroy . . . yet, it is not anger, but reason that separates the harmful from the sound."

Throughout history, as we will see again and again, boys were considered to be of much greater value than girls. Mause (1974:26) says that the few statistics available from antiquity "show large surpluses of boys over girls; for instance, in 79 families who gained Milesian citizenship about 228–220 B.C., there were 118 sons and 28 daughters." What he is implying, of course, is that more girls than boys were put to death at birth. The first born of any family was usually permitted to live, particularly if it was a boy. Girls, however, were less desirable, as the following advice to parents indicates: "If, as may well happen, you give birth to a child, if it is a boy let it live; if it is a girl expose it [leave it outside to die]" (Mause, 1974:26).

Much later in 17th-century France, the same themes were perpetuated (Marvick, 1974:283–284). The desire for children even among the upper classes was a desire for boys. Writers of the time noted the "curious" fact that there had been a universal surplus of boys over girls for three centuries, suggesting, of course, that greater efforts were expended on saving boys than girls. One of many contributing factors was the belief that the milk of women who delivered girls was best for boys. Since boys were valued more highly than girls and since many women of the poorer classes hired themselves out as wet nurses, they had an incentive to abandon their own baby girls so they could nurse the boys of wealthier people.

ABANDONMENT

A practice that was closely related to infanticide was abandonment. In some cases, mothers abandoned their children for profit. In antiquity, for example, both boys and girls were sold into slavery or prostitution or used as security to pay debts (Mause, 1974:33). Likewise, as indicated above, country women throughout much of European history could add to their incomes by abandoning their own children and nursing the offspring of wealthier people.

But, lest any Americans feel smug, it should be recalled that early colonists in this country also traded in children. The first settlements were desperate in their need for laborers. Consequently, large numbers of homeless children were rounded up in the streets of London and other cities and indentured to these settlements as workers. Furthermore, the purchase of black children to act as slaves was common in America until the end of the 19th century. It was not black parents, however, who favored this practice but their white captors of European descent.

In other instances, babies were abandoned because parents could not afford to care for them or simply because all of a couple's children were not equally prized. Infanticide and abandonment, rather than contraception or abortion, were methods of controlling family size. Two sons might be raised, possibly three, but seldom more than one girl (Mause, 1974:26). Similarly, orphaned children might experience a sad fate. Rather than raising the orphaned children of a brother or a sister, relatives often abandoned them and sometimes had them killed (Marvick, 1974:284).

In European towns of the Middle Ages and as late as the 17th and 18th centuries, children could be found abandoned and rotting on city streets, on doorsteps, or on garbage dumps. Destitute mothers or the mothers of illegitimate children sometimes brought their children to a hospital or foundling home, if one was available, but such children were usually filthy and starving and almost inevitably died (Marvick, 1974:286).

In trying to place these practices in some kind of time frame, Mause (1974:51) says that the practice of outright infanticide was most common prior to the 4th century and that abandonment was more the mode from the 4th to the 13th centuries. During these time periods, relatively few questions were raised about these ways of dealing with the young. The deliberate killing of infants appears to have been regarded as casually as abortion is today.

Furthermore, history indicates that infanticide and abandonment were not confined entirely to the periods mentioned above. Longstanding cultural practices do not disappear overnight; rather, they gradually merge into new ones. Thus, infanticide and abandonment continued on into later centuries in guises that appear to have been gradually more acceptable according to our standards.

THE CARE OF INFANTS

Abandonment did not always take the form of leaving a child to die or selling it into slavery, nor were such practices confined to the poor and uneducated. The reverse was often true. Among the wealthier classes, there were institutionalized and widely accepted patterns for rearing children which, according to modern standards, constituted a form of abandonment. To the people who practiced them, however, these patterns defined the most desirable ways for rearing children.

Wet-nursing

The first had to do with the care of small infants. Up to about the 18th century, most children of well-to-do or even average parents spent their earliest years in the care of a wet nurse. Rather than feeding and caring for their own children, mothers who could afford to do so hired other women to perform these tasks (Mause, 1974:32–34; Illick, 1974:308; Robertson, 1974:410–411; Ross, 1974:195). Soon after birth, a baby was taken from its own home and placed in the home of a wet nurse until it was weaned. And, since human milk was believed to be the most appropriate food for infants, weaning often took a long time—anywhere from a few months to three years. Although the use of wet nurses was confined to families who could afford them, it was apparently widespread nonetheless. "As late as 1780 the police chief of Paris estimated that of the 21,000 children born each year in his city, 17,000 were wet-nursed and only 700 were nursed by their mothers" (Mause, 1974:35).

The practice of using wet nurses was apparently denounced by physicians and moralists from the time of the ancient Greeks and Romans onward, but the hold of custom was great. Hence, although some parents may have loved their babies, the evidence suggests that infants sent to wet nurses died at a far higher rate than did the few who remained in their own homes. Wet nurses were often malnourished and disinterested women who had their own children to care for. Further, these women used other commonly accepted child-raising practices that may have contributed to a distressingly high death rate.

Swaddling

One such practice was the practice of swaddling. As described by a 19th-century physician.

[swaddling] consists in entirely depriving the child of the use of its limbs, by endlessly enveloping them in an endless bandage. . . ; and by which the skin is sometimes excoriated; the flesh compressed, almost to gangrene; the circulation arrested; and the child without the slightest power of motion (Mause, 1974:37).

The practice of swaddling was believed to serve many functions. Air, sunlight, and soap were thought to be dangerous for a child (Robertson, 1974:410–412). Hence, by keeping the child wrapped tightly, it could be protected. A relatively late 17th-century account noted that "when the child is seven months old you may (if you please) wash the body of it twice a week with warm water" (Tucker, 1974:242). The account also advised that the bandages should be shifted often so that the "piss" and the "dung" could be taken care of. But in terms of our present concerns with constantly changing and washing a child, it can only be imagined what the results of this advice were in terms of an accumulation of excrement and filth on a baby. It is no wonder that infant death rates were appallingly high.

Swaddling was also thought to be a means of protecting the child from hurting itself and of insuring that it would grow straight. But in addition, it must have been a practice of enormous convenience to wet nurses or mothers who were preoccupied with other tasks. Lacking modern labor-saving devices, they had to devote most of their attention to activities other than cuddling babies or taking them to the zoo. Consequently, while the baby was tied up, it could be left like a parcel in a convenient corner or hanging on the wall. Indeed, both modern research and historical descriptions indicate that "swaddled infants are extremely passive, their hearts slow down, they cry less, they sleep far more, and are withdrawn and inert" (Mause, 1974:37). Clearly, the practice must have survived for centuries (we have all heard about Jesus in swaddling clothes)

both because it was believed helpful to infants and because it was practical for adults.

Toughening infants

From a modern perspective, other child-raising practices also revealed practices that we might define as indifference or cruelty to children. Deformed children and children that cried too much were believed to be possessed of the devil (Mause, 1974:10). The ancient Huns customarily cut the cheeks of newborn males, while adults in Renaissance Italy burned the necks of babies with a hot iron or hot wax in order to prevent "falling sickness' (Mause, 1974:31). Some wet nurses starved infants in order to save money or because they had accepted too many babies for their milk supply (Stone, 1974:29). Adults even amused themselves by playing catch with tightly swaddled infants, sometimes with deadly consequences when the pass catcher did not make a good reception (Mause, 1974:31). Infants were dipped in ice water or rolled in the snow to harden or to baptize them. In other cases they were put to bed wrapped in cold towels. "It is not surprising," concludes Mause (1974:32), "that the great 18th century pediatrician William Buchan said 'almost one half of the human species perish in infancy by improper management or neglect.' "

DISEASE AND DEATH

Indeed, until very recently, life was difficult and brutal. In his novel *Shogun*, James Clavell (1975:697) presents the reflections of an English sea pilot, John Blackthorne, on the premature aging of his wife, Felicity, and on the filth in which they lived in 16th-century England:

> *Felicity.* Dear *Felicity.* A bath once a month perhaps . . . always hidden to the neck and wrists, swathed in layers of heavy woolens all year long that were unwashed for months or

years, reeking like everyone, lice-infested like everyone. . . .

Sleeping most of the time in your dayclothes and scratching like a contented sea dog, always scratching. Old so young and ugly so young and dying so young. *Felicity.* Now twenty-nine, gray, few teeth left, old, lined and dried up.

Captain Blackthorne's lament was accurate. Average life expectancy, as late as the 17th century, was no more than 30 years; from one half to two thirds of all children died before the age of 20 (Bremner, 1970, I:3–4; Gillis, 1974:10–11). Living in filth, lacking a knowledge of such simple (to us) diseases as measles, pneumonia, or the consequences of malnutrition, few children survived, even among the privileged classes.

In America, for example, Cotton Mather went through the trauma of seeing only two of his 15 children survive. In one measles epidemic in 1713, he lost his wife and three children in a two-week period (Bremner, 1970, I:46). Similarly, another American wrote to a friend: "My niece Stukley was lately brought abed of a son, but the joy lasted not longe, for they both vanished soone thereafter" (Bremner, 1970, I:3). "Before they [children] are old enough to bother you," a Frenchman agreed, "you will have lost half of them, or perhaps all of them" (Ariès, 1962:38). As a result, the prevailing situation has been aptly described as a "melancholy procession of cradles and coffins" (Queen and Adams, 1952:211).

In light of this melancholy procession, several historians have suggested that high death rates among the young may have accounted for the indifferences that seemed to characterize existing attitudes toward them:

Under these conditions, no parent could retain his or her sanity if he or she became too emotionally involved with such ephemeral creatures as young children. Aloofness, or the acceptance of God's will, or sending one's children away from home were three natural solutions to this problem of how to deal with their deaths (Stone, 1974:30).

Whatever the explanation, there is evidence that indifference may be the best way to categorize cultural responses to children during most of Western history. Ariès (1962:28–29) notes, for example, that various languages did not even include words to describe childhood and the meaning of age:

In its attempts to talk about little children, the French language of the 17th century was hampered by a lack of words to distinguish them from bigger ones. The same was true of English, where the word "baby" was also applied to big children. . . . People had no idea of what we call adolescence, and the idea was a long time taking shape.

What then, was the nature of family and social life for the children who did survive infancy? What role in the scheme of things did they play?

THE LIVES OF CHILDREN

Today, we live much of our lives in nuclear families in which one set of parents lives with their children, by themselves, in their own dwelling, apart from others. Contact with people from other social classes or even one's blood relatives is often infrequent and sporadic. Parents and children alike live in an environment characterized by ever greater emotional isolation and interdependence.

In the households of earlier times, by contrast, family life was far less intimate and exclusive. While many poor did live in hovels, those who were servants and the well-to-do whom they served lived in large barnlike dwellings where as many as 25 people were housed (Ariès, 1962:393–394; Ross, 1974:195–196; Bremner, 1970, I:5). A child returning from the home of his wet nurse, therefore, might have to compete for the attention of his mother with a great many other people. Mixed together under one roof were his parents, relatives, servants, apprentices, other little children, even slaves, and a host of visitors flowing in and out.

"There were," says Ariès (1962:393–394), "no professional premises either for the judge or the merchant or the banker or the businessmen. Everything was done in the same rooms with his family." No rooms were set aside specifically for dining, or sleeping, or meeting with guests or clients. "In the same rooms where they ate, people slept, danced, worked, and received visitors." Even the beds were collapsible. Though pushed aside during the day, they were pulled out at night for everyone—family and servants alike—to sleep on.

The one major exception to this kind of housing and family existence was a large floating lower-class population whose life, if not less communal, was spent in shacks and on the streets or in the fields. What must not be forgotten, however, is that many lower-class people—adults and children—lived and worked in the large homes of wealthier people as servants and apprentices. Hence, many were not unfamiliar with the communal living and lifestyles of the well-to-do. The point is that whether lower- or upper-class people had little privacy, even in sleeping or making love. There was little segregation of the sexes or of the young and perhaps even less segregation of the classes than today.

In such a setting, the young child might attach himself to an older brother or sister, to an uncle or an aunt, to a female servant, or even to a young slave or apprentice. The social rules of the day apparently did not require that the ties be with his mother. Hence, if he could find someone with whom his physical, social, and psychological needs could be met, all was well. But, if such ties were lacking, then he might suffer. Almost certainly, there were variations in the way children were treated, just as there are today.

Moral rules

Prevailing conditions also meant that the behavioral rules of the time were vastly different from our own. Throughout the 19th and much of the 20th centuries, we have been highly concerned with protecting the moral innocence of children:

> Some months ago I saw two girls, who looked about 12 years old, gaping at and giggling over a magazine in a drugstore. I glanced over their shoulders and saw a color picture of a naked woman holding the penis of a naked man. You may piously defend the First Amendment, but I would rather you defend the right of children not to have their minds infected by such poison (Letter to the Editor, *Los Angeles Times*, February 18, 1977).

Contrast the moral rules implied in this statement with those that prevailed in the 16th and 17th centuries:

> It is easy to imagine the promiscuity which reigned in those rooms where nobody could be alone, which one had to cross to reach any of the communicating rooms, where several couples and several groups of boys or girls slept together (not to speak of the servants, of whom at least some must have slept beside their master, setting up beds which were still collapsible in the room, or just outside the door), in which people foregathered to have their meals, to receive friends or clients, and sometimes to give alms to beggars (Ariès, 1962:394).

This kind of familiarity was not restricted to the poorer classes. It was common among the aristocracy as well. Ariès (1962:100–107) documents its presence with a fascinating series of excerpts taken from the diaries of a man by the name of Heroard, who was the physician of King Henry IV of France. Judged by the rules of modesty that were to develop later, jokes were coarse and gestures obscene. They shocked no one, however, but were taken as perfectly natural.

Consider the treatment of Henry's young son, Louis XIII. According to Heroard's diary, he was apparently seen as a droll little figure by whom adults were amused. "He laughed uproariously when his nanny waggled his cock with her fingers. An amusing trick which the child soon copied. Calling a page, he shouted, 'Hey there!' and pulled up his robe, showing him his cock." Jokes like this were repeated over and over and were made by all members of the extended household, by parents and visitors, by lower-class servants as well as royalty:

> [The Marquise de Verneuil] wanted to play with him [Louis] and took hold of his nipples; he pushed her away, saying: "Let go, let go, go away." He would not allow the Marquise to touch his nipples, because his Nanny [a servant] had told him, "Monsieur, never let anyone touch your nipples, or your cock, or they will cut it off!" (p. 101).

Likewise, by our standards, the queen played immodestly with her son. Grasping his penis at one time, she said, "Son, I am holding your cock" (p. 101). Not to be outdone, the king got into the act. While playing in bed with Louis and his sister, the king asked his son: "Son, where is the Infanta's bundle [Louis' penis]?" Louis showed it to his father saying, "There is no bone in it, Papa." Then, as it did distend slightly, he said, "There is now, there is sometimes" (p. 101).

Later, when Louis was five or six, familiarity with adult women was permitted. The following took place among Louis, his nanny, and Mercier, a female servant, who slept next to Louis. While Mercier was still in bed one morning,

> [Louis] played with her, toyed with her toes and the upper part of her legs. . . . His Nanny asked him: "What have you seen of Mercier?" He replied calmly: "I have seen her arse." "What else have you seen?" He replied calmly and without laughing that he had seen her privates (p. 102).

Louis was married at age 14 and was put into his wife's bed almost by force by his mother, the queen. Young men who were also present told Louis some ribald stories to encourage him. After making love to his wife twice and sleeping a while, he arrived back in the company to report that his cock was all red. Obviously, this kind of behavior and this kind of familiarity between sexes of all ages was due not just to communal living arrangements but to a set of cultural norms that made them socially acceptable.

Ariès (1962:105–106) cites numerous calenders, church pictures, and other forms of art in which children were commonly shown urinating in public places or mothers were shown breast-feeding their children. Neither church nor lay people were offended by such scenes. Likewise, religious iconography commonly depicted the circumcision of young boys "in almost surgical detail." In one church painting, "the scene of the circumcision is surrounded by a crowd of children, some of them with their parents, others climbing the pillars to get a better view" (p. 106). Such scenes may seem shocking to us today, says Ariès, but they were not so to people in 16th or early 17th centuries.

Sex and prostitution

This evidence suggests that children had an intimate knowledge of sex and all other bodily functions. Whatever adults did, children knew about. Indeed, children were sometimes treated as sexual objects, as well as becoming early participants in sex like Louis XIII. It is difficult to say how extensive this treatment was, but there is evidence that beginning in antiquity boy brothels may have been fairly common. Men often kept slave boys for their own pleasure. Even in their own homes, it may not have been uncommon for a father's own children to observe him having intercourse with one of these boys (Mause, 1974). The favorite sexual practice was anal intercourse not fellatio. In Rome, men preferred boys who had been castrated for this purpose. Castration somehow made the sex act more exciting. While still infants, boys destined for a brothel were castrated by placing them in a tub of hot water. When the testicles were softened, they were squeezed until they disappeared (Mause, 1974:46). The other alternative, of course, was simply to cut the testicles out.

Better known, of course, is the fact that girls throughout history have been regularly sold into concubinage and prostitution for the satisfaction of men. Like the boys who were castrated, some of these girls suffered clitoridectomies. Mause (1974:45) describes one recorded instance in which a girl of seven was subjected to intercourse while adult witnesses, both male and female, applauded the procedure. And even under the regulated ritual of marriage, many girls were contracted out as early as age 12 and had often given birth to several children before finishing the age of adolescence.

The literature of the Middle Ages and the Renaissance is full of statements decrying the sexual abuse of children (Mause, 1974:47–49). Servants and nursemaids were often criticized for showing "lewd tricks" to children and for carrying out "all sorts of sexual acts" for their (the women's) pleasure. Some people apparently believed as late as 1900 that venereal disease could be cured by having intercourse with children. Hence, it seems likely that while children may have enjoyed the gratifications of sex at an earlier age, many of them were also exploited.

Children are also exploited today. There are child molesters; incest occurs; young girls become street walkers at an early age; there are even occasional reports of boy brothels. Consequently, it is not as though the exploitation of children is something that occurred only in ages past. Rather, what is being suggested is that it was probably more

the norm the further back in Western history one goes.

We should probably not be too surprised if this were the case. In a population that almost daily witnessed the early death of children, that sometimes observed them lying abandoned and rotting on city streets, that permitted them to be raised by others, that hardly ever washed, and that lived without plumbing amid its own excrement, life was both brutal and cheap. If, as seems likely, children were of relatively less value than now, it follows that their use for the sexual pleasure of adults would also occur. But even if that practice was not universal, it is almost certain that the norms governing child-raising practices were far different from the ones we now observe.

TRAINING OF CHILDREN

The methods used to train children are also at great odds with contemporary practices. The current emphasis upon formal education and the practice of requiring virtually every child to go to school have been confined largely to recent generations. Prior to that time, children received their preparation for adulthood by leaving their own homes usually at age seven to become apprentices, to work, and to serve in the homes of other people. This was their education. In fact, the day of apprenticeship was a major turning point in the life of a child. "Ready for semidependence, they were dressed as miniature adults and permitted to use the manners and language of adult society" (Gillis, 1974:8). Such was true, says Ariès (1962:365), not only of the poor but of the rich, "for everyone, however rich he may be, sends his children into the houses of others, whilst he, in return, receives those of strangers into his own."

In judging this practice according to 20th century standards, says Ariès (1962:366–368), we should not become bogged down in trying to determine whether parents were unfeeling or whether the child was merely a servant or an apprentice. Such distinctions would be anachronistic when evaluated in terms of the norms that prevailed. Children learned how they were expected to behave by serving and working in the homes of others. Consequently, family life was not organized to nourish the profound existential attitude between parents and children which we now emphasize. "This did not mean that parents did not love their children, but they cared about them less for themselves, for the affection they felt for them, than for the contributions those children could make to the common task." Consequently, there was simply no repugnance or degradation associated with the services they performed. Such was a custom common to all classes.

American practices

This medieval orientation to childhood carried over into the settling of America. Although, as we will see in the next chapter, significant changes in the concept of childhood were underway during the colonial settlement, older traditions still carried a great deal of weight. Bremner (1970:I:5) notes, for example, that when the English settled the Middle Atlantic colonies in the 17th century, they did so mainly by individuals, not families. And just as colonial officials sought older artisans or farmers to help in the task, they also sought young children to serve as apprentices. In return for their passage, these children were placed under the total control of new masters.

In some cases, children were signed to indenture contracts by "spirits"—agents who worked in behalf of merchants, shipowners, or settlers to sign up workers. Many young people wished to go to the New World and signed up voluntarily; others, however, were kidnapped. Writing to the Privy Council of England in 1638 the Lord Mayor of London complained that "certain persons called spirits, do inveigle and by lewd subtleties entice away youth against

the consent either of their parents, friends, or masters" (Bremner, 1970, I:9). He requested that something be done to control the spirits, as did other people who also placed charges against them.

Because indentured persons, children or adults, could not pay for their passage, they were bound to serve their new masters for at least four years. The masters, in turn, could sell or reassign the contracts for these indentured persons to anyone they pleased. Dependent children from the streets and asylums of England were indentured for even longer periods and were shipped over in large lots. Consider the request in 1619 to the city of London by the Virginia Company for more children (Bremner, 1970, I:5)

> The Treasurer, Council, and Company of Virginia assembled in their great and general Court the 17th of November 1619 have taken into consideration the continual great forwardness of his honorable City in advancing the plantations of Virginia and particularly in furnishing out one hundred children this last year, which by the goodness of God there safely arrived (save such as died in the way).
>
> And foreasmuch as we have now resolved to send this next spring very large supplies for the strength and increasing of the Colony . . . we pray your Lordship and the rest in pursuit of your former so pious actions to renew your like favors and furnish us again with one hundred more [children] for the next spring. Our desire is that we may have them of twelve years and upward . . . They shall be apprentices, the boys till they come to twenty-one years of age, the girls till they be married, and afterwards they shall be placed as tenants upon the public land with best conditions where they shall have houses with stocks of corn and cattle to begin with, and afterward the moiety of all increase and profit whatsoever.

The treatment of lower-class dependent English children in this way was not totally unlike the treatment of black children who were kidnapped in Africa and also shipped to the colonies. While there was little chance that black children would ultimately receive their freedom as would most of their white counterparts, they were considered to be valuable: 3,000 pounds of tobacco for a black child between the ages of 7 and 11 years; 4,000 pounds for a child between 11 and 15, and 5,000 pounds for a young man over 15 (Bremner, 1970, I:16). Some colonists objected to the capture and sale of small black children, but their objections were often monetary rather than humane; that is, such children were considered to be too young to work efficiently. However, given the extent to which white children were also sought as cheap sources of labor, this kind of objection may not seem too strange. Children were not afforded the highly special protection that they are today.

What these few examples reveal is the vestige of European feudalism in the American colonies. In light of the struggle for survival, childhood was paid little deference. While slave children and the children of the poor were the most likely to be exploited, it was not uncommon for the children of the well-to-do to be sold on indenture contracts as well. What is significant, therefore, is that so many children played an important role in settling the colonies and that they were viewed as sources of labor and service, not as fragile, undeveloped beings who required long periods of special care and freedom from responsibility.

SOCIAL CONTROL OF CHILDREN

The methods that were used to control children throughout the ages and to secure their obedience reveal a legacy of harsh punishment. The evidence, says Mause (1974:40–42), warrants the conclusion that by present standards a large percentage of the children born in the 18th century could be considered "battered children." With rare exceptions, statements of advice from antiquity

to modern times on how to control them approved the use of severe beatings. Even the humanists of the Renaissance, men of relative gentleness and vision, approved of beating children.

The wife of Milton, the poet, complained because she did not like to hear the cries of Milton's nephews as he was beating them; Beethoven used a knitting needle to whip his pupils and sometimes bit them; and Louis XIII, about whose sexual exploits we read earlier, often woke in terror in anticipation of his daily whipping. "I would rather," he said, "do without so much obeisance and honor if they wouldn't have me whipped" (Mause, 1974:41).

Some attempts to temper the violence of child beating were begun during the Renaissance—the transitional period between the 14th and 17th centuries—but these attempts were relative (Mause, 1974:42). Rather than attempting to eliminate the practice, reformers urged adults to use lighter instruments than cudgels and to strike children about the body rather than on the head. It was not until the 18th century that significant decreases in child beating began to occur and not until the 19th century that serious whipping began to go out of style. These changes, as we will see, were probably due to the emergence of the modern concept of childhood; until that concept emerged, children were not protected.

Interpreting history

The interpretations placed by historians upon the history of childhood have varied considerably. The two most divergent perspectives have been stated by Ariès (1962) and Mause (1974). According to Ariès, life in the Middle Ages, if not antiquity, was a happy one for little people. Despite high death rates and exploitation, it was precisely because society was not preoccupied with raising the young and severely restricting their lives that conditions for them were relatively good. Much of the ambiguity and conflict surrounding the separation of child and adult were absent. Communal living and the apprenticeship system constantly brought people of all ages and ranks together more as natural companions than as uniquely different kinds of beings. In lieu of the intergenerational and class conflicts with which we are familiar, these groups mixed together easily and naturally, wore the same clothes, worked together on common tasks, and enjoyed the same pleasures. Rather than repressing, judging, or attempting to protect children with a special set of moral rules, adults shared all aspects of existence with them. The years of littlehood, as a consequence, were sociable and happy.

Mause, by contrast, interprets child-raising practices in Freudian psychological terms and concludes that, while some parents in history may have loved children, they (the parents) were emotionally immature and lodged at a lower stage of human development. Unable to view the child as a person separate from themselves, parents projected or voided on to their children all the evil impulses, superstitions, hostilities, and sexual perversions of which they, the parents, were possessed. Thus, parents were both bad and good, loving and unloving, often to the detriment of the child. When they beat children, killed them in infancy, abandoned them to wet nurses, or played with them sexually, it was not the child to whom they were doing these things, but to themselves. In contrast to Ariès, therefore, Mause believes that the child-raising practices of the past have been a blot on the history of civilization from which, happily, we have begun emerging in the last two or three centuries. In some scheme of human growth, we are at a higher stage of development.

Yet, a third interpretation has been suggested by Gillis (1974) and Stone (1974). First, like most historians, they caution against premature conclusions. The historical study of children has only just begun, good information is sparse, and what sources are available are restricted largely to the wealthier classes. Records chronicling the lives of the poor and such oppressed people as slaves are virtually nonexistent. But, if the children of the better-off were treated with indifference or cruelty, it would not be unreasonable to assume that poor children or those in bondage were subjected to similar, if not worse, treatment.

Beyond that, Stone agrees that we should pay constant attention to the social and cultural contexts in which child-rearing practices occur. To imply, as Ariès does, that life for children used to be happy and sociable but has steadily become more repressive, or to suggest, as Mause does, that the treatment of children has gotten steadily better is to ignore a host of other issues. For a long time, anthropologists have argued that there is no one natural path from infancy to adulthood, nor one universally best method for raising children (Skolnick, 1973:326–327). Ways of treating children do not occur in a social vacuum; rather they must be understood in terms of the larger cultural context in which they occur. What, then, are some of the cultural facts to which we should pay heed?

Cultural adaptions

Perhaps the most important are the demographic facts of life that dominated all Western societies until very recent times. As this chapter has noted, most children were born to die. As late as the 18th century, the odds were two or three to one against a child living until age five (Kessen, 1965). It is not difficult, therefore, to imagine why people in antiquity and in the Middle Ages may have failed to develop strong emotional ties with infants. They could not retain their sanity if they cared too much.

Second, the medieval period in European history has often been called the Dark Ages.

Not only was life expectancy extremely low, but the great masses of people were bound into a feudal economic system which, at best, made life relatively easy for only a few. Intellectual growth, education, art, and medicine were at a standstill. That children were often viewed as a burden or were expected to play a contributing role under the circumstances should not be too surprising. To a population that is half-starved, that lives among its own excrement, that hardly ever washes, and that is ravaged by disease, rules of modesty and solicitude are not of overwhelming importance.

Under conditions like these, the cultural prescriptions that we consider important today were lacking, especially those that make provisions for close ties between parent and child, that stress the importance of the nuclear family, that take delight in the innocence and beauty of children, and that provide long years of total economic support for a phase in the life cycle known as childhood. Perhaps that is why, when judged in terms of these contemporary cultural values, children do not appear to have counted for much throughout much of Western history.

SUMMARY AND CONCLUSIONS

This chapter has indicated that childhood has not always been culturally defined as a special and highly protected phase of the life cycle. *Littlehood*, in other words, is not the same thing as *childhood*. Until the 12th or 13th centuries, the deliberate killing or abandonment of children was regarded as casually as abortion is today. Between the 14th and 17th centuries, infanticide and outright abandonment did not disappear, but their incidence began to decrease, particularly for legitimate children. Nonetheless, newborn babies were still farmed out to wet nurses, and, at age seven, young children were still sent to the homes of others to serve as apprentices and servants. Compared to the present, the attitude of parents toward their children was one of relative indifference and detachment.

Infants were thought to exist ". . . in a sort of limbo, hanging between life and death, more as a kind of animal than a human being, without mental activities or recognizable bodily shape" (Skolnick 1973:333). Childhood was not noteworthy in its own right; many languages lacked words to distinguish babies from those we now call adolescents or young adults; and young humans were not shielded from adult strength or depravity, work, sex, or death. "The cruel truth . . . may be that most parents in history have not been much involved with their children, and have not cared much about them" (Stone, 1974:29).

REFERENCES

Ariès, Phillippe
    1962   *Centuries of Childhood.* Translated by Robert Baldick. New York: Alfred A. Knopf.
Bremner, Robert H., et al., eds.
    1970   *Children and Youth in America: A Documentary History.* 2 vols. Cambridge: Harvard University Press.
Clavell, James
    1975   *Shogun: A Novel of Japan.* New York: Dell.
Gillis, John R.
    1974   *Youth and History.* New York: Academic Press.

Hunt, David
    1970   *Parents and Children in History: The Psychology of Family Life in Early Modern History*. New York: Basic Books.

Illick, Joseph E.
    1974   "Child-rearing in Seventeenth Century England and America." Pp. 303–350 in Lloyd de Mause, ed., *The History of Childhood*. New York: Psychohistory Press.

Kessen, W.
    1965   *The Child*. New York: John Wiley & Sons.

Laslett, Peter
    1972   *Household and Family in Past Time*. Cambridge: Cambridge University Press.

Marvick, Elizabeth W.
    1974   "Nature Versus Nurture: Patterns and Trends in Seventeenth Century French Child Rearing." Pp. 259–302 in Lloyd de Mause, ed., *The History of Childhood*. New York: Psychohistory Press.

Mause, Lloyd de
    1974   *The History of Childhood*. New York: Psychohistory Press.

Queen, Stuart A., and Adams, John B.
    1955   *The Family in Various Cultures*. New York: J. B. Lippincott.

Robertson, Pricilla
    1974   "Home as a Nest: Middle-class Childhood in Nineteenth Century Europe." Pp. 407–431 in Lloyd de Mause, ed., *The History of Childhood*. New York: Psychohistory Press.

Ross, James B.
    1974   "The Middle-class Child in Urban Italy, Fourteenth to Early Sixteenth Century." Pp. 183–228 in Lloyd de Mause, ed., *The History of Childhood*. New York: Psychohistory Press.

Seneca
    1963   *Moral Essays*. Translated by John W. Basone. Cambridge: Harvard University Press.

Skolnick, Arlene
    1973   *The Intimate Environment: Exploring Marriage and the Family*. Boston: Little, Brown.

Stone, Lawrence
    1974   "The Massacre of the Innocents." *The New York Review*, November, 14: 25–31.

Tucker, M. J.
    1974   "The Child as Beginning and End: Fifteenth and Sixteenth Century English Childhood." Pp. 229–258 in Lloyd de Mause, ed., *The History of Childhood*. New York: Psychohistory Press.

William van Mieris, Allegory of the Senses, *Collection of the Art Institute of Chicago*

It was not until the Renaissance that parents began to view children as fragile and innocent and to devote more personal attention to them.

THE DISCOVERY OF CHILDHOOD

We have reviewed historical materials suggesting that in premodern times children, at best, were treated with indifference while, at worst, were cruelly exploited. Modern Americans, by contrast, have been described as child-centered to an extreme degree (Skolnick, 1973:314). "We have set a new record; no other people seem ever to have been so preoccupied with children" (Goodman, 1970:11).

How did this marked change come about? Why are we so concerned with children today?

GLIMMERINGS OF CHANGE

Ariès points out that the art of the Middle Ages—the period roughly from A.D. 500 to A.D. 1400—did not even attempt to portray childhood (1962:33–50). Instead, when an artist showed children in his paintings, they were simply drawn as small adults having none of the characteristics of young people. In a painting portraying biblical stories, for example, "Isaac is shown sitting between his two wives, surrounded by some 15 little men

who came up to the level of the grown-ups' waists: these are their children" (p. 33). They looked like mature midgets.

As Western civilization began to awaken from the intellectual and social stagnation of the Middle Ages, the glimmerings of a new concept of childhood began to emerge, albeit slowly. In 14th-century Italy, people began to exhibit ambivalence over the practice of wet-nursing. A fashionable mother had not wanted to nurse her baby because it stretched her breasts too much, but now at least she began to take greater interest in the selection of the woman who would care for her infant. The new rule was that a wet nurse "should be prudent, well-mannered, honest, not a drinker or a drunkard, because very often children draw from and resemble the nature of the milk they suck" (Ross, 1974:185).

In 15th and 16th century England, the color white was used increasingly to suggest that children were essentially innocent (Tucker, 1974:232). Thus, when they died, children were dressed in white, their coffins were white, and attendants at the funeral wore white. Similarly, children became symbols of godly qualities or of good luck. Their images were placed on gravestones or were used to decorate the fringes of frescoes in the form of little angels.

In the 16th and 17th centuries, art and literature began to attribute a special personality to children. Portraits of well-to-do families began to exhibit children in special costumes rather than in the dress of adults (Ariès, 1962:33–50). It was as though adults had begun to see little people through a different pair of spectacles. Furthermore, women in upper-class homes began to cuddle children somewhat more often, to be more solicitous toward them when they hurt, and to take pleasure from them like we do from kittens or puppies today (Ariès, 1962:129).

Finally, in the late 16th and the 17th centuries, a growing number of reformers began to criticize the ancient treatment of children. Stressing the essential innocence and dependence of children, they argued that what children required was discipline and careful direction, not exploitation or indulgence. The premature induction of children into the adult world, they argued, not only affronted adults but injured the young (Ariès, 1962:130; Bremner, 1970, I; Illick, 1974; Marvick, 1974; Robertson, 1974).

THE MODERN CONCEPT OF CHILDHOOD

Although it had taken several centuries, the modern concept of childhood was beginning to emerge. But as it did, children were perceived as rather odd creatures—fragile, innocent, and sacred, on the one hand, but corruptible, trying, and arrogant on the other. "Unless you give children all they ask for, they are peevish and cry, aye, and strike their parents sometimes; and all this they have from nature. Yet are they free from guilt, neither may we properly call them wicked . . . because wanting the free use of reason they are

exempted from all duty" (Hobbes, 1972:100). Therefore, to insure the proper development of children, the new trend advised, they must be stringently safeguarded, both physically and morally, and must receive a carefully structured education. Only after long years of preparation, in fact, would they be properly prepared for adulthood.

It is difficult to overstate the significance of these seminal ideas. While they were obviously well ahead of the actual practices of the day, they signaled the beginning of the end for age-old tendencies to either ignore children or exploit them. The groundwork was laid for the belief that, until the child had been given distinctive preparation, he or she was not ready for life, that "he had to be subjected to special treatment, a sort of quarantine, before he was allowed to join adults" (Ariès, 1962:411–412).

Sources of change

There are many factors that contributed to the emergence and growth of these ideas: the Renaissance, the Protestant Reformation, the colonization of the New World, and eventually the Industrial Revolution. Most likely, all were important. Nonetheless, several historians imply that the original impetus was given by a relatively small band of moralists, schoolmen, and churchmen, both Catholic and Protestant (Ariès, 1962:330–412; Bremner, 1970; Illick, 1974:316–317; Marvick, 1974:261). It was they more than the intellectual humanists of the Renaissance who became specifically concerned with the young and with the corrupting influence of society upon them. A moralization of society was taking place in which the ethical aspects of religion were gradually taking precedence over the sacred. Heretofore, Catholic Church functions had been largely ritualistic; seriously religious persons had withdrawn into a monastery or a nunnery if they sought escape from a sinful world. Now, efforts were being made to reshape the world and to do so, in part, through children.

Two Puritan reformers, Robert Cleaver and John Dod, in 1621 revealed both the reformist theme and the mixed perceptions of children; that is, that they were both wicked and worth saving:

> The young child which lieth in the cradle is both wayward and full of affections; and though his body be but small, yet he hath a reat [wrongdoing] heart, and is altogether inclined to evil. . . . If this sparkle be suffered to increase, it will rage and burn down the whole house. For we are changed and become good not by birth but by education. . . . Therefore, parents must be wary and circumspect . . . they must correct and sharply reprove their children for saying or doing ill (Illick, 1974:316–317).

John Winthrope, the first governor of the Massachusetts Bay Colony, justified the Puritan migration to America as a method of carrying the gospel to the New World and of permitting the young to escape the corruption of the Old World. The fountains of learning and religion had been destroyed, he said, such that "most children, even the best wits and of fairest hopes, are perverted, corrupted, and uttly overthrown" (Bremner, 1970, I:18–19).

Besides moral training, it should be noted, the remarks of these reformers stressed the importance of education and learning. In medieval Europe, by contrast, interest in education was virtually nonexistent. The schools that did exist were not intended specifically for children nor were they overly concerned with moral, intellectual, and social matters. Rather, they were a kind of technical school designed to prepare people, young or old, for the clergy (Ariès, 1962:330). Hence, the revival of interest in education, beginning in about the 15th century, has been hailed as a significant landmark, as a Renaissance, a rebirth. It marked the time when Western civilization began to come out of the Dark Ages,

when an interest in the arts and literature was revived and when modern science was born.

The intellectual humanists of the Renaissance are generally given credit for the revival of education, but Ariès (1962) maintains that while they were devoted to the spread of learning they were not particularly interested in children. Learning, the humanists felt, should be available to everyone. Indeed, the schools of the 17th century still bore this stamp. School was not reserved just for children, and pupils were not divided as they are today according to age and grade; all attended the same classes together. But the various reformers, by contrast, increasingly stressed the use of formal schooling as a device for preparing children for adult life. They wanted to use the school as a mechanism for moral as well as intellectual preparation.

Finally, the new morality stressed the importance of the family. Greater emphasis was placed upon the role of natural parents in raising their own offspring, seeing that they were educated, and reducing the chances that they would be subjected to undue influence from nonfamily members. John Elliott, 17th-century American churchman, phrased these sentiments well (Bremner, 1970, I:33):

> It is a very false and pernicious principle that many people and parents are trained with, viz., that youth must be suffered awhile to take their swing, and sow their wild oats, to travail into the world, to follow the fashions, company, and manner of the time, hoping they will be wiser hereafter. Oh false principle; God speaks fully to the contrary. Prov. 19:18. *Chasten thy son while there is hope, and let not thy soul spare for his crying.* Prov. 13:24. *He that spareth the rod, hateth his son, but he that loveth him, chasteneth him betimes.*

Besides advocating stern methods of control, such injunctions speak of love for children and the importance of attending to their moral welfare—a sharp contrast to the indifference or easygoing attitudes of the Middle Ages. Over a period of two or three centuries, a slow but obvious transformation in the status of children had taken place. The voices of the first 15th-century reformers were joined by a veritable chorus by those of the 17th century, all attesting to the essential dependence of children and demanding that newer standards of morality for them be enforced. By no means had all older practices ceased, but important trends were underway.

The ideal child

The way children were characterized by the religious moralists of the 17th century reflected highly complicated feelings. By no means had the status of children gone from indifference or disregard to complete acceptance and warmth. As the Puritans Cleaver and Dod had suggested, children had "wrong-doing hearts" and were altogether "inclined to evil." If that inclination was not to "rage and burn," it had to be controlled. Therefore, their injunctions to parents were to be "wary" and to "sharply reprove" their children. Although child raising might have entailed some pleasures for parents, it must also have been an onerous duty.

Based upon the precepts of the new morality, many treatises and manuals were written in the 17th and 18th centuries to guide parents. The principles they set forth were important because implicit in them was the emerging image of the ideal child. Such an image became the standard by which not only conformity but deviance among children was judged. Thus, when 19th century Americans became highly concerned with delinquency, this image still retained a great deal of currency. It was the standard by which undesirable conduct by children and failure by unworthy parents was evaluated. Indeed, there is much about the image that is familiar today (Ariès, 1962:114–119; Bremner, 1970, I:passim).

Supervision.   The first principle emphasized the importance of keeping a close watch over children and never permitting them to be alone. As Benjamin Wadsworth, a clergyman of Boston, put it, "Children should not be left to themselves, to a loose end, to do as they please; but should be under tutors and governors, not being fit to govern themselves" (Bremner, 1970, 1:35).

Discipline.   The second principle stressed the importance of disciplining rather than pampering or coddling children. It is cruelty to allow children to do as they please, to forbid them nothing, to allow them to laugh when they ought to cry, or to permit them to remain silent when an adult speaks to them. They must learn to exercise self-control and to exhibit appropriate manners.

Modesty.   The third principle stressed the importance of modesty. Children should not be permitted to go to bed in the presence of a person of the opposite sex. Young girls should be completely covered and not lie in an immodest position. Children of different sexes should not sleep together. Songs expressing "dissolute passions" should neither be sung nor heard. Language should be pure and wholesome. Only the most chaste of books should be read. Games that were not a part of the educational system should be avoided. "Ordinary entertainments provided by jugglers, mountebanks, and tightrope walkers [are] forbidden" (Ariès, 1962:118). Even puppet shows were beneath contempt.

Diligence.   The fourth principle admonished parents to bring up their children to be "diligent in some lawful business" (Bremner, 1970, I:110). Work for children was not only morally desirable, but economically necessary. Throughout the 18th and 19th centuries, and well into the 20th, the belief of children taking part in the work ethic was a cardinal virtue.

Obedience.   Finally, the fifth principle stressed a virtue that encompassed all others— respect for, and obedience to, authority. Children were warned to honor not only their parents but anyone in authority, because disobedience inevitably led to destruction (Bremner, 1970, I:32; Gillis, 1974:21).

Such admonitions may have been softened somewhat during the 19th century but not markedly. Throughout the century, in fact, key opinion makers felt that children who were not being raised according to these principles should be taken from their unworthy parents and placed in institutions where they could be raised properly. Thus, not being able to govern themselves, children should be obedient, submissive to authority, hardworking, self-controlled, modest, and chaste.

THE ORGANIZATION OF CHILD RAISING

The new concept of childhood was accompanied by alterations in the way society was organized to raise children. This does not necessarily mean that the discovery of childhood caused these changes; more likely, the forces of change were interactive, being both cause and effect.

The family

Part of the fabric of change was the emergence of the *nuclear* family. The nuclear family is the family with which we are most familiar, in which the people living under one roof consist largely of a set of parents and their own children. The families of the Middle Ages had been *extended* because so many people in addition to parents and children had lived under one roof. Now, however, economic and demographic changes were tending to reduce family size. Although all forms of communal living had by no means disappeared, the family became increasingly nuclear during the 17th century, particularly among the middle class (Laslett, 1962:1–89).

Sentiments favoring the nuclear family were also carried to the New World by such groups as the Puritans, who apparently emigrated, not only in the interests of preserving their Protestant religious beliefs, but of liberating their children from the evils of the Old World (Bremner, 1970:128–129). So committed were they to this view, in fact, that the Massachusetts Bay Colony passed a law in 1642 designed to broaden and enforce the educational and socialization functions of the family and to insure that parents carried out these responsibilities. The new law required that each family teach its children a trade and how to read. Parents who failed were to be brought before the authorities, while children who disobeyed their parents could be dealt with severely. Further, the law decreed that no single person, especially a young one, could live outside the confines of some family. The family was to be a guardian of the public as well as the private good (Demos, 1970; Farber, 1972).

Despite these innovations, the Puritans did not discard entirely the practices of the apprenticeship system. Rather, the rules governing it were changed. If the new settlements were to survive, everyone had to work. But rather than working for others, six- or seven-year-olds worked for their own parents. Meanwhile, the age for apprentices to leave home had risen considerably, to ages 14 or 15. Furthermore, parents were warned that, when they did apprentice their children, it should be to a lawful calling in a religious home (Bremner, 1970, I:110–111).

At the same time, beliefs in the innate depravity of children continued to legitimize severe punishment. People took very seriously the notion that to spare the rod was to spoil the child. Consequently, the debate was not whether children should be whipped but at which age it should begin (infancy, age three, or five?), how the whipping should be administered (a birch or leather thongs?), where it should be administered (bare bottom or covered?), and until what age (15 or older?). Most people preferred such methods to isolating the offender, putting him on bread and water, or tying him up. But even these methods were used (Robertson, 1974:414–420).

In summary then, the conflicted character of child-raising principles, emphasizing love and affection, on the one hand, but stern, unyielding punishment for disobedience on the other, seems to have generated considerable ambivalence for families. Lamenting the death of her eight-year-old granddaughter, an 18th-century New England poet by the name of Anne Bradstreet penned the following lines (Illick, 1974:326):

> Farewel dear babe, my heart's too much
>   content,
> Farewel sweet babe, the pleasure of mine eye,
> Farewel fair flower that for a space was lent,
> Then Ta'en away unto Eternity.

But, in another poem, she expressed the prevailing religious belief in child depravity:

> Here sits our Grandame in retired place
> And in her lap, her bloody Cain new born.

Coupled with the high death rates of the times, the new concept of childhood was not without its anxieties.

The school

Possibly the greatest consequence of the Renaissance and the moralists' efforts to reform child-raising practices was the subsequent emphasis placed upon formal schooling for children. Although the colonial schools in America were eventually organized differently from European schools, the emphasis upon education was an Old World derivative.

Virtually all European schools in the 16th and 17th centuries were privately not publicly run, and the children attending them were a mixed lot (Ariès, 1962:269–285). Since not every town or hamlet had a school, school populations were recruited not merely from the towns in which they existed but from other towns and the countrysides as well. As a result,

those students who lived too far from the school to return home each night were forced to take up residence in town, either as boarders, as servants on the school premises, or as lodgers in private dwellings. The majority were of the latter type.

The practices surrounding the schools reflect the transitional character of society as it moved from medieval to modern. There is evidence, for example, that in many of the lodgings boys of all classes and ages were housed. Furthermore, the principal source of discipline and control, when it existed, was exercised by the boys themselves. As a consequence, their lives could scarcely be distinguished from that of single, unfettered adults. Plumb says that students "lived like hippies and wandered like gypsies, begging, stealing, fighting; yet they were always hungry for books" (1972:83). "There remained," says Ariès, "a great deal of the free and easy attitude of the preceding centuries" (1962:254). But it was not long until both schoolmasters and parents were driven by their philosophy to curb this freedom and to exercise stringent controls over pupils.

Landlords apparently did not feed their lodgers. Hence, on market days, the schools closed down so that pupils could go shopping or collect the money and food their parents had sent to them. They lived from week to week, receiving just enough provisions—cheese, bread, fruit, and bacon—to last for that period. It was probably in response to circumstances like these that the boarding school system, so common in Europe, developed. Efforts were made to provide means by which pupils could live on school premises under the strict supervision of schoolmasters. Under this system, which began to flourish in the 18th century, a concerted effort was made to separate pupils from adults and thence to mold them according to the strict moral principles of the reformers.

Reformers in the New World, meanwhile, stressed the importance of schooling, but there were important variations in the way they implemented it (Bremner, 1970, 1:72–102). In the English colonies, at first, the responsibility for education was diffused among parents, the masters to whom older children were apprenticed, and clergymen. As the education movement gained momentum, however, increasing emphasis was placed upon the immediate family and its new ally, the school. Since parents were often ill-equipped to teach their children, special provision had to be made for educating them. Hence, along with family discipline, education became an important means by which the world was to be shaped into a new, and more moral, pattern.

Besides the 1642 law passed in Massachusetts which attempted to coerce parents and masters to exercise their educational responsibilities, the General Court of that state also took the first step in 1647 toward the establishment of a public educational system (Bremner, 1970, I:72–73). Connecticut and New Hampshire followed suit. Towns of 50 households were supposed to provide a schoolmaster for elementary training while larger towns of 100 were expected to have a grammar school. In actual practice, however, these requirements were not always met. Education, especially at the secondary school level, was dependent upon private support and the payment of fees by pupils. Hence, school attendance was not mandatory and tended to favor the middle and upper classes, leaving lower-class children to rely upon their parents and the apprenticeship system for whatever education they might receive. As a result, only a few relatively well-to-do students went beyond an elementary level and even fewer to a university.

Despite these limitations, the New England schools were superior to those in the Middle Atlantic colonies and in the South. With private assistance, Southern and Middle Atlantic churches maintained some elementary schools which the poor could attend, but secondary education was entirely private and confined almost entirely to wealthier pupils. With all these limitations, Bremner maintains that colonial education in the 17th century was unmatched, reaching more children and providing them with a greater ability to read and write than a comparable number of children elsewhere (1970, I:74).

Even more significant is the fact that the foundation was laid for the ultimate development of tax-supported public schools. An experiment in educational democracy was begun that was unparalleled in Europe. But, while the usual inclination has been to focus upon its presumed benefits, its significance in terms of its alteration of the nature of childhood and societal life, in general, often goes unnoticed. In almost unbelievable contrast to Europe in the Middle Ages, the stage was set for the ultimate confinement in the 20th century of children in youth ghettos—the schools—for most of their formative years. More and more, the effects of the apprenticeship system and even those of the family itself would be eroded by the socialization functions of the school. The widespread effects of the discovery of childhood had only just begun to be seen.

Social stratification

In the context in which the modern concept of childhood developed, great changes were introduced into social relationships among the various strata of society—changes whose long-range effects may still be observed today. During the Middle Ages, there were only two principal groups in society—the nobility and the common people. When Western society began to emerge from this period, however, trade and commerce with other parts of the world gradually increased. This trade was associated first with the commercial revolution of the 17th and 18th centuries and later with the Industrial Revolution of the 19th century. In response to both, a whole new middle stratum in society emerged—the entrepreneurs, merchants, traders, and professionals with whom we are now so familiar. Eventually, many of these people became extremely powerful, replacing the aristocracy as the most influential segment of society. The old order was gradually phased out and a new one installed.

Most historians maintain that it was this segment of society, and not its working-class people, to whom the modern concept of childhood, the nuclear family, and the idea of schooling most appealed, at least originally. Businessmen, merchants, and professionals were increasingly inclined to shrink from the indiscriminate mixing of the generations and of the social classes that had probably been common in the Middle Ages. The privacy and special kind of identity provided by the nuclear family and the intellectual and moral skills that were derived from schooling were particularly suited to their special interests.

Various writers have tended to refer to this new segment of society as the *middle class.* Though this term had some meaning in those days when it was useful to view the middle rank of society as intermediate between the nobility and the common people, it has become less useful today as a precise, descriptive term (Gould, 1964:426–428). Most people either describe themselves as *middle class* or use the word *upper class* to denote the powerful executives, the corporate officials, the politicians, or others who are now the most dominant stratum in society. Nonetheless, there is some utility in noting the effects on children of the emergence of merchants, businessmen, and professionals in earlier centuries.

Using the word *middle class* to describe them, Ariès (1962:414) traces this group's progressive separation in the 17th and 18th centuries from its working-class origin:

There came a time when the middle class could no longer bear the pressure of the multitude or the contact of the lower class. It seceded: It withdrew from the vast polymorphous society to organize itself separately, in a homogeneous environment, among its families, in homes designed for privacy, in new districts kept free from all lower-class contamination. The juxtaposition of inequalities, hitherto something perfectly natural, became intolerable to it: The revulsion of the rich preceded the shame of the poor. The quest for privacy and the new desires for comfort which it aroused (for there is a close connection between comfort and privacy) emphasized even further the contrast between the material ways of life of the lower and middle classes. The old society concentrated the maximum number of ways of life into the minimum of space and accepted, if it did not impose, the bizarre juxtaposition of the most widely different classes. The new society, on the contrary, provided each way of life with a confined space in which it was understood that the dominant features should be respected, and that each person had to resemble a conventional model, an ideal type, and never depart from it under pain of excommunication.

Rather strong support for this interpretation may be found in Roberts (1971) recent social history of the lower working classes in England. Until World War I, he says, working-class people lived in a social environment that lay outside the mainstream of English society. Living according to their own provincial standards, they were left without much hope and without much contact with middle- and upper-class people. So separate were their worlds, in fact, that the guardians of public morality—the schools, churches, and courts—generally feared the poorer slum dwellers.

In a similar vein, Bremner (1970, 1:343) and Platt (1969:passim) describe an American scene in which class, ethnic, and religious differences abounded. "What," asks Bremner, "did slave children, immigrant children in city slums, children of a doctor or minister, and the children of a proud aristocrat on a plantation, or those of a wealthy New England merchant really have in common?" They had little in common; the American environment was one of great diversity. As in Europe, therefore, the significance of this diversity lay in the likelihood that children in different social worlds were being socialized in different ways. If the emerging concept of childhood was a possession largely of middle- and upper-class people, its influence on lower-class children would be lessened. Even more important, if the norms associated with that image were those of the rule makers of society, then it is likely that the children of the poor would be penalized. Without proper induction into the world of the successful, they could not compete on an equal footing. Worse still, they might be defined as deviant or unworthy to the extent that they departed from the expectations of teachers, employers, and community leaders. There is considerable evidence, in fact, that this is the kind of situation that developed.

Ariès reports that in 16th- and 17th-century Europe some private scholarships and special schools were organized for the poor (1966:272). Soon, however, both were taken over by students of better means. In some cases, scholarships originally set aside for the poor were actually bought and sold for prices the poor could not afford. Losing such opportunities as these, most poor people could scarcely afford to place their children in lodgings and provide them with food.

Ariès also suggests that, for a much longer time than did the middle class, lower-class people retained their liking for crowds, communal living, and apprenticeship training (1962:413–415). They preferred the old social order and its system of norms. Whether this preference was voluntary or was due to economic discrimination by the middle class is hard to say. Both were likely important. In any event, a single school system in both France and England was eventually replaced by a dual system, one for the lower class and one for the middle class. The school for the lower class, of short duration, indeed, was called *primary* school, while the school for the middle class was called *secondary* education and extended for a much longer period.

To a lesser degree, early American schools also favored well-to-do over poorer children. But Americans were confronted with ethnic as well as class differences—differences that Europe did not face. At first, the predominant minority groups were the native Indians and the blacks, most of whom were slaves. Far more widespread than discrimination by class was discrimination by race.

While dominant white groups in the colonies increasingly stressed the importance of education for their children, they did not do so for the minority groups. Some religious groups, some individuals, and even some colonies made an effort to see that both groups of children were educated, but these efforts produced few results (Bremner, 1970, I:72; 335–339).

Besides the Indians' understandable skepticism about the intentions and cultural ways of the white missionaries, they were constantly subjected to the manipulations of white traders, to massacres, and to the broken promises of settlers. "With so many colonists regarding the Indians as the chief threat to their security and the Indians looking upon the colonists as hypocrites, it is little wonder that attempts to win converts and to educate them should fail" (Bremner, 1970, I:72).

Efforts to extend education to black children were equally dismal, although the opportunities to do so were undoubtedly greater. As with the Indians, colonists were more concerned with the religious conversion of blacks than with their learning in secular terms. Furthermore, the colonists openly confessed to a great deal of ambivalence, even on this score. On the one hand, they felt obligated to carry the Christian message to the slaves, but on the other, they were fearful that if the slaves were baptized they would consider themselves free.

The way this dilemma was resolved is captured in the remarks of a Virginia clergyman in 1724 (Bremner, 1970, I:98):

> But as for the Children of Negroes and Indians, that are to live among Christians, undoubtedly they ought all to be baptized; since it is not out of the power of their masters to take care that they have a Christian education, learn their prayers and catechism, and go to church, and not accustom themselves to lie, swear, and steal, though such (as the poorer sort in England) be not taught to read and write; which as yet has been found to be dangerous upon several political accounts, especially self-preservation.

In other words, both black and Indian children, like the poorer classes in Europe, ought to learn and to adhere to the social rules that would make them willing to accept a subordinate position in society but not to arm themselves with the kinds of educational skills that would make them politically or socially dangerous. As the new concept of childhood grew and spread, therefore, it was applied to all children in moral, but not educational, terms. While the children of dominant groups should receive both moral and secular education, those of subordinate groups should be content with the moral. The logic of this kind of thinking seemed to be that the two could be separated and result in a society without conflict. Such thinking, however, has not been supported by the events of history.

In the next chapter we will discover that the consequences of attitudes like these grew even more troublesome as ever-increasing numbers of different ethnic groups came to America in the 19th century—ethnic groups whose lifestyles and images of childhood were different from those of the Anglo-Saxon middle and upper classes. While some groups were assimilated into the American culture more easily than others and while the class structure of the United States did not become so rigid as that of many European countries, the conflicts engendered by clashes over the appropriate image of childhood were numerous. Many contemporary theories of delinquency, in fact, as well as the actual operation of the juvenile justice system itself, are directly traceable to traditional beliefs about social class differences.

Sexual stratification

Another issue of great interest today is the effect the modern concept of childhood may have had on the treatment of girls. Throughout Western history, girls were considered to be of considerably less value than boys, probably because the family line and family inheritances were traced through the males. Boys were the social security and pension plans of the preindustrial world. They were the best guarantees that parents could provide against the infirmities of sickness and old age. Hence, a failure to produce any sons, or a succession of girls, could destroy the best of well-laid plans (Gillis, 1974:11). After the discovery of childhood, girls were apparently spared some of the neglect and cruelty to which they had been subjected formerly, but this generally improved treatment did not eliminate the sexism of centuries past.

During the 17th century the belief persisted that boys were not only preferable, but more healthy for the expectant mother. "A woman whose color was good and body temperature comfortably warm might expect a boy, while if she were carrying a girl she would be distinguished by 'a pale, heavy and swarthy countenance, a melancholique eye: She is wayward, fretful, and sad . . . her face is spotted with red' " (Illick, 1974:304). Furthermore, even if the mother survived the terrible effects of carrying a girl, her birth would not be especially welcome. After delivering her third girl, for example, Lady Frances Hatton wrote to her husband, saying, "I am sure you will love it though it be a Girle and I trust in God I may live to bring you boys" (Illick, 1974:304).

If aristocrats like Lord Hatton were not happy with girls, neither were peasants. French peasants, says Robertson, were known to declare: "I have no children, monsieur, I have only girls" (1974:409). And in Naples it was customary to hang out a black flag if a girl were born so that neighbors might be spared the terrible embarrassment of coming to see her. People were not crazy about girls. Hence, the treatment of girls under the new child-raising practices probably did not change as much for girls as it did for boys.

European schools, for example, were sexist; that is, they were off-limits to females and remained so for a long time. Despite the outcry over the necessity to improve the intellects as well as the morals of children, it was apparently felt that the needs of girls, as well as that of society, could be fulfilled without using the special ministrations of the school (Ariès, 1962:331–332). Most girls were already little women by the age of 10 or 12, devoting their time to family chores or to domestic service. Little of the education care and training expended on boys was expended on them.

One writer of the 17th century describes and criticizes the results (Ariès, 1962:332).

> How many masters and colleges there are! . . . this shows the high opinion people have of the education of boys. But the girls! It is considered perfectly permissible to abandon girls willy-nilly to the guidance of ignorant or indiscreet mothers. . . . It is shameful but common to see women of wit and manners unable to pronounce what they read. . . . They are even more at fault in their spelling.

If virtual illiteracy was characteristic of "women of wit and manners" (women of the upper classes) think what it was of women in poorer circumstances. Ariès maintains, however, that "girls of good family were no better educated than girls of the lower classes" (p. 334). Efforts designed to improve the skills and morals of boys through formal education were not extended to girls until much later. The thought that girls should receive extensive formal education, in fact, is largely a product of the 20th century. As with social class, therefore, differences in the status and socialization of girls has had lasting consequences.

Age stratification

A final element of social organization on which comment is vital is the extent to which the discovery of childhood resulted in an increasing tendency to stratify people by age—to divide up the life cycle into major segments such as infancy, childhood, adolescence, adulthood, and old age and, then, to further subdivide these by year of birth or grade in school. In antiquity and during the Middle Ages, such age grading, especially where young people were concerned, seemed to be of relatively little importance. As the modern concept of childhood continued to grow, however, grading by age was extended further and further down the ladder. Nowadays, kindergarten children are kept apart from first graders, first graders apart from second graders, and so on—not only in school but elsewhere. We are terribly conscious of the ages of childhood, and our social institutions, our beliefs, and even our scientific theories reflect that consciousness. What is profoundly striking, however, is that such a consciousness is a function of only the last century or two.

Kett, for example, notes that "the word 'adolescence' appeared only rarely outside of scientific literature prior to the 20th century" (1973:97). Instead, it was given prominence in 1890 by G. Stanley Hall, who wrote a two-volume work entitled *Adolescence.* In that work, he described adolescence as "a second birth, marked by a sudden rise of moral idealism, chivalry, and religious enthusiasm" (Kett, 1973:96). Yet, in the short space of less than a century, consider how extensively adolescence has been defined as the last stage of childhood and how adolescents are relegated to a childlike status:

> Following Hall's original work, a parade of books emerged describing adolescence as the "awkward age" and noting its relationship to problems of schooling and delinquency:
>
> Adolescents have been largely eliminated from the job market.
>
> The length of formal education has been stretched out to the late teens and early 20s.
>
> Adolescents have been increasingly segregated from adults and expected to confine their primary relationships to their peers.
>
> Adolescents have become a burden on the family rather than contributing economically to its welfare. Moreover, parents have become less and less capable of imparting specific work skills to their children, since the two no longer work together. (Coleman et al., 1974; Kett, 1973).

Our whole society, in other words, is organized to separate child from adult and to provide a host of ways for taking the presumed developmental stages of childhood into account. The invention of delinquency, the creation of the juvenile court, the drafting of child labor laws, the legal requirements regulating the age for compulsory school attendance, as well as pediatricians, child psychiatrists, and elementary and secondary school teachers are all reflections of our modern construction of childhood.

What is fascinating about this construction is that while our modern norms suggest that we stratify by age in order to take into account the needs of children, they do just the opposite where males and females are concerned. That is, modern norms suggest increasingly that in order to take into account the needs of females we must make them equal with males. Although we must eliminate all stratification by sex, we must not do so by age. Consequently, the implications of such contradictory beliefs are profound and will appear again and again throughout our study.

SUMMARY AND CONCLUSIONS

The modern concept of childhood suggests that children must be stringently safeguarded, must receive a carefully structured education and, only after long years of moral, physical, and intellectual quarantine, can they be allowed to join adults. It took many centuries, however, for this concept to develop and to become a part of the institutional fabric of American society.

Small children became symbols of innocence and purity in the 15th and 16th centuries, when people began to take increasing pleasure in them. New moral standards for the young began to appear in the 16th and 17th centuries, as did a new emphasis upon parental responsibility for the welfare of children. The family became increasingly nuclear in the 17th and 18th centuries and schools, solely for the young, became the norm. Finally, the age segregation of society became an accomplished fact in the late 19th and 20th centuries.

The consequences of this extended process were great. By mid-20th century, childhood had become a long transitional period in the life cycle; family insularity was common; community solidarity across generational and class lines was virtually nonexistent; families, schools, and peer groups had replaced apprenticeship and interaction with adults as the primary sources of socialization; and the new morality for children had stripped them of adult pleasures and responsibilities.

The cost of these changes in economic terms was profound and would have been unbearable had it not been for the labor saving technology introduced by the Industrial Revolution. For the first time in Western history, society eliminated a huge segment of its population—it's children—from productive work in the labor force. Nonetheless, for social as well as economic reasons, the presumed benefits of these changes were not evenly distributed.

Lower-class and minority children were not only kept in the labor force and were denied educational opportunities for a much longer period of time, but were socialized at home in ways that hindered their capacities to adapt to the new standard of childhood. In a similar, but less obvious way, differences between the sexes persisted. While girls were undoubtedly affected by the altered child-raising practices of the family, they remained locked by ancient traditions into domestic roles.

It is clear, as a result, that the institutionalization of childhood has had mixed consequences. On the one hand, infanticide is now rare; most babies are raised and loved by their parents and most children are not exploited. On the other hand, there is also a darker side to the picture. In seeking to moralize the lives of children, reformers looked at age-old behaviors and discovered immorality; in seeking to foster conformity, they defined more of the acts of children as deviant; and in encouraging greater discipline and control, they narrowed the range of acceptable childhood conduct.

In the next chapter, therefore, we will inquire further into this side of childhood. Rather than looking only at the ideal image of childhood, we will be examining its counterpart, delinquency: how delinquency was invented, why it was invented, and who its inventors were. After discovering childhood, society was forced to decide not only how the ideal child might be produced, but how to deal with the children who, for social or personal reasons, appeared to deviate from this ideal.

REFERENCES

Ariès, Phillippe
    1962   *Centuries of Childhood.* Translated by Robert Baldick. New York: Alfred A. Knopf.

Bremner, Robert H., et al., eds.
    1970   *Children and Youth in America: A Documentary History.* 2 vols. Cambridge: Harvard University Press.

Coleman, James S., et al.
    1972   *Youth: Transition to Adulthood.* Chicago: University of Chicago Press.

Demos, John
    1970   *A Little Commonwealth.* New York: Oxford University Press.

Farber, Bernard
    1972   *Guardians of Virtue: Salem Families in 1800.* New York: Basic Books.

Gillis, John R.
    1974   *Youth and History.* New York: Academic Press.

Goodman, Mary E.
    1970   *The Culture of Childhood: Child's-eye Views of Society and Culture.* New York: Teachers College Press.

Gould, Julius
1964   "Middle-class." Pp. 426–428 in Julius Gould and William L. Kolb, eds., *A Dictionary of the Social Sciences.* New York: Free Press.

Hobbes, Thomas
1972   "The Citizen." In T. S. K. Scott-Craig and Bernard Gert, eds., *Man and Citizen.* (1st ed., 1642) Gloucester, Mass.: Peter Smith Publisher Inc.

Illick, Joseph E.
1974   "Child Rearing in Seventeenth Century England and America." Pp. 303–350 in Lloyd de Mause, ed., *The History of Childhood.* New York: Psychohistory Press.

Kett, Joseph F.
1971   "Adolescence and Youth in Nineteenth Century America." Pp. 95–110 in Theodore K. Rabb and Robert I. Rotberg, eds., *The Family in History.* New York: Harper and Row.

Laslett, Peter.
1972   *Household and Family in Past Time.* Cambridge: Cambridge University Press.

Marvick, Elizabeth W.
1974   "Nature Versus Nurture: Patterns and Trends in Seventeenth Century French Child Rearing." Pp. 259–302 in Lloyd de Mause, ed., *The History of Childhood.* New York: Psychohistory Press.

Mause, Lloyd de
1974   *The History of Childhood.* New York: Psychohistory Press.

Platt, Anthony
1969   *The Child Savers.* Chicago: Chicago University Press.

Plumb, J. H.
1972   "The Great Change in Children." *Intellectual Digest* 2:82–84.

Roberts, Robert
1971   *The Classic Slum: Salford Life in the First Quarter of the Century.* Manchester: Manchester University Press.

Robertson, Priscilla
1974   "Home as a Nest: Middle-class Childhood in Nineteenth Century Europe." Pp. 407–431 in Lloyd de Mause, ed., *The History of Childhood.* New York: Psychohistory Press.

Ross, James B.
1974   "The Middle-class Child in Urban Italy, Fourteenth to Early Sixteenth Century." Pp. 183–228 in Lloyd de Mause, ed., *The History of Childhood.* New York: Psychohistory Press.

Skolnick, Arlene
1973   *The Intimate Environment: Exploring Marriage and the Family.* Boston: Little, Brown.

Tucker, M. J.
1974   "The Child as Beginning and End: Fifteenth and Sixteenth Century English Childhood." Pp. 229–258 in Lloyd de Mause, ed., *The History of Childhood.* New York: Psychohistory Press.

The Philadelphia House of Refuge was created in 1828 to care for runaway, delinquent, and neglected children.

THE INVENTION OF DELINQUENCY

Throughout the Middle Ages and as late as the 17th century, children participated in acts which, if committed today, could not only result in their being defined as delinquent but could require that their parents and other adults be charged with contributing to their delinquency. As soon as they could talk, most children learned and used obscene language and gestures; many engaged in sex at an early age, willingly or otherwise; they drank freely in taverns, if not at home; few of them ever went to school, and when they did, they wore sidearms, fomented brawls, and fought duels (Ariès, 1962; Sanders, 1970). In modern society, these same acts occur, but they are illegal, and authorities are charged with curbing them. How did this change come about? How should the modern response be interpreted?

Two major interpretations are possible: either the undesirable behavior of children has increased over the centuries and become more dangerous, or significant modifications have been made in the way that behavior is defined. The latter is probably the more accurate interpretation. As the concept of childhood grew and expanded, the meanings attached to it were significantly altered. The acts of children which in previous centuries were not seen as particularly deviant now became unique problems. New norms and expectations developed as childhood became a special phase in the life cycle.

In this chapter, we will trace the development of those norms and expectations on the American scene. It was during the 19th century that most laws applicable only to children were actually written and a juvenile court created. But in order to understand these social inventions, it is necessary to begin our analysis in the 18th century. Delinquency did not come about suddenly but was the product of a continuing stream of cultural change, demographic upheaval, and institutional experimentation (Schlossman, 1977:55).

EIGHTEENTH-CENTURY CHILDHOOD AND ORGANIZATION[1]

Although Puritan child-raising practices were by no means universal throughout the colonies, the moralist principles they espoused seem to have had great impact upon 19th-century reformers—the 17th-century principles stressing obedience, submission to authority, hard work, modesty, and chastity. Furthermore, the small towns in which the colonists lived were admirably suited to an implementation of these principles.

Few individuals or families in colonial times commanded the kinds of resources, tools, or labor that would free them from dependence upon their neighbors. Life was dominated by a subsistence existence in which cooperation was vital. "Common goals demanded community action" (Rothman, 1971:12). Most people were Protestant and worshiped at the same church. In many parts of the country, particularly New England, there were few outsiders to intrude upon the daily routine of the average citizen. Frequent marriages turned many neighbors into relatives, and daily contacts with a limited number of people fostered a reliance upon strong, informal social control.

In short, the environmental conditions of the time produced a kind of community interdependence and insularity that facilitated local community control, an emphasis upon individual responsibility, and a distrust of outside influence. There were exceptions, of course, especially toward the latter part of the 18th century. But, even then, change was relative. People still had to band together to build water lines, to protect themselves, or to care for the old, the sick, or the poor.

---

[1] The framework for this analysis relies heavily upon David J. Rothman's provocative work, *The Discovery of the Asylum* (1971). Attention is invited to this excellent volume for greater detail and for extended documentation of many of the points made here.

Family, church, and community

Life was dominated by a network of three major social institutions: family, church, and community. "Families were to raise their children to respect law and authority, the church was to oversee not only family discipline but adult behavior, and the members of the community were to supervise one another to detect and correct the first signs of deviancy" (Rothman, 1971:16). The values and beliefs surrounding this network provided whatever explanations or solutions needed to deal with the behavior of both children and adults.

The family was the guardian of the public as well as the private good. The functions it was expected to perform and the rules set forth for doing so were prescribed in the tracts and sermons of the day (Moody, 1715:17–19; Wadsworth, 1719:44–58). Parents should love their children and provide for them. "He that provides not for his own, especially those of his own house, hath denied the faith, and is worse than an infidel" (I Timothy 8). Conversely, as the following catechism indicates, children were expected to reciprocate with obedience and respect (Bremner, 1970, 1:32):

> *Question:* What is the fifth commandment?
> *Answer:* Honor thy father and thy mother, that thy days may be long in the land which the Lord thy God giveth thee.
> *Question:* Who are here meant by father and mother?
> *Answer:* All our superiors, whether in family, school, church, and commonwealth.
> *Question:* What is the honor due to them?
> *Answer:* Reverence, obedience, and (when I am able) recompense.

Disobedience to authority could only lead to destruction. "Appetites and passions unrestricted become furious in youth; and ensure *dishonor, disease,* and an *untimely death*" (Rothman, 1971:17).

These admonitions for children, like most of

the rules for adult conduct, revealed the strength of religious influence. The church tended not only to dominate family discipline and individual behavior, but to provide the core set of values around which community life was organized. The assumption prevailed that the existing social order was not accidental but divinely inspired. The church, as a consequence, set strict standards, stressed the need to observe them, and related obedience to eternal rewards and punishments. The person who came from a well-regulated family, worked hard, and attended church was obviously adhering to God's will. Even the legal codes of the time reflected the influence of religious belief.

Deviance and sin

The colonists were concerned about deviant behavior and adopted harsh methods for dealing with it. But they did not see it as a critical social problem in the sense that they blamed themselves or their communities for it, nor did they expect to eliminate it. Crime and evil, they believed, were inherent in people and, therefore, endemic to society (Rothman, 1971:115). To some Americans later in the 19th century this was a pessimistic and unenlightened view which they rejected. To the colonists, however, it made sense.

The reason lay in their religious explanation for deviance; they equated crime with sin. Hence, their criminal codes defined a wide range of behaviors as criminal—witchcraft, sexual misconduct, disrespect for parents, property crimes, blasphemy, or murder—and drew few distinctions between adults and children or between major and minor offenses. Any offense was a sure sign "that the offender was destined to be a public menace and a damned sinner" (Rothman, 1971:15–17).

At first blush, such thinking might appear to be contrary to the heavy emphasis colonists placed upon family life. If the seeds of crime and sin are present in everyone, why the heavy emphasis upon training children? The answer is that the colonists did not share the modern belief that people can be easily shaped into some desirable form. By nature, they felt, people are forever inclined to the temptations of the flesh. The purpose of training, therefore, is to secure the strict obedience of children to correct conduct, not to assume that evil impulses can ever be totally eliminated. Thus, the colonists were not bothered by a strong impulse to rehabilitate sinners once they had sinned. Rather, their transgressions demanded retribution. If offenders were allowed to escape, others would be implicated in their crimes, and God would be displeased.

The most common punishments were the fine and the whip, but wide use was made of such mechanisms of shame as the stocks, the pillory, and, occasionally, branding. Both the stocks and the pillory were located in a public place. The stocks held the offender while sitting down, with his head and hands locked in the frame. The pillory held him while standing up. In both, he was subject not only to physical pain and discomfort but to public scorn and ridicule. In some instances, he might also be whipped. In others, he might have his ears nailed to the pillory. Occasionally, criminals were driven through town in a cart and then whipped. Offenders were also branded with a *T* for thief, with a *B* for blasphemy, or with an *A* for adultery. In all these instances, shame as well as pain was a source of control (Barnes, 1972:56–67).

Even capital punishment served a protective as well as retributive function. The criminal codes prescribed a long list of death-penalty offenses—arson, horse stealing, robbery, burglary, sodomy, murder, and many others. Sending occasional offenders to the gallows for these crimes was a method of ridding the community of them forever. So was the practice of permanently banishing them from their home communities. And, since the colonists devoted little attention to reform, they built no prisons. Instead, the small jails found in most towns were used primarily to hold offenders awaiting trial or debtors who had yet to meet their obligations. The American invention of the prison was yet to come (Rothman, 1971:48–53).

The child offender

What was the status of the child offender in this 18th-century social system? How did she or he fare?

First, there was no distinct legal category called "juvenile delinquency." Americans still relied on the English common law which specified that children under the age of seven could not be guilty of a serious crime. Between the ages of 8 and 14, they might be presumed innocent unless proved otherwise. Juries were expected to pay close attention to the child, and, if he was capable of discerning the nature of his sins, he could be convicted and even sentenced to death. Anyone over the age of 14, presumably, was judged as an adult, although some colonies made exceptions. In Pennsylvania, for example, only youths over the age of 16 could receive such severe penalties for noncapital offenses as public whipping (Bremner, 1970, I:307–308; Platt, 1969:187–188).

Although the long list of forbidden criminal offenses applied to everyone, there were some that applied only to children: rebelliousness, disobedience, sledding on the sabbath, or playing ball on public streets. In some colonies, the penalty for rebelliousness against parents was death: "If a man have a stubborn or rebellious son of sufficient years of understanding, viz. 16, . . . such a son shall be put to death" (Bremner, 1970, 1:38). In other places, the prescribed punishment was whipping. In actual practice, however, courts and juries were often lenient towards the young. Children were often acquitted after a nominal trial or pardoned if found guilty. Some young children were severely punished or even put to death, but the latest available evidence suggests that it may have been less common that originally thought (Platt, 1969:183).

In many ways, elaborate legal machinery for children was unnecessary in the small-town colonial environment because the family, neighborhood, school, and apprenticeship system served so well as a tight-knit mechanism of social control. Thus, while town members may have shrunk from punishing children as criminals, they did not shrink from punishing them as subservient beings. Caning was a commonly accepted practice and was widely used. Moreover, if a family was unable to control, or to educate its own children to the satisfaction of town officials, it had the power to remove those children from their own home and to place them in others where they would receive a "decent" and "Christian" education (Rothman, 1971:14).

Treatment of poverty

In the nineteenth century, Americans came to view poverty, along with disordered families, as the roots of juvenile misconduct and crime. Eighteenth-century Americans, by contrast, clearly separated the two. They did not believe, as Americans came later to believe, that being poor would almost automatically lead to illegal behavior. Rather, their religious beliefs provided them with a much different view of poverty (Rothman, 1971:7–14).

They accepted the long-standing Christian belief that the poor would always be with us. They did not lament their presence as evidence of a tragic breakdown in social organization but "serenely asserted that the presence of the poor was a God-given opportunity for men to do good" (Rothman, 1971:7). The presence of hungry children or poor widows, for example, was not evidence of God's lack of concern. Quite the contrary. Because of their presence, persons at all levels of society could be benefited. The poor would be given charity, and industrious stewards could do God's work by providing it.

Such pervasive beliefs led to a situation in which people did not fear and distrust the poor as they were later to be feared. By providing spiritual sanction for earthly good works, the more common reactions to poverty were pity and sympathy. The one major exception was the idle ne'er-do-well who might be told to move on to some other town. But the sickly, the elderly, a widow with children, or a family down on its luck received help in one of two forms: "outdoor relief," wherein they received food and care in their own homes, or "indoor relief," wherein they went to live or to board in the homes of others. As a result, poor adults did not live in constant dread of the poorhouse, and children, simply because they were destitute, did not face the prospect of being confined in a state institution. Such institutions, with rare exceptions, did not even exist. It was the duty of townspeople to care for the children.

Treatment of minorities

The historical literature says little about the influence of black people on community organization during this period. This fact is striking in light of the size of the black population. In 1775, there were approximately 500,000 slaves in the colonies, or about one black in every five inhabitants (Bremner, 1970, 1:316). There were a few free Negroes whose ranks were swelled somewhat during the War for Independence, but their impact upon the nature of organized community life appears to have been slight. This meant that while black children were expected to adhere to the legal rules of the white community they benefited little from any advantages it had to offer. Some slaves were taught to read and write, but the legal codes of the 1800s still suggested that slave

children should be kept in utter ignorance and subservience as a means of protecting the security of whites (Bremner, 1970, I:317–318).

Northern states, one after another, began to take steps to free the slaves during the latter part of the 18th century, but a few slaves could still be found in those states on the eve of the Civil War. As a result, slave owners had almost complete legal authority. Short of willful murder, where the state might step in, an owner could do almost anything to a slave. Since the slave family did not exist in a legal sense, it was not protected by the law. Eighteenth-century owners could separate parents and children or keep them together as they wished. There were instances in which kindly owners or authorities would act to protect the needs of a mother and her children, but such practices were the result of informal, not official, practices.

NINETEENTH-CENTURY ENLIGHTENMENT

Colonial social organization did not survive for long into the 19th century. After the War of Independence, Americans were subjected to a series of changes which, on the one hand, were intoxicating but which, on the other, altered irrevocably the tightly knit communities to which they were accustomed.

Changes in belief

Those Americans who framed the Declaration of Independence and the Constitution relied upon the philosophy of the Enlightenment for many of their ideas (Becker, 1932). Whereas the religious doctrine of the moralist and religious reformers of the past two centuries had suggested that people were inherently depraved and foreordained to a particular destiny, the philosophy of the Enlightenment was individualistic and stressed universal and unlimited human progress.

Through the use of reason and the application of the principles of democracy, humanity could achieve unimagined heights. Optimism, not pessimism, was the cornerstone of Enlightenment thinking. Furthermore, newly won independence was in itself evidence that the new philosophy worked. America's destiny, as well as that of its people, was of divine origin.

Just as they began to cast off the strictures of some of their former theological beliefs, Americans began to feel that some of their 18th-century methods of social control were obsolete (Rothman, 1971:57–59). They reasoned that the legal codes of the mother country had stifled their better inclinations and had caused them to imitate the crude customs of the Old World (Bremner, 1970:104). They were encouraged in this belief by such philosophers of the Enlightenment as Francois Voltaire (1694–1778) and Charles de Montesquieu (1698–1775), but particularly by Cesare Beccaria (1738–1794), an Italian. Inspired by Voltaire's and Montesquieu's attacks on the notorious abuses and cruelties of the criminal law, Beccaria proposed a series of reforms in 1764 designed to make the treatment of law violators more equitable, more rational, and more humane (Monachesi, 1960).

The administration of justice, Beccaria argued, could not be left in the hands of the nobility or in those of their judicial minions. Instead, the only hope for a just and equitable system was to write laws that reflected the will of the people, and then to constrain the officials who enforced the laws with systematic procedures. Furthermore, the countries in which punishments had been the most severe were those in which the bloodiest deeds had been committed. A more enlightened society, by contrast, is one in which law and legal procedure take precedence over self-serving, secretive, and arbitrary officials, and in which the severity of punishment is reduced. Moderate punishments, equitably and swiftly administered, will accomplish what severe punishments fail to accomplish.

Such a message may have found fertile soil in the colonies because it seemed to square so well with the revolutionary experience. British legislation, like harsh punishments, had often seemed arbitrary and vengeful to Americans. They had been led to rebellion and had proved successful. Harshly imposed controls on them had not worked. Hence, under the heady influence of their newfound freedoms, they significantly altered their responses to the lawbreaker: criminal codes were rewritten early in the 19th century; steps were taken to make due process a greater part of the administration of justice; the death penalty for robbery, burglary, sodomy, and witchcraft was repealed; penalties for such acts as petty larceny were reduced; and such corporal punishments as burning offenders' hands, cutting off their ears, or nailing them to the pillory were abandoned. In some states, legislation against whipping was also written, and the only crime left punishable by death was murder (Bremner, 1970:106–107). No longer, said a number of influential reformers, could Americans abide the use of barbarous punishments, particularly for children. Americans had a grand mission to fulfill, and one way they could do it was to uplift a formerly hopeless segment of mankind: the criminal class (Rothman, 1971:60–61).

Altered explanations for crime and sin

Ways by which this mission could be accomplished were suggested by the new explanations for deviant behavior that began to emerge in the late 18th and early 19th centuries. More and more, Americans began to reject the older colonial notions that crime and sin were synonymous, and that lawbreaking was the result of inborn tendencies and the handiwork of the devil. Such theological conceptions were losing their currency. In their stead, the belief grew that deviancy could be traced back to early childhood. Almost always, there had been a breakdown in family discipline. Orphaned children or the children of drunks and licentious parents were those most likely to fall prey to temptation and vice. The typical road to crime was paved, first, by a lack of discipline and rudeness, then, drinking and intemperance, and, finally, lawbreaking itself. Criminals were those who were inadequately prepared early in life to take their places as respectable members of the community.

Another social evil—community corruption—was soon added to that of family disorganization (Rothman, 1971:57–59). Between 1790 and 1830, the population of the United States grew markedly, as did the size and density of several cities and states. Massachusetts doubled in numbers, Pennsylvania tripled, and New York increased fivefold. When George Washington became president, most people lived in towns having less than 2,500 inhabitants. By the time Andrew Jackson was inaugurated in 1829, more than 1 million people resided in towns larger than that. Some notion of the trends that were underway can be gleaned from the fact that in 1750 there were only about 1.25 million people in this country. By 1850, the figure had reached over 23 million—an incredible growth (U.S. Bureau of the Census, 1955). Simultaneously, as manufacturing and commerce continued to develop, the simple economic and social organization of the colonies was no longer adequate. Again, there was pressure to reconsider existing methods of social control.

The memories of small tightly knit towns were still fresh in the minds of many Americans so that they retained firm notions about the way a well-ordered community ought to appear. Thus, when they looked about them and saw growth, hordes of new immigrants, change, and instability, they concluded that

these factors also promoted deviant behavior. Community disorder went hand in hand with the disorder of unstable families (Schlossman, 1977: 19–20).

Such ideas demanded a major turnabout in thinking. Rather than preoccupation with the internal evils of sinners, reformers now had to be concerned with the external forces that shaped them—a significant turnabout indeed, and it had paradoxical consequences for children. If, on the one hand, deviant behavior was endemic to societal life and not to the human soul, then it could be rooted out or at least greatly reduced! If the criminal was no longer innately depraved, he could be redeemed! If there were young children in danger of becoming criminal, their misconduct could be prevented! The grounds for optimism were considerable.

On the other hand, the impact of such thinking could do little to alter the child-raising principles derived from the 18th century. Indeed, if families and communities, and not the devil, were at fault, then even greater attention to childhood was required. Parents were warned of the awful consequences of an absence of discipline and admonished to take stern measures against any loss of family control. Likewise, the attention of community leaders was directed toward the sources of vice, evil, and societal corruption:

> Vicious propensities are imbibed at a very early age by children in the crowded population of a city. Parents, whose extreme poverty, casual calamity, or moral turpitude induces a neglect of their off-spring, expose them at once to be caught up by the profligate and knavish, to be made unsuspecting agents in the commission of offenses, and to be trained into habits of idleness, cunning, and predatory vagrancy. . . . Children, too, accomplish petty thefts with ease, and with frequent impunity; they pass unnoticed by the busy or, if detected, are treated with indulgence. Success gradually emboldens; they become proud of their skill, form combinations among themselves, and

grow ambitious to surpass each other in their daily contributions to the hoard of a common guide and pretended protector" (Committee of the Board of Managers of the Philadelphia House of Refuge, 1835:8–12; Sanders, 1970:363–364).

Rothman says that 19th-century Americans were so sensitive to childhood, so concerned with matters moral that "they stripped away the years from adults and made everyone into a child" (1971:76). Yet, they were also faced with serious problems: How was social order to be maintained? What were the best means for reducing the effects on children of poor family discipline and community instability?

THE INSTITUTION AS A PANACEA

In seeking answers to these questions, Americans took a step that was to leave an indelible imprint on the future treatment of both children and adults in trouble, and was to change irrevocably the search for community solutions to deviant behavior that had characterized the social order of colonial society. Out of the many methods that might have been tried to prevent crime and correct offenders, leading reformers chose *confinement*. They built prisons for adults and houses of refuge and orphan asylums for children. Asylums for abandoned children had been used in England and elsewhere in Europe for some time, but the idea was entirely new that places of confinement could be used effectively both to punish and correct criminals and to substitute for the family and community as the best method for raising neglected children. Not only was this idea a social invention of profound significance, but it was viewed as an extremely humane one as well— an answer to the brutality of prior methods of control and punishment (Bremner, 1970, 1:122; Schlossman, 1977).

Pennsylvania led the way in 1790 by converting the old Walnut Street Jail in Philadelphia into a state prison and in 1829 by erecting a huge and striking edifice called Eastern State Penitentiary. Through the mercies of incarceration rather than physical torment, stigma in the stocks, or death on the scaffold, the criminal would learn the errors of his ways. Deterrence, not revenge, would protect the community. Not to be outdone, New York erected the Newgate Prison in Greenwich Village in 1796 and built a rival to Pennsylvania's huge edifice around 1820 at Auburn. Other states soon followed suit (McKelvey, 1968:6–11).

The first houses of refuge, designed to separate children from hardened criminals, were built by private philanthropists in Boston and New York in 1825, and in Philadelphia in 1828. The assumptions that led to their construction were striking.

First, they were designed to house, not merely juvenile criminals, but all problem children: the runaway, disobedient, or vagrant children who were in danger of falling prey to loose women, taverns, gambling halls, or theatres. Given what they considered to be laudatory goals, reformers were not bothered by any thought that they might be infringing on the rights or wishes of these children. "A good dose of institutionalization could only work to the child's benefit" (Rothman, 1971:209).

Second, the people who sponsored and managed the first houses of refuge took the public school, not the family, as the model to be emulated. Children would be saved through education, hard work, and stringent discipline rather than through the loving care of parental surrogates:

> The whole community is deeply interested in its accomplishments. It has for its object . . . employment of the idle;—instruction of the ignorant;—reformation of the depraved;— relief of the wretched;—a general diffusion of good morals;—enlargement of virtuous society;—and the universal protection of

property and life (Committee of the Board of Managers of the Philadelphia House of Refuge, 1835:8–12. See Sanders, 1970:366).

Those who managed the house of refuge, says Schlossman, were very frank in describing it ". . . as an instrument for compelling lower-class children to conform to middle-class standards of behavior." It would deter crime and "would reinforce the crumbling authority of impoverished parents. . . , giving them a potent symbol of fear with which to scare 'ungracious and disobedient' children into humility and quiescence." (1977:24).

Although orphan asylums were not constructed to house young criminals, their mission was much the same. In addition to abandoned and orphaned children, they accepted the children of women without husbands or even those whose parents were alive but poor. Such children, reformers reasoned, should not be penalized merely because they were the offspring of degenerates or paupers (Rothman, 1971:207). Like the house of refuge, the orphan asylum was to become an instrument of the new social order whose purpose it was to produce the ideal child. It caused considerable shock, therefore, when these institutions were branded as failures by a new generation of reformers.

Failures of the panacea

By 1850, criticisms of house of refuge and asylums had begun to mount; by 1870, there was an overwhelming demand for change. Rather than becoming models of care, orphan asylums and houses of refuge had become prisonlike warehouses for ever larger numbers of children from the margins of society. Furthermore, said Elijah Devoe, assistant superintendent at the New York House of Refuge, various means of corporal punishment are "liable to be used everywhere at all times of the day" (Schlossman, 1977:35). Rather than turning out ideal children, therefore, asylums and houses of refuge were producing young things who either marched, thought, and acted like robots, or who were more criminal than ever (Bremner, 1970, I:696–697; Rothman, 1971:258–260).

In response to this state of affairs, one group argued that the examplar for saving children should not be the large institution, but the family; a rural home was "God's reformatory" (Schlossman, 1977:45). Beginning in the 1850s, therefore, thousands of children were sent each year from large cities such as New York to live and work with farmers. Indeed, this movement exemplified the older colonial belief that "the place for the poor in a Christian community is the home of those who are not poor" (Schlossman, 1977:46). But in the face of momentous social change and a large population of children, this movement was destined to fail.

In addition to the Civil War, the last half of the 19th century was marked by ever more urban growth and instability. Immigrant groups, moreover, were seen as contributing disproportionately to this mess. As early as 1850, the children of foreigners constituted almost three quarters of the population of the New York House of Refuge, more than half of that of the Cincinnati Refuge, and two thirds of that of the Philadelphia Refuge (Rothman, 1971:261:2). The parents of these children were often penniless when they arrived in the United States and thus found it necessary to remain in the big cities where they swelled the ranks of the unemployed and often contributed to high crime rates. Furthermore, they alarmed Americans of Anglo-Saxon origin by bringing new customs with them—the Catholic religion, strange sexual habits, and new ways of talking and behaving. And since these traits were deviant by definition, they further contributed to the belief that immigrants were an inferior lot and a threat to social order.

The tendency to depreciate immigrant, poor, and criminal groups was also reinforced by the emergence of new scientific theories in the second half of the 19th century. Americans heard about Charles Darwin's notion that life is a competitive struggle for existence and that only the fittest survive. Applied to the societal realm, such ideas were pessimistic, in contrast to the optimism of the Enlightenment, and suggested that among men, as among the lower animals, nature selects the fittest and weeds out the unfit. Some people are biologically predetermined to succeed, others to fail. The implication was that destitution, poverty, and crime were the result of innate inferiority (Hofstader, 1959:31–50).

An Italian physician named Cesare Lombroso lent further confirmation to such ideas in his study of criminals. He concluded that lawbreakers are born, not made. Some are measurable physical types who are throwbacks to a more primitive level of development; others, while not physically deformed, are mentally defective (Vold, 1958:28–32).

Such ideas appeared in the thinking of leading reformers. Enoch Wines, the most prominent reformer of the 1870s, described the criminal as being the consequence of three great "hindrances": depravity, physical degeneracy, and bad environment (Henderson, 1910:12,19). Peter Caldwell, a reformatory superintendent, said that a typical delinquent is "cradled in infamy, imbibing with its earliest natural nourishment the germs of depraved appetite, and reared in the midst of people whose lives are an atrocious crime against natural and divine law and the rights of society" (Platt, 1969:52).

Institutionalization reaffirmed

It was likely that such reasoning led a new generation of post–Civil War reformers to reaffirm the utility of children's institution, despite their initial failure. The task of saving children, if anything, had taken on more monumental proportions:

This whole mass of pestilent and pestiferous juvenility is already supported at your expense . . . They all have mouths to feed and bodies to be clothed . . . not only at the expense of your purses, but at the far more extravagant and alarming expense of your public and private morals (Report of Joint Special Committee, Hartford, 1863:2–7. See Sanders, 1970:401).

Hence, reformers reasoned that the fault with surrogate places of child raising lay in poor execution, not in concept; the methods, not the goals, had been bad. Furthermore, as the above comment indicates, the literature of the period reveals the persistent ambivalence of people toward the "pestiferous" juveniles of the period. Nonetheless, hope remained.

In the famous Cincinnati Prison Congress of 1870, delegates framed a Declaration of Principles that was to incorporate a new philosophy, not only for children, but for adults as well. This new philosophy was less punitive than the one that prevailed when the first prisons and houses of refuge were built. An institution governed by force and fear, the declaration stated, is an institution mismanaged. Punishment that degrades is a mistake. Degradation "destroys every better impulse and aspiration. It crushes the weak, irritates the strong, and indisposes all to submission and reform." Why not try the effects of reward upon inmates? Cultivate their self-respect, educate them, provide them with honorable labor, and teach them self-control. These are the principles that should govern institutional life (Henderson, 1910:39–63).

Symbolic of these principles, some new names were found for places of confinement—"industrial schools" for destitute, neglected, and disobedient children, and "reformatories" for young criminals. Moreover, new guidelines stressed the importance of locating both of these institutions in the country and of seeing that industrial schools, if not reformatories, emulated the character of the well-disciplined family. "Add to [them] the holy and softening influence of a quiet, moral, and Christian home and family, and we are complete" (Sanders, 1970:404).

Once again, reformers were prepared to keep marginal children for as long as it took to save them. For example, consider that which was prescribed for the "giddy" and "restless" girl (Hart, 1910:72).

> When she reaches the age of 14 or 15, she becomes restless, uneasy, discontented. She chafes under restraint, desires more liberty, wants to choose her own associations and recreations. She wants to go out at night. She craves pretty clothes and admiration. Perhaps she is the recipient of flattering and dangerous attentions from some young man. . . . The girl is not vicious, she does not want to do anything wrong, but she is in a critical and dangerous situation. She is giddy, headstrong, easily influenced. She needs to be kept safe for a few years or two, until she comes to herself, and in the meantime she ought to receive such training as will either enable her to support herself or will make her a more efficient housewife and mother. It is for this class of girls that [industrial] schools are now demanded.

The new reformatory, by contrast, would be more stern, even though it would make use of enlightened principles. Indeed, when the country's model reformatory opened in Elmira, New York, it looked more like a military school than anything else. Z. R. Brockway (1910), its first superintendent, stressed that it should be run like a monarchy so that the offender's life could be stringently regulated according to scientific principles. He devised a marking system for classifying offenders into different categories; an indeterminate sentence which would allow officials to keep delinquents until they were reformed; a strict regimen of education, work, military drill, and hard physical exercise; and supervision upon release to the community. Nothing would be left to chance or to well-meaning but misguided

people who did not understand the systematic controls that were needed.

There were a few dissenters from this renewed faith in institutions, and most southern states did not bother to create them at all (Bremner, 1970, I:672; Platt, 1969:61–62). Otherwise, the movement once again swept the major industrial states. But, by 1900, it had come full circle, just like the refuge movement before it. Institutions were still not a panacea.

From our privileged vantage point, it does not seem surprising that places of confinement should have failed. Not only were they poor devices for socializing people, but even if they had been built on every street corner, it is unlikely that they could have done much to stabilize the effects of immigration, urban growth, industrialization, and ideological change, or to have served as a surrogate parent capable of producing the same kind of offspring as a nuclear family located in a small rural community. The means were totally inappropriate to the goals. But these are not the only reasons that a search began for other alternatives. By the end of the 19th century, child savers were concerned not merely with devices for controlling "pestiferous" juveniles, but with doing more to insure the protected status of all children.

THE "RIGHTS" OF CHILDREN

Through several centuries, the values and beliefs associated with the modern concept of childhood had resulted in the development of a series of "rights" for children. But these rights were not of the constitutional variety—the right to free speech, to freedom from search and seizure, to freedom of assembly, or to freedom of religion. Rather, they were rights of a more fundamental type.

Nurturance rights

In contrast to the indifference which children had experienced during the Middle

Ages, the discovery of childhood gradually led to the acceptance of a number of *nurturance* rights for them: the rights to life, to food, clothing, and shelter, and to proper moral standards to follow. The presence of indoor and outdoor relief for them in the 18th century, or the construction of houses of refuge, asylums, and industrial schools in the 19th century, were evidence of a commitment to those rights. Despite their ambivalence, people no longer accepted the idea that unwanted children, even those of the unworthy poor, could be abandoned or killed at the whim of adults. But much remained to be done.

Since it was clear that all children whose rights were not being protected could not be locked up, reforms of a more dramatic nature were required—reforms designed to protect them from economic exploitation, to see that their parents cared for them properly, to see that they were educated, and to protect them with a new set of laws and legal procedures. Hence, the late 19th and early 20th centuries were marked by efforts to make these reforms a part of the institutional fabric of society.

Mandatory education

Prior to the Civil War, many states had passed laws requiring that children attend school, that those under 12 be prohibited from employment, and that the work day of a child over 12 be limited to ten hours. Although such laws were supposed to provide some protection for the young, they proved largely unworkable. Employers ignored them; many children worked rather than attending school; and parents even joined in circumventing the law. Lower-class children, however, were the ones most likely to be exploited. While hard work was considered morally desirable by most people, it was the poorer classes who found the employment of children, to the exclusion of school, an economic necessity. The reality of circumstance in an entrepreneurial and capitalistic society kept them at a disadvantage (Bremner, 1970, I:559).

As the country industrialized, child employment increased. According to the census of 1870, one in every eight children was employed, but by 1900 the figure had risen to one in six. The greatest increases came in industry: one third of all workers in Southern mills, for example, were children, more than half of them between the ages of 10 and 13. Furthermore, more than half of the children in industry were the children of immigrants.

But in contrast to prior centuries, such practices generated references to "cannibalism," "child slavery" and the "slaughter of the innocents," and led to a crusade against them by lawyers, social workers, various charitable groups, and even some industrialists (Bremner, 1970, I:601–604). By the dawn of the 20th century, therefore, most states had passed laws regulating child labor and requiring that children attend school. "Educate the rising generation mentally, morally, physically," a U.S. senator told his colleagues, "and this nation and this world would reach the millennium within 100 years" (Welter, 1962:151).

Distinctive legal rights

Before education and the other nurturance rights for children could be enforced, however, some legal teeth were required. Experience had indicated that children's rights would not be realized voluntarily. Hence, an entirely new set of legal principles, solely for children, gradually evolved—principles that contrasted greatly with those that governed the constitutional rights of adults, particularly adults who were charged with violating the criminal law.

It will be recalled that the American Constitution and the legal codes rewritten after the War of Independence were designed to insure the protection of adults from unreasonable invasions of their personal privacy and from the arbitrary actions of legal authorities. Furthermore, any adult charged with a crime was assured the protections of due process: the right to legal counsel, a clear statement of charges, proceedings that protected the accused from hearsay and other forms of questionable evidence, and a jury trial. In short, carefully prescribed guidelines, not the arbitrary discretion of authorities, were to govern the legal processing of adults.

The principles that evolved for the legal treatment of juveniles, by contrast, were strikingly different. Because the modern concept of childhood suggested that children were immature, it was assumed that they were incapable of appreciating the consequences of their behavior. They were dependent people, like the mentally defective or the insane. Consequently, the principles of due process did not apply to them. Rather, authorities required broad discretionary powers to act in their behalf, not only to insure their protection but to inquire into the most private of family and personal matters. If children were to be properly raised, and their nurturance rights assured, the state required legal means—part criminal and part civil—by which to make this possible.

In tracing the origins of these principles, legal writers are fond of citing an English doctrine, *Parens Patriae,* which emerged in medieval times and which gave the crown the right to intervene in family affairs as a means of protecting the property rights of juveniles. They are likewise fond of indicating that English Common Law—unwritten traditions based on reason and common sense—also tended to protect young children from the full penalties of the criminal law. But it was not until the 19th century in both England and America that a unique system of justice, solely for juveniles, began to take shape. And even this process took a century to complete.

Throughout much of the 19th century, the laws and legal procedures that granted power to authorities to place neglected and dependent children in asylums and houses of refuge without the benefits of due process were constitutionally questionable and far from clear. As a consequence, they were legally challenged; the most noteworthy case may have been that of *The People* v. *Turner* in 1870 (Schlossman, 1977:11–13).

A boy by the name of Daniel O'Connell had been incarcerated in the Chicago Reform School under an Illinois law which specified that children under age 16 found to be "vagrant . . . destitute of proper parental care of . . . growing up in mendicancy, ignorance, or vice" could be confined until they were reformed or reached the age of 21. Daniel's father sought to have him released.

Mr. Justice Thornton, writing the majority opinion, ordered Daniel discharged from custody. "The disability of minors," he wrote, "does not make slaves or criminals of them. . . . Even criminals cannot be imprisoned for misfortune. Destitution of proper parental care, ignorance, idleness, and vice, are misfortunes, not crimes" (See Bremner, 1970, II:485–487). But the logic of Judge Thornton's argument notwithstanding, the O'Connell case stirred hardly a ripple. Instead, virtually every other higher court decision affirmed the right of the state to intervene in the lives of children without having to insure that their constitutional rights were protected (Schlossman, 1977:11–14). Consequently a conflict over which set of rights should dominate was set in motion which, even today, continues to bedevil us.

At the same time, reformers seemed to grow increasingly uncomfortable with the practice of adjudicating the cases of children in the criminal courts. It was not that they doubted the wisdom of discarding the protections of due process for children. Indeed, their concerns were just the opposite; that is, they were convinced that such procedures, as administered by the criminal courts, were too mechanistic and too insensitive to the child. In 1869, therefore, Massachusetts passed a law requiring agents of the State Board of Charities to attend the trials of children to protect their interests and to make recommendations to the judge. The City of Boston went even further. In 1870, it began holding separate hearings for juveniles under 16, as did New York in 1877 (Bremner, 1970, II:485–501).

In a similar way, the last part of the 19th century was filled with protests over the continued confinement of young law violators in jails and prisons. In 1883, for example, the Chicago Women's Club engaged in an effort to improve jail conditions for adult criminals. But when they began to visit local lockups, they were horrified to find that these places still held a significant number of young children, all the grand talk about special institutions for youth notwithstanding. Consequently, the focus of their efforts changed. Rather than saving criminals, they would save children (Lathrop, 1925).

After failing to provide schooling and other amenities for these incarcerated children, the women were ultimately led to a more radical idea: why not go further than Boston and New York? Why not create a *juvenile* court? Indeed, why not legislate an entirely separate system of justice for juveniles?

CREATION OF THE JUVENILE COURT

In pursuit of these ideas, the Chicago Women's Club drafted a bill in 1895 to be presented to the Illinois Legislature. But when they submitted it to their legal advisor for his approval, he questioned its constitutionality. It was too broad, he suggested, too lacking in procedural safeguards. Like Judge Thornton, 25 years before, he questioned whether the state had the right to intervene in the lives of children for noncriminal offenses, or to deprive them of their liberty without the

protections of due process (Lathrop, 1925).

The club members took this advice to heart, intending to drop the project. But when a number of other influential people learned about it—clergymen, lawyers, judges, and prison wardens—they felt it should be continued. Consequently, when the Illinois Conference of Charities met in 1898, its sole topic was children. After reviewing the proposed court, a new act was drafted by the conference. The Chicago Bar Association then threw its support behind the act, and the Illinois Legislature passed it.

This new legislation was broad and sweeping in character and gave the juvenile court jurisdiction over all children under the age of 16 who were in some kind of trouble. It provided for a special judge, a separate courtroom, and separate records, and it specified that court sessions were to be informal rather than formal. Indeed, the new law was to be "liberally construed to the end . . . that the care, custody, and discipline of a child shall approximate . . . that which should be given by its parents" (*Revised Statutes of Illinois,* 1899, Sec. 21). Consequently, the juvenile court could not be encumbered by all the formalities of the criminal trial. What family could operate effectively if the resolution of its difficulties required official indictments, prosecutors, defense attorneys, strict rules of evidence, and a jury? These features of adult justice would only aggravate the problems of children.

In addition to a justice system tailored to families, moreover, new "detention homes" would be constructed to house children awaiting a hearing, rather than incarcerating them in jails, probation officers would be appointed to investigate and diagnose each child's problems, assist the judge, and supervise children in their own homes; and, if a child had to be incarcerated, it could not be with hardened criminals. In short, the new juvenile justice system was to be nothing less than society's new "superparent," charged with protecting the nurturance rights of all children—delinquent, dependent, or neglected—and with rehabilitating those who neede extended treatment.

Delinquent children

The way this new system was to be applied to juvenile lawbreakers was stated in idealistic terms before the American Bar Association in 1909 by Julian W. Mack, one of the first judges of the juvenile court in Chicago:

> Why isn't it just and proper to treat these juvenile offenders as we deal with the neglected children, as a wise and merciful father handles his own child whose errors are not discovered by the authorities? Why isn't it the duty of the State instead of asking merely whether a boy or a girl has committed the specific offense, to find out what he is, physically, mentally, morally, and then, if it learns that he is treading the path that leads to criminality, to take him in charge, not so much to punish as to reform, not to degrade but to uplift, not to crush but to develop, not to make him a criminal but a worthy citizen. (1910:296–297).

As Judge Mack's remarks indicate, those who invented the juvenile court saw themselves as decriminalizing the misconduct of children, not criminalizing it. First, delinquent behavior would be treated as something less than crime. Second, the court would intervene, not as a harsh and punitive monitor of evil conduct, but as a thoughtful, not unkindly, superparent. Third, the enforcement of rules would be characterized by help, not punishment; juveniles would be lent a hand rather than forced into conformity. The purpose of the court was to discover a child's problems and to correct them, not to respond to the acts he or she had committed as the criminal court did.

Other states were obviously charmed by these ideas because, within 10 years, 20 states and the District of Columbia had enacted similar laws, and within 20 years, all except 3 states had done so. By mid-20th century, in fact, all states and territories, and many foreign countries, had adopted similar laws (Caldwell, 1966:402–403).

Although most of these laws were modeled after the original Illinois statute, relatively few changes were made in them until very recently. For example, the South Dakota statute, which was not revised until 1968, defined a delinquent as:

> any child who, while under the age of 18 years, violates any law of this state or any ordinance of any city or town of this state; who is incorrigible, or intractable by parents, guardian, or custodian; who knowingly associates with thieves, vicious, or immoral persons; who, without cause and without the consent of its parents, guardian, or custodian, absents itself from its home or place of abode; who is growing up in idleness or crime; who fails to attend school regularly without proper reason therefor, if of compulsory school age; who repeatedly plays truant from school; who does not regularly attend school and is not otherwise engaged in any regular occupation or employment but loiters and idles away its time; who knowingly frequents or visits a house of ill repute; who knowingly frequents or visits any policy shop or place where any gaming device is operated; who patronizes, visits, or frequents any saloon or dram shop where intoxicating liquors are sold; who patronizes or visits any public poolroom where the game of billiards or pool is being carried on for pay or hire; who frequents or patronizes any wineroom or dance hall run in connection with or adjacent to any house of ill fame or saloon; who visits, frequents, or patronizes, with one of the opposite sex, any restaurant or other place where liquors may be purchased at night after the hours of nine o'clock; who is found alone with one of the opposite sex in a private apartment or room of any restaurant, lodging house, hotel, or other place at nighttime or who goes to any secluded place or is found

alone in such place with one of the opposite sex at nighttime with the evident purpose of concealing their acts; who wanders about the streets in the nighttime without being on any lawful business or lawful occupation, or habitually wanders about any railroad yards or tracks, or jumps or attempts to jump onto any moving train, or enters any car or engine without lawful authority; who writes or uses vile, obscene, vulgar, or indecent language, or smokes cigarettes or uses tobacco in any form; who drinks intoxicating liquors on any street, in any public place, or about any school house, or at any place other than its own home; or who is guilty of indecent, immoral, or lascivious conduct (Rubin, 1974:1–2).

Few laws could be more inclusive and still be enforceable. In the South Dakota law, for instance, only two or three lines were devoted to prohibiting the kinds of criminal acts for which adults can be charged—those which state that a child should not violate "any law of this state or any ordinance of any city or town of this state." Otherwise, all of the remaining lines were devoted to describing *status offenses*— offenses that apply only to children.

This way of defining delinquent behavior indicates why, even now, such behavior cannot be equated with criminal behavior. It covers much more ground than that. In virtually every case, state laws have represented an attempt to embody in formal language the modern concept of childhood. They have emphasized the dependent status of children and stressed the need to quarantine them from many activities in which adults are free to engage. It is true that these laws have concentrated on what children should *not* be, but, by turning them around, one can get a good picture of what legislators and other child savers have thought they *should* be.

The list suggested by the South Dakota statute, for example, is amazingly similar to those drawn up in the child-raising manuals of the 18th and 19th centuries, suggesting that the ideal child should be submissive to

authority, obedient, hardworking, a good student, sober, chaste, circumspect in habit, language, and associates, and should otherwise avoid even the appearance of evil by staying out late, wandering the street, being alone with a person of the opposite sex, or playing in dangerous places like railroad yards. According to these official rules, the child who avoids these acts and stays within the limits of his quarantine is playing the game of childhood appropriately. The one who commits them and violates his quarantine is delinquent.

This is not a very precise definition of delinquency. So ambiguous is it, in fact, that in 1949, one eminent lawyer-sociologist suggested that "delinquency has little specific behavioral content either in law or in fact." Because the juvenile court's philosophy has traditionally emphasized a child's background more than his or her conduct, and because its procedures have not been systematized, about all that can be said is that "the juvenile delinquent is a person who has been adjudicated as such by a court of proper jurisdiction" (Tappan, 1949:30). Nonetheless, this is the definition that was intended.

The goal of modern child savers was to legislate the morality of children so that the rules governing their conduct would be broader than the list covering adult behavior; otherwise, they could not insure that children would develop properly. And, because the announced goal of the court was assistance, not punishment, benevolence would triumph over any shortcomings in procedure (Platt, 1974):

> The fundamental function of a juvenile court is to put each child who comes before it in a normal relation to society as promptly and as permanently as possible, and that while punishment is not by any means to be dispensed with, it is to be made subsidiary and subordinate to that function. . . . As far as practicable [children] shall be treated, not as criminals, but as children in need of aid,

encouragement, and guidance. Proceedings against children . . . shall not be deemed to be criminal proceedings (Baker, 1910:321).

Dependent and Neglected Children

Attitudes toward, and the rules covering, dependent and neglected children were much the same as those toward delinquent children. That such children were viewed as being similar to delinquent ones is illustrated by the original Illinois statute. "The words dependent and neglected child," it said,

> shall mean any child who for any reason is destitute or homeless or abandoned; or dependent upon the public for support; or has not proper parental care or guardianship; or who habitually begs or receives alms; or who is found living in any house of ill fame or with any vicious or disreputable person; or whose home, by reason of neglect, cruelty, or depravity on the part of its parents, guardian, or other person in whose care it may be, is an unfit place for such a child; and any child under the age of eight years who is found peddling or selling any article, or singing or playing any musical instrument upon the street, or giving any public entertainment. (Bremner, 1970, II:507).

Besides noting that a dependent or neglected child might be homeless or destitute, this law described this child in much the same way that it and other laws also described the delinquent child. For example, it noted that a "dependent" child is one who begs for alms, lives in a house of ill fame, or lives with some vicious person. Yet, any difference between this child and the "delinquent" one who frequents saloons, loiters away his time, or stays out too late at night seems to be purely academic. For most of the century, there has been a tendency to equate the two types of children, probably because of the persistence of the 19th-century belief that poverty and neglect are inevitable precursors of criminal behavior. That is why, in attempting to understand both the meaning

of delinquency and the treatment of children, this broad equation of types must be kept in mind.

One must also keep in mind another important reason for dependent and neglected children to be brought under the umbrella of the juvenile court. Until the 19th century, children were treated as subservient subjects of parental and family government. They had no separate legal status of their own. In 1874, for example, the American Society for the Prevention of Cruelty to Animals was confronted with a case of cruelty to a little girl who had been beaten repeatedly and tormented by a foster mother. To the surprise of this society, it was found that the child had no protection under the law unless someone took up her cause and until the guilt of her foster mother could be established in an adult court (McCrea, 1910). Since no organization existed for the prevention of cruelty to children, new state laws charged the juvenile court with seeing the children whose nurturance rights were not being protected would be given protection and care.

Few people have questioned these functions of the juvenile court. Some serious questions have been raised, however, over the fact that legal rules traditionally have not drawn very sharp distinctions between the dependent or neglected and the delinquent child. In 1914, Flexner and Baldwin argued forcefully that the juvenile court should not have jurisdiction over the children who are not lawbreakers:

> For many years [poverty] was regarded as a valid reason for judicial interference with the family status. It is a sad commentary that we should still be wrestling with this question in our courts. The presence of the dependent or destitute child in court, presenting family or home conditions remediable simply by relief measures, is an injustice to the court, and a worse injustice to the child and to the family. (x–xi).

But comments like this attracted little attention. Instead, views like those expressed by Judge Edward Schoen of the Newark, New Jersey, juvenile court in 1921 were the popular ones:

> The field of the juvenile court is the maladjusted child, whom the State is in duty bound to protect, correct, and develop; and the duty of this tribunal is to follow up the case by ascertaining all the facts and circumstances in the life of the child, to determine in what particulars that child has been deprived of essentials for a full moral and physical development. And if, as is common experience, it is found that certain essentials are lacking in the environment in which the child is being reared, the State, *in loco parentis*, acting through its instrumentality, the juvenile court, must provide the essentials of which the child has thus far been deprived.

Court practices have also been criticized because they have seemed contrary to our older classical concept of justice. If a person is not really criminal, he or she should not even be in court, let alone be confined in an institution with proven offenders. Yet, these criticisms have often missed the point. According to the fundamental premises upon which legal rules for children were drawn, the failure to distinguish between neglected and delinquent children is not bad.

In theory, at least, the juvenile court was created to serve a different and much broader set of functions than the criminal court. It was devised to: raise the standards of child raising for society as a whole; act as a monitor over other societal institutions in order to insure that the young are not exploited or maltreated but are fed, loved, and educated; apply scientific knowledge to diagnose and cure the physical or emotional ills of children; and even prevent crime by serving as a catch basin for the children of poor, uncaring, or licentious parents (Schlossman, 1977:57–63).

Given this awesome but benevolent mandate, society's new superparent enjoyed widespread support for two thirds of the 20th century (Rosenheim, 1962). Although the juvenile court could be a gloved fist at times, the popular opinion was that its desirable aspects outweighted its undesirable ones. Lawyers remained ignorant of, or shied away from, the procedural dilemmas it posed, and when, on occasion, these dilemmas were raised, the constitutionality of the juvenile court was sustained by various appeal and supreme courts (Paulsen and Whitebread, 1974:4).

In recent years, by contrast, dissatisfaction with this concept of juvenile justice has mounted, and revolutionary changes are now being introduced. But since these changes are the product of recent events and ideologies, they will be left for discussion in later chapters. For now, it will be more instructive to recapitulate the long process that led, first, to the creation of the modern concept of childhood and, then, to the invention of delinquency as a direct outgrowth of that concept.

RECAPITULATION: THE EVOLUTION OF CHILDHOOD AND DELINQUENCY

Throughout this and previous chapters, we have seen that childhood and delinquency are social constructions, the products of an ongoing process of cultural change and institutional experimentation that has spanned many centuries. In order to grasp both the length and complexity of that process, it is useful to think of it as being comprised of three major epochs—the indifference to childhood, the discovery of childhood, and the preoccupation with childhood—each of which was characterized by a series of memorable developments.

Indifference to childhood

The first epoch was, at best, an epoch of indifference towards children. At worst, it has been described as a "nightmare" and a "catalog of atrocities":

From antiquity until 1100 or 1200 A.D., the deliberate killing or abandonment of children was regarded as casually as abortion is today. Legitimate but imperfect children, unwanted females, or illegitimate offspring were deliberately killed, were left to die of exposure, or were sold into slavery or prostitution.

Between 1300 and 1600, the incidence of infanticide decreased, but abandonment, if not deliberate killing, persisted in a series of institutionalized and widely accepted practices: newborn babies were farmed out to wet nurses until weaned; family life was not organized to nourish the emotional and physical needs of young children; and those over the age of seven received their educations by being apprenticed to the domiciles of others.

Living in filth and unprotected from the ravages of common childhood diseases, few youngsters survived the first years of life. As a consequence, infants were thought to exist in a sort of limbo, the childhood was not noteworthy in its own right.

Discovery of childhood

The second epoch—the *discovery of childhood*—overlapped the first:

During the 15th and 16th centuries (1400–1500 A.D.), children gradually became symbols of innocence and purity, and the well-to-do began to clothe them in distinctive dress and to take pleasure in their droll behavior.

During the 16th and 17th centuries (1500–1600 A.D.), the modern concept of childhood began to emerge: children were described as guileless, but corruptible; special tracts were written which set forth the new moral standards by which their lives should be governed; and moralists suggested that children should be carefully trained before they took their places in the adult world.

In the 17th and 18th centuries (1600–1700 A.D.), institutional adaptions to these beliefs were apparent: the nuclear family became more common, and schooling began to replace apprenticeship as a second source of early socialization. For the middle class, in particular, these two child-raising institutions comprised the ideal standard.

By the dawn of the 19th century (1800), the values associated with the concept of childhood had resulted in the espousal of a series of nurturance rights for *all* children, even those of the unworthy poor: the right to life, food, clothing, and shelter, and moral standards to follow. The length of childhood had also been extended, and age-segregation was more apparent.

Preoccupation with childhood

During the third epoch—the *preoccupation with childhood*—steps were taken to solidify the rights of children and to make them a part of the legal and bureaucratic structures of society:

The traumas engendered by rapid immigration, industrialization, and the growth of urban society in the 19th century (1800–1900 A.D.) led to the construction of houses of refuge, asylums, and reformatories to control the children of poor and inadequate parents and to act as surrogate families and schools for them.

Late in the same century, the continued exploitation of children resulted in the passage of laws designed to regulate child labor and to make some education mandatory for the offspring of lower- as well as middle- and upper-class families.

The first third of the 20th century (1900s) was devoted to establishing a unique legal system—the juvenile court—by which to enforce these laws and to see that children (and their parents) conformed to the standards that defined the ideal concept of childhood.

By mid-20th century (1950), the status of children was unmistakeably and officially defined as different from that of adults: childhood had become a long and powerless phase in the life cycle; the rights of children reflected their dependent and unequal status; legal, as well as moral, rules defined that which was expected of them; the nuclear family and the public school, not the larger adult community, were charged with socializing children; and, in the event that either failed, or that some children deviated from the ideal concept of childhood, the juvenile court would assume the parental role. Thus, by defining childhood in this way, society also defined and invented delinquency. And while delinquency was viewed as undesirable, it was not to be equated with adult crime. Rather, it represented a form of childish behavior from which both its perpetrator and society would be rescued.

As might be expected, the ideals associated with these constructions of reality have often been at odds with actual events and feelings. Ambivalence toward children persists; the juvenile court, to say nothing of families and schools, has been unable to rescue all dependent and neglected children; and juvenile crime continues to be a major social problem.

In the next section, therefore, we will inquire further into these issues, and will review the extent to which delinquent children continue to slip through the institutional cracks of society, despite its avowed preoccupation with them.

REFERENCES

Ariès, Philippe
　1962　*Centuries of Childhood.* Translated by Robert Baldick. New York: Alfred A. Knopf.

Baker, Harvey H.
　1910　"Procedure of the Boston Juvenile Court." Pp. 318–327 in Hastings H. Hart, ed., *Preventive Treatment of Neglected Children.* New York: Russell Sage.

Barnes, Harry Elmer
　1972　*The Story of Punishment.* 2d ed., rev. Montclair, N.J.: Patterson-Smith.

Becker, Carl
　1932　*The Heavenly City of the 18th Century Philosophers.* New Haven: Yale University Press.

Bremner, Robert H., et al., eds.
　1970　*Children and Youth in America: A Documentary History.* Vol. II. Cambridge: Harvard University Press.

Brockway, Z. R.
　1910　"The American reformatory prison system." Pp. 88–107 in Charles R. Henderson, ed., *Prison Reform and Criminal Law.* New York: Charities Publication Committee.

Caldwell, Robert G.
  1966 "The Juvenile Court: Its Development and Some Major Problems." Pp. 399–423 in Rose Giallombardo, ed., *Juvenile Delinquency: A Book of Readings.* New York: John Wiley & Sons.

Flexner, Bernard, and Baldwin, Roger N.
  1914 *Juvenile Courts and Probation.* New York: Century.

Hart, Hastings
  1910 *Preventive Treatment of Neglected Children.* New York: Russell Sage.

Henderson, Charles R., ed.
  1910 *Prison Reform and Criminal Law.* New York: Charities Publication Committee.

Hofstader, Richard
  1959 *Social Darwinism in American Thought.* New York: G. Braziller.

Lathrop, Julia C.
  1925 "The Background of the Juvenile Court in Illinois." Pp. 290–297, 320–330 in Julia Addams, ed., *The Child, the Clinic and the Court.* New York: New Republic.

Mack, Julian
  1910 "The Juvenile Court as a Legal Institution." Pp. 293–317 in Hastings H. Hart, ed., *Preventive Treatment of Neglected Children.* New York: Russell Sage.

McCrea, Roswell C.
  1910 "Societies for the Prevention of Cruelty to Children." Pp. 194–209 in Hastings H. Hart, ed., *Preventive Treatment of Neglected Children.* New York: Russell Sage.

McKelvey, Blake
  1968 *American Prisons.* Montclair, N.J.: Patterson-Smith.

Monachesi, Elio
  1960 "Cesare Beccaria." Pp. 36–50 in Hermann Mannheim, ed., *Pioneers in Criminology.* Chicago, Quadrangle.

Moody, Eleazar
  1715 "The School of Good Manners." Pp. 33–34 in Robert H. Bremner, ed., *Children and Youth in America.* Vol. I. Cambridge: Harvard University Press.

Paulsen, Monrad G., and Whitebread, Charles H.
  1974 *Juvenile Law and Procedure.* Reno: National Council of Juvenile Court Judges.

Platt, Anthony
  1968 *The Child Savers.* Chicago: University of Chicago Press.
  1974 "The Triumph of Benevolence: the Origins of the Juvenile Justice System in the United States." Pp. 356–389 in Richard Quinney, ed., *Criminal Justice in America.* Boston: Little, Brown.

Revised Statutes of Illinois
  1899 Section 21

Rosenheim, Margaret K., ed.
  1962 *Justice for the Child: The Juvenile Court in Transition.* New York: Free
         Press.

Rothman, David J.
  1971 *The Discovery of the Asylum.* Boston: Little, Brown.

Rubin, Ted
  1974 "Transferring Responsibility for Juvenile Noncriminal Misconduct from Ju-
         venile Courts to Nonauthoritarian Community Agencies." Mimeographed.
         Phoenix: Arizona Conference on Delinquency intervention.

Sanders, Wiley B., ed.
  1970 *Juvenile Offenders for a Thousand Years.* Chapel Hill: University of North
         Carolina Press.

Schlossman, Steven L.
  1977 *Love and the American Delinquent.* Chicago: University of Chicago Press.

Schoen, Edward
  1921 *Participant remarks. Proceedings of the Conference on Juvenile Court Stan-
         dards.* U.S. Children's Bureau Publication, No. 97. Washington, D.C.: U.S.
         Government Printing Office.

Tappan, Paul
  1949 *Juvenile Delinquency.* New York: McGraw-Hill.

U.S. Bureau of the Census
  1955 *Current Population Reports, Population Estimates.* Series P-25, No. 123.

Vold, George G.
  1958 *Theoretical Criminology.* New York: Oxford University Press.

Wadsworth, Benjamin
  1719 "The Well-ordered Family." Pp. 35–36 in Robert H. Bremner, ed., *Children
         and Youth in America*, Vol. I. Cambridge: Harvard University Press.

Welter, Rush
  1962 *Popular Education and Democratic Thought in America.* New York: Colum-
         bia University Press.

EXTENT AND NATURE OF DELINQUENT BEHAVIOR

Introduction: How delinquent behavior is measured

While occasional questions were raised about the awesome power of the juvenile court prior to mid-20th century, it was not seriously challenged until the 1960s. When these challenges did arise, moreover, they were probably due to an apparent rise in the rates of juvenile crime rather than to radical changes in the concepts of delinquency and juvenile justice.

Because of their growing fear of crime, a significant segment of the populace responded positively to a body of rhetoric suggesting that the nation was in dire peril. As Bittner described it:

> A figure of speech that has recently gained a good deal of currency is the "war on crime." The intended import of the expression is quite clear. It is supposed to indicate that the community is seriously imperiled by forces bent on its destruction and calls for the mounting of efforts that have claims on all available resources to defeat the peril. The rhetorical shift from "crime control" to "war on crime" signifies the transition from a routine concern to a state of emergency. We no longer face losses of one kind or another from the depredation of criminals; we are in imminent danger of losing everything! (1970:48).

Beliefs in the imminence of peril were reinforced by the FBI's annual account of traditional crime. During the decade of the 1960s, crimes of violence (murder, forcible rape, robbery, and aggravated assault) per 100,000 population increased 104 percent, while crimes against property (burglary, larceny, and auto theft) increased 123 percent. Overall, the total number of these seven offenses per 100,000 increased 120 percent (FBI., 1969:4). Furthermore, these official statistics implied that if a crime war were to be waged it would have to be directed against the nation's youth. According to the President's Commission on Law Enforcement and Administration of Justice (1967:44), more burglaries, larcenies, and auto thefts were being committed by young people ages 15 to 17 years than by any other group. Fifteen-year-olds were arrested most often, with 16-year-olds a close second. Those from ages 18 to 20 were the most responsible for crimes of violence, with the second largest group in the 21 to 24 age bracket.

Many juveniles were arrested, of course, for acts far less serious than those mentioned. In 1966, it was estimated that between 1 and 1.5 million persons under 18 were arrested, and approximately half of them were referred to court for trial. Overall, the evidence indicated that delinquency was at a very low ebb before the onset of adolescence, rose sharply after its onset, hit its peak at around age 16 or 17, and then declined sharply. Apparently, traditional forms of crime, as well as status offenses, were very much a youthful phenomenon.

Coupled with the campus protests and race riots of the 1960s, this frightening crime information evoked a vision of millions of Americans sitting crouched behind locked doors, fearful that if they ventured forth they would become victims of their own criminally disposed children. Will we, asked the National Commission on the Causes and Prevention of Violence, have to "expect the establishment of the 'defensive city,' the modern counterpart of the fortified medieval city?" Will we "witness frequent and widespread crime, perhaps out of police control?" (1969:xxv). While such questions are noteworthy in their own right, they point to another issue that is even more central to our full understanding of delinquency: sentiments favoring a war on criminals are often opposed to sentiments inherent in the benevolent philosophy of the juvenile court. Our recent past, in other words, has been marked by contradictory trends.

On the one hand, recent years have seen a growing intellectual and legal resistance to the all-embracing character of juvenile court laws and practices. The benevolent assumptions upon which they are based have been questioned and efforts made to reduce their scope and power. On the other hand, mounting public fears over the rising crime and delinquency rates of the young suggest, to some people at least, that delinquents should be subjected to greater, not lesser, legal controls. Perhaps the idea of a strong juvenile court with a wide jurisdictional net is not so bad after all. Perhaps juvenile criminals should be treated like adult criminals. Whatever is done, society should get tougher, not more lenient.

Given these contradictory trends, it is obvious that we must pay attention to the extent of delinquent behavior at the present time, as well as in the past. Are great portions of America's children criminal violators? Are they becoming more delinquent? Are they a threat to the very foundations of society?

We must also pay attention to any clues that crime statistics might provide us regarding important assumed facts that must be explained by theory: Are certain segments of the youth population more delinquent than others? Do boys commit more crimes than girls? Are there any notable differences among the races? What factors stand out, when crime is measured, that require explanation?

Such questions are not easily answered. Valid information on juvenile crime has been difficult to obtain because much of it has gone officially undetected. Moreover, official police and court statistics have often been as much a reflection of what officials do as they have been of what delinquents do. In the recent past, however, important new sources of information have been developed and added to official accounts. In this part of the book, therefore, we will review these new sources of information as well as official accounts:

In *chapter 5*, we will analyze official accounts of delinquent behavior derived from the records of the police and the juvenile courts.

In *chapter 6*, we will utilize confidential self-reports of delinquent behavior derived from young people.

In *chapter 7*, we will utilize accounts from the victims of criminal acts in order to obtain yet a third estimate of the amount and character of crime.

As can be imagined, these three accounts differ markedly. But, by triangulating on delinquent behavior, we should be able to get a reasonably good fix upon it, just as the surveyor does when he attempts to locate a particular position by viewing it from different angles. Once this is done, we will be able to draw some conclusions about current trends in delinquent behavior, what areas are in need of explanation, and where in society it is most heavily concentrated.

REFERENCES

Bittner, Egon
    1970   *The Functions of the Police in Modern Society*. Publication No. 2059. Washington, D.C.: U.S. Government Printing Office.

Federal Bureau of Investigation
    1969   *Crime in the United States: Uniform Crime Reports—1968*. Washington, D.C.: U.S. Government Printing Office.

National Commission on the Causes and Prevention of Violence
    1969   *Crimes of Violence*. Vol. 2. Washington, D.C.: U.S. Government Printing Office.

President's Commission on Law Enforcement and Administration of Justice
    1967   *The Challenge of Crime in a Free Society*. Washington, D.C.: U.S. Government Printing Office.

CHAPTER
5

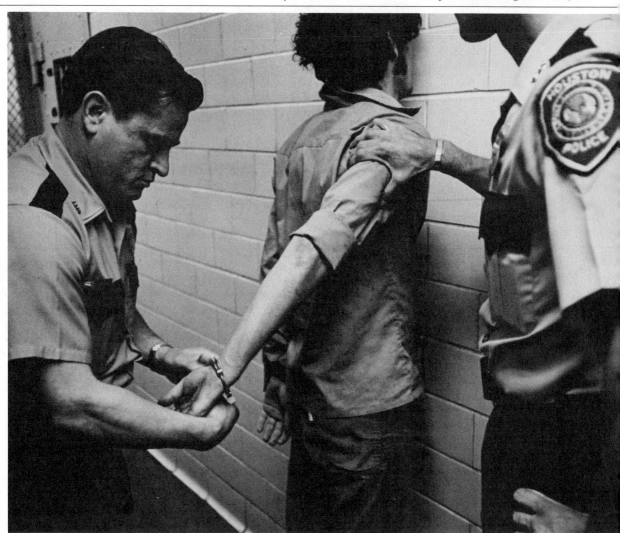

Juveniles do not become official delinquents until they are apprehended.

There are two major sources of official information on the extent of delinquent behavior: (1) the number of juvenile arrests reported to the Federal Bureau of Investigation (FBI) each year by the police; and (2) the number of court cases reported to the National Center for Juvenile Justice (NCJJ) annually by the juvenile courts.

Of the two, police statistics provide the most accurate estimate of the actual number of delinquent acts. "Regardless of how rigorous the court . . . data are intended to be," said the National Commission on the Causes and Prevention of Violence, "they are inherently less useful than police data in profiling the levels and trends of crime" (1969,2:14). The reason is that the juvenile justice system is like a funnel in which estimates of crime grow progressively less accurate the further down the funnel those estimates occur: a crime does not always result in an arrest; an arrest does not always result in a case being referred to court; a referral to court does not always result in a trial; and a trial does not always result in a conviction. At each stage in the process, some accuracy is lost in determining levels of and trends in crime.

POLICE ESTIMATES OF DELINQUENT BEHAVIOR

Police estimates of crime appear yearly in the *Uniform Crime Reports* issued by the FBI. Today, several thousand law enforcement agencies, representing 98 percent of the total national population, voluntarily submit information to the UCR Program (FBI, 1980:3). The latest figures indicate that in 1979 approximately 12.2 million crimes were reported to the police, and that approximately 10.2 million arrests were made (FBI, 1980:37; 187).

As the data in Figure 5–1 reveal, the majority of these arrests involved young people. They show that, while children ages 12 and under comprise almost 20 percent of the population, they constitute less than 3 percent of all arrestees. After puberty, however, the picture changes rapidly: 13- to 15-year-olds make up only about 5 percent of the population, yet they

FIGURE 5–1

Age distribution of arrestees and total U.S. population

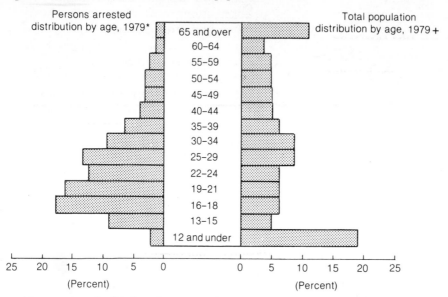

Persons arrested
distribution by age, 1979*

Total population
distribution by age, 1979 +

65 and over
60–64
55–59
50–54
45–49
40–44
35–39
30–34
25–29
22–24
19–21
16–18
13–15
12 and under

25 20 15 10 5 0   0 5 10 15 20 25
(Percent)   (Percent)

* Persons arrested is based on reports received representing 204,622,000 population.
  † The total population is 220,099,000 for the United States, based on Bureau of Census provisional estimates, July 1, 1979.
  Source: FBI, 1980:187.

comprise almost 10 percent of all those arrested. Furthermore, the disparity for 16- to 18-year-olds is even greater. While they constitute only about 6 percent of the population, they comprise almost 20 percent of the arrests; indeed, they are the most arrested segment of the population. Then, with increasing age, the rate of arrest gradually declines; by middle age, subsequent groups of arrestees are progressively a smaller portion of the total criminal population than they are of the total population.

The youthful character of arrestees is further substantiated by the findings of a longitudinal study conducted by Wolfgang, Figlio, and Sellin (1972). These investigators obtained the names of an entire cohort of 9,945 boys, born in 1945, who lived in Philadelphia from the time they

were 10 years old until they were 18. Then, they used official records to determine how many delinquent acts by these boys were recorded during the years they were of juvenile court age.

Official records revealed that 35 percent (3,475) of the 9,945 boys had at least one recorded police contact sometime between their 10th and 18th birthdays, while 65 percent (6,470) had none (p. 54). For every 1,000 boys, in other words, there were approximately 350 who became officially delinquent. Furthermore, these records corroborated the relation between age and arrest mentioned earlier: arrest is at low level at age 10, increases steadily thereafter, reaches its apex at age 16 and then at age 17 begins to decline (pp. 112–118). In short, arrest data suggest that youth of juvenile court age are among the most criminal segments of the population.

"FACTS" THAT MUST BE EXPLAINED

Given this finding, important questions are posed: For what kinds of crime are juveniles most likely to be arrested? What segments of the youth population are arrested most often? Are they boys? Are they girls? Are they the children of the poor? Are they members of minority groups?

When we reviewed the discovery of childhood and the invention of delinquency, we learned that:

The discovery of childhood contributed to the notion that children are in need of special care and supervision. Otherwise, it was assumed, they would grow up to be adults in whom the least, not the most, desirable features of society would be embodied.

The ideal concept of childhood is a product largely of white, middle-class values and experiences. It was the middle class, in particular, which stressed the importance of the nuclear family and formal schooling, in lieu of the communal household and the apprenticeship system, as devices for socializing the young.

While great changes did occur in the methods of raising children, role expectations for girls and boys remained markedly different. Boys were granted more freedom than girls, were encouraged to pursue higher levels of education, and were expected to assume positions in commerce, industry, and the professions. Girls, meanwhile, were expected to be less venturesome, to limit their educations, to marry, and to assume domestic roles in support of their husbands and children. Above all, they were to be more modest, more retiring, and more virtuous than boys.

Opportunities to develop and to adhere to these expectations were limited for black people, American Indians, lower-class whites, and other poor minority groups. Given these limitations, in fact, American beliefs increasingly stressed the idea that the poverty, disrupted family life, and ignorance of minority and lower-class groups were inevitable precursors of crime. In 1967, for example, the President's Commission on Law Enforcement and Administration of Justice concluded that "delinquents tend to come from backgrounds of social and economic deprivation. . . . It is inescapable that juvenile delinquency is directly related to conditions bred by poverty" (pp. 56–57).

The laws which created the juvenile court were a direct reflection of these developments and assumptions. In the interest of saving wayward boys and girls, particularly those who were disadvantaged, the agents of juvenile justice were not only expected to detect and to suppress their crimes, but to compensate for their poverty, their ignorance, their "disrupted" family life, and their failure to heed ideal role expectations.

In short, if there is any validity to this description of historical developments, it should be reflected in arrest statistics. Such factors as age, sex, minority status, and class membership should have some relation to actual juvenile arrests. Indeed, if such relationships do appear, they become "facts" for which criminologists then seek some explanation. Why, they might ask, is age, or sex, or minority status related to arrest, if indeed such a relationship can be demonstrated? In pursuit of such assumed facts, therefore, let us consider in greater detail the relationship between age and crime.

Age and kinds of crime

We have already seen that juveniles, more than any other segment of the population, are likely to be arrested. But for what kinds of crime are they arrested? Are they largely juvenile status offenses, involving sexual misbehavior, running away, drinking, or violation of curfew, or are they the kinds of crimes involving violence or theft?

In order to answer these questions, we will concentrate for now on the population of young people, ages 10 through 17, since children under the age of 10 are not likely to be arrested and youths over the age of 17 are considered to be adults in most states. Relative to this issue, therefore, population estimates by the Census Bureau indicate that juveniles, ages 10 through 17, constitute only about 15 percent of the total population in the United States (Bureau of the Census, 1978:9; 1980:5). Yet, arrest statistics reveal the disturbing fact that they are arrested, year after year, for approximately 40 percent of the eight serious felonies that comprise the FBI's *Index Offenses* (compare FBI, 1971:128 and 1980:196):

1.	Criminal homicide	Willful murder and manslaughter by negligence.
2.	Forcible rape	Rape or attempted rape by force.
3.	Robbery	Stealing or attempted stealing by force.
4.	Aggravated assault	Assault with intent to kill or do severe injury.
5.	Burglary	Breaking and entering to commit a felony or theft.
6.	Larceny-theft	Any theft not involving force and violence except auto theft, forgery, etc.
7.	Motor vehicle theft	Any theft, or attempted theft, of a motor vehicle.
8.	Arson	Any willful or attempted burning of a dwelling, public building, vehicle, or personal property.

1. Violent crimes. Table 5–1 provides a detailed breakdown of the arrests for these offenses. It reveals that juveniles are not as likely as adults to be arrested for violent crimes—murder, rape, robbery, and aggravated assault. Although they do account for approximately one third of all arrests for robbery, arrests for sush acts as murder, rape,

TABLE 5–1

Juvenile arrests for index crimes

Arrest offenses	All ages	Juveniles under 18	Males under 18	Females under 18
Total arrests:				
Number	2,086,487	811,352	664,456	146,896
Percent	100	38.9	31.9	7.0
		Percent of all arrests		
Criminal homicide:				
Murder and nonnegligent manslaughter	17,157	9.4	8.4	1.0
Forcible rape	27,687	15.6	15.4	0.2
Robbery	125,669	31.5	29.3	2.2
Aggravated assault	247,396	15.4	13.1	2.3
Burglary—breaking or entering	450,264	48.8	45.6	3.2
Larceny—theft......................	1,065,830	40.4	29.5	10.9
Motor vehicle theft	138,671	49.4	44.4	5.0
Arson	17,653	49.3	44.6	4.7

Note: Figures based on 11,239 agencies; 1979 estimated population, 197,679,000.
Source: FBI, 1980:195

TABLE 5–2 ━━━━━━━━━━━━━━━

Typical juvenile arrests for non-Index crimes

	Total all ages	Percent of all arrests		
Arrest offenses		*Juveniles under 18*	*Males under 18*	*Females under 18*
Curfew and loitering	75,692	100.0	78.0	22.0
Runaways	146,445	100.0	41.5	58.5
Vandalism	230,825	54.3	50.0	4.3
Liquor laws	371,301	36.3	28.4	7.9
Stolen property:				
Buying, receiving, possessing	102,498	33.2	30.3	2.9
Drug abuse violations	469,792	23.5	19.7	3.8
Other assaults	434,655	18.7	14.9	3.8
Sex offenses except rape and				
prostitution	61,085	18.1	16.8	1.3
Disorderly conduct	690,365	17.7	14.7	3.0
All other offenses except traffic	1,516,099	18.8	15.1	3.7

Note: Figures based on 11,239 agencies; 1979 estimated population, 197,679,000.
Source: FBI, 1980:195.

and aggravated assault are more often committed by young adults, particularly those between the ages of 19 and 21 (Greenberg, 1977:190). Consequently, juveniles account for about one fifth of the total arrests for all violent crimes, an amount that is only about 5 percent greater than their share of the total population.

2. Property crimes. Property crimes are another matter. Juveniles are arrested for 44 percent of all property crimes; 49 percent of all motor vehicle thefts; 49 percent of burglaries; 40 percent of larcenies; and 49 percent of arsons. Furthermore, arrests for most of these acts are likely to peak among juveniles who are 15 or 16 years of age (Greenberg, 1977:190). Consequently, the proportion of all arrests for Index crimes which are juvenile (44 percent) is almost three times the proportion of all people in the population ages 10 through 17.

The yearly publication of official figures like these not only fuels public fear but illustrates the anxieties related to our traditional beliefs about the young. The modern concept of childhood says that, by attending to the moral, economic, and psychological needs of the young, crime could be prevented. These figures suggest either that this assumption is false or that the juvenile justice system has not been very effective. Although arrests of juveniles are more likely to involve property crimes than violent crimes, the *Uniform Crime Reports* provide little support for the belief that serious evils among the young are being prevented by modern methods of child raising.

3. Non-Index offenses. Data for non-Index crimes are also illuminating. These are less violent, usually less serious crimes, ranging from forgery to curfew violation.

The non-Index offenses for which juveniles are arrested most often are shown in Table 5–2. As might be expected, they account for all curfew violations and runaway incidents, since these are status offenses applicable only to children. Yet, it is noteworthy that the total number of juvenile arrests for these offenses is only a fraction of their arrests for such crimes as burglary or theft. Furthermore, juvenile arrest rates are also high for vandalism (54 percent), liquor law violations (36 percent), dealing in stolen property (33 percent), and drug abuse (24 percent).

There are, however, some non-Index crimes for which the number of juvenile arrests are not high, such as forgery, counterfeiting, fraud, embezzlement, and commercial vice, all of which require greater sophistication and opportunity than juveniles possess.

Moreover, some findings with respect to alcohol and drug abuse do not conform to popular beliefs either. While society has been terribly concerned over the increased use of heroin, marijuana, and pills among juveniles, Table 5–2 implies that their use of these drugs may be less frequent than their use of the most abused drug of all, alcohol. Thirty six percent of all those arrested for "liquor law violations"—drinking under age or buying liquor illegally—are juveniles. By contrast, only about 24 percent of those arrested for use of all other drugs are juveniles.

At the same time, other arrest data indicate that, relatively speaking, alcohol abuse may be more of an adult than a juvenile problem, since about 96 percent of those arrested for drunkeness, and about 98 percent of those arrested for drunken driving, are adults (compare FBI, 1975:187 and 1980:195). Nonetheless, the point is clear: alcohol is our most serious drug problem, for adults as well as for juveniles.

4. *Chronic offenders.* A final issue has to do with the possibility that these high rates of arrest are not characteristic of all juveniles but that, instead, they are due to a small group of chronic offenders. Indeed, the Philadelphia Cohort Study mentioned earlier suggests that such is the case (Wolfgang, Figlio, and Sellin, 1972).

It will be recalled that, of the total cohort of 9,945 boys, 35 percent became officially delinquent. However, the data revealed that only 19 percent (1,862 boys) had more than one recorded offense. Yet, this small minority not only accounted for 8,601 arrests, but were more likely to be arrested for serious Index offenses. All told, in fact, they were arrested 2,935 times for such crimes, while one-time offenders were arrested only 330 times (p. 71).

Furthermore, the most chronic of all offenders from the repeater group were selected and studied—those who had *five or more* recorded offenses during childhood. Although there were only 627 boys in this group, they were responsible for *more than half* of all the offenses of the entire cohort of 9,945 boys. In other words, a group comprising only 6 percent of the total birth cohort, and only 18 percent of those who became delinquent, was responsible for more than 50 percent of all arrests. Such findings seem to suggest that the number of young people who become truly serious career offenders may be only a tiny proportion of the total.

5. *Summary.* In summary, our analysis of the relation of age to arrest has revealed that (1) juveniles may be among the most criminal segments of the population; (2) they are more likely to be arrested for serious property crimes than for violent crimes; and (3) a small group of chronic offenders may be accounting for a highly disproportionate share of all juvenile arrests. These findings pose some difficult questions.

On the one hand, the implied criminality of the young runs counter to the assumption that enlightened methods of child raising and the invention of the juvenile court protect children from involvement in the debaucheries, misdeeds, and crimes of adults. On the other hand, this dismal conclusion is softened somewhat by the finding that there may be a small, but highly chronic, group of recidivists who are contributing disproportionately to the high rate of arrests recorded for the young. Although the relationship of age to crime is a powerful one, it may not support the belief that the great majority of juveniles are to be feared because of their criminality.

TABLE 5–3 ▬▬▬▬▬
Arrest rates of girls and boys as proportions of all female and male Index arrests

Type of offense	Girls under 18 (percent of all female arrests)			Boys under 18 (percent of all male arrests)		
	1970	1975	1979	1970	1975	1979
Murder and nonnegligent manslaughter	5.2	6.2	7.5	12.5	10.2	9.7
Forcible rape	—	25.9	27.1	21.5	17.8	16.4
Robbery	39.3	37.2	30.0	34.0	34.9	32.0
Aggravated assault	18.2	21.7	18.9	16.6	17.6	15.9
Burglary	47.8	50.9	50.3	50.9	52.8	48.9
Larceny theft	45.7	41.5	36.2	51.0	47.7	43.0
Motor vehicle theft	57.1	58.3	57.0	54.9	54.3	49.0
Totals	43.3	40.7	36.1	45.3	44.3	39.8

Sources: FBI: 1971:124; FBI, 1976:187; FBI, 1980:193.

Gender and arrest

A second question, in light of traditional differences between the roles of males and females, is whether girls are as delinquent as boys. According to traditional role expectations, juvenile girls should be more law-abiding and virtuous than both their male counterparts and their adult sisters. In order to examine this issue, therefore, two kinds of data are required: (1) information which contrasts the arrest rates of boys and girls; and (2) information which contrasts the arrest rates of girls and adult women.

1. Girls versus boys. By referring again to Table 5–1, it can be seen that arrests of girls comprise only 7 percent of all serious Index offenses, versus 32 percent for boys. In other words, the rate per 100,000 at which boys are arrested is more than four times greater than the rate for girls (compare Bureau of the Census, 1978:9 with FBI, 1980:195). Furthermore, although the most common arrest of girls is for theft (11 percent), that figure lags far behind the proportion for boys (30 percent) for the same offense. In short, arrests for serious traditional crimes are still predominantly male, typically young males—not females.

Table 5–2, showing non-Index crimes, also reaffirms the extent to which delinquency arrests are predominantly male. For only one offense—running away—are girls (59 percent) arrested more frequently than boys (42 percent). This difference may be due, at least in part, to the traditional double standard which allows both society and the police to be more concerned with unsupervised girls than unsupervised boys. Otherwise, girls, like their adult sisters, are arrested less often than boys. Indeed, arrests of females of all ages during the 1970s have constituted only about 15 percent of total arrests, while 85 percent of all arrests have been male (compare FBI, 1971:124 with 1980:193).

2. Girls versus women. When girls are compared with women ages 18 and older, however, the picture changes considerably. The reason is that girls have consistently been responsible for about one third of all female arrests, whereas boys have been responsible for only about 20 to 25 percent of all male arrests (compare FBI, 1971:124; 1976:187; and 1980:193). However, when only serious Index crimes are considered, boys and girls are surprisingly alike in the sense that each group accounts for about 4 out of 10 arrests in their respective populations (see Table 5–3). In other

TABLE 5–4

Number and percent of all juvenile arrests, by ethnic group

	White		Black		Indian		Chinese		Japanese		All others	
	Number	*Percent*	*Number*	*Percent*	*Number*	*Percent*	*Number*	*Percent*	*Number*	*Percent*	*Number*	*Perce*
Index crimes:	574,764	68.9	239,183	28.7	5,973	0.7	824	0.1	800	0.1	12,836	1.5
Violent crime	42,494	48.7	42,756	49.0	531	0.6	122	0.1	33	—	1,296	1.5
Property crime	532,270	71.2	196,427	26.3	5,442	0.7	702	0.1	767	0.1	11,540	1.5
Non-Index crimes ...	1,054,055	81.1	217,455	16.7	9,840	0.8	626	—	611	—	16,659	1.3
Total	1,628,819	76.3	456,638	21.4	15,813	0.7	1,450	0.1	1,411	0.1	29,495	1.4

Source: FBI, 1980:201.

words, their arrest rates for serious crimes are more than 250 percent greater than one would expect, given the sizes of their respective populations. Furthermore, the total number of girls arrested for such crimes as burglary, theft, drug and alcohol use, or disorderly conduct, far exceeds the total, for running away or violating curfew. This is similar to the findings for boys.

3. Summary. In summary, then, an examination of the relation of gender to arrest reveals some paradoxical findings. On the one hand, girls (as well as adult women) are arrested *far less frequently* than boys, suggesting that traditional expectations for females still retain great strength, and that females continue to be far more circumspect and lawabiding than males. On the other hand, girls are arrested *far more frequently* than adult women, again suggesting that society's presumed efforts to nurture and protect its young, particularly girls, have not prevented their becoming more criminal than adult females. Hence, both sets of findings are important issues for theorists to consider.

Minority status and arrest

A third potentially important relationship is that between minority status and arrest. During the 19th century, it will be recalled, children of white minority groups were far more likely to be defined as delinquent, or in need of

institutionalization, than were the children of established, wealthier groups. But now that minority groups are viewed as predominantly black, brown, red, or yellow, does the same pattern exist?

The *Uniform Crime Reports* provide data on all these groups except for Hispanics, whose arrests are apparently included with those of whites. But, as may be seen in Table 5–4, most groups are so small that the arrests among them are dwarfed by the arrests of blacks and whites. American Indians, for example, are the largest of the smaller minority groups. Yet, their Index offenses constitute less than 1 percent of the total. Furthermore, the task of calculating arrest rates per 100,000 juveniles is made impossible for such groups because population estimates by the Census Bureau do not provide detailed, age-specific information on any minority groups other than blacks and whites. Consequently, our analysis will have to be confined to these two groups.

At the present time, blacks comprise about 15 percent of the youth population, ages 10 through 17, while whites constitute about 84 percent (Bureau of the Census, 1978:9). In arrest statistics, however, black juveniles are overrepresented, constituting 21 percent of the total, while whites constitute 76 percent (see Table 5–4). On a general level, therefore, arrest data lend some support to the popular theory that minority youth are the more delinquent.

This conclusion, however, does not begin to

represent the most salient facts. Instead, they are best revealed by detaching Index from non-Index crimes and analyzing them separately. And in order to do this effectively, it is necessary to *standardize* our comparisons; that is, to calculate arrest rates per 100,000 for each race, black and white. The reason is that there are only about 4.4 million blacks, ages 10 through 17, versus 25.2 million whites in the United States. Thus, unless rates are standardized, whites will appear to be the more delinquent, simply because their absolute number of arrests will be the larger. In 1979, for example, 7 in 10 arrests among juveniles for Index crimes were white, while only 3 in 10 were black (Table 5–4). But when rates are standardized, the picture changes because the number of black arrests is compared not to the number of white arrests, but to the size of the black juvenile population. The same is done with whites; their arrest rates will reflect the number of arrests per 100,000 white juveniles.

1. Race and Index crimes. When black and white arrests for Index crimes are standardized and compared for the years 1970 and 1979, they provide some astonishing findings. The results are displayed in Table 5–5.

First, they indicate that the number of black arrests per 100,000 black juveniles is far greater for serious crimes than is the number of white arrests per 100,000 white juveniles. Put another way, the chances that a black juvenile will be arrested for an Index crime are far greater than for a white juvenile: 3.4 to 1 in 1970, and 2.4 to 1 in 1979. Furthermore, these disparities are much greater for violent than for property crimes. In 1970, for example, the ratio of black to white juvenile arrests for murder was 16 to 1; for rape, 10 to 1; for robbery, 18 to 1; and for aggravated assault, 7 to 1.

By 1979, however, these disparities had decreased substantially. While black juveniles were still far more likely to be arrested for violent crimes, the ratios of black to white juvenile arrests had grown smaller: murder, 5 to 1; rape, 7 to 1; robbery, 10 to 1; and aggravated assault, 3 to 1. Nonetheless, these high rates per 100,000 among blacks meant that they were still responsible for 44 percent of all arrests among juveniles for murder, 55 percent for rape, 63 percent for robbery, and 35 percent for aggravated assault, despite the fact that they comprised only about 15 percent of the population of children ages 10 through 17 (FBI, 1980:201).

TABLE 5–5

Arrests for Index crimes per 100,000 ages 10 to 17, by race, 1970 and 1979

	1970			1979		
Type of offense	*Blacks*	*Whites*	*Ratio*	*Blacks*	*Whites*	*Ratio*
Murder and nonnegligent manslaughter	19.5	1.2	16 : 1	17.1	3.5	5 : 1
Forcible rape	38.9	3.9	10 : 1	57.7	7.9	7 : 1
Robbery	371.4	20.7	18 : 1	585.6	57.0	10 : 1
Aggravated assault............	202.3	39.0	7 : 1	313.9	100.0	3 : 1
Burglary	1,020.1	308.4	3 : 1	1,330.9	643.9	2 : 1
Larceny theft	1,882.9	672.2	3 : 1	2,767.8	1,225.5	2 : 1
Motor vehicle theft	500.1	150.2	3 : 1	348.5	209.2	1.6 : 1
Arson	24.9	13.2	2 : 1	29.2	29.8	1 : 1
Total	4,060.1	1,198.9	3.4 : 1	5,450.8	2.276.8	2.4 : 1

Note: estimated population, ages 10 to 17: 1970—blacks, 4,355,000; whites, 27,872,000. For 1979—blacks, 4,388,000; whites, 25,244,000.

Sources: Bureau of Census, 1978:16; FBI, 1971:132; FBI, 1980:201.

Similar findings were reported by the Philadelphia Cohort study mentioned earlier (Wolfgang, Figlio, and Sellin, 1972:65–129; 245–250). While 29 percent of the white boys in the cohort became delinquent, 50 percent of the blacks were so designated. Black boys were also more likely to be recidivists, and of the recidivists, they were more likely to be chronic offenders. They were, in fact, five times more likely than whites to be numbered among the 6 percent who were responsible for over half of all the arrests of the entire cohort. Indeed, of the 14 murders recorded for the entire group, all were committed by blacks. According to the index used by the investigators to measure the seriousness of delinquent offenses, in fact, these 14 homicides alone represented more social harm than all the acts of physical violence taken together committed by white boys.

Consequently, when all of these distressing facts are taken together, they indicate that the conclusion is only partially accurate which suggests that, because white juveniles greatly outnumber black youngsters, their arrests will always be the larger. While this may be true for less serious offenses, arrest data suggest that it is not true where violent crimes are concerned.

This conclusion is supported by data in Table 5–5 which indicate that the ratios of black to white arrests for Index property crimes are much lower than they are for violent crimes, about 3 to 1 in 1970, and about 2 to 1 in 1979. Thus in 1979, the proportion of all black juvenile arrestees for property crimes was much lower than the proportion arrested for violent crimes: 36 percent for burglary, 28 percent for theft, and 14 percent for arson.

In addition to this finding, moreover, the data in Table 5–5 raise a provocative question: Why did the ratio of black to white arrests decrease so drastically between 1970 and 1979? Did the decrease mean that black juveniles were being arrested less often? Ironically, that is not the answer. The arrest rate among black juveniles ages 10 to 17 for all Index crimes increased from 4,060 per 100,000 in 1970, to 5,451 in 1979—an increase of 34 percent. However, the arrest rate among white juveniles increased at an even more rapid pace: from 1,199 per 100,000 in 1970, to 2,277 in 1979— a tremendous increase of 90 percent. Thus, disparities between the two races concerning serious crime rates decreased because the white rate of arrest increased at a more rapid pace than the black rate.

2.   Race and non-Index offenses.   Given the relatively high rate of arrest for serious crimes among black youngsters, ages 10 to 17, Table 5–6 presents a second set of astonishing findings. It shows that, where such crimes as

---

TABLE 5.6

Arrests for selected non-Index crimes per 100,000, ages 10 to 17, by race, 1970 and 1979

Type of offense	1970			1979		
	Blacks	*Whites*	*Ratio*	*Blacks*	*Whites*	*Ratio*
Vandalism	297.5	204.7	1.5 : 1	364.8	438.2	1 : 1.2
Liquor laws	60.8	226.5	1 : 4	72.4	527.7	1 : 7
Drug abuse	164.7	211.2	1 : 1.3	322.4	387.1	1 : 1.2
Sex offenses	62.7	23.3	1 : 3	66.0	32.4	2 : 1
Curfew	420.4	283.6	1.5 : 1	385.3	236.8	1.6 : 1
Running away	455.5	499.3	1 : 1	440.3	508.5	1 : 1.2
Total	1,461.8	1,448.6	1 : 1	1,651.2	2,130.7	1 : 1.3

Note: estimated populations, ages 10 to 17: 1970—blacks, 4,355,000; whites, 27,872,000. For 1979, blacks, 4,388,000; whites, 25,244,000.

Sources: Bureau of Census, 1978:16; FBI, 1971:132; FBI, 1980:201.

vandalism, liquor law violations, drug abuse, or status offenses are concerned, the overall rate of arrest among white juveniles is as great as among blacks. Indeed, in both 1970 and 1979, white juveniles were *more* likely to be arrested for violation of liquor laws and drug abuse, while concerning other non-Index offenses, differences between the races tended to fluctuate and were not great.

These findings also raise a series of provocative questions: Are the modes of behavior of black and white youngsters glaringly different when it comes to serious crimes but virtually alike when vandalism, drug abuse, and running away are involved? Could it be that the police are inclined to be more protective of whites than of blacks when it comes to serious crimes? Is it possible that, where status offenses are concerned, authorities are somewhat more tolerant of black than of white youth? Such is the long list of questions that the arrest data raise, but do not answer.

3. Summary. In summary, this analysis of the relationship between minority status and arrest has shown that (1) the arrests of American Indian and Oriental groups are dwarfed by those of white minority and majority groups and by blacks; (2) black youths are immensely more likely than white youths to be arrested for serious, particularly violent, crimes; and (3) arrest rates for non-Index juvenile offenses are approximately equal for both races.

In light of the legacy of slavery and discrimination in America, and the extended exclusion of blacks from full participation in the economic, political, and social life of the dominant white culture, perhaps such findings should not surprise us. Yet they leave a series of questions which today, if not in the past, literally beg for explanation: To what degree is the relationship between minority status and arrest a reflection of police policy and procedure rather than juvenile behavior? To what degree would the same findings hold for other important minority groups—Hispanics, Asiatics, or Native Americans? To what extent are the behavioral differences implied by arrest statistics due to cultural differences between minority and dominant groups? In short, the relationship between minority status and arrest continues to be an assumed fact much in need of further research, age-specific arrest and population data, and theoretical attention.

Social class and arrest

As we learned earlier, American beliefs have stressed that poverty and membership in the lower class are likely to enhance the chances that children will become lawbreakers. To the extent that this is true, moreover, it should help to explain why black youngsters generate such high arrest rates. They are likely to have been not only historically disadvantaged, but also are today more likely than whites to be residents of urban ghettoes and rural slums. Hence, their disproportionate representation in arrest statistics may be more strongly related to the prejudice, poor schooling, and poverty that they have experienced than to factors that are somehow limited strictly to race.

Unfortunately, this possibility cannot be explored using FBI data, since the relationship between social class and arrest is not analyzed in the *Uniform Crime Reports*. However, data that bear on this issue were gathered in the Philadelphia Cohort Study (Wolfgang, Figlio, and Sellin, 1972:65:129; 245–250). Briefly, its findings were these:

First, socioeconomic status (SES) was found to be related to arrest. Forty six percent of the cohort were classified as living in lower-class census tracts, of whom almost half (45 percent) were delinquent. By contrast, only 27 percent of those who lived in higher-class tracts had police records, although they comprised 54 percent of the cohort.

Second, SES and race appear to intertwine and overlap; that is, black boys were more likely than whites to live in lower-class areas. The double jeopardy in which this placed them, in turn, was reflected in a host of social afflictions. They were more likely not only to be arrested but to have experienced the disruption of a greater number of school and residential moves, to have achieved the lowest IQ scores and other measures of achievement, and to have completed the lowest average grade in school.

Third, boys from lower-class census tracts were more likely than those from higher tracts status to be numbered among the small group of 627 chronic offenders. As a consequence, the double jeopardy experienced by black boys seemed to increase the likelihood that they would be overrepresented in this group.

In short, the Philadelphia study implied three points about the relationship between social class and arrest: (1) membership in the lower class is likely to enhance the chances of arrest; (2) lower-class boys are more likely to be serious chronic offenders than boys of a higher status; and (3) lower socioeconomic status, combined with the status of being black,

is likely to further increase the chances of arrest. Hence, class membership is another "fact" warranting attention in explanations for crime.

Community and arrest

Finally, since the 19th century, Americans have believed that cities are a major source of crime and corruption. While rural areas and small towns are safe and desirable places to live, cities, particularly their urban cores, are ridden with evil.

As may be seen in Figure 5–2, arrest data tend to support this belief. Cities still have the highest rates of arrest, followed by suburban and rural areas. Nonetheless, police statistics also reveal that, since 1973, the arrest rate has increased at a much greater rate in rural areas (36 percent) than in the cities (9.9 percent). But this increase notwithstanding, the relationship of community to arrest continues to remain a "fact" demanding attention. Why *do* cities have higher arrest rates than either rural or suburban areas?

ARREST TRENDS

In addition to the sociological factors associated with arrest, to understand juvenile crime we must also pay heed to arrest trends, and to the extent to which they imply that the crime rate is increasing or decreasing. Hence, if one looks only at the total number of juvenile arrests, the message seems clear: youth crime increased at an astronomical rate during the past two decades. In 1960, for example, the national number of juvenile arrests for all types of crime was only about 587,000, but by 1979, the number had risen to almost 2,488,000—an increase of 324 percent (compare FBI, 1961:92,98 and 1980:195). Such estimates, however, overlook two crucial points: (1) the youth population fluctuates in size; and (2) today's estimates of arrest are based upon a

FIGURE 5–2 ▬▬▬▬▬
Arrest rate per 100,000 by type of community

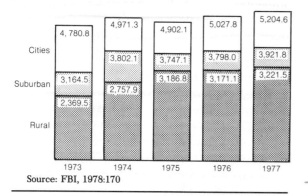

Source: FBI, 1978:170

much larger segment of the total population than they were in 1960. Therefore, a more accurate way to estimate trends is to *standardize* arrest rates, and to compare them over time.[1]

Violent crimes

Arrest trends for violent crimes—murder, rape, robbery, and aggravated assault—are displayed in Figure 5–3. Covering the period between 1960 and 1979, the rate of arrest per 100,000 juveniles of *all* ages, 1 to 17, is compared with the rate for all adults, ages 18 and older. Three observations can be made:

1. The rate at which juveniles have been arrested for violent crimes during the past 20 years has remained lower than the adult rate.

2. Arrest rates for both groups increased considerably between 1960 and 1974, and then began to level out. Since 1974, they have either

remained at about the same level or have decreased slightly.

3. Rates of arrest for violent crimes have increased markedly in both groups. But while the adult rate has increased by 85 percent since 1960, the juvenile rate has increased by 233 percent. Thus, despite signs that the rate of arrest for violent crimes has moderated in recent years, the data suggest that young people are considerably more violent today than they were 20 years ago.

Property crimes

The same kinds of information are displayed in Figure 5–4 for property crimes—burglary, larceny, and motor vehicle theft. However, these findings differ from those for violent crimes:

1. Since 1960, the rate at which juveniles have been arrested for property crimes has remained consistently higher than the adult rate. The gap between adults and juveniles appears to have widened since that time.

2. Rates of arrest for property crimes increased for both groups between 1960 and 1974, as they did for violent crimes, and then began to level out.

3. The juvenile arrest rate for property crimes has increased 124 percent during the past 20 years, versus 108 percent for adults. Thus, when these findings are compared with those for violent crimes, they suggest that while juveniles appear to have become more criminal overall, the greatest increase among them has been in committing violent crimes.

All crimes

Finally, Figure 5–5 shows increases in the rate of juvenile arrests for all crimes—non-Index as well as Index offenses. In this figure, however, juveniles are not compared with adults. Rather, two changes are introduced: (1) only juveniles, ages 10 to 17, are considered, since it is they, and not children below the age

---

[1] In 1960, FBI estimates were based on arrest data covering only 59 percent of the total population. Since that time, the proportion has increased each year, so that it is close to 95 percent today. As a consequence, raw estimates of increases in arrest are inflated, since the further one goes back in time the greater is the underestimation of the actual number of arrests. Because of this fact, and because of fluctuations in the youth population, standardized rates are used in the estimates that follow. However, in order to compensate for underestimations by the FBI, the following adjustment is made:

$$X = \frac{A_o \cdot P_a}{P_o}$$

where

X = Estimated number of actual arrests
A_o = Arrests reported by the FBI
P_a = Actual population of the United States
P_o = Population upon which FBI arrests are based

The use of this adjustment necessitates two assumptions: (1) arrest rates are the same in areas not covered by the FBI as they are in areas that are covered, and (2) the proportions of different segments of the population (i.e., juvenile and adult, or male and female) are distributed the same in uncovered as in covered areas. To the extent that these assumptions are not met, error will be introduced. Nonetheless, it is likely that this error will be less than the error that is inherent in unadjusted, nonstandardized comparisons.

FIGURE 5–3

Arrests for violent crimes per 100,000, juvenile and adult, 1960–1979*

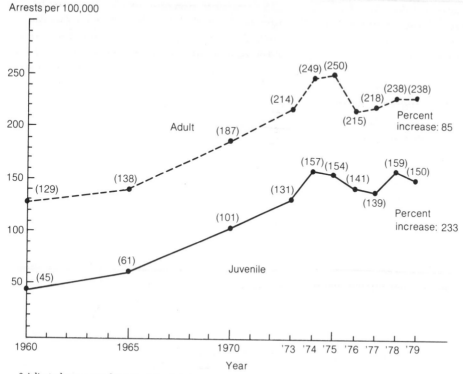

Arrests per 100,000

Year

* Adjusted rates, see footnote 1 for detail.

Sources: FBI, 1961:92,98; 1966:112; 1971:126; 1974:128; 1975:186; 1976:188; 1977:181; 1978:180; 1979:194; 1980:196. Bureau of the Census, 1965:23–24; 1978:9–16; 1980:5.

of 10, who contribute most to the arrest rate; and (2) changes in the size of this particular population (ages 10 to 17) are compared with changes in the arrest rate over time. The following will be observed:

1. The youth population grew steadily in size between 1960 and 1975, and then began to decline. Nonetheless, it was still about 20 percent larger in 1979 than it was in 1960.

2. Although the youth population increased by only 20 percent, the rate at which young people were arrested increased by 94 percent.[2]

---

[2] Nonetheless, this increase (94 percent) is far smaller than the one (324 percent) suggested when raw, unstandardized data were used.

In short, by every yardstick, arrest data suggest that juveniles have become more criminal.

Female crimes

Given these findings, an important question is whether they contain any evidence that, as a result of incipient changes in the female role, comparative arrest rates between boys and girls ages 10 to 17 have also changed. Relative to boys, do girls appear to have become more delinquent?

The answer is provided in Table 5–7. It suggests the following:

1. Boys continue to be arrested at a far

higher rate than girls for all types of crime. Nonetheless, the differences between them have lessened. In 1960, the ratio of male to female arrests for Index crimes was 10 to 1, for non-Index crimes, 4 to 1, and for all crimes, 6 to 1. By 1979, however, these same ratios were 4 to 1, 3 to 1, and 4 to 1 respectively.

2. Since the ratios of male to female arrests have lessened, proportional increases in female arrest rates between 1960 and 1979 have been far greater than increases in male rates: 328 versus 88 percent for Index crimes, 161 versus 117 percent for non-Index crimes, and 202 versus 104 percent for all crimes.

In short, it may well be that there is a connection between alterations in the female role and rates of arrest. It could be that changes are occurring, not only in the attitudes of females toward themselves, but also in the attitudes of society toward females. Since arrest rates reflect the actions of the police, as well as those of the persons who are arrested, it could be that the police are becoming less protective of females, just as females are becoming more assertive in seeking to alter their traditional roles.

Such an interpretation would be paradoxical if it meant that, in order to achieve greater freedom, girls would have to become as criminal as boys. Yet, if present trends continue,

FIGURE 5–4
Arrests for property crimes per 100,000, juvenile and adult, 1960–1979*

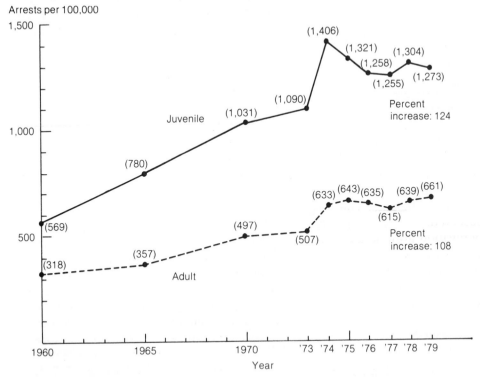

*Adjusted rates. See note in Table 5–3.
Sources: See Table 5–3.

FIGURE 5–5

Trends in arrest and youth population,
10 to 17 years of age, 1960–1979

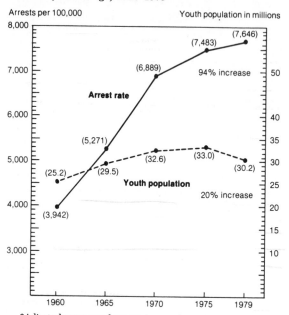

*Adjusted rates, see footnote 1.
  Sources: FBI, 1961:92,98; 1980:196. Bureau of Census, 1965:23–24; 1978:9–16; 1980:5.

that is a possibility. Even worse, if this possibility is tied to arrest trends for youth in general, the paradox grows even greater. Not only has their overall arrest rate accelerated more rapidly than their population growth during the past 20 years, but there is evidence that they have become markedly more violent. Hence, in light of traditional hopes and aspirations for the young, arrest trends are disquieting, if not alarming.

JUVENILE COURT REFERRALS

Following arrest, the next formal step in the processing of arrestees is referral to juvenile court. Therefore, in the pages that follow, the rates and trends of these referrals are analyzed.

Number of referrals

The National Center for Juvenile Justice (NCJJ:7) estimated that approximately 1,355,500 cases were processed by the juvenile courts in 1977, the latest year for which estimates are available. In order to keep this estimate in perspective, it should be known that it constituted only 2 percent of all juveniles that year, and only 4 percent of those ages 10 through 17. The nation, in other words, was not inundated by juvenile court cases.

It should also be noted that this number of court cases was only 62 percent of the 2.2 million juvenile arrests reported by the police in the same year. Hence, according to police estimates, approximately 3.5 percent of all juveniles, and 7 percent of those ages 10 to 17, may have committed illegal acts. But because 40 to 50 percent of all the juveniles picked up by the police are released, and hence are not subjected to further legal action, they do not appear in the estimates reported by the courts (FBI, 1967:110; 1976:42; 1978:210). Instead, approximately half of the original number remain unaccounted for. This fact illustrates the point made at the beginning of this chapter: the further one goes into the juvenile justice system seeking estimates of the numbers of juvenile crimes, the less accurate the estimates become.

Reasons for referral

The kinds of offenses for which juveniles are referred to court are revealed in Figure 5–6. On the one hand, this information tends to sustain the notion that the most common criminal offenses among juveniles are property crimes (40 to 45 percent of all referrals), followed by violent crimes (9 to 10 percent) and the use of drugs and alcohol (8 to 10 percent). On the other hand, the relatively high rate of referrals for status offenses (21 to 25 percent) does not sustain the picture painted

TABLE 5–7
Trends in rate of arrest per 100,000, male versus female, ages 10–17*

Type of offense	Rate, 1960			Rate, 1979			Percent change, 1960–1979	
	Male	Female	Ratio; Male: Female	Male	Female	Ratio; Male: Female	Male	Female
Index	2,557	258	10 : 1	4,801	1,104	4 : 1	88	328
Non-Index	3,259	794	4 : 1	7,068	2,072	3 : 1	117	161
Total	5,816	1,052	6 : 1	11,869	3,176	4 : 1	104	202

* Adjusted rates, see footnote 1, p. 91.
Sources: FBI, 1971:124; 1980:195. Bureau of Census, 1965:23–24; 1978:9–16; 1980:5.

by arrest data; the proportions reported by the police for running away and curfew violations are far lower. Such findings are probably the result of several conditions: (1) the fact that the police do not record many status offenses; (2) the possibility that some juveniles are formally charged with committing status offenses when, in fact, they have been arrested for criminal acts; and (3) the fact that about 20 percent of all referrals to juvenile court are made by agencies other than the police—schools, parents, and welfare departments (NCJJ, 1980:13).

In short, since about one quarter of all court cases involve status offenses, juvenile court records indicate that the court is still continuing to serve as a backup institution, acting as a surrogate parent when families, schools, and communities are considered inadequate, or when juveniles violate the rules for ideal childhood by being truant, incorrigible, a runaway, or sexually promiscuous.

Characteristics of court referrals

Several of the assumed facts about arrest data are also found in court data.

1. Age. Figure 5–7 reveals that the likelihood of being referred to court is closely related to age—the older the juvenile, the greater the likelihood of a referral. But while this finding tends to support arrest data in

general, it also raises some difficult questions. For example, the rate of referral for 17-year-olds (126 per 1,000) is twice as high as the rate for 15-year-olds (65 per 1,000). Yet, it is questionable that 17-year-olds are twice as delinquent. The difference is difficult to explain. Is it because 17-year-olds have longer records and thus are more likely to be defined as chronic offenders? Or is it because authorities are more inclined to hold 17-year-olds responsible for their acts?

Since the answers to such questions are known only to the officials who process juveniles and keep official records, it is clear that their responses to the age and other characteristics of young people may be as important in generating court action and court records as are the acts that young people commit.

2. Gender. Court data also sustain the notion that males are more delinquent than females. For the past several years, in fact, three quarters of all referrals have been male, and only one quarter female (NCJJ, 1980a:1–6). Yet, when one examines the reasons for these referrals, one encounters further evidence of official discretion and possibly a double standard. The reason is that almost three times as many girls (46 percent) as boys (16 percent) are referred to court for status offenses (NCJJ, 1980b:15).

The implication is that, while officials still

look with greater disfavor upon the disobedient and indiscrete girl, they may also be more protective of her when it comes to criminal offenses, since, as we saw earlier, girls are arrested far more often for crimes than for status offenses. Their pattern of criminal arrests is not greatly different from that of boys, although they are arrested much less frequently. Hence, it is clear that tradition continues to exert an important influence upon the actions of legal authorities, the impact of the women's movement notwithstanding.

3. Minority status. An examination of the relation of race to court referral reveals that 7 in 10 referrals are white, 2 in 10 are black, and less than 1 in 10 is of another minority group (NCJJ, 1979; 1980a; 1980b). However, when one considers the smaller size of the black population, it is clear that the chances a black juvenile, age 10 to 17, will be referred to court are greater than the chances of a white (56.6 versus 35.5 per 1,000). Furthermore, blacks are more likely than whites to have had a prior referral (49 versus 40 percent) and to have been

FIGURE 5–7
Referral to court: Rate per 1,000 by age

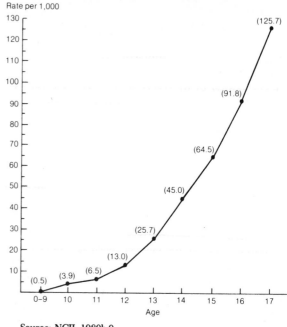

Source: NCJJ, 1980b:9.

FIGURE 5–6
Reasons for referral to juvenile court (percent)

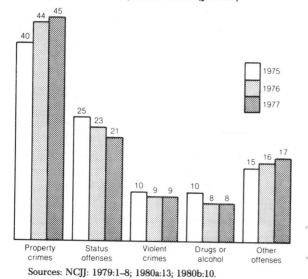

Sources: NCJJ: 1979:1–8; 1980a:13; 1980b:10.

charged with a violent crime (17 versus 7 percent). Thus, while the disparities between blacks and whites in court records are not as great as in arrest statistics, they do suggest either that black youngsters are the more delinquent, or that a racial double standard is continuing to operate, or both.

Trends in referral

Trends in referral to juvenile court, between 1960 and 1977, are displayed in Figure 5–8. Three points may be observed:

1. Referrals increased steadily between 1960 and 1974, as did the number of arrests. Then, in subsequent years, they leveled out.

2. The number of referrals between 1960 and 1977 increased by 108 percent when both

sexes are examined together, a figure that is close to the increase of 94 percent reported in arrest statistics.

3. When the sexes are considered separately, the increase for girls (152 percent) is greater than the increase for boys (97 percent). And since these increases parallel those reported in arrest data—202 percent for girls versus 104 percent for boys—they imply that the delinquent behavior of girls may have increased somewhat more rapidly than that of boys. Indeed, arrest and court data project the same general trends, despite the fact that they differ significantly on a number of specific issues.

SUMMARY AND CONCLUSIONS

Arrest records may be cause to question the extent to which the ideology of child saving has served to quarantine children from involvement in criminal acts. Instead, arrest records suggest that juveniles are among the most criminal segments of the population.

Basic facts

Relative to this finding, certain assumed facts require explanation:

1. *Age. Why is arrest for crime so strongly related to age?* While juveniles are more likely

FIGURE 5–8

Trends in court referral rate per 1,000, ages 10 to 17

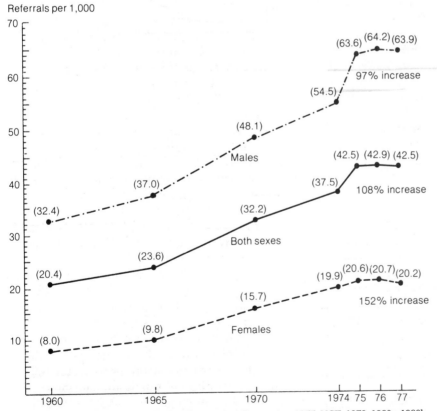

Sources: Office of Juvenile Justice and Delinquency Prevention, 1977; NCJJ, 1979; 1980a; 1980b; Bureau of the Census, 1965:23; 1978:17–24.

to be arrested for property crimes than for violent crimes, and while a small group of chronic offenders may be accounting for a disproportionate share of all juvenile arrests, apprehensions of the young by the police increase steadily during adolescence, peak at age 16, and then decline.

2. *Gender.   Why are arrest rates much higher for males than for females?* It may be that traditional differences between the roles of males and females account for the greater arrest rate of boys. Yet, there is a puzzling corollary question: *Why are girls arrested at a much higher rate than adult women?* Although they are much less delinquent than boys, their youth seems to predispose them to higher rates of arrest and court referral than older persons of the same sex.

3. *Minority status.   Why are arrest rates much higher for black juveniles than for whites?* Arrest data imply that centuries of exclusion from the benefits of American life have had a profound impact on the lives of young black people. While arrest rates for less serious juvenile offenses are approximately equal for both races, black youth are immensely more likely to be arrested for serious, particularly violent, crimes. Moreover, there are findings which suggest that crime rates among Hispanic groups may also be relatively high, while among some Oriental groups they are low. But in the absence of detailed arrest and census data for the country as a whole, it is difficult to present comparative findings.

4. *Social class.   Why are arrest rates higher for lower-class than for middle-class juveniles?* Like membership in the black race, membership in the lower class enhances the likelihood of arrest. Indeed, evidence indicates that these factors are intertwined, and place in double jeopardy those young people who possess both characteristics.

5. *Community.   Why are arrest rates so high in the city?* As Americans have long believed, arrest statistics suggest that crime is greatest in the city, lower in suburban areas, and lower still in rural areas.

Arrest trends

A review of arrest trends also raises important questions because they suggest that juveniles have become more criminal during the past 20 years: Why has their arrest rate grown more rapidly than their population rate? Why do juveniles now appear to be more violent? Why has the arrest of girls increased at a more rapid rate than among boys? Why has the arrest rate leveled out in recent years?

Although arrest rates have not decreased from their unprecedently high levels, at least they have not continued to increase.

Juvenile court referrals

The number of young people referred to juvenile court is much smaller than the number who are arrested, often by as much as half. Court records, as a consequence, are not as accurate an indicator as arrest statistics in reporting the actual incidence of juvenile crime.

This fact notwithstanding, court records raise the same kinds of questions as arrest records: Why does referral to juvenile court increase with age? Why are males referred at a higher rate than females? Why are the chances greater that a black child will be referred to court than a white child? Why have court referrals begun to level out after many years of acceleration?

In response to these difficult questions, the next two chapters are devoted to an analysis of two additional kinds of data: (1) data derived from the self-reported law violations of juveniles rather than from official records; and (2) data derived from the victims rather than from the controllers or the perpetrators of crime. By adding information from these two sources, we can check the validity of official records and determine the accuracy of the questions they raise.

REFERENCES

Bureau of the Census
1965 *Current Population Reports: Population Estimates.* Series P-25, No. 321. Washington, D.C.: U.S. Government Printing Office.
1978 *Current Population Reports: Population Estimates and Projections.* Series P-25, No. 721. Washington, D.C.: U.S. Government Printing Office.
1980 *Current Population Reports: Population Characteristics.* Series P-20, No. 350. Washington, D.C.: U.S. Government Printing Office.

Federal Bureau of Investigation
1961 *Uniform Crime Reports for the United States—1960.* Washington, D.C.: U.S. Government Printing Office.
1967 *Crime in the United States: Uniform Crime Reports—1966.* Washington, D.C.: U.S. Government Printing Office.
1971 *Crime in the United States: Uniform Crime Reports—1970.* Washington, D.C.: U.S. Government Printing Office.
1974 *Crime in the United States: Uniform Crime Reports—1973.* Washington, D.C.: U.S. Government Printing Office.
1975 *Crime in the United States: Uniform Crime Reports—1974.* Washington, D.C.: U.S. Government Printing Office.
1976 *Crime in the United States: Uniform Crime Reports—1975.* Washington, D.C.: U.S. Government Printing Office.
1977 *Crime in the United States: Uniform Crime Reports—1976.* Washington, D.C.: U.S. Government Printing Office.
1978 *Crime in the United States: Uniform Crime Reports—1977.* Washington, D.C.: U.S. Government Printing Office.
1979 *Crime in the United States: Uniform Crime Reports—1978.* Washington, D.C.: U.S. Government Printing Office.
1980 *Crime in the United States: Uniform Crime Reports—1979.* Washington, D.C.: U.S. Government Printing Office.

Greenberg, David F.
1977 "Delinquency and the Age Structure of Society." *Contemporary Crises* 1:189–223.

National Center for Juvenile Justice
1979 *Delinquency 1975: United States Estimates of Cases Processed by Courts with Juvenile Jurisdiction.* Pittsburgh: NCJJ.
1980a *Delinquency 1976: United States Estimates of Cases Processed by Courts with Juvenile Jurisdiction.* Pittsburgh: NCJJ.
1980b *Delinquency 1977: United States Estimates of Cases Processed by Courts with Juvenile Jurisdiction.* Pittsburgh: NCJJ.

National Commission on the Causes and Prevention of Violence
1969 *Crimes of Violence.* Vol. 2. Washington, D.C.: U.S. Government Printing Office.

Office of Juvenile Justice and Delinquency Prevention
1977 *Juvenile Court Statistics—1974.* Washington, D.C.: U.S. Government Printing Office.

Office of Youth Development
    1974   *Juvenile Court Statistics—1973*. Washington, D.C.: U.S. Government Printing Office.

President's Commission on Law Enforcement and Administration of Justice
    1967   *The Challenge of Crime in a Free Society*. Washington, D.C.: U.S. Government Printing Office.

Wolfgang, Marvin E.; Robert Figlio; and Thorsten Sellin
    1972   *Delinquency in a Birth Cohort*. Chicago: University of Chicago Press.

John Thoeming/Dorsey Press

Scientific surveys are used to obtain data on self-reported delinquent behavior from representative samples of American youth.

SELF-REPORTED DELINQUENT BEHAVIOR

Many people are uncomfortable, if not disbelieving, about official accounts of delinquent behavior. This discomfort is due not only to the finding that law violation is much higher for younger than for older people but that it is higher for the poor than for the rich, and higher for blacks than for whites. The probability that the police share in this judgment only adds to the discomfort. It is feared that because they relate crime more to the young, to the poor, and to blacks than to other groups they are more likely to round up these individuals, producing a disproportionate number of youthful, poor, and black offenders in arrest statistics.

FLAWS IN OFFICIAL STATISTICS

In addition to the possibility that official accounts do result in a self-fulfilling prophecy, widespread discomfort is fueled by a number of technical flaws in official statistics:

1. The "dark figure" of crime. Official accounts of delinquency are like the tip of an iceberg. Since many delinquent acts go unobserved or unreported, we have had little knowledge until recently about the size and shape of the iceberg. The National Commission on the Causes and Prevention of Violence (1969:18) called this missing body of information the "dark figure" of crime—the gap between the amount of crime recorded by the police and the amount of crime committed.

The reasons for this gap are numerous. First and foremost is the capacity of most juveniles to keep their illegal acts secret—shoplifting, truancy, fornication, drinking, gambling, vandalism, joyriding, or even burglary. A second reason is closely related. People often fail to report crimes. Some victims are fearful of reprisal; others do not know where to report; and some citizens have little confidence in the police (President's Crime Commission, 1967a:18).

2. The village watchman. A second flaw in the accuracy of official reports of delinquency is the fact that national statistics are collected on the local level by people who may have a vested interest in seeing their reports turn out in a way that favors them. Nettler (1974:45)

103

quotes Sir Josiah Stamp, an English economist, who put his finger directly on the problem. "The government," said Stamp, "are very keen on amassing statistics. They collect them, raise them to the nth power, take the cube root, and prepare wonderful diagrams. But you must never forget that every one of these figures comes in the first instance from the village watchman, who just puts down what he damn pleases."

The reason for Stamp's concern about the village watchman is illustrated by the following comments of a police official:

> The unwritten law was that you were supposed to make things look good. You weren't supposed to report all the crime that actually took place in your precinct—and, if you did, it could be your neck. I know captains who actually lost their commands because they turned in honest crime reports (National Commission on the Causes and Prevention of Violence, 1969:18).

The point is that a variety of city watchmen in police departments, the courts, and in correctional institutions often distort their reports, either through ignorance or for a variety of self-serving reasons. Their commitments to themselves and to their organizations are greater than their commitments to accurate knowledge. Like students cheating on a test or citizens misreporting their income to the IRS, other matters take precedence.

3.   *Changing norms and expectations.* Changing norms for behavior and the social expectations that attend them also contribute to the technical difficulties in interpreting delinquency statistics—difficulties that often appear in an unexpected way. For example, one of the results of political inequality traditionally has been the tendency for the police to ignore many but the most serious crimes in slum areas (President's Crime Commission, 1967b:26). Without political

power, poor and minority people were left to take care of their own problems. As a result, many common delinquent acts went unchecked and unreported. But as poor and minority people acquired some political clout, demands were made that the police take a more active role in suppressing delinquency in the ghetto. The likely consequence, particularly in recent years, has been an increase in the number of reported delinquencies. Lawbreaking behavior that was customary heretofore—particularly status offenses, gang behavior, and petty crimes—now became a matter of public record. It is possible that without a great increase in the actual incidence of delinquent behavior, arrest and court records were inflated considerably.

Changing rules and expectations can alter crime records in other ways. In virtually every state, many forms of sexual conduct—fornication, adultery, prostitution, homosexuality, sodomy, and oral sex—have been against the law. In recent years the sexual revolution has led to increasing demands that such laws be repealed. Nettler notes that once it was anticipated that the Wolfinden Committee would make similar recommendations in England, the number of recorded homosexual offenses dropped by half over the space of a few years (1974:45–46). Yet, the laws during that period were not actually changed. The reduction in official offenses was due to changes in police activity, not to changes in the law or changes in homosexual conduct.

These examples illustrate that laws are selectively enforced, depending in part upon changing circumstance and social definition. Any adequate interpretation of the meaning of official statistics, therefore, requires some knowledge of these changes.

4.   *Police professionalization.*   Those who run the Uniform Crime Reporting System are not unaware of these problems. Both the President's Crime Commission (1967b:26) and the National Commission on Violence (1969:23)

note that significant efforts have been made to correct and to professionalize police reporting practices. For example, now included in the calculation of crime trends are only those police agencies that have had comparable records and reporting practices over the years. Also, the collection of data by the police has been improved and their methods of recording crimes standardized.

Paradoxically, one of the reasons for care to be exercised in interpreting police findings is precisely that their recording practices have improved. As the number of statistical clerks has increased and as reporting systems have become better organized, known crimes are recorded more faithfully than ever before. Undoubtedly, some of the increase in reported crimes is due to these improved methods, a fact that illustrates a sociological truism: as society becomes more aware of a problem and attempts to do something about it, the size of the problem seems to increase.

In summary, "it can be argued that official statistics on crime, whether compiled by the police, the courts, or any other administrative agency, can never provide a definitive measure of crime" (Penick and Owens, 1976:153). They are unsatisfactory, partly because of offenses that are never reported to the police and partly because of wide variations in the way reported crimes are recorded.

THE BASIC ISSUE

The basic issue, then, is this: on one hand, it is clear that official records are less than ideal and possibly misleading; on the other hand, arguments against them are often ideological rather than factual.

Like official records, therefore, these arguments should be considered with a healthy degree of skepticism. In contrast to the cynicism and ambivalence which many people now express, some well-known theorists have argued that these negative feelings are based more on humanitarian inclinations than on facts.

Consider, for example, the argument that official records are biased against lower-class children. While granting that illegal behavior is by no means confined to lower-class children, Cohen maintains that its concentration among them is not an illusion. It is only our "egalitarian proclivities and sentimental humanitarianism," he suggests, "which cause us to think otherwise" (1955:42). Likewise, Cloward and Ohlin maintain that middle-class delinquency is "petty" in comparison with lower-class delinquency (1960:12). They believe that the inclination to violate the law is more deeply ingrained in lower-class youngsters and that they possess a greater potential for the development of criminal careers. Given the urgency of these contrasting points of view, therefore, alternative ways for measuring delinquent behavior have been sought. One of the more important has been self-reported delinquent behavior.

SELF-REPORTED LAW VIOLATION

In contrast to official methods of collecting data on delinquent behavior, a growing number of social scientists have gone to juveniles themselves to discover how many law violations they have committed and what led them to crime. They have done this by administering anonymous questionnaires, interviewing youngsters, and simply observing their behavior. Their findings help to answer a series of crucial questions.

1. How prevalent is law violation among juveniles? The *prevalence* of law violation is measured by determining what proportion of all juveniles report having violated the law. When delinquent behavior is measured in this way, self-report studies find that almost all juveniles have been delinquent (Ageton and Elliott, 1978; Erickson and Empey, 1963; Gold, 1966, 1970; Gould, 1969; Illinois Institute for

Juvenile Research, 1973; Murphy et al., 1946; Short and Nye, 1958; Williams and Gold, 1972). This finding, moreover, is not limited to the United States, but has been reported in other countries as well (Christie, 1965; Elmhorn, 1965). Law violation among juveniles is very common.

2. *What kinds of offenses are most commonly reported?* In order to answer this question, a series of tables have been constructed which show the prevalence of law violation when (1) juveniles are asked if they have *ever* committed any one of a long list of different offenses, and (2) juveniles are asked if they have committed these same offenses *during the past year.* These tables were derived from a variety of studies spanning 20 years, which were conducted in both rural and urban areas and which used different methods of gathering data.[1] Yet, their findings paint a fairly consistent picture.

a. Status offenses. Table 6–1 reveals several points about the commission of undetected status offenses—offenses that are generally illegal for children but not for adults. First, it suggests that, whether the time period is a lifetime or the previous year, significant proportions of all juveniles, male and female, admit to having committed a number of status offenses at least once: truancy, drinking, and driving without a license rank first; defying

parents and fornication rank second; and running away ranks last. Second, although girls are consistently less delinquent than boys, their pattern of offenses is much the same. Almost as many girls as boys report having been truant from school, having used alcohol, and having run away from home. Third, the only difference of any magnitude between girls and boys has to do with sexual intercourse. Fewer girls report having engaged in sex, suggesting that the sexual partners of boys may be smaller in number, and somewhat more promiscuous, than the general population of girls.

b. Crimes against property. When young people are asked whether they have *ever* committed property offenses, Table 6–2 suggests that petty theft, shoplifting, and destroying property are about as common as drinking and truancy, involving considerable numbers of girls as well as boys. Breaking and entering is also quite common: sometimes it merely involves illegal entry into homes, public buildings, or businesses for the purpose of "having fun" or "messing around"; other times, illegal entry is made for the purpose of burglary. Finally, auto theft, which often involves taking a car to go joyriding, is the least common of these kinds of offenses. Only about 10 percent of all boys and about 3 percent of all girls report ever having committed this offense.

---

[1] These studies include the following:

Area	Community	Sample	Method	Investigators	Published
Midwest	3 communities: rural, rural/urban, suburban	596	Question-naire	Short & Nye	1958
Washington	3 communities: 10,000 to 40,000	2,350	Question-naire	Short & Nye	1958
Utah	Community of 40,000	180	Interview	Erickson & Empey	1963
Illinois	Statewide	3,100	Question-naire	Institute for Juvenile Research	1972
Michigan	Community of 200,000	522	Interview	Gold	1970
United States	Probability Sample of all young people ages 11 to 17	1,725	Interview	Elliott & Ageton	1978; 1980

TABLE 6–1

Prevalence of self-reported *status* offenses

	Truancy	Drinking	Type of offenses			
			Defying parents	Fornica-tion	Running away	Driving without license
Percent *ever* committing offense:						
Midwest,						
Boys	54	68	22	39	13	81
Washington,						
Boys	53	57	33	40	13	75
Utah,						
Boys	66	52	40	—	22	72
Illinois,						
Boys and girls	47	61	—	—	—	43
Michigan,						
Boys	30	55	—	19	6	—
Girls	17	43	—	5*	6	—
Percent committing offense *during past year:*						
United States,						
Boys	34	49	—	18	6	—
Girls	29	43	—	7	5	—

Note: Blank columns indicate no information collected.
* Validation information suggests that this figure would be more accurate estimate if it were doubled (Gold, 1970:4).

When juveniles are asked to report only on the *preceding year,* the prevalence of property offenses drops off considerably. In other words, the data suggest that chronic criminality is not characteristic of most young people. Petty larceny and vandalism are the only acts for which the prevalence of law violation remains relatively high.

Furthermore, only about one boy in a hundred, and no girls, reported having deliberately stolen a motor vehicle in the preceding year, although 6 and 3 percent, respectively, said they had taken a vehicle to go joyriding.

c. Crimes against persons. Table 6–3 tends to support official records which suggest that, overall, crimes against persons are much less common among adolescents than are status offenses or property crimes. There are some exceptions, however—fist fighting, gang fighting and, to a lesser degree, assault, are quite common. But while fighting is one

activity that has long been a part of adolescent life and apparently continues to be as common as drinking, petty theft, or destroying property, deliberate assault on others for the purpose of doing them serious harm is another matter.

According to Table 6–3, serious assault is less prevalent than other personal offenses, as is carrying a concealed weapon. Even less common is armed robbery or "strong-arming" someone to obtain money or goods. Nonetheless, the proportions of these kinds of offenses reported during the past year as well as for several years earlier remain considerably higher than those ordinarily reported by the police. Furthermore, the fact that *any* girls were involved in these acts, to say nothing of about 1 in 10 boys, runs contrary to the traditional belief that it is adults who are more likely to commit violent acts.

d. Drug use. Comprehensive data on the prevalence of drug use have been provided by the Institute for Social Research at the University of Michigan (Johnston et al., 1979). Each year, from 1975 through 1979, the institute gathered information from a probability sample of several thousand high school seniors throughout the United States. Table 6–4 summarizes the levels of illegal use of nonprescription drugs reported by the graduating class of 1979. Several points are noteworthy:

Alcohol and cigarettes are the most popular drugs among young people. Indeed, almost as many seniors reported having used alcohol in the past month (72 percent) as having ever used it (93 percent).

Considerable proportions reported having tried other drugs during their lifetimes: stimulants (24 percent), inhalants (19 percent), hallucinogens (19 percent),

tranquilizers (16 percent), cocaine (15 percent), sedatives (14 percent), and opiates other than heroin (10 percent). However, except for stimulants (10 percent), the proportions who reported having used these drugs during the past month drops off considerably, suggesting that the numbers of regular users is relatively small (2 to 6 percent).

The prevalence of reported heroin use among high school students, despite the media attention given to it, is small (1 percent lifetime and 0.2 percent last month). However, this estimate, along with those for other drugs, does not take into account the extent of heroin use among school dropouts. It is likely somewhat higher, perhaps as high as 3 percent (Illinois Institute for Juvenile Research, 1972:25–28).

TABLE 6–2

Prevalence of self-reported crimes against *property*

	Offenses					
	Less than $2	Larceny $2–$50	Shoplifting	Destroying property	Breaking and entering	Auto theft or joyriding
Percent *ever* committing offense:						
Midwest						
Boys	63	17	—	61	—	11
Washington						
Boys	61	16	—	45	—	15
Utah						
Boys	92	22	—	66	32	2
Illinois						
Boys and girls	56*	16	50	31	13	10
Michigan						
Boys	60†	—	50	27	38	10
Girls	30†	—	25	6	23	3
Percent committing offense *during past year:*						
United States						
Boys	22	7‡	—	24	6	6 (1)
Girls	13	3‡	—	10	2	3 (0)

Note: Blank columns indicate no information collected.
* Petty theft.
† Theft by stealth.
‡ $5 to 50.
( ) Refers to auto theft.

TABLE 6–3

Prevalence of self-reported crimes against *persons*

	Offenses				
	Fist fighting	Gang fighting	Assault	Carrying concealed weapon	Armed robbery or strong-arming
Percent *ever* committing offense:					
Midwest					
Boys 87		24	16	—	6
Washington					
Boys 81		23	14	—	—
Utah					
Boys 52		—	—	—	0
Illinois					
Boys and girls 50		21	—	25	13
Michigan					
Boys .... —		23	11	13	6
Girls .... —		5	2	1	0
Percent committing offense *during past year:*					
United States					
Boys .... —		17	9	10	4
Girls .... —		7	3	2	2

Note: Blank columns indicate no information collected.

The Survey Research Institute has also studied trends in drug use among high school seniors between 1975 and 1979. Its findings reveal the following (Johnston et al., 1979:23–30).

The use of two drugs—marijuana and cocaine—showed a dramatic increase between 1975 and 1979. The proportion who reported having ever used marijuana increased by 13 percent, and cocaine by 6.4 percent. Furthermore, the monthly use of these drugs increased 9.4 percent and 3.8 percent respectively.

The reported use of several other drugs also increased, but at a lower rate: alcohol, 2.7 percent lifetime and 3.6 percent monthly; stimulants, 1.9 percent lifetime and 1.4 percent monthly; and inhalants, 2.4 percent on an annual basis.

Finally, the reported use of still other drugs declined slightly: sedatives, −3.6 percent lifetime and −1.0 percent monthly; heroin, −1.1 percent lifetime and −0.2 percent monthly; and tranquilizers, −0.7 percent lifetime and −0.4 percent monthly.

In short, these findings on young people's drug use provides a virtual mirror image of drug use in society at large: (1) alcohol and cigarettes are the most popular drugs; (2) the use of marijuana and cocaine is increasing; (3) experimentation with a host of new drugs, as they arrive on the scene, is considerable; and (4) reliance upon drugs for the purposes of both recreation and escape is widespread.

THE DARK FIGURE OF CRIME

Given the fact that many more juveniles report having violated the law than official statistics would indicate, some crucial questions are raised: How large is the dark figure of crime? What proportion of all offenses reported by juveniles become a part of the official record.

Studies indicate that at least 9 out of 10 illegal acts either go undetected or unacted upon by anyone in authority (Erickson and Empey, 1963, Gold, 1966; Murphy et al., 1946; Williams and Gold, 1972). This conclusion is based upon two kinds of information: (1) statements by young people concerning how often they have been caught, and (2) official records regarding how often the names of self-confessed offenders appear in them. For example, after having checked the official record against the self-reports of a national sample, Williams and Gold found that "less than 1 percent of the chargable offenses committed in the three years prior to the interviews were recorded as official delinquency. . . . And when offenses do come to the attention of the police, they often result in warnings, 'station adjustments,' and a host of other police actions that fall short of delinquency records for teenagers" (1972:221).

These outcomes are particularly true with respect to so-called minor violations: traffic violations, petty theft, buying and drinking alcohol, destroying property, skipping school, and so on. There is some evidence, however, that the picture changes with respect to more serious violations—felonious theft, auto theft, breaking and entering, and armed robbery. Fewer of these offenses go undetected and unacted upon. Yet, even in these cases, 8 out of 10 violations remain undetected, and 9 out of 10 do not result in court action (Erickson and Empey, 1963:465; Williams and Gold, 1972:221–222).

So striking are such findings that one is reminded of the statement made over 30 years ago by Murphy et al. when they first encountered the large gap between actual lawbreaking and officially recorded delinquency. "Even a moderate increase in the amount of attention paid to [it] by law enforcement authorities," they said, "could create a semblance of a 'delinquency wave' without there being the slightest change in adolescent behavior." (1946:696). If all, or even

---

TABLE 6–4

Prevalence (percent ever used) and recency of drug use among high school seniors (15,500)

Type of drug	Ever used	Past year	Past month	Never used
Alcohol	93.0	88.1	71.8	7.0
Cigarettes	74.0	—	—	26.0
Marijuana (pot, hash, grass)	60.4	50.8	36.5	39.6
Stimulants (uppers, amphetamines, bennies, speed)	24.2	18.3	9.9	75.8
Inhalants (glue, aerosol, poppers)	18.7	9.2	3.1	81.3
Hallucinogens (LSD, PCP, acid, mescaline, peyote)	18.6	12.8	5.5	81.4
Tranquilizers (Librium, Valium, Miltown)	16.3	9.6	3.7	83.7
Cocaine (coke, snow)	15.4	12.0	5.7	84.6
Sedatives (downers, ludes, reds, goofballs, yellows)	14.6	9.9	4.4	85.4
Opiates other than heroin (opium, codeine, paragoric, morphine)	10.1	6.2	2.4	89.9
Heroin (horse, smack)	1.1	0.5	0.2	98.9

Note: Blank columns indicate information not available.
Source: Johnston et al., 1979:11.

a significant part, of law violations became a part of the official record, the result would be unprecedented: a large majority of adolescents would be official delinquents.

In light of current efforts to improve crime reporting by the police, such findings raise some important and provocative questions: To what degree might the youthful crime wave of the 1960s and 1970s be a result of better police records? To what extent are the frightening rises in official crime rates the results of tapping more successfully the high degree of juvenile lawbreaking that has always existed?

It is difficult to be conclusive about these questions. But after comparing the results of two national surveys, Gold and Reimer found no overall increase in self-reported illegal behavior when information gathered in 1972 was compared with the same kind of information gathered in 1967. Rather than an increase in law violation, they found a change in both the nature of the offenses committed and who it was that had committed them:

> Specifically, more of the '72 male respondents reported more frequent use of illicit drugs—mostly marijuana—than the 1967 respondents did and less larceny, threatened assault, trespassing, forcible and nonforcible entry, and gang fighting. The girls in '72 also reported greater use of drugs—mostly marijuana but including alcohol—than did girls in '67, while reporting less larceny, property destruction, and breaking and entering. But the decline of the latter kinds of offenses among girls in 1972 does not balance their greater use of drugs, so the girls in '72 reported more delinquent behavior overall (Gold and Reimer, 1974:13).

In short, illegal behavior among boys may actually have declined, while among girls it may have risen due to their increased use of marijuana.

Since these unofficial findings conflict sharply with official reports indicating that youth crime is on the increase, they must be treated with considerable caution. While Gold and Reimer (1974:29) contend that their findings may approximate the actual levels of delinquent behavior more closely than official records, their two surveys, which were based on relatively small samples and were separated by an interval of five years, cannot be taken as definitive. However, some attempts are being made to remedy this problem. The national survey of youth by Elliott and Ageton, which was noted on page 106, was but the first of five annual surveys which they are now conducting. Therefore, some definitive findings on trends in juvenile law violation may be available a few years hence (Elliott and Ageton, 1980:98).

CHRONIC DELINQUENT BEHAVIOR

In the previous chapter, we reviewed the Philadelphia study of official delinquents by Marvin Wolfgang and his associates (1972) which suggested that there may be a small group of young chronic offenders who pose the greatest threat to other persons and properties. A basic question, therefore, is whether any confirmation for this conclusion can be found in self-report studies: Do all young people report being equally delinquent or are some of them more delinquent than others?

In order to answer this question, we must examine not merely the *prevalence* of delinquent behavior—how many juveniles have violated the law, but also its *incidence*—how many delinquent acts youth report having committed. Every study in which this measure is used suggests that the delinquent behavior of individuals varies greatly. It is not an either-or variation like having the mumps or measles, but is a more-or-less variation. Young people are distributed by their behavior along a continuum running from high to low (Elliott and Ageton, 1980; Elmhorn, 1965; Erickson and Empey, 1963; Gold, 1970; Nettler, 1974;

Short and Nye, 1958; Williams and Gold, 1972).

On one end of the continuum are the majority of young people, most of whom have committed a number of minor acts, although an occasional serious offense may appear. Further along the continuum, one encounters fewer and fewer juveniles who, at the same time, tend to be more and more delinquent. Their illegal acts tend to increase not only in frequency but in seriousness. Thus, at the extreme end of the continuum are a small minority of individuals who are both frequent and serious offenders. All young people who are delinquent are not equally delinquent.

But this is not all we need to know in order to answer the question about chronic offenders. We must also consider the fact that relatively few law violators are caught and punished. In order to determine whether any confidence can be placed in the Wolfgang findings, therefore, two additional questions must be answered: Is being arrested entirely a chance thing? Are official records at all accurate in identifying those who, by their own admission, are the most delinquent?

Some evidence suggests that the possession of an official record is not entirely a chance thing—that those individuals who admit to being the most delinquent are somewhat more likely to have been arrested, to have appeared in court, and, particularly, to have been confined to a training school.

Consider arrest first. In their nationwide study, Williams and Gold found a small but nonetheless significant relationship between frequency of offense and likelihood of arrest (1972:219). The greater the number of violations, the greater the chance of apprehension. To a lesser degree, seriousness of offense was also associated with getting caught. Crimes against persons, in particular, were those which increased the likelihood of arrest. Yet, despite these findings, the evidence indicated that the odds are still greatly on the side of the lawbreaker. Even though the most frequent and serious violators are somewhat more likely to be arrested, the risks they take are small.

Once offenders are involved in the juvenile justice system, however, the picture begins to change. For a first offense, especially if it is a petty or status offense, the risks are not so great that the offender will be sent to court since the police are inclined to counsel and release a large number of first offenders (FBI, 1976:177). But when some of these individuals get caught more than once in the police net, the likelihood increases that they will be sent to court. The evidence suggests, moreover, that the reason they reappear is because they have been more delinquent. Indeed, Erickson (1972:394–95) found a correlation of .95 between self-admitted law violation and appearance in court (see also Erickson and Empey, 1963:147). Boys who admit to having been highly delinquent are those most likely to be sent before a judge.

Once in court, the same process begins all over again. Like the police, most judges and probation officers, in seeking to treat rather than to punish children, are inclined to be lenient with the individuals they see for the first time (National Center for Juvenile Justice, 1977:14). If these first offenders have not committed a grievous offense, and if they are not dependent and neglected, they are usually warned and informally supervised.

Indeed, this kind of response seems to work for the majority. But for a few individuals, partly because they continue to defy the gods of chance, another court appearance will follow. When that occurs, court officials tend again to react like the police; that is they are inclined to respond negatively to official repeaters and to send them further on into the system. They are the ones, therefore, who are most likely to end up in a training school. But are they the most delinquent, or are they just the most unlucky?

The evidence on this issue is telling. Self-report studies indicate that incarcerated delinquents or those who have a record of several court appearances are by their own admission individuals who fit on the most delinquent end of the adolescent continuum (Erickson and Empey, 1963; Short and Nye, 1958). Not only have they committed more offenses, most of which are unknown to authorities, but those offenses are of a more serious variety. The evidence regarding them, in fact, is very much like that presented in the Wolfgang cohort study (1972). Just as these investigators found that a small but chronic group of offenders were unusually delinquent, so these self-report studies find that incarcerated offenders or those with repeated court appearances are not only more delinquent than juveniles who have no official record, but more delinquent than those who have appeared in court only once.

For example, Erickson and Empey (1963:462) found that if non- and one-time offenders are combined—because their offense rates are more alike than different—and compared with the chronic repeater group, the cumulative violations of the latter group exceed those of the former by thousands: theft (2,851 versus 20,836); violations of property (1,450 versus 10,828); violations of person (457 versus 8,569); and violations involving the purchase and drinking of alcohol (564 versus 21,134). In addition, far smaller proportions of non- and one-time offenders committed serious crimes than did official repeaters or boys who were confined: theft of articles worth more than $50 (2 percent versus 50 percent); auto theft (2 percent versus 52 percent); forgery (0 percent versus 25 percent); and armed robbery (0 percent versus 9 percent).

A study of an entirely different population in Washington State by Short and Nye (1958:44) showed virtually the same thing: far smaller proportions of nondelinquents, when compared with incarcerated boys, reported having committed various illegal acts: theft or

articles worth more than $50 (5 percent versus 91 percent); auto theft (15 percent versus 75 percent); strong-arming (6 percent versus 68 percent); and destruction of property (45 percent versus 84 percent). Furthermore, many of these differences continued to appear when status rather than criminal offenses were considered: skipping school (53 percent versus 95 percent); running away (13 percent versus 68 percent); and buying and using alcohol (57 percent versus 90 percent).

What these findings suggest, in short, is that the juvenile justice system is like a coarse net that is dragged in a large ocean (Nettler, 1974:90). The chances are small that most fish will be caught. And even when some are caught, they manage to escape or are released because they are too small. But because a few fish are much more active than others, and because they are bigger, they are caught more than once. Each time this occurs, moreover, the chances that they will escape or be thrown back decrease. At the very end, therefore, they form a very select group whose behavior clearly separates them from most of the fish still in the ocean.

FACTS THAT MUST BE EXPLAINED

In light of this finding, a key question is whether these chronic law violators possesses any characteristics that differentiate them from the less delinquent segment of the youth population. Official records suggest that they are more likely to be adolescent than preadolescent, male than female, black than white, and lower- than middle-class. Indeed, if self-report studies confirm the existence of these differences, then they become assumed facts which criminologists must seek to explain in their theories of delinquent behavior.

Age

According to official data, age is highly related to delinquent behavior. It will be recalled that the incidence of arrest is low for juveniles, ages 10 to 12, but that at age 13 it accelerates sharply and peaks at about age 17.

The results of a national survey by Ageton and Elliott (1978), only partially confirm these figures. They found that, while the prevalence of assault and robbery generally increases with age, it tends to peak between ages 13 to 15 for many offenses. While 16- to 17-year-olds are more inclined to commit aggravated or sexual assaults, 13- to 15-year-olds are just as likely to hit parents and teachers, and more likely to hit and strong-arm their fellow students. Furthermore, the average frequency with which a small number of 11- to 12-year-olds report having hit or strong-armed parents, teachers or fellow students is often as high as the frequency with which older groups report having done so.

These findings reveal, in short, that some juveniles are inclined to prey upon those with whom they interact the most—members of their families, their fellow students, and their teachers.

Much the same picture reappears when one considers property crimes. It is among 13- to 15-year-olds, rather than older juveniles, where the incidence, as well as the prevalence, of these acts seem to peak. Finally, it is only when status offenses are examined that a linear progression upward, from lower to higher ages, seems to occur. Juveniles ages 16 to 17 are more likely than younger to have run away, been truant, had intercourse, used alcohol and drugs, or been suspended from school during the past year.

It is still too early to say whether these kinds of findings will hold up in future surveys, but if they do, they may require more attention than they have received in the past. While they do not take issue with the idea that juveniles are often inclined to break the law, they suggest that many offenders are somewhat younger than arrest statistics would indicate. Either the authorities are inclined to be more lenient with younger children, or they are concentrating more on the criminal acts of older adolescents which, rather than involving friends, parents, or teachers, involve strangers who are burglarized, robbed, or attacked on city streets.

Gender

As we learned in the previous chapter, records maintained by the police and courts have suggested that gender is a second fact that should be taken into account in explaining delinquent behavior because (1) official rates of delinquency have been much higher for boys than for girls, and (2) official records suggest that girls are more likely to commit such "female" offenses as running away, being sexually promiscuous, or defying parents rather than to commit serious personal or property crimes. But are these findings accurate? Are girls less delinquent than boys? Are their patterns of self-reported law violation different from boys?

When Gold (1966) sought answers to these questions, he discovered that female offenses accounted for only about 8 to 11 percent of the law violations reported by girls. Considerably more common, by contrast, were drinking, shoplifting, truancy, theft and illegal entry; property destruction, and even fighting were about as common as female offenses. What is more, these findings have since been confirmed by a series of subsequent studies (Elliott and Ageton, 1980; Hindelang, 1971; Jensen and Eve, 1976; Williams and Gold, 1972; Wise, 1967). The pattern of female delinquent behavior is much the same as that of boys (see Tables 6–2, 6–3, 6–4 and 6–5).

The same is not true, however, either for the *prevalence* or the *incidence* of delinquent behavior. Not only does a larger proportion of the male population report having violated the law, but the frequency with which it does so is far greater. In Table 6–5, for example, it can be seen that the ratio of female to male offenses

TABLE 6–5

Mean number of self-reported delinquent acts by gender

Type of offense	Girls	Boys	Approximate ratio
Aggravated assault	.05	.28	1 : 5
Sexual assault	.07	.01	1 : 7
Strong-armed others	.04	.18	1 : 4
Burglary	.03	.22	1 : 7
Larceny:			
$5 to $50	.24	.29	1 : 1
Over $50	.01	.11	1 : 11
Motor vehicle theft:			
Stole vehicle	.00	.03	—
Joyriding	.07	.15	1 : 2
Damaged property	.20	1.48	1 : 7
Prostitution	.02	.14	1 : 7
Sexual intercourse	2.04	3.43	2 : 3
Use of drugs:			
Alcohol	5.50	9.24	1 : 1.7
Marijuana	6.64	7.73	1 : 1
Hallucinogens	.12	.15	1 : 1
Amphetamines	.35	.63	1 : 1.8
Barbiturates	.39	.43	1 : 1
Truancy	2.61	5.43	1 : 2
Running away	.08	.10	1 : 1

Source: Ageton and Elliott, 1978: table 2.

is low: aggravated assault, 1:5; sexual assault, 1:7; strong-arming others, 1:4; damaging property, 1:7. Even prostitution (1:7) and truancy (1:2) follow this pattern. The only major exceptions are theft of items worth $5 to $50 (1:1), alcohol and drug use (1:1 to 1:2), and running away (1:1). Otherwise, the strong relationship between being male and committing delinquent acts suggests, once again, that traditional expectations for females may have continued to dampen their delinquent behavior, even though they commit some delinquent acts commonly attributed to boys.

Finally, there is the related question as to whether female delinquency is increasing, as official accounts have suggested. As a result of its survey in Illinois, the Institute for Juvenile Research (1972) concluded that such is the case. Girls, it suggested, are "reporting a higher level of delinquent involvement than has ever been reported in the past." While tending to agree with that conclusion, Gold and Reimer (1974:15–17) suggest the need for qualification. While they did find national increase in reported female delinquency of 22 percent between 1967 and 1972, this was related primarily to the use of alcohol and drugs. The frequency of drinking among girls nearly doubled during those years, and the per capita use of marijuana and drugs was nine times greater among females in 1972 over 1967.

Other investigators disagree, contending that the purported rise in female crime is a myth (Steffensmeier and Steffensmeier, 1980). Nonetheless, if their disagreement is taken to mean that illegal acts among females are inconsequential and need not be taken into account in forming theories of crime, a serious error is being made. While males *do* report having committed a greater range of delinquent acts, and more frequently than females, differences between the sexes are not universal concerning all delinquent acts. Even though the *incidence* of alcohol and drug use among girls, for example, is generally somewhat less than among boys, its *prevalence* is almost as great (Johnston et al., 1979:31–35); (see also Table 6–5). Furthermore, while girls are not as delinquent as boys overall, they do report having committed a long list of illegal acts which historically have been viewed as "male" offenses. Thus, while explanations are needed to account for the greater delinquency of males, they are also needed to account for a picture of female behavior that is far different from that suggested by tradition.

Minority status

As we learned when reviewing official accounts of delinquency, arrest data have tended to confirm the long-held assumption that minority groups have contributed disproportionately to the juvenile crime rate. But is this assumption true? Are minority

TABLE 6–6

Average incidence of self-reported delinquent acts by race

Race	Total self-reported delinquent acts			Crimes against persons		Crimes against property		Illegal service crimes		Public disorder crimes		Hard drug use		Status offenses	
	N	$\bar{X}$	SD	$\bar{X}$	SD	$\bar{X}$	SD	$\bar{X}$	SD	$\bar{X}$	SD	$\bar{X}$	SD	$\bar{X}$	SL
White	1357	46.79	161.37	7.84	58.42	8.93	42.87	1.85	22.36	14.98	62.37	1.26	14.03	14.84	49
Black	259	79.20	277.38	12.96	76.59	20.57	106.27	1.71	22.83	16.50	67.78	.18	1.35	16.19	53
F		6.68		1.50		8.79		.09		.13		1.55		.16	
Probability		≤.01		NS		≤.001		NS		NS		NS		.16	

Source: Elliott and Ageton, 1980:102.

children more likely than others to be chronic offenders?

Unfortunately, these questions cannot be answered for all minority groups, since very few self-report studies have been made of such important groups as Mexican-Americans, Puerto Ricans, other Latin American groups, several Oriental groups, or even many different Caucasian groups in American society (see Voss, 1966, for an exception). Any conclusions, therefore, will have to be limited once again to contrasts between black and white Americans.

1. Prevalence. Official records have suggested consistently that the *prevalence* of delinquent behavior is much greater among blacks than among whites. Hirschi (1969:43), for example, found that 53 percent of the black and 29 percent of the white boys in Richmond, California had official police records. These figures, in turn, were strikingly similar to those reported in the Wolfgang study (1972) in Philadelphia (50 percent for blacks and 29 percent for whites). Thus, at opposite ends of the country, official records have implied that black boys are far more likely to violate the law than white boys.

But when Hirschi (1969:75–76) compared official with self-report accounts of delinquent behavior, he found the difference between blacks and whites greatly diminished. For example, 49 percent of the blacks and 44 percent of the whites reported having

committed at least one delinquent act during the previous year. Yet, while this was only a difference of 5 percent, the official records cited above indicated a difference of 24 percent (53 versus 29 percent).

Such findings are not unique. Along with Hirschi, most self-report studies, local or national, have indicated that the overall prevalence of law violation does not differ significantly between the races. The proportion of whites who report having violated the law at least once is about the same as the proportion of blacks (Elliott and Ageton, 1980; Elliott and Voss, 1974; Gold and Reimer, 1974; Institute for Juvenile Research, 1972; Williams and Gold, 1972).

2. Incidence. The *incidence* of delinquency is another matter. When Elliott and Ageton (1980:102–103) examined the whole range of frequencies in their recent national study, they found that the ratio of black to white total offenses was nearly two to one; that is, black youngsters reported having committed many more delinquent acts (Table 6–6). Furthermore, this differential was due primarily to the greater involvement of blacks in serious predatory crimes, not in drug use, illegal service crimes, public disorder crimes, or status offenses.

Other studies report remarkably similar findings. While they have not always agreed that the overall incidence of delinquent acts is greater among black youth, they have agreed that blacks are more likely to report serious crimes. In Illinois, for example, the Institute for Juvenile Research found that "black adolescents are approximately twice as likely to report an act of violence as white adolescents" (1972:23–24). Similarly, Gold and his associates found in their two national surveys that "assaults, burglary, and theft—in that order—account for the greater seriousness of the delinquent behavior of black compared to white boys" (Williams and Gold, 1972:217; Gold and Reimer, 1974:17). Indeed, about the only major exception has to do with cars: whites, not blacks, are more likely to steal autos, to go joyriding, or to drive recklessly (Illinois Institute for Juvenile Research, 1972; Higgins and Albrecht, forthcoming).

3. *Chronic offenders.* Elliott and Ageton (1980:103–104) also found that differences between the races seem to be due to a relatively small number of *chronic offenders* (10 percent or less). As may be noted in Table 6–7, ratios of blacks to whites on the low (less delinquent) end of the frequency continuum for all delinquent acts are close to 1 to 1, but at the high (more delinquent) end the ratios are greater than 2 to 1. Furthermore, these differences are even greater for serious property crimes. While the majority of juvenile blacks and whites rate virtually the same at the low end, they differ by more than 2 to 1 at the high end.

The findings of Elliott and Ageton (1980:104) were also illuminating when they analyzed three different types of assault offenses: simple assault, aggravated assault, and sexual assault. They found that the mean number of simple assaults reported by juvenile whites was two times greater than that reported by blacks. But for aggravated and sexual assault, the ratios of whites to blacks (1:5 and 1:4) were in the opposite direction—surprisingly like those reported in arrest statistics. Even though the incidence of these serious crimes was much less common among all youth, blacks were considerably more inclined to report having committed them.

These findings suggest, then, that minority status is a third issue that should be taken into account in an attempt to explain delinquency. Yet, there is also need for caution in the way these statistics are interpreted. On the one hand, they tend to support official accounts, which suggest that the incidence of delinquent acts among black children may be greater than the incidence among whites, particularly where serious crimes are involved. On the other hand, there are few findings in which the self-reported discrepancy between the two races approaches the discrepancy reported in official data. While official accounts indicate a large difference between blacks and whites, self-report studies suggest not only that the discrepancy is much smaller, but that much of

TABLE 6–7

Percentage of juveniles reporting different levels of law violation by race

| | Total self-reported delinquency | | | | Crimes against property | | |
| | Race | | | | Race | | |
Number of offenses reported	Black percent	White percent	Ratios	Number of offenses reported	Black percent	White percent	Ratios
0–24	67.6	71.8	1 : 1.1	0–4	70.7	70.6	1 : 1
25–49	8.1	11.0	1 : 1.4	5–29	24.1	22.7	1 : 1.1
50–199	15.4	13.1	1.2 : 1	30–54	2.4	3.4	1 : 1.4
200+	9.8	4.1	2.4 : 1	55+	4.2	1.9	2.2 : 1

Source: Elliott and Ageton, 1978:104.

it may be due to the activities of a small group of chronic offenders. How, then, does one account for the large racial differences reported in official data?

The explanation is probably similar to our explanation when we considered arrest statistics. To be sure, apprehension for a serious offense is likely to increase the probability of arrest and trial. But beyond that, characteristics other than law-violating behavior will increase the likelihood that black children will be processed through the juvenile justice system. Because they are more likely to be poor, to come from single-parent families and to be school dropouts, the chances they will be processed officially are increased. Almost inevitably, their official delinquency rates will be higher. Furthermore, since these conditions may apply to other minority groups, particularly those who are Spanish-speaking, the need to gather more self-report data on their actual behaviors seems to be particularly urgent.

Social class

As late as 1967, the President's Crime Commission concluded that "there is still no reason to doubt that delinquency, and especially the most serious delinquency, is committed disproportionately by slum and lower-class youth." (p. 57). But is the conclusion true? Do lower-class juveniles, by their own admission, confess to being more delinquent than their middle- or upper-class peers?

When the findings of the first self-report studies on this subject were revealed, they hit like a bombshell: investigation after investigation indicated that the presumed relationship between social class and law-violating behavior was either small or nonexistent (Akers, 1964; Dentler and Monroe, 1961; Empey and Erickson, 1966; Hirshi, 1969; Illinois Institute for Juvenile Research, 1972; Short and Nye, 1958; Tittle et al., 1978; Voss,

1966; Williams and Gold, 1972). While a few studies did suggest that lower-class children might be slightly more delinquent (Clark and Wenninger, 1965; Empey, 1967; Gold, 1966; Reiss and Rhodes, 1961), others suggested just the opposite (Voss, 1966; Williams and Gold, 1972). But since the relationship in either direction was usually very weak, the best scientific conclusion seemed to be that social class membership was not a good way to separate chronic law violators from others. Indeed, one group of investigators concluded that the assumption that lower-class children were the more delinquent was a myth (Tittle et al., 1978).

Since many criminologists were inclined to accept this conclusion, efforts were made to explain why the myth had persisted for so long. One explanation was that the police and courts, indeed society at large, had been guilty of unadulterated prejudice. The juvenile justice system had been deliberately designed by those in power to discriminate against the children of the poor. Even though they were not more delinquent, they were future members of society's "dangerous classes," and had to be controlled (Platt, 1974; Quinney, 1970; Turk, 1969). A second possibility was that, while social class may have been an important factor in the past, it was no longer important. Law violators today, if not in the 19th century, are scattered throughout the class structure (Tittle et al., 1978:654). Finally, a more technical explanation suggested that official records may have been misinterpreted, not only by lay persons but by scientists. The assumption that lower-class children are the more delinquent has persisted because people have failed to distinguish between *law-violating behavior*— that which self-report studies measure, and *official delinquency*—that which police and court records measure.

This last explanation deserves some further consideration. While it is clear that self-report studies are designed to measure only the delinquent acts of juveniles, official records reflect several highly complicated phenomena: (1) the acts that bring children to the attention of authorities; (2) the social backgrounds of these children; and (3) the reactions of officials to both their acts and their backgrounds. Official delinquency, in other words, is a reflection of the way officials interpret and react to the behavior and backgrounds of children as well as to the children's actions. Hence, law-violating behavior should not be equated with official delinquency.

At the same time, it would be unwise to assume that self-report studies are free from error. One possible weakness lies in the fact that most studies have been based upon data derived from local samples which might not be representative of the youth population at large. A second problem involves difficulties of recall and accuracy of information provided when juveniles are questioned about their delinquent acts. Third, many studies have failed to obtain data on the most serious forms of criminal behavior, particularly rape, robbery, and aggravated assault. Finally, analyses of self-report data by various investigators have often been characterized by serious methodological problems (Hindelang et al., 1979).

In the past decade, however, self-report studies have grown more sophisticated. Indeed, by comparing the results of three relatively recent national surveys, it is possible to be more precise about the relationship between social class and law-violating behavior (Elliott and Ageton, 1980; Williams and Gold, 1972; Gold and Reimer, 1974).

Several items concerning these studies should be noted.

1. Prevalence. Although these surveys were conducted at different points in time—1967, 1972, and 1977—they lead to the same conclusion as earlier local surveys: the *prevalence* of delinquent behavior among lower-class juveniles is not greater than among higher-class juveniles. "A comparison of the proportions of youth reporting one or more offenses . . . reveals no statistically significant class differences . . ." (Elliott and Ageton, 1980:103).

2. Incidence. The same is not true, however, when the *incidence* of delinquent acts is considered; that is, when juveniles are asked *how many times* they have violated (not *have they ever* violated) the law during the past year. In their national studies of this phenomenon, Gold and his associates concluded that there are no class differences (Williams and Gold, 1972; Gold and Reimer, 1974). But in reaching this conclusion, they collapsed the frequencies reported by juveniles and used the number *3* to represent the hundreds of acts reported. In their more recent analysis, by contrast, Elliott and Ageton (1980) did not collapse frequencies but analyzed the full range of acts reported, and in doing so found some significant differences.

In order to explore these differences, it is necessary to note that they divided their respondents into three class levels: (1) a *lower-class group* made up of the children of unskilled or semiskilled parents who, at best, had completed high school; (2) a *working-class group* whose parents were skilled manual workers, clerical workers, salespersons, or owners of small businesses who were high school graduates and who might have had some college; and (3) a *middle-class group* whose parents filled professional or managerial occupations and were college-educated. Their findings are displayed in Table 6–8.

First, the table indicates that the average number ($\bar{X}$) of *delinquent acts* reported by lower-class juveniles (60.42) was greater than that reported by working-class (50.63) or middle-class (50.96) youths. While the incidences of crime in the latter two groups were approximately equal, that for the lower-class group was higher. Furthermore, the chances were only about 5 in 100 that this difference was not real and could not be viewed with confidence.

Second, the average number (X̄) of *crimes against persons* (sexual assault, aggravated assault, simple assault, and robbery) reported by lower-class juveniles (12.02) was 1.5 times greater than that reported by the working-class group (8.04), and nearly four times greater than that reported by the middle-class group (3.32). As might be expected, therefore, the probability was high that these differences were also real.

Third, the average number of reported *crimes against property* (vandalism, burglary, auto theft, larceny, stolen goods, fraud, and joyriding) was also higher for lower-class (13.50) than for working-class (8.04) or middle-class youths (7.25). This difference, however, was not statistically significant (NS). Furthermore, the same was also true with respect to such crimes as prostitution, disorderly conduct, hard drug use, and status offenses.

Thus, while the overall incidence of delinquent acts is apparently greatest among lower-class youths, this is not true for all kinds of crime. Rather, it is confined mostly to predatory crimes against persons and, possibly, crimes against property (Elliott and Ageton, 1980:102–103).

3. Chronic offenders. The frequency with which young people reported violating the law varied widely among these studies.

Hence, it is possible that differences among the classes might be due, at least in part, to a large numbers of crimes being committed by a small group of people. Indeed, the findings displayed in Table 6–9 tend to confirm that idea.

The table's total self-report measure shows that less than 6 in 100 juveniles reported committing 200 or more delinquent acts during the previous year. By contrast, 70 in 100 reported committing from 0 to 24 acts. Second, lower-class youth were most likely to be represented on the most delinquent end of this spectrum. For example, they reported over 1.5 times the offenses of middle-class youth on the total self-report measure (scores 200+) and nearly three times as many offenses on the crimes against persons measure (scores 55+). In short, while the data indicate that there are small numbers of chronic offenders in all social classes, they are most heavily concentrated in the lower-class.

This set of findings, then, did suggest that there is a relationship between class membership and delinquent behavior. However, the relationship is qualitatively different from the global one implied by official records. Rather than indicating that all lower-class juveniles are more delinquent than their peers, it suggests instead that theorists should seek to answer three questions: Why are there chronic offenders in all social classes? Why is the group of chronic offenders largest in the

TABLE 6–8

Incidence of self-reported delinquent acts by social class

Class	N	Total self-reported delinquent acts		Crimes against persons		Crimes against property		Illegal service crimes		Public disorder crimes		Hard drug use		Status offenses	
		X̄	SD	X̄	SD	X̄	SD	X̄	SD	X̄	SD	X̄	SD	X̄	SD
Lower	717	60.42	220.24	12.02	72.68	13.50	78.60	2.19	30.29	14.32	58.75	1.20	14.64	14.27	46.5
Working	509	50.63	186.19	8.04	67.12	9.40	38.68	1.36	10.92	16.21	78.92	.73	4.02	14.47	42.3
Middle	494	50.96	79.88	3.32	11.31	7.25	23.17	1.56	14.07	13.81	42.44	1.37	15.68	15.66	58.3
F		2.94		3.11		1.94		.25		.22		.35		.13	
Probability		≤.05		≤.05		NS		NS		NS		NS		NS	

Source: Elliott and Ageton, 1980:102.

TABLE 6–9
Percentage of juveniles reporting different levels of law violation by social class

Number of offenses reported	Total self-reported delinquency (Social class)			Number of offenses reported	Crimes against persons (Social class)		
	Lower	Working	Middle		Lower	Working	Middle
0–24	71.7	72.3	70.9	0–4	77.3	80.0	84.6
25–49	10.6	9.4	11.5	5–29	18.2	16.1	13.8
50–199	11.4	14.4	14.4	30–54	1.7	2.1	.8
200 + ...	6.3	3.9	3.2	55 + ...	2.8	1.8	.8
	100.0	100.0	100.0		100.0	100.0	100.0

Source: Elliott and Ageton, 1980:104.

lower-class? And why are lower-class chronic offenders more inclined to commit serious crimes?

Relative to these issues, Clark and Wenninger (1962) suggest that variations in the social climates or social networks of different neighborhoods might help to explain the existence of chronic offenders in all classes. In those neighborhoods in which everyone tends to be more delinquent, this factor, and not class membership as such, will be the determining influence. Furthermore, Johnstone (1978) maintains that it is being a "have-not" in a neighborhood of "haves" that causes lower-class juveniles to be more delinquent. Rather than coming from neighborhoods in which everyone is lower-class, the most serious delinquents are lower-class juveniles who live in a mixed neighborhood, where they are confronted with their own poverty. It is a sense of relative deprivation, then, which leads them to commit greater numbers of delinquent acts.

Whatever the answer, it is clear that, while class membership remains important, it is not in itself sufficient as an explanatory variable. For example, we have seen repeatedly that its effects are so intertwined with racial status in American society that both factors need careful attention before the influence of one or the other can be sorted out.

Group delinquency

The final issue for which theories must account is the group nature of delinquent behavior. Because offenders are processed through the juvenile justice system one by one, official records often fail to acknowledge the extent to which illegal acts usually occur in the company of others, a fact which criminologists have noted for more than 50 years (Shaw and McKay, 1931; Healy and Bronner, 1936; Glueck and Glueck, 1952; Cohen, 1955; Scott, 1956).

In recent years, Maynard Erickson (1973a; 1973b) and his associate Gary Jensen (Erickson and Jensen, 1977) have documented this phenomenon using self-report data. Table 6–10 shows that, whether male or female, whether in urban settings or small towns, young people tend to follow herd instincts when they violate the law. Alcohol and drug offenses tend to have the highest group violation rates (from 78 to 93 percent); personal and property crimes rank next (from 44 to 90 percent); and status offenses such as defying parents or running away rank last (from 11 to 44 percent). Furthermore, females are similar to males in this respect, and there are no significant differences by social class. Indeed, the gregarious and companionate character of law-violating behavior is a strikingly pervasive issue

TABLE 6–10

Group violation rates (GVR) by community and gender*

| | Urban | | | | Small town | | | |
| | Male | | Female | | Male | | Female | |
Type of offense	GVR	Frequency	GVR	Frequency	GVR	Frequency	GVR	Frequency
Drunk	91	13,535	94	6,072	93	5,561	94	2,991
Drinking	86	22,036	95	10,302	86	8,684	92	4,593
Marijuana	85	15,075	93	8,229	87	7,222	89	6,346
Drugs	82	2,452	78	1,260	78	779	84	1,622
Vandalism	81	1,068	84	119	72	294	90	51
Burglary	74	659	87	279	81	122	86	34
Grand theft	69	220	33	2	68	23	50	1
Smoking	67	11,713	71	10,055	61	5,846	66	6,188
Auto theft	67	152	69	56	52	54	66	42
Truancy	63	8,151	73	3,819	65	851	80	1,037
Petty theft	60	593	54	464	45	105	54	69
Armed robbery	52	124	100	2	58	11	—	—
Robbery	48	179	67	8	53	44	50	1
Shoplifting	45	1,446	59	488	42	438	61	497
Runaway	38	32	33	384	44	13	11	4
Assault	25	213	36	386	23	31	6	2
Fights	23	309	21	32	14	58	21	14
Defy parents	23	2,898	30	2,373	16	648	42	2,855

* Coefficient of concordance (w) = .94 (p $\leq$ .000): Mean rank order correlation coefficient ($\bar{R}$) = 88.

Source: Erickson and Jensen, 1977:267. Reprinted by special permission of the Journal of Criminal Law and Criminology © 1977 by Northwestern University School of Law, Vol. 68, No. 2, and by the authors, Maynard L. Erickson and Gary F. Jensen.

for which official data not only fail to account but to which many theories have paid scant attention.

LIMITATIONS OF SELF-REPORT STUDIES

Before summarizing what we have learned in this chapter, it is important to be aware of the limitations of self-report studies:

1. Nationwide surveys of law-violating behavior are limited in number. Hence, caution must be exercised in generalizing about all youths from the data now available.

2. Although a few investigators are now collecting self-report data from the same panels of respondents over a period of a few years, no permanent mechanisms have been devised by which to gather self-report data on an annual basis—data that would be analagous to those published in the *Uniform Crime Reports*. It is

difficult, as a result, to know whether crime rates are increasing or decreasing, or whether patterns of law violation are changing.

3. Perhaps most important, questions have been raised about two features of self-report studies: (1) their *reliability*—that is, whether repeated administrations of a questionnaire or interview will elicit the same answers from the same juveniles when they are queried two or more times; and (2) their *validity*—that is, whether self-report studies measure what they purport to measure, namely, actual delinquent behavior (Reiss, 1975).

Fortunately, their exhaustive study of these issues has led Hindelang et al. to conclude that "reliability measures are impressive, and [that] the majority of studies produce validity coefficients in the moderate to strong range" (1981:126). The only major difficulty has to do with *validity,* primarily because those juveniles most likely to have serious police records, problems in school, and low scores on their knowledge of everyday affairs are less inclined to answer questions accurately. As a result, Hindelang et al. conclude that self-report studies are likely to underestimate the illegal behavior of those who are most likely to be seriously delinquent (1981:295).

4. Self-report studies have gathered little information from adults, discouraging efforts to make valid comparisons of the relative criminality of both age groups.

In short, self-report studies, like other measures of delinquent behavior, have their limitations. Nonetheless, they are probably the single most accurate source of information on the actual illegal acts of the young.

SUMMARY AND CONCLUSIONS

In response to dissatisfaction with official accounts of delinquent behavior, self-report studies have been conducted. The conclusions for which they provide the greatest support are these:

1. The *prevalence* and the *incidence* of juvenile lawbreaking are far greater than official records indicate. Because these records reflect official reaction as well as juvenile behavior, and because they sample only a fragment of the youth population, they grossly underestimate the extent of lawbreaking by young people.

2. The dark figure of crime may be as much as nine times greater than the official figure, since approximately 9 out of 10 law violations either go undetected or unacted upon.

3. While most juveniles are law violators, only a small minority are chronic offenders who violate the law with great frequency and seriousness.

4. Although the juvenile justice system is far from totally effective in apprehending all law violators, it does seem to operate like a coarse net. Those youngsters who have had the most court appearances or who are incarcerated are the most delinquent, by their own admission.

5. Official records have suggested that certain issues should be taken into account in trying to explain delinquent behavior. Self-report studies suggest the following:

a. Age. Self-report studies do not suggest that crime increases uniformly between the ages of 11 and 17. Rather, there are numerous offenses, some of them serious, for which 13- to 15-year-olds are the most delinquent.

b. Gender. Both the *prevalence* and the *incidence* of delinquent behavior are greater among boys than among girls. However, the pattern of offenses reported by girls is not confined to female crimes but approximates that of boys. Furthermore, the prevalence, if not the incidence, of alcohol and drug use among girls is beginning to approximate that of boys.

c. Minority status. While conclusions cannot be reached about all minority groups, there is a need to qualify the findings of official records with respect to blacks. On the one hand, self-report studies do not support the idea that the *prevalence* of delinquent behavior is greater among black juveniles than among whites. On the other hand, they do support the finding that its *incidence* is greater among blacks, particularly where serious crimes are involved. However, they also suggest that this variation is due more to the unusual number of delinquent acts committed by a small group of chronic offenders than to all black youth taken as a whole.

d. Social class. The same sorts of conclusions apply to the relationship between class membership and law-violating behavior. While self-report studies do not agree with police and court records, which imply that the *prevalence* of law violation is greater among lower- than middle-class youths, they do suggest that the *incidence* is greater among lower-class juveniles. Although chronic offenders appear in all social classes, lower-class youths are the most likely to be represented on the highest end of the delinquency continuum and most likely to have engaged in serious criminal acts.

e. *Group delinquency.* Although official records report nothing about the phenomenon, self-report studies strongly support the idea that the preponderance of delinquent acts are committed in groups.

In terms of their social and scientific implications, then, these findings suggest that, while important qualifications need to be added to the picture of delinquent behavior painted by official records, that picture is far from totally inconsistent with the findings of self-report studies. Hence, it will be interesting to determine whether these conclusions are confirmed or discredited in the studies on victimization discussed in the next chapter.

REFERENCES

Ageton, Suzanne S., and Elliott, Delbert S.
   1978   *The Incidence of Delinquent Behavior in a National Probability Sample of Adolescents.* Boulder, Colorado: Behavioral Research Institute.

Akers, Ronald L.
   1964   "Socio-economic Status and Delinquent Behavior: A Retest." *Journal of Research in Crime and Delinquency* (January): 38–46.

Christie, Nils, et al.
   1965   "A Study of Self-reported Crime." In K. O. Christiansen, ed., *Scandinavian Studies in Criminology.* Vol. 2. London: Tavistock Publications.

Clark, John P., and Wenninger, Eugene P.
   1962   "Socio-economic Class and Area as Correlates of Illegal Behavior Among Juveniles." *American Sociological Review* 27 (December):826–834.

Cloward, Richard A., and Ohlin, Lloyd E.
   1960   *Delinquency and Opportunity: A Theory of Delinquent Gangs.* New York: The Free Press.

Cohen, Albert K.
   1955   *Delinquent Boys: The Culture of the Gang.* New York: The Free Press.

Dentler, Robert A., and Monroe, Lawrence J.
   1961   "Social Correlates of Early Adolescent Theft." *American Sociological Review* 26 (October):733–43.

Elliott, Delbert S., and Ageton, Suzanne S.
   1980   "Reconciling Race and Class Differences in Self Reported and Official Estimates of Delinquency." *American Sociological Review* 45 (February):95–110.

Elliott, Delbert S. and Voss, Harwin L.
   1974   *Delinquency and Dropout.* Lexington, Mass.: D.C. Heath.

Elmhorn, K.
   1965   "Study in Self Reported Delinquency Among School Children in Stockholm" In K. O. Christiansen, ed., *Scandinavian Studies in Criminology.* Vol. 2. London: Tavistock Publications.

Empey, LaMar T. and Erickson, Maynard L.
  1966 "Hidden Delinquency and Social Status." *Social Forces* 44 (June):546–54.
Empey, LaMar T.
  1967 "Delinquency Theory and Recent Research." *Journal of Research in Crime and Delinquency* 4 (January):28–42.
Erickson, Maynard L., and LaMar T. Empey
  1963 "Court Records, Undetected Delinquency, and Decision-making." *Journal of Criminal Law, Criminology and Police Science* 54 (December):456–69.
Erickson, Maynard L.
  1972 "The Changing Relationship Between Official and Self-reported Measures of Delinquency: an Exploratory-predictive Study." *Journal of Criminal Law, Criminology and Police Science* 3 (September–October):388–95.
  1973a "Group Violations, Socioeconomic Status and Official Delinquency." *Social Forces* 52 (September):41–52.
  1973b "Group Violations and Official Delinquency: The Group Hazard Hypothesis." *Criminology* 11 (August):127–60.
Erickson, Maynard L., and Jensen, Gary F.
  1977 "Delinquency is Still Group Behavior: Toward Revitalizing the Group Premise in the Sociology of Deviance." *Journal of Criminal Law and Criminology,* 68:262–73.
Federal Bureau of Investigation
  1976 *Crime in the United States: Uniform Crime Reports—1975.* Washington, D.C.: U.S. Government Printing Office.
Glueck, Sheldon, and Glueck, Eleanor
  1952 *Delinquents in the Making.* New York: Harper.
Gold, Martin
  1966 "Undetected delinquent behavior." *Journal of Research in Crime and Delinquency* 3 (January):27–46.
  1970 *Delinquent Behavior in an American City.* Belmont, Calif.: Brooks/Cole Publishing Company.
Gold, Martin, and Reimer, Donald J.
  1974 "Changing Patterns of Delinquent Behavior Among Americans 13–16 Years Old: 1967–1972." *Crime and Delinquency Literature* 7:483–517.
Gould, LeRoy C.
  1969 "Who Defines Delinquency: a Comparison of Self-reported and Officially-reported Indices of Delinquency for Three Racial Groups." *Social Problems* 16 (Winter):325–36.
Healy, William, and Bronner, Augusta F.
  1936 *New Light on Delinquency and Its Treatment.* New Haven: Conn.: Yale University Press.
Higgins, Paul C., and Albrecht, Gary L.
  1981 "Cars and Kids: a Self-reported Study of Juvenile Auto Theft and Traffic Violations." *Sociology and Social Research* 66 (October):29–41.
Hindelang, Michael J.
  1971 "Age, Sex, and the Versatility or Delinquency Involvements." *Social Problems* 18 (Spring):527–35.

Hindelang, Michael J.; Hirschi, Travis; and Weis, Joseph
   1981   *Measuring Delinquency.* Beverly Hills: Sage.

Hirschi, Travis
   1969   *Causes of Delinquency.* Berkeley: University of California Press.

Illinois Institute for Juvenile Research
   1972   *Juvenile Delinquency in Illinois.* Chicago: Illinois Department of Mental Health.

Jensen, Gary, and Eve, Raymond
   1976   "Sex Differences in Delinquency." *Criminology* 13 (February): 427–48.

Johnston, Lloyd D.; Bachman, Jerald G.; and O'Malley, Patrick M.
   1979   *Drugs and the Nation's High School Students.* Rockville, Md.: U.S. Department of Health, Education and Welfare.

Murphy, Fred J., et al.
   1946   "The Incidence of Hidden Delinquency." *American Journal of Orthopsychiatry,* October, 686–96.

National Center for Juvenile Justice
   1977   *Juvenile Court Statistics, 1974.* Pittsburgh: National Council of Juvenile Court Judges.

National Commission on the Causes and Prevention of Violence
   1969   "American Criminal Statistics: An Explanation and Appraisal." *Crimes of Violence,* Vol. 2. Washington, D.C.: U.S. Government Printing Office.

Nettler, Gwynn
   1974   *Explaining Crime.* New York: McGraw-Hill.

Penick, Bettye K. Eidson, and Owens, Maurice E. B. III, eds.
   1976   *Surveying Crime.* Washington, D.C.: National Academy of Sciences.

Platt, Anthony M.
   1974   "The Triumph of Benevolence: the Origins of the Juvenile Justice System in the United States." Pp. 356–89 in Richard Quinney, ed., *Criminal Justice in America.* Boston: Little, Brown.

Porterfield, Austin L.
   1946   *Youth in Trouble.* Fort Worth: Leo Potishman Foundation.

President's Commission on Law Enforcement and Administration of Justice
   1967a   *Task Force Report: Crime and its Impact.* Washington, D.C.: U.S. Government Printing Office.
   1967b   *The Challenge of Crime in a Free Society.* Washington, D.C.: U.S. Government Printing Office.

Quinney, Richard
   1970   *The Social Reality of Crime.* Boston: Little, Brown.

Reiss, Albert J., Jr., and Rhodes, Albert L.
   1961   "The Distribution of Juvenile Delinquency in the Social Class Structure." *American Sociological Review* 26 (October):720–32.

Scott, Peter
   1956   "Gangs and Delinquent Groups in London." *British Journal of Delinquency* (July):4–26.

Shaw, Clifford R., and McKay, Henry D.
    1931   *Social Factors in Juvenile Delinquency.* Report of the National Commission on Law Observance and Enforcement. Vol. 2. Washington, D.C.: U.S. Government Printing Office.

Short, James F., Jr., and F. Ivan Nye
    1958   "Extent of Unrecorded Delinquency, Tentative Conclusions." *Journal of Criminal Law, Criminology and Police Science* 49 (November–December):296–302.

Steffensmeier, Darrell J., and Steffensmeier, Renee H.
    1980   "Trends in Female Delinquency: an Examination of Arrest, Juvenile Court, Self-report, and Field Data." *Criminology* 18 (May):62–85.

Tittle, Charles R.; Villemez, Wayne J.; and Smith, Douglas A.
    1978   "The Myth of Social Class and Criminality: An Empirical Assessment of the Empirical Evidence." *American Sociological Review* 43 (October):643–56.

Turk, Austin T.
    1969   *Criminality and the Legal Order.* Chicago: Rand McNally.

Voss, Harwin L.
    1966   "Socio-economic Status and Reported Delinquent Behavior." *Social Problems* 13 (Winter):314–24.

Williams, Jay R., and Martin Gold
    1972   "From Delinquent Behavior to Official Delinquency." *Social Problems* 20 (Fall):209–29.

Wise, Nancy B.
    1967   "Juvenile Delinquency Among Middle Class Girls." Pp. 179–88 in Edmund W. Vaz, ed., *Middle Class Juvenile Delinquency.* New York: Harper & Row.

Wolfgang, Marvin E., et al.
    1972   *Delinquency in a Birth Cohort.* Chicago: University of Chicago Press.

Luis Medina

The most likely victims of violent crime are adolescents.

VICTIM ACCOUNTS OF DELINQUENT BEHAVIOR

This is the third and final chapter on the extent and nature of delinquent behavior. It seeks its information in a series of surveys on criminal victimization in the United States. These surveys have an interesting history.

In July 1965, President Lyndon Johnson established a Commission on Law Enforcement and Administration of Justice and charged the commission with providing a more coherent picture of crime in American society and making recommendations as to what should be done about it (1967a:v). Almost immediately, knowledgeable staff members and consultants expressed the conviction that information on the extent and nature of crime and delinquency required improvement. Their concerns stemmed from the well-known difficulties with police statistics that we have already discussed. Before sensible recommendations could be made, new information was required. Consequently, the decision was made to conduct a national survey of 10,000 representative American households to determine what experiences with crime their residents had had, whether they had reported those experiences to the police, and how those experiences had affected their lives.

The findings of the survey were striking. Like self-report studies, they indicated that there is far more crime than is ever officially reported. Rape, for example, appeared to be four times as frequent as police reports had indicated (Ennis, 1967:9). Likewise, many other crimes were underreported. The commission report noted that:

> Burglaries occur about three times more often than they are reported to police. Aggravated assaults and larcenies over $50 occur twice as often as they are reported. There are 50 percent more robberies than are reported. In some areas only one tenth of the total number of certain kinds of crimes are reported to the police. Seventy-four percent of the neighborhood commercial establishments surveyed do not report to police the thefts committed by their employees (President's Commission on Law Enforcement and Administration of Justice 1967a:v).

As a result of such findings, the commission expressed the fear that crime was eroding the

129

quality of American life. This fear was fed by another commission study (1967a:*v*) which was conducted in the high-crime areas of two cities. It found that:

43 percent of the respondents say they stay off the streets at night because of their fear of crime.

35 percent say they do not speak to strangers any more because of their fear of crime.

21 percent say they use cars and cabs at night because of their fear of crime.

20 percent say they would like to move to another neighborhood because of their fear of crime.

Nationwide, the same fears were expressed. More than one third of all Americans, in fact, say they keep firearms in the house for protection against criminals. Almost that many keep watchdogs for the same reason.

The commission (1967a:*vi*) was also concerned over the fact that young people commit a disproportionate share of all crime. It not only warned that 15- and 16-year-olds have the highest arrest rate in the United States but also that during the late 1960s the number of children was growing at a much faster rate than other age groups in the population. "The problem in the years ahead," it said, "is dramatically foretold by the fact that 23 percent of the population is 10 and under."

The significance of this fact, reported in 1967, should not be lost on us. This large population of young people was moving through its most crime-prone years during the period on which this and foregoing accounts of delinquent behavior are based. This fact has undoubtedly contributed to the increasing numbers of official crimes that have been noted. Although official delinquency has increased more rapidly than the juvenile population has grown, the mere fact that there were more juveniles would also increase the total number of crimes.

It was for this and other reasons—most

notably the questionable accuracy of police reports—that the crime commission (1967b:2) recommended that further victim surveys be conducted and made a part of the nation's regular data-gathering procedures. Likewise, a more recent commission—the National Advisory Committee on Criminal Justice Standards and Goals—noted that it is unrealistic to expect any single measure of crime to be completely accurate (1973:32). Therefore, victim surveys might be useful in evaluating police crime statistics and vice versa.

THE NATURE OF VICTIM SURVEYS

After several years of preparation and pilot study, the first National Crime Survey under governmental auspices was conducted in 1973 by the U.S. Bureau of the Census in conjunction with the Law Enforcement Assistance Administration's newly created National Criminal Justice Information and Statistics Service (NCJISS: 1975a:*iii–vii*). Information was gathered from a sample of approximately 125,000 people located in 60,000 households and 15,000 businesses throughout the nation. Current plans are to continue the National Crime Survey on a regular basis.

Data collected

The types of crimes on which data were originally collected in 1973 were crimes against persons, crimes against households, and crimes against commercial establishments. The collection of data on commercial crimes, however, was suspended in 1977 (NCJISS, 1979a:iii). But this is not a serious limitation for our purposes, since we are concerned primarily with personal crimes against individuals and with crimes against households. Briefly, these latter types of crimes are as follows:

1.   Crimes against persons.   These are crimes in which individuals are the victims—

rape, robbery, assault, and personal theft. Such violent crimes as rape or robbery always involve confrontation between victim and criminal. Theft, however, is of two types: *(a)* larceny *with contact,* in which criminal and victim meet; and *(b)* larceny *without contact,* in which the theft is not discovered until a later time.

2. *Crimes against households.* These are crimes in which dwelling units rather than individuals are the victims. They include three acts: burglary, household larceny, and motor vehicle theft. If the criminal should come into direct contact with one of the inhabitants of a household, however, the act is considered a personal crime.

Limitations of victim surveys

Victim surveys have certain limitations. One of the most important is that they deal only with one dimension of delinquent behavior, that is, with criminal offenses rather than juvenile status offenses, or with cases of cruelty and neglect to small children.

The victim surveys also omit the collection of information on a long list of other crimes—murder, for example, where victims cannot be interviewed, or kidnapping, where victims are rarely found. Other types of crimes such as drunkenness, drug use, gambling, and prostitution, like juvenile status offenses, do not usually have immediate victims and thus are not measured. Finally, a third set of crimes, difficult to document from the victim's standpoint, are employee theft, shoplifting, income tax violations, or even blackmail where the victim as well as the blackmailer has something to hide. The victim surveys, therefore, do not collect data on illegal acts of these types.

Some of these omissions are serious in the sense that they tend to focus attention on youthful and lower-class crimes while ignoring the crimes of affluent, powerful, and older people—embezzlement, bribery, fraud, violation of antitrust laws, stock swindles, income tax evasion, and so on. While it is true that these are difficult to document in an interview—because the victim is unaware of them, because he may join in covering them up if his losses will be recovered, or because the "victim" is all of us—neither our knowledge of crime nor our social trust will be improved until something is done to measure them more effectively (Penick and Owens, 1976:134). In fact, the failure of the National Criminal Information Service (NCIS) to collect information on crimes like this is surprising in light of the fact that the victim survey conducted for the President's Crime Commission in 1967 did so (Ennis, 1967). Too often, attention is focused on the extent of personal robbery or household burglary at the expense of knowing to what extent and to what cost to society are the more sophisticated white-collar crimes.

A final set of limitations has to do with the survey method for collecting victim data. One question that is often asked is whether accurate estimates of crime can be obtained by interviewing only a sample of Americans rather than all of them. Why not interview everyone over age 12—more than 160 million people? The answer is that the expenses would outweigh the benefits; the yearly cost would be astronomical. Furthermore, it is unnecessary. By carefully selecting a representative sample of the entire population, it is possible to estimate what that population would have said had everyone been interviewed. That is what the Censes Bureau and the Office of Criminal Justice Information did.

In the latest survey available,

> Information . . . was derived from interviews with about 136,000 occupants of some 60,000 housing units. The housing units were representative of those in the 50 states and the District of Columbia. Respondents . . .

were interviewed at 6-month intervals during the course of the appropriate data collection period (NCJISS, 1979a:iii).

Once the data were collected, steps were taken to generalize from the sample to the entire population, using scientific procedures to estimate the amount of sampling error and to report its size to the public. In the latest survey, for example, it is reported that, where comparisons of victimization rates between two groups are made, "the chances are at least 95 out of 100 that each difference . . . did not result solely from sample variability" (NCJISS, 1979a:iii). In other words, the chances are quite high that any observed differences in the survey are real.

The most serious problems are probably inherent in the actual process of interviewing people—gaining the cooperation of suspicious respondents, overcoming language and communication barriers, and determining whether people are telling the truth or whether they are accurately recalling the events surrounding the crimes in which they were victimized. Sometimes memories or perceptions are unintentionally, if not deliberately, faulty (Penick and Owens, 1976: 27–28). Those who conducted the survey attempted to deal with the problems of recall by asking people to describe only those events taking place within the last six months because they can be recalled most accurately. But there is no way of knowing for certain the extent to which other kinds of distortions are present in the survey findings. After the survey has been run several times, some distortions will be located and eliminated, but others will always remain. Hence, we can never be satisfied that survey findings are totally accurate.

Benefits of victim surveys

Despite their limitations, the expectation is that victim surveys will do much to improve our knowledge of crime and delinquency, not only because they avoid the filtering process through which the gathering of police and court statistics must pass, but because they will provide new kinds of information that have simply been unavailable heretofore:

Better information on the number of crime victims as contrasted to the number of crimes reported by the police. Normally, the number of victims is greater than the number of crimes because more than one victim may be involved in the commission of any crime. We will now have a better estimate of how many victims exist.

The risks of being victimized. What are the chances of being robbed, assaulted, or having one's house or business broken into? When and where are these likely to occur? Over a period of time, year-by-year victim surveys can detect increases or decreases in these probabilities.

Variations in vulnerability to crime. Who are the most likely victims of crimes— males or females, young people or old, blacks or whites, poor or well-to-do? Does the risk of becoming a victim vary according to one's sex, age, or status in society? Do the victims of one type of crime differ from the victims of another?

Crime trends. Victimization data are now available for a five-year period, from 1973 through 1977. Thus, these data are beginning to provide us with a valuable assessment of crime trends, that is, information as to whether crime rates are increasing or decreasing.

Increasing objectivity in crime reporting. The victim survey will provide a most valuable addition to our measurement of crime. Along with official and self-report accounts, it will permit us to speak with a great deal more objectivity, not only with respect to crime rates and trends, but with respect to the facts with which theorists must be concerned in their attempts to explain crime.

Annual victim surveys, in short, have considerable potential. Their value is by no means exhausted by the few examples just cited. The information they provide, though limited in some respects, may not only throw new light on the nature and extent of delinquent behavior, but help to pinpoint both weaknesses and strengths in the ways we explain and respond to that behavior.

Number of victims

The National Crime Survey (NCS) estimated that there were 40.3 million victims of successful or attempted crimes in 1977 (NCJISS, 1979a:20). As may be seen in Table 7–1, about 56.6 percent of the victims were individuals, ages 12 and over, and 43.4 percent were households.

Two points about these overall figures are noteworthy. First, as Table 7–1 shows, the most common victimizations did not involve the direct use of threat or violence. Instead, most prevalent were crimes of theft against individuals (42 percent)—such acts as stealing money, picking pockets, or property loss where force was not involved. The next most common crime was household larceny (23.4 percent)—

a theft or attempted theft from a home in which neither forcible nor unlawful entry occurred. Burglary, which ranked next (16.8 percent), does involve unlawful entry but not direct confrontation between victim and criminal. Thus, such violent crimes as assault (11.6 percent), robbery (2.7 percent), or rape (0.4 percent) rank relatively low in terms of overall frequency. Even though they are abhorrent crimes and terribly frightening to their victims, they are by no means the most common.

The second important finding is less consoling. If there were 40.3 million victims of crimes in 1977, as was estimated, that figure is approximately four times larger than the number of similar crimes (10.9 million) reported by the police for the same year (FBI, 1978:35). This large discrepancy must be discounted to some degree because of differences in the way police and victim data are collected. Yet, even when this is taken into account, victim surveys join self-report accounts in suggesting that police records grossly underestimate the number of criminal incidents.

THE RISKS OF BEING A VICTIM

Since the risks of becoming a victim of crime are probably greater than police records

TABLE 7–1

Number and percent of personal and household crimes

Type of offense	Number	Percent within type*	Percent of all crimes*
All crimes	40,315,000	—	100.0
Crimes against persons	22,835,000	100.0	56.6
Rape	154,000	0.7	0.4
Robbery	1,083,000	4.7	2.7
Assault	4,664,000	20.4	11.6
Crimes of theft	16,933,000	74.2	42.0
Crimes against households	17,480,000	100.0	43.4
Burglary	6,765,000	38.7	16.8
Household larceny	9,418,000	53.9	23.4
Motor vehicle theft	1,297,000	7.4	3.2

* Percents may not add to total because of rounding.
  Source: NCJISS, 1979a:20.

indicate, it is useful to examine those risks in two ways: (1) to examine what the risks are that the "average" person will be a victim of crime; and (2) to examine variations in the risks of being victimized depending upon one's social class position, sex, race, and age.

In this section, we will be concerned with the risks faced by the average person. Some review of them is important because of prevailing beliefs that crime rates are increasing and that the ordinary citizen is in great danger. Newspaper accounts like the following, for example, are far more important in constructing our social image of the dangers we face than any number of statistical accounts issued by the federal government.

THREE TEENAGERS HELD IN SLAYING OF MAN, WOMAN FOR $13 LOOT

Three Teenaged boys were held by Inglewood police Wednesday after a violent night in which a housewife was beaten and shot to death for $3 and a man was killed for $10. Each of the victims had been shot in the eye.

The first murder victim was . . . apparently dragged from her car in her driveway . . . about 8 P.M. Tuesday after taking her husband to night school.

Neighbors heard her screams and called police. She had been beaten around the head and shot through the eye. Her car and purse containing $3 were gone.

An hour later . . . near Dodger stadium residents heard shots. A short time after that, the body of an unidentified Latin man was found by strollers. Police said this victim, too had been shot through one eye. They said $10 was believed taken from him (*Los Angeles Times,* May 9, 1974).

Even though the findings of statistical studies can never be so dramatic as newspaper accounts, they can help to put crime into a larger perspective. Table 7–2 is constructed for that purpose. It contrasts the rates of various personal crimes reported by victims in the National Crime Survey with those reported

TABLE 7–2

Violent and property crimes: Contrasts between victim and police accounts

Type of offense	Victim survey*	Uniform crime report*
Crimes of violence	17.1	4.7
Murder	—	0.1
Rape	0.9	0.3
Robbery	6.2	1.9
Aggravated assault	10.0	2.4
Crimes against property	—	45.9
Burglary	88.5†	14.1
Larceny-theft	—	27.3
Personal larceny	97.3	—
Household larceny	123.3†	—
Motor vehicle theft	17.0†	4.5

* NCS rate per 1,000 population, age 12 and over. UCR Rate per 1,000 population, all ages.
† Rate per 1,000 households.
Note: Blank columns indicate data not collected or calculated in a way that permits comparison.
Sources: NCJISS, 1979a:22;32; FBI, 1978:35.

by the police in the *Uniform Crime Reports.*

The table illustrates once again the disparity between police and citizen reports of crimes. According to the police, there were about 4.7 victims of violent crimes per 1,000 people in 1977. By contrast, the victim survey puts the rate at about 17.1 per 1,000, more than four times as great. For crimes against property, the disparities are even greater, with victimizations exceeding police crimes by large amounts: burglary, 6.3 times; personal larceny, 3.6 times; auto theft, 3.8 times.

Indeed, since the victim survey calculates many of its rates in terms of crimes per 1,000 households, while police rates are calculated in terms of crimes per 1,000 persons, it is likely that these disparities would be even greater if a common base was used. Taken at face value, then, such findings could be interpreted to suggest that the risks of being victimized are overwhelming. But there is another side to the picture.

If the national victim surveys are interpreted to assess the chances that the average American will suffer from a violent crime during any given year, they indicate that the odds are about 98 to 2 against it. In 1977, for example, the chances that a person would be murdered were 1 in 10,000; raped, 1 in 1,000; robbed, 6 in 1,000; or assaulted, 1 in 100. However, the chances were greater that that person might suffer from personal theft (10 in 100), burglary (3 in 100), or car theft (2 in 100). But even then, the odds for the average citizen are not catastrophic.

SPECIAL VULNERABILITY: FACTS TO BE EXPLAINED

Since we are inclined to breathe a sigh of relief upon discovering that the odds are not "catastrophic," we should know that all people are not equally vulnerable to crime. Rather, some people are more likely to be victimized than others based upon their age, gender, ethnicity, social class, and place of residence. Indeed, the same set of issues that required explanation when we reviewed official and self-report data tend to reappear when victimization data are examined.

Age

Because of our concern with the young, it is significant that age is highly related to the chances of becoming a victim of crime. As may be seen in Figure 7–1, the people most likely

FIGURE 7–1

Victimization rates for personal crimes by age of victim, 1977 (rate per 1,000 in each age group)

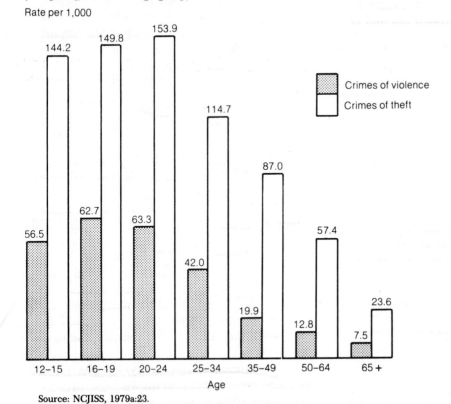

Rate per 1,000

Legend:
- Crimes of violence
- Crimes of theft

Age	Crimes of violence	Crimes of theft
12–15	56.5	144.2
16–19	62.7	149.8
20–24	63.3	153.9
25–34	42.0	114.7
35–49	19.9	87.0
50–64	12.8	57.4
65 +	7.5	23.6

Age

Source: NCJISS, 1979a:23.

to suffer from personal crimes—rape, robbery, assault, and theft—are young people.

Indeed, what is striking about Figure 7–1 is that it so closely parallels the overall rate at which youth are arrested for crime. While, on the one hand, the rates of victimization reported by 12- to 15-year-olds are almost as high as those ages 16 to 19 or 20 to 24, the rates reported by middle-aged and elderly people, on the other hand, are only a fraction of those reported by adolescents. Sixteen- to 19-year-olds, for example, suffered from violent crime at a rate five times higher than that of 50- to 64-year-olds, and eight times higher than that reported by people age 65 and older.

Some striking findings surface when we consider the types of crimes for which juveniles are victimized. In both police and self-report statistics, we saw that young people are more likely to commit property than violent crimes. As may be seen in Figure 7–1, the victim survey parallels these findings. Victimization in crimes

of theft is by far the most common, with the youngest groups having the highest rates, while each older group has successively lower rates. But the victim survey findings do not parallel police and self-report accounts where violent crimes are concerned. As mentioned earlier, it is younger, not older, people who are most likely to be victimized in cases of rape, robbery, and assault.

Furthermore, a growing body of evidence suggests that violence against the young may be common in many families. Parent-child violence, says Straus, is "truly ubiquitous" (1977:718). Besides being spanked, whipped or punched, infants and children are often burned with cigarettes, bitten, cut, locked in dark closets, or are subjected to tortures in which their hands are placed over a gas burner or inserted into a pot of boiling water.

Consequently, victimization data suggest that, if any segment of our society is close to living in a predatory jungle, it is the young. Not only may they be more likely to commit

FIGURE 7–2

Victimization rates for violent crimes by gender and age (rates per 1,000 in each age group)

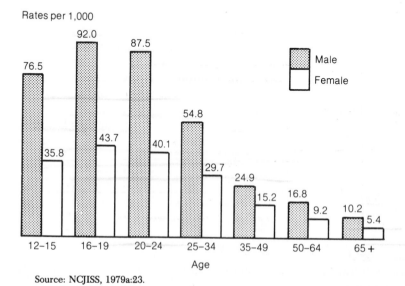

Source: NCJISS, 1979a:23.

crime but also more to suffer its consequences.

Gender

Special vulnerability to crime does not end with age; gender is also important. Its effects can be demonstrated in two ways. First, the general effects of gender can be considered. Who runs the greater risks of being victimized—males or females? Second, the effects of gender and age can be combined to determine how they interact to alter the chances of victimization. Are young females more likely to be victimized than older males or older females? Who run the greater risks?

1. Violent crime. Figure 7–2 indicates that when violent crimes are considered, the ratio of male to female victimizations is about 2 to 1. The only exception is rape. Otherwise, men are much more likely than women to be the victims of robbery and assault.

This conclusion remains true, however, only when age is held constant; that is, only when males and females of the same age are compared. For example, the victimization rate for 16- to 19-year-old girls is 43.7 per 1,000, while that for boys is 92.0; the chances that boys of this age will be victimized are more than twice as great (Figure 7–2). Yet, observe what happens when 16- to 19-year-old girls are compared with males, 65 and over. The rate for girls is more than four times as great—43.7 versus 10.2 per 1,000. Indeed, girls of this age have higher rates than middle-aged males, age 25 to 49 (43.7 versus 24.9). In short, middle-aged and elderly men, as well as women, live much safer lives than the young of either sex.

2. Crimes of theft. Crimes of theft present a somewhat different picture. On the one hand, Figure 7–3 shows that, while younger males are somewhat more likely to be victimized than females of the same age, differences between the sexes tend to diminish for middle-aged people and then to widen

again for males and females over age 50. As a result, growing older does not always mean that differences between the genders will persist. Between ages 25 to 49, women seem to run about the same risks for theft as men. Furthermore, differences between the sexes throughout the life cycle are not so great for crimes of theft as they are for crimes of violence.

On the other hand, Figure 7–3 does demonstrate the extent to which victimization declines with age, for males as well as females. While the victimization rate for people, age 65 and older, is 30.2 for males and 19.0 for females, it is 165.5 for 16- to 19-year-old males and 134.2 for females. In short, the rate for young males is not only 5 to 8 times greater than that for elderly men and women, but the rate for young females is also 4.7 to 7 times greater.

Equally significant is the rate at which young people are victimized in their own homes. Table 7–3 shows that, as people grow older, the chances of being burglarized, having household goods stolen, or losing an automobile to thieves decline steadily. Thus, the ratios of household victimization for 12- to 19-year-olds versus people age 65 and older are also high: burglary, 4.5 to 1; household larceny, 3 to 1; motor vehicle theft, 6 to 1. Whether on the streets or at home, youth are the most vulnerable to victimization.

Given these findings, two conclusions seem warranted: (1) when age is held constant, males generally have higher victimization rates, particularly for violent crimes; but (2) when the effects of age and sex are combined, young people, whether male or female, have higher rates than middle-aged or older people. In fact, the National Victim Surveys indicate that, *if we were to rank different groups according to their vulnerability to crime, they would rank as follows: (1) young males; (2) young females; (3) older males; (4) older females.*

Such findings are contrary to popular belief. While there seems to be widespread awareness

FIGURE 7–3

**Victimization rates for personal crimes of theft by gender and age
(rates per 1,000 in each age group)**

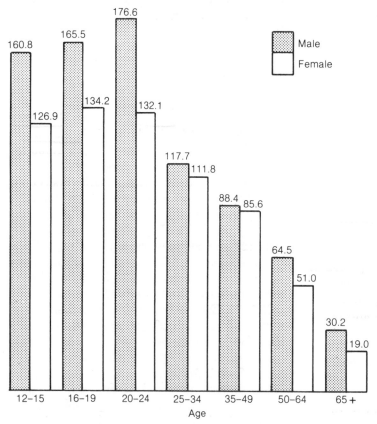

Rate per 1,000

Source: NCJISS, 1979a:23

of the disproportionate contribution of the young to the commission of crime, the opinion is not widely held that the young are the most likely to be victimized. A more common belief is that it is older people who run the greatest risks—the defenseless old lady whose purse is snatched or the reputable business person who is terrorized on a city bus by a street gang.

Actually, these and studies of the public schools indicate that a more likely scenario is one in which a frightened child is backed up

against the wall in the school lavatory and is robbed of his lunch money by his peers (McDermott, 1979; National Institute of Education, 1978). Indeed, in rare instances, extortion occurs in which children rob other children of sizeable sums of money:

> Four [17-year-old] students . . . faced criminal charges Thursday for allegedly extorting $1,686 from a 14-year-old pupil. . . .
> The young victim told officials the "terrorizing" began after he accidentally

stepped on the shoes of one of the suspects.

Demands were made for "damages," police said, first in amounts of $3 to $10 and later increasing to $50 and $100.

"This kid said he got the money to pay them by draining his bar mitzvah account," the police investigator said.

The victim went to [the police] last week after he was allegedly taken to a rest room, threatened with a knife and told to give the four $1,000 by February 14.

When he said he did not have that kind of money, the suspects reportedly punched him and threatened to kill his parents. . . . (*Los Angeles Times*, February 4, 1977).

Finally, some juvenile crimes have deadly consequences. Many killings, for example, particularly in our larger cities, are gang-related or a function of the kinds of subcultural environments in which the poor live. In one bizarre case, three boyfriends of the same teenage girl were shot to death in a period of four months (*Los Angeles Times*, November 22, 1974). The chances that such a sequence of events could occur without the girl and her boyfriends being tied to a unique, but unusually deadly, social network are small. In another case, the members of a rival gang tortured, and ultimately killed, a 16-year-old boy by tying him to the underside of a car and dragging him to death (*Los Angeles Times*, November 3, 1974).

Even though such cases are statistically rare, they are much more a part of everyday life in some of the neglected areas of our central cities than in some of the more affluent. Indeed, since minority status and poverty are characteristic of such areas, they imply that both might be important facts in attempting to understand victimization.

Minority status

Since their inception, the victim surveys have shown that (1) whites are more likely than blacks to report having been victimized in crimes of theft (98.2 versus 90.0 per 1,000 in 1977); and (2) blacks are more likely to have suffered from violent crimes (41.9 versus 33.0 per 1,000 in 1977). Furthermore, the latest survey indicates that disparities between Hispanics and non-Hispanics are virtually the same as those between blacks and whites. While Hispanics reported fewer crimes of theft than non-Hispanics (89.8 versus 97.6 per 1,000), they suffer more from violence (40.1 versus 33.6 per 1,000) (NCJISS, 1979a:24–25). Whether measured in terms of race or ethnicity, therefore, minority status seems to be important in helping to explain differential rates of victimization.

Having demonstrated this fact, however, the National Crime Surveys fail to provide specific information by gender and age for any minority group except blacks. As a consequence, our analysis of the effects of minority status must once again be confined largely to racial comparisons between blacks and whites.

1. Race and gender. Table 7–4 has been constructed to demonstrate the general effects of race and gender on victimization. Two points will be observed. First, it will be noted that males, whether black or white, usually report higher victimization rates than females. Black males suffer most, followed by white males, black females, and then white females.

Second, Table 7–4 shows that, while black and white women report identical rates for

TABLE 7–3
Household victimization rates by type of crime and age of head of household (rate per 1,000 households)

Age	Burglary	Household larceny	Motor vehicle theft
12–19	234.6	193.5	26.3
20–34	120.0	169.4	24.1
35–49	91.9	143.8	20.2
50–64	69.6	95.4	15.1
65 and over......	49.7	57.4	3.8

Source: NCJISS, 1979a:24.

TABLE 7–4 ━━━
Victimization rates for personal crimes by race and gender (rate per 1,000)

Type of offense	Male		Female		Ratio of black to white victims	
	Black	White	Black	White	Males	Females
Crimes of violence	57.4	45.3	29.0	21.7	1.3:1	1.3:1
Rape	0.4*	0.1*	1.6	1.6	4:1*	1:1
Robbery	19.8	7.5	7.4	3.5	2.6:1	2.1:1
Assault	37.3	37.7	20.0	16.6	1:1	1.2:1
Aggravated assault	19.8	15.1	9.0	4.5	1.3:1	2:1
Simple assault	17.5	22.6	11.1	12.2	0.8:1	0.9:1
Crimes of theft	104.6	108.1	77.7	89.0	0.9:1	0.9:1
Theft with contact	5.9	2.0	5.6	2.4	3:1	2.3:1
Theft without contact	98.7	106.2	72.2	86.5	0.9:1	0.8:1

* Estimate is based on 10 or fewer cases and is unreliable.
Source: NCJISS, 1979a:24

rape (1.6 per 1,000) the rates at which both black men and women are victimized by robbery and aggravated assault are about twice as great as for their white counterparts. Furthermore, while whites report slightly higher theft rates overall, these are due primarily to incidents in which they do not have personal contact with the criminal, whereas the reverse is true for blacks. Not only do blacks suffer more from violent crimes but also from personal contact with the criminal when something is stolen from them.

2. *Race and age.* Figure 7–4 shows that the two groups that suffer most from violent crimes are black youngsters, ages 12 to 15, and white youth, ages 16 to 24. However, there are some differences between the races when types of victimization are considered. While black teenagers (as well as black adults) are likely to report higher rates of robbery and aggravated assault, white people are more likely to report higher rates of simple assault. Consequently, it is blacks, not whites, who suffer more from the most violent of crimes.

With respect to the higher rates of theft which whites experience, Figure 7–5 indicates that, while the rates of blacks and whites are about equal among older adults, it is white youths, ages 12 to 24, who bear the brunt of

this kind of victimization. And while black youths report less theft than white youths, their rates are also higher than those for older adults of either race. Once again, therefore, age proves to be an accurate predictor of victimization.

3. *Race and murder.* The foregoing rates of victimization are important, but they pale into insignificance when the ultimate of all crimes is analyzed—murder. Consider the following:

Murder presently accounts for more than 1 percent of all deaths in the United States. "Because younger people tend to be murdered, its impact upon the life span is greater than that of all infectious diseases, tuberculosis, diabetes, or arteriosclerosis" (Farley, 1980:186; U.S. National Center for Health Statistics, 1975:table D).

The murder rate among blacks of all ages and genders is staggeringly high. Although blacks comprise only about 11 percent of the population, they constitute from 40 to 50 percent of all murder victims (FBI, 1974–1978). In some cities, the percentage may be even higher. Between 1965 and 1970, for example, more than 7 out of 10 homicide victims in Chicago were black (Block and Zimring, 1973:3).

The most likely victims of these staggering rates are black males (Table 7–5). Even as small children, ages 1 to 4 their victimization rate is four times higher than that for white males, and more than seven times higher for those ages 25 to 44. As a consequence, "homicide has a greater impact upon the life expectation of nonwhite men than all but three ailments—heart diseases, malignant neoplasms (cancer), and cerebrovascular diseases" (Farley, 1980:186).

For most types of crimes, males are the most likely victims. But where murder is concerned, this generalization breaks down. Until middle age, if not throughout life, the victimization rate for black females exceeds that of white females, and white males as well (Table 7–5).

Since murder rates are highest between the ages of 25 and 35, homicide is also the leading cause of death among young white men (Farley, 1980:186; U.S. National Center for Health Statistics, 1979, table 1–9). In short, the murder rate among white males is terrible, but among blacks it is catastrophic.

Such findings suggest that the isolated and depressing ghettos to which American society has confined its black citizens have become places of crime and terror to many of them, particularly to young black men. In his classic work, *Manchild in the Promised Land,* Claude Brown (1965:126–128), supposedly a hardened delinquent at age 13, describes what it means to be a "bad nigger" in Harlem and how heartsick he was over the expectations associated with that status:

> I was growing up now, and people were going to expect things from me. I would soon be expected to kill a nigger if he mistreated me, like Rock, Bubba Williams, and Dewdrop had. . . . I knew now that I had to keep up with

FIGURE 7–4
Victimization rates for violent crimes by race and age
(rates per 1,000 in each age group)

Rate per 1,000

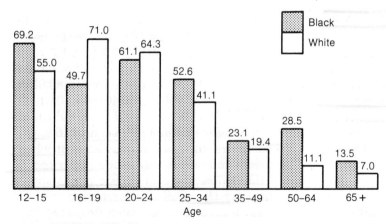

Source: NCJISS, 1979a:25

FIGURE 7–5

Victimization rates for crimes of theft by race and age
(rates per 1,000 in each age group)

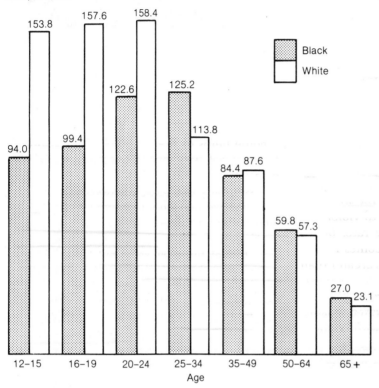

Rate per 1,000

Black
White

153.8 157.6 158.4 122.6 125.2 113.8 94.0 99.4 84.4 87.6 59.8 57.3 27.0 23.1

| 12–15 | 16–19 | 20–24 | 25–34 | 35–49 | 50–64 | 65+ |

Age

Source: NCJISS, 1979a:25

these cats; if I didn't, I would lose my respect in the neighborhood. . . . It made life seem so hard. Sometimes I just wanted to give it up.

Then, to a correctional counselor who had befriended him, Brown made a fatalistic remark that is not uncommon among ghetto gang members: "I don't think I'm gonna stay on the street, Papanek, not for much longer. I don't think I'll see Christmas on the streets." Why plan for the future? Violent death is more likely.

To make matters worse, it is not just from personal crimes that black people suffer the most. With few exceptions, they also suffer the highest victimization rates in crimes against households (NCJISS, 1975–1979a). In 1977, for example, the burglary rate for black households was 122.4 per 1,000 for blacks versus 83.9 for whites; for motor vehicle theft it was 21.1 versus 16.4. Only in household thefts did whites have the higher rates, 124.0 versus 116.2. Furthermore, the same disparities exist when Hispanics and non-Hispanics are compared (NCJISS, 1979a:32–33). Thus, for blacks and perhaps for Hispanics, these rates are prescriptions for disaster when projected over a lifetime.

TABLE 7–5

Rates of murder victimization in the United States by race, gender, and age (rate per 100,000 population)

	Death rate		Black Percent male of female death rate	Percent of all causes of death		Death rate		White Percent male of female death rate	Percent of all causes of death		Ratio of blacks to whites	
Age	*Male*	*Female*		*Male*	*Female*	*Male*	*Female*		*Male*	*Female*	*Male*	*Female*
1–4	8.2	6.3	130	7.6	7.2	1.9	1.6	119	2.7	2.9	4.3:1	3.9:1
5–14	2.9	2.4	121	5.5	7.7	0.9	0.9	100	2.2	3.6	3.2:1	2.7:1
15–24	65.5	16.9	388	31.9	21.1	11.5	3.9	295	6.9	6.8	5.7:1	4.3:1
25–44	109.1	19.7	554	21.4	8.9	14.2	3.9	364	6.7	3.8	7.6:1	5.0:1

Source: Metropolitan Life Insurance Co., 1980:6.

Income

As might be anticipated, income is a fourth factor to consider in studying victimization. The data show that families with the lowest incomes are the most vulnerable to violent crimes (NCJISS, 1975–1979a). The rates of victimization for families with incomes less than $3,000 are often several times greater than the rates of those with incomes of $15,000 and over—rape, 1.8 versus .5 per 1,000; robbery with injury, 5.6 versus 1.5; aggravated assault, 15.7 versus 8.9; personal larceny with contact, 4.6 versus 1.8. Conversely, the higher a family's income, the more likely it will suffer from personal theft without contact (106.3 versus 87.6). In short, poverty is associated with greater violence while affluence is associated with impersonal theft (NCJISS, 1979a:28).

Survey findings also show that race interacts with income in ways that are important. On the one hand, the general pattern just described is characteristic of blacks as well as whites when comparisons are made *within* races; that is, poor people, whether black or white, suffer the highest rates of violent victimizations when compared to their more affluent counterparts. Conversely, the greater the income, the greater the impersonal larceny (NCJISS, 1975–1979a). On the other hand, comparisons *across* races reveal that no matter what their income, blacks tend to suffer more from crime—particularly violent crime—than do whites with comparable incomes. Increased

income helps to shelter blacks from crime, but it is not sufficient to overcome racial disparities.

Essentially the same relationships characterize household victimizations. When income levels *within* races are considered, families in the lower-income brackets tend to have higher burglary rates but lower larceny and motor vehicle rates (NCJISS, 1975a–1979a). But, as with personal crimes, comparisons *across* races reveal that black households on all income levels tend to suffer more from crime than do white households on the same levels. Whether poor or well-to-do, blacks are much more heavily victimized by burglary than their white counterparts, and the rate of motor vehicle theft among affluent blacks is approximately twice that of affluent whites. Only on household larceny do victimization rates begin to approach equality (NCJISS, 1979a:35–36).

As a consequence, it is clear that while many poor whites suffer excessively from violent and household crimes, the effects of poverty combined with minority status for blacks makes them even more vulnerable to these crimes.

Community

The final factor associated with vulnerability to crime is community—the place where one lives. Official accounts by the police have long tended to support the 19th-century belief that the greatest amount of crime is spawned in the city. The victim surveys now lend further confirmation to that idea.

Running on a continuum from city centers to nonmetropolitan areas, the rates per 1,000 for violent crimes are as follows: central cities, 47.2; outside central cities, 33.7; nonmetropolitan areas, 22.1. The same linear trend also characterizes crimes of theft: central cities, 112.9; outside central cities, 107.2; nonmetropolitan areas, 70.9. There is a steady decline in crime from central cities outward, and the rate of violent crime decreases by over 200 percent (NCJISS, 1979a:31).

Such findings lend support to current fears over crime in the city, and lend substance to the assumption that the deteriorating conditions of our urban centers are related to the high rates of victimization experienced by poor and minority people.

TRENDS IN VICTIMIZATION

Police and court statistics have suggested that crime increased considerably during the 1960s and early 1970s. A fundamental question, therefore, is whether victim surveys provide any evidence to show that these trends have continued on until the present.

Over the six years during which victimization has been measured (1973–78), the following conclusions can be reached: for many of the more serious crimes, victimization rates have declined significantly (robbery, burglary, and motor vehicle theft) or have remained about the same (rape, aggravated assault, and personal larceny without contact). Meanwhile, the only rates that have increased significantly are those for simple assault, larceny with contact, and household larceny. Hence, while these findings do not provide assurances that crime is decreasing rapidly, at least they do not support the popular assumption that violent and serious crimes, in particular, are continuing to accelerate at unprecedented rates (NCJISS, 1979b; 1979c).

SUMMARY OF VICTIMIZATION FINDINGS

By using scientific procedures to sample the public at large, yearly victim surveys have provided a valuable new source of information on crime. Since 1973, they suggest the following:

1. Extent of crime. The number of victim-reported crimes greatly exceeds the number reported by the police or courts. Nonetheless, the chances that the "average" citizen will be victimized in any given year, particularly in a violent crime, are not great.

2. Vulnerability to crime. Victimization surveys do not support the common belief that it is older people, or members of the white middle and upper classes, who are the most vulnerable to crime. Instead, they suggest that certain other segments of the population are far more vulnerable:

Young people are more vulnerable than older people.

Males are more vulnerable than females.

Blacks are more vulnerable than whites.

Poor people are more vulnerable than the affluent, at least to violent crimes.

City dwellers are more vulnerable than country dwellers.

In summary, when all of these factors interact, they indicate that the prototypical victim, particularly of violent crimes, is the young, poor, black male who lives in an urban ghetto. The young, poor, white male is not far behind, followed closely by the young, poor, black female.

There is irony in such findings. Despite the notion that special steps are taken to nurture and to protect the young, they are far more likely than middle-aged or older adults to be the victims of crime. Furthermore, the findings show that those members of our population that are the most disadvantaged economically and culturally are also those who suffer most from violent crimes. Clearly, then, these are important facts to which theorists must pay attention in their attempts to explain, not only the commission of crime, but its distribution.

3. *Trends in crime.* The National Crime Surveys reveal that, since 1973, victimization rates have either remained about the same or have decreased slightly for several types of crime: rape, robbery, personal larceny with contact, burglary, and motor vehicle theft. The only exceptions are simple assault, personal larceny without contact, and household larceny (NCJISS, 1979b:1–6). Furthermore, where decreases have occurred, they are most pronounced among the young. As a consequence, victimization data do not support the widespread assumption that the high crime rates of the 1960s and early 1970s have continued upward in an unbroken chain. While they have not declined, as one might hope, at least they have not continued to escalate.

CONCLUSIONS: CONGRUENCE OF OFFICIAL, SELF-REPORT, AND VICTIM ACCOUNTS OF CRIME

In light of the findings on victimization, it is important that we proceed now to examine the extent to which they are congruent with official and self-report accounts of crime. Using all three measures, what conclusions can be reached regarding the extent of the juvenile crime problem, the important facts that must be explained by theory, and the increase or decrease in juvenile crime?

Extent of juvenile crime

Compelling data indicate that there are far more juvenile law violators and crime victims than there are official delinquents. Self-report studies suggest that only about 10 percent of all crimes are actually recorded, while victim surveys indicate that the figure may be as high

as 25 percent. But whatever the precise figure, both estimates lead to the same general conclusion: police and court records grossly underestimate (1) the actual number of criminal acts committed by juveniles, and (2) the instances in which they are victims of crime.

Facts that must be explained

The three methods of measuring crime are in surprising agreement on the facts to which theorists must attend. Consider first the similarities between official and victim accounts of crime:

Police records show that arrest rates are higher for the young than for the old, higher for males than for females, higher for blacks than for whites, higher for low-income than for high-income persons, and higher in the country than in the city.

Victimization studies paint an identical picture: young people are more vulnerable to victimization than older people; males are more vulnerable than females; blacks are more vulnerable than whites; poor people are more vulnerable than affluent people; and city dwellers are more vulnerable than country dwellers.

In short, while arrest reports represent only a portion of those who violate the law, and while victim accounts represent only those who are willing to report having been victimized, they seem to be tapping a common universe of behavior. Despite their differences over the size and precise characteristics of that universe, they are in general agreement on many of the variables for which theory is needed.

The picture painted by self-report studies, while similar in general terms, suggests the need for qualification. For example, while these studies strongly support the idea that crime is disproportionately concentrated among the young, and that males are more heavily involved than females, they also suggest that the pattern of female offenses is much more like that of males than was previously believed. Furthermore, they question whether differences in law-violating behavior between low- and high-income persons, and between blacks and whites, are as great as arrest statistics indicate. Instead, they suggest that theorists pay heed to the distinction between the prevalence and incidence of illegal behavior.

On the one hand, the prevalence of delinquent behavior does not seem to be greater among low-income or black juveniles: about equal proportions of young people from all classes and races report having violated the law. On the other hand, the incidence of delinquent behavior does seem to be greater among low-income and minority juveniles: although there are chronic offenders in all classes and racial groups, lower-class and black youths are the most likely to be represented on the highest end of the delinquency continuum and to have engaged in the most serious criminal acts.

It is noteworthy, as a result, to find that the National Crime Surveys paint a similar picture from the perspective of the victim. That is, while victimization is prevalent throughout society, it is poor and minority people who suffer the highest incidence of violent crimes and from thefts in which they are confronted personally by the criminal. The most extreme illustration of this phenomenon, of course, is murder. Not only are black men and women more likely to be its victims, but their killers are generally relatives, friends, or acquaintances. Meanwhile, white and upper-income people are more likely to suffer from instances of theft in which they do not experience direct contact with criminals.

In short, all three measures of crime agree that its prevalence is widespread, while pointing, at the same time, to those segments of society where its incidence is the greatest.

Finally, we must consider the group nature of delinquent behavior. Since the preponderant majority of all delinquent acts are committed in groups—whether male or female, black or white, middle- or lower-class—this phenomenon becomes a fact that should be added to those just listed. Indeed, when that is done, some of the questions for which theories are needed are the following:

1. Why are the young the most likely victims as well as the most likely perpetrators of crime?
2. Why are their illegal acts likely to occur in groups?
3. Why are males more delinquent and more victimized than females?
4. Why are there chronic offenders (and perhaps chronic victims) in all classes and racial groups?
5. Why are lower-class and black youths more likely to be represented on the highest end of the delinquency continuum and to have engaged in, or to have suffered from, the most serious criminal acts?
6. Why are both victimization and illegal behavior more heavily concentrated in urban centers?

Any society which aspires to improve its quality of life requires answers for questions like these.

Crime trends

Between 1960 and 1974, arrest and court records implied that (1) crime rates among juveniles had increased at a steady, if not alarming, rate; (2) violent acts committed by the young had increased at a much more rapid pace than by adults; and (3) while official delinquency was still predominantly male, it had increased at a faster pace among girls than boys.

With the advent of the *National Crime Surveys* in 1973, a second source of data became available with which to assess trends. In general, they tend to agree with the *Uniform Crime Reports* of the FBI. Since 1974, they suggest that (1) juvenile crime rates have remained about the same, or have decreased slightly; (2) decreases have occurred in violent as well as property crimes; and (3) the crime rate among girls has followed the same trend as that among boys.

In short, while youth crime escalated rapidly during the 1960s and early 1970s, it has now leveled out. Nonetheless, these findings do not provide grounds for uncontrolled joy, since they fail to show that rates of violence and theft are now retreating to more modest levels.

Furthermore, the juvenile crime problem is exacerbated by the fact that those members of the population who are most victimized are also those most likely to commit crime: juveniles tend to prey upon juveniles, males upon males, blacks upon blacks, ghetto dwellers upon ghetto dwellers (Mulvihill et al. 1969:207–17). As a result, some neighborhoods and schools are much more treacherous and unsafe than others.

In the next section, therefore, we will turn our attention to theories of crime, and will seek to determine the degree to which they are able to explain these phenomena and to suggest ways for dealing with them.

REFERENCES

Block, Richard, and Zimring, Franklin E.
   1973   "Homicide in Chicago, 1965–1970." *Journal of Research in Crime and Delinquency* 10 (January):1–12.

Brown, Claude
   1965   *Manchild in the Promised Land.* New York: Signet Books.

Ennis, Philip H.
   1967   *Criminal Victimization in the United States: A Report of a National Survey.* University of Chicago: National Opinion Research Center.

Farley, Reynolds
   1980   "Homicide Trends in the United States." *Demography* 17 (May):177–88.

Federal Bureau of Investigation
   1974   *Uniform Crime Reports for the United States—1973.* Washington, D.C.: U.S. Government Printing Office.
   1975   *Uniform Crime Reports for the United States—1974.* Washington, D.C.: U.S. Government Printing Office.
   1976   *Uniform Crime Reports for the United States—1975.* Washington, D.C.: U.S. Government Printing Office.
   1977   *Uniform Crime Reports for the United States—1976.* Washington, D.C.: U.S. Government Printing Office.
   1978   *Uniform Crime Reports for the United States—1977.* Washington, D.C.: U.S. Government Printing Office.

McDermott, M. Joan
   1979   *Criminal Victimization in Urban Schools.* Washington, D.C.: U.S. Government Printing Office.

Metropolitan Life Insurance Company
   1980   "Mortality Differentials Favor Women." *Statistical Bulletin* 61 (April–June):3–7.

Mulvihill, Donald J.; Tumin, Melvin M.; and Curtis, Lynn A.
    1969   *Crimes of Violence: A Staff Report Submitted to the National Commission on the Causes and Prevention of Violence,* Vol. 2. Washington, D.C.: U.S. Government Printing Office.

National Advisory Committee on Criminal Justice Standards and Goals
    1973   "Victimization Surveying: Its History, Uses, and Limitations." *Report on the Criminal Justice System.* Washington, D.C.: U.S. Government Printing Office.

National Criminal Justice Information and Statistics Service
    1975a *Criminal Victimization in the United States: 1973.* Advance Report, 1 (May). Washington, D.C.: Law Enforcement Assistance Administration.
    1975b *Criminal Victimization Surveys in the Nation's Five Largest Cities.* Washington, D.C.: U.S. Government Printing Office.
    1976   *Criminal Victimization in the United States: A Comparison of 1973 and 1974 Findings.* Washington, D.C.: Law Enforcement Assistance Administration.
    1976   *Criminal Victimization in the United States, 1974.* Washington, D.C.: U.S. Government Printing Office.
    1977   *Criminal Victimization in the United States, 1975.* Washington, D.C.: U.S. Government Printing Office.
    1978   *Criminal Victimization in the United States, 1976.* Washington, D.C.: U.S. Government Printing Office.
    1979a *Criminal Victimization in the United States, 1977.* Washington, D.C.: U.S. Government Printing Office.
    1979b *Criminal Victimization in the United States: A Description of Trends from 1973 to 1977.* Washington, D.C.: U.S. Government Printing Office.
    1979c *Criminal Victimization in the United States: Summary of Findings 1977–78, Changes in Crime and Trends in 1973.* Washington, D.C.: U.S. Government Printing Office.

National Institute of Education
    1978   *Violent Schools—Safe Schools.* Washington, D.C.: U.S. Government Printing Office.

Penick, Bettye K. Edison, and Owens, Maurice E. B., III
    1976   *Surveying Crime.* Washington, D.C.: U.S. Government Printing Office.

President's Commission on Law Enforcement and Administration of Justice
    1967a *The Challenge of Crime in a Free Society.* Washington, D.C.: U.S. Government Printing Office.
    1967b *Task Force Report: Crime and Its Impact—An Assessment.* Washington, D.C.: U.S. Government Printing Office.

Straus, Murray A.
    1977   "Societal Morphogenesis and Intrafamily Violence in Cross-cultural Perspective." *Annals of the New York Academy of Sciences* 285:717–30.

U.S. National Center for Health Statistics
    1975   *United States Decennial Life Tables for 1969–71, United States Life Tables by Causes of Death: 1969:71.* Vol. 1. No. 5.
    1979   *Vital Statistics of the United States: 1975.* Vol. 2. Part A.

SCIENTIFIC EXPLANATIONS FOR DELINQUENT BEHAVIOR

Introduction: The role of science in the construction of delinquent behavior and juvenile justice

In prior sections of this book, we learned that (1) the discovery of childhood led to the invention of the juvenile court, and (2) certain facts associated with the delinquent behavior of juveniles require explanation. In this section, we will review the relation of scientific criminology to both of these phenomena.

Given the gradual awakening of Western civilization from the stagnation of the Middle Ages, it is no accident that strong parallels formed between the invention and growth of the juvenile court and the invention and growth of modern science. Indeed, the latter did much to justify a separate system of justice for juveniles. Its increasingly complex explanations for delinquent behavior not only provided a highly prestigious rationale for treating children differently from adults, but also lent much-needed support to the notion that the juvenile court should implement an entirely new concept of justice for them—a *rehabilitative concept*.

In order to grasp the role that scientific criminology played, it is necessary to contrast its approach to the understanding and control of delinquent behavior with the classical approach, which dominated legal thought and practice prior to the invention of the juvenile court. By way of setting the stage for that task, consider again the beliefs about the sources of crime that were dominant in the 18th century. It will be recalled that American colonists, like their European cousins, tended to believe supernatural explanations for criminal or delinquent behavior. People who got into trouble, young or old, were thought to be possessed by the devil and cursed by God. Any transgressions of the law, therefore, demanded stern punishments: whipping, hanging, mutilation, branding, banishment, or the use of the stocks and the pillory.

It will also be recalled that this view and treatment of crime began to change as a result of the philosophy of the Enlightenment—the set of 18th-century beliefs which stressed human reason, equal justice for all, and the belief that, by applying the principles of democracy, unimagined heights of human welfare could be achieved. Indeed, Enlightenment philosophy was largely responsible for what we now call the *classical school of criminology* (Monachesi, 1960; Radzinowicz, 1966).

CLASSICAL CONSTRUCTION OF CRIME

Led by Cesare Beccaria (1738–1794) late in the 18th century, this school attacked the systems of criminal justice in all Western countries for their arbitrary, cruel, and oppressive practices, and set out to reduce the severity of existing punishments and to achieve equal justice for everyone, noble or commoner (Beccaria, 1963). But basic to the pursuit of these goals was a set of beliefs that eventually contributed to a new concept of justice—the *classical concept*. Installed shortly after the American Revolution, it dominated legal practice throughout the 19th century.

Human nature

This new concept of justice incorporated a natural, rather than a supernatural, view of human nature. According to Beccaria, and to Jeremy Bentham (1748–1832), an English philosopher, human nature is possessed of three distinguishing features: (1) people are not bound by original sin but have freedom of choice; (2) people are rational, and rather than being controlled by supernatural forces, they are entirely capable of using reason to govern their own lives; and (3) people are self-seeking, and are motivated, if given the chance, to pursue their own selfish interests at the expense of others.

Consequently, Beccaria and Bentham believed that it is the free exercise of human reason in the pursuit of pleasure, not supernatural forces, which dictates human conduct, be it law-abiding or criminal (Geis, 1960:56–57).

Social order

Having defined people as reasonable and free, classical theorists then envisioned a democratic society in which the criminal law would be the product of a social order characterized by value consensus. Reasonable people would agree that the protection of private property and personal welfare is desirable, that individuals are responsible for their own actions, and that excuses for committing crime are unacceptable. Hence, if society were run on democratic principles, its citizens would willingly enter into a social contract with the state to refrain from crime and to preserve the peace (Monachesi, 1960:40).

Criminal behavior

Given their concepts of human nature and social order, members of the classical school were not much interested in seeking complex explanations for criminal behavior, since they already knew the answers. The answers were inherent in their beliefs about human nature: lawbreaking is due to a free and rational decision to violate the law in pursuit of personal satisfaction. If a criminal act appears to have greater utility for the individual than the pain he will suffer from committing it, he will engage in it (Bentham, 1948:2). Hence, classical theorists were most concerned, not with the reasons that people violate the law, but with reforming the administration of justice.

Administration of justice

They believed that, if the tyrannies of past centuries were to be overcome, the methods of trying, sentencing, and punishing offenders had to be revolutionized. Consequently, they stressed the following reforms (see Monachesi, 1960:41–43):

1. *Democratic lawmaking.* Criminal codes should be written by democratically elected legislators not by arbitrary rulers. Furthermore, it is these codes and not their own biases and self-interests, which judges should be required to follow in trying and sentencing offenders.

2. *Simplicity of law.* Laws should be written in terms that are understandable to ordinary people. The better they are understood, the less likely people will be to violate them.

3. *Independent judges.* The judiciary should be an independent arm of government so that they are not subject to the daily whims of unscrupulous leaders or citizens.

4. *Equality before the law.* The laws should apply equally to all members of society, no matter what their social standing.

5. *Strict rules of due process.* The administration of justice should be governed by procedures which assure that the accused is given a fair trial.

In short, law and procedure, not the power of the accused or the discretion of the judge, should govern all criminal proceedings. An enlightened system of justice is one which incorporates all of the constitutional protections with which we are familiar—freedom from unreasonable search and seizure, freedom from torture and self-incrimination, the idea that a person is innocent until proven guilty, and all the protections of due process during the conduct of a trial. Only when these are instituted are citizens protected from self-serving, secretive, or arbitrary officials.

Crime control

If, after just procedures have been followed, a person is found guilty of a crime, society has the right—indeed, the obligation—to punish him. Not only is this obligation inherent in the social contract theory of social order, but it also makes sense in terms of human nature. Since people are rational and seek to avoid pain, punishment will deter them from crime. Hence, lawbreaking can be controlled if certain principles are followed (Monachesi, 1960:40–41):

1. *Make punishment certain.* People who break the law should know that they cannot escape responsibility for their acts.

2. *Make punishment prompt.* Punishment should be speedily imposed. The sooner it takes place, the more effective it will be.

3. *Grade punishments.* Punishments should be graded according to the seriousness of criminal acts—minor punishments for minor crimes and major punishments for major crimes. But in no instance is brutality or the death penalty necessary. People do not have to be scourged, disemboweled, or have their heads cut off to get the idea that crime does not pay. Instead, they will be deterred from crime if they grasp the simple fact that the pleasure to be gained from any illegal act will not be sufficient to override the pain it will cause.

In summary, classical criminologists were far more concerned with rationalizing and justifying means by which to reform the tyrannical and brutal systems of justice of the 18th century than with conducting studies into the causes of crime or the best methods for rehabilitating offenders.

Hence, classical criminologists are best remembered for two ideas: (1) the administration of justice should be blind to the social standing and the power of offenders, and (2) it should respond quickly, but fairly, to the acts they commit. Otherwise, the criminal codes and the administration of justice will favor the rich and the powerful, while they severely punish the poor and the meek. That is why, according to classical dictates, an enlightened system of justice is one which responds uniformly and equitably to *crimes*, not to criminals.

Legacy

It is difficult to overstate the impact of classical criminology on Western thought and legal practice. As a part of the general growth of democratic institutions, the criminal codes of many countries were rewritten in the late-18th and early-19th centuries; an independent judiciary became a separate arm of government; steps were taken to make due process a regular part of the administration of justice; punishments were reduced in severity and graded according to the seriousness of criminal acts; and newly designed prisons were constructed as more humane places for punishing offenders.

Indeed, many of these elements remain locked in our legal system today. The classical concept of justice continues as a powerful article of faith for many people in its insistence that justice should be blind, and that punishments should be allocated according to the crimes that people commit, and not according to their backgrounds or reasons for committing them.

SCIENCE: THE POSITIVE SCHOOL OF CRIMINOLOGY

The legacy of classical criminology notwithstanding, changes took place during the 19th century which tended to erode its influence. One of these was the growth of science, ironically no less a product of Enlightenment philosophy than the classical school. But while classical criminology partook of the emphasis of Enlightenment philosophers upon overthrowing the autocratic regimes of the 18th century, the growth of science reflected their emphasis upon seeking knowledge by inductive means, and then using that knowledge to accelerate human progress. As a consequence, a new school of criminology began to take shape—the *positive school*.

Intrigued by the growth of the physical and natural sciences in the 18th and 19th centuries, a number of philosophers suggested that the methods of science should be applied to the study of human affairs as well. In 1813, for example, Henri de Saint-Simon, a French philosopher, argued that science, not religion, should become the new spiritual power in Western civilization. The studies of morals and politics—heretofore limited to religious and philosophical discourse—should become *positive* sciences. The application of scientific methods to the study of human affairs could then serve to guide the development of modern industrial society (Barnes, 1948:73–74).

By the latter quarter of the 19th century, such beliefs had become widespread and had been applied to the study of crime and criminals. Indeed, the century between Beccaria's statement on the principles of classical criminology in 1764 and the statements of a growing number of scientific positivists late in the 19th century was marked by "a shift in man's thinking about himself that is of such magnitude that it can well be considered an intellectual revolution" (Vold and Bernard, 1979:35). Beccaria had taken for granted the idea that human behavior is due to the rational exercise of free will, and that the "social contract" is responsible for social order. But an increasing number of positivists began to question these assumptions: "What sort of creature is the human animal?" they asked. And "how is society organized and maintained?" But rather than turning to philosophical speculation for the answers, they turned to the positive methods of science—observation, experimentation, and comparison.

Basic doctrines

The application of these methods, in turn, meant that a much different approach to the understanding and control of crime would be required. Whereas classical criminologists had assumed that they knew why people commit crime and, thus, had made reform their transcendent goal, positivists were tentative, and tended to shy away from suggesting solutions until they could verify their worth. By the time the juvenile court was firmly established in the 20th century, therefore, a new set of doctrines tended to dominate criminology.

1.   *Empirical documentation.*   Positivists contended that, as in the natural and physical sciences, the application of reason to any problem is not enough. Classical theories may be plausible; they also may be false. Therefore, if empirical support for them cannot be documented, they should be revised or discarded. The job of criminologists is to test, as well as to formulate, theories of delinquent behavior and social control.

2.   *The doctrine of determinism.*   Reflecting the exciting ideas of Charles Darwin and other scientists, positivists also argued that crime, like any other phenomenon, is determined by prior causes. It does not just happen. The emphasis of the classical school upon reason and free will, for instance, is too simple, they said. People are not free to do as they wish; much, if not all, of their behavior is determined by biological, psychological, social, and environmental forces over which they have little personal control. Furthermore, natural laws govern the operation of these forces. Hence, a second major task of criminology is to discover these laws with respect to crime.

3.   *Value neutrality.*   Finally, positivists held that until they could provide verified information, criminologists should remain neutral with respect to the conduct of social policy. Just as they were skeptical with regard to various theories of delinquent behavior, so they were skeptical about its proposed reforms. Indeed, science should use experimental methods to determine whether punishment, or any other approach, actually accomplishes the good that it is supposed to accomplish.

As a reflection of the widespread acceptance, and growth of these doctrines, the *Dictionary of the Social Sciences,* in 1964, defined criminology as the discipline which attempts "to formulate and test theories as to *why* criminal law becomes law, *why* people break such law, *why* societies do what they do to those who break such law, and *what* the effects of varying modes of intervention are" (Gilmore, 1964:148, emphasis added). The implication was clear: criminologists should remain impartial in their search for understanding, skeptical about the nature of their findings, neutral with respect to social reforms, and humble in the assertions they make. As a result, the scientific beliefs that eventually helped to justify a rehabilitative concept of justice for juveniles were much different from those which were used to justify the classical concept of justice a century earlier.

Human nature

First, scientific study in a variety of disciplines suggested that the concept of human nature be altered. In addition to the biological study of the effects of genetics, physiology, and anatomy upon human behavior, anthropologists began to inquire into the astounding array of cultures in the world, psychologists studied the nature of human emotions and individual development, and sociologists sought to define the complex web of ethnic, institutional, and class relationships and to determine its effect on the people living in it. Following the turn of the 20th century, therefore, criminology partook of an increasing flood of new ideas regarding the concept of human nature.

In light of these new ideas, the classical view of human nature soon appeared to be naive and simplistic. Theories from a variety of disciplines suggested that human nature is not comprised of some universal free will and capacity for reason which somehow transcend all cultural boundaries or individual experiences. Instead, it is the product of a uniquely complex biological endowment which may be shaped into any number of different forms—by varying experiences in contrasting cultures, family patterns that differ from society to society, variations in secular and religious education, or membership in different subcultural or class groups within the same society. In contrast to classical criminology, therefore, positivistic criminology suggested that human nature is characterized by two distinguishing features:

1. *Human nature is learned.* People must be trained to be human. While their basic needs for survival—food, procreation, the elimination of waste—are necessary to be human, they are not sufficient. Until people have also learned to behave in accordance with the values and standards of their own society, they are not human.

2. *Human nature varies.* There is not be just one, but many, human natures. Since both social expectations and the process of socialization vary from society to society, and from time to time, human nature will also vary (Volkhart, 1964:306–307).

Social order

The scientific study of varying cultures also suggested that there is no universal social order. If human nature varies from society to society, so does the concept of social order. Furthermore, there may be subcultural variations within the same society. In America, for example, differences in custom might be expected between Southerners and Northerners, among different ethnic groups, or among the lower, middle and upper classes. Hence, to the degree these variations exist, the social order may be characterized by diversity, competition, and even conflict.

Given their growing awareness of this diversity, in fact, positivists were confronted with a dilemma: how could they explain the regularity and persistence of order in complex, 20th-century society, though it was characterized by rapid change and a great deal of ethnic, class, subcultural, and regional variation? Two general explanations were forthcoming.

1. *Value consensus.* The first suggested that, despite subcultural differences within any given society, order is maintained by a common agreement on basic values, general definitions of right and wrong, and the kinds of laws that are needed to control crime. While all the parts of any complex society are never fully integrated, they do tend toward a condition of stability and equilibrium (Merton, 1968:73–136; van den Berghe, 1963). Society, in short, is held together by a general *value consensus* (Davis, 1948:3, 52–82).

2. *Coercion.* The second explanation suggested that society is characterized by conflict, and that order is maintained through the *coercion* of the weak by the powerful. While different ethnic groups or social classes may have their own subcultural values and customs, those which dominate social relations and lawmaking will usually belong to the most powerful groups (Dahrendorf, 1958; Turk, 1969). Despite social conflict, therefore, social order and the operation of the criminal justice system will result from coercion of the weak by the powerful.

Despite the presence of these contrasting views of social order, it is probable that, until very recently, most criminologists favored the consensus model. They have felt that people are generally bound together by their opposition to crime, and that they continue to be motivated by Enlightenment values which suggest that, while all societies are not yet equal, science may yet discover and initiate universal laws, which will promote a consensual social order based on democratic principles. Once these laws are known and applied, efforts to improve social law and legal practice will insure greater equality, security, and happiness for everyone (Pound, 1942).

Criminal behavior

The positivistic construction of criminal behavior clearly reflected these scientific assumptions about human nature and social order. As we will soon see, the most popular theories of the late 19th and early 20th centuries suggested that crime is due to biological causes—physical degeneracy, inherited genetic weaknesses, or defective intelligence. Following shortly thereafter, psychological theories were added which indicated that children who violate the law are likely to suffer from emotional conflicts that are poorly understood and poorly handled—conflicts that originate in the family, the result of inadequate socialization in the first few years of life. Finally, 20th-century sociologists and anthropologists theorized that the primary causes of delinquent behavior are poverty, ignorance, discrimination, social disorganization, and the delinquent subcultures, all produced by an unequal society. Lawbreaking is a consequence of the way society is organized.

Given these various explanations, it is clear that positivistic criminology has been, and continues to be, divided along disciplinary lines regarding the accuracy and practicality of its theories. Yet, despite its internal dissonance, it is unified by an overall image of the delinquent that is stunningly different from the image projected by the classical school.

Rather than suggesting that delinquents are rational persons who freely and deliberately calculate the pros and cons of law-violating behavior, the positivistic view suggests that they are virtually driven to criminal acts by complex forces over which they have little control. Thus, whether these forces are biological, psychological, sociological, or a combination of the three, they tend to shape offenders in ways that leave little room for conscious and enlightened decision making. As the 19th-century physician Henry Maudsley put it, criminals "go criminal, as the insane go mad, because they cannot help it" (Scott, 1969:147).

Maudsley's conclusion not only reflected the deterministic character of scientific theory, but it was highly compatible with the set of beliefs that motivated the child saving movement of this and previous centuries. The belief that children are innocent and fragile and that they must be quarantined from adult vices while they are carefully trained was deterministic in character. Like positivistic science, therefore, it seriously questioned the classical belief that human behavior is rational and suggested, instead, that it is determined by forces over which children have little control. How can young people who are poverty-stricken, poorly socialized, or mentally deficient be deterred by punishment if they do not know the difference between right and wrong? The only hope for controlling their antisocial behavior is to discover, and then treat, its causes.

ADMINISTRATION OF JUSTICE AND CRIME CONTROL

This way of viewing the law violator implied the need to profoundly alter the classical concept of justice, at least for children. If the causes for crime were not the same for all people, and if they were due to factors which law violators could not control, then any system which uniformly punished them for the acts they had committed would be unjust, not just. A more reasonable system, by contrast, would be one which reacted to *criminals,* not to crimes.

As English scientist Charles Goring put it (1913:11):

> All thinking people today, legislators and judges, as well as the general public, the morality of the age, as well as the voice of science, attest to the truth . . . that it is the criminal and not the crime we should study and consider; that it is the criminal and not the crime we ought to penalize.

Rather than relying upon the strategy of classical criminology, the new scientific strategy was supposed to individualize justice and reduce delinquent conduct by identifying and eliminating its causes.

Implications for evaluating theories

During most of this century, the juvenile justice system is supposed to have exemplified this strategy in its purest form. Therefore, it is imperative that we carefully examine the theories of delinquent behavior which, along with the modern concept of childhood, have been instrumental in justifying its existence. But before we do so, we should pay heed to an important lesson inherent in this brief review of criminological history: the positive construction of crime, no less than the classical construction which preceded it, is a reflection of cultural values and trends that are much broader than science itself. In fact, we have already seen that some of the same trends which gave birth to the juvenile court also gave birth to science.

The implications of this fact are profound. What they suggest is that, even though the game of science does subject scientists to stricter demands for detachment and objectivity than do most other social games, they are inevitably affected by nonscientific values, obligations, and points of view. Indeed, William Graham Sumner, one of the pioneers of American sociology, once commented that "it is vain to imagine that a 'scientific man' can divest himself of prejudice or previous opinion, and put himself in an attitude of neutral independence toward the mores. He might as well try to get out of gravity or the presence of the atmosphere" (1907:521–522).

Since Sumner was quite correct, a caution is suggested relative to our examination of the theories that follow: rather than examining them as pristine statements of reality, which somehow transcend all cultural boundaries or measures of time, we should recognize that they, too, are artifacts of culture and history. Indeed, if we were to draw a diagram showing the relation of either classical or positive constructions of crime to their place in the history of Western culture, it might look something like this:

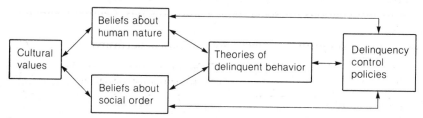

The diagram indicates that cultural values lead to certain assumptions about human nature and social order. These, in turn, contribute both to the construction of theories of delinquent behavior and to the policies designed to control it. But the relationship holds in both directions. While theories of delinquent behavior are affected by prevailing values and beliefs, they also tend to alter these beliefs in return. In fact, it is often difficult to tell whether changes in belief reflect new theories or whether new theories merely reflect old beliefs.

Since both cases are often true, theories play an important role not only in the scientific game of accumulating knowledge, but also in constructing new social values and ways of responding to delinquent conduct. Moreover, it is not always the scientific quality of any theory that will determine its uses but rather, its capacity to capture and to give expression to emerging cultural trends. How well a theory conforms to emerging beliefs and delinquency control policies may determine its popularity every bit as much, if not more, than the actual evidence that can be brought to bear upon it.

Classification of theories

Given this state of affairs, two steps will be taken to sort out the many theories that exist and to draw some overall conclusions about them.

First, they will be classified into major types, ranging from the deterministic theories of the late 19th century, which tended to locate the sources of delinquent behavior in the inherent characteristics of defective children, to the most recent theories, which are no less deterministic but which describe society as being at fault. The historical progression of these ideas across the societal stage and the changes they have wrought in our construction of delinquency will be described.

Second, the examination of each of these bodies of theory will be organized to answer a series of fundamental questions:

1. What are the beliefs about human nature and social order upon which the theory is constructed? What values does it reflect and what pictures of children and society does it portray?
2. What is its underlying logic and basic content? What are the facts upon which it concentrates in trying to explain delinquent conduct? Are any of these facts among those which are enumerated when we examined the various measures of delinquent conduct: age, gender, social class, minority status, or the group nature of delinquent behavior?
3. What are its implications for social policy, and how has it actually affected policy?
4. How well does it stand up to logical and empirical scrutiny?

Once these steps have been taken, we will be in a position to draw some conclusions about the overall contribution of scientific and scholarly communities to our social construction of delinquency and to the policies designed to prevent and control it.

REFERENCES

Barnes, Harry E.
 1948 "Social Thought in Early Modern Times." Pp. 29–90 in Harry E. Barnes, ed., *An Introduction to the History of Sociology.* Chicago: University of Chicago Press.

Beccaria, Cesare
 1963 *On Crimes and Punishments.* Translated by Henry Paolucci. Indianapolis: Bobbs-Merrill.

Bentham, Jeremy
 1948 *An Introduction to the Principles of Morals and Legislation.* Edited by Laurence J. Lafleur. New York: Hafner.

Dahrendorf, Rolf
 1958 "Out of Utopia: Toward a Reorientation of Sociolgoical Analysis." *American Journal of Sociology* 67:115–27.

Davis, Kingsley
 1948 *Human Society.* New York: Macmillan.

Geis, Gilbert
 1960 "Jeremy Bentham." Pp. 51–67 in Hermann Mannheim, ed., *Pioneers in Criminology.* Chicago: Quadrangle.

Gilmore, Harlan W.
    1964   "Criminology." P. 148 in Julius Gould and William L. Kolb, eds., *A Dictionary of the Social Sciences.* New York: Free Press.
Goring, Charles
    1913   *The English Convict.* London: His Majesty's Stationery Office.
Merton, Robert K.
    1968   *Social Theory and Social Structure,* Enlarged edition. New York: Free. Press.
Monachesi, Elio
    1960   "Cesare Beccaria." Pp. 36–50 in Hermann Mannheim, ed., *Pioneers in Criminology.* Chicago: Quadrangle.
Pound, Roscoe
    1942   *Social Control Through Law.* New Haven: Yale University Press.
Radzinowicz, Leon
    1966   *Ideology and Crime.* New York: Columbia University Press.
Scott, Peter
    1969   "Henry Maudsley." Pp. 144–167 in Hermann Mannheim, ed., *Pioneers in Criminology.* Chicago: Quadrangle.
Sumner, William
    1907   *Folkways.* New York: Ginn and Co.
Turk, Austin T.
    1969   *Criminality and the Legal Order.* Chicago: Rand McNally.
van dan Berghe, Pierre L.
    1963   "Dialectic and Functionalism: Toward a Theoretical Synthesis." *American Sociological Review* 28:695–705.
Vold, George B., and Bernard, Thomas J.
    1979   *Theoretical Criminology.* 2d ed. New York: Oxford University Press.
Volkhart, Edmund H.
    1964   "Human nature." Pp. 306–307 in Julius Gould and William L. Kolb, ed., *A Dictionary of the Social Sciences.* New York: Free Press.

Psychological control theory began with Sigmund Freud. In this caricature, he analyzes himself.

CONTROL THEORY: BIOLOGICAL AND PSYCHODYNAMIC

The earliest kinds of scientific theory were "control" theories, either biological or psychodynamic in character. They are defined as control theories because of their emphasis upon the idea that both conformist and delinquent behavior are products of the ability or inability of children to *control* their antisocial impulses. They become delinquent either because they are inherently incapable of exercising control over their drives or because they have not been properly trained to do so.

BIOLOGICAL CONTROL THEORY

The earliest biological theories were "kinds-of-people" theories—theories which suggested that delinquents are innately inferior, while those who obey the law have inherited the ability to control their aggressive impulses and to behave in responsible ways.

While several theorists of the 19th century advanced such ideas, Cesare Lombroso (1835–1909), an Italian physician, is generally considered the first person to apply the "positive" methods of science in an attempt to test these theories. During his student days, Lombroso found himself increasingly at odds with the free will philosophy of classical criminology, intrigued by the doctrines of positivistic philosophy, and excited by the implications of human evolution (Wolfgang, 1960:170).

Since Lombroso's medical training was in comparative anatomy, he was quick to accept the importance of empirical measurement in his studies of brain pathology, mental illness, and criminal behavior, and to postulate a possible relationship among these disorders. Hence, in contrast to the emphasis of classical criminology upon criminal acts and legal procedure, Lombroso stressed the importance of examining the characteristics of criminals and of the conditions under which they commit crime (Vold and Bernard, 1979:35–40).

Physical degeneracy

Lombroso came into prominence in 1876 when he published a book entitled *The Criminal Man.* As a result of his empirical

163

observations of Italian soldiers and prisoners, he concluded that criminals are "atavistic types"—born lawbreakers who are subhuman throwbacks to an earlier, more primitive stage of evolutionary development. The essence of his theory can be captured in the following three propositions:

1. Law violators are a distinct physical type at birth.
2. Law violators possess physical features, or stigmata, characteristic of an earlier form of evolutionary development—imbalanced regions of the brain; an asymmetrical face and cranium; an abnormal nose; fleshy, protruding lips; excessively long arms; abundant wrinkles; abnormal sex organs, insensitivity to pain; and other physical anomalies.
3. People who possess at least five of these physical characteristics lack adequate personal control and are predisposed to crime (Sutherland and Cressey, 1974:53).

Inherent in Lombroso's propositions were a series of assumptions which today are considered racist and sexist:

1. Race and crime. Lombroso (1911) contended that habitual white criminals possess many of the characteristics which, he said, were found among the "colored" races—receding foreheads, low cranial capacity, enormous jaws, broad faces, thick curly hair, insensitivity to pain, indolence, lack of remorse, and total moral insensibility. His theory appears to reflect the views of many 19th-century Europeans who, in observing African peoples, the Australian Aborigines, or American Indians, concluded that, because their cultures were different and less developed technologically, these people were innately inferior—lower on the scale of evolutionary development. Consequently, Lombroso tended to use some of the physical features of the "colored" races as his standard of primitiveness and then concluded that white criminals looked like

them. Their criminal behavior was due to their reversion back to the levels of these more primitive peoples.

2. Sex and crime. In his book entitled *The Female Offender,* Lombroso (1920) also attributed differences among males and females to variations in evolutionary development. Females, he contended, are more primitive than males—naturally revengeful, jealous, insensitive to pain, and lacking any sense of morality. Nonetheless, they have lower rates of crime than men because their natural deficiencies "are neutralized by piety, maternity, want of passion, sexual coldness, weakness, and an undeveloped intelligence" (1920:151). Indeed, women are so "monotonous and uniform," when compared with men, that they not only fail to become artists, scientists, and political leaders, but they are less inclined to be criminal (1920:122). Why, then, do any women violate the law?

Ironically, it is only when women inherit male characteristics—a "virile" cranium, excessive body hair, moles, and other gross features—that they become criminal. The reason is that masculinity among women is, itself, an anomaly. Usually, if women are born with feminine features, their innate physiological limitations will protect them from crime and will predispose them to unimaginative, dull, and conformist lives (Klein, 1973:9).

Cloaked in the mantle of science, and buoyed by the widespread popularity of evolutionary doctrines, Lombroso's ideas attracted international attention. Nonetheless, it was not long before he and his students began to soften them. By the time of his death in 1909, in fact, he had decided that *born* primitives constitute only about 40 percent of the total criminal population, and that the remaining 60 percent are comprised of two additional types: *insane* offenders whose crimes are the result of any one of a number of complex mental disorders, and *criminaloids* whose personalities have somehow been warped by a host of environmental factors (Vold and Bernard, 1979:38).

A study published in 1913 by Charles Goring, an English physician further discredited Lombroso's ideas. After comparing several thousand criminals and noncriminals, he concluded that there is no such thing as an atavistic, physical criminal type (Goring, 1913:19). Nonetheless, the biological seed had been planted and was growing rapidly.

Hamilton Wey, a physician at the Elmira Reformatory for juveniles in New York, agreed with Lombroso. Young law violators, he maintained, are born with distinctive features: they have big ears; the heads of thieves are small; the heads of murderers are large; and some crafty offenders have yellow irises which give them a snakelike appearance (Vold, 1958:58).

Even more important, Arthur McDonald, an employee of the U.S. Department of Education, appealed to Congress in 1908 for funds to establish a laboratory for the physical study of delinquents. He was particularly concerned with their height and weight; hair and skin color; nationality; size of hands, ears, and mouth; thickness of lips; sensitivity to heat and pain; and whether, as a result of parental death or drunkenness, they had been subjected to "hereditary taint" or to the "stigmata of degeneration." McDonald told Congress: "There is little hope of making the world better if we do not seek the causes of social evils at their beginnings" (Bremner, 1971, 562–563).

Defective intelligence

It is significant that McDonald should suggest that "hereditary taint," as well as the "stigmata of degeneration," should be taken into account in studying delinquents. His concern reflected an awareness of another variation in biological thinking that had been progressing parallel to Lombroso's for several years: the possibility that poor heredity rather than physical degeneracy leads to delinquent behavior. Indeed, this was the conclusion of Charles Goring (1913:369). Even though his study of English convicts had convinced him that there is no such thing as a physical criminal type, he concluded that the tendency to be delinquent is inherited and that environment plays little part in producing it. Defective intelligence, due to poor heredity, is the cause of delinquent behavior.

This theory of feeblemindedness was given greatly increased respectability by the growth of experimental psychology in the late 19th century and its subsequent attempt to measure intelligence scientifically. After several years of investigation, French scholars, Alfred Binet and Theodore Simon, published a scale for measuring intelligence in 1905. Then, in 1908, they published a revised scale based upon the ideas that (1) childhood is characterized by developmental stages; and (2) "mental age" can be measured by taking these developmental stages into account (Vold, 1958:79–81). The concept of mental age suggests that intelligence grows with age and peaks at about age 16—ideas that are now widely accepted. Thus, it should be possible not only to measure the average or normal intelligence for children of different ages, but to determine, as well, which ones are feebleminded. Those whose IQs fall below the norm for their age are mentally defective.

It should come as no surprise that intelligence testing was soon applied to delinquent populations. In 1914, Henry Goddard, an American psychologist, published the results of several studies in which he concluded that at least 25 percent of all delinquents, and perhaps as much as 70 percent, are defective (Goddard, 1911:563; 1914:569; 1921). Hence, in the heyday of biological thinking, the implication was that defective genes, far more than society at large, were responsible for producing problem children—children who were incapable of learning right from wrong. But this belief suffered a near fatal blow when, during World War I, intelligence tests were used to determine the fitness of Armed Forces draftees.

In testing convicted offenders, Goddard had concluded that anyone whose mental age was 12 or under should be considered feebleminded. This standard, therefore, was applied to thousands of young men entering military service. But, after having tested them, officials were astounded to find that about one third would have to be considered feebleminded if Goddard's standard were retained (Zeleny, 1933).

To his credit, Goddard agreed with others that such a conclusion would be absurd. A large proportion of all young men were not feebleminded. Furthermore, when the test scores of delinquents and draftees were compared, the data indicated that these two groups were more alike than different; in fact, only about 5 percent of all delinquents could be considered feebleminded. Thus, the prevailing standard proved incorrect not only for draftees, but for delinquents as well.

Intelligence testing continued as a device for classifying offenders for several years following these discoveries, but its use was short-lived. In 1931, Edwin H. Sutherland, perhaps the most eminent of all American criminologists during the mid-20th century, wrote an essay debunking "mental testers"—a response that has represented the thinking of most criminologists since that time (Sutherland, 1931). Even though intelligence tests have improved markedly since World War I, sociologists, in particular, have objected to their use with offenders on two grounds.

First, they object to the idea that intelligence tests can measure innate ability. "So-called intelligence tests measure only 'test intelligence' not innate intelligence" (Clinard, 1968:170). Furthermore, test intelligence is a product of culture, not heredity. "So-called intelligence tests tend to measure the degree to which the individual has assimilated and internalized middle-class values rather than intelligence" (Haskell and Yablonsky, 1971:71).

The second objection is to the Lombrosian idea that something defective within the individual produces delinquent behavior. Sociologists are inclined to argue that such behavior, like conformist behavior, is a product of learning. Motivations to violate the law are socially produced and are a characteristic part of normal life. The idea that delinquent behavior is predominantly a product of idiots who are unable to understand the difference between right and wrong is nonsense.

BIOLOGY: TWENTIETH-CENTURY VINTAGE

The fate of intelligence testing was symptomatic of a general tendency to discard physical and hereditary explanations for delinquent behavior as society moved ever further into the 20th century. Then, in the 1930s, Earnest A. Hooton (1931; 1939), a Harvard anthropologist, published a series of volumes which quickly put both physical inferiority and defective intelligence back on the agenda of scientific discussion.

After measuring 13,000 inmates in jails and reformatories and comparing them with 3,203 noncriminals—college students, firemen, policemen, and patients in regular and mental hospitals—Hooton concluded once again that offenders are physically and mentally inferior. His long list of findings can be distilled into three major propositions (1939, 1:229; 301–08):

1. Criminals are physically inferior to noncriminals.
2. Physical inferiority is associated with mental inferiority.
3. The basic cause of both types of inferiority is poor heredity.

Like Lombroso, Hooton also asserted that offenders are characterized by physical stigmata—low foreheads, long thin necks, sloping shoulders, compressed faces, narrow jaws, speckled eyes, and small protruding ears. He also asserted that different types of criminals have different physiques: tall, heavy men are killers and commit forgery and fraud; tall, thin men also murder but are inclined to be robbers; rapists are squat, heavy persons; undersized men are thieves; and men of mediocre physique have no specialty because their delinquent acts are like their physical makeup—characterless (1931:376–78).

Unlike its reception in the 19th century, the publication of this type of theory stirred up a great deal of controversy in the 1930s. By now, the social sciences had grown in stature, and their emphasis upon cultural and environmental, as contrasted to biological, factors had assumed increased importance. Unfavorable and critical reviews were made by sociologists in particular, the most telling of which was Hooton's poor use of scientific procedures and circular reasoning (Vold, 1958:63; Sutherland and Cressey, 1974:119). First, he used conviction of a crime as a method of separating criminals from noncriminals. Then he measured the criminal group and concluded that they were inferior. Having done that, he turned around and used their inferiority to account for their criminality.

From a scientific standpoint, this procedure is unacceptable. There must be independent evidence that physical characteristics are proof of inferiority before their relationship to delinquent behavior can be demonstrated. Indeed, by what criterion can it be said that a low forehead, a long neck, or small ears are evidence of organic inferiority? The desirability of one set of physical characteristics over another is more often a product of cultural definition than of some universal biological standard.

So convincing were these and other criticisms that only a few investigators felt inclined to pursue the biological quest. One was William Sheldon, who, like Hooton, argued that body type and mental type go together and that both are inherited (1949:352). But his scheme for classifying individuals was markedly different.

After comparing the physical measurements of 200 boys in a private institution with those of 200 college boys, he reported that the body types of these samples fell into three major categories: (1) *endomorphs*, who are fat and round; (2) *mesomorphs*, who are large-boned and muscular; and (3) *ectomorphs*, who are lean and delicate (Sheldon, 1949:14–30). While rarely pure in form, Sheldon argued that these body types are genetically determined and that each produced a different personality and temperament. *Mesomorphs* are aggressive, insensitive, quick to translate impulse into action, and inherently deficient in internal controls. By contrast, *endomorphs* are easygoing, sociable, and comfort-loving, while *ectomorphs* are introverted, sensitive, and nervous. Hence, Sheldon concluded, *mesomorphs* are most likely to be delinquent.

In a study that was far more defensible than Sheldon's, the Gluecks (1956) reported findings that supported Sheldon, as did Cortes and Gatti (1972). But such findings have not been widely accepted. Indeed, the derisive comments of S. L. Washburn, a physical anthropologist, sum up the feelings of most criminologists today. Suggesting that Sheldon's work had now brought us full circle to the days of phrenology, he described it as a "new phrenology in which the bumps of the buttocks take the place of the bumps on the skull" (1951:563).

Impact on social policy

Most people would now agree with Washburn, but, in their day, biological theories had considerable impact on social policy. As the first scientific representatives of the positivistic philosophy, they seriously questioned the classical emphasis upon free will and the use of punishment. How could physical degenerates or mental defectives be deterred from illegal behavior if they were the product of genetic forces over which they had no control? The only hope for controlling their behavior was to neutralize its causes.

This could be done in two ways. The first was for the state to remove defective children from their degenerate parents and to care for them itself. Consider the suggestions for public policy made by a University of Kansas sociologist in 1897:

> It is seen at once that families of this class . . . are the most difficult to deal with, because they have no place in social life, and it is difficult to make a place for them. . . . The principle of social evolution is to make the strong stronger that the purposes of social life may be conserved, but to do this the weak must be cared for or they will eventually destroy or counteract the efforts of the strong. We need social sanitation, which is the ultimate aim of the study of social pathology (Blackmar, 1897:499–500).

Though this call for "social sanitation" was a stern one, it still retained a humane flavor, suggesting that defectives should be cared for rather than eliminated. These sentiments were also echoed by Henry Goddard, who said that the defective delinquent should not be turned loose in the streets, but neither should he be locked up in a jail or in prison. Rather, "He must be cared for . . . in a place we care for irresponsibles" (1911:564). Goddard also believed that delinquency could be prevented by using the Binet test in the public schools to pick out defectives at an early age. "When we have learned to discriminate and recognize the ability of each child and place upon him such burdens and responsibilities only as he is able to bear, then we shall have largely solved the problem of delinquency."

In short, the earliest scientific theories

helped to perpetuate the 19th-century belief that state intervention and institutional confinement were the best methods for dealing with delinquents. But rather than suggesting that punishments be graded according to their crimes, these theories suggested that social controls should be graded to fit their levels of biological incompetence.

A second, and perhaps more questionable, method was suggested for preventing delinquent behavior. This could be accomplished by the proper application of eugenics. Eugenics was defined as a "science" concerned with improving the quality of the human race by controlled breeding. Its basic rationale was well stated by Hooton. Since offenders are organically inferior, "it follows that the elimination of crime can be effected only by the extirpation of the physically and morally unfit; or by their complete segregation in a socially aseptic environment" (1939, 1:309). Likewise, Sheldon suggested that since delinquency "is mainly in the germ plasm" (1949:872), the only hope for control is selective breeding to weed out harmful constitutional types.

Actually, a eugenics movement designed to realize these objectives had begun several years before Hooton and Sheldon stated these opinions. Though this movement was by no means universally supported, it gained some importance in the first two decades of this century. It was concerned not merely with weeding out the "mental defectives" and "physical degenerates," but with avoiding the pollution of the race by people who masturbated excessively or overindulged in sex (Shannon, 1916:160). In pursuit of these objectives, 31 states passed laws between 1907 and 1937 permitting the sterilization of the feebleminded, the mentally ill, and epileptics. As late as 1973, 21 states still retained such laws (McCaghy, 1976:20). Moreover, those eligible for sterilization are often described in terms with which Lombroso and Hooton would have been at home: "hereditary criminals," "degenerates," and "moral degenerates" (Kittre, 1973:314). Incredibly, an estimated 70,000 people have been sterilized as a result of the eugenics movement (McCaghy, 1976:21).

In short, this method of trying to prevent delinquent and other undesirable behavior is a sobering illustration of the extent to which scientific theories can be applied to the control of human conduct without much proof that they are accurate. Between the first appearance of biological theories in the late 19th century and the time they were disavowed by scientists in the 1920s and 1930s, they gained considerable lay support and were translated into social policy—policy which is still in effect in some states.

Scientific adequacy

We have already seen that 20th-century criminologists have been inclined to discredit biological theories. The reasons for this tendency are several:

1. Prevalence of delinquent behavior. Only if lawbreaking were rare could biological defects take a prominent role in explaining it. Yet, as our analysis of self-reported delinquent behavior indicated, its prevalence is great; virtually every young person is delinquent at one time or another, and many have broken the law several times. Hence, unless defective heredity and feeblemindedness are also highly prevalent, other factors must play a prominent role in causing delinquent behavior.

2. Ignorance of culture. Biological theorists often revealed almost total ignorance of social, economic, and cultural factors in relation to their studies. Lombroso's theory, for example, reflected deep-seated and ethnocentric views of both race and sex. Not only did his ideas on race reflect the attitudes of 19th-century Europeans toward less developed societies, but his emphasis upon the passivity and piety of women failed to pay heed

to the fact that relations between the sexes at this time were often initiated and dominated by males, allowing females to appear passive, conformist, or inferior (Klein, 1973). Thus, he took social relationships for granted and used biological evolution to explain them.

3. Poor research. Given the benefit of hindsight, it is obvious that much of the research designed to test biological theories was poor (Cohen, 1966:53; Sutherland, 1951). The inability of early theorists to design controls for, or even to acknowledge, the effects of environment made their findings suspect.

4. Ideological bickering. The limits of research notwithstanding, criminologists have continued to divide along disciplinary lines regarding the adequacy and utility of their theories. Like Lombroso, an eminent, mid-20th century biologist contended that genes, not culture, determine human behavior: "The materials of heredity contained in the chromosomes are the solid stuff which ultimately determines the course of history" (Darlington, 1953). Meanwhile, an equally eminent anthropologist maintained that ". . . from the standpoint of human behavior . . . all evidence points to the utter insignificance of biological factors as compared with culture in any consideration of behavior variations" (White, 1949).

In short, biologists and social scientists have engaged in a fruitless, and nonscientific, argument over the effects of *nature* versus *nurture* (Shah and Roth, 1974). Such bickering has overlooked the fact that complex and continuous interactions between nature and nurture are inevitable byproducts of human existence. Few modern geneticists, for example, believe that genes, by themselves, determine behavior, but that genes only help to determine a person's potential, and the development of that potential is dependent upon the social environment.

Furthermore, the way in which biological and environmental factors interact may be intimately related to two of the facts concerning delinquent behavior: the overrepresentation of poor and minority children in both arrest statistics, and in victimization statistics. Recent studies have shown that these children run much greater risks of biological impairment and mental retardation than do other children (Shah and Roth, 1974:126–129). But rather than indicating that these impairments are always genetic in origin, the evidence suggests that often they are due to an unfortunate series of environmental events: poverty and ignorance reduce the likelihood that poor mothers will receive adequate nourishment and prenatal care while they are carrying their children; the lack of prenatal care, in turn, leads to an excessive number of premature births; and premature births then further enhance the likelihood of even greater impairment. Furthermore, the first few months of life are crucial to growth and maturation. The cells of the brain are not fully developed but continue to grow and to divide after birth. Other key developments take place in these early months. Thus, it is not merely genetic inheritance, but the interaction of that inheritance with the environment that spells the difference in a child's physical makeup.

A preliminary report by Britain's National Child Development Study helps to illustrate this very point. After following the subsequent growth and development of every child born in Britain during a seven-day period in 1958, investigators found that (1) disadvantaged children, on the average, were three years behind ordinary children in school; (2) they were notably smaller and more likely to suffer physical defects; and (3) 1 in 11 had had contact with the juvenile justice system as contrasted with only 1 in 300 of the other children (*Time*, 1973:88).

In the same vein, other investigators continue to point out that intelligence tests, which have improved markedly since the days of Goddard, tend to reveal a persistent, though relatively small, difference in IQ between delinquents and nondelinquents (Gordon, 1976; Hirschi and Hindelang, 1977). In this country and elsewhere, delinquents—official and self-reported—tend to score somewhat lower than do nondelinquents. How, then, shall these findings be interpreted?

A strictly biological interpretation would suggest that delinquents, particularly those who are chronic offenders, are genetically inferior. A strictly social interpretation, by contrast, would suggest that IQ scores are reflective of the individual's environment, that those who score poorly on IQ tests are those who have been subjected to environmental deprivations which limit their verbal and problem-solving skills (Simons, 1978).

Yet a third interpretation would suggest that both genetic and environmental factors are important and that differences over the meaning of low IQ scores among delinquents cannot be resolved until an integrated, "biosocial" approach is taken. Indeed, a recent resurgence of interest in biosocial research suggests several other possibilities as well: because of "sluggish" nervous systems, some persons may not readily learn to inhibit undesirable behavior or to benefit from punishment; injury to parts of the brain can contribute to uncontrollable fits of rage; or chemical imbalances in the brain may dispose some people to greater aggression than others (Mednick and Christiansen, 1977).

From a positivistic view, in short, these unresolved questions suggest that "it would be incorrect to draw the conclusion that the case for biology has been refuted, or that further research along this line would be fruitless" (Cohen, 1966:53). The most objective conclusion would be that no final conclusions can be drawn. Nonetheless, we do know that, while efforts must be made to sort out the complex ways in which biological and environmental factors interact to produce human behavior, the prevalence of delinquent conduct is so great that we should not anticipate that biological factors alone will prove to be of overriding importance in explaining it. While some linkages between biology and the various expressions of delinquent behavior may exist, they will not be anything like the direct and powerful ones postulated by early biological control theories.

PSYCHODYNAMIC CONTROL THEORY

Following the gradual decline of biological theories during the first third of this century, the next group of control theories to gain widespread popularity were psychodynamic in nature. These are theories which locate the sources of delinquent behavior in the psychological development of the individual rather than in his genetic makeup. Much of the credit for their formation goes to Viennese psychiatrist Sigmund Freud (1856–1939). Though his ideas have since been modified in many ways, they remain strikingly important as the cornerstone upon which many later theories have been built.

Freud was far less concerned with explaining how delinquent behavior is produced than with explaining how children can be made good. The reasons for his concern become obvious when one considers the main elements of his theory.

1. Human nature is inherently antisocial. Unlike the biologists who believed that only delinquents are born bad or defective, Freud theorized that *every* child possesses a set of primitive and antisocial instincts which he called the *id.* "The primitive, savage, and evil impulses of mankind," Freud wrote, "have not vanished in any individual, but continue their existence, although in a repressed state" (Freud, 1963:14). Children are not gentle, friendly creatures who simply defend themselves if attacked. They possess a measure of aggression that will cause them to exploit

their neighbor "to use him sexually without his consent, to seize his possessions, to humiliate him, to cause him pain, and to torture and to kill him" (Hughes, 1961:143). In short, all of us, not just delinquents, are born with ample capacity to be bad.

2. Good behavior requires effective socialization. Given this pessimistic view of human nature, Freud believed that the capacity of the individual to renunciate the antisocial instincts of the id can come about only through socialization—the process by which internal controls are cultivated within children by their parents. In order to describe how this process takes effect, Freud posited the existence of two other elements within the mind and personality besides the id.

The first is called the *superego.* In layman's terms, it is the individual's conscience—a nonreflective shell of inhibition, reflecting the moral rules of society, which prevents the free expression of primitive impulses. To the degree that the superego develops, therefore, it becomes an internalized mechanism for keeping antisocial drives in the person's unconscious, preventing them from coming into action, and threatening punishments if they do (Freud, 1963:121).

Freud's remaining psychic element is the *ego.* It is the conscious organizer of the personality, that part of the person's makeup which permits him or her to reflect on available alternatives and to make discriminating choices among them. Hence, its main purpose is to act as a rational intermediary between the person's drives and the demands of the external world. In one instance, it may suggest that the individual should suppress his drives in his own self-interest, while in another, it may encourage him to release them and to manipulate others.

Along with the superego, therefore, the ego is a second means by which basic instincts are directed and controlled. But while the superego is unreflective and repressive, the ego facilitates a greater exercise of reason and choice (Freud, 1963:15).

3. ***The life-long features of the personality are registered in infancy.*** Freud theorized that by the age of five all of the essential features of a child's adult personality will have been determined. Whether the anti-social and aggressive instincts of the id are to become dominant, or whether the ego and superego are to be effective in controlling them is the product of parental socialization during the first few years of life (Aichorn, 1936).

This socialization occurs in a series of developmental stages (Freud, 1963, Abraham, 1927, Abrahamsen, 1960, Freud, 1965). The first is called the *oral* stage because the mouth is the principal source of gratification to the newborn infant in its sucking, swallowing, gurgling, and kissing. If it is fondled, fed on time, and weaned at the right time, the child will feel loved and will develop properly. But if not, the child will experience a sense of deprivation and frustration that may last a lifetime.

The second stage is the *anal* stage, which lasts from about ages one to three. During this stage, two things happen. First, the infant begins to gain erotic satisfaction from the evacuation of urine and bowels rather than from oral activities. Second, the superego begins to receive particular attention because of the importance of toilet training. If children are trained improperly, difficulties will result. Rigid training—too much emphasis upon superego controls—can either produce a person who is stubborn and sadistic or one who is totally subdued and passive. Indifferent training, on the other hand, will result in a child who is sloppy, careless, and dirty. Only if training is just right will the child be freed from an anal fixation later in life.

The third stage is the *phallic* stage.[1] It lasts

---

[1] Freud postulated the existence of two additional stages of development—the *latency* and *genital* stages—but they are seen as less crucial than the first three.

from about the third to the sixth year. Whereas the child previously sought pleasure from mouth and anus, it now switches to the genitals. Masturbation, voyeurism, and sex play are common. More important, the male child unconsciously develops intense incestuous cravings for his mother (the Oedipus complex) and begins to hate his father who stands in his way. The reverse is true for the female, except that her problem is compounded. According to Freud, the girl envies those who have a penis, desires to possess one, and so turns to the adult figure who has one—her father (the Electra complex). She now experiences sexual attraction for him and perceives her mother as a rival. But, since both she and her brother still require love from both parents, their incestuous cravings soon arouse intense guilt feelings, the result of a developing superego. If both children are socialized properly, therefore, they can overcome their negative feelings and learn to identify with the parent of the same sex. But if not, emotional illness or delinquent behavior may result. For example, the boy who never gets over his hate for his rival father will grow up to hate all authority. Later in life, delinquent acts will be committed which reflect spite for this parent and an immature fixation at the phallic stage.

Hence, the implications are clear: the future behavior of any individual is not the result of personal choice, cultural differences, or changing social conditions. Rather, it is the product of parental training imposed upon the antisocial instincts of the infant.

Sources of delinquent behavior

Because Freud believed that delinquent tendencies are inherent in everyone, he devoted little attention to the many ways they might be manifested. His followers, however, have outlined at least four ways by which ineffective socialization might allow them to slip through (Feldman, 1969).

1. **Delinquent behavior is neurotic behavior.** Neurotic delinquents suffer from a compulsive need for punishment because they feel intolerably guilty over some unconscious, but socially unacceptable, drive, such as a boy's incestuous craving for sex with his mother. Though his superego tells him that such a craving is wrong, his ego is not sufficiently strong to rationalize and to manage it. Hence, he may commit any one of a number of delinquent acts—theft, robbery, or even rape— so he can be caught and punished. Punishment will help to expiate his overwhelming sense of guilt.

2. **Delinquent behavior is the result of a defective superego.** Some delinquents are poorly socialized. Failing to develop internal controls, they readily succumb to primitive impulses. Constantly preying upon others, they are psychopathic persons who are both asocial and amoral—guiltless, affectionless, callous, and aggressive individuals who have failed to internalize any standard of moral conduct (McCord and McCord, 1956).

3. **Delinquent behavior is the result of a gap in superego training.** Closely related is the notion that delinquent behavior can occur in children who have been properly socialized in the sense that they identify with the appropriate parent. But because their parents have failed to teach them appropriate values and expectations, they become delinquent. They have not had the opportunity to learn what is expected of them.

4. **Delinquent behavior represents a search for compensatory gratifications.** Children who were deprived at some early stage of development still seek the gratifications which they missed. For example, some adolescents may become alcoholics in order to satisfy an oral craving, or they may be sadistic and cruel because of poor toilet training at the anal stage. Their delinquent behavior will reflect deeply hidden needs that remained unsatisfied in infancy.

Psychodynamic theory and females

These sources of delinquency apply to girls as well as to boys. Yet, females are a special case, requiring additional explanation. Freud, like Lombroso, believed that women are inferior to men; that women are destined to be wives and mothers rather than captains of industry or even heads of the Mafia; and that nature has dictated that women be passive and compliant rather than aggressive and domineering. But what is his evidence for this conclusion?

The evidence, Freud said, is revealed by the differences between the sex organs of the male and female. Those of the female are obviously inferior, a fact that boys as well as girls recognize instinctively. Indeed, that is why

> Women are exhibitionistic, narcissistic, and attempt to compensate for their lack of a penis by being well dressed and physically beautiful. Women become mothers trying to replace the lost penis with a baby. Women are also masochistic . . . because their *sexual* role is one of receptor, and their sexual pleasure consists of pain (Klein, 1973:16).

Given the obvious inferiority of girls, the major problem for parents in socializing them is that of helping them to overcome their sense of castration. During the phallic stage of development, it will be recalled, the girl recognizes her lack of a penis, may be traumatized by it, and is envious of those who have one. That is why it is so important that she be taught to identify with her mother and to accept her inferiority. Otherwise, in her anger and frustration, she will behave in masculine ways, and masculinity among girls, according to Freud, is synonymous with being delinquent (Simon, 1975:5). Indeed, "the deviant woman is one who is attempting to be a *man*" (Klein, 1973:17).

Such an attempt is bad not only because of the female delinquent's rebellious defiance of society but because of her obvious immaturity, her state of arrested development, fixed still at the phallic stage. Hence, as was true of boys, Freud's explanation of female delinquency is a highly deterministic one, suggesting that delinquent behavior is always much more than it appears to be. He felt that it can never be understood as the simple product of traditional economic and social relationships or of rational decision making. Rather, it is always symbolic behavior that has been determined by unconscious motives which lie deep within the individual and which continue to defy easy detection.

Freudian theory would suggest that the only hope for understanding and correcting these motives is some kind of psychotherapy. In the case of the delinquent girl, for example, the goal would be to uncover the sources of her repressed, but forbidden, desires and then to bring them to her conscious awareness so that she could examine them and subject them to the controls of her ego and superego. Were the effort successful, she could then withdraw from the competitive strife of the masculine world (for which she is inherently unfitted anyway), could marry, and could take her place in the calm serenity of a loving home.

Social impact of Freudian theory

The impact of Freudian theory on our social construction of delinquency has been profound, probably because it captured and gave expression to a host of ideas about childhood and human development which, until Freud came along, had not been articulated.

On the one hand, many of his ideas were by no means radical. For example, his notions about human nature departed little from age-old religious traditions which suggested that children are inherently inclined to evil. Freud merely stated in secular and psychological terms what the Puritans had said long before

in religious terms: "Children become good, not by birth, but by education." Furthermore, he reaffirmed the validity of traditional sex roles by suggesting, like the biologists, that such roles are instinctive and not due to culture. His view of appropriate behavior for girls, for instance, could scarcely have been more conservative.

On the other hand, Freud's preoccupation with childhood and his tremendous emphasis upon the importance of parental child-raising practices reflected a set of middle-class concerns that had been emerging for centuries. Not only was the formulation of his theory coincident with the disappearance of apprenticeship as a method of raising children, but also because a growing urban populace found itself increasingly cut off from extended family ties and isolated in emotionally packed small family units. Never before had parents and children been left so completely to their own resources, nor in such an all-consuming way (Laslett, 1973).

Hence, Freud's theory contributed to a modern school of thought which suggests that the life-long characteristics of the human personality are determined almost exclusively by a combination of organic nature and the relation of a child to its parents. It had tremendous impact because it reflected social trends and seemed to provide a highly sophisticated scheme for making sense of them, particularly of indicating to the white middle class the terrible consequences of poor child-raising practices.

This is not to suggest that Freud's complex ideas were published in the *Reader's Digest* and read by everyone. Rather, they gradually filtered into public awareness and, more important, into the organization of societal life via intellectual, academic, and professional circles. Later theoretical variations on the Freudian theme are too numerous to list in detail, but certain ones have found repeated expression:

The first few years of life are critical. If an infant does not secure satisfying relationships with affectionate, nurturant parents, the damage will be irreversible (Abrahamsen, 1960; Cohen, 1966:54). The child will linger on as a selfish infant, failing to develop as a self-sufficient, responsible person.

The ego and superego, if not the id, remain key concepts in most psychodynamic theories. When both are weak, the child is unable to subordinate antisocial impulses, to defer gratifications, and to adhere to rational and moral courses of action (Redl and Wineman, 1951).

Moral maturity is attained when the child has successfully moved through a series of developmental stages and is no longer fixated at infantile levels (Piaget, 1932; Kohlberg, 1964). According to one theory, there are seven stages of interpersonal maturity, but most delinquents remain fixed between the second and fourth stages. Almost half of them are neurotics whose emotional disturbance is characterized by feelings of guilt and inadequacy (Warren, 1969).

Early childhood experiences produce in every individual a deeply ingrained and enduring personality. It is this personality which spells the difference between troublemakers and well-adjusted children. Troublemakers possess personality traits that predispose them to antisocial conduct (Healy and Bronner, 1936; Abrahamsen, 1960; Glueck and Glueck, 1950).

In short, most psychodynamic theories tend to remain in the Freudian tradition, sharing with it

> the idea that the wellsprings of behavior, and especially deviant behavior, are largely irrational, obscure energies relatively inaccessible to observation and conscious control by the actor (Cohen, 1966:54).

They have helped to perpetuate a deterministic tradition that has tended to grow stronger, not weaker, over time.

Impact on social policy

Even more than biological theory, psychodynamic ideas found fertile soil in 20th-century American society. In general terms, they did much to solidify and maintain traditional, middle-class sex roles, suggesting that, while males are naturally rational, aggressive, and outgoing, females are inherently passive, compliant, and feeling— the gender determined by destiny to be the heart of a loving home. Hence, when it came to describing delinquent acts, it should not be surprising that certain offenses—robbery, assault, and burglary—continued to be defined as male offenses, while such acts as sexual promiscuity, running away, or defying parents were known as female offenses. Not only did the behavior of boys and girls help to sustain these definitions, but they were reinforced by the responses of legal authorities to their actions.

In more specific terms, the Freudian notion that delinquent behavior is not a deliberate defiance of social norms but rather an unconscious response to a combination of antisocial instincts and to poor parental practices helped greatly to legitimize the ideology of the court. Delinquents are sick, not wicked. Their acts are not the disease that must be cured, only the symptoms of the disease.

Translated into public policy, these ideas strongly supported the belief that judges should not sentence delinquents according to the crimes they had committed but according to the diagnosis of their ills by psychological experts. Treatment could then be carried out throughout the whole correctional process— girls to be trained as girls and boys to be trained as boys. Such treatment, moreover, would require the use of professional counseling, psychotherapy, and medical care, as well as the more traditional academic and vocational training.

This need for psychological treatment, in turn, contributed to a growing professionalism among those who worked with delinquents. Rather than well-intentioned lay persons, specialists were required—psychiatrists, clinical psychologists, and social workers. Schools of social work, which, ironically, had traced their origins to 19th-century muckrakers and settlement workers, now began to take on a new identity. Much more than previously, their prestige was associated with their capacity to turn out students with a psychodynamic orientation. These changes lead not only to an emphasis upon psychological cures for known delinquents, but also to the creation of a child guidance movement designed to neutralize the presence of "latent delinquency" in young children. The assumption was that since "predelinquent traits" can be identified at a very early age, professional treatment should begin at that time.

> If children were intelligently examined and treated during the course of their school attendance, it would be no difficult matter to predict which ones, upon graduation, would be likely to continue to have emotional difficulties resulting in deviant behavior. The most seriously disordered children could be treated and trained in special clinics (Banay, 1948:186).

During the 1950s, numerous influential groups—the United States Children's Bureau, the World Health Organization, and the United States Senate—made similar recommendations (Hakeem, 1957:488–89). And, for more than ten years, the New York City Youth Board ran a prevention program for first-graders who had been identified as "predelinquents" (Craig and Glick, 1963). Though such efforts stirred up much controversy (Toby, 1965), considerable enthusiasm was exhibited over the idea that

the potential carriers of delinquency disease might be identified early and an antitoxin successfully administered.

On the other side of the coin, many jurisdictions have not been able to afford treatment programs based on a psychodynamic model. They are very expensive because of the assumption that therapy may require years of effort by a highly skilled staff. Nonetheless, the treatment model suggested by psychodynamic theory has remained the standard to which most courts and correctional agencies have aspired until very recently. As a professional ideology, if not a vehicle, for the proper treatment of children, therefore, few bodies of theory have enjoyed widespread popularity like that of psychodynamic theories.

Scientific adequacy

Despite their widespread social impact, most psychodynamic theories have not received a great deal of empirical support. The major reason is that they are not readily amenable to scientific test. For example, some investigators have used retrospective case studies as a method of testing them. After obtaining the life histories of delinquents, analyzing their dreams, or putting them under hypnosis, an attempt is made to explain their behavior (Alexander and Healy, 1935; Lindner, 1944). Most such studies, however, have had a fatal flaw.

The flaw is produced by the kind of reasoning that is associated with clinical, hindsight methods of investigation. It goes something like this:

1. Delinquent behavior is the product of psychological abnormality.
2. Joe is a delinquent.
3. Therefore, Joe is psychologically abnormal.

This is circular reasoning. For example, until Joe becomes delinquent, he is not defined as abnormal. But, once he has gotten into trouble, this abnormality is used to explain his behavior (Wootton, 1959:250). Yet, the only behavioral evidence that he is abnormal is the delinquency that his abnormality is supposed to explain.

A far more defensible attempt to test psychodynamic theories has come about through the use of personality tests—tests designed to measure the various traits that different persons are assumed to possess (McCord, 1968). In contrast to the case study method, personality tests have permitted psychologists to seek independent proof that some people are abnormal and then to see whether his abnormality is linked to delinquent behavior.

Alas, the results have not been encouraging. Schuessler and Cressey (1950) reviewed 113 studies conducted prior to 1950 and concluded that they did not demonstrate a direct link between delinquency and specific personality traits. Later reviews, covering scores of more recent studies, reaffirm the same basic conclusion (Waldo and Dinitz, 1967; Tannenbaum, 1977). While personality abnormality may be present in relatively rare, bizarre cases of criminality, there is little evidence that it is related, strongly and consistently, to law violation in general. Indeed, the latest review concludes that current testing not only fails to reflect the multidimensional differences between criminals and noncriminals but it also "allows for more differences to be found *within* groups of criminals and noncriminals than *between* them" (Tannenbaum, 1977:228).

One of the better studies of the problems of personality testing illustrates this very conclusion. Hathaway et al. (1960) selected nearly 2,000 ninth-graders who were first tested with the Minnesota Multiphasic Personality Inventory (MMPI) to determine their personality configurations. Then, the investigators checked both public and private records two years later to determine how many

of the students had become official delinquents. If differences in personality were related to official delinquency, they should appear in this followup. Though some differences were uncovered, Hathaway et al. expressed disappointment over the results. Personality measures, they said, "are much less powerful and apply to fewer cases . . . than would be expected if one reads the literature on the subject. . . . Surely we cannot say that these data put us very far ahead either in understanding or prediction." (1960:439).

Several problems may have contributed to these inconclusive findings. In the first place, it is a gross oversimplification simply to equate psychological abnormality and delinquent behavior, to state that child is disturbed so he or she commits a delinquent act. By their own accounts, most young people have been delinquent, but it is unlikely that all are abnormal.

Second, any relationship between abnormality and delinquent behavior is probably a limited one. Hathaway et al. found, for example, that while psychopathy, schizophrenia, and hypomania were associated with higher rates of delinquent behavior, such traits as introversion, depression, and masculinity-femininity were associated with *lower* rates (1960:434). In short, abnormality is not a unidimensional phenomenon that is universally associated with delinquent behavior. Sometimes, in fact, it may be associated with excessive or compulsive conformity, not delinquency.

Third, there are theoretical problems associated with the concept of personality. Its use as a predictor of behavior rests upon the assumption that it is an enduring characteristic that will affect the individual in much the same way throughout life. It suggests, for example, that a child who possesses personality tendencies toward delinquency will possess the same tendencies as an adult. Yet, as we have seen, delinquent acts among people tend to peak at about age 16 and to decline thereafter. Few young people become adult criminals. Why is this? If psychodynamic theory were correct, it suggests that the pattern should be just the opposite, that delinquent acts should continue. But since they tend to decline, there are grounds for suspecting that a person's behavior, and thus the psychological motivations that give rise to it, are likely to change markedly throughout life.

Despite these limitations, it would be unwise to dismiss all psychological factors as irrelevant. If nothing else, Freudian psychology has convinced most people that, in the process of growing up and devleoping independent personalities, they must learn to subordinate some of their most powerful and aggressive drives. Otherwise, the mere existence of society would be impossible. Furthermore, the idea persists that, in the process of learning to control these drives, many of them are driven underground, below conscious level, where they are repressed at considerable personal cost. Yet, despite this cost of repression, inner conflict is inseparable from living and is part of every personality.

Also widely accepted is the Freudian idea that the people least capable of handling the strains of living are those whose childhoods were marred by unhappy circumstance. Indeed, numerous scientific studies indicate that children who grow up in brutal homes, mental hospitals, orphanages, or concentration camps, where warmth and nurturing are lacking, are more likely to suffer psychological and social damage (Nettler, 1974:237–238). But while some of these children become abnormally aggressive and do not exhibit any guilt over outrageous behavior, others are so overly controlled and submissive that they appear to have no ego at all (Redl and Wineman, 1951). Thus, while an unhappy childhood may not always lead to delinquent

behavior, it may lead to other kinds of behavior which, though not predatory, are deviant in another sense.

Quay and Werry for example, contend that "the vast majority of deviant behaviors of children and adolescents can be subsumed under four major patterns: conduct disorder, anxiety-withdrawal, immaturity, and socialized aggression" (1979:36). Yet, only two of these patterns—conduct disorder and socialized aggression—include behaviors that are delinquent; the others exhibit such deviant conditions as fear, depression, withdrawal, passiveness or inability to concentrate. In short, as was pointed out earlier, psychological abnormality is not a one-dimensional phenomenon that is universally associated with delinquent behavior.

Nonetheless, so long as one is concerned with the questions, "Why is she delinquent?" or "Why did he do it?", one must deal with matters of psychological motivation. Indeed, as Cohen points out, "sociologists . . . are no less interested in internal motivation than are psychologists, but they are interested in it from a special point of view" (1966:65). What they want to understand, in addition to family factors, is how such variables as class membership, minority status, age, gender, and peer relationships also affect a person's psychological state. Just as forces within the family can shape one's way of viewing and responding to the world, so forces outside of it can do so also. Thus, as psychiatrist Seymour Halleck (1971) has noted, persons who are interested in the relationship between personality and delinquency must take into account this larger body of forces.

SUMMARY AND CONCLUSIONS

Biological and psychodynamic control theories have contributed to our social construction of delinquent behavior in unique ways. That contribution can be summarized by

FIGURE 8–1

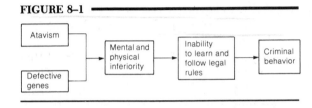

reference to the basic questions that will be asked about all theories:

1. *What assumptions do control theories make about human nature and social order?*. Biological theories assume that delinquents and nondelinquents are different kinds of people at birth. Delinquents possess genetic traits or depraved tendencies which predispose them to antisocial behavior. Nondelinquents, however, are inherently good people, predisposed to good conduct.

Psychodynamic theories, by contrast, assume that *all* children are animals at birth—impulsive, self-centered, and lacking the ability to control themselves in socially approved ways. Their tendency to be antisocial "is as original as sin" (Rieff, 1959:274).

Given these views of human nature, both kinds of theory tend to take the social order for granted; that is, to assume that its various elements reflect a high degree of consensus, that morality is self-evident, and that it is the delinquent individual on whom attention must

be focused, since the social order does not create problems that might contribute to the commission of delinquent acts.

2. *What is the underlying logic and content of control theories?*. The general logic and content of biological theories can be diagrammed as shown in Figure 8–1.

According to Lombroso, many, if not most, criminals are born to be criminal—atavistic throwbacks to primitive man. Hence, their inability to learn and to adhere to social rules causes them to be criminal. Other biologists, however, traced delinquent acts to genetic deficiencies which, like atavism, were thought to inhibit learning and to encourage criminal behavior.

Psychodynamic theory, by contrast, was as concerned with explaining why children conform to social rules as why they are inclined to break them. This body of theory, therefore, could be diagrammed as shown in Figure 8–2.

Early in life, the child's primitive drives (id) encounter the child-raising practices of the home. If, out of the interaction that occurs, socialization is effective, a well-developed ego and superego will result, the child will have conscious control over his or her primitive drives, and mature, conformist behavior will result. But if the process of socialization is ineffective, poorly developed controls will result in an unconscious search for

FIGURE 8–2

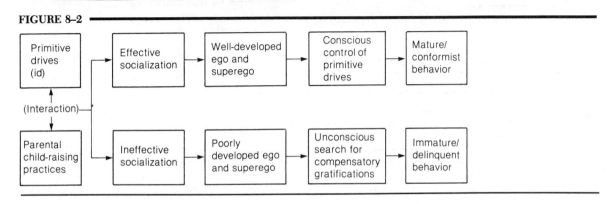

compensatory satisfactions and immature, delinquent behavior.

3. What are the implications of control theories for social policy, and what impact have they had?.   Biological theories imply the need to forbid defective people from reproducing, and to incapacitate those already born. Such theories fostered a eugenics movement and led to the passage of laws which permitted the sterilization of "degenerate" or "defective" people.

Psychodynamic theories imply the singular importance of early child-raising practices. If those fail, predelinquent or delinquent children should be diagnosed and placed in correctional settings for long-term treatment. As a professional ideology for the juvenile court, this doctrine has probably been the most influential of all theoretical doctrines.

4. How well do control theories stand up to logical and empirical scrutiny?.   The fact that control theories have been heavily applied to the conduct of social policy is striking when contrasted with their lack of acceptance among positivistic criminologists. Biological theories have not been well received because (1) as originally stated, they were logically inadequate and lacked empirical support; and (2) ideological bickering took place between social and biological scientists over the role of *nature* versus *nurture*. As a result, current theories of delinquency have failed to reflect a growing body of knowledge which documents profoundly complex relations among many biological and environmental factors.

Many of the same conclusions apply to psychodynamic theories: (1) most of them are impossible to falsify; (2) the assumption that life-long behavior patterns are set within the confines of the family in early infancy is overly simplistic; and (3) the tendency to equate personality abnormality with delinquent behavior has not been confirmed by empirical evidence.

Yet psychological motivation can scarcely be ignored. What has been lacking in the psychodynamic approach, therefore, are postulates which link motivation to social and cultural factors, as well as to those which are familial.

Indeed, like biological theory, psychodynamic theory has failed to address many of the facts which measures of delinquent behavior suggest are in need of explanation. In the chapters that follow, however, we will discover that criminologists soon began to attend to some of these facts, even as contol theories reached the apex of their popularity.

REFERENCES

Abraham, Karl
    1927   *Selected Papers on Psychoanalysis*. London: Hogarth.

Abrahamsen, David
    1960   *The Psychology of Crime*. New York: Columbia University Press.

Aichorn, August
    1936   *Wayward Youth*. New York: Viking Press.

Alexander, Franz, and Healy, William
    1935   *Roots of Crime*. New York: Alfred A. Knopf.

Banay, Ralph S.
    1948   *Youth in Despair*. New York: Coward-McGann.

Blackmar, F. W.
    1897   "The Smoky Pilgrims." *American Journal of Sociology* 2 (June):490–500.

Bremner, Robert H., et al., eds.
    1971   *Children and Youth in America: A Documentary History.* Vol. 2. Cambridge: Harvard University Press.

Clinard, Marshall B.
    1968   *Sociology of Deviant Behavior.* New York: Holt, Rinehart & Winston.

Cohen, Albert J.
    1966   *Deviance and Control.* Englewood Cliffs: Prentice-Hall.

Cortes, J. B., and Gatti, F. M.
    1971   *Delinquency and Crime: A Biopsychosocial Approach.* New York: Seminar Press.

Craig, Maude M., and Glick, Selma J.
    1963   "Ten Years of Experience with the Glueck Prediction Table." *Crime and Delinquency* 9 (July):249–61.

Darlington, D. C.
    1953   *The Facts of Life.* London: Allen and Unwin.

Feldman, David
    1969   "Psychoanalysis and Crime." Pp. 433–42 in Donald R. Cressey and David A. Ward, eds., *Delinquency, Crime and Social Process.* New York: Harper & Row.

Freud, Anna
    1965   *Normality and Pathology in Childhood: Assessments of Development.* New York: International Universities Press.

Freud, Sigmund
    1963   *An Outline of Psychoanalysis.* New York: W. W. Norton.

Glueck, Sheldon, and Glueck, Eleanor T.
    1956   "Early Detection and Future Delinquents." *Journal of Criminal Law, Criminology and Police Science* 47 (1956):169–81.

Goddard, Henry H.
    1911   "The Treatment of the Mental Defective Who Is Also Delinquent." Pp. 563–564 in Robert H. Bremner et al., eds., *Children and Youth in America: A Documentary History.* Vol. 2. Cambridge: Harvard University Press.
    1914   *Feeblemindedness: Its Causes and Consequences.* New York: Macmillan.
    1921   *Juvenile Delinquency.* New York: Dodd.

Gordon, Robert A.
    1976   "Prevalence: The Rare Datum in Delinquency Measurement and Its Implications for the Theory of Delinquency." Pp. 201–284 in Malcolm W. Klein, ed., *The Juvenile Justice System.* Beverly Hills, Calif.: Sage.

Goring, Charles
    1913   *The English Convict.* London: His Majesty's Stationery Office.

Hakeem, Michael
    1957   "A Critique of the Psychiatric Approach to the Prevention of Juvenile Delinquency." *Social Problems* 5 (Winter):194–205.

Halleck, Seymour
    1971   *Psychiatry and the Dilemmas of Crime.* Berkeley: California University of California Press.

Haskell, Martin R., and Yablonsky, Lewis
    1971   *Crime and Delinquency.* Chicago: Rand McNally.

Hathaway, Starke R.; Monachesi, Elio D.; and Young, Laurence A.
    1960   "Delinquency Rates and Personality." *Journal of Criminal Law, Criminology, and Police Science* L (February):433–40.

Healy, William, and Bronner, Augusta F.
    1936   *New Light on Delinquency and Its Treatment.* New Haven, Conn.: Yale University Press.

Hirschi, Travis, and Hindelang, Michael J.
    1977   "Intelligence and Delinquency: A Revisionist Review." *American Sociological Review* 42 (August):571–87.

Hooton, Ernest A.
    1931   *Crime and the Man.* Cambridge: Harvard University Press.
    1939   *The American Criminal: An Anthropological Study.* Vol. 1. Cambridge: Harvard University Press.

Hughes, H. Stuart
    1961   *Consciousness and Society: The Reorientation of European Social Thought 1890–1930.* New York: Vintage Books.

Kittre, Nicholas N.
    1973   *The Right to be Different: Deviance and Enforced Therapy.* Baltimore: Penguin Books.

Klein, Dorie
    1973   "The Etiology of Female Crime: A Review of the Literature." *Issues in Criminology* 8 (Fall):3–30.

Kohlberg, Lawrence
    1964   "Development of Moral Character and Moral Ideology." Pp. 383–431 in Martin Hoffman and Lois Hoffman, eds., *Review of Child Development Research.* Vol. 1. New York: Russell Sage.

Laslett, Barbara
    1973   "The Family as a Public and Private Institution: An Historical Perspective." *Journal of Marriage and the Family* 35 (August):480–92.

Lindner, Robert M.
    1944   *Rebel Without Cause.* New York: Grune and Stratton.

Lombroso, Cesare
    1911   *Crime, Its Causes and Remedies.* Boston: Little, Brown.
    1920   *The Female Offender.* New York: Appleton.

McCaghy, Charles H.
    1976   *Deviant Behavior.* New York: Macmillan.

McCord, William
    1968   "Delinquency: Psychological Aspects." Pp. 86–93 in David L. Sills, ed., *International Encyclopedia of the Social Sciences,* Vol. 4. New York: Macmillan and Free Press.

McCord W., and McCord J.
    1956   *Psychopathy and Delinquency.* New York: Grune and Stratton.

Mednick, Sarnoff A., and Christiansen, K.O., eds.
    1977   *Biosocial Bases of Criminal Behavior.* New York: Gardner Press.

Nettler, Gwynn
    1974   *Explaining Crime.* New York: McGraw-Hill, Inc.

Piaget, J.
    1932   *The Moral Judgment of the Child.* London: Routledge and Kegal Paul.

Quay, Herbert C. and Werry, John S.
    1979   *Psychopathological Disorders of Childhood.* New York: John Wiley & Sons.

Redl. Fritz and Wineman, David
    1951   *Children Who Hate.* Glencoe: The Free Press.

Rieff, P.
    1959   *Freud: The Mind of the Moralist.* New York: Viking Press.

Schuessler, Karl F., and Cressey, Donald R.
    1950   "Personality Characteristics of Criminals." *American Journal of Sociology* 55 (March):476–84.

Shah, Saleem A., and Roth, Loren H.
    1974   "Biological and Psychophysiological Factors in Criminality." Pp. 101–73 in Daniel Glaser, ed., *Handbook of Criminology.* Chicago: Rand McNally.

Shannon, T. W.
    1916   *Eugenics.* Marietta, Ohio: S. A. Mullikin.

Sheldon, William H.
    1949   *Varieties of Delinquent Youth.* New York: Harper & Row.

Simon, Rita James
    1975   *The Contemporary Woman and Crime.* Washington, D.C.: U.S. Government Printing Office.

Simons, Ronald L.
    1978   "The Meaning of the IQ–Delinquency Relationship." *American Sociological Review* 43 (April):268–70.

Sutherland, Edwin H.
    1931   "Mental Deficiency and Crime." Pp. 357–75 in Kimball Young, ed., *Social Attitudes.* New York: Holt, Rinehart & Winston.

Sutherland, Edwin H., and Donald R. Cressey
    1974   *Criminology.* 9th ed. Philadelphia: J. B. Lippincott.

Tannenbaum, David J.
    1977   "Personality and Criminality: A Summary and Implications of the Literature." *Journal of Criminal Justice* 5:225–35.

Time Magazine
    1973   "Born to Fail." *Time* 102 (November 12):88.

Toby, Jackson
    1965   "An Evaluation of Early Identification and Intensive Treatment Program for Predelinquents." *Social Problems* 13 (Fall):160–75.

Vold, George B.
    1958   *Theoretical Criminology.* New York: Oxford University Press.

Vold, George B., and Bernard, Thomas J.
    1979   *Theoretical Criminology.* 2d ed. New York: Oxford University Press.

Waldo, Gordon P., and Dinitz, Simon

    1967   "Personality Attributes of the Criminal: An Analysis of Research Studies, 1950–1965." *Journal of Research in Crime and Delinquency* 4 (July):185–201.

Warren, Marguerite Q.

    1969   "The Case for Different Treatment of Delinquents." *The Annals* 381 (January):47–59.

Washburn, S. L.

    1951   Review of *W. H. Sheldon, Varieties of Delinquent Youth. American Anthropologist* 53 (December):561–63.

White, L.

    1949   *The Science of Culture.* New York: Grove Press.

Wolfgang, Marvin E.

    1960   "Cesare Lombroso." Pp. 168–227 in Hermann Mannheim, ed., *Pioneers in Criminology.* Chicago: Quadrangle.

Wootton, Barbara

    1959   *Social Science and Social Pathology.* New York: Macmillan.

Zeleny, L. D.

    1933   "Feeblemindedness and Criminal Conduct." *American Journal of Sociology* 38 (January):564–76.

Cultural deviance theory grew out of the early 20th-century study of white minority groups.

CULTURAL DEVIANCE THEORY

In this chapter, we will be dealing with a body of knowledge called *cultural deviance theory*. This type of theory is noteworthy because of its sharp contrast with control theory. Control theory suggests that since the impulse to be delinquent is present in everyone, delinquent acts are made possible by the *absence* of effective controls over them. By contrast, cultural deviance theory rejects the notion that delinquent impulses are universal and suggests that delinquent acts are caused by learned beliefs that *require* them. Delinquent behavior is an expression of conformity to cultural values and expectations that run counter to those of the larger society. *The delinquent is a social individual who is behaving in accordance with the values and norms of his particular group.*

ORIGINS

The origins of cultural deviance theory can be traced to the pioneering work of two Chicago sociologists, Clifford R. Shaw and Henry D. McKay. When Shaw and McKay began their work in the 1920s, they were confronted with a confusing, often contradictory, welter of explanations for delinquency. On the one hand, religiously oriented social reformers were preoccupied with the waves of foreign-born immigrants and rural native-born Americans who ended up as industrial workers in our burgeoning cities. High rates of urban delinquency, poverty, and vice led the reformers to bemoan the corruption of the cities and to see them as major sources of trouble. Their commonsense explanations suggested that the moral standards of rural civilization were being destroyed and that children were being led into debauchery and sin. On the other hand, prevailing scientific theories reflected the thinking of biological and psychological determinists. The delinquent was innately inferior, psychologically abnormal, or both. Street-smart and sexually precocious working-class youths were not merely deviant but inherently psychopathic.

By contrast, the theory eventually advanced by Shaw and McKay took exception to both

187

the commonsense and scientific points of view, particularly the idea that delinquents were biological and psychological misfits. Furthermore, these investigators approached the task of constructing theory in an empirical way. Rather than merely formulating ideas based on what they already knew, they used extensive research to establish the factual character of delinquency in the city. Only after this was accomplished did they set about trying to explain the facts they had uncovered.

Because they were schooled in the fields of sociology and demography—fields that are concerned with social organization, and the density and distribution of people in the city—they sought to answer two fundamental questions:

1. How are official delinquents geographically distributed in the city? Shaw and McKay gathered information on all official delinquents in Chicago who had police records, court hearings, and correctional commitments during various periods between 1900 and 1940—over 60,000 cases in all (Shaw et al., 1929; Shaw and McKay, 1942). In order to determine how these thousands of cases were geographically distributed, Shaw and McKay plotted the address of each of them on city maps. What they found, over and over again, was that official delinquents were highly concentrated in particular areas of the city: adjacent to the central business district, around the railroads and stockyards, and in the industrial and steel districts. They lived in the most dilapidated, least desirable portions of the cities.

The extent of this concentration is illustrated in Figure 9–1. It is a radial map which breaks Chicago into a series of concentric zones. Near the center of the city, the rate of official delinquency per 100 boys was 24.5. By contrast, it declined to a rate of 3.5 in the outer areas. Not only were male delinquents concentrated near the core of the city, but their rate declined progressively the further one moved from this core.

Such findings were not confined to boys. Shaw et al. found that, while rates of delinquency were not as high among girls as among boys, female delinquents were also

FIGURE 9–1
Rate of delinquents based upon the 8,056 male juvenile delinquents, by mile zones surrounding the Loop.

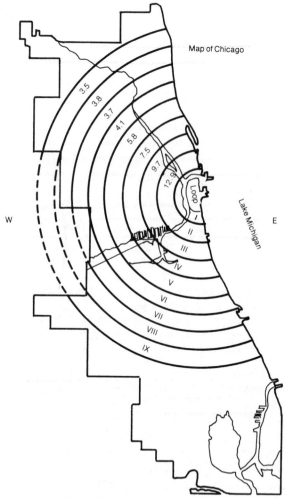

concentrated in deteriorated areas adjacent to the center of the city and to industrial districts (1929:158). And like boys, the delinquency rate for girls, though much lower, declined as one moved from city center to periphery.

These initial findings were not destined to remain unique. Between the mid-1920s and 1940, Shaw and McKay studied the distribution of delinquents from almost every conceivable angle. They plotted the locations of truants, juveniles with police records, juveniles committed to correctional schools, and juveniles who became recidivists (repeat offenders); they plotted the locations of delinquents, male and female, in Philadelphia, Boston, Cincinnati, Cleveland, and Richmond. Finally, after Shaw's death, McKay continued to update delinquency data in Chicago for additional time periods up to 1966 (Shaw and McKay, 1929; 1931; 1942; 1969). Yet, for three quarters of a century and in different locations, the findings remained the same: official delinquents were concentrated in the overcrowded and deteriorated areas of the city. Of crucial importance, therefore, became the second question they sought to answer.

2.   *What are the social conditions associated with high-delinquency areas?*
Shaw and McKay found that certain clear-cut social conditions are associated with high-delinquency areas.

a.   Physical deterioration and population loss. As the city expands outward, commercial and industrial enterprises continue to invade areas formerly used for residential purposes. As a result, living conditions grow progressively worse, from which a decreasing population flees as soon as it can.

b.   Economic segregation. The low rents in old, dilapidated buildings and deteriorated neighborhoods attract the population with the lowest income (Shaw and McKay, 1969:147–149). Sometimes the straits for children can be desperate. In his extraordinary autobiography,

Claude Brown (1965:34) describes an event that happened in Harlem when he was a child of six or seven. He had gone to the home of his friend Bucky and found Bucky choking his younger sister Debbie. Meanwhile, Bucky's older sister Dixie was hitting Bucky over the head with a broom trying to free Debbie. All three were crying. When finally the fight stopped, Brown saw what it was over. "The three of them had been fighting over one egg, and the egg was broken in the scuffle." There was nothing else in the house to eat.

c.   Racial and ethnic segregation. Delinquency areas have a high percentage of foreign-born and minority populations who come to American cities seeking the promised land (Shaw and McKay, 1931:79):

> I want to talk about the first Northern urban generation of Negroes. I want to talk about the experiences of a misplaced generation, of a misplaced people in an extremely complex, confused society. . . .
>
> The characters are sons and daughters of former Southern sharecroppers. These were the poorest people of the South, who poured into New York City during the decade following the Great Depression. These migrants were told that unlimited opportunities for prosperity existed in New York and that there was no "color problem" there. They were told that Negroes lived in houses with bathrooms, electricity, running water, and indoor toilets. To them, this was the "promised land.". . .
>
> One no longer had to wait to get to heaven to lay his burden down; burdens could be laid down in New York (Brown, 1965:vii).

Black people were not the first to seek salvation in American cities. In the 1880s, the central city in Chicago was occupied largely by German, Irish, and English immigrants. These groups gradually gave way to Scandinavian, Polish, Italian, and Jewish immigrants around the turn of the century. Only after the 1920s did the large migration of southern blacks begin. In each case, the newest immigrants were the poorest, and helped to push the earlier inhabitants into more stable working-class areas (Shaw et al., 1929:17–18).

In the process, the central city became an incredible mixture of people and cultures. "In my naborhood," said one delinquent, "there were jews, polocks and irish, mostly foreigners and a poor class of people that could hardly read or write but had a flock of kids" (Shaw, 1931:19). Today, the cast of characters has changed, but the play remains the same. Earlier groups of white migrants—foreign- or native-born—have been gradually replaced by the more recent groups of rural blacks, Latins, Mexicans, or Puerto Ricans.

  d. High incidence of social ills. In the areas in which delinquency rates are the highest, the rates of other problems are also highest: truancy, infant mortality, mental disease, tuberculosis, and adult crime. In every instance, these problems vary together; that is, they are highest near the center of the city and become progressively lower as one moves toward the periphery (Shaw and McKay, 1969:105–6).

In summary, Shaw and McKay conclusively demonstrated that official delinquency rates vary widely and consistently across the city and that high-delinquency areas are characterized by poverty, segregation, and disease. Hence, the significance of their findings could hardly be overstated. Rather than implying that the deranged makeup of biological or psychological misfits was responsible for delinquent conduct, they implied that the spatial, economic, and social distribution of people in deteriorated urban areas was somehow at fault. Furthermore, the facts they uncovered were virtually the same as those we encountered when we reviewed arrest, self-report, and victimization statistics: the facts of gender, minority status, socioeconomic standing, group deviance, and community are related to

delinquency. What, then, was the nature of the theory which Shaw and McKay constructed to explain these facts?

THE SHAW-MCKAY THEORY

Before trying to answer that question, Shaw and McKay had to deal with a provocative and highly significant finding. On the one hand, their studies tended to support 19th-century belief that delinquency is associated with the corruption of American cities. On the other, they did not support the belief that delinquency is due to the moral or biological depravity of particular ethnic and racial groups (Shaw and McKay, 1969:153–54). They rejected this conclusion because they discovered that the population composition of high-delinquency areas had changed again and again as successive, but highly different, groups had moved through them. Yet the delinquency rates remained the same—changes in race and nationality did not alter them. Moreover, as each successive ethnic group moved outward into more desirable areas, its delinquency rate declined.

Thus, Shaw and McKay concluded that delinquency rates—high or low—are associated more with the kinds of neighborhoods in which juveniles live than with their racial or ethnic backgrounds. Hence, they theorized that the explanation for delinquency—particularly the high rates exhibited by boys—lies in the kind of community life that deteriorated neighborhoods produce, not in the kinds of people who live in them. The following postulates capture the essence of that explanation.

  1. The deteriorated areas of the city produce social disorganization. Shaw and McKay argued that there is an almost total absence of a sense of community in slum areas. They agreed with Frederic Thrasher, another pioneer investigator, that the cultural standards of different immigrant and racial groups not only conflicted with each other, but that these groups were beset with a host of additional ills: "inadequate family life, poverty, deteriorating neighborhoods; ineffective religion, education, and recreation" (Thrasher, 1927:339). These problems, moreover, were compounded by the constant threat of invasion by business and industry and by high levels of population mobility which only made conditions worse. In short, slum conditions produce socially disorganized neighborhoods (Shaw et al., 1929:204–205; 1969: 171–172).

2. Socially disorganized neighborhoods lead to a lack of social control over children. "The absence of common community ideals and standards prevents cooperative social action . . . to . . . suppress delinquency" (Shaw and McKay, 1931:102). Children who grow up in disorganized neighborhoods have little access to the cultural heritage of the larger society (Shaw, 1931:15). Under such conditions, parents are relatively helpless to control or to help their children, though they often try:

Mama soon realized that hiding my clothes would not keep me in the house. The next thing she tried was threatening to send me away until I was 21. This was only frightening to me at the moment of hearing it. Ever so often, either Dad or Mama would sit down and have a heart-to-heart talk with me. These talks were very moving. I always promised to mend my bad ways. I was always sincere and usually kept the promise for about a week. During these weeks, I went to school every day and kept my stealing at a minimum. By the beginning of the second week, I had reverted back to my wicked ways, and Mama would have to start praying all over again (Brown, 1965:21)

In brief, then, demoralized slum parents are unable either to provide direction for their children or to control their delinquent tendencies.

3. Loss of social control encourages the development of street gangs. Shaw and McKay (1969:173) found that approximately 8 in 10 delinquent boys had committed their offenses in groups. Hence, they concluded that

membership in such groups is an important contributing factor in delinquency, since it is found that very often the boy's contact with the delinquent group marks the beginning of his career in delinquency and that his initial delinquencies are very often identical with the traditions and practices of his group (1931:256).

So I grew old enough to go out on the street. The life in the streets became fascinating and enticing. I had two close companions that I looked up to with childish admiration and awe. One was William, my stepbrother. The other was Tony, a dear friend of my stepbrother William. They were close friends, four years older than me and well versed in the art of stealing (Shaw, 1966:50).

But where did William and Tony learn to steal? Where do delinquent traditions come from? Does each small group of boys develop its own? The answer is no. Delinquent traditions have a broader base of support in slum communities.

4. Delinquent traditions are transmitted from one generation of gang boys to the next:

The heavy concentration of delinquents in certain areas means . . . that boys living in these areas are in contact . . . with groups which sanction such behavior and exert pressure upon their members to conform to group standards. . . . This means that delinquent boys in these areas have contact not only with other delinquents who are their contemporaries, but also with older offenders, who in turn had contact with delinquents preceding them, and so on, back to the earliest history of the neighborhood. This contact means that the traditions of delinquency can be and are transmitted down through successive generations of boys in much the same way that language and other social forms are transmitted (Shaw and McKay, 1931:256).

What this suggests, then, is that a child's immediate play group becomes a vehicle for perpetuating delinquent traditions and forcing adherence to them, but such traditions are actually learned from older groups and individuals:

> Whenever the boys got together they talked about robbing and made more plans for stealing. I hardly knew any boys who did not go robbing. The little fellows went in for petty stealing, breaking into freight cars, and stealing junk. The older guys did big jobs like stick-ups, burglary, and stealing autos. The little fellows admired the "big shots" and longed for the day when they could get into the big racket. Fellows who had "done time" were big shots and looked up to and gave the little fellows tips on how to get by and pull off big jobs (Shaw, 1966:54).

Although Shaw and McKay wrote mostly about boys, their life history documents imply that girls were also caught up in delinquent gangs and traditions:

> Tony had two sisters who always played with us and went on our stealing adventures. They could steal as good as any boy. Also they had sex relations openly with all the boys in the neighborhood. I remember how the boys boasted that they had had sex relations with each of them. All the boys talked about it and the girls didn't care; they seemed to be proud of it and expect it. The funny thing about it was that Tony knew all about his sisters and their behavior and only made merry of it (Shaw, 1966:50).

According to this postulate, then, conventional values have relatively little salience for slum children because of the demoralization of their parents and the lack of consensus in the neighborhood. Instead, unsupervised play groups and delinquent traditions fill the void.

5. *Delinquent traditions produce high delinquency rates.* In the disorganized vacuum of the central city, delinquent traditions are the culmination of a long series of contributing community conditions: deteriorated areas produce social disorganization; social disorganization leads to a loss of control over children; loss of control encourages the existence of street gangs; street gangs perpetuate delinquent traditions; delinquent traditions produce high delinquency rates. In short, delinquents are portrayed as inherently sociable people whose response to parental indifference and neighborhood demoralization is the development of alternative forms of organization. These alternate activities happen to be delinquent according to the standards of the larger society (Kobrin, 1971:124).

Implications and impact on policy

The implications of this kind of theory were profound. Rather than some racial or biological defect in children, delinquency was attributable to the way society was organized. Indeed, Shaw and McKay stressed the idea that poverty, deteriorating neighborhoods, and ethnic conflict were important in producing delinquency only if they result in social disorganization. It is the absence of social control, more than poverty per se, that is the source of delinquent gangs and illegal conduct.

In interpreting their theory, however, two national commissions—The National Commission on Law Observance and Enforcement (1931) and the President's Commission on Law Enforcement and Administration of Justice (1967)—placed the greater stress on poverty, and recommended that it should become the primary focus of social policy.

"It is inescapable," said the President's Commission "that juvenile delinquency is directly related to conditions bred by poverty"

(1967:57). It suggested, therefore, that the most promising method for dealing with delinquency would be to ameliorate the conditions that "drive" juveniles toward it: strengthen the ability of lower-class families to guide and control their children, reduce unemployment, improve housing, enrichen slum schools, combat racial and economic segregation, put more personnel on the streets to work with gangs, and establish youth service bureaus in slum areas (1967:58–77). "The commission doubts that even a vastly improved criminal justice system can substantially reduce crime if society fails to make it possible for each of its citizens to feel a personal stake in it—in the good life it can provide" (1967:58).

In some ways, these recommendations reflect the efforts of Shaw himself for the prevention of delinquency. But rather than advocating a radical reconstruction of society, as Karl Marx did in the 19th century, followed by many socialists today, Shaw stressed the importance of helping slum dwellers, most of whom were recent, largely rural, immigrants, to do a more effective job of running their own lives—to develop a better sense of community in their neighborhoods, foster greater opportunities for their children, and find more effective ways for adjusting to an alien, highly complex, urban culture. Hence, in the 1930s, Shaw fathered the Chicago Area Project which sought to realize three goals: (1) to induce the residents of slum areas to take up the cause of prevention; (2) to assist them in gaining greater influence over their children by organizing local programs and resources for them; and (3) to foster cooperative action among local residents, the schools, the police, and the courts.

Shaw was a charismatic leader who threw himself into the Chicago Area Project for more than a quarter of a century. Solomon Kobrin (1959:584–586), a later colleague of Shaw and McKay, concludes that the results of the project vindicated Shaw's untiring efforts. Not only was

he highly respected among different generations of various ethnic groups, but also, his Chicago Area Project is still in operation. It has been applied in Chicago over the years, and special legislation was passed in Illinois and a Juvenile Delinquency Prevention Commission created so that the model developed by Shaw could be utilized and applied throughout the state. In no other locale has such a feat been duplicated, combining both theoretical and applied work over such a long period of time

In light of this outcome, it is significant that today's theorists, to be discussed in subsequent chapters, would argue that Shaw's efforts represented nothing more than the application of a Band-Aid when radical surgery was required. Since it is the poverty, the overcrowding, and the misery of modern capitalist society that are the real sources of delinquency, not social disorganization, the Chicago Area Project did nothing more than address symptoms, not basic causes. Radical economic and political changes are required, not efforts to help victims of society to adjust more effectively to unacceptable conditions.

The magnitude of the effort required is indicated by the fact that the sweeping recommendations of the two presidential commissions may have had even less effect than Shaw's efforts. Our largest cities are now closer to bankruptcy than ever before; their urban cores continue to deteriorate; unemployment rates among ghetto dwellers remain staggeringly high; racial and economic segregation persist; and delinquent gangs are omnipresent. Indeed, the desperate problems of many of today's immigrants sound like they could have been taken from the pages of Shaw's biographies, written 50 years ago:

> Those who knew Jose Salcido say he was a good man whose life was plagued by tragedies.
> In 1974, a roving gang in a "hit car" shot and killed 18-year-old Hector Salcido. Another son,

Frank, now 20, was wounded and partially paralyzed on his left side in another gang-related shooting in Los Angeles in 1976.

Mrs. Salcido became ill in 1976. She was found to have terminal cancer and died after about six months of pain . . .

In 1977, Danny Salcido, 14, . . . was drowned.

The final tragedy in Salcido's life occurred early Thursday morning. . . . At about 5:45 A.M., Salcido was unloading two boxes of frozen foods from the delivery truck he had parked in an alley. . . . The truck suddenly began to move, trapping Salcido between the door and the brick wall in the alley. He was crushed to death (Billiter, 1979:1).

In short, many contemporary critics would argue that the most fundamental implications of the Shaw-McKay theory have never really been implemented.

Scientific implications

The scientific legacy left by Shaw and McKay falls into two categories. The first is their set of empirical findings. They have never been excelled, and little subsequent research has altered the picture they presented (Short, 1972).

The second is their theory. It could be interpreted in two ways. In one sense, it could be described as a sociological control theory (in contrast to the psychological control theories reviewed in the last chapter).[1] That is, the theory of Shaw and McKay could be interpreted as stressing the disorganized character of impersonal modern cities and the need to foster more effective means of raising and controlling the children in them. But, rather than seeking to alter the internal states of these children, one by one, the task would be that of understanding and developing more effective social institutions by which to socialize

them—modern counterparts of the families, churches, and communities which were so effective in the small rural towns of 18th-century America.

Indeed, the fact that Shaw and McKay worked so hard to foster the Chicago Area Project suggests that it was this interpretation of their theory that they preferred. To them, delinquent traditions among lower-class youth seemed to have been analogous to Freud's unrestrained, but potentially evil, tendencies in individuals, only in collective form. But, in this case, effective socialization would require the concerted efforts of all social institutions, not just the family.

This interpretation, however, is not the one that most modern theorists have placed upon the theory. For many years, the concept of social disorganization was a popular one, but it has declined in popularity in recent decades. Instead, contemporary theorists have picked up and expanded upon the role played by poverty in fostering delinquent gangs and traditions. When seen in this light, as Kobrin (1971:117) points out, the theory becomes totally deterministic and evokes an image of delinquency that has an all-or-nothing character. The influence of the gang in the slum areas exceeds the influence of the family, the school, and other conventional groups, "requiring and demanding that its members follow its norms and take on its attitudes" (Clark, 1972:2). Even more striking, it implies that virtually all lower-class children will become young criminals, wed only to the traditions of their peers.

This method of constructing delinquency has had immeasurable impact during the past quarter of a century. On the one hand, it has reinforced long-standing beliefs that the primary threat to social order comes from lower-class groups and ethnic minorities. Indeed, the idea has been accepted as an established fact by many people, lay and scientific. On the other hand, when Shaw and

---

[1] I am indebted to James F. Short, Jr., for bringing this interpretation to my attention.

McKay began their work, the scientific tendency was to view the delinquent as a different kind of person—genetically inferior, mentally deficient, or psychologically abnormal. By contrast, their theory suggested that delinquent responses were the only ones available to inherently social children, given the environmental circumstances to which they must adapt.

Although Shaw and McKay never used the word *culture* to describe the ties that bind lower-class children, their emphasis upon gang traditions has since been a major source of many subsequent theories, all stressing the idea that delinquency is the product of unique cultures or subcultures. A major question, therefore, is whether this construction of delinquency is an accurate one. Let us consider some issues that have been raised concerning this construction.

1.   Social disorganization in deteriorated areas.   Shaw and McKay attributed the development of delinquent traditions to the disintegration of community controls in blighted areas. Yet, they offered no direct evidence that the residents of higher-income areas in the city engage in collective problem solving any more effectively than do residents in low-income areas (Kobrin, 1971:128–129). Furthermore, they did not provide direct evidence that the population in outlying areas is any less heterogeneous than in the central city. Hence, their assumption that inner city areas are more disorganized than other areas was not supported by compelling evidence, though such may be the case.

Because of this possibility, it became fashionable among sociologists to suggest that what we should look for in high delinquency areas is differential social organization, not social disorganization (Cohen et al., 1956:21; Kobrin et al., 1967; Whyte, 1943). While our society is often divided by competing subcultural norms, slum communities are not necessarily jungles, continuing high rates of crime, victimization, and lowered life expectancy notwithstanding. Instead, there is an awareness of community in slum areas and a concern among individuals about their reputations in that community:

> The organization which exists may indeed not be adequate for the effective control of delinquency and for the solution of other social problems, but the qualities and defects of organization are not to be confused with the absence of organization (Cohen, 1955:33).

2.   Delinquency as a lower-class phenomenon.   Shaw and McKay documented the existence of heavy concentrations of *official* delinquents in slum areas. Yet, their own findings do not support the all-or-nothing concentration of their theory on lower-class children. The reason is that their data do not show that official delinquency disappears outside of deteriorated areas. Instead, they show that official rates decline as one moves from the central city outward (Figure 9–1). Although the rates in deteriorated areas are the highest, they are also present in middle-class and suburban areas.

Even more questionable was their construction of a theory based exclusively on official measures of delinquency. On the one hand, repeated studies have confirmed the Shaw-McKay finding that lower-class children are overrepresented in official statistics (see Chapter 5). It is an accurate finding. On the other hand, official data are not accurate measures of law-violating behavior. Yet, Shaw and McKay treated them as if they were because their theory is concerned primarily with explaining why slum children violate the law, not how official rates are created. Yet, as we have already learned, official data not only represent the way children behave, but the way society in general, and legal agents in particular, respond to the children of different classes and colors.

Furthermore, studies of self-reported

delinquency suggest that the relation between social class and law-violating behavior may not be nearly so strong as the relation between social class and official delinquency (compare Chapters 5 and 6). For these reasons, it is now clear that the Shaw-McKay theory possesses two additional limitations: (1) it is not a complete explanation of official delinquency because the defining role of officials is not included in it; and (2) it is not a complete explanation of law-violating behavior because it is built on official data.

3. *The group nature of delinquency.* This finding has remained considerably more stable than the one suggesting that law-violating behavior is a lower-class phenomenon. Repeated studies have confirmed it (Erickson, 1973; Erickson and Empey, 1965; Eynon and Reckless, 1961; Glueck and Glueck, 1950; Hindelang, 1971; Short, 1957). Consequently, an important issue is not so much whether delinquent acts are committed in groups, but how one interprets such findings.

Shaw and McKay suggest that delinquent norms become widespread in disorganized areas because of the high prevalence of unsupervised play groups. Yet, Kobrin found that "approximately half the boys of a high delinquency rate area did not participate at all in its juvenile street life" (1971:130). Because some children are unsupervised, all need not be. Many lower-class parents supervise their children rather carefully, and a life of crime is not the only future open to them.

There are also some problems in assuming that young children have the capacity to develop the sense of group purpose necessary to maintain delinquent traditions in the face of a disapproving society (Kobrin, 1971:130). Whereas Shaw and McKay suggest that deteriorated areas are so demoralizing to lower-class adults that they cannot maintain a sense of community, they proceed to reach the rather startling conclusion that lower-class children are able to do so. Apparently, they

can establish a community where adults cannot.

This point of view, whether intended or not, started a trend which portrayed lower-class gangs as possessing strong *esprit de corps,* a free and easy life, and members whose commitments to the purposes of the gang exceed their commitments to any other purpose (Thrasher, 1927). Yet, a number of recent investigations, along with tragedies like those of the Salcido family, have questioned this nostalgic view of lower-class gangs.

Klein and Crawford (1967:63) argued that such groups are not close-knit and internally strong. Were it not for the external pressures of police and other officials or the threats of rival groups, delinquent gangs would have little to unify them. By themselves, gangs do not develop the kind of group goals and instrumental activities indicative of a high degree of organization.

Similarly, Short and Strodtbeck report that "the capacity of lower-class gangs to elaborate and enforce norms of reciprocity is very much below what might be required to sustain the group if alternative forms of gratification were available" (1965:233). They found that gang boys were characterized by a long list of social disabilities: unsuccessful school adjustment, limited social and technical skills, a low capacity for self-assertion, low intelligence scores, and a tendency to hold other gang members in low esteem (p. 331). Interaction within the gang seemed to be characterized by an omnipresent tone of aggression rather than by close personal ties. In short, there is real uncertainty regarding the extent to which adolescent street groups have developed widely shared and mutually supported norms, to say nothing of a lifestyle that could qualify as a unique and independent culture.

What is missing in most discussions of this issue, however, is a sense of history demonstrating the extent to which lower-class culture, in general, has either remained different from or has modified middle-class culture in response to modern urban life. Some of the descriptions of lower-class youth by Shaw (1931; 1936; 1966), and by his contemporary, Frederick Thrasher (1927), are quite consistent with descriptions of lower-class groups of earlier centuries (Gillis, 1974). In the crowded, teeming streets of the slum, children are attracted by innumerable exciting opportunities for fun and adventure. They swipe fruit, tip over garbage cans, stay out all night, and roll drunks. To be sure, they are unsupervised by middle-class standards, but does this mean that their behavior is entirely inconsistent with lower-class traditions? According to Shaw and McKay and Thrasher, it is.

They imply that the standards of lower-class adults may have become more middle class during the 20th century, even though those same adults are ineffective in enforcing their beliefs. That is why, as youth groups develop and solidify, they are increasingly at odds with parental expectations.

But this interpretation may be incorrect. It could be that lower-class children are not at odds with their parents. It could be that their behavior is consistent with norms shared by all lower-class people. Indeed, there are those who argue that such is the case and that lower-class communities, those existing today at least, do not fit the Shaw-McKay description of them.

DELINQUENCY AS A PRODUCT OF INTEGRATED LOWER-CLASS CULTURE

In 1958, Walter Miller, an anthropologist, gave voice to a theory which suggests that delinquency is the product of a united, not a divided, lower-class culture. The picture that he painted is as follows:

1.   The slums are organized by a distinctive lower-class culture.   According to Miller (1958), delinquent groups are neither the product of disorganized communities nor are they isolated from adult influence. Adults and children in lower-class communities share a common set of values. In response to the processes of economic and social segregation in American society, "there is emerging a relatively homogeneous and stabilized native American lower-class culture" (Miller, 1959:225). Such a culture is the result of many years of immigration and internal migration to which several ethnic populations have contributed. This culture now represents a common adaption of *unsuccessful* whites and blacks to the American system.

2.   Lower-class culture emphasizes membership in single-sex peer groups.   A key to understanding this culture lies in the way it organizes family life and relations between the sexes. Family life is dominated by the female. Men do not usually play a consistent and predictable role in it, nor do they provide it with reliable economic support. After generations of failure, conventional work and family roles no longer attract them. Instead, new values have emerged which tend to separate males and females into different groups. Except for transitory relations between the sexes, males and females lead relatively separate lives. As a result, the lower-class family does not possess the close, intimate ties supposedly found in the middle-class family. Responsibility for raising children falls to the mother, and they may be the offspring of different men.

This means that children spend the first few years of life under the domination of women, during which time they receive mixed messages about the male role. They learn from their mothers that men are rogues: simultaneously despicable and desirable, luring but hateful, irresponsible but very attractive on Saturday night. This message poses some problems for girls but is particularly difficult for boys. They are faced with a problem of sexual identity: a mother does not want her boy to grow up like his father, but anticipates that he will.

This problem is resolved during adolescence. While girls continue to identify with their mothers, boys take up membership in male street gangs, a natural outcome of the lower-class emphasis upon single-sex peer groups. These gangs are a haven for simultaneously escaping female domination and learning how to be a man. Indeed, Miller suggests that gang members are probably the most able young members of the community. Why, then, do they tend to get into trouble? What motivates them?

3. *Single-sex peer groups are organized by a unique set of "focal concerns".* The answer lies in the unique focal concerns of lower-class culture: trouble, smartness, toughness, fate, and autonomy:

> Adult status [for males] is defined less in terms of the assumption of "adult" responsibilities than in terms of certain symbols of adult status—a car, ready cash, and, in particular, a perceived "freedom" to drink, smoke, and gamble as one wishes, and to come and go without external restrictions (Miller, 1958:17).

The lower-class street group is merely an adolescent expression of these adult focal concerns. Whereas a major dimension for evaluating a man's status in middle-class culture is achievement in education and work, criteria in the lower class suggest that hard work and deferred gratification are for suckers. Consequently, young members of street gangs gain a sense of belonging and acquire status by demonstrating physical prowess, committing delinquent acts which demonstrate the ability to live by their wits, resisting authority, and avoiding the drudgery of a daily job. Thus, while lower-class people, young and old, are aware of middle-class norms, they do not value them. They may express verbal support for them, but they do so to escape getting into trouble with the police, not because they are committed to middle-class standards (Miller, 1958:8).

4. *Adherence to lower-class "focal concerns" produces delinquency.* What this suggests, then, is that the closer the members of lower-class gangs conform to the values and beliefs of their culture, the more likely they are to be defined as officially delinquent. They are delinquent merely because of their faithful conformity to lower-class values, which by middle-class standards are deviant.

Compared with the Shaw-McKay theory, then, Miller's cultural deviance theory has two distinctive features. On the one hand, it is like that of Shaw and McKay in that it suggests that delinquency is predominantly a lower-class group phenomenon and that deviant behavior is due to cultural values and beliefs which condone it. On the other hand, it departs widely from the Shaw-McKay theory in the location of delinquent traditions. Whereas Shaw and McKay suggest that such traditions are the sole possession of unsupervised gangs and play groups, Miller indicates that they belong to the entire lower-class community. Delinquent behavior is an expression of a distinctive culture in which effective socialization by adults results in deviant values which everyone shares.

Perhaps even more important, Miller "alerts us to a possible historical development that has received relatively little attention—the emergence of something like a stable American lower class" (Bordua, 1961:131). Although few people, until recently, have made such an argument, in 1976 Bayard Rustin, a long-time black civil rights activist, argued that "the future advancement of blacks and other poor in this country has very little to do with the color of their skin" (*L.A. Times*, Aug. 11, 1976). Instead, poverty (and the assorted ills associated with it), has become a class, not a race problem. Because technology has phased out the need for the muscle power of the laboring man, a class of "economic untouchables," made up of blacks, browns, and whites, has been created. Similarly, some social scientists have presented research findings which suggest that blacks as well as whites are polarized, more and more, into middle- and lower-class groups (Sampson and Milam, 1975; Wilson, 1978). While racism continues, it is no longer the deciding economic factor it once was.[2] Rather, the real and substantial gains made by middle-class blacks have increasingly separated them from the American underclass trapped in the ghetto, just as affluence has separated middle-class whites from that same underclass. Like Miller, therefore, these observers imply that American society has become increasingly stratified and may some day be witness to the development of a lower-class with a distinctive culture of its own.

As we will see in later chapters, some theorists take strong exception to this conclusion, arguing that the goal of success is still shared by all Americans. Middle-class values stressing the importance of education, hard work, and deferred gratification, they argue, have filtered down to members of the lower class and are highly motivating to them. Furthermore, Miller's argument may be faulty because he

> also forgets that none of the lower status groups in the society, with the possible exception of lower status Negroes, has any history of his female-based household, at least not in the extreme form he describes (Bordua, 1961: 130–31).

Such households are under continuous pressure from welfare workers and other officials to conform to the patterns of middle-class families.

Miller's position, of course, is that lower-class families successfully resist these pressures. That is why lower-class adolescents become delinquent. They get into trouble because they

remain faithful to cultural standards learned from their parents. Again, however, this position has been disputed by control theorists who point to contradicting research findings. Regardless of class background, they find that the closer juveniles are to their parents, the less likely they are to commit delinquent acts (Dinitz et al., 1962; Hindelang, 1973:475; Hirschi, 1969:97). Furthermore, Hirschi (pp. 215–20) has found that there is little disagreement among adolescents from different social classes on what people ought to do: whether they should obey the law, whether it is right to con others, or whether it is fate rather than personal competence that determines a person's destiny. Hence, Hirschi concludes that "those lower-class boys committing delinquent acts are not finding support for their actions from their parents or from their 'class culture'" (p. 97).

Such findings notwithstanding, much of the delinquency literature continues to stress the idea that society is divided into competing class cultures and that these cultures are intimately linked to the commission of delinquent acts. This is true not only of theories of lower-class but also middle-class delinquency. They paint a picture that is strikingly at odds with the theories of lower-class delinquency we have just reviewed. They seem to suggest that American youths on different class levels live in totally different cultural worlds, and that to understand their delinquency, we must understand those worlds.

MIDDLE-CLASS SUBCULTURE THEORY

Cultural theories of middle-class delinquency stem from two traditions in social science. The first is a concern with adolescence in general. It is seen as an ill-defined period in the life cycle in which peer relationships take on unusual significance. Because adolescents are segregated from the adult world, a hedonistic and irresponsible youth subculture

---

[2] The Association of Black Sociologists has expressed "outrage" at this conclusion, and contends that it is a gross misrepresentation of the black experience (ABS, 1978:4).

is created (Coleman, 1961; Davis, 1944; Glaser, 1971; Parsons, 1942).

The second tradition is a direct concern with delinquency. Shortly after mid-20th century, the first of the self-report studies and some official data suggested that the middle-class delinquency might be increasing. These findings led to scattered efforts to explain the deviant acts of more affluent youths (Bloch and Niederhoffer, 1958; Bohlke, 1961; England, 1960; Scott and Vaz, 1963).[3]

Though these two bodies of theory came from different traditions and though the first was ostensibly concerned with all adolescents, they are remarkably alike. The reason is that they are constructed from the world view of the middle class, the world view that most social scientists hold. In fact, these theories are so consistent with the middle-class concept of childhood, and with the historical values surrounding that concept, that they clearly apply more to middle-class than to lower-class youths—those whose families are intact, who are attending school, and who are preparing for college and a white-collar job.

Furthermore, both groups of theorists are not inclined to view middle-class delinquency as particularly serious. Rather, they tend to describe the values of middle-class delinquents as being a parody of the worst features of adult values. Thus, as Kvaraceus and Miller

---

[3] Parenthetically, a noteworthy feature of these bodies of theory is their failure to distinguish between youths of the "middle" and "upper" classes as they do between those of the "middle" and "lower" classes. The reasons are two-fold. The first has to do with the meaning of the term *middle class*. It is used uncritically and usually includes all youths whose family backgrounds are white-collar but whose incomes range from modest to affluent. Thus, the children of schoolteachers and small businessmen are lumped together with those whose parents are highly prestigious professionals and corporate executives. Second, almost no theoretical attention has been paid to the upper-class children of wealthy people, revealing once again the bias of existing theory toward the lower class. As a result, such children are either ignored in existing theories or are included in formulations of middle-class subculture theory.

(1959:234) put it, middle-class delinquency appears less as a "social problem" than as a "home problem." The main theme of this construction of delinquency is captured in the following postulates.

1. The social status of middle-class adolescents is ill-defined. Reflecting historical changes in the status of children, most theorists point out that adolescents do not possess a clear-cut and responsible position in society. The groundwork for this state of affairs

> was laid a century and more ago when youngsters were gradually removed from functional roles in the economy through restrictive apprenticeship codes, protective labor legislation, the compulsory education movement, and the withdrawal of children from agricultural activities attendant upon urbanization. However diverse the forces were which led to this removal from productive roles, the result was that for probably the first time a major society deactivated a large and energetic segment of its population without clearly redefining the status and function of that segment (England, 1960:536–537).

As a result, adolescents find "an absence of definitely recognized, consistent patterns of authority," and are "subjected to a confusing array of competing authorities" (Davis, 1944:13). They are barred from productive labor, but are expected to be hardworking; they attend school to develop their intellects, but are not expected to challenge the opinions of parents and teachers; they are sexually mature and encouraged to be socially skilled, but are supposed to refrain from adult vices; they are expected to be civic-minded, but cannot hold public office or serve on juries; they are often separated from the direct supervision of parents and are granted considerable freedom, but lack the kinds of ties to other adults by which privilege and freedom can be prevented from deteriorating into license (England, 1960:537). As they attempt to deal with these ambiguous directives, therefore, "boys and girls

. . . often find it difficult to tell when and how 'adult' behavior is expected" (Williams, 1952:71).

This problem has worsened in recent years because middle-class parents have been enjoined to pay greater heed to new theories of child development which question the wisdom of premature responsibility for children and recommend that they be allowed to develop at a slower, less pressured pace (Scott and Vaz, 1963:210–13). Concomitantly, opportunities for ambitious young people to become proprietors of their own small businesses have also declined. Instead, more and more young people have been corralled into large corporations and industries. As a result, the work skills required of middle-class youth have also changed. "We used to look primarily for brilliance," said one corporation president in the 1950s. "Now . . . we don't care if you're a Phi Beta Kappa or a Tau Beta Phi. We want a well-rounded person who can handle well-rounded people" (quoted by Whyte, 1956:150).

These changes have produced a situation in which the standards of right and wrong for young people are less certain. About all that can be said is that some admixture of technical skill and social competence will produce satisfaction and success. As a result, both parents and educators have become gradually more permissive and have placed more stress on personality development and peer adjustment than upon strict adherence to carefully defined rules.

2. *An ill-defined social status separates adolescents from the adult world.* To further complicate matters, the ill-defined adolescent period has been growing longer (Flacks, 1971; Keniston, 1972), and this extension has further diminished the contact of young people with the adult world (Coleman, 1961; Berger, 1971). As recently as 1950, many students did not even finish high school (Glaser, 1971:34). Rather, at about age 16 or 17, they moved into an adult

role because jobs were available to them. But since that time, increasing numbers have been confined to society's youth ghetto—the school. In the 1960s, for the first time in history, a majority of American high school graduates entered college. Indeed, many more students extended their studies into graduate school. As a result, the upper limit of adolescence has increased from around age 16 or 17 a few years ago to around age 21 or 22 today. Hence, more than ever before, young people are separated from adult work roles and civic responsibilities.

3. *Social separation produces middle-class youth subculture.* Virtually all theorists agree that the separation of adolescents from adult responsibility produces new customs and values. However, they tend to disagree over the extent to which these new standards are at odds with those of middle-class adults.

One group of theorists suggests that the difference is dramatic. "A fundamental law of sociology and anthropology," says Glaser, "is that social separation results in cultural differentiation. The more adolescents interact exclusively with each other, the more their customs and values become different from those of other age groups" (1971:35). A youth culture develops which (1) is isolated, (2) fosters a psychic attachment among the young to others their own age, (3) rejects adult standards and presses for autonomy, (4) develops an unusual regard for the underdog, and (5) seeks to foster change (Coleman et al., 1974:116–25).

"The so-called youth subculture . . . sharply cuts off adolescent experience from that of the child and from that of adult" (Green, 1952:95). Eventually, it becomes intolerant for young people to be different from their peers (Parsons, 1950). "So extreme is the gap [between the generations] that parents and their adolescent children literally represent [different] subcultures" (Williams, 1952:73). Yet, the development of a unique culture by youth "is their natural response to the somewhat unnatural position in which they find themselves in society" (Coleman et al., 1974:125).

A second group of theorists take a much softer position, suggesting that any youth subculture is likely to reflect a great many adult expectations and teachings. For example, middle-class parents want their children to be skilled socially because their success, both as adolescents and as adults, depends upon it (Berger, 1963). Hence, for parents as well as for adolescents, successful involvement with the youth crowd becomes a moral imperative (Scott and Vaz, 1963:211; Whyte, 1956:434). Not only do parents exhibit great concern over the popularity of their children, but look to the school as the central agency for facilitating it. Indeed, says Cohen, "status in the school is increasingly defined in terms of the standards and values of adolescent peer groups, and the role of the adult becomes to create a benign atmosphere in which every child can integrate happily with some group" (1957:205). In other words, parents help to facilitate youth relations rather than feeling totally alienated from them.

4. Middle-class youth subculture produces delinquent behavior. Despite differences over the uniqueness of adolescent subculture, most theorists suggest that (1) it helps to produce an adolescent world of hedonism and irresponsibility, and (2) the more adolescents are involved in it, the more likely they are to be delinquent. At the same time, most theorists argue that the delinquent acts the subculture encourages are not likely to be very serious because they evolve from legitimate activities that are sanctioned and supported by adults as well as by peers: dates, parties, athletics, extracurricular activities, owning automobiles, and following the latest fads (England, 1960; Scott and Vaz, 1963). The only reason these activities lead to delinquent behavior is that the youth subculture is peopled by immature and inexperienced persons:

Delinquent motivations among middle-class teenagers arise from [an] adaptive process in which the teenage world, peopled by immature and inexperienced persons, extracts from the adult world those values having strong hedonistic possibilities, with the result that the values of the teenage culture consist merely of distorted and caricatured fragments from the adult culture (England, 1960:539).

Thus, the dominant forms of middle-class delinquent conduct are joy riding, drinking, smoking pot, staying out late, gambling, or engaging in sex—acts that are scarcely unknown to middle-class adults in their hedonistic moments.

Occasionally, parties or athletic contests, combined with alcohol or drugs, result in destructive acts such as letting the air out of tires, pitched battles, breaking street lights, ripping antennae off cars, or vandalizing the local school. But, while these activities are tolerated by the standards of middle-class youth subculture, such acts as assault, armed robbery, or burglary stand outside its boundaries. In fact, according to Kvaraceus and Miller, when serious delinquency is committed by a middle-class adolescent, it probably represents "pathological" rather than group-supported behavior (1959:241). Hence, most prevailing theories construct an image of middle-class delinquency that is comprised of status offenses and misdemeanors, not of dangerous felonies. At the same time, such theories are like other cultural deviance theories in that they suggest that delinquent behavior is motivated by shared beliefs that it the desirable thing to do.

Implications for social policy

The social implications of this kind of theory are readily apparent and apply as much to lower-class as to middle-class adolescents. Society can reduce delinquency by taking one or both of two steps: (1) cease to define such acts as drinking, smoking pot, engaging in premarital sex, joy riding, staying out late, or skipping school as delinquent offenses; and (2) seek to reduce the social separation of adolescent and adult worlds by giving adolescents a greater stake in conformity (Toby, 1957). To some extent, both steps have been recommended and are being tried.

1. "Decriminalizing" status offenses. For almost two decades, a growing number of influential organizations and social theorists have recommended that juvenile status offenses should be "decriminalized" (Empey, 1973). In part, these recommendations imply the emergence of a new middle-class morality. Morris and Hawkins express its policy implications:

> We must strip off the moralistic excrescences on our [juvenile] justice system so that it may concentrate on the essential. The prime function of the criminal law is to protect our persons and our property; these purposes are now engulfed in a mass of other distracting, inefficiently performed legislative duties. When the criminal law invades the spheres of private morality and social welfare, it exceeds its proper limits at the cost of neglecting its primary task. . . . Man has an inalienable right to go to hell in his own fashion, provided he does not directly injure the person or property of another on the way (1970:2).

This new philosophy is based upon the assumption that individual morality has become situational and peer-related rather than sacred and universal, as it was thought to be in the 19th century. Hence, while various states have not yet eliminated status offenses from the jurisdiction of the juvenile court, there are pressures in that direction.

Furthermore, this process is being speeded up by expansion of the legal rights of children: the Supreme Court has granted the right of abortion to teenage girls without parental consent—a revolutionary step in light of our traditional concept of childhood; school

attendance laws are being relaxed; and the legal drinking age has been lowered in many states. These are simply an extension of rights that have already been granted to slightly older youths. Not long ago, colleges and universities were expected to guard the morals of students in their parents' absence. They are no longer charged with that responsibility. Dorms have been sexually integrated, and curfews have been abandoned. Other changes of this type have taken place clearly making the statement that there should be less official interference in the private moral conduct of young people.

At the same time, society may be hoping that these changes will produce some kind of sociological magic. On the one hand, they imply a greater tolerance for a number of acts that have long been common among adolescents— skipping school, being incorrigible, engaging in sex, and drinking. A legal response has done little to prevent them. On the other hand, a refusal to police these acts does not mean that some of their more serious consequences will disappear—being poorly educated, running away from home, having an unwanted pregnancy, or becoming an adolescent alcoholic. Changing their legal definition will not eliminate these problems.

Furthermore, the decriminalization of status offenses will do little to reduce the gap between adolescent and adult worlds. If, as existing theory suggests, adolescents are alienated because they lack a meaningful role in society, then the changes now taking place will do little to solve that problem. For example, allowing teenagers to leave school at age 16 will not assure that they can find employment if jobs do not exist (and they do not). It is likely, therefore, that the status of out-of-school youths will remain ambiguous. Indeed, the possibility that "desirable" reforms can have unanticipated, negative consequences leads us to the second implication of this body of theory.

2. *Providing adolescents with a stake in conformity.* If delinquent subculture is due to the separation of adolescents from responsible middle-class adults, then the following remedies are implied: *(a)* eliminate the ambiguity and lack of purpose inherent in the adolescent status; *(b)* close the generation gap; and *(c)* provide adolescents with socially desirable adult roles—a productive place in the economy, civic responsibilities, and the power of decision making.

Theoretically, if these steps were taken, the functions served by the youth culture would no longer exist; because they are inherently social, adolescents would develop a sense of competence and belonging; generational conflict would be eliminated; and youth would exhibit a firm attachment to the aims, values, and norms of a unified adult-youth culture (Polk and Kobrin, 1972).

In recent years, society has taken some hesitant steps in this direction: the voting age has been lowered to age 18; work-study programs, combining school and work have been initiated; and more young people are becoming active in the political process. Yet, when all is said and done, these steps are far short of those necessary to integrate adolescent and adult roles.

In the first place, it is difficult to imagine that either adolescent misconduct or the adult belief that adolescents are inherently disposed to deviant behavior will be eliminated by these attempts to neutralize the presumed effects of a middle-class youth culture. Delinquency—the making and enforcing of rules as well as the behavior those rules proscribe—will continue, at least if history is any criterion. We have already seen that in the 18th and 19th centuries relations between the generations were far more integrated than they are today. Work roles for adolescents were plentiful, and their labor was much in demand. Yet, youth deviance and adult complaints about it were widespread. Furthermore, many people who now seek to undo the effects of child labor laws and other protective devices for children are the same ones who loudly decry the apprenticeship system of earlier times and the employment of children in factories. They fail to see that children cannot be both protected from and equal to adults at the same time.

Industrial technology in this century has compounded the problem. Not only has adolescent labor become superfluous in our technically sophisticated and affluent society, but our economy is unable to employ all of its adults. This problem will have to be solved before policy makers, labor unions, and other powerful groups can become serious about more work opportunities for teenagers. Furthermore, the most desirable jobs still require levels of literacy and training that only schooling can provide. Indeed, artificially devised and demeaning roles for teenagers might only increase their sense of separation.

Scientific questions

Several important questions have been raised in the scientific literature regarding middle-class subculture theories and their implications for policy. The first has to do with their deterministic character. The original statements about this kind of theory suggested that it would be the exceptional adolescent indeed who was not programmed to follow the hedonistic dictates of the adolescent subculture. To be sure, there is some disagreement between the generations, but recent evidence suggests that it may have been exaggerated. At the very least, there is considerable "selective continuity" between young and old (Bengston et al., 1974; Kandel and Lesser, 1972). While adults and youth may differ on some issues—child-raising practices or authority relationships—they agree considerably on others—educational goals, occupational aspirations, even religious affiliations (Elkin and Westley, 1955; Hill, 1970).

It would be difficult, for example, to convince adolescents who are planning middle-class careers in medicine, law, classical music, or science that the older values of delayed gratification, hard work and self-discipline always defer to adolescent group norms.

The point is that, while differences between the generations surely exist, the beliefs and practices of adolescents are neither uniformly hedonistic and irresponsible nor uniformly conforming and responsible. There are many exceptions.

A second question is closely related. Middle-class subculture theories assert that the more adolescents are involved with their peers, the more likely they are to be delinquent. As indicated earlier in the chapter, indirect support for this hypothesis has resulted from repeated studies which found delinquency to be a group phenomenon. But there are more subtle issues to be considered. Why do middle-class adolescents commit delinquent acts in groups? Is it because they are strongly attached to each other, because they are so concerned with acceptance that they will do whatever the group demands, or for some other reason?

Evidence for the answer to this question is mixed. On the one hand, Hirschi (1969) found that admiration and respect for peers acted as a barrier to delinquent behavior: the greater the attachment, the less the delinquency. Hindelang by contrast, found just the opposite, that attachment to peers is more likely to lead to delinquency (1973).

In their attempt to resolve this issue, Jensen and Erickson could find strong support for neither position (1976). It was not clear whether group violations were due to strong feelings of attachment among friends or whether they were situational acts committed by people who merely went along with the group. Matza (1964:27–30) maintains that it is the latter. The majority of delinquents are "drifters" who are committed neither to conventional nor delinquent values. If so, this is another case in which the deterministic character of delinquent subculture is called into question. It may not be so all-consuming in its scope and power as some theories suggest.

Finally, there is the assertion that middle-class adolescents do not ordinarily commit serious delinquent acts, that virtually all of their offenses are status offenses. Such an assertion is not supported by the facts. It is true that recent victim studies have tended to support official accounts of crime which suggest that the highest rates of serious crime are located among the poorest segments of society (Chapter 6). But our review of self-report studies also indicated that this relationship has been exaggerated and that middle-class adolescents commonly commit some serious property, if not personal, crimes. Hence, while middle-class theorists have been partially right, they have overemphasized class differences. Furthermore, in assuming that most middle-class offenders are status offenders, they have failed to account theoretically for such middle-class offenders as the following:

> RIVERSIDE—Nine of 13 teen-agers charged here with the setting of hundreds of fires that caused more than $500,000 damage were identified Friday as present or former members of an Explorer Scout post sponsored by the Riverside City fire department.
>
> Capt. Russ Leland of the California Division of Forestry said five youths were members of Explorer Post 101 when they were arrested and four other suspects had "dropped out of the post" (*L.A. Times*, Jan. 22, 1977).

SUMMARY AND CONCLUSIONS

In opposition to the individualistic theories of early biologists and psychologists, some sociologists and anthropologists have constructed an entirely different image of delinquent conduct, taking into account the following points.

1. Assumptions about human nature and social order. Cultural deviance theories assume that human nature is inherently social. No less than conventional behavior, delinquent behavior is an expression of a universal tendency to behave in accordance with the values and beliefs of one's own culture. But while human nature is essentially good, the social order is disrupted because competing cultures are found in it. There is no overriding standard of good and bad. Moral values range from those that are strictly conventional to those that are unconventional and delinquent.

2. The underlying logic and content of cultural deviance theories. Cultural deviance theories represent an ideological, as well as theoretical, reaction to biological and psychodynamic theories. Yet, some of them are no less deterministic. Delinquents are socialized in cultural settings which justify, make attractive, and, eventually require delinquent behavior. Such behavior is as normal and as moral to the members of delinquent cultures as law-abiding behavior is to members of conventional cultures. However, the various versions of cultural deviance theory differ in indicating the source of delinquent traditions.

a. Lower-class theory. This is comprised of two versions. The Shaw-McKay version indicates that delinquent culture is produced in disorganized slum communities by unsupervised play groups and adolescent gangs. The only coherent traditions perpetuated from one generation to the next in these communities are delinquent and criminal traditions, as demonstrated by this diagram:

Slum   Social   Loss of   Street
areas → disorganization →   adult   → gangs →
                            control

         Delinquent   Delinquent
            youth   →   behavior
           culture

By contrast, the Walter Miller version suggests that American society has become progressively stratified and has witnessed the development of a lower class with an increasingly distinctive culture of its own. Adolescent misconduct, therefore, is merely a reflection of widely shared lower-class values, as shown in this diagram:

Slum   Lower-   Single-sex   Unique   Delinquent
area → class →   peer   →   focal → behavior
         culture   groups   concerns

b. Middle-class theory. This suggests that delinquency is a subcultural variation of the middle class. This kind of delinquency is not very serious and is merely a distorted caricature of adult values and standards, as shown in this diagram:

Ill-defined   Separation   Middle-class   Delinquent
adolescent →   of   →   youth   → behavior
  status   generations   subculture

3. Policy implications. The Shaw-McKay version of lower-class theory implies the need for radical economic and social changes: full employment, improved housing, enriched schools, elimination of economic and ethnic segregation, and more effective control by family and neighborhood over children—in short, a full assimilation of lower-class people into the middle-class way of life.

Miller's version implies even more. Either society must accept and tolerate a unique, but seemingly deviant, culture among lower-class people, or it must seek ways for reasserting the importance of the American Dream among them. If they no longer value the things that middle-class people value, then they not only require realistic opportunities, but a change in the lower-class values that no longer define middle-class goals as goals worth pursuing. A restructured society, along with a mass conversion, is implied.

Middle-class theory suggests two possible remedies for the delinquency of privileged youth: (1) the acceptance of a new morality in which juvenile status offenses are no longer defined as delinquent offenses, and (2) means by which adolescents can be given a greater stake in the rewards of conformity—closer ties with adults and a greater involvement in socially desirable and productive roles.

4.   Logical and empirical adequacy. Several of the facts upon which some or all cultural deviance theories are constructed have continued to receive empirical support: (1) law-violating behavior occurs most frequently among adolescents; (2) official delinquency is concentrated in the most overcrowded, deteriorated areas of the city; (3) delinquent behavior tends to be committed in groups; and (4) there is some discontinuity between the generations.

Unless one takes the position that all these conditions are due to inherently antisocial or pathological tendencies among large numbers of youngsters, then one must pay attention to the possible existence of cultural values and standards that are deviant. Yet, important questions can be raised about the excessive determinism of cultural deviance theories and the utopian solutions they imply.

Some part of delinquent behavior is due to the ambiguous or class status of adolescents in American society. Delinquency is often an expression of either status and of an attempt to establish oneself in a social context in which peers play an important role. But it is a gross oversimplification, except in Miller's case, to suggest that the single most important source of direction and acceptance for adolescents— lower- or middle-class—is that afforded by peers. Young people are not programmed like computers to conform only to delinquent peer standards. Conventional adults and institutions also perform a socializing role. Indeed, even the most delinquent of adolescents behave conventionally most of the time.

The point is that American society is a complex and pluralistic culture in which people are confronted with alternative guides for behavior—some conventional, some deviant. And, while certain individuals or groups may be influenced by one more than the other, both determine behavior to a considerable degree. Hence, what is needed from cultural deviance theories is specification of the conditions under which some individuals or groups resist temptation and remain wedded to conventional alternatives, while others accept it and join in the commission of delinquent acts. Control processes exerted by interested adults, as well as pressures by peers to be delinquent, operate in any setting, and reasonable theories should acknowledge the presence of both factors (Rivera and Short, 1967). At the present time, however, cultural deviance theories make little provision for this situation—individual or group choice is ignored.

In attempting to deal with these issues while reflecting the social character of delinquency, other theorists, some of whom were contemporaries of Shaw and McKay, tended to proceed in one of two directions. Those in the first group continued to suggest that delinquency is largely a group phenomenon, but discarded the notion that it is the function of any particular class culture. Instead, they suggested that it can occur on any class level in response to learning and reinforcement in small groups. This kind of theory is called *symbolic interactionist theory* and will be discussed in the next chapter.

Those in the second group followed the lead of Shaw and McKay by suggesting that delinquency is predominantly a lower-class phenomenon. But rather than theorizing that it arises in cultural isolation from middle-class values, members of this group suggest that delinquent acts result from the very attractiveness and pursuit of those values. This is called *strain theory* and will be reviewed in Chapter 11.

REFERENCES

Association of Black Sociologists
1978   "ABS Statement Assails Book by Wilson." *ASA Footnotes.* 6:4.

Bengston, Vern L., et al.
1974   "Time, Aging, and the Continuity of Social Structure: Themes and Issues in Generational Analysis." *Journal of Social Issues* 20 (No. 2):1–30.

Berger, Bennett M.
1963   "Adolescence and Beyond." *Social Problems,* Spring, 10:394–408.
1971   *Looking for America: Essays on Youth, and Suburbia and Other American Obsessions.* Englewood Cliffs, N.J.: Prentice-Hall.

Billiter, Bill
1979   "Man Stalked by Tragedy—The Final Act." *Los Angeles Times* March 3, Part II:1, 4.

Bloch, Herbert A., and Niederhoffer, Arthur
1958   *The Gang: A Study in Adolescent Behavior.* New York: Philsophical Library.

Bohlke, Robert H.
1961   "Social Mobility, Stratification Inconsistency and Middle-Class Delinquency." *Social Problems* 8 (Spring):351–63.

Bordua, David J.
1961   "Delinquent Subcultures: Sociological Interpretations of Gang Delinquency." *The Annals of the American Academy of Political and Social Science* 338 (November):119–36.

Brown, Claude
1965   *Manchild in the Promised Land.* New York: New American Library.

Clark, Robert E.
1972   *Reference Group Theory and Delinquency.* New York: Behavioral Publications.

Cohen, Albert K.
1955   *Delinquent Boys: The Culture of the Gang.* New York: Free Press.
1957   "Middle-class Delinquency and the Social Structure." Pp. 203–7 in Edmund W. Vaz, ed., *Middle-class Juvenile Delinquency.* New York: Harper and Row.

Cohen, Albert K.; Lindesmith, Alfred; and Schuessler, Karl
1956   *The Sutherland Papers.* Bloomington: Indiana University Press.

Coleman, James S.
1961   *The Adolescent Society.* New York: Free Press.

Coleman, James S., et al.
1974   *Youth: Transition to Adulthood.* Chicago: University of Chicago Press.

Davis, Kingsley
1944   "Adolescence and the Social Structure." *Annals of the American Academy of Political and Social Sciences* 236 (November):1–16.

Dinitz, Simon; Scarpitti, Frank R.; and Reckless, Walter C.
1962   "Delinquency Vulnerability: A Cross Group and Longitudinal Analysis." *American Sociological Review,* 27 (August):515–17.

Elkin, Frederick and Westley, William A.
    1955   "The Myth of Adolescent Culture." *American Sociological Review* 20 (December):680–84.

Empey, LaMar T.
    1973   "Juvenile Justice Reform: Diversion, Due Process and Deinstitutionaliza-tion." Pp. 13–48 in Lloyd E. Ohlin, ed., *Prisoners in America*. Englewood Cliffs, N.J.: Prentice-Hall.

England, Ralph W.
    1960   "A Theory of Middle-class Juvenile Delinquency." *The Journal of Criminal Law, Criminology, and Police Science* 50 (April):535–40.

Erickson, Maynard L.
    1973   "Group Violations and Official Delinquency." *Criminology* 11 (August): 127–60.

Erickson, Maynard L., and Empey, LaMar T.
    1965   "Class Position, Peers, and Delinquency." *Sociology and Social Research,* 49 (April):268–82.

Eynon, Thomas G., and Reckless, Walter C.
    1961   "Companionship at Delinquency Onset." *British Journal of Criminology* 2 (October):162–70.

Flacks, Richard
    1971   *Youth and Social Change*. New York: Markham.

Gillis, John R.
    1974   *Youth and History*. New York: Academic Press.

Glaser, Daniel
    1971   *Social Deviance*. Chicago: Markham.

Glueck, Sheldon, and Glueck, Eleanor
    1950   *Unraveling Juvenile Delinquency*. Cambridge: Harvard University Press.

Green, Arnold
    1952   *Sociology*. New York: McGraw-Hill.

Hill, Reuben
    1970   *Family Development in Three Generations*. Cambridge: Schenkman.

Hindelang, Michael J.
    1971   "The Social Versus Solitary Nature of Delinquent Involvements." *British Journal of Criminology* 11 (August):127–60.
    1973   "Causes of Delinquency: a partial replication and extension." *Social Problems* 2 (Spring):471–87.

Hirschi, Travis
    1969   *Causes of Delinquency*. Berkeley: University of California Press.

Jensen, Gary F. and Erickson, Maynard L.
    1976   "Peer Commitment and Delinquent Conduct: New Tests of Old Hypothe-ses." Unpublished. Tucson: University of Arizona.

Kandel, Denise B., and Lesser, Gerald S.
    1972   *Youth in Two Worlds*. San Francisco: Jossey-Bass.

Keniston, Kenneth
    1972   *"Youth: A 'New' Stage of Life."* In Thomas J. Cottle, ed., *The Prospect of Youth*. Boston: Little, Brown.

Klein, Malcolm W. and Crawford, Lois Y.
    1967   "Groups, Gangs and Cohesiveness." *Journal of Research in Crime and Delinquency* 4 (January):63–75.

Kobrin, Solomon
    1959   "The Chicago Area Project—a 25-year Assessment." *The Annals of the American Academy of Political and Social Science* 322 (March):20–29.
    1971   "The Formal Logical Properties of the Shaw-McKay Delinquency Theory." Pp. 101–32 in Harwin L. Voss and David M. Petersen, eds., *Ecology, Crime and Delinquency*. New York: Appleton-Century-Crofts.

Kobrin, Solomon; Puntil, Joseph; and Peluso, Emil
    1967   "Criteria of Status Among Street Corner Groups." *Journal of Research in Crime and Delinquency* 4 (January):98–118.

Kvaraceus, William, and Miller, Walter B.
    1959   "Norm-violating Behavior in Middle-class Culture." Pp. 233–41 in Edmund W. Vaz, ed., *Middle-Class Juvenile Delinquency*. New York: Harper & Row.

Matza, David
    1964   *Delinquency and Drift*. New York: John Wiley & Sons.

Miller, Walter B.
    1958   "Lower-class Culture as a Generating Milieu of Gang Delinquency." *Journal of Social Issues* 14 (Summer):5–19.
    1959   "Implications of Urban Lower-class Culture for Social Work." *The Social Service Review* 33 (September):219–36.

Morris, Norval and Hawkins, Gordon
    1970   *The Honest Politician's Guide to Crime Control*. Chicago: University of Chicago Press.

National Commission on Law Observance and Enforcement
    1931   *Social Factors in Juvenile Delinquency*. No. 13, Vol. 2. Washington, D.C.: U.S. Government Printing Office.

Parsons, Talcott
    1942   "Age and Sex in the Social Structure of the United States." *American Sociological Review* 7 (October):604–16.
    1950   "Psychoanalysis and the Social Structure." *Psychoanalytic Quarterly,* 19:371–84.

Polk, Kenneth, and Kobrin, Solomon
    1972   *Delinquency Prevention Through Youth Development*. Washington, D.C.: U.S. Government Printing Office.

President's Commission on Law Enforcement and Administration of Justice.
    1967   *The Challenge of Crime in a Free Society*. Washington, D.C.: U.S. Government Printing Office.

Rivera, Ramon J. and Short, James F., Jr.
    1967   "Significant Adults, Caretakers, and Structures of Opportunity: an Exploratory Study." *Journal of Research in Crime and Delinquency* 4 (January): 76–97.

Sampson, William A., and Milam, Vera
    1975   "The Intraracial Attitudes of the Black Middle Class: Have They Changed?" *Social Problems* 23 (December):153–65.

Scott, Joseph W., and Vaz, Edmund W.
    1963   "A Perspective on Middle-class Delinquency." Pp. 207–22 in Edmund W. Vaz, ed., *Middle-class Juvenile Delinquency*. New York: Harper & Row.

Shaw, Clifford R.
    1931   *The Natural History of a Delinquent Career*. Chicago: University of Chicago Press.
    1936   *Brothers in Crime*. Chicago: University of Chicago Press.
    1966   *The Jack-Roller: A Delinquent Boy's Own Story*. Chicago: University of Chicago Press.

Shaw, Clifford R., and McKay, Henry D.
    1931   *Social Factors in Juvenile Delinquency*. Report of the National Commission on Law Observance and Enforcement (Wichersham Commission). No. 13, Vol. 2. Washington, D.C.: U.S. Government Printing Office.
    1942   *Juvenile Delinquency and Urban Areas*. Chicago: University of Chicago Press.
    1969   *Juvenile Delinquency and Urban Areas*. rev. ed. Chicago: University of Chicago Press.

Shaw, Clifford R., et al.
    1929   *Delinquency Areas*. Chicago: University of Chicago Press.

Short, James F., Jr.
    1957   "Differential Association and Delinquency." *Social Problems* 4 (January): 233–39.
    1972   "Introduction to the Revised Edition." Pp. xxv–liv in Clifford R. Shaw and Henry D. McKay, *Juvenile Delinquency and Urban Areas*. Chicago: University of Chicago Press.

Short, James F., Jr., and Strodtbeck, Fred L.
    1965   *Group Process and Gang Delinquency*. Chicago: University of Chicago Press.

Thrasher, Frederick M.
    1927   *The Gang*. Chicago: University of Chicago Press.

Toby, Jackson
    1957   "Social Disorganization and a Stake in Conformity." *Journal of Criminal Law, Criminology, and Police Science* 48 (May–June): 12–17.

Whyte, William E.
    1943   *Street Corner Society*. Chicago: University of Chicago Press.

Whyte, William H., Jr.
    1956   *The Organization Man*. New York: Simon & Schuster.

Williams, Robin
    1952   *American Society*. New York: Alfred A. Knopf.

Wilson, William J.
    1978   *The Declining Significance of Race: Blacks and Changing American Institutions*. Chicago: University of Chicago Press.

Symbolic interactionist theory stresses the importance of learning and identity in small intimate groups.

SYMBOLIC INTERACTIONIST THEORY

Symbolic interactionist theory grows out of the larger field of social psychology which is shared both by sociologists and psychologists. This fact gives us some clue as to its character. Symbolic interactionists believe that both parental training and broad cultural standards affect behavior. But they do not believe that children are cast into a permanent mold by either set of forces. Instead, they theorize that human behavior reflects changing concepts of self and social order.

Initially, children acquire a view of themselves based upon their relations with their parents. Over time, however, these views change, acquiring new forms as the children interact with new groups and learn new definitions of behavior. Because of this unique perspective, therefore, symbolic interactionist theory suggests methods for locating the motive for delinquency and defining human nature and social order that are different from those of other theories.

These differences can be illustrated by recalling the major premises of other theories. While control theories suggest that the motive for delinquent behavior lies in a human nature that is either warped or inherently antisocial, cultural deviance theories assume just the opposite: human nature is social and that the motive for delinquent behavior lies in the organization of society and the cultural adaptations that people make to that organization.

In opposition to both of these perspectives, symbolic interactionists view human nature and social order as opposite sides of the same coin. Neither is permanent; both are plastic and subject to change. On the one hand, individuals are constantly being modified, taking on the expectations and points of view of the people with whom they interact in intimate small groups. On the other hand, these same individuals contribute to the process of change, helping to shape the groups of which they are a part. Thus, it is from this ongoing process of interaction that the motive for delinquent behavior arises, not from permanent antisocial impulses or broad cultural imperatives that require it.

Furthermore, since any individual

213

participates in intimate groups in several different settings, the roles he or she plays will often be inconsistent and conflicting. For example, a high school girl who is known as a pot-smoking makeout artist among her friends would not exhibit the same kind of "self" at home. The self-conception and rationalizations that make such a role acceptable in one group of intimates would not make it acceptable in another.

This is a significant point of view because it not only implies a human nature that is malleable, but suggests that the social order is contradictory: society is not organized by a monolithic set of conventional values on which there is universal consensus. Rather, all people are exposed to deviant as well as to conformist traditions. Both are a part of culture, and people are aware of them. Whether or not they are delinquent, therefore, will depend upon the kinds of groups in which they participate on an intimate basis. If one or more is a delinquent group, it may provide the individual with all the justifications he or she needs for violating the law. If none is delinquent, conformist traditions will be supported.

In short, symbolic interactionist theory assumes three things: that (1) human nature is plastic and changing; (2) a changing social order presents deviant as well as conformist guides for behavior; and (3) the motive for delinquency resides in the rationalizations and techniques supplied to the individual by intimate, personal groups.

ORIGINS

Delinquency was originally constructed in this way by Edwin H. Sutherland in 1939. But, as a broader theory of human behavior, symbolic interactionism owes its origins to others. The first was Charles H. Cooley (1902), a sociologist who penned his ideas at the turn of the century. As Cooley observed his own children, he concluded that they began to develop a self-image very early in life. It was his opinion, however, that this image is not something with which the child is born. Rather, it is the product of involvement and communication with others. It emerges, first, as the result of interaction within the family; later, it is further developed in play groups, the school, and other social settings.

In the first years of life, the voices, facial expressions, and moods of parents are largely indistinguishable from other phenomena surrounding infants. Gradually, however, young children begin to attach special significance to other people and to perceive themselves as being different. They also become aware that others are judging them, responding positively to certain behaviors and negatively to others. They begin to realize that these responses are patterned and that their conduct and appearance are evaluated in terms of predictable standards.

Over time, therefore, children learn to make increasingly significant judgments about themselves and the reactions of others to them. A *self-image* emerges that is primarily the product of social interaction and communication. Without group interaction, in fact, the human self might never develop.

In order to illustrate the importance of interpersonal interaction, Cooley used an interesting metaphor. He likened the responses of others to our selves as a mirror. Just as we can look in the mirror and be pleased or displeased with what we see, so we can see the way people respond to us and judge ourselves in those terms. We develop what Cooley called the *looking glass self*. We imagine how others perceive our appearance, our clothes, our manners, and our behaviors and we evaluate ourselves accordingly. If the reflection appears to be a favorable one, we are pleased; but if it appears to be an unfavorable one, we are mortified and attempt to change our image. This image, in other words, is a social product, the result of the responses of others to us.

This way of describing the emergence of the self represented a radical departure from the biological and psychodynamic theories that prevailed during Cooley's life. It suggested that human nature is the product of social interaction, not the product of biological endowment or fixed, but unconscious, psychological drives. To Cooley, it was the imagination of oneself which a person develops in response to the social mirror that constitutes the essence of human nature.

· Furthermore, the process by which the looking glass self is developed does not end in childhood. As the person moves through successive stages in the life cycle—from childhood, to adolescence, to adulthood, and, then, to old age—the social mirror reflects an ever-changing image. According to this perspective, then, human nature is not a fixed attribute—social or antisocial—but is a mirror, capable of reflecting many faces.

THE SYMBOLIC ELEMENT

It fell to another theorist, George Herbert Mead (1934), to expand upon the symbolic element in symbolic interactionism. Mead stressed the importance of symbols as the basis for human interaction and communication. A symbol is a word or a gesture that acts as a shorthand way of representing something else—an idea, a person, or a thing. Some symbols are amazingly complex. Take the word *culture*. Though it is now familiar to the average lay person, this single symbol is used to represent the total way of life of a people—their beliefs, knowledge, values, technology, tastes, and prejudices. We take for granted the idea that the contrasting lifestyles of Eskimos, Turks, or Chinese are due in large part to their indoctrination into contrasting cultures.

What is significant about such complex symbols is that only humans, among all the animals, are capable of using them to construct reality. Once a symbol has become conventional in a given group, each person using it can experience the same general meaning from it. Even more important, a person can respond to a symbol in much the same way as one does to the thing or idea it represents. Once having learned what a "cow" is, one does not have to see it again when the symbol is used. The three-letter word will do.

Mead was concerned with symbols because, collectively, they become language, and language is essential to the process of communication by which human nature is developed. Other animals can communicate on a primitive level, but only through the use of language can people acquire a concept of self, engage in systematic thought, or deal in complex and abstract ideas. Therefore, language becomes the means by which the world view of children is constructed. The way symbols are tied together and the images they conjure up are crucial in determining not only how children see other things and people, but also how they see themselves.

Like Cooley, Mead also believed that the self is not a fixed entity but is pliable and subject to change. At the same time, he was somewhat unclear on just how plastic the human self is. According to one interpretation, Mead saw the self as a process and not as a structure— something that is constantly being shaped and reshaped, something that is never cast into a permanent mold, as some other theories might suggest (Blumer, 1969:2).

According to a second interpretation, however, Mead considered the self to be both a process *and* a structure; it has some stability and is not totally plastic but rather is the result of the accumulation of one's experiences as well as of recent social interactions. While the self does change over time, therefore, it also develops a structure of attitudes and perspectives that are relatively permanent and which move with the individual from group to group (Mead, 1974:158–174).

This is not an idle issue because of its importance in trying to understand human behavior. If we are inclined to believe that people are totally plastic, then we can determine what they might do only by looking at their immediate situation, who is present, and how the interaction of the moment results in a particular outcome. Little could be gained by assuming that an individuals's behavior will be relatively constant from situation to situation or that it can be predicted in advance.

If, by contrast, we believe that people are both a structure and a process, attempts to understand their behavior would have to be concerned with that which is relatively permanent in their makeups as well as with the outcomes of their interactions with others. Both would help to determine how they behave and why they behave that way.

As will be seen later, the validity and implications of symbolic theory are affected by the way this issue is resolved. For now, however, the thing to be remembered is that this body of theory, much more than others, stresses the importance of seeing the human being as an active organism which, on the one hand, is subject to modification by social interaction but which, on the other, contributes to change in the self conceptions and behaviors of others. In other words, the social relations and self-conceptions of a particular group of people will reflect a continuous process of change in which new ideas and courses of action emerge which may not have existed before they came together.

THE THEORY OF DIFFERENTIAL ASSOCIATION

When Edwin H. Sutherland applied these ideas to crime and delinquency, his theory was a direct reflection of the thinking of theorists like Cooley and Mead. He considered their

points of view to be far superior to the views of biological and psychodynamic control theorists, against whom he was a powerful and persuasive anatagonist. His theory consists of nine propositions which have remained unchanged since the fourth edition of his *Principles of Criminology* was published in 1947, three years before his death. However, later statements by Donald R. Cressey, Sutherland's student and coauthor, have helped to clarify the propositions. As stated by both authors, (Sutherland and Cressey, 1955:77–80), therefore, they are as follows:

1. Criminal behavior is learned. People are not inherently antisocial, nor do they possess permanent personality traits that predispose them to delinquent behavior. Rather, if they violate the law, it is because they have learned to do so.

2. Criminal behavior is learned in interaction with other persons in a process of communication. "What . . . we should study if we are going to establish a theory for explaining criminal conduct is, in a word, *words*" (Cressey, 1965:90). It is not enough to say that delinquent acts are made possible by the absence of effective constraints over human nature, as control theory suggests. People require positive motives or justifications for deviant behavior. These are supplied by symbols, by language. Gestures and nonverbal communication contribute to the process but are much less important. It is the symbolic learning of deviant values, attitudes, norms, and techniques that leads a person to commit delinquent acts.

3. The principal part of the learning of criminal behavior occurs within intimate personal groups. "The person (personality) is not separable from the social relationships in which [the individual] lives. . . . Criminal behavior is, like other behaviors, attitudes, beliefs, and values which a person exhibits, the *property of groups,* not of individuals" (Cressey, 1965:90). Consequently, such impersonal sources of learning as movies, television, and newspapers are relatively unimportant. While they might provide the individual with some delinquent ideas, these ideas are not likely to be carried out unless they receive the sanction and support of an intimate group of associates.

4. *When criminal behavior is learned, the learning includes (a) techniques of committing the crime, which are sometimes very complicated, sometimes very simple; (b) the specific direction of motives, drives, rationalizations, and attitudes.* People do not become mechanics, school teachers, or quarterbacks until they learn the necessary techniques. The same is true of delinquents. It takes training to hot-wire a car, to become a successful shoplifter, or even to smoke marijuana properly. Even more important, the commission of illegal acts requires the development of appropriate motives, attitudes, and rationalizations. These are derived from group definitions which make delinquent behavior acceptable: "Everybody cheats. Why shouldn't we?" "What your parents don't know won't hurt them." "Stealing from a crooked company like this is no crime." "Those guys had it coming to them." Without rationalizations like these, delinquent behavior is not likely to occur. "It is the presence or absence of a specific learned verbal label in a specific situation which determines the criminality or noncriminality of a particular person" (Cressey, 1952:44).

5. *The specific direction of motives and drives is learned from definitions of the legal codes as favorable or unfavorable.* Sutherland called his theory a "theory of differential association" (1956:20–21). He did this, he said, because the social order is characterized by cultural conflict. Reactions to the criminal law are not uniform in any modern society. Instead, people associate in groups which put them in contact with two kinds of culture, one kind whose norms favor adherence to law and the other whose norms encourages

law violation. This is "differential association." Individuals are confronted with mixed definitions for behavior, some conformist, some deviant. Whether they become delinquent, therefore, will depend on what they learn from the particular groups they encounter, and how those groups define the legal codes. If they define them favorably, the person will be motivated to obey the law. If they define them unfavorably, delinquent motives will be supplied.

6. *A person becomes delinquent because of an excess of definitions favorable to violation of law over definitions unfavorable to violation of law.* This is the proposition that defines the crucial condition for delinquent behavior to occur. If people become delinquent, it is because their contacts with delinquent patterns exceed their contacts with those that are nondelinquent. Some individuals, in fact, are almost completely isolated from antidelinquent groups and definitions. Hence, delinquent behavior on their parts is a virtual certainty since there is nothing to counter the delinquent self-concepts, values, and norms which their groups perpetuate.

7. *Differential associations may vary in frequency, duration, priority, and intensity.* These four elements explain the nature and effects of association in different groups. Sutherland did not explain them well, but, presumably, *frequency* refers to how often a person associates with delinquent groups, while *duration* refers to the length of the associations. Hence, the greater the frequency and/or the duration of delinquent associations, the more likely delinquent conduct will occur. *Priority*, meanwhile, has to do with the time in life when delinquent associations begin—the earlier they develop, the more likely they will persist. Finally, *intensity* has to do with "such things as the prestige of the source of a criminal or anticriminal pattern and with emotional reactions related to the associations" (Sutherland and Cressey, 1955:78). If a group

favoring law violation has high prestige and is emotionally satisfying to its members, the more likely its members are to become delinquent.

8. *The process of learning criminal behavior by association with criminal and anticriminal patterns involves all the mechanisms that are involved in any other learning.* Sutherland considered the meaning of this proposition to be self-evident: the same mechanisms that are involved in learning nondelinquent behavior—reward, punishment, imitation, coercion, or search for self-acceptance—are involved in learning delinquent behavior.

9. *While criminal behavior is an expression of general needs and values, it is not explained by those general needs and values since noncriminal behavior is an expression of the same needs and values.* The pursuit of money, success, and prestige does not help to explain delinquent behavior. Thieves generally steal in order to secure money, but likewise honest laborers work in order to secure money. The attempts by many scholars to explain criminal behavior by general drives and values—the happiness principle, the drive for social status, the money motive, or simple frustration—have been and must continue to be futile, since they explain lawful behavior as completely as they explain criminal behavior (Sutherland and Cressey, 1955:79). Consequently, the delinquent motives and rationalizations learned in small groups which justify the pursuit of money and prestige through illegal means create the delinquency, not the desire to be successful.

Implications and impact on policy

Sutherland's theory for constructing delinquency is more optimistic than most of the theories we have discussed thus far. In contrast to control theories, for example, it suggests that people may be easily affected by others. They are not cast into psychological or biological molds that are relatively impervious to outside influence. Instead, they are changeable, being so subject to the opinions and values of others. If one wants to reduce delinquency, moreover, one does not have to change an entire society, as cultural deviance theory suggests. Rather, the chief task is that of paying attention to the small groups in which children associate and insuring that prosocial values are constantly taught and reinforced.

Despite these implications, Sutherland said relatively little about them, leaving their discussion to Cressey, who expanded upon them in considerable detail (1954; 1955; 1965). He suggests that if delinquent behavior is the result of deviant motives, values, and rationalizations acquired in intimate groups, then intimate groups should be used to change that behavior. Indeed, one of the most significant implications of interactionist theory is its suggestion that the practice of keeping delinquents separate from nondelinquents, in detention centers and correctional institutions, may do more to encourage delinquent behavior than to discourage it. When they are isolated from law-abiding juveniles and locked up only with each other, the strength of delinquent norms, rationalizations, and identities can only increase.

Interactionist theory, in other words, lends support to the commonsense assumption that separate institutions for delinquents can only become schools of crime, since delinquents housed in them continue to associate only with other delinquents. By contrast, if we want them to become like nondelinquents, the two groups must be integrated, not kept apart. Delinquents must learn from nondelinquents that criminal conduct is wrong, and that the continued justification of predatory behavior is evil. Furthermore, delinquents require social support before they can adopt conventional social images and lifestyles.

Despite the theoretical attractiveness of this

view, Cressey seems to prefer a second alternative—that of using delinquents to change delinquents. In the first place, he argues, efforts to reintegrate them with nondelinquents would be impractical. Community leaders and conventional parents would not stand for it, fearing that the good children would be corrupted by the bad ones, rather than the reverse. In addition, Cressey feels, delinquents and criminals would actually be more effective as agents of change for each other than people who have never been serious offenders, particularly such professionals as social workers, group therapists, or probation and parole officers. Delinquents share a better rapport with each other, they trust each other more, and they have a greater sense of belonging to the same group.

Even more important, any delinquent who attempts to change someone else is more likely to be changed himself than he is to change the other person. Cressey calls this "retroflexive reformation" (1955:119). If a delinquent is serious in his attempts to reform others, he must automatically accept the common purpose of the reformation process, identify himself closely with others engaged in it, and grant prestige to those who succeed in it. In so doing, he becomes a genuine member of the reformation group and, in the process, is alienated from his former, delinquent group. A good example of a setting in which this is presumed to occur is in Alcoholics Anonymous. That organization depends upon alcoholics, not outsiders, to "cure" other alcoholics.

These principles, says Cressey, have not been applied on any wide scale in correctional organizations because they are governed by other theories of delinquency: (1) classical deterrence theory, which suggests that punishment will reform offenders and deter others; and (2) psychodynamic theory, which stresses individualized treatment and the need to alter unconscious drives, pathological fixations, and psychological frustrations. Even

when group therapy has been used, group leaders have been concerned more with changing the psychological makeup of the individual than with changing the values, standards, and rationalizations of the group with which he identifies. In traditional group therapy, the goal is to give offenders insight into the unconscious forces that are presumed to be at the roots of their separate disorders. Psychodynamics are stressed and the individual is treated in the group rather than through it. By contrast, Cressey's principles suggest that the group, itself, should become both the target and the medium of change. His assumption is that once the group becomes antidelinquent, individual change will follow.

Although these ideas have not been widely applied in public agencies, they have been used in small, private, or experimental programs. Perhaps the best known is Synanon, a program for drug addicts run by drug addicts (Yablonsky, 1965). Synanon was founded in 1958 by a member of Alcoholics Anonymous. Under his direction, a few addicts began living together voluntarily in an abandoned store. Since that time, the organization has expanded to several other cities and now owns its own residential property and several businesses run by its members.

In recent years, Synanon seems to have lost some of its original sense of purpose and to have become more of a self-seeking cult than an organization with a mission to help others. Nonetheless, in its early years, it was an ideal example of Cressey's suggestions that offenders should be isolated from people who view themselves as delinquents and surrounded by those who view themselves as antidelinquents. Addicts were free to join Synanon only if they were willing to adhere to a stringent set of group demands: give up drugs, have their hair cut off, give up all their money, take up permanent residence at Synanon, and sever all former ties that might prevent the Synanon group from assimilating them entirely. All personal desires had to be subverted to the antidelinquent, antidrug group.

The following excerpt from an admission interview illustrates the kinds of language used at Synanon to stress the stupidity of drug addiction and to introduce a sense of guilt over it:

> We ask him things like "What do you want from us?" "Don't you think you're an idiot or insane?" "Doesn't it sound insane for you to be running around the alleys stealing money from others so's you can go and stick something up your arm?" . . . We tell him, "We don't need you." "You need *us.*" And if we figure he's only halfway with us, we'll chop off his hair (Volkman and Cressey, 1963:132).

Synanon first helped addicts to kick their habits and then required that they participate in regular group meetings and perform other tasks when they were able. They could remain at Synanon as long as they stayed away from crime, drugs, and alcohol. Indeed, Synanon was unrelenting in its implementation of the principle that no other goal in life was so important as becoming a noncriminal nonaddict.

Other examples of experimental programs which have applied Cressey's principles of symbolic interactionism are Highfields (McCorkle, Elias, and Bixby, 1958), the Provo Experiment (Empey and Erickson, 1972), and the Silverlake Experiment (Empey and Lubeck, 1971b). All of these programs, however, were for convicted delinquents, not volunteer addicts. And, although they were like Synanon in their attempts to develop an antidelinquent group culture, they were different in other ways.

First, delinquents did not join them voluntarily. Instead, they were assigned by the juvenile court. Second, these programs were organized and run by conventional adults who, though they gave considerable power to the delinquent group to make decisions and to enforce norms, were still officially responsible

for the program. Third, these experiments could not use some of the coercive techniques that Synanon used, such as forcing delinquents to cut off their hair, demanding money from them, or requiring that they give up all former associates. Even then, one of the programs—the Provo Experiment—was accused of using "Communist brain-washing techniques" because of the methods it did use (Empey and Rabow, 1962; Gordon, 1962). Finally, unlike Synanon, where addicts might take up lifelong residence, the goal of these programs was to get delinquents back home, in school, or on the job as soon as possible. Indeed, in the Provo Experiment, delinquents continued to live at home and came to the program only during the day.

With all these differences, however, there was evidence of support for some of Cressey's ideas. One of these ideas, as expressed by a delinquent himself, was that offenders may be better agents of change than official reformers:

> **Boy:** Boys know more about themselves than grownups do. The first couple months [in this program] don't do any good. Then you find out that the meetin' knows you better than you know yourself. They can tell when you're lyin'. They can tell you things about yourself an' find out what your problems are . . . I jus' don't like to listen to adults lecturing . . . it is boring as hell. All the help I got, I got from other guys in the meetin'—nine other guys instead of one stupid adult talkin' to you. I felt they done the same things I done, an' know exactly how I feel, an' why I do them things (Empey and Erickson, 1972:58–61).

Another plausible generalization from Cressey's approach is that a delinquent group which makes use of the principle of symbolic interactionism might be more successful in producing change than traditional punishment.

> **Boy:** I mentioned that being locked up won't help a guy out of trouble. Understanding why you got there might, but the jail itself

won't. You have to get the understanding, an' that comes in group meetings.

Adult: Looking back, did the boys in your group do anything that helped you?

Boy: They helped me most when they put me in jail for not showin' up. When I got out, I said I wanted to get drunk that night an' the meeting talked to me about it.

Adult: How did that help?

Boy: Well, for one thing, I didn't go out an' get drunk. They talked to me quite a bit. They pointed out to me I was playing a tough role, an' that going on a blast now was the same ol' thing with me.

Adult: So what happened?

Boy: I can't say I was a goodie-goodie right off, but one thing that stuck with me was when they showed me that how I was acting was the way I was talking and treating my mother and my girl. I was being a hard-ass. I thought a lot of my girl an' I saw I was only makin' things worse, not better. Her ol' man don't like me anyhow, an' gettin' drunk wouldn't help (Empey and Erickson, 1972:57).

Besides impressionistic comments like these, systematic research has also indicated that a group-oriented program may produce a greater sense of commitment to correctional goals than do traditional programs. The members of such programs are less likely to be split into competing adult and delinquent groups and are more likely to reinforce antidelinquent values and points of view (Shichor and Empey, 1974). Yet, despite such findings, there is also evidence that the principles of symbolic interactionism are something less than a panacea.

Some limitations. Programs which develop a strong and demanding antidelinquent group are unable to hold onto many potential members. At Synanon, 72 percent of 263 persons who joined that organization during a three-year period dropped out after a short stay. Fifty nine percent of the dropouts left within one month,

90 percent within three months (Volkman and Cressey, 1963:142). In the Silverlake Experiment, the same phenomenon was observed among delinquents, though it was not so marked (Empey and Lubeck, 1971b:chap. 10). Located in the open community, this program had 37 percent of its members run away, most of them during the first month or two of residence. As a result the findings suggest that delinquents are not so malleable as symbolic interactionist theory suggests. Many persist in old patterns of behavior and do not readily accept prosocial values from their peers.

Likewise, group-centered programs may not be strikingly more successful in inducing criminals and delinquents to refrain permanently from new offenses. At Synanon, only about 29 percent of the addicts who joined the organization remained free from drugs for any appreciable length of time. However, the longer they stayed there, the higher their success rate became—after staying one month, 48 percent remained drug-free; after three months, 66 percent; and after seven months, 88 percent (Volkman and Cressey, 1963:142). The evidence seems to indicate that if a person is successful in actually becoming a member of an anticriminal antidrug group, the probability is increased that he or she will remain prosocial. The problem, however, is that in the early days of Synanon approximately 7 in 10 members did not stay long enough to become committed to the program.

Among delinquents in the Silverlake and Provo Experiments, long-range success rates were much higher (Empey and Lubeck, 1971b: chap. 12; Empey and Erickson, 1972: chaps. 9–10). Approximately 60 percent had no recorded arrests after being released for one year, and about 80 percent had no more than one arrest. Furthermore, their commission of serious offenses declined markedly following group involvement. Yet, when the delinquents in all these experiments were compared with control groups of delinquents assigned to regular probation or traditional places of incarceration, their postprogram success rates were not markedly higher. The only time they remained significantly less delinquent was when they were still in the experimental program and still members of the antidelinquent group (Empey and Erickson, 1972: chap. 5). Once removed from it, their behavior was much like that of delinquents who had never had contact with it.

Policy implications. Such findings raise some serious questions about the relevance of symbolic interaction theory for public policy. Early in this chapter, it was noted that, according to interactionist theory, the human self can be viewed in two ways: (1) nothing more than a process that undergoes constant modification; or (2) both a structure and a process in which the self retains considerable continuity. The research findings described above do not totally resolve the issue.

On the one hand, many of the members of Synanon and of the Provo and the Silverlake Experiments resisted involvement in prosocial groups. They were not easily changed; they seemed to possess self-concepts that were rather structured and resistant to change. On the other hand, those who did become participating members in these programs were not much more inclined than nonmembers to remain faithful to group standards once they left the programs' influence. This finding, therefore, could be said to confirm the plasticity of human nature. What success Synanon has had, for example, seems to be based on the necessity for addicts to remain in the program for their entire lives if they are to remain free from drugs. They can never plan on leaving it because, once they do, they are easily converted back to drug use.

Given this set of inconsistent findings, one policy alternative would be to organize more programs like Synanon. Offenders would choose to live voluntarily in their own miniature communities, totally isolated from the rest of society. But such an alternative, particularly for children and adolescents, is not likely to receive public endorsement. Not only is it reminiscent of the ideas that led to the asylums of the 19th century, but also it is contrary to the democratic values that govern our concept of childhood. Furthermore, it is not likely that anywhere near a majority of offenders, if given a choice, would choose this alternative.

A second policy alternative would be to reconsider the way Sutherland's theory has been implemented, particularly taking into account Cressey's suggestion that offenders are the best agents of change. It will be recalled that this theory could just as well be interpreted as suggesting that offenders should be totally separated from other offenders and integrated into prosocial groups instead. What if delinquents were placed on an individual basis into conventional groups in schools, neighborhoods, and places of recreation rather than in correctional programs with other offenders? Two possible outcomes are suggested.

First, nondelinquent groups might be confronted with the need for some kind of change on their parts. Cressey's reading of the principles of symbolic interactionism overlooks this need. If the individual and the group are two sides of the same coin, then group as well as individual change is implied. Conventional adolescents might be involved in the task of changing delinquents.

Second, delinquents might not only encounter an excess of definitions unfavorable to violation of law in normal group settings, but they would also have a greater chance to participate in activities that might help to reinforce those definitions. The evidence seems clear that words, attitudes, and rationalizations alone will not do the trick. This would be particularly true for those delinquents, described by control and cultural deviance theories, who lack social skills, are behind in their educational development, or have no access to the means for success. These factors require attention as well.

There has been a growing attempt in recent years to address some of these problems by locating correctional programs in the open community. Yet, officials remain more concerned with changing offenders than with changing the networks of adolescent relations with local neighborhoods, schools, and clubs so that delinquents might be integrated more effectively with nondelinquents. Consequently, if the implications of symbolic interaction theory are to be assessed more thoroughly, public policies are needed which would cease separating official delinquents from conventional adolescents and help to reduce the sea of social distance which still separates these two groups.

SCIENTIFIC LEGACY

The scientific legacy of Sutherland's theory of differential association can be assessed by considering: (1) the extent to which it meets scientific criteria for a good theory and is supported by evidence; and (2) its impact on the scientific construction of delinquency.

Scientific adequacy

According to Sutherland, the theory of differential association was designed to explain why an individual becomes delinquent.[1] If it is to accomplish that task, however, it must possess a set of propositions that enable one to predict delinquent behavior under a clearly specified set of conditions, and it must be readily amenable to scientific test.

Most criminologists agree that Sutherland's theory does not meet these criteria. It does not provide a clear statement on the process by which an individual becomes delinquent. While it stresses the existence of competing norms in the community and suggests that a person learns to be delinquent through excessive contact with delinquent patterns, it does not provide a set of deductive statements indicating how this comes about: how membership in delinquent groups occurs, how delinquent behavior is learned and reinforced, or at what point definitions favorable to law violation override definitions unfavorable to it and lead to actual delinquent behavior. The propositions, as presently stated, simply do not permit one to predict this sequential series of events.

As a result, Cressey (1969:420) suggests that Sutherland's propositions should be "viewed as a set of directives about the kinds of things that ought to be included in a theory of criminality, rather than as an actual statement of theory." His propositions are a valuable starting point for the development of precise theory, but by themselves they do not yet accomplish that task.

The theory of differential association does not lend itself to rigorous scientific test (Short, 1960). For example, how does one determine when a person has been subjected to an "excess of definitions" favorable to violation of law? Can it be shown that this excess actually precedes delinquent behavior, or that all people define "excess" in the same way?

In the same vein, Sutherland said that "differential associations vary in frequency, duration, priority, and intensity." Yet, he neither defined these terms carefully nor did he indicate how, when combined in some way, their relationship to delinquent conduct could be measured. Indeed, he noted that a "formula" by which this could be accomplished would be extremely difficult to develop (Sutherland and Cressey, 1955:79). He was

---

[1] A host of investigators have raised questions about the theory of differential association. For a comprehensive review of their questions and of a critique of them by a proponent of the theory, see Donald R. Cressey (1969). The following analysis is indebted to that review.

right. No one has been able to construct one.

Drawing upon the broader field of symbolic interactionism, the theory of differential association suggests that beliefs, attitudes, and rationalizations provide the motive for delinquent behavior. Yet, an increasing number of studies find that beliefs and attitudes are poor predictors of actual human conduct (Deutscher, 1973). Words do not always lead to action. As a result, there is reason to suspect that verbal symbols and attitudes alone do not constitute the only reasons for law-violating acts. If people often behave in ways that are contrary to their expressed attitudes and values, then other factors—a disinterest in conformity, a sense of strain, or, in the case of heroin users, a physical addiction—may also be important.

In the same vein, the theory of differential association provides little help in explaining the delinquent conduct of the lone individual who invents and carries out an illegal act by himself or who, in a fit of rage, attacks a loved one. There are many instances in which delinquent acts cannot be traced to a former group of associates who endorse and teach this kind of behavior.

The theory of differential association suggests that the motives for delinquent behavior are solely the product of membership in delinquent groups. Virtually every other theory, by contrast, suggests that motives, at least in part, are due to other factors: Control theory emphasizes the role of biological factors or early training; cultural deviance theory stresses class position and societal organization; and still more factors are stressed by theories not yet discussed here. In each instance, some condition in the life of the individual is thought to motivate *both* delinquent behavior *and* membership in delinquent groups, which are seen as a combined method of solving some problem of adjustment.

These theoretical differences are most apparent when one contrasts control and differential association theories. Most control theorists argue that membership in delinquent groups occurs only *after* an individual becomes delinquent, not before (Glueck and Glueck, 1950:163–64; Hirschi, 1969:135–38). In other words, it is only following their involvement in delinquency that delinquents, like birds of a feather, flock together. According to this view then, their flocking is a byproduct of their delinquent behavior, not the primary cause of it. Delinquents take up with other delinquents because they have already lost their stakes in conformity and because they have already become detached from parents and conventional friends and have nowhere else to turn for support and confirmation. As a basic cause of delinquent behavior, therefore, peer relations are of secondary importance.

Which explanation is correct, the one suggested by Sutherland or the one suggested by control theorists? Existing evidence suggests that neither is entirely accurate (Hirschi, 1969:152–160; Empey and Lubeck, 1971a:chap. 9; Jensen, 1972). Both disinterest in conformity and membership in groups make independent contributions to the commission of delinquent acts; that is, a child's lack of attachment to family and school can lead to delinquent behavior as well as to membership in a delinquent group. Either, or both, may contribute. Hence, even if there is some support for Sutherland's theory in this finding, it certainly does not constitute a full affirmation of it. The evidence suggests that factors other than group associations are sources of delinquent behavior.

In summary, then, a number of serious questions have been raised about the scientific adequacy of Sutherland's theory and about symbolic interactionism in general. Like most other explanations of human conduct, both are extremely difficult to verify or to disprove, and both leave many questions unanswered.

Scientific construction of delinquency

Despite the scientific inadequacies of Sutherland's theory, its new and stimulating way of constructing delinquency gave it immense popularity. For an entire generation of sociologically oriented criminologists, his statement, like Darwin's theory of evolution among biologists, became the orienting schema around which new theories were organized. Cohen (1955) and Cloward and Ohlin (1960) drew upon it in constructing the strain theories that are to be discussed in the next chapter, particularly the idea that delinquent behavior reflects group norms and support. Indeed, Cloward and Ohlin expressed their indebtedness to Sutherland by dedicating their book to him.

Other criminologists have attempted to reformulate Sutherland's theory to account for some of the criticisms made of it (De Fleur and Quinney, 1966). Daniel Glaser (1956:440–41) argues that its organizing principle should be "differential identification" rather than "differential association." In essence, his point of view suggests that "a person pursues criminal behavior to the extent that he identifies himself with real or imaginary persons from whose perspective his criminal behavior seems acceptable" (p. 440). In other words, Glaser suggests that people often identify with persons or groups with whom they have had little intimate contact. Actual group associations are not necessary. They might identify with a deviant TV hero or a group of peers, though they have had close associations with neither. Although this emphasis upon *identification* is much different than Sutherland's emphasis on *association,* it is more consistent with a body of theory which suggests that the roles we play are often dictated by our reference groups rather then by the many less important groups in which we hold membership. Only those to which we look for normative direction are those that influence our behavior.

In quite a different way, Burgess and Akers (1966) reformulated Sutherland's theory to make it more consistent with recent developments in psychological learning theory. They attempted to account for research findings which suggest that neither symbolic interaction nor Glaser's differential identification are enough by themselves to reinforce delinquent behavior. Other kinds of rewards and punishments must also be present—money, a personal sense of accomplishment, or excitement. Nonetheless, their final set of propositions are like Sutherland's in the sense that they provide a set of organizing principles for enlarging the scope of differential association theory rather than a deductive set of statements which would allow one to predict delinquent behavior.

Finally, several theorists have amplified and added some new dimensions to three of Sutherland's basic ideas: (1) the social order is characterized by cultural conflict; (2) delinquent behavior is a situational phenomenon; and (3) verbal symbols provide both the motive and justification for delinquent behavior. Now we will consider their contributions to the original scheme.

Culture conflict

Sykes and Matza argue that there is a subculture of delinquency in American society, but that this subculture is not something that is possessed only by adolescent groups (1957; 1964). American culture, they believe, is not a simple puritanism exemplified by middle-class norms. Instead, it is a complex and pluralistic culture in which, among other subcultural traditions, there are "subterranean," deviant traditions. These traditions do not represent ignorance of the law nor even general negation of it. Rather, they have a complex relationship to law that is symbiotic rather than oppositional: they do not represent a separate set of beliefs which distinguish delinquents from other youths or youths from adults. Instead, deviant traditions make up that part of the overall culture which consists of the personal, less conventional, and less publicized version of existing standards for behavior. The two sets of traditions—conventional and deviant—are held simultaneously by almost everyone, and, while certain groups may be influenced more by one than the other, both determine behavior to a considerable degree.

Daniel Bell's (1953) analysis of crime as an American way of life is probably a good illustration of Sykes and Matza's point. Bell notes that Americans are characterized by an "extremism" in morality, yet they also have an "extraordinary" talent for compromise in politics and a "brawling" economic and social history. These contradictory features form the basis for intimate and symbiotic relationships—not oppositional relationships—between crime and politics, crime and economic growth, and crime and social change. The tradition of cheating to get ahead in school or of using any means to succeed in business or politics is no less an ethic than wanting to observe the law.

Illegal acts have been a major means by which a variety of people have achieved the American success ideal and obtained respectability. Sykes and Matza suggest, therefore, that deviant traditions contribute more than we realize to the behavior of younger as well as older people. A delinquent subculture, rather than being uniquely the property of adolescents, may have its roots in the broader culture. Everyone is aware of deviant traditions, as Sutherland suggested, and everyone resorts to them when it seems expedient to do so.

Situational quality of delinquent behavior

Though stressing the idea that delinquent acts are a product of social interaction, David Matza (1964) places far less emphasis than did Sutherland on the constraining influences of group relations. He considers the theory of differential association (as well as all other theories in the positivistic tradition) to be too deterministic and calls attention to the uncertain status of adolescents in our society. Given their ambiguous social position, it should not be too surprising that they commit delinquent acts. Law violators may be a little bit out of the ordinary—but not by much. Hence, in order to understand their behavior, it is necessary to recognize that they exist in a condition of "drift":

> The image of the delinquent I wish to convey is one of drift; an actor neither compelled nor committed to deeds nor freely choosing them; neither different in any simple or fundamental sense from the law-abiding, nor the same; conforming to certain traditions in American life while partially unreceptive to other more conventional traditions. . . .
>
> Drift stands midway between freedom and control. . . . The delinquent *transiently* exists in a limbo between convention and crime, responding in turn to the demands of each, flirting now with one, now with the other, but postponing commitment, evading decision. Thus, he drifts between criminal and conventional action (p. 28).

The line of analysis suggested by Matza is consistent with symbolic interactionism because it asserts that human behavior emerges out of a continuous process of interaction. But the process suggested by Matza is far more fluid and open than the one suggested by Sutherland. In the first place, adolescents have a modicum of choice in deciding whether to violate the law. In the second place, that choice will be determined not by some prior set of causes, but by an intermix of factors present in the situation when a choice is made—who is present, what the risks are, and so on. According to this view, then, nobody *has* to be delinquent. If an adolescent does break the law, it will depend upon a process that is dictated more by immediate circumstance than by conditions that are predetermined by personality, social position, or membership in a deviant subculture.

Recently, for example, a young Amish family in Indiana was driving home from a party in their horse-drawn buggy. As they did so, a pickup truck drove alongside, and a rock was thrown at them. To their horror, they discovered that it had hit the head of their seven-month-old daughter, asleep on her mother's lap. The baby seemed to stretch twice, and then relaxed. She was dead of a fractured skull and a massive brain injury.

Shortly thereafter, four teenagers were picked up by the local sheriff, all of them sons of "good families," none of whom had a criminal record or had been drinking or using drugs. When asked why they had thrown the rock at the peaceful religious family, one replied that they had simply decided to go out and get some "clapes," a derogatory local term for the Amish. When asked further why they wanted to harass clapes, another told the sheriff, "I don't even know" (Siegel, 1980:1).

As it turned out, this explanation was not entirely true. People acquainted with the four boys testified that they often bragged about "getting" the Amish, and that they did so every weekend as a diversion, like going to the local movie. Nonetheless, as the case unfolded, it served as a classic illustration of symbolic interactionist theory. Not only was the group commission of the act an example of this theory, but so were the efforts made by townspeople to rationalize the killing of the baby. They employed what Sykes and Matza (1957) call "techniques of neutralization"—verbal statements which serve to lessen the impact of, if not to justify, the commission of the crime:

1. Denial of responsibility. One such technique is to deny the responsibility of the offender. Local townspeople, for example, contended that the "death of the baby was just a matter of 'kids fooling around,' of a prank that had gone awry. Certainly, 'the boys' did not intend to kill anyone" (Siegel, 1980:6).

2. Denial of the victim. Similarly, moral indignation over a crime may be neutralized by transforming the victim into someone who, if not deserving injury, could be an understandable target. Although contending that the attacks on Amish people were not motivated by religious bigotry, the local sheriff said that they "just happen to be the best and easiest target. In the buggies, they are a slow-moving target, and young people know they won't retaliate by chasing them or filing charges" (Siegel, 1980:4). Indeed, if the worth of this particular target—a peaceful Amish family—could be further lessened or completely denied, think how effective the rationalization would have been had it been applied to a homosexual, the town drunk, or a newly arrived Iranian family.

Other techniques of neutralization might have been used—denying that real injury was done, condemning those who wanted to punish the boys, or contending that loyalty to one's friends takes precedence over loyalty to "strange" people like the Amish—but these techniques were ultimately made unnecessary by the Amish themselves. Being pacifists, they joined with other local people by suggesting that the boys should not go to jail. Instead, they recommended that the best punishment would be to require the boys to attend the baby's funeral. "We wouldn't push for jail," they said. "We just hope they never do it again" (Siegel, 1980:9).

In summary, then, this local drama illustrated two major features of symbolic interactionist theory. First, it illustrated the contention of interactionists that adolescents, if not most people, tend to drift between conventionality and criminality. Hence, when the boys in question did commit a delinquent act, it was made possible by their membership in a small intimate group, and by the group's collective use of momentary rationalizations—

"having fun," "getting some clapes," or "doing what everybody does." But rather than representing a permanent commitment to a distinctive delinquent subculture, the group's crime was the result of its use of subterranean traditions in a transitory situation. Delinquents, in other words, are not divorced entirely from conventionality, as other theories suggest, but move back and forth between conventionality and deviance, as the situation dictates.

Second, the Amish incident illustrated the extent to which other people—law-abiding townspeople as well as delinquents themselves—will resort to subterranean traditions in order to explain away criminal acts. But rather than suggesting that such traditions should dominate social conduct, or that they should replace legal rules, these people contend that the legal rules should not be rigorously applied *in this case*. Since it is an exception, the delinquents in point should not be viewed as bad people, only people who made a momentary slip.

The criminals in this case were good boys, the children of respected families. Yet, Short and Strodtbeck provide data which suggest that interactionist ideas might be applied to lower-class boys in ghetto areas. They point out that there is considerable support for conventional values among the members of lower-class urban gangs: "fidelity in marriage, small families, hard work and thrift, and keeping one's son in school" (1965:250). Yet, these same gang members are often participants in delinquent acts, school dropouts, job failures, and fathers of illegitimate children for whom they assume no responsibility. Why?

Short and Strodtbeck (1965:263) conclude that gang member behavior is not satisfactorily explained by irrational tendencies, neurotic drives, or a commitment to totally deviant values. Rather, situational elements play a key part, such as a serious threat to the status of a gang leader, which can be avoided only by his willingness to engage in a delinquent act; the advantages to be gained from a delinquent act, which can be realized without entailing much risk of detection; or perceived threats from outside groups, which might require an aggressive response.

In most instances, therefore, delinquent acts occurred in situations in which the range of choice was narrowed and focused due to the presence of others. But contrary to the notion that gang members always feel compelled to commit crimes, some choose to avoid them, as Matza theorizes, while others choose the delinquent alternative. Furthermore, it is relatively easy for boys to rationalize either choice by drawing from conventional as well as subterranean traditions.

SUMMARY AND CONCLUSIONS

Symbolic interactionist theory was instrumental in establishing a new tradition in our social construction of delinquency. It suggested that delinquent behavior is the product of learning and communication in small intimate groups, not the product of biological endowment, unconscious psychological drives, poverty, or small societies of deviants who have their own unique way of life. As a consequence, it added new assumptions and hypotheses to our explanations for delinquent behavior:

1. Assumptions about human nature and social order. Symbolic interactionists assume that human nature is the product of social interaction rather than something with which people are born. The mind and the self develop in response to the processes of communication among small groups of intimate associates. Furthermore, the human self is not a permanent attribute but rather an entity that is undergoing constant change as the person moves through the life cycle or from one group to another.

In a sense, the social order is seen as the reverse side of the same coin. Like human nature, it is not a fixed and monolithic set of values characterized by a high degree of consensus. Rather, all members of society are confronted with contrasting and emergent definitions for behavior, some deviant, some conformist. Along with conventional traditions, therefore, there are subterranean traditions to which people may resort depending upon circumstance and the way any situation is defined by significant others.

2. *The underlying logic and content of symbolic interactionist theory.* Sutherland's theory of differential association is the most completely developed criminological version of symbolic interactionism. While it does not provide an adequate description of the process by which an individual becomes delinquent, it does imply something akin to the following sequence:

All young people are confronted with conflicting standards for behavior. Whether or not they become delinquent, however, will depend upon the groups with which they associate. If, by chance, they happen to establish intimate contacts with a group of delinquent companions, they will encounter an excess of definitions favorable to the violation of law, learn techniques for committing crime, and acquire the necessary motives and rationalizations by which delinquent behavior is made possible. (This sequence might be diagrammed as in Figure 10–1.)

Matza suggests, however, that this process will provide a greater degree of choice for the individual and will be more fluid and open than Sutherland suggested.

3. *Policy implications.* Since people are easily subject to change, the theory of differential association implies that delinquent behavior can be unlearned by the same process it is learned. Delinquents should be surrounded by associates who define illegal behavior as immoral and conventional behavior as desirable. Deliberate attempts by public agencies to apply these ideas have not been extensive; when used by private, experimental programs, they have achieved only partial success. Experiments like those at Synanon, Provo, and Silverlake raise questions about the plasticity of the human self and suggest that reinforcements other than words are necessary to sustain conventional behavior.

4. *Logical and empirical adequacy.* Sutherland's theory possesses many inadequacies: it does not provide a clear statement of the process by which a person becomes delinquent; it is very difficult to translate it into propositions that are testable; it fails to account for crimes in which intimate associates and shared definitions are lacking; and it probably overdoes the extent to which rationalizations, by themselves, provide the necessary motive for delinquent behavior. The available evidence suggests that some of the factors stressed by other theories also play an important role in producing delinquent behavior. With all these inadequacies, the theory has had immense impact on the construction of other theories, directing our attention to the possibilities that society is characterized by cultural conflict, delinquent acts are highly situational, and verbal definitions do help to neutralize delinquent conduct and make it possible.

FIGURE 10–1

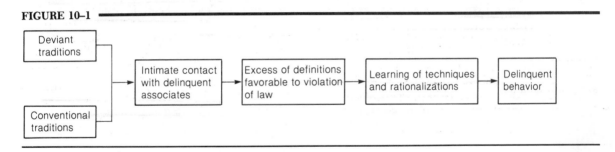

REFERENCES

Bell, Daniel
1953   "Crime as an American Way of Life." *Antioch Review* 12 (Summer): 131–53.

Blumer, Herbert
1969   "Sociological Implications of The Thought of George Herbert Mead." Pp. 62–65 in Blumer, ed., *Symbolic Interactionism*. Englewood Cliffs, N.J.: Prentice-Hall.

Burgess, Robert L., and Akers, Ronald L.
1966   "Differential Association-reinforcement Theory of Criminal Behavior." *Social Problems* 14 (Fall):128–47.

Cloward, Richard A., and Ohlin, Lloyd E.
1960   *Delinquency and Opportunity: A Theory of Delinquent Gangs.* New York: Free Press.

Cohen, Albert K.
1955   *Delinquent Boys: The Culture of the Gang.* New York: Free Press.

Cooley, Charles H.
1964   *Human Nature and the Social Order.* First published 1902. New York: Schocken Books.

Cressey, Donald R.
1952   "Application and Verification of the Differential Association Theory." *Journal of Criminal Law, Criminology, and Police Science* 63 (May–June):43–52.
1954   "Contradictory Theories in Correctional Group Therapy Programs." *Federal Probation* 18 (June):20–26.
1955   "Changing Criminals: The Application of the Theory of Differential Association." *American Journal of Sociology* 61 (September):116–20.
1965   "Theoretical Foundations for Using Criminals in the Rehabilitation of Criminals." *Key Issues* 2 (January):87–101.
1969   "Epidemiology and individual conduct." Pp. 557–77 in Donald R. Cressey and David A. Ward, *Delinquency, Crime and Social Process.* New York: Harper & Row.

DeFleur, Melvin, and Quinney, Richard
1966   "A Reformulation of Sutherland's Differential Association Verification." *Journal of Research in Crime and Delinquency* 3 (January):1–11.

Deutscher, Irwin
1973   *What We Say/What We Do: Sentiments and Acts.* Chicago: Scott, Foresman.

Empey, LaMar T., and Erickson, Maynard L.
1972   *The Provo Experiment: Evaluating Community Control of Delinquency.* Lexington, Mass.: D. C. Heath.

Empey, LaMar T., and Lubeck, Steven G.
1971a   *Explaining Delinquency.* Lexington, Mass.: D. C. Heath.
1971b   *The Silverlake Experiment: Testing Delinquency Theory and Community Intervention.* Chicago: Aldine.

Empey, LaMar T., and Rabow, Jerome
   1962   "Reply to Whitney H. Gordon." *American Sociological Review* 27 (April):256–58.

Glaser, Daniel
   1956   "Criminality Theories and Behavioral Images." *American Journal of Sociology* 61 (March):433–44.

Glueck, Sheldon, and Glueck, Eleanor
   1950   *Unraveling Juvenile Delinquency.* Cambridge: Harvard University Press.

Gordon, Whitney H.
   1962   "Communist Rectification Programs and Delinquency Rehabilitation Programs: A Parallel?" *American Sociological Review* 27 (April):256.

Hirschi, Travis
   1969   *Causes of Delinquency.* Berkeley: University of California Press.

Jensen, Gary F.
   1972   "Parents, Peers, and Delinquent Action: A Test of the Differential Association Perspective." *American Journal of Sociology* 72 (November):562–75.

Matza, David
   1964   *Delinquency and Drift.* New York: John Wiley & Sons.

McCorkle, Lloyd W.; Elias, Albert; and Bixby, F. Lovell
   1958   *The Highfields Story.* New York: Holt, Rinehart & Winston.

Mead, George H.
   1974   *Mind, Self and Society.* Chicago: University of Chicago Press, 1934.

Shichor, David, and Empey, LaMar T.
   1974   "A Typological Analysis of Correctional Organizations." *Sociology and Social Research* 58 (April):318–34.

Short, James F., Jr.
   1960   "Differential Association as a Hypothesis: Problems of Empirical Testing." *Social Problems* 8 (Summer):14–25.

Short, James F., Jr., and Strodtbeck, Fred L.
   1965   *Group Process and Gang Delinquency.* Chicago: University of Chicago Press.

Siegel, Barry
   1980   "Killing Forces Amish to Face Outside World." *Los Angeles Times,* March 23, Part 1:1–9.

Sutherland, Edwin H.
   1956   "Development of a Theory." Pp. 20–31 in Albert K. Cohen et al., eds., *The Sutherland Papers.* Bloomington: Indiana University Press.

Sutherland, Edwin H., and Cressey, Donald R.
   1955   *Principles of Criminology.* 5th ed. Philadelphia: J. B. Lippincott.

Sykes, Gresham M., and Matza, David
   1957   "Techniques of Neutralization: A Theory of Delinquency." *American Sociological Review* 22 (December):664–70.

Volkman, Rita and Cressey, Donald R.
   1963   "Differential Association and the Rehabilitation of Drug Addicts." *American Journal of Sociology* 29 (September):129–42.

Yablonsky, Lewis
   1965   *The Tunnel Back: Synanon.* New York: Macmillan.

Strain theory suggests that in the absence of legitimate opportunities for success, delinquency will result.

STRAIN THEORY

Strain theory is the third major body of sociological theory to deal with juvenile delinquency. Formulated in the 1950s, it draws upon the earlier perspectives of both Shaw and McKay (cultural deviance theory) and Sutherland and Cressey (symbolic interactionist theory) (Cloward and Ohlin, 1960:X).

Strain theory assumes that human nature is either inherently social or is the product of interaction in intimate groups. It also sees delinquent behavior as an expression of conformity to shared values and standards. When young people violate the law, their behavior represents an effort to adjust collectively to society's organization and structure. Finally, strain theory supports the contention of Shaw and McKay, if not Sutherland and Cressey, that chronic delinquent behavior is limited largely to lower-class gangs.

At the same time, strain theory departs from both of its predecessors in locating the basic motive for criminal conduct. Rather than suggesting that delinquents are motivated by deviant values unique to their particular gang or subculture, it maintains that their criminal conduct can be explained by values that all Americans share, young or old, black or white, lower or middle class. The reason is that the social order is characterized by widespread consensus on the importance of achievement and success. When lower-class youth violate the law, therefore, it is because they are angry and frustrated over their lack of opportunity to fulfill the American Dream. They are people whose legitimate, widely prized aspirations have been blocked by the prevailing American class structure.

This way of locating the sources of deviant behavior can be traced to Robert Merton, an eminent American sociologist. In a series of statements, beginning in 1938, Merton first discounted Freudian explanations of deviant behavior and then formulated an alternative view (1938; 1957; 1968):

> Until recently . . . one could speak of a marked tendency in psychological and sociological theory to attribute the faulty operation of social structure to failures of social control over man's

imperious biological drives. . . . In the beginning, there are man's biological impulses which seek full expression. And then there is the social order, essentially an apparatus for the management of impulses, for the social processing of tensions, [and] for the "renunciation of instinctual gratifications," in the words of Freud. Nonconformity . . . is thus assumed to be anchored in original nature. . . . And by implication, conformity is the result of a utilitarian calculus or of unreasoned conditioning (1968:185).

Such a view, said Merton, is faulty (1968:185–248). Humankind is not, by nature, inherently deviant. Deviant impulses are socially induced. In American society, for example, a great emphasis is placed upon monetary success and the achievement of high social status. Yet, at the same time, society does not provide all of its citizens with equal opportunities for this success. For lower-class people, in particular, "culturally induced" goals cannot be realized; they lack the means. As a result, they are faced with a cruel dilemma: either they must give up the pursuit of that which everyone values, and thus appear to be morally inferior, or they must seek out illegal means for success, even though they again face the risk of censure. But, should they choose the latter course, it will be the product, not of an inherently evil nature, but of the discrepancy between culturally valued goals and socially available means. "A cardinal American virtue, 'ambition,' promotes a cardinal American vice, 'deviant behavior' " (1957:146).

Two versions of this general view have been applied specifically to juveniles, the first by Albert K. Cohen in 1955 and the second by Richard A. Cloward and Lloyd E. Ohlin in 1960. So provocative were their statements, ideologically as well as scientifically, that throughout the 1960s they had considerable impact upon the formulation of social policy as well as the conduct of scientific investigation. Each version therefore, is set forth below.

COHEN: STATUS FRUSTRATION AND DELINQUENCY

Cohen's introduction to his theory (1955) reveals the extent to which, by the middle of this century, cultural explanations of delinquency had gained widespread acceptance, at least among sociologists. His theory, he says, is designed to explain two sets of "known facts": (1) the existence and content of delinquent subculture; and (2) the concentration of this subculture among the male working-class segments of American society.

To him at least, both of these facts were not arguable. The prevalence of delinquent traditions was widely accepted, and the prevailing opinion was that female delinquency was not serious:

> Authorities are agreed that female delinquency, although it may appear euphemistically in the records as "ungovernability" or "running away" is mostly sex delinquency. Stealing, "other property offenses," "orneriness" and "hell-raising" . . . are primarily practices of the male (p. 45).

It was upon this foundation, then, that Cohen advanced the following propositions to explain delinquent subculture and the functions it serves for lower-class boys:

1. Lower-class Americans embrace the middle-class success ethic. Cohen rejects the notion that a distinctive culture has been perpetuated or has developed among lower-class Americans. The middle-class values which have played such an important part is shaping the American character and our concept of childhood have now established a foothold in the lower class. Its members watch television, go to the movies, listen to the radio, and attend schools dominated by the middle class. Thus, over time, they have come more and more under the spell of a set of norms which stress ambition, resourcefulness, achievement, respect for property, and, above all, the desire for material success. The American Dream is a valued goal of the lower class.

This acceptance of the American Dream has been encouraged by the democratic belief that every child should be free to compete with every other, regardless of background. "The cards are not dealt and the hands all played . . . before the child appears on the scene" (p. 85). Instead, each child should be judged as an individual, and it should be his achievement that determines his future status, not the social position into which he was born. However, since every individual should be encouraged to compete, there can only be one standard for measuring success: *the middle-class measuring rod,* which is the ability to get ahead. Hence, no less than middle-class children, each lower-class boy should be expected to compete for success with all comers.

2. The socialization of lower-class children hinders their capacity to compete. Unfortunately, the desire to share in the American Dream does not mean that all children have an equal ability to compete. Lower-class parents, for example, do not have the economic resources and social power that middle-class parents have—money, clothes, a home in the right neighborhood, or the capacity to intercede effectively with schools or influential employers.

Even more important, lower- and middle-class parents socialize their children in different ways. Middle-class parents are rational, deliberate, and demanding. They leave little to chance, stressing self-discipline and close adherence to the age-graded demands of childhood. They abhor physical violence and prefer reason and diplomatic maneuver. They surround their children with books and toys that are selected for their educational value. They budget the time of their offspring, and fill their days with participation in the Boy Scouts, Junior Achievement, and music or tennis lessons. Finally, they teach their children that love from and acceptance by parents and

teachers are earned by disciplined effort and achievement. Neither comes automatically. Rather, the child must show that he deserves them.

By comparison, lower-class parents are easygoing and permissive. Their children receive less training in self-discipline and are granted greater latitude with respect to the use of their time. They have much less contact with books and highly structured recreational and educational activities. Instead, much earlier in life they are thrown into the company of their peers where they are freer to play in the streets or to get into trouble. Fighting as a method of settling problems is more acceptable, and the love of parents is less dependent upon achievement and self-discipline. In short, lower-class children are handicapped in terms of their ability to compete because they are still socialized in ways that reflect the lower-class traditions of centuries past—communal living, earlier induction into adult activities, and immediate rather than deferred gratification.

3. Decreased ability to compete produces strain. Despite the vast differences in the way they are socialized, lower-class children both expect, and are expected, to compete with middle-class children when they enter school. Indeed, the school is a mirror reflection of the larger society: its goals are avowedly democratic, and it idealizes the development of each child's potential. Yet, throughout history, the school has been a middle-class institution that is designed to foster and reward middle-class character, skills, and manners. Hence, because the lower-class child lacks these skills and manners, it is he who is found most wanting.

Like everyone else he wants status and acceptance, but the techniques he has learned for acquiring it are not those of the middle class: his boisterous behavior destroys the order and routine of the classroom; he does not read well; he has little experience in being studious, docile, and obedient; and he lacks interest in intellectual matters. In short, he is placed in an arena in which he must compete for status against all others, but for which his prior training is inappropriate. More than others, therefore, he is programmed to fail.

This programming carries over to other middle-class institutions as well—youth centers, church groups, or settlement houses. Although the people who run such places often have special regard for the "rough" boys of the slums, they are still drawn to the occasionally polite, personable, and mannerly child. The reason is that, like teachers, they feel compelled to sponsor and to reward desirable (middle-class), not disruptive (lower-class), behavior.

Hence, in these settings, as well as in the school, lower-class boys find themselves at the bottom of the status ladder, not only among adults but among their peers. Even worse, this loss of social status is accompanied by a growing sense of personal failure—a feeling that would not be a problem if lower-class boys did not believe in the legitimacy of middle-class goals. But having adopted the middle-class measuring rod for judging themselves, they share the view that they are failures. Falling short of their own expectations, their sense of self-worth is lowered, and they experience a growing sense of frustration and ambivalence. As Cohen puts it, they face a serious problem of adjustment and are in the market for a solution. How shall their sense of strain be resolved?

4.   Increased strain produces delinquent subculture.   Cohen argues that most people adjust to strain by joining with others to seek a solution, not by going it alone or by becoming psychologically unstable. Hence, one of three possible role adjustments is likely: the corner boy; the college boy; or the delinquent boy.

a.   The corner boy.   First, most lower-class boys are likely to deal with their sense of frustration and failure by accepting their lower-class status, disengaging themselves

psychologically from competition, and withdrawing into a sheltering community of like-minded peers—the "corner boy" society of the lower class. By so doing, they avoid rupturing their ties with parents and neighbors and incurring intense hostility from middle-class persons. They may have a few minor scrapes with the law, but, in the main, they will acquire a limited education, a blue collar job, and a family, and will eventually become stable members of working-class society. To the degree that they still aspire to the American Dream, they will be saddled with a chronic load of frustration, but at least they will have the satisfaction of living in a world with which they are familiar and in which they are not continually confronted with failure.

b.   The college boy.   The second alternative involves the relatively few boys who rupture their ties with the corner boy society and accept the challenge of the middle-class status system. This solution, the "college boy" alternative, entails considerable sacrifice on their parts, requiring the acquisition of unfamiliar linguistic, academic, and social skills. But, by hard work and deferred gratification, they can be among the few lower-class boys who go on to college and who play the game of life according to middle-class rules.

c.   The delinquent boy.   The third alternative involves the delinquent boy, who turns to the standards of the delinquent subculture for a solution. According to Cohen, the delinquent subculture is *nonutilitarian, malicious,* and *negativistic.* Ordinarily, he says, people steal things because they can use them, buy something with them, or wear them. But the delinquent acts of lower-class boys usually do not appear to have a useful purpose. Instead, they steal things "for the hell of it"—clothes they do not wear, food they do not eat, or articles they do not use. They delight in terrorizing "good" kids or older people. They vandalize, even destroy, their own schools. They dump garbage on their neighbors' doorsteps, deface public buildings, or defecate on their teachers' desks.

Such behavior makes no sense to middle-class people, but it is precisely for this reason that it makes sense to those who feel rejected by others and who view themselves as failures. Hence, says Cohen, "The hallmark of the delinquent subculture is the explicit and wholesale repudiation of middle-class standards and the adoption of their very antithesis" (p. 129). Its appeal lies in the fact it does not temporize with middle-class values. An ordinary lower-class boy skips school because it is dull and unrewarding, but a member of the delinquent subculture does so because "good" boys are not supposed to play truant. A corner boy steals some hubcaps to dress up his car, but a member of the delinquent subculture merely destroys them because he disdains the middle-class love of property.

In short, the delinquent subculture is appealing to lower-class boys because it rejects everything valued by the middle class and compensates for the humiliation that middle-class institutions cause them. It serves a valuable personal function because it helps delinquents to deal psychologically with the shame and degradation that they have experienced in middle-class settings.

Cohen implies that delinquents are boys who, perhaps more than the majority, continue to prize middle-class goals. Thus, the only way they can handle their own sense of failure is to deny middle-class values completely. Their behavior is a collective expression of reaction-formation: an exaggerated, disproportionate, abnormal reaction against repressed desires that continue to press for attention. Only by "irrational," "malicious," "unaccountable" hostility to these middle-class desires can delinquents remain free of their seductive blandishments.

Cohen says that membership in the delinquent subculture is not the only road to delinquency, but, given the problems that

lower-class boys face and the group support that delinquency provides, it is the most likely road. Lone individuals could not handle the personal and social tensions inherent in rejecting the moral imperatives of society. But the delinquent subculture compensates for these problems: it provides the support of like-minded peers; it grants status for nonconformity to middle-class standards; and it sets the successful delinquent on a higher pedestal than the ordinary corner boy or the upward-bound college boy. In short, it becomes a sort of substitute society for the delinquent, providing an alternative for the middle-class dominated society in which he has failed.

5. Delinquent subculture produces delinquent behavior. Since the hallmark of the delinquent subculture is the wholesale repudiation of middle-class standards, the delinquent behavior of its members will reflect this spirit. Delinquent boys are resistant to the efforts of home, school, or community to regulate their behavior. They are impulsive and impatient, seeking fun without regard to long-range gains or costs. Their delinquent acts are not well planned nor highly specialized. They may steal anything from tomatoes to cars; they may disobey parents and defy teachers; they may vandalize graveyards, public buildings, or churches; or they may attack their conventional peers or outsiders who invade their turf. In short, the delinquent subculture is a *contraculture;* that is, a way of life opposed to everything conventional. As an alternative means of avoiding failure, achieving recognition, and acquiring status, it rewards almost any behavior that attacks the morality of the middle class.

Cohen says that the circumstances are obscure which lead some boys to choose a delinquent adjustment and others to choose a corner boy or college boy adjustment. Nonetheless, when the delinquent adjustment is chosen, boys respond in a collective, but irrational and malicious, way to the society that has humiliated them and denied them status. This humiliation, then, provides the motive for delinquent behavior, while the delinquent subculture provides the means for translating that motive into action and for granting status to those who act on it.

CLOWARD AND OHLIN: DELINQUENCY AND OPPORTUNITY

Cloward and Ohlin's version of strain theory (1960) possesses some of the same features as Cohen's. Like Cohen, they assume that delinquent subcultures and gangs "are typically found among adolescent males in lower-class areas of large urban centers" (p. 1). Hence, their goal is to explain how these subcultures arise and persist. They also assume the premise that virtue promotes vice; that is, that the desire to get ahead promotes delinquent behavior.

But beyond these similarities, their theory possesses some distinctive features of its own. While Cohen's delinquents are irrational and malicious—the opposite of everything middle class—Cloward and Ohlin's law violators are rational and utilitarian. When legitimate channels for success are closed to them, they simply turn to illegitimate ones, if at all possible. But conventional goals, if not conventional means, continue to guide them.

Consider the propositions that carry this theme.

1. The success ethic is a prized possession of all Americans. Cohen suggests that middle-class values have only established a recent and somewhat tenuous foothold in the lower class. Cloward and Ohlin go much further. To them, the success ethic in our democratic society is so widely shared that it scarcely deserves to be called "middle class." America has been the Promised Land to all its people; everyone wants to get ahead. In fact, lower-class people feel a relatively greater need for upward mobility than persons already

higher in the social structure. Because their problems are greater, the pressures to escape them are impelling.

2. Opportunities for success are not equally distributed throughout the class structure. No less than Cohen, Cloward and Ohlin indicate that education is an indispensable tool for upward mobility. They also suggest that the early socialization of lower-class children may inhibit their capacity to do well in school. But, to them, this is not the most serious problem. Educational achievement is not just a matter of a favorable attitude or the ability of the child to sit still in school and to put off immediate needs. The more serious problems are "structural"—the result of the American class system. Many lower-class families simply cannot afford to keep their children in school, particularly beyond high school. This is the major reason so many lower-class children drop out—not because they devalue education, but because they and their parents cannot afford it. If and when lower-class children scale down their educational expectations, therefore, it is not because they want to—they know full well that education is vitally important. It is because they must. For them, opportunities to climb upward are blocked.

3. Blocked opportunities produce strain. A serious condition of strain is produced when a society submits some of its people to confusing, conflicted, and impossible demands. When it stresses the importance of achieving certain goals, but denies the legitimate means by which to realize those goals, discontent can be expected:

> The disparity between what lower-class youth are led to want and what is actually available to them is the source of a major problem of adjustment. . . . Faced with limitations on legitimate avenues of access to conventional goals and unable to revise their aspirations downward, they experience intense frustrations (p. 86).

However, unlike Cohen's, Cloward and Ohlin's boys do not see themselves as failures. It is the system that is the failure. Consequently, the strain they feel is not due to a lowered sense of self-esteem but to a sense of injustice.

4. Strain produces delinquent subcultures. When people feel that existing norms are unjust, they are likely to withdraw support from them and to search for alternatives. Indeed, Cohen suggested that when delinquents do this they not only reject the norms governing access to major goals, they also reject the goals themselves. That is why, according to Cohen, delinquent subculture is so malicious and negativistic—it rejects *everything* middle class.

Cloward and Ohlin advance a much different thesis. As they see it, the American Dream rarely loses its hold on lower-class boys. Hence, when they are frustrated by limited access to legitimate means, they merely turn to ones that are illegitimate. They do not give up easily. Yet, even in this endeavor, they often fail. Whether their dream ever comes true depends upon the way their slum communities are organized.

a. The criminal subculture. Some slum neighborhoods provide opportunities for success through criminal means. There are close ties between adults and children, and the adults transmit traditions that are criminal and career-oriented. In other words, a *criminal* subculture exists which provides illegitimate, if not legitimate, means for success. Thus, while middle-class youngsters are learning to be bankers, lawyers, or businessmen, lower class youngsters may be learning to be professional burglars, numbers runners, bookies, or professional fences. Furthermore, they learn the importance of building strong political ties and hiring the best lawyers, so they can avoid prosecution and conviction. Thus, in neighborhoods where criminal subcultures are found, delinquent behavior is rational and utilitarian, not the opposite as Cohen

suggested. Indeed, where adults and youngsters are linked in criminal activities, the wild, untrammeled delinquent gang is frowned upon because it interferes with business by bringing the attention of the police to the neighborhood.

b. The conflict subculture. As a consequence, the closest thing to Cohen's subculture, according to Cloward and Ohlin, occurs in totally disorganized neighborhoods like those described by Shaw and McKay. In these neighborhoods, young people can find neither legitimate *nor* illegitimate means. They are deprived of both kinds of opportunity. To be sure, there are criminals in these neighborhoods, but they tend to be the unorganized, petty, poorly paid members of the criminal world, not the sophisticated, well-organized members found in neighborhoods where a criminal subculture exists. The result, for juveniles, is a second form of delinquent subculture—a *conflict* subculture characterized by malicious and violent activities that symbolize protest against the meaninglessness of the social experience. This is where one will find the aggressive fighting gangs that people so often associate with lower-class delinquency. Actually, however, their behavior is a way of calling attention to the futility of a life in which opportunity is lacking.

c. The retreatist subculture. Disorganized neighborhoods also produce a third delinquent subculture—a *retreatist* subculture. This is made up of juveniles who have given up on the struggle for success and have turned to drugs. They are double failures, individuals who have failed in the use of both legitimate and illegitimate means. But rather than blaming society, they blame themselves, retreat from the struggle, and seek solace in escape. It is a mistake, however, to view drug users as total isolates. Even in drug use, where kicks become the purpose for existence, one needs other people to learn how to use drugs, to gain access to a steady supply, and to obtain group support for denying the validity of conventional behavior. In other words, drug use, no less than other forms of delinquent behavior, is subcultural behavior.

In summary, all three modes of adaption—criminal, conflict, and retreatist—are symbolic of blocked opportunities, not the repudiation of fundamental societal goals. In each case, illegitimate activity and subcultural standards develop as alternative means for the satisfactions which all people seek.

5. *Delinquent subcultures produce delinquent behavior.* In describing three kinds of delinquent subculture, Cloward and Ohlin have suggested that such subcultures are specialized. For that reason, they imply that we should guard against the tendency to see all delinquent behavior as representing responses to subcultural requirements. For example, drinking, truancy, destroying property, petty theft, or disorderly conduct are all delinquent acts. Yet, say Cloward and Ohlin: "We would not necessarily describe as delinquent a group that tolerated or practiced these behaviors *unless they were the central activities around which the group was organized*" (p. 7, emphasis added).

This is the key distinguishing factor: Delinquent norms and activities must have a relatively narrow focus before they can be considered subcultures. For example, the members of a *criminal* subculture are rational and commit delinquent acts for material gain and social status. To them, the fighting of conflict gangs or the drug use of retreatist groups might not even be tolerated. By contrast, the members of a retreatist subculture are preoccupied only with the next fix and the means by which it can be obtained. Using delinquent means to get ahead is of little concern to them. Hence, *"a delinquent subculture is one in which certain forms of delinquent activity are essential requirements for the performance of the dominant roles supported by the subculture"* (p. 7).

This emphasis is a crucial one because it is at odds with other subculture theories. According to Cloward and Ohlin's definition, the delinquent acts of middle-class groups could not be considered to be expressive of delinquent subculture unless they are the central concerns of these groups. If their major concerns are with school, dating, and going to college, then their delinquent behavior is incidental to other concerns and does not deserve to be called subcultural delinquency. Likewise, even the Shaw-McKay theory or Cohen's definition of lower-class delinquent subculture would be too broad for Cloward and Ohlin. To them, delinquent subcultures and the acts they endorse are relatively narrow and specialized. This is why the only really serious delinquency arises in the lower class, since it is only in lower-class communities that tightly knit, narrowly focused subcultures exist.

IMPLICATIONS AND IMPACT ON SOCIAL POLICY[1]

The idea that delinquency is a failure of American society was enough to assure the popularity of strain theory. But, as luck would have it, the Cloward-Ohlin version in particular was destined to become a rationale for some of society's most ambitious attempts at social engineering. The reason is that it is a prime example of a case in which a new theory gives expression to long-standing and widely shared beliefs. It is quintessentially American; it is a better reflection of American culture than apple pie.

> A half century of international sociology had produced a set of propositions not far from Father Flanagan's assertion that "there is no such thing as a bad boy." Cloward and Ohlin argued that delinquents were resorting to

---

[1] This discussion of implications is drawn from three major sources: Daniel P. Moynihan (1969), Peter Marris and Martin Rein (1973), and James F. Short, Jr. (1975).

desperately deviant and dangerous measures in order to *conform* to the routine goals of the larger society. If that society wished them to conform not only in their objectives but in their means for achieving them, it had only to provide the *opportunity* to do so. Opportunity was the master concept. *And what else was America all about?* (Moynihan, 1969:51, emphasis added in last sentence).

The processes by which earlier generations of immigrants were assimilated into the mainstream of American life had now broken down, and the remedy must lie in the reopening of opportunity.

Mobilization for youth

Cloward and Ohlin did not stand aloof from the implications of their theory. Instead, they set about seeing its principles translated into programs for lower-class boys. While writing their book on delinquency, they worked with the Henry Street Settlement on the Lower East Side in New York to draw up a large action research program which would utilize its ideas. To be called Mobilization for Youth, this program was outlined in a 617-page volume entitled *A Proposal for the Prevention and Control of Delinquency by Expanding Opportunities*. Among other things, Mobilization for Youth was designed to accomplish the following objectives:

To improve education: Improve teacher training and curriculum, provide preschool programs for young children, and improve other educational service.

To create work opportunities: Organize an Urban Youth Service Corps, a Youth Jobs Center, and better vocational training.

To organize the lower-class community: Take steps to reach and organize unaffiliated persons, organize neighborhood councils, and establish the Lower East Side Neighborhood Association.

To provide specialized services to adolescent groups: Initiate a detached worker program for gangs, an Adventure Corps, and a Coffee Shop Hangout.

To provide specialized services to individuals and their families: Organize Neighborhood Service Centers that would provide counseling, assistance to families, and other services of this type.

This ambitious endeavor was not conceived solely as a service program. It was to be a social experiment, carefully conceived and systematically evaluated. Indeed, says Moynihan, the proposal "is one of the more remarkable documents in the history of efforts to bring about 'scientific' social change: lucid, informed, precise, scholarly, and, above all, candid" (1969:51).

A major problem with the proposal, however, was its price tag of several million dollars. But the early 1960s was a time of opportunity for scholars as well as for delinquents. A new president, John Kennedy, had just been elected. His campaign slogan had been "The New Frontier." Change was in the wind and new ideas were being sought. And, since Cloward and Ohlin's ideas were better formulated than most, they soon came to the attention of the new administration.

The Kennedy family had a long-standing interest in the problems of youth. Soon after the president was inaugurated, therefore, efforts were made to develop a new federal initiative against delinquency. A high-powered committee entitled the President's Committee on Juvenile Delinquency and Youth Crime was created by executive order on May 11, 1961. Its chairman was Robert Kennedy, the president's brother and the new attorney general. Other committee members included Abraham Ribicoff, the secretary of health, education, and welfare; and Arthur Goldberg, the secretary of labor. David Hackett, a friend and close associate of Robert Kennedy's, was named as executive director for the committee.

Hackett sought to inform himself on the latest thinking on delinquency and was introduced to strain theory and the philosophy of Mobilization for Youth by officers of the Ford Foundation, for whom both Cloward and Ohlin were consultants. Their innovative and stimulating ideas, along with those of Albert Cohen, appealed to the spirit of the New Frontier, and Hackett was soon persuaded that the President's Committee should be pushing opportunities for lower-class youth. Hence, he invited Ohlin to help him develop the federal program.

Accepting Ohlin's notion that delinquency reduction required large-scale effort, the President's Committee stressed the need to bring all possible resources to bear upon the delinquency problem. Therefore, one of its first efforts was to promote the coordination of several federal departments and agencies relating to delinquency. Hopefully, they would cooperate with each other and encourage the same process at state, local, and private levels. New delinquency legislation was also written and passed. The preamble to this legislation bore the unmistakable stamp of strain theory:

> Delinquency and youth offenses occur disproportionately among school dropouts, unemployed youth faced with limited opportunities and with employment barriers, and youth in deprived family situations. . . . Prevention and contol of such delinquency and and youth offenses require intensive and coordinated efforts on the part of private and governmental interests (Marris and Rein, 1973:22).

The new legislation authorized the expenditure of $10 million a year for three years. The key concepts in the disbursement of this money were *opportunity, coordination,* and *community action.* Communities throughout the nation were invited to submit proposals, but they had to indicate how they would mount an interdisciplinary, broadly based attack on delinquency in which the goal was institutional, not personality, change. The federal government would provide planning and seed money, but communities must commit local resources and indicate how those resources would be reallocated in an effective manner. Furthermore, they had to involve members of the target population—poor people themselves—in the planning process, and they had to use research to evaluate their efforts.

Because Mobilization for Youth had served as the blueprint for the entire effort, it only made sense that it should be among the first programs funded. Indeed,

> a singular consortium consisting of the Ford Foundation, the city of New York, and the federal government was put together to provide a three-year $12.5 million grant. In round terms, Ford put up 15 percent, the city of New York 30 percent, and the rest came from Washington (Moynihan, 1969:58).

This was the New Frontier at its best. Hence, the launching of Mobilization for Youth was accomplished with great fanfare.

> The program was launched in a sunny ceremony in the White House garden on May 31, 1962. . . . The Democratic Party, the Chief Executive of the nation, and the mayor of its largest city were sponsoring the project. "New York's program," the President declared, "is the best in the country at this time and is the furthest along." He thanked the members of Congress who had worked on this problem of juvenile delinquency, which, he added, "is really perhaps not the most descriptive phrase; it's really a question of young people and their opportunity" (Moynihan, 1969:58–59).

The war on poverty

Mobilization for Youth and the President's Committee had scarcely gotten under way when opportunity theory became the rationale for social intervention on even a grander scale. A nationwide War on Poverty was declared. In October 1963, the President's Council of Economic Advisers asked David Hackett to submit a proposal for a series of community programs, something like Mobilization for Youth, which would cost $500 million in the first year of operation.

But then President Kennedy, who was ultimately responsible for this innovation, did not live to see it fulfilled, when on a political trip to Dallas, he was assassinated.

The shock and mourning that engulfed the nation might have spelled the end of the War on Poverty, but the new President, Lyndon Johnson, not only decided to go ahead with it, but also to expand it. Furthermore, in order to see it carried out, he turned to the senior staff members who had run the President's Committee on Juvenile Delinquency and Youth Crime and placed them in charge of the War on Poverty. They simply took many of the ideas originally outlined in the Mobilization for Youth proposal and transferred them to the new agency. The staff also retained the notion of scientific planning and urged that local communities prepare carefully for the new experiment.

As any protracted war would require, the War on Poverty was to be fought in stages, as communities gained knowledge, trained their troops, and gradually improved their skills. But President Johnson was impatient, and tended to eschew a protracted approach. Hence, as Commander in Chief, his orders were carried out: an all-out attack was made (Piven and Cloward, 1971).

Space precludes a detailed analysis of what happened to the War on Poverty and its precursors, Mobilization for Youth (MFY) and the President's Committee. Suffice it to say that between 1965 and 1970, billions of dollars were spent in an endeavor to assimilate the poor into the opportunity structure of American society and, thereby, to reduce delinquency and its attendant problems. What, then, were the results?

Those who have chronicled the history of this effort have concluded that, at best, it had mixed results and, at worst, it was a failure.

Even before the poverty program got underway in 1964, Mobilization for Youth was described by the *New York Daily News* as an organization that was infested with "Commies and Commie sympathizers." Some of its staff members were also accused of misappropriating funds (Moynihan, 1969: chap. 6). Actually, these accusations were levied more because MFY had become involved in a political struggle with city hall than because there was much substance to them. Hence, some important forces rallied to the defense of MFY and calm was restored. Nonetheless, the damage was done. "The logic of scientific problem solving collapsed in piecemeal pragmatism" (Marris and Rein, 1973:214). Despite its auspicious launching, MFY slowly sank in a sea of conflict.

The President's Committee also withered away. From the beginning, it encountered resistance from established old-line departments in the federal bureaucracy. Then, influential members of Congress made it clear that the mandate of the President's Committee was to reduce delinquency, not to reform urban society or to try out sociological theories on American youths. Finally, interest in the committee simply shriveled as interest was transferred to the grander strategy of the War on Poverty.

The War on Poverty, meanwhile, initiated numerous new programs, among them Head Start, the Job Corps, Vista, and Neighborhood Legal Services, but the heart of its effort was the Community Action Program (CAP). Modeled after MFY, it was designed to establish in every local community an organization in which the poor would join with members of the establishment in planning and operating the poverty program. It was this feature of the federal effort, however, that encountered the greatest difficulty.

Moynihan (1969) argues that CAP did much harm to the true interests of the poor because it was based on unproven theory, was poorly conceived and poorly run, and, most of all, because it resulted in a dogma about the evils of powerlessness and a strategy for stirring up trouble. As did Mobilization for Youth, CAP enjoined the poor to engage in rent strikes, organize social protests, and attack the political and welfare establishments.

The obvious goal was to let political leaders know that the poor were an increasingly organized constituency to which they would have to respond with jobs, better housing, improved education, and extended social services. But the organized protests apparently had the opposite effect than was intended. Both Congress and local politicians withdrew support from the War on Poverty, as well as from Mobilization for Youth.

Given the dismal conditions under which the poor were living, these actions were certainly questionable. Unfortunately, however, they were given credence by other segments of the poverty program that were even more ill-advised and naive. For example, a younger brother of CAP was Youth Organizations United, (YOU), an enterprise made up of streetwise gang members (Poston, 1971).

Based upon the romantic myth that these members of delinquent gangs could transform the ghetto—from a place of misery, crime, and poverty to a place of enterprise, safety, and economic well-being—many of the nation's newspapers, TV networks, and fashionable leaders threw their support behind YOU. They editorialized, idolized, and otherwise supported the notion that these uneducated, unskilled, even depredatory, youths could lead the way in changing the slums of America. It was too much.

Not only were members of YOU feared and disliked by the law-abiding and hard-working members of their own neighborhoods, but also their actions helped to legitimize the withdrawal of much-needed political support for other, more desirable, segments of the War on Poverty. As a result, says Moynihan ". . . an immense opportunity to institute more or less permanent social changes—a fixed full employment program [and] a measure of income maintenance—was lost while energies were expended in ways that very probably hastened the end of the brief period when such options were open" (p. 193). In other words, the wrong tactics were used. Efforts should have been concentrated on using practical political means to provide economic resources for the poor rather than trying to force them by outright attack.

In some ways, Marris and Rein (1973) agree. They point out that neither sociologists nor the poor have political constituencies. Moreover, "when intellectuals take over policy, they lack the professional politicians' sense of the constituency for reform and are likely to attempt the impossible. They not only spoil the opportunity for practical interventions, but raise expectations [among the poor] which cannot be met" (p. 244). At the same time, say Marris and Rein there is real question regarding the extent to which there was ever full political support, even among the Kennedys, for the kinds of radical social changes that the philosophy of strain theory implied (pp. 244–46). One does not easily alter the basic structure of society—economically, politically, and socially—without incurring great opposition.

Despite these problems, some useful fallout resulted from the War on Poverty. Perhaps the most significant was the formation and training of a strong cadre of minority leadership in the CAP program. Far more than ever before, blacks, Mexican-Americans, and Puerto Ricans took up places in the structure of American political life and have since organized their constituencies into potent political forces. Thus, "if [their] rights can be secured and applied at every level of government to a more open process of arbitrating the allocation of resources, then the experiment of community action may be vindicated after all" (Marris and Rein, 1973:296). Furthermore, preschool programs initiated by Mobilization for Youth and Head Start have become more or less permanent fixtures in our educational system, as have medicaid or Neighborhood Legal Services for the poor. These types of programs are central to any effort to achieve equality of opportunity and, therefore, may contribute to the goals that the War on Poverty sought.

To those of a more radical persuasion, such results are far too little and come far too late. Indeed, as we will see in the chapter on radical theory, some writers believe that the philosophy of MFY and the War on Poverty was far too conservative, little more than a sop to the oppressed masses. Such programs were destined to fail because they did not really mount an attack on American capitalism and the class structure if perpetuates; these are at the root of all our troubles, and delinquency will never be eliminated until they are eliminated. Indeed, the real criminals are not those who protest oppression, but the capitalist exploiters who perpetuate it.

SCIENTIFIC ADEQUACY OF STRAIN THEORY

Given the questionable success of MFY and the War on Poverty, an examination of the scientific adequacy of strain theory becomes all the more important, because of the deterministic picture it paints of lower-class youth. While the boys in the Shaw-McKay groups had a great deal of fun running the streets, dumping over garbage cans, and stealing from the neighborhood grocery, those described by Cohen and by Cloward and Ohlin "are driven by grim economic and psychic necessity into rebellion" (Bordua, 1961:136). Delinquency is no fun for them. They are

virtually forced to use desperate measures, either to overcome a gnawing sense of inadequacy or to open up new avenues to success. But is this construction of delinquents an accurate one?

The answer to that question requires attention to three issues: (1) the idea that serious delinquency is limited largely to lower-class youth; (2) the complex series of events that are supposed to produce delinquent behavior—internalization of the American Dream, failure in school, a sense of strain, and the discovery of a solution in one or more delinquent subcultures; and (3) the failure of strain theory to address female delinquency.

The class foundation

The assumption that serious delinquency is primarily a lower-class phenomenon probably requires modification. On the one hand, all accounts of delinquent behavior indicate that conventional crime and its victims are concentrated most heavily in the poorer segments of society. Furthermore, there are chronic offenders in those segments whose serious and repeated crimes do require explanation, as strain theory suggests.

On the other hand, those same accounts indicate that illegal conduct is prevalent throughout the class structure, and that chronic offenders, perhaps smaller in number, exist on all levels. Indeed, as Clelland and Carter (1980) point out, we must find new ways for thinking about the relation of socioeconomic status to crime. First, it is a gross oversimplification to divide our complex status system into only two strata—lower and middle—and then to assume that juvenile behavior is largely explainable in those terms. Second, several studies have suggested that delinquency may be more strongly related to children's relationships with their parents, or their progress in school, than to class membership (Aultman and Wellford,

1976; Empey and Lubeck, 1971; Hindelang, 1973, Hirschi, 1969).

In short, while the proponents of strain theory are correct in suggesting that a focus upon male gangs in the poorest segments of society is crucial, the subcultures and behaviors of those gangs are not the only subjects that require explanation. Furthermore, other factors may be more predictive of delinquent behavior than is class membership.

The theoretical chain

Consistent with this conclusion, the theoretical chain postulated by strain theory itself suggests that class membership should be only slightly related to delinquent conduct, since it is but the first of a long series of events leading to that conduct—from class membership, to high aspirations, to failure in school, to a sense of strain, to membership in a delinquent gang, to the commission of delinquent acts. Causal inference, in other words, suggests that, as we move down the causal chain, each subsequent variable should have a higher direct relationship to delinquency than the variable(s) that preceded it (Blalock, 1964). Furthermore, while each variable is necessary, it is not sufficient, by itself, to explain delinquency. What, then, does research reveal about these other variables?

1.   The American Dream.   There is considerable evidence that, on a superficial level at least, the American Dream is widely shared, as strain theory indicates. Research studies suggest that lower-class children, male and female, are more likely to internalize the conventional desires for money, recognition, and status than to adopt a set of values somehow unique to the lower-class. Likewise, they are aware that the legitimate steps for realizing these goals involve education and a place in the labor force (Empey, 1956; Gold, 1963; Gordon et al., 1963; Gould, 1941; Kobrin, 1951).

What research has not documented, however, is the degree of sophistication which lower-class boys, in particular, possess in their awareness of these values and means.

Strain theory, particularly the Cloward-Ohlin version, implies that they are highly sophisticated—that they recognize that long years of schooling will be required for success, that immediate gratifications will have to be deferred in the interest of completing college as well as high school, and that hard work will be entailed before they are able to marry, buy a house in the suburbs, and acquire both a station wagon and a Porsche. But has their socialization been that complete?

If Cohen is correct, it has not. Lower-class boys have received little schooling in the methods of middle-class success, little exposure to books about science, social studies, or the arts, and little training in deferring immediate impulses or budgeting their time. Moreover, there are many ghetto boys in Los Angeles who have never been inside the Museum of Science and Industry, many in New York who know nothing about Wall Street, many in Chicago who have never seen the University of Chicago campus, though it resides in their neighborhood.

Hence, when suggestions are made that these boys are delinquent because they are fully aware of the disparity between their lofty aspirations and their chances for success, questions must be raised. Should such an awareness be lacking, then other reasons for difficulties in school, for feelings of alienation, and, eventually, for delinquent conduct must be explored. Indeed, that is why, as the following sections indicate, criminologists are divided over this issue.

2.   School failure and blocked opportunities.   Research findings do confirm that school performance is highly related to delinquent behavior. Study after study indicate that those who do the worst, or who most strongly believe that their chances for graduating are low, are the most likely to be delinquent (Elliott and Voss, 1974; Empey and Lubeck, 1971; Hirschi; 1969; Polk and Halferty, 1966; Polk and Schafer, 1972; Rankin, 1980; Stinchcombe, 1964).

After having documented this side of strain theory, however, research also raises more questions about it. First, research indicates that higher rates of delinquency are associated with school failure on all class levels, not just on the lower-class level (Empey and Lubeck, 1971; Hirschi, 1969; Rankin, 1980; Stinchcombe, 1964). Second, failure in school is associated with the delinquency of girls as well as of boys (Elliott and Voss, 1974; Rankin, 1980). Third, Bordua admonishes us to consider the possibility that failure in school may sometimes be the *result* of delinquent behavior, not always the cause of it. Boys who use the school as a battleground, he says, or who treat its property as "arts and crafts material do not meet the criteria for advancement" (1961:134). In short, while programs in school are important, as strain theory suggests, they are not only due to a lack of economic resources or to class discrimination.

3. Strain. Strain theorists suggest that the concept of strain is a condition of psychological dissonance which is a necessary bridge between failing in school and joining a delinquent group. In order to determine whether this is true, several questions must be answered.

The first asks whether failure in the middle-class institution of the school produces a sense of frustration and inadequacy. There is limited evidence that such is the case. Among middle- as well as lower-class students, school failure seems to result in a loss of self-esteem and the belief that one's occupational chances are lowered (Empey and Lubeck, 1971:50). Furthermore students who report that they are unlikely to finish high school, or to go to college, are more likely to be delinquent (Cernkovich and Giordano, 1979; Datesman et al., 1975; Rankin, 1980).

Relative to such findings, however, Stinchcombe (1964) argues that it is middle-class, not lower-class, children who are the more rebellious and troublesome because of frustration over failure in school. Since they are more fully socialized relative to its long-range importance, an inability to achieve not only represents a threat to their upward mobility but actually confronts them with a loss of social status and respect. Of all children, therefore, they experience the greatest pressures to succeed or, failing that, to seek out alternative, delinquent means.

Such contentions notwithstanding, one cannot really pinpoint the dimensions of strain, or among whom it is the greatest, because criminologists rarely attempt to document its existence in psychological terms—they simply assume its presence. For example, when students report that their chances of graduating from school are poor, investigators assume that they must feel badly because they have not lived up to the standards of the middle-class measuring rod. They further assume that this failure produces a gnawing sense of inadequacy which leads to rebelliousness and delinquency. But because psychological measures of strain are rarely used, we do not really know whether these assumptions are true.

For that reason, findings by Hirschi (1969), Johnson (1979:105–08), and Rankin (1980) are all the more provocative. They found that high aspirations among juveniles, lower- or middle-class, are associated with *low* rates of delinquent behavior, not the reverse. Delinquents, in other words, are not highly ambitious. How, then, could it be said that their misbehavior is due to a sense of failure, in middle-class terms, and to frustrated occupational ambitions? Hirschi's answer is straightforward: *"Frustrated occupational ambitions . . . cannot be an important cause of delinquency"* (1969:182–83, emphasis added). Delinquents must be marching to the beat of a different drummer; strain, if it does exist in them, must not be due to the frustration of lofty aspirations (Johnson, 1979:108).

Along a different dimension, Cernkovich and Giordano (1979) indicate that racial differences may exist for which strain theory has failed to account. Contrary to the suggestion that blacks should experience greater frustration over blocked opportunities than whites and thus should be more delinquent, they found the opposite: blocked opportunities were more strongly associated with the delinquent behavior of whites than of blacks. They speculate, that such findings may be due to a tendency for blacks to develop an attitude of resignation regarding future occupational goals. Given the racial and economic discrimination they have experienced, they may be less inclined than whites to judge themselves by the middle-class measuring rod. Once again, however, these investigators did not attempt to measure strain in psychological terms. Hence, we cannot know if their speculations are accurate. Furthermore, we cannot afford to ignore the possibility that those who do poorly in school are, in fact, inclined to have a poor image of themselves.

Given this possibility, some investigators have provided an alternative explanation for the source of strain. They maintain that it is due not to the frustration of long-range goals, but to the pressures and tensions generated by the school itself (Elliott and Voss, 1974; Frease, 1973; Polk and Schafer, 1972):

> The curriculum and status reward systems of high schools are chiefly oriented toward producing students who will attend college. The teachers unwittingly instill their educational values in students by encouraging the development of college-oriented personalities and rewarding the proper "orderly" and "cooperative" behavior (Rankin, 1980:423 on Frease, 1973).

For those students lacking long-range educational aspirations, therefore, the school becomes a setting for boredom and even degradation. In turn, their negative feelings lead to rebellion and truancy—acts that, in legal terms, are technically delinquent. According to this explanation, however, strain is created not by frustration of deeply held conventional goals, but by the interaction of students who *lack* such goals with teachers and principals who think they ought to have them.

Relative to this conclusion, some studies have suggested that student achievement depends more on the child's family than on the school (Coleman, 1966). Students who fail are those who have been poorly socialized or prepared for achievement by their parents. Moreover, Hirschi (1969) contends that the problems of these students stem not only from being lower class or failing to please teachers. Instead, they are lower- or middle-class people whose *commitments* to legitimate means for success— long-range plans, hard work, and deferred gratification—are minimal. And so, Hirschi would turn strain theory upside down.

It is not that failing and delinquent students do not want money, material goods, and personal pleasures. Indeed, they want them. But rather than experiencing strain because the avenues to these desirable goals are blocked, they get into trouble because they are not willing to use legitimate means to achieve them. Consequently, if they experience strain, it is produced not by the frustration of long-range plans, but by an unwillingness to pay the conventional price for autonomy and privilege.

Although the issues raised by these alternative views cannot be resolved with certainty, they do question the concept of strain as projected by strain theory. At least three possibilities might be considered.

First, if strain were carefully measured and documented, it could be due to the frustration of lofty, but blocked, ambitions, as strain theory indicates. But should that be the case, it may also be present among middle- as well as lower-class juveniles.

Second, it is possible that strain and deviant behavior are due more to the degradation and loss of status within the youthful arena of the school itself than to the frustration of long-range goals. After all, juveniles may not be the highly utilitarian and goal-oriented individuals that Cloward and Ohlin project, particularly those whose fathers and mothers are poorly educated, unemployed, and unable to provide much insight into the nature of success in a highly technological society. In fact, some studies suggest that lower-class juveniles may not view the use of time, the future, and the need to defer gratification in middle-class terms (Davis, 1946; Horton, 1967).

Third, if delinquents are people who have not been socialized concerning the importance of committing themselves to legitimate means for success, and who do not judge themselves by the middle-class measuring rod, then strain may be of little help in explaining their delinquent behavior. Law violators would then simply be viewed as young people who feel that ordinary rules do not apply to them and who couldn't care less that they do not fit the conventional mold.

4. Delinquent subculture. These puzzling conclusions are also relevant to the concept of delinquent subculture, since strain theory postulates that it is the means by which shared feelings of strain are resolved. Furthermore, they are made all the more puzzling by the fact that we have seen repeatedly that delinquent behavior tends to be a group phenomenon. In fact, the stability and persistence of this group phenomenon is a persuasive indicator that delinquent subcultures actually exist (Empey and Lubeck, 1968; Erickson and Empey, 1965; Erickson and Jensen, 1977; Hindelang, 1973). Nonetheless, some problems remain when strain theory is used to explain the existence of such subcultures.

First, neither Cohen nor Cloward and Ohlin included any indication as to why, in response to strain, some boys choose to identify with delinquent subculture, while others select a corner boy or a college boy adjustment. Although these theorists were more concerned with accounting for the content and nature of delinquent subculture than with answering this crucial question, some clarification is desperately needed. What are the psychological or sociological mechanisms that affect the direction a boy chooses? Why do some boys choose a deviant adjustment, presumably in response to strain, while others do not?

Second, there is a puzzling lack of evidence that delinquent subculture does much to compensate for the serious problems of adjustment which lower-class boys are supposed to possess. Strain theory implies that delinquent groups become a substitute society for lower-class boys, easing the pains produced by frustration and a loss of self-esteem. But repeated studies indicate that gang members, like inmates in prison, are held together not by feelings of loyalty and solidarity, but by forces much less attractive. Delinquent groups possess a structure, but it is not one that provides much understanding and warmth. Gang members tend to hold each other in low esteem (Hirschi, 1969:159; Short and Strodtbeck, 1965:chaps. 10, 12). Their relationships are characterized by aggression and insult and by a constant need to protect their status and to assert their masculinity (Matza, 1964:33; Miller, 1958). The highly stylized, even threatening, kind of interaction found in gangs is not of the type that is ordinarily associated with internally strong and emotionally satisfying groups (Yablonsky, 1959). Instead, what emerges is a picture which suggests that delinquent groups may stay together simply because they have no other alternative or because they have more to lose than to gain by any breach in their ranks. While they may appear to the outsider to be dogmatic, rigid, and unyielding in their loyalty to each other, the sources of this loyalty are not internal but external. Remove the threats of rival gangs and of the authorities, and you remove the ties that bind (Klein and Crawford, 1967).

Since this empirical picture is so different from the almost romantic one painted by strain theory, there is serious doubt as to whether delinquent groups serve the psychological needs of rejected lower-class boys. If such groups are their only sources of understanding and respect, they face a lamentable life indeed. What is more, if delinquent groups are not cohesive and internally gratifying, it is questionable whether they even provide the personal motivation or the organizational skills necessary to promote and maintain a deviant subculture that is in total opposition to prevailing values.

Rather than indicating that members of delinquent gangs are eventually led to reject such values, several studies indicate just the opposite. Cohen, it will be recalled, argued that in response to humiliation and a loss of status, delinquent boys completely repudiate middle-class values. The only way they can handle their sense of failure and frustration is to react against them. The same would also be true, perhaps, of Cloward and Ohlin's conflict and retreatist gangs. Yet, as discussed earlier, that is not a finding that studies support.

The members of delinquent gangs do not seem to be alienated from the goals of the larger society (Gold, 1963; Gordon et al., 1963). "Even the gang ethic is not one of 'reaction-formation' *against* widely shared conceptions of the 'good' life" (Short and Strodtbeck, 1965:271). Gang, lower-class, and middle-class boys, black and white, evaluate "images representing salient features of the middle-class style of life equally high[ly]" (Short and Strodtbeck, 1965:59).

There is little evidence, in short, that lower-class delinquent boys eventually become alienated from conventional goals. Indeed, if they continue to view these goals as desirable,

the motive for delinquency is not the repudiation of everything middle class, as Cohen suggested. Other motives must be at work, some of which are shared by middle-class boys, since they also tend to commit delinquent acts in groups (Empey and Lubeck, 1968; Erickson, 1973).

Finally, it is necessary to know whether delinquent subcultures of the type described by strain theories actually exist. Cohen suggests the presence of a "parent" delinquent subculture characterized by malicious and negativistic behavior, a subculture in which delinquents are not specialized. Cloward and Ohlin, by contrast, theorize that delinquent subcultures are specialized, falling into three types: criminal, conflict, and retreatist. Before a delinquent subculture can be said to exist, they say, it has to be organized around a specific activity.

Studies of this issue provide some support for the Cohen version but little for the Cloward and Ohlin version (Short and Strodtbeck, 1965:13). In the first place, even the most delinquent groups of boys spend most of their time in nondelinquent activities (Short, 1963:xlvii). Even in what are considered violent gangs, few boys actually become involved in acts of assault (Miller, 1965). Finally, when delinquent behavior does occur, it does not tend to follow any particular pattern. Delinquent boys drink, steal, burglarize, damage property, smoke pot, or even experiment with heroin and pills, but rarely do they limit themselves to any single one of these activities (Erickson and Empey, 1963; Gold, 1966; Illinois Institute for Juvenile Research, 1972).

Thus, while there is little support for the idea that delinquent subcultures are autonomous and highly specialized, there is some support for the notion of a ubiquitous parent subculture which encourages a "garden variety" of delinquent acts (Cohen and Short, 1958). About the only time that highly organized criminal gangs appear is when they are linked to the criminal rackets of adults, and these associations are rare (Kobrin et al., 1967; Spergel, 1961).

At the same time, it would be unwise to assume that all delinquent acts are malicious and without any useful purpose. If one understands the nature of street life, then some acts take on a utilitarian character, at least from the view points of their perpetrators:

> If a group of boys lives days or even weeks away from home, then the theft of food or of things which are sold to buy food is hardly nonutilitarian. If such a group steals from freight cars, peddles the merchandise to neighbors for movie money, . . . this can hardly be considered nonutilitarian. . . .
> Such youngsters may, of course, spend the two dollars gained from selling stolen goods entirely on doughnuts and gorge themselves and throw much of the food away. [But] this largely indicates that they are children, not that they are nonutilitarian (Bordua, 1961:121–22).

Indeed, the finding that most delinquent behavior is of a garden variety is consistent with the idea that delinquent subculture is characterized more by the pursuit of immature and vaguely formulated beliefs than by sophisticated and focused values. It must be remembered, after all, that delinquent groups are peopled by young and inexperienced adolescents. Thus, when questions about the character of delinquent subculture are combined with those about the concept of strain, the implication is that the construction of delinquency suggested by strain theory may be overdrawn and excessively deterministic. This construction implies a sophistication with respect to cultural goals and the organization of delinquent subculture among lower-class boys that does not seem to square with their meager education, poor organizational skills, and lack of respect for one another.

Strain theory and female delinquency

Finally, there is the question of female delinquency. When strain theory was formulated in the late 1950s, the general assumption was that female crime was nonserious and primarily sexual in nature. Since that time, feminist writers have attacked this and other theories, and have suggested that they tend to stereotype, and thus to ignore, the real problems faced by women (Adler and Simon, 1979; Crites, 1976; Klein, 1973; Smart, 1976). The roles that women have been expected to play, both in conventional and criminal worlds, have been characterized by a sex-determined *lack of opportunity*. Girls have been more passive, more law-abiding, and more acquiescent than boys, not because they are inherently predisposed to this behavior, but because they have not been accorded the same degree of autonomy and opportunity.

But the world is changing. Females, says Adler (1975:14–30), are becoming more like men—more competitive, more "macho." Changes in the roles of adolescent girls have also "virilized" this formerly docile segment of the population (p. 87). As a consequence, girls should now face more strain than boys. Not only must they compete on an equal footing for a scarce number of prestigious positions, but also they are

> denied access, on the basis of gender, to those legitimate opportunities which are essential for successful achievement. The various pressures associated with this sex-role convergence and competition simply make girls *more vulnerable to delinquency* (Cernkovich and Giordano, 1979:146, emphasis added).

Figueira-McDonough and Selo (1980:334) do not agree that the strain experienced by females will make them more vulnerable to delinquency, but they do contend that equality of opportunity will lead to similar behavior among males and females. In contrast to the traditional idea that "lower rates of female delinquency can be explained by lower aspirations among females" (p. 341), they hypothesize that "the illegal activities engaged in by girls with high success aspirations and low access to material and legitimate opportunities will be similar to the misbehavior of boys, attributed to strain" (p. 338).

At the same time, Figueira-McDonough and Selo add a new concept to their propositions, heretofore absent in strain theory—the concept of *social control.* "Low levels of control, under conditions of strain, result in similar delinquent behavior among males and females" (p. 340). This addition seems to impose a significant qualification on strain theory because it implies that high levels of frustration will produce delinquent, "male" behavior only to the extent that girls are no longer constrained by traditional expectations, and that they have internalized the same ambitions as boys. Since the norms that govern female behavior are now in a transitional phase, older patterns may still continue to exercise considerable influence.

Given these contrasting positions, what does research suggest? Are the misbehaviors of girls and boys alike? Is crime among girls attributable to a denial of opportunity and resultant feelings of frustration and alienation?

Female versus male crime. We need only recall our review of arrest and self-report studies to know that young girls have not yet become completely macho or virilized. On the one hand, it is true that the pattern of female offenses does not fit, and may never have fit, the stereotyped version of the passive female. Furthermore, during the past 20 years, the rate of arrest among girls appears to have increased at a more rapid pace than among boys (for a contrary conclusion, see Steffensmeier, 1978).

On the other hand, gender remains among the strongest and most reliable indicators of crime: boys are still much more delinquent than girls. Although differences between the sexes may have lessened in recent years, the incidence of male crime, overall, is four to six times greater, and where violent crimes are concerned, may be greater still.

Such findings cannot be interpreted as suggesting that girls never commit crimes because of high aspirations and blocked opportunities. But if they do, two qualifications must be taken into account: that (1) girls are not yet more vulnerable to crime than boys, and (2) given lower rates of female crime, it is likely that any sense of strain among girls due to blocked opportunities must still contend with some extremely effective forms of social control that are traditional in nature. With these qualifications in mind, therefore, let us review the theoretical chain of strain theory as it applies to females.

Female aspirations. There can be little doubt that the feminist movement has had a marked impact on the aspirations of well-educated and sophisticated women. Yet, contentions concerning the virilization of all females cannot be confirmed or denied because the delinquency literature is remarkably bereft of studies comparing the aspirations of boys and girls across all social strata and ethnic groups. Consequently, we cannot say for certain whether the same lofty aspirations are shared equally by the two sexes; and we cannot then go on to determine whether lofty aspirations are perceived as being blocked and whether, in turn, these events are followed by a sense of strain and the commission of delinquent acts. Instead, we can only use existing research to shed a very weak and diffuse light on the subject of female aspirations.

Blocked opportunities. Earlier in this chapter, we learned that, regardless of sex, delinquents are more likely than nondelinquents to fail in school and to believe that their chances of graduating are poor (Elliott and Voss, 1974; Rankin, 1980). The difficulties generated in the educational arena are no less a problem for girls than for boys. But does this mean, then, that girls are delinquent because they have already experienced a sense of strain, particularly that which might be due to sex discrimination?

Strain. In attempting to answer this question, we encounter the same problems that were encountered when strain among boys was examined, the greatest of which has been the failure of investigators to measure strain in psychological terms. A few investigators, however, have skirted the fringes of this issue.

Datesman et al. found that "white female delinquents regarded their opportunities less positively than did their nondelinquent counterparts" (1975:120). It might be concluded, therefore, that aspirational strain must have been present. But this was not what Datesman et al., actually found. Instead, they discovered that white female delinquents "seemed to fare no better and no worse in terms of self esteem than nondelinquents" (p. 119). Hence, they concluded that, in lieu of aspirations similar to those of boys, followed by self-degradation, delinquent girls retained a reasonable sense of self-respect because their offenses were primarily sexual in nature. These girls were conforming to traditionally feminine, not masculine, expectations. "Sexual behavior . . . may represent an attempt to gain male attention for either immediate dividends or possible marriage" (p. 120).

Not only was this conclusion the opposite of that anticipated by feminist strain theory, but Datesman et al. discovered that black females who had committed serious, masculine offenses fared worse than nondelinquent black girls in terms of self-esteem. In other words, it may have been masculine, rather than traditional feminine, behavior that resulted in a poor self-image. However, this finding could also have been due to unexplained factors related to differences between the races rather than differences between male and female roles, because black girls who had not

committed serious crimes were just as likely as those who had to have lower levels of self-worth.

Nonetheless, there was precious little evidence in this study to support the notion that aspirational strain played a key role in the delinquent behavior of girls, black or white. In fact, Datesman et al. (1975) concluded that any loss of self-esteem by delinquent girls was due more to the stigma of being defined as delinquent than to the blockage of opportunity. Indeed, if that is so, delinquent conduct may precede a sense of self- and social degradation rather than follow it, as strain theory suggests.

Cernkovich and Giordano (1979) have taken umbrage with this conclusion, hypothesizing instead that delinquent behavior among girls is a means of striking back at an unfair sexist system. But when they examined their data, they found no evidence to support their hypothesis. Girls who were inclined to say that females experience discrimination in hiring, firing, and promotion were no more likely to be delinquent than those who did not. Instead, it was those who believed that they were unlikely to finish school or to get a good job who were the most delinquent—girls, in fact, whose responses to this issue were similar to those of male delinquents.

But Cernkovich and Giordano, like investigators mentioned earlier, failed to measure strain in psychological terms, to clarify its precise sources, and to determine its sequence in the theoretical chain; so it is difficult to interpret their findings. Instead, we must continue to entertain the possibility that such findings could have been due to any one of, or a combination of, the following factors: (1) the frustration of ambition and the blockage of opportunity, as strain theory suggests; (2) the stigma associated with failure in school; (3) the lack of commitment to long-range educational and occupational goals; and/or (4) the stigma that results from being delinquent. In short, research on strain among girls is like that on strain among boys: it raises more questions than it answers. Until it is improved, therefore, its sources and character will remain very much a matter of debate.

Delinquent subculture. Despite the group nature of female delinquency, it is astonishing that no mention is made by newer strain theorists of the possible role of delinquent subculture in resolving the strain that girls are presumed to experience. It is as though they are solitary creatures who are bereft of moral support when they commit delinquent acts. Indeed, Datesman et al. suggest that there is a "relative absence of subcultural support for female delinquency" (1975:112). Perhaps that is why black girls experience a loss of esteem when they are delinquent. "Female delinquency is largely individualistic, and not buttressed by the support and approval of others to as great an extent as male delinquency" (Datesman et al., 1975:112).

This is certainly a provocative conclusion because it implies that unless girls are an auxiliary appendage to their parents or to male groups, they are without social support from other girls when they are deviant. This projects a highly traditional image of the female. By contrast, the logic of feminist strain theory would suggest that frustrated and oppressed females should begin to generate subcultural support for their struggles against a sexist society, even if those struggles involve illegal conduct. But since recent additions to strain theory have not projected a subcultural outcome of this type, let alone examining it, we must look to the future for further clarification.

SUMMARY AND CONCLUSIONS

When, at mid-20th century, strain theory was first formulated, it represented an attempt to explain certain phenomena which had become accepted as facts: that delinquency is predominantly a male phenomenon, concentrated in the lower class, occurring in groups, and representing the existence of delinquent subculture. But because it emphasized the idea that delinquent behavior is a product of the discrepancy between culturally valued goals and limited means to achieve them, its scope has been broadened in recent years, and now it has been applied to the feminist movement. Girls may now be more vulnerable to delinquency than males because they not only face the problems of class and racial discrimination, but the gender-based prejudice of a sexist society.

1. Assumptions about human nature and social order. Strain theory is like cultural deviance and symbolic interactionist theories in that it assumes that human nature is inherently social, that the delinquent is a moral animal who prefers to follow conventional rules, given reasonable opportunity to do so. Unlike the other two theories, however, strain theory paints a more complicated picture of the social order.

Both cultural deviance and interactionist theories imply that the social order is characterized by conflict because there is no overriding standard of good and bad. Since American culture includes both deviant and conformist traditions, there is no consensus on appropriate rules for behavior. Strain theory, by contrast, implies that there is a moral consensus, particularly on basic values and goals. Everyone hails these as desirable and lends support to legitimate means for achieving them. Ironically, this very consensus promotes conflict and deviance because some persons cannot achieve success by obeying cultural rules. Yet, the impression is pervasive throughout strain theory that there would be no conflict, and no deviance, if only society were organized differently. Were there no structural impediments to self-esteem and material success, the inherently social natures of all females and males would allow them to be law-abiding.

2. Underlying content and logic of strain theory. As originally formulated, strain theory possessed four distinguishing features: (1) it assumed that while females are conditioned to be passive and law-abiding, males are expected to be status strivers—autonomous, hard driving, and preoccupied with success; (2) it assumed that these expectations are universal across class and ethnic lines; (3) it assumed that because of their socialization, it will be males, not females, who will experience a sense of strain if opportunities are blocked; and (4) it assumed that lower-class males, given their disadvantaged position in the social structure, are those most vulnerable to strain. That is why, in fact, the latter are the most delinquent segment of the population. In an effort to resolve the intense pressures they feel, they turn to illegitimate means, and to like-minded peers, for a solution. Delinquent subculture(s) and behavior are the result.

The two expressions of this kind of theory are as shown in Figure 11–1.

In response to the women's movement, recent versions of strain theory appear to have modified some, if not all, of the earlier assumptions. They now suggest that (1) females as well as males are expected to be autonomous and preoccupied with success; (2) these expectations cut across class and ethnic lines; but (3) it is now females, not males, who are in the greatest bind, since they must not only confront the existence of limited opportunities, common to both sexes, but must also face the gender-based restrictions of a sexist society. As a consequence, less emphasis is placed upon the restrictions of social class and ethnicity and more upon the disadvantages of being female. Hence, this way of formulating strain theory may be diagrammed as follows:

American   Sexual   Delinquent
Dream   → discrimination → Strain → behavior

Significantly, few, if any, recent theorists have hypothesized that a female delinquent subculture, or one of both sexes, will emerge as a means to resolving strain and supporting the use of illegitimate actions for achieving success.

FIGURE 11–1

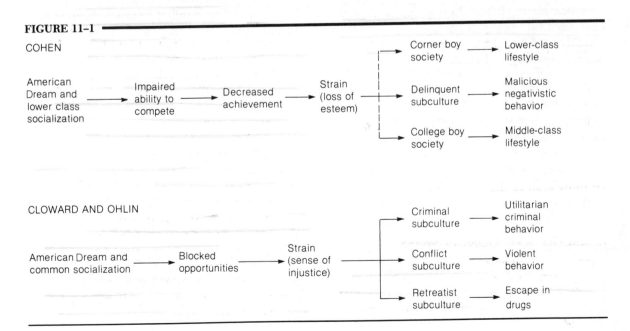

3. *Policy implications.* Strain theory implies that there is no such thing as a bad boy or girl. If delinquency occurs, it is because of the failure of the social order. Hence, that order must be changed.

This construction of delinquency resulted in some of the most deliberate and comprehensive efforts yet tried to address such "root causes" of deviant behavior as poverty, inadequate education, economic segregation, and powerlessness in lower-class communities. It has not, as yet, resulted in similar efforts to reduce sexual discrimination. Nonetheless, it is a part of a more general movement which is certainly pointed in that direction.

4. *Logical and empirical adequacy.* Strain theorists have made highly valuable contributions to the delinquency literature by focusing originally upon lower-class boys, and by suggesting that delinquent subculture(s) may result from the problems they face. It was Cohen, in fact, who first used the term *delinquent subculture* to refer to the delinquent traditions that Shaw and McKay wrote about. And it was Cloward and Ohlin who first alerted us to the possibility that different kinds of subcultures may be linked to the opportunity structures of different kinds of communities. Their stress upon these matters highlights the likelihood that lower-class boys have a more difficult transition from childhood to adulthood than middle-class boys. But do they handle that transition in the way that strain theory suggests? Are many of them virtually driven to membership in delinquent subculture(s)?

The elements of strain theory that have measured up best to empirical scrutiny are those which suggest that (1) lower-class boys probably want the same goods, pleasures, and status that others want; (2) failure in such middle-class institutions as the school provokes serious problems; and (3) delinquent behavior is a group, possibly a subcultural, phenomenon. By contrast, the elements of strain theory about which there is the greatest question are those which indicate that (1) serious delinquent behavior is restricted to the lower class; (2) it is a boy's position in the class structure, rather than his relation to his parents or even his unwillingness to pay the legitimate price for success, which is likely to produce problems in school; and (3) delinquent subculture is capable of solving the serious problems of adjustment which failure in school produces.

Similar difficulties arise with the application of various elements of strain theory to girls. Although there can be little doubt that gender-based discrimination is a serious problem, there is little evidence that it has made girls more, or even equally, vulnerable to delinquency. First, the limited research now available supports an idea which academics should note: fundamental alterations in the roles of males and females take generations to accomplish, not a decade or two. Second, when caught up in the ideology of a social upheaval, like the feminist movement, academics often overlook the fact that changes in the female role cannot occur in isolation, but must inevitably alter the male role. Why, then, should it be anticipated that the strain it produces will inevitably be greater for females than for males? Third, until the current transition in roles is accomplished, any attempt to understand delinquency will require that we continue to pay attention to traditional expectations and controls, as well as to a more diffuse, emerging set of norms.

In short, strain theorists may have attempted to account for too much. In their construction of delinquency, they seem to have forgotten that delinquents are young and immature people whose understanding of social inequality and pressing contemporary issues is limited. Rather than reflecting an attempt to redress some of society's most serious inequities, therefore, their group behavior may represent little more than an unfettered, irresponsible, and sometimes predatory pursuit of childish desires. To be sure, the deprivations, disillusionments, and frustrations of being lower class or female may contribute heavily to their problems. But Cohen's humiliated, irrationalistic angry boys, Cloward's and Ohlin's hard-driving rationalistic criminals, and Adler's "macho" girls seem to be extreme. As Bordua puts it, "It seems peculiar that modern analysts have stopped assuming that 'evil' can be fun and see gang delinquency as arising only when boys [or girls] are driven away from 'good.'" (1961:136).

REFERENCES

Adler, Frieda
　1975　*Sisters in Crime: The Rise of the New Female Criminal.* New York: McGraw-Hill.

Adler, Frieda, and Simon, Rita James, eds.
　1979　*The Criminology of Deviant Women.* Boston: Houghton Mifflin.

Aultman, Madeline, and Wellford, Charles F.
　1976　"Evaluations of Major Sociological Theories of Delinquency." Paper presented at the Annual Meetings of the American Society of Criminology. November 1976. Tucson, Arizona.

Blalock, Hubert M., Jr.
　1964　*Causal Inference in Non-experimental Research.* Chapel Hill: University of North Carolina Press.

Bordua, David J.
　1961　"Delinquent Subcultures: Sociological Interpretations of Gang Delinquency." *Anals of the American Academy of Political and Social Science* 338 (November):119–136.

Cernkovich, Stephen A., and Giordano, Peggy C.
　1979　"Delinquency, Opportunity, and Gender." *Journal of Criminal Law and Criminology* 70:145–151.

Clelland, Donald, and Carter, Timothy J.
　1980　"The New Myth of Class and Crime." *Criminology* 18 (November):319–336.

Cloward, Richard A., and Ohlin, Lloyd E.
　1960　*Delinquency and Opportunity: A Theory of Delinquent Gangs.* New York: Free Press.

Cohen, Albert K.
　1955　*Delinquent Boys: The Culture of the Gang.* New York: Free Press.

Cohen, Albert K. and Short, James F., Jr.
　1958　"Research in Delinquent Subcultures." *Journal of Social Issues* 14 (Summer):20–36.

Coleman, James S.
　1966　*Equality of Educational Opportunity.* Washington, D.C.: U.S. Government Printing Office.

Crites, Laura, ed.
　1976　*The Female Offender.* Lexington, Mass.: D. C. Heath.

Datesman, Susan K., and Scarpitti, Frank R.
  1975 "Female Delinquency and Broken Homes: A Reassessment." *Criminology* 13 (May):33–55.

Davis, Allison
  1946 "The Motivation of the Underprivileged Worker." Pp. 84–106 in William F. Whyte, ed., *Industry and Society*. New York: McGraw-Hill.

Elliott, Delbert S., and Voss, Harwin L.
  1974 *Delinquency and Dropout*. Lexington, Mass.: D. C. Heath.

Empey, LaMar T.
  1956 "Social Class and Occupational Aspiration: A Comparison of Absolute and Relative Measurement." *American Sociological Review* 21 (December):703–709.

Empey, LaMar T., and Lubeck, Steven G.
  1968 "Conformity and Deviance in the 'Situation of Company.' " *American Sociological Review* 33 (October):760–774.
  1971 *Explaining Delinquency*. Lexington, Mass.: D. C. Health.

Erickson, Maynard L.
  1973 "Group Violations, Socioeconomic Status and Official Delinquency." *Social Forces* 52 (September):41–52.

Erickson, Maynard L., and Empey, LaMar T.
  1963 "Court Records, Undetected Delinquency, and Decision Making." *Journal of Criminal Law, Criminology, and Police Science* 54 (December):456–469.
  1965 "Class Position, Peers and Delinquency." *Sociology and Social Research* 49 (April):268–282.

Erickson, Maynard L., and Jensen, Gary F.
  1977 "Delinquency is Still Group Behavior: Toward Revitalizing the Group Premise in the Sociology of Deviance." *Journal of Criminal Law and Criminology* 68:262–273.

Figueira-McDonough, Josefina, and Selo, Elaine
  1980 "A Reformulation of the 'Equal Opportunity' Explanation of Female Delinquency." *Crime and Delinquency* 26 (July):333–343.

Frease, Dean E.
  1973 "Delinquency, Social Class, and the Schools." *Sociology and Social Research* 57 (July):443–459.

Gold, Martin
  1963 *Status Forces in Delinquent Boys*. Ann Arbor: Institute for Social Research, University of Michigan.
  1966 "Undetected delinquent behavior." *Journal of Research in Crime and Delinquency* 3 (January):27–46.

Gordon, Robert A., et al.
  1963 "Values and Gang Delinquency." *American Journal of Sociology* LXVIX (September):109–128.

Gould, R.
  1941 "Some Sociological Determinants of Goal Striving." *Journal of Social Psychology*, 13 (May):461–473.

Hindelang, Michael J.
1973 "Causes of Delinquency: A Partial Relication and Extension." *Social Problems* 20(Spring):471–487.

Hirschi, Travis
1969 *Causes of Delinquency*. Berkeley: University of California Press.

Horton, John
1967 "Time and Cool People." *Transaction* 4 (April):5–12.

Illinois Institute for Juvenile Research
1972 *Juvenile Delinquency in Illinois*. Chicago: Illinois, Department of Mental Health.

Johnson, Richard E.
1979 *Juvenile Delinquency and Its Origins*. New York: Cambridge University Press.

Klein, Dorie
1973 "The Etiology of Female Crime: A Review of the Literature." *Issues in Criminology* 8 (Fall):3–30.

Klein, Malcolm W., and Crawford, Lois Y.
1967 "Groups, Gangs and Cohesiveness." *Journal of Research in Crime and Delinquency* 1 (January):63–75.

Kobrin, Solomon
1951 "The Conflict of Values in Delinquency Areas." *American Sociological Review* 16 (October):653–661.

Kobrin, Solomon; Puntil, Joseph; and Peluso, Emil
1967 "Criteria of Status Among Street Corner Groups." *Journal of Research in Crime and Delinquency* 4 (January):98–118.

Marris, Peter and Rein, Martin
1973 *Dilemmas of Social Reform*. 2d ed. Chicago: Aldine.

Matza, David
1964 *Delinquency and Drift*. New York: John Wiley & Sons.

Merton, Robert K.
1938 "Social Structure and Anomie." *American Sociological Review* 3:672–682.
1957 *Social Theory and Social Structure*. 2d ed. New York: Free Press.
1968 *Social Theory and Social Structure*. Enlarged ed. New York: Free Press.

Miller, Walter B.
1958 "Lower-class Culture as a Generating Milieu of Gang Delinquency." *Journal of Social Issues* 14 (Summer):51–119.
1965 "Violent Crimes in City Gangs." *Annals of the American Academy of Political and Social Science* 324 (March):105–115.

Moynihan, Daniel P.
1969 *Maximum Feasible Misunderstanding: Community Action in the War on Poverty*. New York: Free Press.

Piven, F. F. and Cloward, Richard A.
1971 *Regulating the Poor*. New York: Pantheon Press.

Polk, Kenneth and Halferty, David S.
1966 "Adolescence, Commitment and Delinquency." *Journal of Research in Crime and Delinquency* 4 (July):82–96.

Polk, Kenneth and Schafer, Walter E. (Eds.)
1972   *School and Delinquency.* Englewood Cliffs, N.J.: Prentice-Hall.

Poston, Richard W.
1971   *The Gang and the Establishment.* New York: Harper & Row.

Rankin, Joseph H.
1980   "School Factors and Delinquency: Interactions by Age and Sex." *Sociology and Social Research* 64 (April):420–434.

Short, James F., Jr.
1963   "Introduction to Abridged Edition." Frederick M. Thrasher, *The Gang.* Chicago: University of Chicago Press.
1975   "The Natural History of an Applied Theory: Differential Opportunity and Mobilization for Youth." Pp. 193–210 in N.J. Demerath, III et al., eds., *Social Policy and Sociology.* New York: Academic Press.

Short, James F., Jr., and Strodtbeck, Fred L.
1965   *Group Process and Gang Delinquency.* Chicago: University of Chicago Press.

Smart, Carol
1976   *Women, Crime and Criminology: A Feminist Critique.* Boston: Routledge and Kegan Paul

Spergel, Irving
1961   "An Exploratory Research and Delinquent Subculture." *Social Service Review* 35 (March):33–47.

Steffensmeier, Darrell J.
1978   "Crime and the Contemporary Woman: An Analysis of Changing Levels of Female Property Crime, 1960–75." *Social Forces* 57 (December):566–584.

Stinchcombe, Arthur L.
1964   *Rebellion in High School.* Chicago: Quadrangle Books.

Yablonsky, Lewis
1959   "The Delinquent Gang as a Near-group." *Social Problems* 7 (Fall):108–117.

Control theory suggests that delinquent behavior is more likely when young people are not strongly attached to home and school.

SOCIAL CONTROL THEORY

In Chapter 8, we reviewed a number of *control* theories—theories which suggest that delinquent behavior is due to underlying genetic or intrapsychic forces over which children have little control. Even though these uncontrollable forces cannot be observed, they are instilled in children by their parents, either by genetic inheritance or by improper training.

In this chapter, by contrast, we will examine a more recent control theory that is social in nature. But while this theory continues to suggest that the family is important in shaping personal controls within the individual, it also suggests that these controls should be observable and verifiable, rather than hidden and difficult to verify. Indeed, unless their impact can be documented, science will not be able to prove or to disprove their existence.

HISTORICAL BACKGROUND

In order to set the stage for our examination of this newer control theory, we need to review a bit of history. It will be recalled that during the 19th century, Americans became convinced that, of all the causes of juvenile misconduct, the most important was broken or depraved families—families that were incapable of controlling their own children. That is why child-saving institutions were invented—to get the children of disrupted families off the street and into a moral environment.

In her analysis of the impact of this traditional view upon 20th-century criminology, Wilkinson (1974) notes that, from 1900 until 1932, the relation between broken homes and delinquency was widely accepted in the scientific community. Impressed by the revolutionary views of Freudian psychology as well as by the cultural beliefs of their time, many investigators were convinced that divorce and desertion were threats to the very foundation of society, to say nothing of the problems created by delinquent boys and girls.

Then, from about 1933 until 1950, a new generation of criminologists, most of whom were sociologists, rejected the broken home explanation because (1) many in this generation were urban dwellers who saw less danger in divorce and social change; (2) these sociologists had a growing disdain for Freudian theory; (3) most studies of broken homes were of dubious scientific quality; and (4) the division of families into two categories—broken and unbroken— gave absolutely no clue as to the quality of life within either of them. A child in a broken home might have a parent who is still loving and supportive, while one in a home that is intact might be subjected to destructive experiences. But instead of improving the methods for investigation of family life, most criminologists either ignored or rejected its importance altogether.

Finally, after mid-century, renewed interest in the family was shown by a few investigators. Their findings continued to suggest not only that broken or disrupted families were important, but also that they were based upon more defensible methods of research (Chilton and Markle, 1972; Monahan, 1957; Nye, 1958). By then, however, the sociological theories that we reviewed in previous chapters had become transcendent. Criminology was preoccupied not with family relationships, but with the implications of cultural deviance and symbolic interactionist and strain theories. Furthermore, most investigators were absorbed with the fact that males are far more delinquent than females. Consequently, their now-familiar theories tended to suggest that delinquent behavior is a kind of normal social functioning for aggressive, lower-class males whose behavior is dictated by the deviant values of the delinquent subcultures and groups to which they belong.

In a telling commentary on this preoccupation, Bordua contended that

> the discussion of delinquency in recent sociological theory seems to be distinguished more by a desire to avoid "psychologizing" than by a desire to understand delinquency. If a boy is humiliated by his teacher, then that is social class and is admissable, but if he is

humiliated by his father, that is child psychology and is inadmissable (1962:249– 250).

Meanwhile, most theories of female delinquency remained frozen in time. When, eventually, some explanations were forthcoming—some as late as 1970—it was as though they had turned the clock back to the days of Lombroso and Freud (Klein, 1973). As in the past, these explanations were concerned less with the effects of race, class, and culture on female behavior than with those that were biological and intrapsychic in origin.

In 1950, for example, Otto Pollack theorized that female arrest rates are low, not necessarily because females are less criminal than males, but because they are *naturally* more deceitful and manipulative. Used to hiding their menstrual cycles each month, and coldly pretending to enjoy sex when they get no pleasure from it, they have developed concealment, stealth, and misrepresentation to a high art. They are able to blackmail men, shoplift from their stores, or manipulate them into committing serious crimes, all the while avoiding personal responsibility for such acts. Furthermore, when females are caught, male chivalry protects them from prosecution, unless, of course, they have been guilty of sexual indiscretion.

Pursuing the idea that "anatomy is destiny," Cowie et al. (1968) suggested that although upbringing may play a part in initiating delinquent conduct among girls, *chromosomal* factors exert the greatest influence. Ordinary women are constitutionally disinclined to be delinquent. But should they be born with masculine traits, the predisposition will be implanted. Aggression and rebellion among females can be traced to atypical features that are decidedly masculine.

Gisela Konopka (1966) was more Freudian in her critique. Almost inevitably, a delinquent girl's problems are "deeply personalized," she suggested. "Whatever her offense—whether shoplifting, truancy or running away from home—it is usually accompanied by some disturbance or unfavorable behavior in the sexual area" (p. 41). Above all she is lonely. Unlike her better-adjusted peers, she is unable to establish a satisfactory relationship with a person of the opposite sex, and thus unable to fulfill the roles for which her biological inheritance has destined her—helpmate, wife, and mother.

About the only exceptions to these more traditional points of view were those advanced by sociologists who agreed with Sutherland and Cressey (1955:112–113) that differences between the sexes are significant in the causation of delinquency only to the extent that they reflect the social roles that males and females are expected to play (Vedder, 1979). If girls were less supervised than boys, if they were permitted to occupy the same social roles, and if they had the same opportunity to associate with delinquent peers, they would be as delinquent. In other words, it is not innate differences but the different way males and females are socialized and controlled which form the gap between the sexes.

But whether stress was placed upon social or constitutional factors, most theories continued to imply that innate or acquired personality traits are the determining factors. Males are more criminal than females because they are "assertive" and "aggressive," while females obey the law because they are "passive" and "dependent." But as Shover and Norland (1978) point out, such explanations come perilously close to being tautologies,—that is, spurious circular arguments. With regard to males, for example, the argument would be that "crime [is a] 'masculine' [activity] because males are involved in [it] more often than females; therefore, males should be *expected* to commit more crime because crime is a 'masculine' domain" (p. 116). Conversely, the same argument would suggest that law-abiding behavior is a feminine activity because females are involved in it more often than males; therefore, females should be *expected* to be less criminal because law-abiding behavior is a female domain.

Given the questionable quality of these arguments, it is clear that the theories of the past 50 years have left us with a host of unresolved problems. On the one hand, these theories are valuable precisely because of their diversity and because they leave open a much-needed window to the past. Furthermore, although more recent theories underscore the importance of adding the effects of social and cultural factors to those that are biological and intrapsychic in origin, the persistence of the latter frameworks suggest that we should continue to entertain the possibility that differences in crime rates between males and females may be due, not merely to the gender roles and cultural traditions of an ancient past, but to the genetic heritage of a history that is even more ancient.

On the other hand, it is equally clear that the theories of this century have been characterized by a great deal of disciplinary provincialism and cultural ethnocentrism. That is why sociologists' interests in the family have waxed and waned over time, and why biological and intrapsychic theories of female crime now seem outdated. Scientific perspectives, as well as cultural values, have changed so greatly that it is difficult for us to determine the degree to which existing theories reflect those factors that are actually associated with delinquent conduct and those which merely portray the changing interests and disciplinary concerns of criminologists.

In light of this dilemma, the most recent version of control theory is provocative indeed. It suggests that we should not only draw upon the past in attempting to understand delinquency, but also rediscover the importance of the family.

CONSTRUCTION OF CONTROL THEORY

In 1969, Travis Hirschi, a sociologist, not only reasserted the importance of many 19th-century beliefs about the family but also tied them to the importance of schooling. Furthermore, he based his theory upon a series of assumptions about human nature and social order that were older still—beliefs that most 20th century theorists had long since discarded.

Hirschi (1969:31–34) observes that it has now become fashionable to disdain the assumptions made by philosophers like Hobbes, religionists like the Puritans, or theorists like Freud that human nature is inherently antisocial. Most moderns prefer to believe that people are inherently moral at birth or, at worst, that they are a blank slate on which nothing, good or bad, has been inscribed. Hirschi rejects both points of view, however, and asserts that control theory remains what it has always been—a theory which suggests that it is not criminals and delinquents alone who are animals "but that we are all animals, and thus all naturally capable of committing criminal acts" (1969:31). If we strip away the veneer of civilization, we will find that all people are subject to animal impulse.

If that is true, then there is nothing to be explained when the question, "Why did they do it?" is asked. Since human nature is inherently antisocial, all children would commit delinquent acts if they dared. Hence, the central questions which theory should be designed to answer is: "Why don't they do it?" (Hirschi, 1969:34). "Why do most children stay out of serious trouble?"

The social bond

Hirschi (p. 16) answers these questions by suggesting that it is an individual's *bond* to society that makes the difference (see Reckless, 1961, for a similar statement). He cites the French sociologist, Emile Durkheim to illustrate what he means. "The more weakened the groups to which the individual belongs, the less he depends on them, the more he consequently depends only on himself and recognizes no other rules of conduct than what are founded on his private interests" (1951:209). In short, we are moral beings to the extent that we have internalized the norms of society and have become sensitive to the needs of others. Indeed, sensitivity to others *is* the social bond:

> To violate a norm is . . . to act contrary to the wishes and expectations of other people. If a person does not care about the wishes and expectations of other people—that is, if he is insensitive to the opinion of others—then he is to that extent not bound by the norms. He is free to deviate (Hirschi, 1969:18).

This way of defining the bond to society requires that one make certain assumptions about the social order. Like other control theorists, Hirschi is disinclined to see value conflicts in society as being responsible for an individual's insensitivity to the wishes of others. Instead, he assumes that the members of society are tied together by a common value system, at least where predatory crimes are concerned (Hirschi, 1969:18,23).

This is a crucial assumption. First, it means that Hirschi's theory is not a gender, a class, or a racially based theory. Rather, since most people share the feeling that they should not kill, rob, or steal, it is only delinquent individuals who defy convention and threaten social stability. Second, it implies that deviant values are not widely shared. While most people remain committed to basic standards of right and wrong, delinquents are insensitive persons who do not adhere to the moral standards of any group, deviant or conformist. They violate the law not because they feel obligated to others, but because their natural human impulses remain unrestrained by a lasting bond to any group.

Elements of the Bond

Hirschi theorizes that the *social bond is* made up of four major elements, which are defined in such a way that their presence can be observed and verified, thus avoiding the weaknesses of Freudian theory.

1. Attachment. The first element is *attachment.* This refers to the ties of affection and respect between children and such key persons as parents, teachers, and friends. A strong bond with all three will be a major deterrent to delinquency. Attachment to parents, however, is the most important, since children are first socialized by parents. Furthermore, it is not whether families are broken by divorce or desertion that is of greatest importance, but the quality of the relationship between children and their parent(s). If children are strongly attached to their parents, they are much more likely to internalize the norms of society and to develop feelings of respect for persons in authority, such as teachers, or for peers, such as friends. But if they are alienated from their parents, they will likely be alienated from others. They will not learn or feel responsible for moral rules, nor will they develop an adequate conscience (Hirschi, 1969:86).

In a sense, Hirschi's attachment is analogous to Freud's super-ego. But it locates ". . . the 'conscience' in the bond to others rather than making it a part of the personality" (p. 19). In other words, one does not need to rely upon hidden intrapsychic forces to know that the conscience exists. If it can be demonstrated that a person is attached to others and respects their wishes, then one can assume that the conscience exists.

2. Commitment. The second element of the bond is *commitment.* This is a rational component similar to Freud's ego, but it also has roots in long-standing traditions. It has to do with the extent to which children are committed to the ideal requirements of childhood—getting an education, postponing participation in adult activities like drinking and smoking, or dedicating themselves to long-term goals. If children commit themselves to these activities, they will develop a stake in conformity, and will be disinclined to engage in delinquent behavior. To do so would be to endanger their futures (p. 21). And, though commitment refers to an internalized set of expectations, it, too, is amenable to observation and measurement, since one can measure how strongly a person is dedicated to the pursuit of conventional means and goals.

3. Involvement. The third element is *involvement.* This is the equivalent of the traditional belief that "idle hands are the devil's workshop." It is a concept that has particular relevance for adolescents, since they are in that phase of the life cycle when they are neither totally under parental domination nor totally free to behave as adults. Instead, they are in a limbo where expectations are not as clear-cut as they might be. Hence, large amounts of unstructured time may decrease the effectiveness of the social bond and increase the likelihood of delinquent behavior. By contrast, adolescents who are busy doing conventional things—duties around the home, studying, or engaging in sports—do not have time to be delinquent. Furthermore, the degree to which an individual is involved in conventional activities is another variable that can be readily measured (pp. 21–23).

4. Belief. The fourth element is *belief.* Some persons simply have not been trained to respect the law. They are people who feel no obligation whatsoever to conform to the expectations of others. However, this is not to say that such persons do not know when they are breaking the law, or that they fail to recognize that they may incur the wrath of others when they do. It is just that their consciences are not offended by deviant behavior; lacking any moral constraints, they are free to deviate. Hence, the less juveniles believe in the morality of law, the greater the likelihood they will be delinquent (pp. 25–26).

In summary, Hirschi's theory, like Freud's, is more a theory of conformity than of delinquency. Since it assumes that all of us are animals at birth, and will rob, cheat, and steal unless restrained, delinquent conduct needs no explanation. Rather, what we must seek to understand is why, to some people, morality appears good and desirable. As Durkheim suggested, many of us "find charm in the accomplishment of a moral act prescribed by a rule that has no other justification than that it is a rule. We feel a . . . pleasure in performing our duty simply because it is our duty" (1963:45). But why? Since the performance of duty inevitably requires effort, why do we find it attractive?

Hirschi implies that it is because we have a *stake in conformity* (Toby, 1957). If we enjoy the respect of our parents, our teachers, and our friends, and are committed to long-range goals, we are threatened with a loss of those valuable possessions if we fail to do our duty, particularly if we commit criminal acts. That is why the social bond is so important. We have learned that we have more to lose than to gain from doing anything so stupid as committing a crime and getting arrested. Not only will it bring stigma upon us, but it will threaten whatever chances we have of completing school, launching a career, and earning the esteem of respectable people.

IMPLICATIONS FOR SOCIAL POLICY

It cannot be said that Hirschi's version of control theory has had a direct impact on social policy that is anywhere near the striking impact of strain theory. Nevertheless, it has continued to reinforce a set of beliefs and practices that are deeply rooted in our culture.

To begin with, it appeals to common sense (Nettler, 1974:247). For example, a well-known black writer, William Raspberry (1980), notes that when black leaders talk about the difficult problems that black youths face, they sound like strain theorists; they blame "the system." But,

> when it comes to *their* children, these leaders do not waste time railing against "the system." Instead, they work at getting their children ready to take advantage of the opportunities that exist. They tell their children to modify their language, dress and behavior to create favorable impressions. . . . They tell them to show initiative and ambition, to be punctual and dependable, to make employers believe that they are worth having around.

In other words, when most people concentrate on their own children, rather than on children in general, they sound like control theorists. The same is no less true of legal authorities. Contrary to academic criminologists, they actually encounter delinquents, one by one. Furthermore, because of the way these delinquents are filtered through the system, they are much less likely than most children to have apparent ties to anyone, even to their parents. For example, consider the comments of a physician about the delinquents who end up in the hospital because of their wounds in street battles:

> The kids we get are real rough kids. They make you feel afraid. You know they wouldn't hesitate to take a knife to your throat. But when they come in here for care, they've been hurt so badly that they have no fight left. They have been stabbed or shot, but they never ask for anyone. They expect to die and would just as soon die as live.
>
> The thing that shocks me is that many of their parents never show up to see them. They just watch with a hopeless attitude; they've given up on their children. They ask questions like, "Why did you call me in?" "Why do I have to sign this paper?" "Isn't he a ward of the court?" The parents don't want anything to do with their children and the children seem to have lost all sense of caring (unpublished personal interview).

Given their repeated confrontations with distressing problems like these, authorities are inclined not only to sound like control theorists but also to agree with one study of official delinquents which indicates "(1) that children charged with delinquency live in disrupted families substantially more often than children in the general population, and (2) that children referred for more serious delinquency are more likely to come from incomplete families than children charged with minor offenses" (Chilton and Markle, 1972:93). It takes no stretch of the imagination for them to believe that disrupted families and a broken bond are associated with delinquent behavior.

Consequently, while Freudian personality theory may have served as a kind of sophisticated and legitimizing rationale for their roles as professionals, Hirschi's theory does a far better job of capturing the common-sense side of the problems they face. They can readily understand the need to (1) *reattach* delinquents to some kind of family; (2) *recommit* them to the long-range conventional goals that childhood demands; (3) *involve* them in school and other constructive activities; and (4) have them acquire *beliefs* in the morality of law.

In short, whether authorities are aware of Hirschi's control theory or not, it is the kind of explanation which makes sense to them and upon which they base many of their interventions. A most important question, therefore, is whether the theory is adequate from a logical and scientific standpoint.

LOGICAL AND EMPIRICAL ADEQUACY

With regard to this matter, Hirschi (1969) did an unusual thing: he tested his own theory. He selected a representative sample of over 4,000 junior and senior high school students—male and female, black and white, lower, middle, and upper class—ranging in age from 13 to 18. From this sample, he obtained three types of information: (1) independent measures of the four elements of the social bond; (2) measures of self-reported criminal behavior—petty theft, auto theft, vandalism, and assault; and (3) measures of official delinquency. Then, by relating the elements of the bond to both measures of delinquent conduct, he hoped to determine whether his four elements could explain the difference between conformity and deviance.

Although approximately half of Hirschi's sample was female, he did not include girls in his analysis. However, this unfortunate ommission has now been rectified, at least in part, by other investigators. Some have analyzed Hirschi's original data on females, and others have added data from other samples as well. What, then, has research shown?

Basic assumptions

Given the differences between Hirschi and other social scientists concerning the concept of human nature, much could be gained if we could test his assumption that people are inherently antisocial. But since there are no practical or ethical means by which this can be done, the issue remains unresolved.

The assumption that the *social order* is characterized by value consensus is another matter. Hirschi did make an indirect test of it. Like other investigators, he found that there is considerable verbal agreement among students from different classes and races on the importance of getting an education, obeying the law, and refusing to take advantage of others (compare Hirschi, 1969:215 with Gold, 1963; Short and Strodtbeck, 1965:59; 271). Additional studies have found that, whether black or white, middle or lower class, educated or uneducated, most people are inclined to rate the seriousness of various crimes in about the same order, and to believe that those who commit crimes that involve harm to others should be condemned and punished (Chilton and DeAmicis, 1975; Rossi et al., 1974; Wellford, 1975).

Insofar as criminal acts are concerned, therefore, there seems to be at least some agreement on basic definitions of right and wrong. But since many criminals would readily agree that people should not hurt each other, a most important question is whether the elements of the social bond—attachment, commitment, involvement, and belief—are able to spell the difference between those who actually conform to basic expectations and those who do not. Several studies, in addition to Hirschi's, can be used to examine this question.

Attachment

It will be recalled that attachment refers to the ties of affection and respect between children and such key persons as parents, teachers, and friends. If present, attachment is supposed to act as an insulator against delinquency; if absent, children should be free to deviate.

1. Attachment to parents. With regard to this variable, Hirschi's theory includes two basic hypotheses: (1) the quality of the relationship between a child and one or both parents will determine the strength of their attachment to each other, not whether the home is broken by divorce or desertion; and (2) the weaker the attachment, the greater the delinquency.

Several studies, based on a comparison of official delinquents and nondelinquents, tend to question these hypotheses, suggesting that broken homes are more important than quality of relationship (Chilton and Markle, 1972; Cockburn and Maclay, 1965; Cowie et al., 1968; Datesman and Scarpitti, 1975; Monahan, 1957; Rodman and Grams, 1969). Not only are officially delinquent boys and girls more likely to come from broken homes, but among girls "the proportions from incomplete families are so high that there can hardly be any doubt as to the importance of parental deprivation to them" (Monahan, 1957:258).

A major problem with most of these studies, however, is their use of official data. When comparisons are made between official delinquents and nondelinquents, there is always the danger that the high incidence of broken homes among the delinquents will be due more to the fact that authorities are charged with remedying their home conditions than to the fact that they have actually committed more criminal acts. Indeed, studies using self-reported law violation to distinguish the amount of delinquent behavior among young people, tend to support Hirschi's argument.

This research indicates that the children *least* likely to report having violated the law are those who feel loved, who identify with their parent(s), and who respect their wishes (Hindelang, 1973; Johnson, 1979; Nye, 1958). By contrast, *lawbreakers* are more likely to come from homes, intact as well as broken, in which (1) cruelty, neglect, erratic discipline, and parental conflict are present (Farrington and West, 1981; Glueck and Glueck, 1968); (2) parental supervision is low (Hirschi, 1969; Jensen, 1972); and (3) communication and mutual support are lacking (Hirschi, 1969; Poole and Regoli, 1979). Furthermore, while occasional studies indicate that parental conflict may have a somewhat greater negative effect on girls than on boys (Norland et al., 1979), most indicate that gender makes strikingly little difference (Jensen and Eve, 1976). Family conflict is about as likely to produce delinquent behavior among boys as among girls.

Given these findings, the existing evidence suggests two basic conclusions with respect to the family. First, because of the problems associated with official data, most investigators are inclined to support Hirschi's hypothesis "that the presence or absence of parents is less relevant to an understanding of delinquency than the quality of the parent-child relationship" (Jensen and Rojek, 1980:199). Second, whether based on official or self-reported data, virtually all studies suggest that the juveniles who are most likely to be delinquent—whether male or female, black or white, lower or middle class—are those whose attachment to their parents is weak (Dinitz, 1962; Hirschi, 1969; Norland et al., 1979). Conversely, the stronger their attachment, the greater their conformity.

2. *Attachment to school.* In assessing attachment to school, Hirschi alludes to the significant place that education has come to occupy in the lives of children. Insofar as this "eminently conventional institution is able to command their attachment," he says, "they are . . . presumably able to move from childhood to adulthood with a minimum of delinquent acts" (1969:110). Indeed, as discussed in prior chapters, the evidence is overwhelming in its support of this conclusion.

First, as Jensen and Rojek indicate, the school has commanded the attention of an ever-increasing number of young people:

> The dropout rate in 1924 was so high that in the 10th grade less than 50 percent of students were still in school and only 39 percent of the 1924 cohort graduated from high school. By 1962 we find a dramatic increase in school retention rates, with over 90 percent entering the 10th grade and over 75 percent of that cohort graduating from high school. In fact, 45 percent of the 1962 cohort entered college and 22 percent earned a college degree in 1975 (1980:201–202).

Second, research indicates that the results can be devastating for those young people who fail in school. Whether male or female, black or white, lower or middle class, those who do the worst in school are most likely to be delinquent (Elliott and Voss, 1974; Empey and Lubeck, 1971; Hirschi, 1969; Johnson, 1979; Polk and Schafer, 1972; Rankin, 1980; Stinchcombe, 1964).

But delinquency is not the only problem. Estimated unemployment rates for all adolescents who are not in school run anywhere from 20 to 40 percent, but for black and Hispanic teenagers they are as high as 50 or 60 percent (National League of Cities, 1977). The basic question, therefore, is not whether attachment to school is important but to what its absence shall be attributed. Why is it that delinquents are more likely than nondelinquents to have broken their ties to the educational system?

Strain theory suggests that the break is due to frustration over blocked opportunities, or to a growing sense of inadequacy because of failure to live up to the standards of the middle-class measuring rod. Control theory, by contrast, suggests that the break represents insensitivity to the opinions of teachers, parents, and conventional friends, followed by a lack of commitment to long-range goals. Students who fail in school simply do not care about the opinions of others, and are not interested in the hard work that conventional success demands.

The available evidence relative to these contrasting interpretations is not entirely clear. On the one hand, much of it appears to support control theory by indicating that students who fail in school, and who become delinquent, tend to have lower, not higher, aspirations, thus questioning the idea that poor attachment is due to frustrated ambitions (Hirschi, 1969; Rankin, 1980; Shover et al., 1979). By contrast, boys and girls who have higher aspirations are not only more closely attached to parents and teachers, but also they are less delinquent.

On the other hand, research does not clearly indicate whether lack of attachment to school precedes or follows the possession of lower aspirations. If control theory is correct, lowered aspirations should be preceded by lack of attachment. But Cohen (1955) has theorized that, while lower-class boys start out with high aspirations, it is the loss of status they suffer in the school that eventually causes them to reject everything middle class, including long-range goals. In other words, the lack of attachment follows the frustration of aspirations rather than preceding it.

Unfortunately, research cannot completely resolve this difference of opinion because it has not documented the sequence in which these events occur. Nevertheless, it is possible that, for some youths at least, poor attachment to others is the result rather than the cause of lowered aspirations. Although perhaps interested in school as elementary students, these youngsters have become alienated from it by the time they reach adolescence. Their lack of attachment and their delinquent conduct are certainly real, as control theory suggests, but their problems may not be due to a life-long disregard for conventional people and conventional goals. Instead, it may be due to unpleasant experiences which the school itself has fostered.

In the same vein, there is the question of intellectual ability. Since those days in which people assumed that most delinquents must be mentally deficient, theorists have been inclined to reject the notion that intellectual impairment could play any role in contributing to delinquent behavior. Hirschi and Hindelang (1977) argue, however, that it may have a weak and indirect, but nonetheless important, influence. If children have the capacity to do well in school, the chances are greater that they will become attached to it. But if they lack that capacity, their poor performance will lead to a dislike of school, followed in turn by a rejection of authority, followed by delinquent behavior.

Again, however, the kinds of longitudinal research needed to explore this question are not yet available. Nonetheless, a variety of studies indicate that (1) delinquents may be less competent in social and organizational terms than nondelinquents (Dinitz et al., 1962; Toby and Toby, 1962:27; Reiss and Rhodes, 1961:723;

Short and Strodtbeck, 1965:237–238); (2) regardless of their socioeconomic or racial status, delinquents do less well on achievement tests (Hirschi, 1969:113–115; Wolfgang et al., 1972:245–250; Jensen, 1976); (3) delinquents get poorer grades in school (Empey and Lubeck, 1971:96–97; Hirschi, 1969:117–118; Polk, 1967; Wolfgang et al., 1972); and (4) delinquents are more likely to reject school authority (Hindelang, 1973:478; Hirschi, 1969:123–124; Stinchcombe, 1964).

Given such findings, control theorists argue that we should continue to investigate the possible role of intelligence, even if its effects on school problems and delinquent conduct are indirect. Other theorists, by contrast, maintain that, since intelligence tests can never be expected to separate the effects of inherited ability from the effects of environment, we should shy away from the dangerous implication that intelligence may be genetic in origin, particularly where poor children are involved (Simons, 1978). We should recognize instead that it is their disadvantaged position in the social structure that produces their problems, not any impaired capacity on their parts (Cloward and Ohlin, 1960).

In summary, research regarding this aspect of control theory has been inconsistent—both definitive and unclear. On the one hand, it leaves little doubt that attachment to school is crucial in separating delinquents from nondelinquents, and that high aspirations are more likely to act as barriers to delinquency than as motivators for it. The data, in other words, support control rather than strain theory. On the other hand, research does not permit us to determine whether delinquents have always been insensitive to conventional goals and people, or whether they acquire such feelings as a result of the school experience. Moreover, it is even less clear as to whether lowered intelligence plays a role in contributing, first, to failure in school and, second, to delinquency.

3. *Attachment to friends.* Affinity with friends is the final dimension of attachment. As we have seen, control theory suggests that young people who do not like and respect their parents and teachers are those most likely to be delinquent. But the theory also suggests that these individuals are not likely to develop respect for their friends either. The reason is that they have never developed feelings of compassion and responsibility for anyone. These theorists believe that while delinquents may join together in groups or gangs, their relations will be exploitive rather than warm and supportive.

This aspect of control theory has been one of the most difficult to confirm or to deny. On the one hand, delinquent behavior among females as well as among males is overwhelmingly a group phenomenon (Erickson and Jensen, 1977; Gold, 1970). Furthermore, as Johnson (1979:109) demonstrates, the school seems to be an arena in which adolescents are sifted and sorted into different groups—some deviant, some conformist. In an attempt to explain these phenomena, cultural deviance and strain theorists have suggested that, in the deviant groups, friends become a sort of substitute society for delinquent youths, providing the satisfactions that nondelinquents find through conventional associates. These theorists believe that because they are outsiders, delinquents are more dependent upon their friends than are nondelinquents and, thus, are more attached to them.

On a superficial level, at least, several studies have implied that this may be the case. When ties are weak to parents and school, peer approval increases in importance (Johnson, 1979:101; Friday and Hage, 1976). And while girls do not form the street gangs so common among boys (Miller, 1975), they are rarely loners either (Thompson and Lozes, 1976). When they use alcohol and drugs, girls often respond to the expectations of their boyfriends more than to those of their girlfriends (Bowker, 1978:63). But in other circumstances, the support of female associates is of undeniable importance (Giordano, 1978; Norland et al., 1979).

Delinquent boys, meanwhile, are more likely to form all-male groups and to exhibit a greater tendency to be affected by the demands of their peers than nondelinquents (Empey and Lubeck, 1968; Erickson and Empey, 1965; Hindelang, 1973; Jensen and Rojek, 1980). Hence, this body of research implies that Hirschi underestimated the role played by peer support in helping to justify and make possible delinquent acts. A person in a group is a much different entity from a person alone. Indeed, if delinquents were psychopaths—people who feel no obligation to others—one might anticipate that they either would be loners or would use the group solely to satisfy their own selfish interests. But given what we know about delinquents, this portrait certainly does not seem accurate for all of them.

On the other hand, the fact that delinquents are more inclined than conventional adolescents to go along with their peers in committing delinquent acts does not necessarily mean that they are as inclined as others to hold their associates in high esteem. With regard to this issue, in fact, Hirschi (1969:145–152) found that those boys who were least respectful of their friends were most likely to have committed delinquent acts.

And while this was not always true, his findings did tend to support the contentions of others that delinquent groups are not groups in which one feels "laid back" or relaxed. Given their unrelenting emphasis upon protecting status and demonstrating toughness, male groups, in particular, are characterized more by aggression, threat, and insult than by warmth, respect, and solidarity (Matza, 1964:33; Short and Strodtbeck, 1965:221–34; Yablonsky, 1963:196). In fact, Klein and Crawford (1967) argued that, were it not for the external pressures of rival groups, neighbors, and police, ordinary street gangs would have little to hold them together. Their highly prized loyalty to each other is more an expression of the need to resist outside pressure than to repay internal debts of kindness and mutual esteem. They may, in fact, be relatively asocial individuals.

In light of these conflicted findings, two conclusions are in order. On the one hand, Hirschi's theory appears to overlook the crucial role played by peers in the commission of delinquent acts. On the other hand, his contention that delinquents are less attached to their friends than conventional adolescents is by no means disproven. Indeed, definitive research on the precise character of delinquent, as contrasted with conventional, groups is desperately needed.

Commitment

As the second element of the social bond, *commitment* assumes that the motivation to adhere to the ideal concept of childhood and to strive for conventional goals is a built-in constraint on delinquent behavior. Such an individual has a stake in conformity which he or she feels will be jeopardized by deviant conduct. For example, Hirschi theorizes that those children who engage in such adult activities as smoking, drinking, using drugs, dating, and driving at an early age are more likely to commit criminal acts. By claiming the right to do these things, they deny their status as children, express contempt for the expectations of parents and teachers, and free themselves from the norms governing childhood.

The evidence in support of these contentions has been rather consistent. Whether male or female, rural or urban, juveniles who willingly violate the expectations of childhood at an early age are more likely to commit delinquent acts (Hirschi, 1969:166–169; Hindelang, 1973).

Furthermore, such acts as drinking, using drugs, and being obsessed with cars are cumulative in their effect: the more juveniles are involved in these activities, the greater their involvement in delinquency (Hindelang, 1973:481).

So much for the deviant side of the coin. What about the conformist side? What effect does a commitment to an education or a career have on delinquency?

We have already seen that ambition, with its implied commitment to long-term educational and occupational goals, is more likely to operate as a barrier to than a cause of delinquency. Therefore, it is not difficult to anticipate the results of research. They indicate that those girls and boys who are committed to staying in school and who otherwise conform to the requirements of childhood are the least likely to rob, steal, or fight (Briar and Piliavin, 1965; Hindelang, 1973; Hirschi, 1969; Johnson, 1979). Indeed, Shover et al. (1979) found that the more faithful girls remain to traditionally feminine roles, the less likely they are to commit property crimes. In short, a commitment to traditional expectations seems to have a dampening effect on the criminal conduct of both genders.

Involvement

The third concept, *involvement*, predicts that participation in conventional activities should also deter delinquency. The evidence, however, is mixed. On the one hand, the greater the involvement in studying or doing homework, the lower the delinquency (Hirschi, 1969:191–192; Hindelang, 1973:481–483). On the other hand, participation in sports, intercollegiate athletics, hobbies, or even a job does not seem to have the dampening effect that was predicted. Young people who engage in these activities are almost as likely to be delinquent as those who do not (Hirschi, 1969:189–90; Jensen and Rojek, 1980:181–82).

Consequently, of these types of activities, it is involvement in academic activities rather than other conventional pursuits that serves as the greatest deterrent to delinquency.

Belief

As the final concept, control theory suggests that *beliefs* are relatively stable attributes of a person and are generally impervious to transitory relationships. They are a part of the conscience. Hence, if girls and boys have been trained to believe in the morality of law, they will be less inclined to be delinquent, no matter what groups they encounter.

By contrast, symbolic interactionist theory suggests that beliefs are relatively transitory attitudes which can be readily shaped and reshaped, depending upon the groups with whom one associates. Even though one might have been a member of law-abiding groups in the past, differential association with a deviant group in which there is an excess of definitions favorable to the violation of law can lead one to alter one's beliefs and to commit delinquent acts.

Research designed to examine these opposing points of view has lent total support to neither. On the one hand, a number of studies appear to lend some support to control theory. Boys and girls who are not closely attached to parents and school are those who have the least respect for the law and the police. These same juveniles, in turn, are the ones most likely to be delinquent (Dinitz et al., 1962; Hindelang, 1973; Hirschi, 1969:200–203).

On the other hand, some investigators have sought to separate the effects of parental supervision, or peer group associations, from the effects of beliefs about the law (Jensen, 1972). In doing so, they have found that beliefs tend to be of secondary importance: although they have some effect on delinquent behavior, parental controls or involvement with delinquent peers have a more direct and powerful effect.

For example, juveniles who do not express beliefs in the morality of law, but who are attached to their parents and are carefully supervised by them, will likely be less delinquent than juveniles who say they believe in the law, but are unsupervised. Conversely, if such controls are lacking, deviant peers can influence them to be delinquent without necessarily causing them to discard their prosocial beliefs. In short, there seems to be a hierarchy of influences on delinquency, with parental controls ranking first, peer relationships second, and beliefs last. In any social situation, therefore, beliefs will rank below the other two in determining behavior.

SUMMARY AND CONCLUSIONS

The publication of Hirschi's control theory in 1969 was valuable because it helped to rectify a striking anomaly in academic criminology: the tendency to downgrade the importance of intrafamily relationships. Although a host of social scientists in other disciplines had long felt that these relationships were vital in determining the course of child development, criminologists had argued, for almost half a century, that they were relatively unimportant when compared to socioeconomic, racial, and subcultural factors. They contended that delinquency results not from the way families are organized, but from the way society is structured. Indeed, when considering the most serious problem of all—lower-class male delinquency—intrafamily relationships are of little importance. Instead, no less than the delinquent boys who are members of them, families are but pawns in the larger scheme of human affairs.

Following the publication of Hirschi's theory, however, research on the family began to increase. Nonetheless, it sparked reactions that were negative as well as positive, ideological as well as scientific. It is a reconstruction of the delinquency problem that remains very much in contention today.

1. ***Assumptions about human nature and social order.*** This contention stems, in no little part, from Hirschi's resurrection of some old, very conservative points of view about human nature; namely that all people would be delinquent if given the chance. Without adequate socialization, or the presence of social control, delinquent conduct would be common. Rather than working for years to pay for a car, for example, people would simply steal one. What children must be taught, therefore, is not how to break the law but how to restrain their natural impulses and how to be law abiding.

Meanwhile, Hirschi, like other control theorists, also assumed that the social order is characterized by value consensus. People are not divided into subcultures according to differing values; rather, most people agree that crime is bad. Hence, it is only delinquents (and adult criminals) who defy convention and threaten social stability.

2. ***Logic and content of control theory.*** Social control theory is as much a theory of conformity as of delinquency. Since all of us are animals at birth who will prey upon others unless restrained, we must seek to explain what spells the difference between deviance and conformity.

The answer is the social bond. If the process of socialization is effective—if children are attached to others, committed to long-range goals, involved in conventional activities, and believe in the morality of law—the social bond will develop, a stake in conformity will be created, and conformist behavior will result. But if socialization is ineffective, natural human impulses will remain unrestrained, children will be free to deviate, and delinquent conduct will be the consequence. (See Figure 12–1.)

3. ***Policy implications.*** Hirschi's assumption about human nature aside, his version of control theory is the kind of explanation which makes sense to authorities and upon which they base many of their interventions. They can readily understand the need to reattach delinquents to some kind of family, recommit them to long-range goals, involve them in constructive activities, and cultivate their belief in the morality of law.

4. ***Logical and empirical adequacy.*** Hirschi contends that social control theory will predict delinquency across the lines of gender, class, and race. Relative to the concepts of attachment, commitment, and involvement, this contention has held up rather well. Those elements of the theory which have best stood the test of logical and empirical scrutiny are those which (1) stress the idea that attachment to family and school is crucial in

FIGURE 12–1

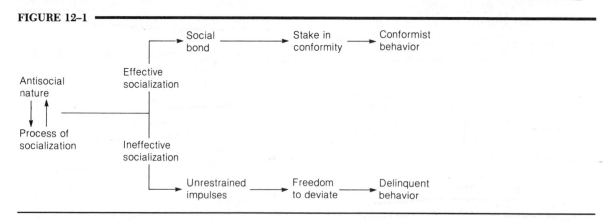

spelling the difference between conformity and deviance; (2) indicate that commitment to long-term educational and occupational goals is a barrier to, rather than a cause of, delinquent behavior; and (3) suggest that involvement is academic pursuits, if not other conventional activities, is useful in promoting conformity.

By contrast, the areas most in question are Hirschi's concepts of human nature and social order, and his view of the delinquent as a psychopath who lacks compassion and feeling for anyone. Just as cultural deviance, strain, and interactionist theories were extreme in painting delinquents as moral and gregarious people who violate the law only because they feel compelled to adhere to the expectations of others, social control theory probably goes too far in the opposite direction. When it indicates that delinquents are unsocialized predators, it underestimates the role of peers in generating support for delinquent conduct, overstates the importance of acquired beliefs as barriers to delinquent behavior, and leaves unaddressed the issues raised by the economic, political, and racial organization of society.

Although attachment, commitment, and involvement are barriers to delinquency, it cannot be said that all juveniles share an equal opportunity to experience these civilizing influences. Why, for example, is the prototypical perpetrator of violent crime synonymous with the prototypical victim— a young minority male who is a ghetto dweller?

Control theory is probably correct in suggesting that he is neither well attached to a stable home life, nor committed to conventional long-range goals, nor involved in academic pursuits. Furthermore, control theory is probably more realistic than cultural deviance, strain, or interactionist theories in painting the destructive consequences of a disrupted social bond. Life for the young urban street dweller is not a romantic odyssey, characterized by warm companionship and a carefree life. As Claude Brown put it so eloquently,

> I remember Johnny saying that the only thing in life a bad nigger was scared of was living too long. This just meant that if you were going to be respected in Harlem you had to be a bad nigger; and if you were going to be a bad nigger, you had to be ready to die. I wasn't ready to do any of that stuff. But I had to. I had to act crazy.
>
> Sometimes I used to get headaches thinking about it. I used to get sick. I couldn't get up. And sometimes I'd just jump out of bed and run out and say, "C'mon, man, let's go steal somethin'!" I'd get Turk, I'd get Tito, I'd get anybody who was around. I'd say, "C'mon, man, let's go pull a score." It seemed like the only way I could get away (1965:127).

Although Brown, was, in fact, poorly attached to home and school, control theory is still unable to encompass the range of forces which contributed to his delinquent conduct. Being aware of his need for greater love and understanding from his parents, we also need to know that they were saddled with a legacy of racial descrimination, poverty, and injustice. Hence, if they were to do a better job of insulating him against the destructive influences that surrounded him, they had to somehow sublimate their own feelings of anger, demoralization, and inadequacy, arm him against the chaos that so often characterizes ghetto schools, and make algebra and social studies more attractive than life on the streets. Clearly, theirs was a herculean task for which better intrafamily relations were not the only answer. At the root of their problems were economic, political, and cultural forces that extended well beyond the limits of their immediate family—forces about which control theory does not provide us with adequate understanding.

In addition, research suggests that more

privileged families also have problems of a more general type, generated by the impersonal character of modern society, the constant struggle for status and belonging, and the economic and ideological changes that can make the role of being a parent seem increasingly less rewarding.

In short, whether we seek to understand the delinquent behavior of either privileged or underprivileged youth, we must combine the insights provided by control theory with those provided by broader, more structural, theories. Beyond the study of intrafamily and school relationships, we must also explore the effects on these institutions by political, economic, and demographic forces. Childhood in American society is designed and organized by all of these social forces.

REFERENCES

Bordua, David J.
  1962   "Some Comments on Theories of Group Delinquency." *Sociological Inquiry* 33 (Spring):245–260.

Bowker, Lee H.
  1978   *Women, Crime and the Criminal Justice System.* Lexington, Mass.: D. C. Heath.

Briar, Scott and Piliavin, Irving
  1965   "Delinquency, Situational Inducement and Commitment to Conformity." *Social Problems* 8 (Summer):35–45.

Brown, Claude
  1965   *Manchild in the Promised Land.* New York: Macmillan.

Chilton, Roland and DeAmicis, Jan
  1975   "Overcriminalization and the Measurement of Consensus." *Sociology and Social Research* 59 (July):318–329.

Chilton, Roland J., and Markle, Gerald E.
  1972   "Family Disruption, Delinquency Conduct and the Effect of Subclassification." *American Sociological Review* 37 (February):93–99.

Cloward, Richard A., and Ohlin, Lloyd E.
  1960   *Delinquency and Opportunity: A Theory of Delinquent Gangs.* New York: Free Press.

Cockburn, J. J. and Maclay, I.
  1965   "Sex Differentials in Juvenile Delinquency." *British Journal of Criminology* 5 (July):289–308.

Cohen, Albert K.
  1955   *Delinquent Boys: The Culture of the Gang.* New York: Free Press.

Cowie, John; Cowie, Valerie; and Slater, Eliot
  1968   *Delinquency in Girls.* London: Heineman.

Datesman, Susan K., and Scarpitti, Frank R.
  1975   "Female Delinquency and Broken Homes: A Reassessment." Criminology 13 (May):33–55.

Dinitz, Simon et al.
  1962   "Delinquency Vulnerability: A Cross Group and Longitudinal Analysis." *American Sociological Review* 27 (August):515–517.

Durkheim, Emile
    1951   *Suicide.* Translated by John A. Spaulding and George Simpson. New York: Free Press.
Durkheim, Emile
    1963   *Sociology and Philosophy.* Glencoe, Ill.: Free Press.
Elliott, Delbert S., and Voss, Harwin L.
    1974   *Delinquency and Dropout.* Lexington, Mass.: D. C. Heath.
Empey, LaMar T., and Lubeck, Steven G.
    1968   "Conformity and Deviance in the Situation of Company." *American Sociological Review* 33 (October):761–774.
    1971   *Explaining Delinquency.* Lexington, Mass.: D. C. Heath.
Erickson, Maynard L. and Empey, LaMar T.
    1965   "Class Position, Peers and Delinquency." *Sociology and Social Research* 49 (April):268–82.
Erickson, Maynard L., and Jensen, Gary F.
    1977   "Delinquency is Still Group Behavior: Toward Revitalizing the Group Premise in the Sociology of Deviance." *Journal of Criminal Law and Criminology* 68:262–273.
Farrington, D. P., and West, D. J.
    1981   "The Cambridge Study in Delinquent Development." In S. A. Mednick and A. E. Baert, eds., *Prospective Longitudinal Research: An Empirical Basis for Primary Psychosocial Disorders.* New York: Oxford University Press.
Friday, Paul C. and Hage, Jerald
    1976   "Youth Crime in Postindustrial Societies." *Criminology* 14 (November):347–67.
Giordano, Peggy C.
    1978   "Girls, Boys and Gangs: The Changing Context of Female Delinquency." *Journal of Criminal Law and Criminology* 69:126–132.
Glueck, Sheldon and Glueck, Eleanor
    1968   *Delinquents and Nondelinquents in Perspective.* Cambridge: Harvard University Press.
Gold, Martin
    1963   *Status Forces in Delinquent Boys.* Ann Arbor: Institute for Social Research, University of Michigan.
    1970   *Delinquent Behavior in an American City.* Monterey, Calif.: Brooks/Cole.
Hindelang, Michael J.
    1973   "Causes of Delinquency: A Partial Replication." *Social Problems* 21 (Spring):471–87.
Hirschi, Travis
    1969   *Causes of Delinquency.* Berkeley: University of California Press.
Hirschi, Travis, and Hindelang, Michael J.
    1977   "Intelligence and Delinquency: A Revisionist Review." *American Sociological Review* 42 (August):571–587.
Jensen, Gary F.
    1972   "Parents, Peers, and Delinquent Action: A Test of the Differential Association Perspective." *American Journal of Sociology* 78:562–575.

1976   "Race, Achievement and Delinquency: A Further Look at Delinquency in a Birth Cohort." *American Journal of Sociology* 82 (September):379–387.

Jensen, Gary F., and Eve, Raymond
1976   "Sex Differences in Delinquency: An Examination of Popular Sociological Explanations." *Criminology* 13 (February):427–448.

Jensen, Gary F., and Rojek, Dean G.
1980   *Delinquency: A Sociological View.* Lexington, Mass.: D. C. Heath.

Johnson, Richard E.
1979   *Juvenile Delinquency and its Origins.* New York: Cambridge University Press.

Klein, Dorie
1973   "The Etiology of Female Crime: a Review of the Literature." *Issues in Criminology* 8 (Fall):3–30.

Klein, Malcolm W., and Crawford, Lois Y.
1967   "Groups, Gangs and Cohesiveness." *Journal of Research in Crime and Delinquency* 4 (January):63–75.

Konopka, Gisela
1966   *The Adolescent Girl in Conflict.* Englewood Cliffs, New Jersey: Prentice-Hall.

Matza, David
1964   *Delinquency and Drift.* New York: John Wiley & Sons.

Miller, Walter G.
1975   *Violence by Youth Gangs and Youth Groups as a Crime Problem in Major American Cities.* Washington, D.C.: U.S. Government Printing Office.

Monahan, Thomas P.
1957   "Family Status and the Delinquent Child: A Reappraisal and Some New Findings." *Social Forces* 35 (March):250–258.

National League of Cities
1977   *CETA and Youth: Programs for Cities.* Washington, D.C.: National League of Cities and U.S. Conference of Mayors.

Nettler, Gwynn
1974   *Explaining Crime.* New York: McGraw-Hill.

Norland, Stephen; Shover, Neal; Thornton, William E.; and James, Jennifer
1979   "Intrafamily Conflict and Delinquency. *Pacific Sociological Review* 2 (April):223–240.

Nye, Ivan
1958   *Family Relationships and Delinquent Behavior.* New York: John Wiley & Sons.

Polk, Kenneth
1967   "Urban Social Areas and Delinquency." *Social Problems,* Winter, 14:320–325.

Polk, Kenneth, and Schafer, Walter E., eds.
1972   *School and Delinquency.* Englewood Cliffs, N.J.: Prentice-Hall.

Pollack, Otto
1950   *The Criminality of Women.* Philadelphia: University of Pennsylvania Press.

Poole, Eric D., and Regoli, Robert M.
　　1979　"Parental Support, Delinquent Friends and Delinquency: A Test of Interaction Effects." *Journal of Criminal Law and Criminology* 70:188–193.

Rankin, Joseph H.
　　1980　"School Factors and Delinquency: Interactions by Age and Sex." *Sociology and Social Research* 64 (April):420–434.

Raspberry, William
　　1980　"Joblessness: System Isn't the Only Culprit." *Los Angeles Times* December 12, 2:5.

Reckless, Walter C.
　　1961　"A New Theory of Delinquency and Crime." *Federal Probation* 25 (December):42–46.

Reiss, Albert J., Jr., and Rhodes, Albert L.
　　1961　"The Distribution of Juvenile Delinquency in the Social Class Structure." *American Sociological Review* 26 (October):720–732.

Rodman, Hyman, and Grams, Paul
　　1969　"Juvenile Delinquency and the Family: A Review and Discussion." President's Commission on Law Enforcement and Administration of Justice. *Task Force Report: Juvenile Delinquency and Youth Crime.* Washington, D.C.: U.S. Government Printing Office.

Rossi, Peter H. et al.
　　1974　"The Seriousness of Crimes: Normative Structure and Individual Differences." *American Sociological Review* 30 (April):224–237.

Short, James F., Jr., and Strodtbeck, Fred L.
　　1965　*Group Process and Gang Delinquency.* Chicago: University of Chicago Press.

Shover, Neal, and Norland, Stephen
　　1978　"Sex Roles and Criminality: Science or Conventional Wisdom?" *Sex Roles* 4 (February):111–125.

Shover, Neal; Norland, Stephen; James, Jennifer; and Thornton, William
　　1979　"Gender Roles and Delinquency." *Social Forces* 58 (September):162–175.

Simons, Ronald L.
　　1978　"The Meaning of the IQ-Delinquency Relationship." *American Sociological Review* 43 (April):268–270.

Stinchcombe, Arthur L.
　　1964　*Rebellion in High School.* Chicago: Quadrangle Books.

Sutherland, Edwin H., and Cressey, Donald R.
　　1955　*Principles of Criminology.* 5th ed. Chicago: J. B. Lippincott.

Thompson, R. J., and Lozes, J.
　　1976　"Female Gang Delinquency." *Corrective and Social Psychiatry and Journal of Behavior Technology Methods and Therapy* 22:1–5.

Toby, Jackson
　　1957　"Social Disorganization and Stake in Conformity." *Journal of Criminal Law, Criminology and Police Science* 48:12–17.

Toby, Jackson, and Toby, Marcia L.
　　1962　"Low School Status as a Predisposing Factor in Subcultural Delinquency." Mimeographed. New Brunswick: Rutgers University.

Vedder, Clyde
    1979   *Juvenile Offenders.* Springfield, Ill.: Charles C Thomas.

Wellford, Charles
    1975   "Labelling Theory and Criminology: An Assessment." *Social Problems* 23 (February):332–345.

Wilkinson, Karen
    1974   "The Broken Family and Juvenile Delinquency: Scientific Explanation or Ideology?" *Social Problems* 21 (June):726–739.

Wolfgang, Marvin E.; Figlio, Robert; and Sellin, Thorsten
    1972   *Delinquency in a Birth Cohort.* Chicago: University of Chicago Press.

Yablonsky, Lewis
    1963   *The Violent Gang.* New York: Macmillan.

Research on theories of delinquency makes use of the latest computer technology.

POSITIVE THEORIES OF DELINQUENT BEHAVIOR: SOME CONCLUSIONS

In our review of positive theories, we encountered a bewildering array of ideas, images, and research findings. If we are to benefit from that review, therefore, we must now seek to summarize what we have learned. This can be done by pursuing the answers to four questions: (1) What major images of the delinquent have been portrayed by the theories of positive criminology? (2) How well do these theories actually predict law-violating behavior? (3) What are the problems associated with predicting delinquent behavior? and (4) What are the implications of positive theory and research for the prevention and control of delinquent behavior?

IMAGES OF THE DELINQUENT

Classical criminology theory did not draw sharp distinctions between delinquents and nondelinquents. Instead, it pictured delinquents as free and rational individuals who violate the law in pursuit of self-satisfaction. Positive criminology theory, by contrast, pictures juvenile lawbreakers as abnormal people, fundamentally different from nondelinquents. Theoretical images are created which suggest that they are atypical, either because they are *unsocialized* and lack a conscience, or because they have been *socialized* into a delinquent, though related, subculture.

The unsocialized delinquent

The image of delinquents as unsocialized people is derived primarily from control theory. It suggests that they are unsocialized (or undersocialized) because they are "relatively free of the intimate attachments, the aspirations, and the moral beliefs that bind most people to a life within the law" (Hirschi, 1977:329). They lack a conscience, are insensitive to others, have no stake in conformity, and are free to deviate.

Although other theorists might disagree, Hirschi (1977) maintains that this image of the delinquent comes not only from his version of control theory, but also from other theories. First, there are the psychological and biological

285

control theories which stress the importance of cultivating *internal* controls within the individual. The child-raising practices of the nuclear family are certainly necessary to accomplish this; but to the degree that a low IQ or a faulty physiology interfere with the process of socialization, children will not learn to inhibit their antisocial inclinations, will not become attached to family and school, and will not acquire the moral and academic skills necessary for a stake in conformity (Hirschi, 1977; Hirschi and Hindelang, 1977; Mednick and Christiansen, 1977).

Second, there are sociological theories, parts of which stress the need for *external* controls over children—controls whose absence can help to account for high rates of juvenile crime and sizable differences in delinquency rates across communities. One such theory is the cultural deviance theory of Shaw and McKay. Although this theory suggests that delinquent peer groups can eventually become important in the commission of delinquent acts, it derives from the premise that such groups might not even exist were the families and neighborhoods of our central cities better organized. But because they are disorganized—because they are characterized by poverty, ethnic discrimination, transiency, and ignorance—children grow up in a social climate of institutional breakdown and failure.

In addition to control theory, therefore, the Shaw-McKay theory might be used to construct an image of the delinquent as an undersocialized individual whose conscience is weakened by the absence of internal controls and whose bond to society is not fully developed due to inadequate or disorganized external controls.

The socialized delinquent

Several theories construct an image of delinquents as *socialized*, even highly motivated, individuals. Best known for this construction are sociological theories, which stress the roles of strain and delinquent subculture in the lives of young people. Strain theory, for example, suggests that delinquents not only share with all good people a universal belief in the importance of ambition and success, but also suffer acute and intense frustration when they are denied legitimate access to these desires. Hence, only when their opportunities are blocked by cruel circumstance do that they turn to delinquent subcultures for guidance and to illegitimate means for success.

In the same vein, middle-class cultural deviance theory suggests that delinquency is a subcultural variation of middle-class culture. In response to age stratification, a distinctive youth subculture develops which is nothing more than an immature, and somewhat distorted, caricature of adult values and standards. Likewise, slum youths in Miller's version of cultural deviance theory become delinquent because of their faithful adherence to a distinctive lower-class culture organized around single-sex peer groups. Their conduct, differing from middle-class behavior, is merely a reflection of widely shared lower-class values. Indeed, the peers who are the carriers of delinquent traditions in these theories are to the subculture theorist what families are to the control theorist (Matza, 1964:19). They provide the intimate setting within which highly motivated individuals generate and transmit alternative, albeit delinquent, standards for behavior.

In summary, then, socialized delinquents are people whose behavior represents conformity to an ethical code which makes their deviant conduct mandatory. Through no fault of their own, they have simply been thrust outside the pale of ordinary life because of the way society is organized. The only reason they are delinquents is because they "belong to what is essentially a different though related culture" (Matza, 1964:18).

Underlying assumptions

In seeking to understand the implications of these two images, it is necessary to recall the positivistic assumptions upon which they are based: that (1) whether delinquents are unsocialized or socialized, their behavior is determined by forces over which they have little or no personal control; (2) if crime is to be understood, our primary attention should be focused upon delinquents and their behavior, not upon the law; and (3) delinquents are fundamentally different from nondelinquents.

In reflecting on these assumptions and the images they project, Matza concludes that they have created "a distorted and misleading picture of the delinquent and his enterprise" (1964:21). Self-report studies, for example, indicate that the great majority of all young people commit delinquent acts. Yet, these and other accounts of crime also indicate that law breaking peaks at about age 16, and then begins to decline. Most young people grow up and become progressively less delinquent; Matza calls this "maturational reform."

If this reform is taken into account, it implies that the hard determinism of positive criminology may possess serious logical weaknesses. Biological theories would be the hardest hit, since they imply that a lawbreaker possess some relatively permanent neurological disorder, an endocrine imbalance, or some other biological anomaly. Why, then, would the effects of such disorders begin to decline at about age 16? Why would they not continue to cause people to commit crimes throughout the remainder of their lives?

By the same token, it could be asked, if delinquents are unsocialized and thus compelled by their asocial tendencies to violate the law, why are most of them only intermittently delinquent while young and eventually live relatively conventional lives as they grow older?

Finally, if juveniles are socialized members of a delinquent subculture whose beliefs make crime mandatory, why do so many of them apparently set these beliefs aside when they reach adulthood? Do they experience a sudden conversion to conventional morality? Or are subcultural and strain theories overdrawn and excessively deterministic?

In short, the maturational reform of many, probably most, young people, coupled with the fact that their delinquent conduct has been intermixed with a great deal of commonplace adolescent behavior, suggests that the assumptions and implications of positive theories need reexamination.

An alternative image: Delinquent as "drifter"

Matza (1964) suggests that we should consider an alternative image of the delinquent—one that comes closer to that painted by symbolic interactionist theory than to any other, but which is even less deterministic.

1. Soft determinism. First of all, this image requires that we discard the assumption of hard determinism. In its stead, a doctrine of soft determinism is substituted—a doctrine that stands somewhere between the emphasis of classical criminology upon *free will* and that of positive criminology upon *constraint.* The point is that almost all juveniles exercise some degree of choice in deciding whether to violate the law.

2. The delinquent and the law. Second, lawbreaking cannot be understood by concentrating solely upon delinquents and assuming that their behavior represents unqualified opposition to either conventional morality or the law. Instead, there is a complex interaction between the two. For example, there are times when the offender "sees his offense as prompted by virtue and justifies it accordingly" (Matza, 1964:155–156). Such behavior, however, would not be sophisticated and political. More likely, it would be childish—it would represent an effort by immature youth to express their version of adulthood.

Adolescent males, for example, "stand at the threshold of manhood, and consequently they are more obsessed by the postures and poses that symbolize and confirm it" (Matza, 1964:156). They attempt to exhibit a kind of precocious manhood by being flamboyant, reckless, and defiant. They think that by being "macho" they express the more mature virtues of honor, valor, and loyalty. For example, some boys steal a car to go joyriding not because stealing is right, but because one's reputation, and possibly one's loyalty to friends, is at stake and occasionally takes precedence over the law.

And while Matza did not say it, the same would presumably be true of the female delinquent. In an endeavor to be accepted, she is often torn between conventional and peer group morality. Hence, if she becomes delinquent, she justifies her drug use, shoplifting, or vandalism by noting that "everyone was doing it," or that she could do no less than "go along."

In short, if we are to understand delinquents, we must recognize that they drift in a limbo between the formal demands of the law and the more informal, more childish, prescriptions of adolescent groups.

3. *Delinquents as more or less normal.* Given their uncertain status, Matza (1964:28–30) suggests that it is an error to assume that delinquents are fundamentally different from nondelinquents. First, the delinquent enterprise is manned, for the most part, by the majority of all adolescents. As self-report studies indicate, it is the typical, not the atypical, adolescent who has violated the law. Second, adolescents have a unique role in modern society. Given their ambiguous and uncertain status, adolescents are neither child nor adult, neither free nor controlled. Instead, they stand on a continuum midway between freedom and control.

On the free end of the continuum are those people who have "a sense of command over [their own destinies], a capacity to formulate programs or projects, a feeling of being [agents] in [their own] behalf. Freedom is self control" (Matza, 1964:29).

On the control end are the relatively small number of chronic delinquents who have virtually no self-control over their lives. Instead, they are compelled to commit crime by their own neuroses or their commitment to delinquent values. But rather than representing the majority of young law violators, these delinquents represent a tiny minority.

Consequently, most delinquents are neither free, like older and more responsible people, nor are they constrained, like the chronically delinquent few. Instead, they are "drifters":

> The image of the delinquent I wish to convey is one of drift; an actor neither compelled nor committed to deeds nor freely choosing them; neither different in any simple or fundamental sense from the law-abiding, nor the same; conforming to certain traditions in American life while partially unreceptive to other more conventional traditions (Matza, 1964:28).

This image is important because of the profound questions it raises concerning other images of positive criminology. If, for example, the behavior of delinquents is highly determined, as most theories suggest, then it should be possible for science to isolate its causes and predict its occurrence with considerable accuracy. But if the delinquent is merely an unconstrained and uncommitted adolescent who drifts in and out of delinquency by choice, then specific causes for his behavior will be less pronounced and its occurrence will not be readily predicted.

PREDICTING DELINQUENT BEHAVIOR

When we reviewed the evidence regarding various theories, many questions were raised about their power to predict delinquent behavior. It could be, therefore, that Matza is correct when he suggests that delinquent behavior cannot be readily predicted because most young people are neither consistently good nor bad. In order to determine whether this is true, however, it is necessary to consider two criteria: (1) whether, across the dimensions of gender, race, and social class, theories have identified any causes that actually predict delinquent behavior; and (2) whether those causes predict law violation with a high degree of accuracy.

Variables that predict delinquent behavior

As a matter of fact, there are some variables, suggested by several theories, that actually do predict illegal conduct.

1. *Attachment to parents.* To a greater or lesser degree, several theories indicate that the ties between parents and child are important. If families lose control over their children (Shaw-McKay theory), if they are unable to prepare them to achieve in middle-class institutions (strain theory), or if the quality of their interpersonal relations is poor (social control theory), delinquent behavior will be more likely to occur.

Much more information is needed on the techniques used by concerned parents to train their children to succeed in a businesslike way. But research does indicate that if children have been disciplined with love and concern and if they like and respect their parents, they will be less delinquent. Consequently, an hypothesis for which there is considerable empirical support is this: *The weaker the attachment between parents and child, the greater the delinquent behavior.*

2. *The school.* Difficulties in school may be the best predictors of delinquency in

American society. Hence, many theories stress their central importance.

If schools are disorganized or unduly segregate juveniles from adult role models (cultural deviance theory), if schools frustrate students or subject them to a loss of self-esteem (strain theory), or if children do not respect their teachers and the authority of the school (control theory), delinquent behavior will be more likely to occur. In general, research has tended to confirm these arguments: *The weaker the attachment to the school, the greater the delinquent behavior.*

But attitudinal and emotional ties are not the only predictors to emerge from research on the school. An even stronger one is academic achievement. Those children who do less well on achievement tests, get poorer grades, and are not considered "college material" are those most likely to be delinquent. Hence, a second, school-related hypothesis has been indicated: *The lower the academic achievement, the greater the delinquent behavior.*

3. *Commitment to the means for success.* Both social control and strain theories suggest that the lack of achievement in the school, as well as delinquent behavior, are somehow related to the long-range plans and goals of juveniles. In seeking to explain these relationships, however, both theories cite concepts that are ambiguous and unclear.

Strain theory stresses *aspirations* and *means.* It hypothesizes that virtually all children possess lofty aspirations and are highly motivated to achieve them. Hence, if they become delinquent it is because legitimate means for success have been blocked or frustrated.

Control theory, by contrast, places greater stress upon *commitment* to success *goals.* All students are not possessed of high aspirations. Instead, those who fail in school and become delinquent do so because of a lack of commitment to long-range goals.

Scientific studies suggest that before we can

resolve these theoretical differences, we must clarify the meaning of these concepts and then use them more efficiently. For example, research indicates that aspirations can be viewed in two ways. On the one hand, if juveniles are asked what the important goals are in American society, virtually all of them will express the conventional view that a good job, wealth, material possessions, and prestige are important. In this sense, therefore, it could be said that they recognize and endorse American definitions of the "good life."

On the other hand, if these same juveniles are asked whether they aspire to complete high school, get a college education, and pursue a demanding career, some will not share these aspirations. Indeed, when defined in these terms, high aspirations appear to be an insulator against delinquency; that is, the higher the aspirations, the lower the delinquent conduct.

The problem with defining aspirations in terms of going to school and getting a job is that they become virtually synonymous with the means for success. That is, if people are to become wealthy and prestigious, most will have to use these conventional means by which to achieve them. Hence, both strain and control theories introduce confusion when they use aspirations and means interchangeably.

Finally, the concept of *commitment*, in conjunction with the other concepts, is also used ambiguously in strain and control theories. First, it is employed to reflect the degree to which juveniles aspire to the good life (strain theory), then it is used to determine the degree to which they are committed to the means for success (control theory).

In short, the same confusion concerning aspirations and means is perpetuated, but with the third concept of commitment added. Fortunately, steps can be taken to eliminate this confusion. Research suggests that, if we take *aspirations* to such general *goals* as wealth, happiness, and prestige for granted, since most

juveniles say they aspire to them, we can safely eliminate those concepts. Then we can concentrate on using the other two—*means* and *commitment*—more effectively. Various studies indicate that, if the conventional means for success are defined to include such activities as studying hard, getting as much education as possible, and finding a job, and if commitment is defined as including personal obligation and desire to employ these means in the pursuit of success, a third hypothesis can be derived for which there is empirical support: *The weaker the commitment to conventional means for success, the greater the delinquent behavior.* Despite aspiring to the good life, those individuals who are unwilling or unable to pay the conventional price for it are the most likely to become delinquent.

4. Identification with delinquent peers. Finally, there is the matter of peer influence. Cultural deviance, strain, and interactionist theories all suggest that disorganized or age-stratified communities, along with schools, seem to act as arenas where children are sifted and sorted into different groups—some deviant, some conformist. Consequently, this sorting process eventually culminates in the creation of delinquent subculture. The traditions and associates it generates become a sort of substitute family for marginal youths, providing the satisfactions that nondelinquents find through conventional means.

Scientific study has provided only partial support for these ideas. On the one hand, it has not supported two ideas that are central to several theories: (1) that delinquent peers are an effective family substitute for deviant adolescents, or (2) that these adolescents possess the organizational skills by which to develop and maintain a coherent system of deviant values, beliefs, and practices. Instead, delinquent groups tend to be loosely structured systems, characterized more by the pursuit of immature, transient, and vaguely formulated values than by subcultural traditions that make delinquent behavior inevitable, specialized, and mandatory.

On the other hand, peer relations are important. Research reveals that the juveniles most likely to be delinquent are those who (1) have a preponderance of deviant associates; and (2) are inclined to adhere to the situational demands of those associates, even if this places them in serious conflict with parents, teachers, or the law. While the majority of adolescents will defy authority some of the time, the more delinquent youngsters persist in doing so in the face of serious and repeated conflict. As a result, the following hypothesis is suggested: *The greater the identification with peers in the face of serious conflict with authority, the greater the delinquent behavior.*

In summary, this review portrays delinquents as young people whose bonds are weak and who lack a stake in conformity. Their attachment to parents and school is tenuous, their academic achievement is poor, their commitment to the conventional requirements of childhood is low, and their identification with delinquent peers often places them in serious conflict with authority.

As a consequence, this portrayal appears to conform more closely to the *undersocialized* image of delinquents, painted by social control theory, than to the highly motivated socialized image, painted by strain and subcultural theories. Judged by conventional standards, at least, delinquents conform less readily to the ideal requirements of childhood than do other children.

Predictive power of positive theory

This portrayal might be viewed as discounting Matza's negative critique of positive theories. However, such a conclusion would be premature, since we have not yet considered the second criterion for judging scientific evidence: its ability to predict delinquent behavior with a high degree of accuracy.

The predictive power of the variables in any theory is based upon the strength of their relationships to delinquent behavior. If those variables are able to explain that behavior with complete accuracy, if they can separate delinquents from nondelinquents without error, it is said that they account for 100 percent of the "variance."

Whether in the physical, natural, or social sciences, few, if any, theories approach this degree of perfection. But compared to those in some of the other sciences, criminological theories are relatively inefficient. Even when their effects are combined, for example, such variables as attachment to parents and school, academic achievement, commitment, and identification with delinquent peers account for only about 25 to 30 percent of the variance (Johnson, 1979; Hirschi, 1969). This means that, while we can say that certain juveniles are more likely than others to violate the law, we must also be aware that about two thirds of the variance goes unexplained. Why is this? Why is the predictive power of positive theory so low?

There are three possible answers. The first is that Matza is correct when he suggests that delinquency is due, in part, to the exercise of free will. If that is true, delinquent behavior may never be explained. Indeed, it is a contradiction in terms to suggest that science can indicate the factors that determine the exercise of will, since by definition will is unconstrained and therefore outside the province of science. "Though we may explore and perhaps specify the conditions that activate the will to crime, we cannot definitively say that a crime will be committed" (Matza, 1964:191).

The second possibility is that the complexities of delinquent behavior make it extremely difficult for science to conceptualize and to measure it. At present, our theories and our methods are simply inadequate and insufficient for the task. Hence, criminology needs more time by which to improve its knowledge and its techniques.

The third possibility is that the use of the physical and natural sciences as a model for research in criminology is inappropriate. These models stress the importance of measuring observable facts. But since human thought and consciousness cannot be readily observed, other models must be sought by which to study these phenomena.

In light of these answers, positive criminology is left with but two possibilities with which it can work: (1) it might improve its theories and its methods; (2) it might find other ways for exploring human thought and consciousness. With these two possibilities in mind, therefore, let us consider the problems associated with the construction and measurement of theory.

CONSTRUCTING AND MEASURING THEORIES

In reviewing the evidence bearing on existing theories, we isolated five hypotheses for which empirical support tends to be the strongest:

1. *The weaker the attachment between parents and child, the greater the delinquent behavior.*
2. *The weaker the attachment to the school, the greater the delinquent behavior.*
3. *The lower the academic achievement, the greater the delinquent behavior.*
4. *The weaker the commitment to conventional means for success, the greater the delinquent behavior.*
5. *The greater the identification with peers in the face of serious conflict with authority, the greater the delinquent behavior.*

In attempting to test or to improve the predictive power of these hypotheses,

criminologists have access to three models: independent, interdependent, and reciprocal.

Independent predictors

The first model is designed to treat each hypothesis as an *independent* explanation for delinquent behavior. If that is done, one assumes that the effect of each variable—attachment to parents, attachment to school, academic achievement, commitment to conventional means for success, and identification with peers—is independent of the effects of all other variables. A child's academic achievement, for example, is not affected by his or her attachment to parents; a child's identification with peers is not affected by his or her bond to the school. Each has a separate and independent effect. Research which utilizes this model is diagrammed in Figure 13–1.

There are grounds for using this model as a guide for research because it is not only clean and convenient, but because each of the variables *is* independently related to delinquency. Yet, one needs only look at it to see that it grossly oversimplifies the processes by which children become delinquent. For example, besides being related to delinquent behavior, it is likely that weak attachment to parents will also weaken attachment to the

FIGURE 13–1

Independent predictors of delinquent behavior

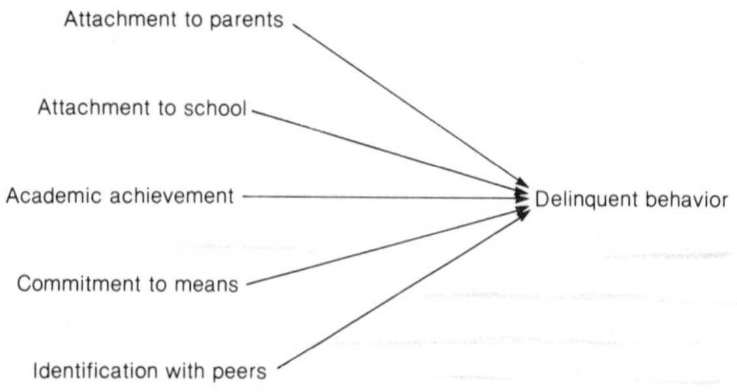

- Attachment to parents
- Attachment to school
- Academic achievement
- Commitment to means
- Identification with peers
- Delinquent behavior

school, will affect academic achievement, and will even hasten identification with delinquent peers. Consequently, most investigators recognize the need for a second, more complex, model for the conduct of research.

Interdependent predictors

This second model suggests that many of the influences in a child's life are *interdependent*. Although this interdependence may be portrayed in numerous ways, one way is to state a series of formal postulates that reflect it.

P1. *The weaker the attachment between parents and child, the weaker the attachment to the school.*

P2. *The weaker the attachment to the school, the weaker the academic achievement.*

P3. *The weaker the academic achievement, the weaker the commitment to conventional means for success.*

P4. *The weaker the commitment to conventional means for success, the greater the identification with peers.*

P5. *The greater the identification with peers, the greater the delinquent behavior.*

When stated in this way, the postulates of the theory may now be diagrammed as follows:

Weak attachment to parents → Weak attachment to school → Weak commitment →

Poor academic achievement → Identification with peers → Delinquent behavior

This model implies that the process of becoming delinquent is a long and complex one in which a whole series of events culminate in law violating-behavior. It further implies that each variable in the chain is not only dependent upon those preceding it, but also is linked to delinquency only through the variables following it. For example, a child whose

attachment to parents and school is weak, and whose achievement and commitment are poor, becomes delinquent only after identifying with peers. Unless each step is present, a child will be unlikely to violate the law.

But what of the evidence that variables in the chain have an independent as well as interdependent effect on delinquency? This evidence suggests that weak ties to parents not only lead directly to delinquency, but also may be affected by other variables in the chain— poor achievement, a weak commitment, or delinquent peers. Hence, since both kinds of effects are very possible, our theory and research must be designed to take both into account. Indeed, if that is done, a model would have to be used as shown in Figure 13–2.

When testing the implications of this model, we would assume that, while weak attachment to parents affects a child's attachment to the school, and that the attachment to school affects achievement, and so on through the steps that lead to delinquency, each step is also related independently to delinquency.

The variables exert effects that are both independent and interdependent. In testing this assumption, however, investigators often run into complex methodological problems. For example, they may be unable to separate independent from interdependent effects unless they are able to obtain a sample of juveniles and to follow them for several years. But since that is a most difficult and costly task and is rarely accomplished, they must attempt to test the model through less defensible procedures. Furthermore, no matter what procedures they use to gather their data, the task of separating one effect from the other by statistical means is most difficult.

To make matters more complicated, these investigators must also face the possibility that the sequence of interdependent effects just outlined may be incorrect. For example, it is possible that a weak commitment to

FIGURE 13–2

Independent and *inderpendent* predictors of delinquent behavior

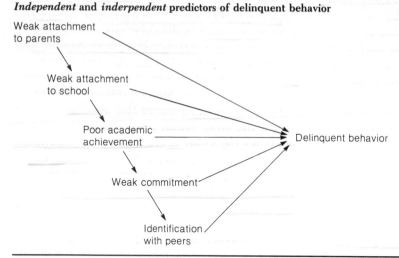

conventional means for success is the result of weak attachment to parents rather than the result of failure in school. If so, it would have to appear earlier in the sequence. Likewise, some theorists have suggested that strong identification with delinquent peers is more likely to occur after a youth has gotten into trouble rather than before. Consequently, investigators must be prepared to test alternative sequential models, such as that shown in Figure 13–3.

Reciprocal predictors

Were these problems not sufficient, we now have reason to believe that not only independent and interdependent effects lead to delinquent behavior, but also *reciprocal* effects—effects that are cyclical and move backward as well as forward. For example, it seems likely that children whose attachments to their parents are already weak may further weaken those ties by getting into trouble at

FIGURE 13–3

An alternative model for examining *independent* and *interdependent* predictors

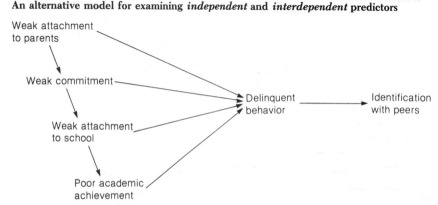

school, failing to pass their courses, and running around with delinquent friends. The same might be true of children's relations to their teachers. The more new problems they cause, the greater their old ones become, creating a steadily worsening situation. A model that combines all three kinds of effects is shown in Figure 13–4.

When it comes to research, this model presents all the problems to investigators mentioned earlier and adds more of its own. The double arrows in Figure 13–4 are used to illustrate the reciprocal as well as the independent and interdependent effects of the various predictors of delinquency. These variables not only contribute directly and indirectly to illegal behavior, but the original effects—trouble at home and school—are made worse by them. As a result, their existence again implies the need for longitudinal studies of juveniles, covering years of data gathering, in which the effects of getting into trouble, as well as the factors that lead to it, can be studied.

In short, this review of the difficulties associated with constructing and testing theories illustrates why it is impossible to know whether, or how much, their predictive power might be increased. On the one hand, it is virtually certain that scientific research will never be able to predict delinquent behavior without error. Since most juveniles violate the law at one time or another, law violation must be viewed as a more-or-less phenomenon, not an either-or phenomenon. For that reason, causes can never be identified which place law-violating juveniles into one distinct category and law-abiding juveniles into another.

On the other hand, even Matza acknowledges that there are chronic offenders who, though they may not differ completely from infrequent violators, may indeed be possessed of characteristics that are relatively distinctive. Hence, if some of the bewildering complexities associated with testing theories could be overcome, their predictive power might be improved. While we could never say that, given a certain set of variables, delinquent conduct would inevitably occur, we might be able to increase the probability that we could identify those people most likely to display it.

With this possibility in mind, let us consider the implications of positive theory and research for the prevention and control of delinquent behavior. It will be recalled that, since its inception, the ideology of juvenile justice has stressed the need to apply scientific principles to programs or rehabilitation and prevention. Hence, it is important, first, to make those

FIGURE 13–4
Independent, interdependent, and *reciprocal* predictors of delinquent behavior

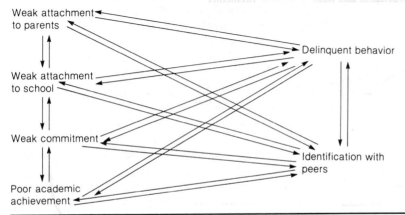

principles explicit and, then, to use them as a backdrop against which we can highlight the system's actual operation since 1899.

PRINCIPLES OF PREVENTION AND CONTROL

In reviewing positive theories one by one, we learned that most of them have had some impact on the operation of the juvenile justice system. But since empirical evidence for many of them was weak or lacking, we will be concerned here with the implications of the five hypotheses for which support has been the greatest.

Drawn from several theories, these hypotheses suggest that chronic delinquents are more likely than other young people to lack a *stake in conformity:* their attachments to the basic child-rearing institutions of home and school are weak or disrupted, their academic achievement is low, they are not committed to conventional means for success, and they are inclined to defy authority by identifying with delinquent peers. This description suggests that the best way for authorities to protect society, as well as to serve marginal youth, is to construct programs that are based upon three interrelated principles:

1. The primary focus of efforts to prevent and control delinquency should be upon the establishment of a stake in conformity in young people.
2. A stake in conformity is most likely to occur if children are effectively socialized.
3. Effective socialization is a product of institutional design and process—a result of the way homes, schools, and communities are organized.

The implication of these principles is significant: rather than indicating that delinquents should be punished, removed from society, or isolated in clinical programs, they indicate that programs of prevention and control should be a part of the ongoing processes of the community.

Guidelines for prevention

With regard to prevention, for example, the following guidelines are implied. Authorities should seek to:

a. Strengthen families so that a strong attachment between parents and children is insured.
b. Design educational programs so that children learn to respect their teachers, the authority of the school, and the importance of learning.
c. Promote academic achievement as a means of insuring that children are prepared for the assumption of adult roles.
d. Commit children to the means by which conventional success is gained—hard work, deferred gratification, and job preparation.
e. Help children to identify with conventional peers and thus avoid conflict with authority.

Guidelines for rehabilitation

The guidelines for rehabilitating official delinquents differ only in terms of emphasis. Instead of punishment, they stress the need to undo the effects of improper or inadequate socialization, to:

a. Reestablish and reinforce the weakened attachment of delinquents to home and school.
b. Provide delinquents with renewed opportunities for education—opportunities that not only appeal to their present levels of learning but also pose the probability of later sources of reward and satisfaction.
c. Turn delinquents away from illegitimate sources of satisfaction and recommit them to conventional means.
d. Assimilate delinquents into those groups favoring law-abiding behavior and alienate

them from groups favoring delinquent behavior.

In short, the principles of positive criminology suggest that programs designed to promote a stake in conformity and the adoption of legitimate roles will be most successful if the home, the school, and the community are involved in the process. It is these institutions, and not jails, reformatories, or training schools, that must be responsible for keeping marginal children on the road that leads from childhood to adulthood. To lock them up with other delinquents, or to further isolate them from conventional pursuits, makes their behavior worse rather than better, and acts to postpone the needed reforms rather than hasten them.

Limitations of positive principles

Despite their apparent attractiveness, however, positive principles have their flaws. To begin with, they provide little guidance for the agents of juvenile justice regarding the psychology of delinquent behavior—little insight into the feelings of alienation, stigma, or the anger which delinquents often feel. Hence, those who organize and run correctional programs are left to put flesh on the bones of scientific findings. While those bones direct them to the problems that must be solved, they do not indicate how to solve them. How does one improve the attachment of marginal or delinquent children to conventional institutions, give them a stake in conformity, and decrease their ties to delinquent groups?

Not only must delinquents be psychologically engaged in this process, but so must their parents, their schools, and their neighborhoods. Thus, difficult organizational tasks are also implied: To what degree will it be necessary to alter the "natural" practices and structures of difficult families, schools, local neighborhoods, even places of employment?

How are clients to be treated when they continue to violate the law? What methods are most likely to produce the desired results?

To further illustrate the difficulty of answering these questions, let us consider the effects of an additional, but crucial, set of variables. In reviewing the various measures of delinquent behavior, we learned that age, gender, minority status, social class, and type of community were all related to delinquent behavior, but in different ways. Yet, these variables do not appear in the principles just outlined or in many of the theories that gave rise to them. Nonetheless, they are contingent conditions that can sharply alter the meaning of those theories and the applicability of any principles derived from them.

Age. The hypotheses outlined above imply that the process of becoming seriously delinquent may cover a period of several years. For example, 11- or 12-year-olds are less likely than 17-year-old gang members to have severely disrupted their ties to home and school and to have identified with delinquent peers. Consequently, an intervention program for this group might have to concentrate more heavily on salvaging their remaining ties to home and school than on attacking ties to delinquent peers and commitments to serious delinquent activities.

By contrast, a program for the 17-year-olds may have to do just the opposite. Unless their rejection of conventional means and their involvement with other gang members is addressed at the outset, any effort to reconstitute their families, reinvolve them in educational programs, or help them find jobs is less likely to succeed. In short, the applicability of positive theory and principles may vary greatly depending upon the ages of the delinquents in question.

Gender. If anything, gender poses an even more complex set of problems. On the one hand, the importance of academic achievement and commitment to a career for females has steadily increased in importance throughout this century. As a result, efforts to liberate women now suggest that programming for girls and boys should be alike. No less than delinquent boys, delinquent girls should be academically disciplined and career-oriented, thus prepared for emancipation.

On the other hand, males are still considerably more delinquent than females, current increases in the female crime rate notwithstanding. How then can unified programming be assured? Since males may constitute a greater danger to the community than females, a more secure environment for them may be required.

But this is not the only issue. What about those who favor traditional roles for females, including not only legal and correctional authorities, but also many delinquent girls themselves? These girls not only remain less aggressive than males, but they are often more traditional in outlook than their better-educated and more sophisticated female peers. Consequently, they are relatively more dependent upon some kind of family ties than are delinquent boys, and they are more interested in pursuing traditional female roles than are nondelinquent girls.

The resulting dilemma for correctional planners is obvious. Since the contingent effects of gender are great, the methods for application of scientific principles to delinquent boys and girls are in a state of flux. Indeed, the problems they create are further illustrated when we consider the effects of minority status.

Minority status. The task of socializing minority children has been a major problem for the juvenile justice system since its inception. Because minority groups come from diverse cultural backgrounds, and because poverty, segregation, and discrimination have inhibited the socializing impact of conventional institutions upon them, the task for correctional programs has been exceedingly difficult.

Consider, for example, the problems still faced by black girls as well as black boys. Partly as a result of the American experience, the black family has always tended to be matriarchal, but in recent years, that tendency has become more marked. In 1950, 18 percent of all black families were headed by women; by 1969, the proportion had risen to 27 percent; by 1977, it had reached 41 percent (Bronfenbrenner, 1974; Davis, 1980; Monahan, 1957). Indeed, if present trends continue, more than half of all American black households will be headed by a single female in 1985, versus 19 percent of all white households.

The implications of such trends are nothing short of profound. First, the majority of unmarried mothers are not successful liberated women, as so much of the popular literature would lead us to believe, but rather uneducated, unemployed teenagers, many as young as 13 or 14 years old. Second, it is among these mothers and their offspring that the rates of infant mortality, school failure, joblessness, mental and physical disease, and criminal victimization are the highest. Third, high rates of illegitimacy, particularly in our urban ghettos, are less a symbol of disgrace than a means of survival. Unacquainted with other means, the daughters of the poor regard pregnancy as a way to welfare, and welfare as a way to independence. For them, the American Dream has been reduced to these proportions.

What does it mean, then, to suggest that the primary focus of intervention programs should be upon the establishment of a stake in conformity among poor black children, and that they should be taught to pursue legitimate roles? Surely, such admonitions would have a much different meaning to them than it would to many other delinquents.

First, it is clear that they are locked far more securely into powerless and unpromising positions than are more affluent blacks or whites. Lower-class black girls, in particular, are being forced by overwhelming economic and social forces into traditional domestic rather than liberated career roles. Second, it seems likely that the distinctions between delinquent and nondelinquent behavior are far less clear for these young people than for those who take for granted a two-parent family, an education, and a job. Indeed, Short and Strodtbeck contend that

> Negro gang delinquency tends *not to be clearly differentiated from nondelinquent behavior*— that participation in the "good" aspects of lower-class Negro life (responsibility in domestic chores and organized sports activities) is closely interwoven with "bad" aspects (conflict, illicit sex, drug use and auto theft). . . . As compared with lower-class white communities, delinquency among lower-class Negroes is more of a total life pattern in which delinquent behaviors are not likely to create disjunctures with other types of behavior (1965: 105–106).

In short, even though poor attachment to family and school, low academic achievement, weak commitment, and identification with delinquent peers do, in fact, predict delinquent behavior among black juveniles, those predictions makes full sense only when they are interpreted in the context of the black experience. Furthermore, it is questionable whether remedial programs designed to apply scientific principles can adequately address the problems that black children face, since they are rooted in economic and political structures which themselves require change. Indeed, when these problems are added to those of Hispanic, American Indian, and Oriental groups, the difficulties become even more horrendous.

Social class. Social class also complicates the meaning of scientific findings and principles. It is quite clear, for example, that these principles strongly reflect a middle-class construction of reality, with its emphasis upon the importance of the nuclear family, education, and a commitment to conventional

pursuits requiring many years of deferred gratification. As a consequence, they pose two major dilemmas.

First, they suggest that lower-class juveniles who fail to live up to the middle-class image are deviant by definition, quite apart from any crime they may have committed. Indeed, if they belong to both a minority and the lower class, they are often placed in a position of triple jeopardy, being different by virtue of their minority backgrounds, by their lower-class life styles, and their criminal reputations.

Second, scientific principles often fail to point explicitly to the political, economic, and cultural factors that are responsible for this triple-jeopardy. It is not merely that underclass children are sometimes in conflict with their parents, or that their academic achievement is low, but that they are caught in an economic and political system in which they are superfluous. Who needs them?

Since the unemployment and welfare roles would be diminished by hundreds of thousands if they disappeared tomorrow, society is confronted with questions for which positive theories have no answer: should abortion be encouraged for unmarried pregnant teenagers or should two-parent families be taxed at a higher rate to support them? Should the immigration of poor people into this country be halted, in an effort to support our own poor more effectively, or should it be encouraged? Should state aid to dependent children be stopped or increased? In an effort to prevent underclass delinquency, in short, should we be tougher or more compassionate?

Community. Since the 19th century, scientists and laypersons alike have lamented growing evidence of physical deterioration, dispossessed groups, and high rates of crime, disease, suicide, and infant mortality in our central cities. Indeed, investigators have concluded, like Shaw and McKay, that prevailing conditions for the poorer segments of society are "suggestive of a social process which leads to demoralization in the person and consequent abandonment or denial of generally recognized social obligations" (Schuessler and Slatin, 1964:147).

But urban decay and ghetto life are not the only problems. Crime is rising in suburban and rural areas at a rate that is relatively greater than in the central cities. As a consequence, anonymity, depersonalization, and lack of community control appear to be increasingly characteristic of all American communities.

Some positive theories and research findings allude to these problems, but, again, scientific principles to little to suggest solutions. If crime is to be controlled, communities require an integrated network of familial, educational, economic, political, and religious institutions by which the generations can be integrated and a common set of expectations developed and reinforced. It is one thing to imply that prevention and control programs should be a part of the ongoing community, and quite another to indicate how this can be accomplished, particularly in a pluralistic society like ours.

What all of this means, in short, is that positive principles provide more of a skeleton than a fully fleshed body of ideas by which to prevent and control delinquency. While they may be useful in suggesting guidelines for intervention, they leave policy makers, judges, and other authorities to reconcile the demands they impose with the demands that an even greater body of social, political, legal, and economic factors impose—factors for which the guidelines are often inadequate.

SUMMARY AND CONCLUSIONS

This chapter has been devoted to a review of the contributions, limitations, and practical implications of positive theories of delinquency.

Images of the delinquent

The construction of positive theories has been predicated upon the basic assumptions that (1) delinquent behavior is determined; (2) the control of that behavior depends upon our knowledge of the offender; and (3) delinquents are fundamentally different from nondelinquents. Consequently, positive criminology has portrayed delinquents as atypical people, either because they are unsocialized and lack a conscience, or because they have been socialized into a delinquent subculture.

Matza argues that these images are distorted and overly deterministic. Except for a tiny minority, delinquents are not constrained but are drifters who exercise free choice in deciding whether to commit crime.

Predicting delinquent behavior

When these differences of opinion are examined, the evidence provides full support for neither. On the one hand, some causes can be identified that do predict delinquent behavior: attachment to parents, attachment to school, academic achievement, commitment to conventional means for success, and identification with delinquent peers. Consequently, the notion that all delinquent conduct is unconstrained, and therefore unpredictable, is not supported.

On the other hand, these causes do not predict delinquent conduct with a high degree of accuracy, possibly supporting Matza's belief that the majority of delinquents are drifters who ultimately reform with age.

Given these findings, some softening of positive doctrines and goals seems appropriate. But while all law violators cannot be viewed as atypical and without choice, there are some chronic offenders whose behavior may be determined. Hence, there remains the hope that, by improving scientific methods, the power of theory to explain their behavior can be improved.

Construction and testing of theory

If this hope is pursued, scientists face a number of difficult tasks: isolating the most likely causes; determining whether their effects are independent, interdependent or reciprocal; and indicating which of several possible models is the most appropriate. But even if prediction is increased, positivists will be limited to probabilistic, not absolute, statements regarding the likelihood that delinquency will occur. Even where chronic offenders are involved, delinquent conduct must be viewed as a more-or-less phenomenon, not an either-or phenomenon. Causes can never be identified which will place delinquents into one exclusive category and nondelinquents into another.

Implications for prevention and control

The limitations of positive theory notwithstanding, the ideology of juvenile justice has stressed the need to apply scientific principles to programs of rehabilitation and prevention. They suggest that, since delinquent behavior is determined, efforts must be made to socialize youth more effectively. By strengthening their families, promoting their attachment to the school, improving their academic achievement, committing them to legitimate roles, and avoiding their identification with delinquent peers, they can be given a stake in conformity.

The statement of scientific principles, however, often fails to anticipate the problems associated with organizing intervention programs. The varying ages of delinquents, conflicts over gender roles, the economic and social factors that affect the opportunities of minority groups, the sorting of people into different social classes, and the disorganization and depersonalization of community life all complicate and further complicate any attempt to apply scientific principles. Nevertheless, our knowledge now places us in the unique position to use these principles and problems as a backdrop against which we can highlight and evaluate the actual organization and operation of the juvenile justice system since its inception.

REFERENCES

Bronfenbrenner, Urie
  1974   "The Origins of Alienation." *Scientific American* 231:48–59.

Davis, Kingsley
  1980   "Demographic Changes and the Future of Childhood." Pp. 112–37 in Lamar T. Empey, ed., *The Future of Childhood and Juvenile Justice.* Charlottesville: University Press of Virginia.

Hirschi, Travis
  1969   *Causes of Delinquency.* University of California Press.
  1977   "Causes and Prevention of Juvenile Delinquency. *Sociological Inquiry* 47:322–341.

Hirschi, Travis, and Hindelang, Michael J.
  1977   "Intelligence and Delinquency: A Revisionist Review." *American Sociological Review* 42 (August):571–587.

Johnson, Richard E.
  1979   *Juvenile Delinquency and Its Origins.* New York: Cambridge University Press.

Matza, David
  1964   *Delinquency and Drift.* New York: John Wiley & Sons.
Mednick, Sarnoff, and Christiansen, Karl O., eds.
  1977   *Biosocial Bases of Criminal Behavior.* New York: Gardner Press.
Monahan, Thomas P.
  1957   "Family Status and the Delinquent Child: A Reappraisal and Some New
         Findings." *Social Forces* 35:250–258.
Schuessler, Karl, and Slatin, Gerald
  1964   "Sources of Variation in U.S. City Crime, 1950 and 1960." *Journal of Re-
         search in Crime and Delinquency* 1 (July):127–148.
Short, James F. Jr., and Strodtbeck, Fred L.
  1965   *Group Process and Gang Delinquency.* Chicago: University of Chicago Press.

THE TRADITIONAL CONCEPT OF JUVENILE JUSTICE

Introduction: The ideology of child saving

In this section of the book, we move to an analysis of another part of the delinquency picture—the juvenile justice system. From 1899 until well into the 1960s, that system remained relatively unchallenged. The ideology of child-saving was transcendent, and reformers, legislators, and judges remained secure in the knowledge that the new system was not only desirable but was downright revolutionary.

The invention of the juvenile court in the state of Illinois was hailed universally as a triumph of benevolent progressivism over the forces of reaction and ignorance (Aichhorn, 1964; Chute, 1949; Mead, 1918; Platt, 1971). By 1920, all except three states had enacted juvenile court laws, although it was not until almost mid-century that Wyoming became the last state to join the movement. Meanwhile, the juvenile court became the model in many other countries as well as in this one (Caldwell, 1961:496).

The rehabilitative philosophy of the court not only spread geographically but its jurisdiction was extended up the ladder of age as well (Caldwell, 1961:496–497). Most states raised the upper limit of childhood from 16 to 18 years of age, and a few raised it to 21. The definition of delinquency was broadened to include cases of illegitimacy and mental or physical defectiveness. Adults could be brought into court charged with contributing to the delinquency of a minor. Some cities created family or domestic relations courts designed to deal with family problems of any kind: dependency and neglect, illegitimacy, adoption, nonsupport by a father, or crimes committed by one family member against another.

Meanwhile, California and Minnesota created youth authorities whose purpose was to diagnose ills and provide unique correctional procedures for youths, many of whom were more than 21 years old. The notion of presentence investigation, diagnosis, and treatment found its way into adult courts and became an accepted part of procedure. During the first half of this century, in short, the philosophy of the juvenile court movement enjoyed ever-widening acceptance and greatly reduced the popularity of the classical concept of justice.

THE REHABILITATIVE IDEOLOGY

The beliefs and assumptions that sustained this movement are best understood as an ideology—a kind of visionary theorizing about the best way to nurture and protect children. For example, the modern concept of childhood assumed that children are qualitatively different from adults, that their immaturity makes them more malleable, and that their uncalculating innocence renders them more susceptible to reform programs. Meanwhile, the positive school of criminology assumed that, because delinquent behavior is due to forces over which children have little control, they simply cannot anticipate the consequences of their acts. Hence, when these two sets of assumptions were combined in positive theories of delinquency, they led to the conclusions reviewed in the previous chapter; namely, that new devices for controlling juvenile lawbreaking were required: *rehabilitation* and *crime prevention*. Indeed, the juvenile court could accomplish these goals simultaneously.

Rehabilitation would work for those who had gone so far as to commit delinquent acts. They could be restored to conditions of health and social repute by scientifically designed programs of care and treatment. Furthermore, by using the same techniques, crime could be prevented among those who were still at the dependent and neglected stage or were status offenders. In pursuit of these twin goals, in fact, there was little need to draw subtle distinctions between the child who was neglected, rude, or intemperate, and the child who had broken the criminal law. Rather, the purpose of the court was to eliminate the factors that caused children to violate the law, not to judge their criminal acts.

Until well after the middle of this century, the theories of delinquency which contributed most to these ideas were biological and psychological in character—theories that concentrated on the defects of the individual. Hence, in addition to suggesting that delinquent behavior is due to causes over which the child has little control, they also suggested that the primary problems were defective intelligence, uncaring parents, and an unacceptable home life. Relatively little thought was given to the possible effects of differential opportunities, delinquent peers, or the pluralistic nature of American culture.

According to the rehabilitative ideology, differential responses to children were the only rational way to protect society. Short of killing off all delinquents, or permanently incarcerating them, the only way the citizenry could be protected was to cure law violators of their criminal tendencies. In pursuit of this goal, moreover, the juvenile court was not viewed as unconstitutional if it denied juveniles the due process rights that were guaranteed for adults.

Indeed, rather than taking issue with this ideology, important higher court decisions served only to sustain it:

> To save a child from becoming a criminal, or from continuing in a career of crime, to end in maturer years in public punishment and disgrace, the legislatures surely may provide for the salvation of such a child, if its parents or guardians be unable or unwilling to do so, by bringing it into one of the courts of the state without any process at all, for the purpose of subjecting it to the state's guardianship and protection. . . . The act simply provides how children who ought to be saved may reach the court to be saved (*Commonwalth* v. *Fisher,* 1905).

Although this judicial statement was made in 1905, the ideology it reflected had changed little by 1962. In that year, Orman Ketcham, judge of the juvenile court in Washington, D.C., observed that "the juvenile in America may [still] be brought within the protective power of the juvenile court without the operation of legal safeguards customarily offered to a person accused of law violation" (1962:25). Caldwell added that "the balance between rights, on the one hand, and duties and responsibilities, on the other, which every court must seek to maintain, has been upset as the juvenile court has been pushed more and more into the role of a social work agency." (1961:497).

Almost to the present day, then, the view of the juvenile court as a rehabilitative instrument has provided the agents of juvenile justice not only with a broad mandate but with awesome responsibilities. On the one hand, this trend has suggested that problem children should be treated in a much more thoughtful and humane way than adult offenders. Retribution, in particular, should be avoided; the care, custody, and discipline provided for delinquents should approximate that of loving parents. On the other hand, officials should not wait until children become criminal in taste and habit before they act. Rather, they should respond at the first sign of parental neglect or of departure on the part of any child from accepted moral and legal standards, even if stern and arbitrary methods are required.

So pervasive was this benevolent ideology that little thought was given to the possibilities that its basic assumptions might be faulty or that the interventions by the court might be more harmful than helpful. Consequently, the development of sociological theories of delinquency had relatively little impact on court philosophy and practice until after 1960. It was not until 1961, for example, that strain theory became the rationale for the creation of both the President's Committee on Juvenile Delinquency and Youth Crime, and Mobilization for Youth. But since these programs were concerned more with preventing delinquency than with judging or correcting known delinquents, they did not have much impact on the practices of judges and correctional people. Little attention was paid to the implications of positive theories which suggested that programs designed to promote a stake in conformity will be most successful if homes, schools, neighborhoods, and conventional peers, as well as probation officers and correctional authorities, are involved in the process.

Partly as a result of this neglect, the juvenile justice system is now in a state of ferment. Its rehabilitative ideology is being challenged, its effectiveness is being questioned, and its basic procedures are being altered. But since these changes are a product of the last few years, they will be discussed in the last section of the book. For now, we will limit our attention to the traditional concept of juvenile justice and how it was reflected in the behaviors of policemen, judges, and correctional personnel.

> *Chapter 14* will be concerned with the police: their historical development in this country; their perceptions of the rehabilitative ideology and its impact upon them; and their responses to a highly conflicting set of social expectations as they actually processed juveniles.
>
> *Chapter 15* will conduct the same sort of analysis of the juvenile court: the historical expansion of its benevolent ideology; its procedures for dealing with juveniles; and the events, scientific findings, and ideologies which eventually tarnished its image and led to cries for reform.
>
> *Chapter 16* will be concerned with the history of society's efforts to reform delinquents, from the time when they were whipped, disfigured, or banished from the country to the mid-20th century when they were placed in programs of diagnosis and treatment. Although the prevailing approach stressed rehabilitation, attitudes toward it began to change in the 1960s. People not only began to question whether rehabilitation was effective but whether it had even been tried.

In short, the following three chapters will be devoted to an analysis of society's efforts to realize a splendorous set of aspirations for children and how, as time went on, optimism was replaced by dismay. Indeed, as we will see, this transformation eventually led to new bodies of theory which, in turn, were critical of the very concept of juvenile justice, and which radically altered the treatment of delinquent children.

REFERENCES

Aichhorn, August
> 1964   "The Juvenile Court: Is It a Solution? Pp. 55–79 in *Delinquency and Child Guidance: Selected Papers.* New York: International Universities Press.

Caldwell, Robert G.
> 1961   "The Juvenile Court: Its Development and Some Major Problems." *Journal of Criminal Law, Criminology, and Police Science* 51 (January–February) 493–507.

Chute, Charles L.
> 1949   "Fifty Years of the Juvenile Court." Pp. 1–10 in *National Probation and Parole Association Yearbook.* New York: National Probation and Parole Assn.

Commonwealth v. *Fisher*
> 1905   213 Pa. 48, 62 Atl. 1. 198.

Ketcham, Orman W.
    1962   "The Unfulfilled Promise of the American Juvenile Court." Pp. 22–43 in Margaret K. Rosenheim, ed., *Justice of the Child*. New York: Free Press.

Mead, George H.
    1918   "The Psychology of Punitive Justice." *American Journal of Sociology* 23 (March) 577–602.

Platt, Anthony
    1971   "Introduction to the Reprint Edition." Pp. v–xvi in *History of Child Saving in the United States*. Montclair, N.J.: Patterson-Smith.

United Press International Photo

Police see themselves as the first line of defense in the war on crime.

POLICING JUVENILES: FIGHTING CRIME VERSUS SOCIAL WORK

The police are the most visible symbol of the juvenile justice system. Whenever a crime, a family fight, or some other disturbance occurs, it is the police to whom most citizens turn. Hence, most of the juveniles entering the juvenile court are referred by the police.

In order to understand how the police have played this crucial role, one must be aware of not only the rehabilitative ideal for juveniles, but also the history and organization of police work, prevailing public perceptions of the police, and the self-image of the police. Taken together, these issues create a view of the delinquency problem which is unique to the police and which, for much of this century, determined how they responded to juveniles.

HISTORY OF POLICE WORK

What may be surprising to the average person is that large, organized police forces, as we know them, have not been in existence for much longer than the juvenile court.[1] Like the juvenile court, in fact, they seem to have arisen in response to the growth of large cities, technology, and industrialization. As the informal controls of rural civilization gradually broke down, society turned increasingly to more impersonal, secondary kinds of control—juvenile institutions and the juvenile court as well as the police.

The origin of the police forces in this country can be traced to earlier developments in Western European countries, particularly England. France and several other European countries had professional police forces of a sort as early as the 17th century. England, however, did not begin to create such a force until the 19th century. This delay was due, in part, to the changing nature of English life and, in part, to the fear of police oppression. "During the period of absolute monarchy the police came to represent the underground aspects of

---

[1] Except where indicated, this brief history is drawn from the Task Force report: *The Police.* President's Commission on Law Enforcement and Administration of Justice (1967a:3–7).

tyranny and political repression, and they were despised and feared even by those who ostensibly benefited from their services" (Bittner, 1970:6–7). Thus, in lieu of a large police force, England had long used the "mutual pledge" system for apprehending criminals. Local citizens were encouraged to maintain law and order, and were responsible for their own actions and those of their neighbors. Hence, when a crime was committed, citizens were expected to raise the "hue and cry," to collect their neighbors, and to pursue the criminal. If citizens failed in this task, they could be fined.

These efforts were coordinated by a local constable or sheriff who performed three functions: organizing citizens into groups of ten families to enforce the laws; supervising the "watch and ward"—a group of people who were expected to protect property against fire, to guard city gates, and to arrest criminals between sunset and daybreak; and inquiring into offenses, serving summonses, taking charge of prisoners, and otherwise assisting the local justices who were responsible for judging cases in each county.

So long as England was a rural country, this system was viewed as adequate. But with the advent of the Industrial Revolution, accompanied by the migration of thousands of people to factory towns, it was no longer sufficient. Anonymity increased, neighborhood networks disappeared, and the people were no longer willing to or capable of enforcing the law. In the second quarter of the 19th century, therefore, England's first professional police forces were organized.

AMERICAN POLICE

The same pattern characterized the development of the police in this country. American colonists in the 17th and 18th centuries brought the mutual pledge, the watch and ward, and the constable systems

with them and installed them in the small colonial towns discussed earlier. These systems were sufficient to supplement the informal controls of family, church, and community. But, as some of these towns began to expand in the late 18th and early 19th centuries, informal methods could no longer cope with increasing disorder:

> New York City was alleged to be the most crime ridden city in the world, with Philadelphia, Baltimore and Cincinnati not far behind. . . . Gangs of youthful rowdies in the larger cities . . . threatened to destroy the American reputation for respect for the law. . . . Before their boisterous demonstrations the crude police forces of the day were often helpless (Cole, 1934:154–155).

Then as now, the most crime-ridden communities were the large urban centers, not the small towns.

In response to this state of affairs, several cities, led by New York, Boston, and Philadelphia, created police forces in the 1830s and 1840s. By the 1870s, all major cities had full-time police forces. But they proved to be less than a panacea: police officers were drawn from the least-educated segments of society and were ill-trained and poorly paid. Worse still, police forces often became instruments of political corruption when elected officials used them for personal gain and political advantage:

> Rotation in office enjoyed so much popular favor that police posts of both high and low degree were constantly changing hands, with political fixers determining the price and conditions of each change. . . . The whole police question simply churned about in the public mind and eventually became identified with the corruption and degradation of the city politics and local governments of the period (Smith, 1960:105–106).

The police, in short, became objects of disrespect. Ancient fears of political corruption and repression were confirmed.

These feelings were encouraged by the

fierce independence and mobility of settlers on the American frontier. The development of police forces in the small towns and mining communities of the West was much later in coming than it was in the larger eastern cities. The same was true of the rural South. In both areas of the country, modern police forces did not begin to develop on any scale until the turn of the 20th century. Until then, the local constable or sheriff, along with the citizenry, were responsible for maintaining law and order.

The real expansion of police forces and citizens' interest in them began after World War I. By that time, most state legislatures had created state police forces because local departments could not, or would not, enforce laws beyond their own jurisdictions. Then, in 1924, J. Edgar Hoover organized the Federal Bureau of Investigation to deal with federal crimes. Finally, in 1931, the first National Commission on Law Observance and Enforcement (pp. 5–7) called for the reform of a growing number of police problems: the average police chief was too subject to political manipulation and control; there was a lack of competent, honest patrolmen; little effort was being made to educate, train, and discipline officers; and the police lacked the necessary equipment, skill, and personnel to enforce the flood of new laws produced by an increasingly complex, industrial society.

In recent decades, some progress has been made in correcting earlier problems, much of it since 1967 when, in response to a second Presidential Commission (the President's Commission on Law Enforcement and Administration of Justice), federal legislation was passed and large sums of money were expended in an effort to improve police training and record-keeping systems, and to expand crime control techniques. As a result, there are approximately 40,000 police agencies in the United States today: 50 on the federal level, 200 on the state level; and 39,750

dispersed throughout counties, cities, towns, and hamlets. By far, the most significant of these, insofar as the policing of juveniles is concerned, are the thousands of municipal police departments.

PUBLIC PERCEPTIONS OF THE POLICE

Given the long-standing distrust and spotty history of the police, experts allude repeatedly to the public's ambivalence about them (Bittner, 1970; Niederhoffer and Blumberg, 1973; Wilson, 1968a). Ben Whittaker, a lawyer who studied the English police system, described this ambivalence as follows:

> The public use the police as a scapegoat for its neurotic attitude toward crime. Janus-like we have always turned two faces toward a policeman. We employ him to administer the law, and yet ask him to waive it. We resent him when he enforces the law in our own case, yet demand his dismissal when he does not elsewhere. We offer him bribes, yet denounce his corruption. We expect him to be a member of society, yet not to share its values. We admire violence, even against society itself, but condemn force by the police in our behalf. We tell the police that they are entitled to information from the public, yet we ostracize informers. We ask for crime to be eradicated, but only by use of "sporting" [i.e., constitutional methods] (Morris and Hawkins, 1969:89).

Whittaker's description is valuable because it indicates that police behavior, good or bad, usually mirrors public attitudes. To be sure, mixed feelings are inevitable as a result of the storm-trooper image that the police often project. Dressed in jodhpurs and boots, wearing a helmet and dark glasses, with a pistol and club strapped to their belts, their approach creates a tinge of panic in even the most innocent of citizens. But for many citizens who are themselves law-violating hypocrites, the suspicion cannot be allayed that the police are likewise less than law-abiding and hypocritical. The notion lingers that "those who do battle against evil cannot themselves live up fully to the ideals they presumably defend" (Bittner, 1970:7).

Sometimes these suspicions are confirmed. In one recent case, for example, criminal charges were levied against five policemen for alleged sexual misconduct with 16- and 17-year-old girls who were members of a police-sponsored Explorer Scout Program. Unconfirmed reports stated that the police had seduced the girls on out-of-town camping trips or had established sexual liasons with them in private (*Los Angeles Times,* October 8, 1976). As can be imagined, public indignation over the matter was considerable. Though the police are certainly not the only citizens—young or old—who engage in premarital or extramarital affairs or who read *Playboy, Playgirl,* or *Penthouse,* they are judged by standards applied only to such guardians of public morality as ministers and teachers. As Whittaker says, we have always turned two faces toward policemen: on the one hand, distrusting them, but on the other, expecting exemplary behavior from them.

This attitude is only worsened by the conflicting roles that the police are expected to play: the tough crime fighter when dealing with human predators versus the thoughtful social worker when responding to the citizens' cries for help.

The crime fighter

In a rather remarkable document, a group of policemen once analyzed, from their perspective, the media-created image of the main protagonists in the war on crime: the criminal versus the crime fighter. First, they noted the fact that criminals are often far more famous than are the police who fight them. Stretching over the past four decades, many famous criminals could be listed:

John Dillinger, "Baby Face" Nelson, "Pretty Boy" Floyd, "Machine Gun" Kelly, [Bonnie and Clyde], "Willie the Actor" Sutton, the Boston Strangler, nurse killer Richard Speck, Charles Whitman of University of Texas notoriety, Charles Manson and his family, Lindbergh Kidnapper Bruno Hauptmann, Alcatraz "Birdman" Robert Stroud, Caryl Chessman, Hickok and Smith of *In Cold Blood* infamy, San Francisco's Zodiac killer, farmhand killer Juan Corona, . . . Charles Starkweather and a host of Mafia-type hoodlums including "Scarface Al" Capone, "Lucky" Luciano, Frank Costello, Albert Anastasia, Joseph "Bananas" Bonnano, and Vito Genovese (Carter et al., 1971:80).

One could add some recent names of those who have become famous: Patricia Hearst, former Attorney General John Mitchell, and former White House advisors H. R. Haldeman and John D. Erlichman. "The list," as the policemen noted, "is seemingly endless" (p. 80).

But who remembers real-life crime fighters? Who are they? At best, people can name only a few: J. Edgar Hoover (who, today, is as notorious as he is famous), Elliott Ness of "Untouchables" fame, and perhaps O. W. Wilson, August Vollmer, and William Parker. Even though the latter were chiefs-of-police, they are not well known outside of law enforcement circles. Instead, most policemen are known to the public as a series of stereotypes: the dumb Irish cop, the flatfoot, the dick, the gumshoe, the fuzz, or the pig. "Sad, but true, the 'good guys' are not very good" (Carter et al., 1971:80).

This is ironic in light of the fact that the crime problem has usually been portrayed in American folklore as black and white, as the good guys versus the bad guys. But, if regular policemen are distrusted and unknown, who are the good guys?

The good guys are not ordinary policemen; they are fictional, and Carter et al. called them SUPERcrime fighters: Dick Tracy, Bruce Wayne, Batman, Superman, the Saint, the Lone

Ranger, Nero Wolfe, the FBI in Peace and War, Barnaby Jones, the Mod Squad, Chief Ironside, Baretta, Wonder Woman, Kojak, the Six Million Dollar Man and the Bionic Woman, Steve McGarrett, Charlie's Angels, Starsky and Hutch, and even Mighty Mouse, Johnny Quest, and Chester Rabbit (Carter et al., 1971:81–86).

Since ordinary policemen are incapable of fighting the war on crime, SUPERcrime fighters have been created to fill the void. Moreover, there are certain themes running through America's crime-fighting mentality which suggest that unusual characteristics and techniques are required of SUPERcrime fighters (Carter et al., 1971:82–88):

SUPERcrime fighters are no mere mortals. They are possessed of exceptional intuition, intelligence, toughness (and even bionic limbs like the Six Million Dollar Man) which make them indestructible and all-powerful.

Crime is best stamped out by gimmicks, hardware, and the products of science. Dick Tracy has a two-way wrist radio; Batman's belt is loaded with scientific devices; James Bond's Aston-Martin has a bullet-proof shield, machine guns, an ejection seat, and a device for spewing oil on the road in front of evil pursuers; and Steve McGarrett has computers that can spill out the most detailed information on crooks anywhere in the world.

The SUPERcrime fighters always triumph over evil; the bad guys are always caught; crime does not pay.

Violence is inevitably present in crime and its control. Most comic strips and TV shows portray heroes and villains who are involved in an almost endless orgy of violence. Even Mighty Mouse dispatches cat villains by punching them in the nose, to say nothing of the brawls in which James Bond, Charlie's Angels, Starsky and Hutch, or Boy Wonder become engaged.

It is usually necessary for SUPERcrime fighters to operate outside the law in order to control crime. As Chester Gould, the creator of Dick Tracy, noted:

The trend of the times seemed to be exactly right for a straight shoot-'em down detective. We had a crime situation . . . that was beyond coping with legally—or what we would call legally today. So I brought out this boy Tracy and had him go out and get his man at the point of a gun, and, if necessary, shoot him down (*Orange County Register,* January 17, 1971).

It is not surprising, therefore, that most SUPERcrime fighters burglarize in order to collect evidence, use illegal wiretaps, obtain confessions through threats or brutality, and engage in a long list of other activities that are contrary to law.

Given this stereotyped construction of the way crime is successfully fought, ordinary policemen are losers. The image of the successful crime fighter cannot possibly fit a law-abiding policeman who is constrained by constitutional provisions protecting the rights of the individual. As a New York precinct captain stated, "A [policeman] out to violate people's rights will have to answer for his actions . . . In real life, a Clint Eastwood character . . . wouldn't last two weeks" (*Los Angeles Times,* March 23, 1977). Furthermore, the popular image of what it is that policemen do has little resemblance to the actual nature of their work.

The social worker

Studies of police behavior reveal that at most 20 to 30 percent of all calls from citizens involve crimes of some sort, even in those areas where crime rates are the highest (Cumming et al., 1973:186; Reiss, 1971:15). The tour of duty for the average policeman, in fact, does not even include the arrest of a single person (Reiss,

1971:15). Unlike TV heroes, most policemen never fire a shot from their weapons during a total career of 25 or 30 years, nor do they engage in wild conflicts involving karate chops and judo holds with bullets zinging through the air (Carter et al., 1971:86). How, then, *do* policemen spend most of their time?

They spend much of it doing social work or, as Cumming et al. (1973) describe it, playing "philosopher, guide, and friend." After monitoring hundreds of calls from citizens to the police, these investigators found that about half of them were requests for some sort of assistance in difficult personal and interpersonal situations:

> A man, reported by his ex-wife as dangerous and perhaps mentally ill, is found asleep. But, since the ex-wife was in the man's home, the police asked her to please leave.
> A car accident severely injures a woman, and the police supervise her removal to a hospital.
> A woman calls because neighborhood children are bullying a small boy who wears glasses. After doing a little shouting and getting shouted at in return, the police watch the problem wither away and leave.
> A woman complains that her husband doesn't bring home enough money to feed the kids. The police advise her to go to children's court.
> A slightly drunk man is an unwelcome visitor in his ex-wife's home. Police send him home in a cab (pp. 189–90).

In short, the closest television has come to portraying this consuming side of police work is in "Adam 12," a TV show which, like police work, is often filled with tedium. Jim Reed and Pete Malloy "spend endless hours on patrol . . . , eat chili and hamburgers . . . , rescue cats from trees and break up family disturbances" (Carter et al., 1971:88).

For the poor, in particular, the police must often play this kind of amateur social worker role—calming unruly children, feeding information into a troubled situation, or acting as counselors in interpersonal conflicts. Other resources or problem-solving networks are simply unavailable to them. "All citizens can count on emergency help from the police when there is sudden illness at night, but only a certain kind of citizen takes his marital troubles to them" (Cumming et al., 1973:192). Perhaps efforts to deal with problems like these counteract some of the negative public perceptions of the police, but the evidence is by no means clear that it does:

> Most citizens express attitudes that are highly inconsistent with the actual demands that they place on the police. They want them to be SUPERcrime fighters, not social workers. Eight in ten citizens say they want policemen to be "tougher than they are now in dealing with crime and lawlessness" (Hindelang, 1975:11).
>
> While approximately six in ten Americans hold generally favorable views of the police, significant proportions of them do not, particularly poor and minority people (Ennis, 1967:52–58; Hindelang, 1975:10). At least half of the latter group view the police as intruders who are too often unfair, racist, and brutal in ghetto neighborhoods (Ennis, 1966:66–67; Skolnick, 1973).
>
> Large proportions of victims of and witnesses to crimes do not report them to the police (Hindelang et al., 1976:338–39). This failure is due, not only because people feel that the police will be of little help, but also because they do not want to become involved in the dirty, time-consuming work of the police: identifying offenders, going to court, or testifying as witnesses.

Given this state of affairs, how do the police respond to the public view that their work is "tainted" and the public feelings about them that are highly ambivalent?

POLICE VIEWS OF POLICE WORK

The police seem to view themselves in two ways: as *social outcasts* and as *crime fighters*.

Social outcasts

The police share the public view that theirs is a tainted occupation. They see themselves as pariahs, as outcasts:

> [The policeman] regards the public as his enemy, feels his occupation to be in conflict with the community, and regards himself to be a pariah. The experience and the feeling give rise to a collective emphasis on secrecy, an attempt to coerce respect from the public, and a belief that almost any means are legitimate in completing an important arrest (Westley, 1975:35).

The police, as a result are extremely sensitive to criticism and are impatient with high-flown academic definitions of their work. Consider the response of a Los Angeles police sergeant to one such definition by well-known academician Egon Bittner (1970:46):

> **Bittner:** The role of the police is best understood as a mechanism for the distribution of nonnegotiably coercive force employed in accordance with the dictates of an intuitive grasp of situational exigencies.
>
> **Sergeant:** What the fuck does that mean? (Carter, 1976:121).

Some words that the police do understand and which Carter (1976:131) says characterize their feelings about their work are *frustration, anger, anxiety, alienation,* and *hostility:*

> People don't like cops. Now, maybe some cops did some stupid things, but most of us are trying to do good. . . . You wonder why we stick together; you almost have to. . . . Nobody understands; noncops can't understand it. Maybe we don't understand it ourselves. Next time you're in a bar, tell the dude next to you that you're a cop. Watch him

come apart. Or try to make it with some broad and tell her you're a cop. Shit. Nothing. People want you around and they don't want you around. They love you, they hate you. They need you, they don't need you. God, if the role is fuzzy, it's probably because no one really knows what they want from police (Carter, 1976:122–23).[2]

Crime fighters

Despite their feelings of frustration and anger, the police also share the public view that they should be crime fighters, not social workers. As a Philadelphia police inspector put it, "Once a police officer becomes a social worker, he isn't any good anymore as a policeman" (Ennis, 1966:139). Speaking explicitly of work with juveniles, a second officer expressed precisely the same point of view:

> The juvenile bureau is not always in step with [the rest of the police]. A lot of guys with a lot of time in the Department don't believe in all this prevention activity, except what is crime related. . . . They'll tell you they didn't join the Department to become a social worker. They want to work patrol or detective bureau, out on the streets. And that is the majority of the people in the Department (Carter, 1976:130).

It is for reasons like these that 8 in 10 calls for assistance are regarded by the police as a waste of time (Reiss, 1971:73). Even though citizens consider their own family disputes and neighborhood disturbances as requiring police attention, the police tend to resent them. "You ought to talk to Sergeant _____ . . . . He'll tell you straight out that prevention isn't our job:

---

[2] This and excerpts on p. 316 from "The police view of the justice system" by Robert M. Carter is reprinted from *The Juvenile Justice System,* vol. 5, Sage Criminal Justice System Annuals, Malcolm W. Klein (Ed.), 1976. By permission of the author and of the publisher, Sage Publications, Inc., Beverly Hills/London.

Parents ought to be doing more, the schools ought to get rid of the fuckups, and people ought to go to church" (Carter, 1976:130).

The police, in short, see themselves as the last "guardians of the morals of the community" (Carter, 1976:131). Since ordinary citizens are so often ambivalent and hypocritical about crime, the first job of the police is to fight it. They are the " 'thin blue line' against the forces of evil" (Carter, 1976:131).

POLICE ATTITUDES TOWARD JUVENILE WORK

Given this perception of themselves, it is not difficult to imagine police views on the rehabilitative concept of justice for juveniles— and the criminology professors whom they feel herald it:

> Nothing personal, but most professors don't know what they are talking about. They sit on the campus putting out all this good shit about rehabilitation and causes of crime. Most of them haven't ever been on the street; and if you want to know what's happening, you have to be on the street. They haven't seen these assholes after the sun goes down, laughing and scratching, shucking and jiving. Instead of them telling us about crime, we ought to be telling them. If they would spend a couple of days with us, they might find out what's happening. No, they don't want to do that; it might upset all their theories. I've heard some of those theories in school. Bullshit! What has toilet training got to do with anything? Nothing. They ought to be teaching stuff we can use, not all that sociology and social work. Like they say in the army: they don't know shit from shinola. It's a shuck (Carter, 1976:123).

To many, probably most, policemen, the traditional concept of juvenile justice is distorted and unrealistic. It has forced them to play a social worker role with large groups of neglected children and status offenders while

hindering their attempts to control serious crime among young "hoodlums" and "pukes":

> I don't want to sound like a hardass, but we have some really bad young hoodlums on the streets in L.A. These aren't the nickel and dime kid shoplifters; they are hardcore. Some of them have dozens of arrests, but they're still out there ripping off people. Some of them have killed people, but they are still out there. These pukes are into juvenile hall and out 20 minutes later; seriously, some of these hoodlums are back on the street before I finish the paperwork. If you are going to correct kids they have to get their hands whacked the first time they put them in the cookie jar, not six months later. Juvenile justice is slow. Jesus, the rights these kids have got. They have more rights than I have. . . . I'm not talking about the Mickey Mouse cases; I mean the hoodlums (Carter, 1976:124).

Given these reactions, two things are clear: policemen regard any responsibility for status offenders as "shit work," and they feel their hands are tied when it comes to dealing with young criminals. Faced with serious juvenile crime on the one hand, and a soft-headed rehabilitative system on the other, they have been engaged in a battle they cannot win. Indeed, as one officer suggested, the juvenile justice system on the streets does not include kindly judges or probation officers, only two lonely men in a squad car:

> When you turn a corner, drive into an alley, or respond to a 211 IP or 459 silent, you don't know what's going to happen. It might be a psycho, a street junkie, some kid on speed, or even some dude who wants to waste a cop. Might not be anything. You don't know. But let me tell you what the justice system is then. It is me and my partner. We have a car, a radio, a backup unit, two .38s, one shotgun in the rack. That is the justice system on the street. To make it complete, you add one criminal (Carter, 1976:123).

It is significant that, in recent years, more and more people have tended to side with the police, although for various reasons. American society is in a transitional phase in which laws and procedures with respect to children are being radically altered. But since these changes are a product of the last few years, and since their effects are only now being widely felt, we will devote our attention in this chapter to the way the police have processed juveniles during most of this century. In later chapters we will contrast traditional treatment with that which is now being mandated by new laws and procedures.

HOW POLICE HAVE PROCESSED JUVENILES

Evidence from a variety of sources suggests that, from the birth of professional police forces until about 1975, the treatment of juveniles by the police has remained relatively unchanged. This treatment can be illustrated by seeking answers to the following questions:

1. How have the police responded to widespread law violation by juveniles? In Chapter 6, we learned that the amount of undetected law violation among juveniles is enormous. Almost every child breaks the law, sometimes repeatedly and sometimes seriously. Have the police been all aware of this state of affairs?

The evidence seems to indicate that they have, but that they have not regarded much of juvenile lawbreaking as particularly serious and, therefore, have not taken formal action against it. Instead, the police have exercised a tremendous amount of discretion in deciding which of the many children who came to their attention would be arrested (Levine, 1973:558). For example, Bordua (1967) found that patrolman in Detroit had contacts with juveniles nine times more frequently than they made arrests. Of well over 100,000 "encounters" or "interviews" with juveniles, only 5 percent (5,282) resulted in actual arrest. Findings of the same sort were reported by

Terry (1967) in Racine, Wisconsin. Of 9,023 offenses known to the police, only 8 percent (755) were referred to the probation department and only 3 percent (246) actually resulted in court hearings.

Such figures vary from department to department but, overall, they suggest that the police have been disinclined to arrest many juveniles who might otherwise have been sent to court for disposition there (Black and Reiss, 1967; Goldman, 1963; Klein, 1970; Williams and Gold, 1972).

2. How many juveniles have actually been arrested each year? In relation to their part of the total population, the proportion of juveniles actually arrested each year has not been great. In 1975, for example, there were approximately 33.3 million juveniles in the United States between the ages of 10 and 17 (National Center for Juvenile Justice, 1977:3); yet there were only about 1.7 million juvenile arrests (FBI, 1976:177). If each arrest represented one juvenile, the percentage of those arrested would be 5.1 percent of the total. But since an individual could be arrested more than once, it is likely that the proportion of all juveniles who were arrested in 1975 was smaller than the 5.1 percent.

It is obvious, however, that when yearly arrest rates are accumulated over a period of several years, the proportion of juveniles who are arrested increases considerably. In their study of a birth cohort in Philadelphia, for example, Wolfgang et al. (1972:54) found that 35 percent of the 9,945 boys in the cohort had at least one official police contact some time between the ages of 10 and 18. But since a contact may not always lead to an arrest, and since almost half of the boys had only one police contact, it is likely that the formal arrest rate was lower than 35 percent. Furthermore, only about 17.5 percent of the total cohort were recidivists, that is, juveniles with two or more police contacts.

3. *For what kinds of offenses have juveniles been arrested most often?* The laws in most states have empowered the police to take custody of neglected children and status offenders as well as those who violate the criminal law (Levine, 1973:556–57). Given this power, official statistics are revealing.

In 1975, juveniles under the age of 18 were arrested for 48 percent of all serious, property crimes—burglary, larceny, and motor vehicle theft—and 23.1 percent of all violent crimes—homicide, rape, robbery, and aggravated assault (FBI, 1976:188). Yet, although juveniles accounted for more than their share of serious arrests, these made up but a small part of the total. They were arrested far more frequently for ". . . petty larceny, fighting, disorderly conduct, liquor related offenses, and conduct not in violation of the criminal law such as curfew violation, truancy, incorrigibility, or running away from home" (President's Commission on Law Enforcement and Administration of Justice, 1967b:56).

The extent to which this was true is revealed in Table 14–1. It is a record of the rates of juvenile arrest in California between 1960 and 1970 (Lerman, 1979:6).

The table shows two things. First, only slightly more than one third of all juvenile arrests were for criminal offenses. Almost two thirds were for "delinquent tendencies"— truancy, incorrigibility, malicious mischief, drinking, disturbing the peace, glue sniffing, and other status offenses—and for using drugs (mainly marijuana). Second, while rates of arrest increased between 1960 and 1970—from 8,631 per 100,000 in 1960 to 12,417 in 1970— they were due more to increases in arrest for delinquent tendencies and drug use than for specific personal and property crimes. As a result, there is little doubt that the traditional concern of American society with the moral behavior of young people had retained its vigor. Indeed, Table 14.1 shows that while the rate of arrests for delinquent tendencies increased between 1960 and 1970, the proportion of all arrests for specific criminal offenses decreased slightly during that period, from 37.4 percent in 1960 to 33.9 percent in 1970.

4. *What have the police done with the arrested juveniles?* Theoretically, legal rules should have applied equally to all juveniles.

TABLE 14–1 ▬▬

Juvenile arrests: specific rates for 1960, 1965, and 1970 (in rates per 100,000 youth ages 10 to 17 and percent distribution for each year)

Arrest category	Rates per 100,000 youth, ages 10 to 17			Percent distribution		
	1960*	1965*	1970†	1960	1965	1970
Specific crime offenses ..	3,232	3,636	4,214	37.4	35.8	33.9
Drugs only	59	87	1,189	0.7	0.9	9.6
Delinquent tendencies ..	5,340	6,421	7,014	61.9	63.3	56.5
Total arrest rates..	8,631	10,144	12,417	100.0	100.0	100.0
(Number of arrests) ...	(182,715)	(277,649)	(382,935)			

* Numbers arrested and computed rates for 1960 and 1965 can be found in *Crime and Delinquency in California,* 1960 (Sacramento: Bureau of Criminal Statistics, 1969), Table 1–2, p. 10, and Table 1–14, p. 44.

† Numbers arrested used in rate computations can be found in *Crime and Arrests: Reference Tables, 1970* (Sacramento: Bureau of Criminal Statistics, 1970), Table 6, p. 61; population figure used in computations can be found in *Juvenile Probation and Detention: Reference Tables, 1970* (Sacramento: Bureau of Criminal Statistics, 1970), Table 1, p. 5.

This table is reproduced by permission of the author, Paul Lerman, and the Kenyon Public Affairs Forum, Kenyon College (Lerman, 1979.)

Once arrested, a child should have been uniformly processed through the system. But that is not what has actually happened. Instead, the police have been inclined to make use of a number of dispositional alternatives, some of which were not prescribed in the law. They have (1) taken the child to the stationhouse and released him to the custody of his parents; (2) referred the child to the juvenile bureau of the police department (if it had one) and have left further decisions to the officers working there; (3) referred the child to some community welfare agency; and (4) referred the child directly to the juvenile court. The police in some jurisdictions have also had the right to place a child in detention, while in others that decision has been made by probation officers acting as an arm of the juvenile court.

On the average, the police have not referred the majority of arrestees to court, but have handled about half of them entirely within their own departments (FBI, 1976:177; California Bureau of Criminal Statistics, 1968:215). This procedure is known as "counsel and release"—the juvenile's parents are summoned to the stationhouse and, if they seem interested and willing, both they and the child are warned about the evils of bad conduct and urged to take steps to see that it does not happen again.

This practice, however, seems to have been used more often for petty and status, than for serious criminal, offenders. In a single year in California, for example, less than one third of all juvenile criminal violators were counseled without referral to court (California Bureau of Criminal Statistics, 1968:208). The police also have had the option of referring a child to a private or public welfare agency, but, historically, the number of children thus referred has not been large. In 1974, for example, the proportion referred to such agencies was only 2.5 percent nationwide (FBI, 1975:177).

5.   What about the questioning of juveniles? Have they been warned of their rights, and protected against self-incrimination?   According to the provisions of the Fifth Amendment of the Constitution, any person charged with a crime should be protected from self-incrimination; that is, that person is not required to answer questions which might result in prosecution and conviction. For most of this century, however, children have not enjoyed the protection of this amendment. Since the presumed purposes of the juvenile justice system were treatment, not punishment, ordinary protections were not guaranteed, and the practices of the police and juvenile courts were not subjected to the scrutiny of the higher courts.

In the mid-1960s, however, the Supreme Court seriously reviewed the practices of this system for the first time (*Kent* v. *United States,* 1966; *In re Gault,* 1967; *Miranda* v. *Arizona,* 1966). As a consequence, the police and juvenile courts were ordered to change their practices, to advise juveniles that (1) they need not answer any questions; (2) anything they might say could be used against them; (3) they had the right to have an attorney present during any discussion with the police; and (4) if they could not afford an attorney, one would be provided. Even further, the Supreme Court noted that juveniles might not appreciate the meaning of a warning, or the consequences of their waiving their rights. Because they were immature and likely incapable of resisting a threatening or persuasive adult, mere warning was not enough. Instead, the court ruled, the child's parents should be notified of any proposed interrogation and should be present when one occurred (Levine, 1973:559).

This decision has had great implications. But since there is always a considerable lag between the time a decision is handed down and the time the police in every hamlet and city precinct put it into practice, its full effects are only now being felt. In fact, this is one reason the juvenile justice system is now in a state of transition—The old practice of ignoring the rights of juveniles is gradually being replaced.

6.   *What criteria have contributed to police decision making?*   Our findings thus far raise some perplexing questions. We have seen that the police have been more inclined to avoid arresting juveniles than to arrest them and have not always insured juveniles the protection of their constitutional rights. Yet, because they have been granted a great deal of discretion, the police have counseled and released half of those whom they have arrested. Even more perplexing, we have seen that about two thirds of all juveniles who have been arrested, and many of those who have been referred to juvenile court, have been charged with petty and status offenses. How, then, can one reconcile such seemingly contradictory findings? Are there no criteria by which to make sense of police behavior? The answer is that there are criteria, other than those which are strictly legal, which have influenced, and continue to influence, police decision making:

a.   Offense seriousness.   We have already seen that the seriousness of an offense is a key factor in determining the course of police response. Virtually all alleged felony encounters end in arrest, while only a fraction of those who are apprehended for rowdiness or status offenses—5 to 15 percent—are arrested (Black and Reiss, 1970; Goldman, 1963; Lundman et al., 1978; Piliavin and Briar, 1964; Terry, 1967).

b.   Citizen complainants.   Many potential arrest situations are the result of complaints from citizens, not of police patrol (Black and Reiss, 1970; Terry, 1967). It is citizens who initiate many of the contacts (Lundman et al., 1978). And when they do, police decisions may well hinge on whether the complainants are present and what their wishes are. "In not one instance," report Black and Reiss, "did the police arrest a juvenile when the complainant

lobbied for lenience" (1970:71). But, if the citizen demanded action, it was taken (Emerson, 1969:42). As a result, it is clear that the sensitivity of the police to the presence of a citizen complainant plays a key role in their processing of juveniles. A child who might be warned and released in one setting might be arrested and processed in another.

c.   Departmental policy.   Police practices vary widely from community to community, depending not upon differences in law, but differences in departmental policy. In his study of four Pennsylvania communities, for example, Goldman (1969) found that the proportion of juvenile arrests referred to court varied from a low of 9 percent in one community to a high of 71 percent in another. Klein (1970) found much the same thing in his study of 46 police departments in southern California. In one department, virtually all juveniles were counseled and released while in another, four in five juveniles were referred to court.

These widely varying policies often reflect the sentiments of the community in which the departments are located. Sometimes, however, they are associated with internal departmental policies and structures (Lundman et al., 1978). In one highly professionalized department, Wilson (1968b) found that the police were very impersonal toward juveniles, went strictly by the book, arrested many of them, and released very few. In another city, he found a much less professionalized department in which officers were permitted a wide latitude of personal choice, often lived in the neighborhoods in which they worked, dealt with juveniles in a highly personal manner, and viewed their arrests as "Mickey Mouse," low-status arrests.

Such findings once again illustrate that justice is not a monolithic concept which operates uniformly throughout the land. Instead, it takes on widely different meanings, depending not only upon varying policies among departments, but also upon community sentiments, the wishes of complainants, the kind of offense committed, and other criteria such as the sex or social status of the offender.

d. Sex of the offender.   Theoretically, legal rules are supposed to apply equally to girls and boys. Realistically, their application tends to reflect a double standard of justice. This double standard has had striking and paradoxical consequences. Since for centuries the sex roles of males and females have been different, the police have not reacted to their offenses in similar ways. On the one hand, our analysis of self-reported delinquent behavior revealed that while girls usually report fewer delinquent acts than do boys, the kinds of offenses they commit are not strikingly different (see chapter 6). Like boys, they commonly drink, shoplift, skip school, destroy property, commit theft, and even burglarize. Indeed, these kinds of offenses—not female offenses such as fornication, running away from home, and incorrigibility—are the most common. Yet, because criminal offenses have traditionally been defined as male offenses, girls have been much less likely to be arrested and referred to court for them. Instead, they have received chivalrous treatment from the police (Armstrong, 1977; Chesney-Lind, 1977). In Honolulu, for example, Chesney-Lind found that "only 6.1 percent of the girls arrested for the most serious offenses and 12.7 percent of the girls arrested for less serious adult offenses were referred to court, compared with 33.7 percent of those arrested for juvenile [status] offenses" (1977:124).

These figures reveal that girls have been far more likely to be taken into custody for violating traditional expectations—running away from home, failing to obey their parents, or being sexually promiscuous—than for violating the criminal law (Chesney-Lind, 1974; 1977; Perlman, 1970).

In the early 1970s, Sarri and Vinter (1975:47) found that 75 percent of the girls processed in the juvenile justice system nationwide were charged with status, not criminal, offenses. This high percentage was not due entirely to police action, since parents often brought their ungovernable and promiscuous girls to the attention of officials. Nonetheless, when the police were asked to intercede, their responses were likely to reflect the views of complaining parents; namely, that girls should be modest and chaste and protected from unladylike behavior.

This kind of thinking was also reflected in figures released by the Children's Bureau (1967) comparing the numbers of boys and girls officially charged with committing status offenses. While girls made up only about one third of those arrested for such offenses, they comprised about half of those referred to juvenile court. By contrast, only about 20 percent of the boys charged with status offenses were referred to court. Clearly, then, our society has tended to perpetuate traditional sex roles requiring girls to be obedient and chaste, while looking the other way if boys "sow their wild oats" (Chesney-Lind, 1977:129). This traditional perspective is changing, but it has had, and continues to have, considerable impact on police decision making in processing juveniles.

e. Race and socioeconomic status.   The race and socioeconomic status of a juvenile are additional criteria that undoubtedly affect police decision making. It is uncertain, however, whether the effects of such criteria are due to a kind of bigotry unique to the police or are reflections of far more pervasive attitudes in our society.

Throughout our history, minority children have been overrepresented in arrest statistics and in courts and correctional institutions. Numerous social scientists, as a result, have concluded that they are the scapegoats of frustrated policemen (Clinard, 1963:440–51; Glaser, 1960:12; Lemert, 1951:311). Furthermore, many ghetto dwellers would agree with this conclusion. To them, the police have been the most obvious symbols of white oppression:

> Their very presence is an insult, and it would be, even if they spent their entire day feeding gum drops to children. They represent the force of the white world, and that world's criminal profit and ease, to keep the black man corralled up here, in his place. The badge, the gun in the holster, and the swinging club, make vivid what will happen should his rebellion become overt (Baldwin, 1962:65–66).

Furthermore, Wilson believes that unusual attention paid to young ghetto dwellers by the police is justified:

> The patrolman believes with considerable justification that teenagers, Negroes, and lower income persons commit a disproportionate share of all reported crimes. . . . Patrolmen believe that they would be derelict in their duty if they did not treat such persons with suspicion, routinely question them on the street, and detain them for longer questioning if a crime has occurred in the area (1968a:40–41).

It should come as no surprise, then, that youthful ghetto dwellers and the police have often viewed themselves as mortal enemies. Anyone familiar with the war mentality that characterizes their relationships knows that minor incidents can easily escalate into major battles. Each group fears and distrusts the other, and it does little good to realize that in earlier times the same kinds of relationships existed between white police and white gang members. But, because our ghettos are now populated largely by browns and blacks, battles can be interpreted as race wars and the police charged with instigating much of the combat.

Likewise, it provides little solace to find that studies have not always confirmed the notion that the police are biased against minority and lower-class juveniles. On the one hand, one group of investigators has concluded that this is the case. After controlling for offense seriousness and prior record, they found that the police were more inclined to arrest minority and low-income juveniles, particularly black boys (Ferdinand and Luchterland, 1970; Goldman, 1963; Thornberry, 1973; Wilson, 1968a). Piliavin and Briar (1964) concluded that boys whose race, group affiliations, grooming, and language suggest to the police that they are "tough" guys are more likely to be arrested. These characteristics, perhaps more than any offense they might have committed, determine police response.

On the other hand, a second group of investigators has failed to find much evidence of bias (Black, 1970; Eaton and Polk, 1961; Hohenstein, 1969; Lundman et al., 1978; Shannon, 1963; Terry, 1967; Weiner and Willie, 1971). However, most of them point out that one can reach this conclusion only by taking into account that (1) arrest rates vary widely from one community to another; (2) the highest rates of arrest occur in minority and low-socioeconomic areas; and (3) police actions are strongly related to the offense histories of offenders and the seriousness of the acts they commit; and (4) black complainants are even more insistent than white complainants that juvenile law violators be arrested.

But, when one sorts through all of these factors, one finds that race and social status are not the major determinants of arrest. Rather, higher rates of arrest in low-income areas are due to the fact that the juveniles living in them are somewhat more likely to be recidivists and to commit serious offenses. Furthermore, it will be recalled from our analysis of self-reported delinquency that the juveniles arrested most often are persons who, by their own admissions, are the most frequent and serious law violators (chapter 6). Even though minority and low-status juveniles are overrepresented in our courts and institutions, therefore, it may be that they are more likely to be numbered among the tiny minority who are chronic offenders.

But, since the scientific community is

divided over this issue, we are faced with a dilemma in interpreting existing evidence. Gibbons resolves the dilemma by concluding that one cannot generalize about police bias. Rather, "what these divergent findings reflect is real differences among communities and police departments" (1976:43). Just as other policies vary from department to department, so practices with respect to poor and minority youths also vary. This conclusion may be accurate, but unfortunately it does not begin to exhaust the complexities of the issue.

Throughout our history, American beliefs have stressed the notion that the poverty, disrupted families, and ignorance of minority and poor people are the inevitable precursors of child neglect and juvenile lawbreaking. As a consequence, laws were written and the juvenile court was created to locate dependent and neglected, as well as law-violating, children, and to bring them into conformity with the ideal concept of childhood.

Given this construction of the nature and causes of delinquency, it should not be surprising that minority and lower-class children have become the special targets of the police and other agents of juvenile justice. These children are more likely to be members of one-parent families, to be neglected, malnourished, and otherwise deprived, and the police have been conditioned to expect higher rates of delinquency among them. As a result, we may be confronted with a self-fulfilling prophecy: the very problems the police and citizens have been conditioned to expect actually occur.

If generations of minority and poor people have not shared the economic, familial, and educational advantages that lead to success in our culture, we should expect the consequences to be evident among their children. Indeed, they are: poor and minority children have higher infant death rates, run much greater risks of biological impairment due to environmental deprivation, and are victimized

in serious crimes far more often, than affluent children (Shah and Roth, 1974:126–129). This disastrous circle is finally completed when these children experience difficulties in social adjustment, fail to achieve in school, and turn to street gangs for alternative sources of satisfaction and protection. Not having been socialized according to the dictates of the ideal concept of childhood and lacking a stake in conventional society, they exhibit behaviors that are not only socially debilitating to themselves, but also contrary to law.

If there is merit in this interpretation, it is clear that the tendency of the police to find and report higher rates of law-violating behavior, child abuse, and neglect among poor and minority children is not just the product of a bigotry peculiar to them. Rather, it is a function of real conditions for which the police are not solely responsible. Instead, the police are merely the front-line troops of conventional society who are expected to mop up ghetto communities after a long war of attrition in which racism and social segregation have taken a heavy toll. Though they often try to play diplomat, social worker, and child saver, in addition to crime fighter, their status in these communities is like that of naive draftees in an occupied country:

> It is hard . . . to blame the policeman, blank, good-natured, thoughtless, and insuperably innocent, for being such a perfect representative of the people he serves. He, too, believes in good intentions and is astounded and offended when [his good intentions] are not taken for the deed. He has never, himself, done anything for which to be hated, which of us has? And yet he is facing daily and nightly, the people who would gladly see him dead, and he knows it. There is no way for him not to know it: There are few things under heaven more unnerving than the silent accumulating contempt and hatred of a people. He moves through Harlem, therefore, like an occupying soldier in a bitterly hostile country; which is precisely what, and where he is, and is the

reason he walks in twos and threes (Baldwin, 1962:66–67).

It is no wonder, then, that the policeman often feels like a pariah. He is distrusted by society's affluent members and hated by its ghetto dwellers for symbolizing and failing to resolve a host of profound problems which he alone did not create.

The actions of the police and the criteria they use in processing offenders are a striking reflection of our cultural history and the kind of society it has produced. The ambivalent attitude of the police toward juveniles, their differential treatment of boys and girls, and their behavior in ghetto communities are the result, not only of their own views, but also of the way delinquency is defined and constructed in our society. If we are to understand how and why the police behave as they do, therefore, we must look not merely at them, but at the role into which they have been cast by the society they serve. During the last century, that role has become increasingly important while the social control functions of the family, age-integrated places of work, and the community have declined. So long as new social inventions do not reverse this trend, the role of the police will continue to increase in importance and will likely become more, not less, controversial.

SUMMARY AND CONCLUSIONS

Throughout history, the police have been viewed with a great deal of public ambivalence: on the one hand, distrusted and feared, but on the other, expected to play social worker as well as crime fighter. Police views of themselves have reflected this attitude: their chosen profession has been tainted and they have seen themselves as outcasts, particularly in ghetto communities where they are viewed as hated symbols of social oppression. Hence, while much of their time has been spent rendering assistance to adults, or processing

neglected children, they have received relatively little recognition for this side of their work.

This conflicting situation has been directly reflected in the way the police have handled and processed juveniles under the original concept of juvenile justice.

1.   The police have exercised a tremendous amount of discretion in deciding whom to arrest and whom to refer to juvenile court.   This discretion has produced a filtering process, graphically portrayed in Figure 14–1. Based upon what we learned in this and previous chapters, it presents an estimate of the actual number of juveniles who violated the law in 1974, and the action the police took concerning them.

Briefly, the evidence summarized in Figure 14.1 is this:

Since most juveniles, ages 10 to 17, report having violated the law, the actual number of offenders probably numbered several millions nationwide in 1974.

The police had contacts with many of these law violators. Although the exact number is not known, they could have legally arrested many of them. Yet, they released the majority with a warning.

The number of juveniles who were actually arrested in 1974 (1.7 million), was only a fraction of all those who had contacts with the police.

Of those arrested, only about 50 percent were actually referred to court (about 867,000 in 1974). Most of the remainder were counseled and released.

2.   This police filtering process has not been a random one. Instead, it has been affected by several criteria that helped determine who would be arrested and for what reasons.

Police practices have reflected society's concern with enforcing traditional moral rules for children. Even though the police have been more likely to arrest serious than petty offenders, the latter have still outnumbered the former.

The police have been highly sensitive to public attitudes, arresting or releasing offenders according to the wishes of citizen complainants.

FIGURE 14–1

The traditional police filtering process (estimates for 1974)

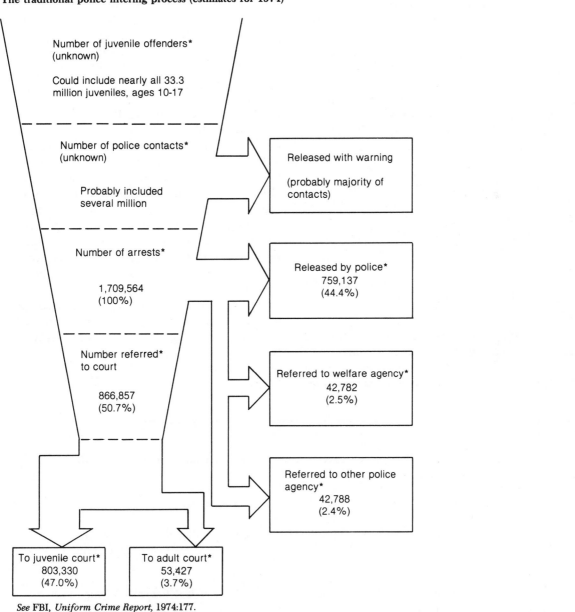

Number of juvenile offenders*
(unknown)

Could include nearly all 33.3 million juveniles, ages 10-17

Number of police contacts*
(unknown)

Probably included several million

Released with warning

(probably majority of contacts)

Number of arrests*

1,709,564
(100%)

Released by police*
759,137
(44.4%)

Number referred*
to court

866,857
(50.7%)

Referred to welfare agency*
42,782
(2.5%)

Referred to other police agency*
42,788
(2.4%)

To juvenile court*
803,330
(47.0%)

To adult court*
53,427
(3.7%)

See FBI, *Uniform Crime Report,* 1974:177.

The police have applied a double standard in making decisions about girls and boys. They have been less inclined to process girls than boys for criminal offenses but have done just the reverse where status offenses are involved.

The actions of the police have helped to produce higher rates of arrest and court referral among lower-status and minority youth. These rates may be partially due to a higher incidence of crimes actually committed by these youths, but they are also a reflection of the tendency of the police to respond to the greater incidence of dependency and neglect in these populations, as well as law-violating behavior.

3. The police have been pragmatic labeling theorists. Within the constraints of the criteria imposed upon them, the police have been more likely to avoid taking official action against juveniles than to take it. Contrary to popular belief, they have long had a tradition of warning and releasing many juveniles rather than referring them to juvenile court.

4. Many, probably most, of the important decisions made by the agents of juvenile justice have been made by the police—on the streets and in the stationhouses—not by judges or probation officers in their paneled chambers. Given the discretion exercised by the police, their actions could be said to have been contrary to the original child-saving philosophy of the juvenile court; namely, that all children with problems should have been uniformly referred to court, not just the ones whom the police chose to refer. It should have been a wise, deliberative judge, with his or her supporting cast of experts, who should have decided whether intervention was required—not the ordinary cop on the street.

The actions of the police, however, have reflected the ambivalent attitudes of our society and the practical problems of day-to-day police work. Indeed, if the police had followed the letter of the law, the courts would have been inundated with "offenders" and the rise in official delinquency rates would have been unprecedented—without the slightest change in juvenile behavior. Whether right or wrong, therefore, the police have probably played the most crucial role in determining the nature and character of juvenile justice during much of this century.

In response to recent changes in ideology, law, and legal practice, however, the role of the police is being altered. In later chapters, therefore, we will review those changes and discuss their impact on the official processing of juveniles.

REFERENCES

Armstrong, Gail
    1977   "Females Under the Law—'Protected' but Unequal." *Crime and Delinquency* 23 (April):109–120.

Baldwin, James
    1962   *Nobody Knows My Name.* New York: Dell Publications.

Bittner, Egon
    1970   *The Functions of the Police in Modern Society.* National Institute of Mental Health. Publication No. 2059. Washington, D.C.: U.S. Government Printing Office.

Black, Donald J.
    1970   "Production of Crime Rates." *American Sociological Review* 35 (August): 733–748.

Black, Donald J., and Reiss, Albert J., Jr.
  1967 "Patterns of Behavior in Police and Citizen Transactions." Section 1 of
       Studies of Crime and Law Enforcement in Major Metropolitan Areas. Vol.
       2. Washington, D.C.: U.S. Government Printing Office.
  1970 "Police Control of Juveniles." *American Sociological Review* 35 (Feb-
       ruary):63–77.

Bordua, David J.
  1967 "Recent Trends: Deviant Behavior and Social Controls." *Annals of the
       American Academy of Political and Social Science* 359 (January):149–163.

California Bureau of Criminal Statistics
  1968 *Crime and Delinquency in California, 1967.* Sacramento: Department of
       Justice.

Carter, Robert M.
  1976 "The Police View of the Justice System." Pp. 121–32 in Malcolm W. Klein,
       ed., *The Juvenile Justice System.* Beverly Hills, Calif.: Sage.

Carter, Robert M., et al.
  1971 "SUPERcop and SUPERcriminal: The Media Portrait of Crime." *Daily Vari-
       ety* 153, 38th Anniversary Issue (October):80–88.

Chesney-Lind, Meda
  1974 "Juvenile Delinquency: The Sexualization of Female Crime." *Psychology
       Today* 8 (July):43–46.
  1977 "Judicial Paternalism and the Female Status Offender." *Crime and Delin-
       quency* 23 (April):121–130.

Children's Bureau
  1967 *Statistics on Public Institutions for Delinquent Children.* Washington, D.C.:
       Department of Health Education and Welfare.

Clinard, Marshall B.
  1963 *Sociology of Deviant Behavior,* rev. ed. New York: Holt, Rinehart & Winston.

Cole, Arthur C.
  1934 "The Irrepressible Conflict, 1859–1865." Pp. 154–155 in Arthur M. Schle-
       singer, Sr., and Dixon R. Fox, eds., *A History of American Life.* Vol. 8.
       New York: Macmillan.

Cumming, Elaine; Cumming, Ian; and Edell, Laura
  1973 "Policeman as Philosopher, Guide and Friend." Pp. 184–192 in Arthur Nied-
       erhoffer and Abraham S. Blumberg, eds., *The Ambivalent Force: Perspectives
       on the Police.* San Francisco: Rinehart Press.

Eaton, Joseph W., and Polk, Kenneth
  1961 *Measuring Delinquency.* Pittsburgh: University of Pittsburgh Press.

Emerson, Robert H.
  1969 *Judging Delinquents: Context and Process in Juvenile Court.* Chicago: Al-
       dine.

Ennis, Philip H.
  1966 *The Police and the Community.* Vol. 2. Washington, D.C.: U.S. Government
       Printing Office.
  1967 *Criminal Victimization in the United States: A Report of a National Survey.*
       Washington, D.C.: U.S. Government Printing Office.

Federal Bureau of Investigation
> 1975   *Crime in the United States: Uniform Crime Reports—1974.* Washington, D.C.: U.S. Government Printing Office.
> 1976   *Crime in the United States: Uniform Crime Reports—1975.* Washington, D.C.: U.S. Government Printing Office.

Ferdinand, Theodore N., and Luchterland, Elmer G.
> 1970   "Inner-city Youths, the Police, the Juvenile Court, and Justice." *Social Problems* 17 (Spring):510–527.

Gibbons, Don C.
> 1976   *Delinquent Behavior.* 2d ed. Englewood Cliffs, N.J.: Prentice-Hall.

Glaser, Daniel
> 1960   As quoted in Richard A. Cloward and Lloyd E. Ohlin, *Delinquency and Opportunity.* New York: Free Press.

Goldman, Nathan
> 1963   *The Differential Selection of Juvenile Offenders for Court Appearance.* New York: National Council on Crime and Delinquency.
> 1969   "The Differential Selection of Juvenile Offenders for Court Appearance." Pp. 264–90 in William Chambliss, ed., *Crime and the Legal Process.* New York: McGraw-Hill.

Hindelang, Michael J.
> 1975   *Public Opinion Regarding Crime, Criminal Justice, and Related Topics.* Washington, D.C.: U.S. Government Printing Office.

Hindelang, Michael, et al.
> 1976   *Source Book of Criminal Justice Statistics—1975.* Washington, D.C.: U.S. Government Printing Office.

Hohenstein, William F.
> 1969   "Factors Influencing the Police Disposition of Juvenile Offenders." Pp. 138–49 in Thorsten Sellin and Marvin E. Wolfgang, ed., *Delinquency: Selected Studies.* New York: John Wiley & Sons.

In re Gault
> 1967   387 U.S. 1.

Kent v. *United States*
> 1966   383 U.S. 541.

Klein, Malcolm W.
> 1970   "Police Processing of Juvenile Offenders: Toward the Development of Juvenile System Rates." Los Angeles County Sub-Regional Board, California Council on Juvenile Justice, Part III.

Lemert, Edwin M.
> 1951   *Social Pathology.* New York: McGraw-Hill.

Lerman, Paul
> 1979   "Order Offenses and Juvenile Delinquency." In LaMar T. Empey, ed., *Juvenile Justice: The Progressive Legacy and Current Reforms.* Charlottesville: University Press of Virginia.

Levine, Martin
> 1973   "The Current Status of Juvenile Law." Pp. 547–606 in Gary B. Adams et al. eds., *Juvenile Justice Management.* Springfield, Ill.: Charles C Thomas.

Lundman, Richard J.; Sykes, Richard E.; and Clark, John P.
    1978   "Police Control of Juveniles: A Replication." *Journal of Research in Crime and Delinquency* 15 (January):74–91.

Miranda v. *Arizona*
    1966   384 U.S. 436.

Morris, Norval, and Hawkins, Gordon
    1969   *The Honest Politician's Guide to Crime Control.* Chicago: University of Chicago Press.

National Center for Juvenile Justice
    1977   *Juvenile Court Statistics, 1974.* Pittsburgh: National Center for Juvenile Justice.

National Commission on Law Observance and Enforcement
    1931   *Report on the Police.* Washington, D.C.: U.S. Government Printing Office.

Niederhoffer, Arthur and Blumberg, Abraham S., eds.
    1973   *The Ambivalent Force: Perspectives on the Police.* San Francisco, Rinehart Press.

Perlman, I. Richard
    1970   "Antisocial Behavior of the Minor in the United States. Pp. 35–43 in Harwin L. Voss, ed., *Society, Delinquency and Delinquent Behavior.* Boston: Little, Brown.

Piliavin, Irving, and Briar, Scott
    1964   "Police Encounters with Juveniles." *American Journal of Sociology* 70 (September):206–214.

President's Commission on Law Enforcement and Administration of Justice
    1967a   *Task Force Report: The Police.* Washington, D.C.: U.S. Government Printing Office.
    1967b   *The Challenge of Crime in a Free Society.* Washington, D.C.: U.S. Government Printing Office.

Reiss, Albert J., Jr.
    1971   *The Public and the Police.* New Haven: Yale University Press.

Sarri, Rosemary C., and Vinter, Robert D.
    1975   "Juvenile Justice and Injustice." *Resolution* 18 (Winter):43–51.

Shah, Saleem A., and Roth, Loren H.
    1974   "Biological and Psychophysiological Factors in Criminality." Pp. 101–73 in Daniel Glaser, ed., *Handbook of Criminology.* Chicago: Rand McNally.

Shannon, Lyle W.
    1963   "Types and Patterns of Delinquency Referral in a Middle-sized City."*British Journal of Criminology* 10 (July):206–214.

Smith, Bruce, Sr.
    1960   *Police Systems in the United States.* 2d ed. New York: Harper & Bros.

Skolnick, Jerome H.
    1973   "The Police and the Urban Ghetto." Pp. 223–38 in Arthur Niederhoffer and Abraham S. Blumberg, eds., *The Ambivalent Force: Perspectives on the Police.* San Francisco: Rinehart Press.

Terry, Robert M.
  1967   "Discrimination in the Handling of Juvenile Offenders by Social-Control Agencies." *Journal of Research in Crime and Delinquency* 4 (July):218–230.

Thornberry, Terence P.
  1973   "Race, Socioeconomic Status and Sentencing in the Juvenile Justice System." *Journal of Criminal Law and Criminology* 64 (March):90–98.

Weiner, Norman L., and Willie, Charles V.
  1971   "Decisions by Juvenile Officers." *American Journal of Sociology* 76 (September):199–210.

Westley, William A.
  1975   "Violence and the Police." *American Journal of Sociology* 59 (July):34–41.

Williams, Jay R., and Gold, Martin
  1972   "From Delinquent Behavior to Official Delinquency." *Social Problems* 20 (Fall):209–228.

Wilson, James Q.
  1968a   *Varieties of Police Behavior: The Management of Law and Order in Eight Communities.* Cambridge: Harvard University Press.
  1968b   "The Police and the Delinquent in Two Cities." Pp. 9–30 in Stanton Wheeler, ed., *Controlling Delinquents.* New York: John Wiley & Sons.

Wolfgang, Marvin E.; Figlio, Robert; and Sellin, Thorsten
  1972   *Delinquency in a Birth Cohort.* Chicago: University of Chicago Press.

The care and treatment of children in the traditional juvenile court was supposed to approximate that which should be given by their parents.

JUVENILE COURT: THE TARNISHED SUPERPARENT

This chapter, like the previous one on the police, is devoted to a review and critique of the original juvenile court, and to its operation until, as a result of severe attacks in the 1960s and 1970s, it began to change.

It will be recalled that the modern concepts of both childhood and the juvenile court resulted from trends spanning centuries of change in both Europe and America. By the 19th century, people no longer accepted the idea that unwanted children, even those of the unworthy poor, could be abandoned or killed at the whim of adults. Instead, a series of *nurturance rights* should be assured for them. Not only should they be guaranteed the right to life, and to food, clothing, and shelter, but also they should be raised and loved by their own parents, permitted to attend school to learn moral principles as well as reading and writing, and protected from the evil blandishments of city streets, immoral associates, and places of vice and corruption.

Such beliefs meant that the social status and influence of children would inevitably be subordinate to that of adults. They could not be both protected from and equal to adults. Persons who are supposedly guileless and immature cannot enjoy equal rights with those who know what is best for them and who are expected to safeguard and discipline them. Thus, throughout much of the 19th century, children were committed to houses of refuge, asylums, and industrial schools, not merely to preserve order and protect society, but to serve their best interests.

Then, in 1899, when such commitments proved to be less than a panacea and it became clear that children were still being exploited, the juvenile court was invented. Where other means had failed, it would succeed.

JURISDICTION OF THE JUVENILE COURT

Although new state laws varied somewhat in their definitions of the powers of the juvenile court, all agreed that it would have jurisdiction over four kinds of children:

1. *Delinquent children.* Those who committed an act which, if committed by an adult, would be a crime.

2. *Status offenders.* Those who were beyond the control of their parents or were engaged in conduct thought to be harmful to themselves.

3. *Neglected children.* Those whose parents failed to provide them with proper care and guidance although they were able to do so.

4. *Dependent children.* Those whose parents, through no fault of their own, were unable to care for them (Paulsen and Whitebread, 1974:32).

In short, new laws endowed the juvenile court with unprecedented powers. Whereas the Constitution of the United States protected adults from unreasonable invasions of their privacy and governed any criminal proceedings against them with carefully prescribed procedures, such would not be the case where children were concerned. Instead, the concept of juvenile justice implied that such procedures would simply frustrate the child-saving functions of the court.

FUNCTIONS OF THE COURT

As envisioned by its inventors, the juvenile court would fulfill several important functions. It would (1) enforce the modern concept of childhood; (2) act as a surrogate for the family and the school; (3) prevent delinquency; (4) decriminalize children; and (5) rehabilitate juveniles.

Enforcing the modern concept of childhood

To begin with, the court was expected to enforce the modern concept of childhood—the ideas that (1) children go through several stages of development; (2) throughout these stages,

they are qualitatively different from adults; and (3) until their full emotional, moral, physical, and rational skills are cultivated, children should be quarantined from adult vices and responsibilities.

The school attendance and child labor laws of the late 19th century, as well as the creation of the juvenile court, represented an embodiment of these assumptions in the legal as well as the cultural fabric of society. That is why, until almost the present day, children have been referred to court not only for violating the criminal law, but for idle conduct, intractability, associating with lewd or lascivious persons, being truant, being alone with someone of the opposite sex at night, or committing one of a host of other possible offenses. Legal definitions of child deviance were simply the obverse of the moral principles inherent in the modern concept of childhood; namely, that the ideal child should be obedient, submissive, self-controlled, hard-working, modest, and chaste. A paternalistic court was expected to insure that children were stringently safeguarded, formally educated, and carefully protected from adult behavior until they had outlived the quarantine associated with childhood.

Acting as a surrogate for family and school

The second function of the juvenile court was closely related to the first. Its creators firmly hoped that it would become a benevolent surrogate for uncaring families and ineffective schools. That is why the first juvenile court act in Illinois specified that the law should be "liberally construed to the end . . . that the care, custody and discipline of a child shall approximate . . . that which should be given by its parents" (*Revised Statutes of Illinois,* 1899, Sec. 21).

By way of illustrating this expectation, the Educational Commission of Chicago complained, in 1899, that its Compulsory

School Attendance Act was not adequate to insure schooling for marginal children caught in the vortex of cultural conflict and social change: "They cannot be received or continued in the regularly organized schools; . . . their parents cannot or will not control them; teachers and committees fail to correct their evil tendencies and vicious conduct. What shall be done with them?" (Harpur, 1899:161).

The answer, of course, was that the juvenile court would discipline them. It would rescue them from their dissolute parents and see that they were properly educated: "The welfare of the city demands that such children be put under restraint. . . . We should rightfully have the power to arrest all the little beggars, loafers, and vagabonds that infest our city, take them from the streets, and place them in schools where they are compelled to receive education and learn moral principles" (Harpur, 1899:163–164). In short, the juvenile court would act as a helpful parent and a stern parent, stepping in when all else had failed.

Preventing delinquency

By taking up the jobs of inadequate parents, teachers, and communities, the juvenile court could not only keep children in school but also perform a much grander function: it could prevent delinquency. As the Chicago Bar Association put it, the court should not have to wait until a child is "criminal in tastes and habits," or "is in jails, bridewells and reformatories" before it acts. Instead, the court should "seize upon the first conditions of neglect or delinquency" and thereby prevent innocent children from wandering down the path that leads to criminality (Platt, 1969:138–39). Furthermore, in fulfilling this role, the court would not be encumbered with all the inhibiting strictures of due process, since its primary goal was in surrounding children with good, not punishing them for evil.

Decriminalizing children

Besides using the juvenile court to prevent delinquency, reformers believed that it also could be used to decriminalize the conduct of young lawbreakers. In the past, as Judge Julian W. Mack put it, children were generally "huddled together" with older criminals in the station houses, jails, and work houses of America. "Instead of the state training its bad boys so as to make of them decent citizens, it permitted them to become outlaws and outcasts of society; it *criminalized* them by the methods it used in dealing with them" (1910:293, emphasis added).

Judge Mack's lament reflected the fact that the actual treatment of children throughout the 19th century had not caught up with the belief that they were qualitatively different from adults and should be so treated. Instead, "children tried for committing crimes were routinely processed primarily by lower municipal courts, which presumably did not adhere to the most libertarian conceptions of due process and adversary rights. . . ." (Schultz, 1974:248). At the discretion of their parents and guardians, as well as the police and courts, children were committed to industrial and reform schools for being ". . . destitute of proper parental care, or growing up in mendicancy, ignorance, idleness or vice" (Platt, 1969:103). Many were also committed to adult jails and prisons for the blanket charge of "disorderly conduct," covering anything from assault with a deadly weapon to building bonfires in the street or playing on the railroad tracks (Lathrop, 1916:2). In order to correct these problems and avoid making outlaws out of children, the juvenile court would destigmatize them by calling them "delinquents" rather than "criminals," and it would devise a set of remedies that were better suited to their particular needs.

Rehabilitating juveniles

The idea that juvenile crimes should be decriminalized and their perpetrators reformed was symptomatic of the growing popularity of the concept of rehabilitation. Indeed, the growth of positive criminology only enhanced this popularity. Since crime in the streets and misconduct in the school were presumed to be due to causes over which children had no control, each misbehaving child required personal attention. Reflecting these ideas, William Healy, an influential psychiatrist who directed the Psychopathic Institute of the first Chicago Juvenile Court, argued that only by a detailed analysis of each offender could suitable remedies be found (Rothman, 1979). Poverty, alone, does not cause bad behavior, he concluded. Rather, it is due to "bad habits of mind" and "mental imagery of low order," both of which result from some combination of defective interests, depraved parents, poverty, and bad companions.

Indeed, when studying an urban juvenile court in 1969, Emerson (p.249) noted the persistence of psychodynamic theory in the court. "Illegal behavior," he observed "is held to be 'pathological' and to reflect psychological conflicts which the psychiatrist can identify." His quotation from the guidelines of the court's psychiatric clinic illustrates this belief:

> The commission of an offense must, by its antisocial nature, indicate some breakdown, overpowering, or remission of that facility which human beings have, or are expected to have, to maintain their status as law-abiding citizens. In a sense, then, an offense may be seen as symptomatic of an inner conflict which the ego is not able to effectively deal with (p. 250).

Such a doctrine suggests that the only solution to delinquency is to attempt to discover, case by case, the causative factors in each child. Fortunately, the juvenile court could act as the screening mechanism for the process.

In summary, then, the needs to be served, and the remedies for meeting them, were clear. The juvenile court would be endowed with all the discretion and power it needed to save America's children. In so doing, there was little need to draw sharp distinctions between 7-year-olds and 16-year-olds, or between children who committed crimes and those who were poor, neglected, or failing in school. As Judge Julian Mack of Chicago proudly proclaimed, it is the duty of the state not to ask merely whether a boy or a girl has committed a specific offense but

> to find out what he is physically, mentally and morally, and then, if it learns that he is treading the path that leads to criminality, to take him in charge, not so much to punish as to reform, not to degrade but to uplift, not to crush but to develop, not to make him a criminal but a worthy citizen (1910:297).

THE IDEAL PROCEDURES

In pursuit of this noble objective, the procedures of the juvenile court have generally been divided into three major steps: *intake, adjudication,* and *disposition.* A simplified version of these steps is displayed in Figure 15–1. By reviewing each of them, we can determine how, according to proponents, each child is supposed to have been treated by the juvenile court.

Intake

Intake was to be the process during which a juvenile referral was received by the court and a series of important decisions made as to whether the court should (1) hold the child in detention while his case was being investigated; (2) release the child with a warning; (3) file a petition for a formal court hearing; or (4) refer

FIGURE 15–1
Juvenile court processing

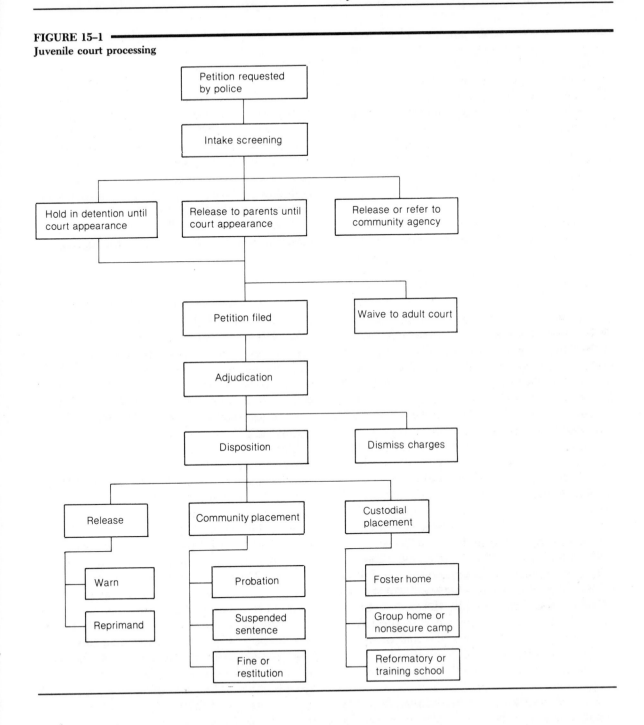

the child to some other agency or the adult court if the offense committed was serious.

One of the major innovations of the juvenile court was the appointment of probation officers to conduct this screening process as well as to supervise juveniles following court action. Indeed, early judges were eloquent in their praise of this invention. "The ideal probation officer," said Judge Baker, "should have all the consecration of the devoted clergyman, all the power to interest and direct of the efficient teacher, and all the discernment of the skillful physician" (1910:326). Likewise, Richard Tuthill who, along with Julian Mack was one of the first judges in Chicago, called probation "the cord upon which all the pearls of the juvenile court are strung. . . . Without it, the juvenile court could not exist (Rothman, 1979).

The intake inquiry conducted by the probation officer was designed to fulfill two major functions. The first was diagnostic. He or she was charged with obtaining detailed information on the background, character, and needs of the child, information that would enable the judge to look behind the offense to the child's condition. As a result, the probation officer was given unfettered authority to obtain case history data from police, parents, teachers, neighbors, welfare workers, and any other relevant persons. He was also expected to seek information from court-appointed experts— psychologists, physicians, and social workers. Depending upon the probation officer's findings, he or she might dismiss the case, authorize a full court hearing, or dispose of it by informal methods such as the "counsel and release" procedures used by the police. As Judge Baker of Boston described it, the role of the probation officer was like that of the medical technician who gathers the information necessary to make a diagnosis and recommend a cure. (1910:322).

The second major function of the probation officer was that of deciding, prior to a court hearing, whether the juvenile should be held in detention. This was a key function because one of the major goals of juvenile court legislation was to get juveniles out of adult jails and into special institutions for children. This need was all the more important because few states extended the right of bail to the young; therefore, it fell to the probation officer to decide which children should be retained in custody. If, in his judgment, parents or guardians were unfit to supervise their children, or if the children were viewed as a serious threat to themselves or the community, they were to be detained. Otherwise, they could be released pending court action.

Adjudication

For those juveniles for whom the intake procedures resulted in a court hearing, *adjudication* refers to the legal process conducted by the judge, with the probation officer assisting. The judge was to determine whether the allegations in the petition were sustained, and whether the child should be defined as delinquent or as dependent and neglected.

Since, in theory, the juvenile court was charged with exploring the mental and social condition of a child, every state moved to relax the style of the adjudicatory proceedings. Judges were supposed to be selected on the basis of their special qualifications—their knowledge of child psychology and social problems, perhaps—more than their legal training. Thus, though they were not technically empowered to banish lawyers from their courts, that, in effect, was what happened. It was done on the grounds that the hearing of a case should be similar to that which thoughtful parents might administer. Hence, judges were inclined neither to adhere to accepted rules of evidence designed for adult proceedings nor to restrict admissions of guilt by youthful defendants. As Judge Orr of Minnesota put it, "The laws of evidence are sometimes forgotten or overlooked" (Rothman, 1979).

In 1910, the Russell Sage Foundation fostered the publication of a volume entitled *Preventive Treatment of Neglected Children.* In it were articles by leading reformers, among them Judge Baker of Boston. The following is his description of the way he, and presumably any enlightened judge, should run his court:

> [T]he judge excludes all newspaper reporters and all other persons having only a general interest in the proceedings. The sheltered location of the room, the absence of decoration, the dispensing with attendants, and the exclusion of outsiders give the simplicity which is necessary to gain the undivided attention of the child and give the quiet which is indispensable for hearing clearly what the child says and speaking to him in the calmest tone.
>
> When the judge is ready to hear a case, the probation officer brings in the child from the waiting room. The child does not stand in front of the desk, because that would prevent the judge from seeing the whole of him, and the way a child stands and even the condition of his shoes are often useful aids to a proper diagnosis of the case. The child stands at the end of the platform, where the judge can see him from top to toe, and the judge sits near the end, so he is close to the child and can reassure him if necessary by a friendly hand on the shoulder. The platform is just high enough to bring the average child's eye about on a level with the eye of the judge (Baker, 1910:319).

While these general procedures should prevail, boys and girls were treated somewhat differently. Judge Baker wanted to see a boy alone at first to spare him the embarrassment and the fear "which he often feels in speaking the truth in the presence of the parents" (p. 319). The judge's objective, if possible, was to get the boy to admit his guilt. "The child is told . . . that in this court there is only one thing worse than stealing (or whatever the child is supposed to have done) and that is not telling the truth afterward" (p. 320). If the boy continued to deny his guilt, Judge Baker, like a good father, continued to reason with him, pointing out why such a denial was harmful. Lying to protect oneself, one's friends, or one's parents only made things worse. Indeed, all these pains were taken to get an admission of guilt because it would enhance the effectiveness of treatment. After the boy had unburdened himself to an understanding judge, he would be ready to accept the helpful intervention of the court.

It is significant that this set of beliefs and practices has been neither exceptional nor isolated throughout this century. In 1962, Judge Paul W. Alexander, a former president of the National Council of Juvenile Court Judges, agreed with Judge Baker in virtually the same terms, though their careers were half a century apart:

> To help the child change his attitude, a confession is a primary prerequisite. Without it the court is aiding the child to build his future on a foundation of falsehood and deceit, instead of on the rock of truth and honesty. [A]nything that may tend to discourage a child from making a clean breast of it, that may tend to encourage him to try to escape the consequences of his actions by denial and other means, must retard, and possibly defeat, the court's efforts to correct the child (p. 88).

If the child persisted in denying his guilt, parents, police, and sometimes defense counsel, could be brought in, and the case would be formally heard. But to both judges this was not the most desirable procedure. As Judge Alexander put it, "The question is almost never 'Did he or didn't he?' but rather 'What is the best way to change his wrong attitude and correct his unlawful behavior?' " (1962:89). Or as Judge Baker indicated, a confession of guilt would enable the child to say to parents, police, and aggrieved parties; "John says it is true that he took Mrs. Doe's money, and I adjudge him delinquent, and he has the right to appeal" (1910:322).

By contrast, Judge Baker was more chivalrous with girls (p. 325). He warned that every step should be taken to protect their reputations and, by implication, that of the judge. From the time of arrest, therefore, a girl should be turned over to an "accredited" woman. "When [the girl] comes into the judge's chamber she is attended by a woman. . . . The judge never talks with girls alone as he does with boys." With the chaperone present, however, he could go on to conduct his informal, fatherly hearing.

In some instances, cases were dismissed for lack of evidence, but the major concern of a judge was not with establishing guilt or innocence but with using the court hearing to begin reforming the delinquent. The general reasoning seemed to be that, if children were in enough trouble to be in court, they probably needed help regardless of whether they were technically guilty of a criminal act.

Disposition

Disposition refers to the process by which a judge decided what should be done with a juvenile for whom some guilt was established— whether the child should be released to his or her parents or separated from them, and whether the child should be placed on probation or committed to a correctional facility.

When an adult is tried, the disposition hearing is separated from the adjudicatory process so that decisions regarding the guilt or innocence of a person will not be confused with those having to do with sentencing and disposition. But, since the inventors of the juvenile court were concerned less with the guilt of a child than with his condition, the two hearings were often intermixed:

> Of course the court does not confine its attention to just the particular offense which brought the child to its notice. For example, a boy who comes to court for some such trifle as failing to wear his badge when selling papers may be held on probation for months because of difficulties at school; and a boy who comes in for playing ball in the street may (after the court has caused more serious charges to be preferred against him) be committed to a reform school because he is found to have habits of loafing, stealing, or gambling which cannot be corrected outside (Baker, 1910:322).

The differences between these procedures and those carried on in adult courts are obvious: an adult cannot be brought to court on one offense and found guilty of another; an adult is defended by a lawyer and protected against self-incrimination; an adult could not be incarcerated upon the initial charge of "playing ball in the street." Furthermore, the decision as to what will be done with an adult once the case has been adjudicated is made in a separate disposition hearing. A few juvenile courts have followed this procedure, but most have not (President's Commission, 1967A:5). Instead, as Judge Baker described it, the procedure should follow that of the medical clinic:

> The judge and the probation officer consider together, like a physician and his junior, whether the outbreak . . . was largely accidental, or whether it is habitual or likely to be so, whether it is due chiefly to some inherent physical or moral defect of the child, or whether some feature of his environment is an important factor; and then they address themselves to the question of how permanently to prevent a recurrence (Baker, 1910:322).

If the child was thought to suffer from feeblemindedness, bad adenoids, or poor eyesight, he would be sent to a specialist, but, if the environment seemed to be at fault, "a change is secured through the parents by making them realize that the child will be taken from them if they do not make the change" (Baker, 1910:322).

The indeterminate sentence

Another striking feature of the juvenile court has been its use of the indeterminate sentence. In order to secure the best possible long-term care for children, most states have empowered the court to maintain supervision over them until age 21. In the event of some trifling matter, such as throwing stones in the street, a child might be given a light punishment, such as copying the laws governing the proper use of public thoroughfares. Once this was done, the probation officer or the judge could check his work, "just as a physician might do in the case of a burn or a bruise" (Baker, 1910:323). If the "burn" had healed, the patient could be released. But, if the offense was serious and likely to lead to a bad breakdown, the child "was seen by the judge at frequent intervals, monthly, weekly, or sometimes daily, just as with the patient and the physician in case of tuberculosis or typhoid." A disease such as delinquency might take a long time to cure.

Judge Baker noted that the only aspect of the medical analogy which was not quite appropriate for the juvenile court was its voluntary character. "The patient attends the dispensary of his own volition," he said, "but the offender is compelled to court and obeys the orders of the officials on pain of the loss of his liberty for disregarding them" (1910:323). Whatever had to be done to secure a child's compliance would be done, even if it meant reform school.

PUBLIC ACCEPTANCE

Early reactions to the juvenile court and its rehabilitative ideology were overwhelmingly favorable; opposition was weak and divided. Some municipal judges objected to their loss of jurisdiction over juveniles, and a few police departments expressed fears that probation would send many serious offenders back to the streets. A leading scholar, Roscoe Pound, also warned in 1913 that "the powers of the court of star chamber were a bagtelle compared with those of American juvenile courts. . . . If these courts chose to act arbitrarily and oppressively they could cause a revolution quite as easily as did the former" (Rothman, 1979). Yet, when he addressed the annual meeting of the National Council of Juvenile Court Judges in 1950, Pound described the juvenile court as "the greatest forward step in Anglo-American jurisprudence since the Magna Charta!" (National Probation and Parole Association, 1957:127).

As a result of this kind of acceptance, the philosophy and procedures just described were those that dominated the operation of the juvenile court until well after mid-century. As Judge Orman Ketcham of the District of Columbia put it, "The first two decades of the juvenile court movement produced a wealth of philosophical comment so sound in conception and so modern in tone that it has scarcely been modified or improved upon since that time" (1962: p. 26). In short, the concern of most authorities was not with protecting children from possible arbitrary procedures but with finding ways by which those procedures could be made more effective. The juvenile court was not an agency that needed to be fettered.

THE ACTUAL PROCEDURES

In any social institution, whether it be the family, church, school, or political system, there is always a great difference between expressed ideals and actual practices. The same was true of the juvenile court. Between 1960 and 1975, as a result, reformers grew increasingly critical of the institution. The gap between its stated ideals and its actual practices, they contended, had grown so large that it could no longer be tolerated. In the remainder of this chapter, therefore, we will seek to determine the precise character and sources of this gap, and the criticisms it generated. In later chapters, we will examine the impact of these criticisms upon the juvenile court and the changes that took place as a result of them.

Intake

Between 1958 and 1974, the number of cases processed by the juvenile court nationwide increased substantially. Consider the way that increase was reflected in its intake procedures:

1. Number of delinquency cases referred to court. As may be seen in Table 15–1, in 1958, approximately 470,000 juveniles, were received at intake at a rate of about 20 children per 1,000. By 1974, the overall number had increased to about 1,252,700, and the rate to 37.5 per thousand. Clearly, then, the number of juveniles referred to court had increased much faster than the growth in the youth population. Indeed, the rate of referrals per thousand increased by 87.5 percent between 1958 and 1974.

It is probably significant that the largest increase occurred between 1966 and 1970 (31 percent). Those were the years during which civil rights protests, campus riots, and demonstrations against the Vietnam War were

at their highest, and during which juvenile crime rates per 100,000 increased by two-thirds. It is also of interest that, between 1958 and 1974, the majority of court cases came from urban areas—between 62 and 69 percent; less than one third were from semiurban areas; and only about 1 in 10 were from rural areas (National Center for Juvenile Justice, 1977:10).

2. Number of dependency and neglect cases. In sharp contrast to the number of delinquency cases (criminals and status offenders), only about one tenth as many juveniles (151,300) were referred to court for dependency and neglect. This means that, in contrast to the rate of 37.5 delinquency cases per 1,000 in 1974, the rate of dependency and neglect cases was only 2.2 per 1,000. This rate, moreover, had remained strikingly unchanged since 1958, rarely fluctuating much below or above the 2.0 figure (NCFJJ, 1977:14). While it seems unlikely that this number of cases, in a child population of over 33.3 million, reflects the true incidence of dependency and neglect, one thing remained certain: the juvenile courts of the country have been involved far more with delinquency than with dependency and neglect.

TABLE 15–1

Estimated number and rate of delinquency cases disposed by juvenile courts, United States, 1958–1974

Year	Estimated delinquency cases*	Child population 10 to 17 (in thousands)†	Rate per thousand‡	Percent increase in rate
1958	470,000	23,443	20.0	
1962	555,000	26,989	20.6	3
1966	745,000	30,124	24.7	20
1970	1,052,000	32,614	32.3	31
1974	1,252,700	33,365	37.5	16
Total percent increase in rate				87.5

*Data for 1958–1968 estimated from the national sample of juvenile courts. This sample represents 60 percent of the population of the United States.

† U.S. Bureau of Census, *Current Population Report,* 1974.

‡ Based on the number of delinquency cases per 1,000 U.S. child population, 10 to 17 years of age.

Source: National Center for Juvenile Justice, *Juvenile Court Statistics,* 1974. Pittsburgh: National Council of Juvenile Court Judges, 1977:14.

TABLE 15–2

Estimated number and percent distribution of delinquency cases disposed by juvenile courts, by sex, United States, 1958–1974

	Boys		Girls	
Year	Number	Percent	Number	Percent
1958......	383,000	81	87,000	19
1962......	450,000	81	104,500	19
1966......	593,000	80	152,000	20
1970......	799,500	76	252,000	24
1974......	927,000	74	325,700	26

Source: National Center for Juvenile Justice, *Juvenile Court Statistics,* 1974. Pittsburgh: National Council of Juvenile Court Judges, 1977:14.

3. Distribution of delinquency cases by sex. Table 15–2 documents the rising number of female cases being referred to juvenile court. Between 1958 and 1966, there was little change: about one fifth of all cases throughout those years were female. Between 1966 and 1974, however, the proportion of female cases rose from 20 to 26 percent, an increase of almost one third in the space of a decade. This growth, moreover, was relatively constant across urban and semiurban courts; as a result, about one fourth of all delinquency cases have been female in recent years (NCFJJ, 1977:10).

4. Sources of court referrals. In the previous chapter we learned that, in 1974, the police reported referring 866,857 juveniles to court. This was about 70 percent of the 1.25 million cases that the juvenile courts reported receiving that year. A similar figure for police referrals (73 percent), was reported by a research team at the University of Michigan as a result of its survey of several hundred juvenile courts (Sarri and Hasenfeld, 1976). The remaining referrals were made by parents and relatives (9.7 percent), the schools (7.7 percent), social service agencies (4.4 percent), and a variety of other community sources and court jurisdictions (5.1 percent) (Hasenfeld, 1976:4).

These figures suggest that one of the major functions of the juvenile court had remained virtually unchanged: that of acting as a backup institution designed to help the community enforce the moral rules governing childhood (Emerson, 1969:269). Parents, schools, and welfare agencies have made referrals to the court when their authority was seriously challenged or when they were sufficiently concerned about the insubordination and misconduct of troublesome youths.

5. Reasons for court referral. The reasons for which juveniles have been referred to court further substantiates the point just made. Based on additional findings of the Michigan research group, Table 15–3 reveals that the greater part of court referrals in were for status (37.2 percent) and property (36.2 percent) offenses. While the latter were clearly alleged cases of criminal conduct, the former were not. Indeed, about 6 in 10 status offenses involved runaways, incorrigibles, and curfew violators. When status offenses figures were added to those for drug violations, therefore, they constituted almost half of all court referrals (Hasenfeld, 1976:68).

6. Use of detention. Some unsettling findings have been provided by studies which have sought to determine how many juveniles have been held in detention while awaiting disposal of their cases by court personnel. First, these studies indicated that, in the mid-1970s, approximately 530,000 young people were admitted to juvenile detention centers each year, for an average stay of 10 days (Poulin et

TABLE 15–3

Reasons for court referral

Type of offense	Percent of total
Offenses against persons	7.3
Offenses against property	36.2
Drug offenses	7.3
Status offenses	37.2
All others	12.0

Source: Hasenfeld, 1976:68.

al., 1980:5–6; LEAA, undated:62 and 20). But this was not all.

Since some counties and states did not have any juvenile detention centers, many were detained in adult jails and police lockups— about 120,000 annually (Poulin et al., 1980:11). Overall, therefore, in the mid-1970s, about 650,000 young people were separated from their families and held in custody while the court was deciding what to do with them.

Furthermore, research revealed wide disparities among the states in the rates at which they detained juveniles (Poulin et al., 1980:5–11). For example, five states (California, Ohio, Texas, Washington, and Florida) accounted for *one half* of all young people being held in juvenile facilities nationwide, although less than 20 percent of the juvenile population, ages 5 to 17, lived in those states. Indeed, the rate per 100,000 in Nevada (4,734) was *100* times greater than the rate in North Dakota (45). Worse still, the same pattern prevailed in the use of jails: more than half of all the juveniles detained in these facilities were from 10 states that included less than 20 percent of the juvenile population.

Such findings were disconcerting because the National Probation and Parole Association had set standards, in 1958, which suggested that "the number of children admitted to a detention facility should normally not exceed 20 percent of the total number of juvenile offenders referred to the probation department of the court . . ." (1959:18). Then, in 1961, it had revised these standards to suggest that the figure should be reduced to 10 percent (NCCD, 1961:10). Such figures notwithstanding, the evidence has revealed that, in 1975, only seven states remained within the 20 percent guideline, to say nothing of the 10 percent level. Indeed, some states were detaining more than 90 percent of all referrals; the percentage for the country as a whole was about 50 percent (Poulin et al., 1980:23–24). Yet, these were but a few among many problems with detention.

a. Age and detention. Studies have indicated that children under age 12 are less likely to be detained than adolescents. Nonetheless, in 1971, 3 percent of the nation's detention centers were holding children under 6 years of age; 9 percent were holding children from ages 6 to 8; and 43 percent of all detainees were children from ages 9 to 11 (Law Enforcement Assistance Administration, undated:12–13). In one jurisdiction, 33 percent of all detainees were children under age 12 (Cohen, 1975a:20). In some communities, there were no other facilities for children who were neglected or abused, but the idea of housing them in detention centers was repugnant to many people nevertheless. To make matters worse, these same children were often housed with adolescents charged with crimes (LEAA, undated:12–13). As in the institutions of the 19th century, therefore, all types of children were still "huddled together" in places of confinement.

b. Detention of status offenders. Generally, the courts have been more likely to detain juveniles with prior criminal records than neglected children or first offenders (Cohen, 1975a; Pawlack, 1977). This generalization, however, should not be interpreted to mean that only those juveniles who committed crimes were numbered among the repeater group. Many of this group were also status offenders; indeed, these juveniles were often detained as frequently as were those with specific criminal offenses (Cohen, 1975a; Pawlack, 1977; Sarri, 1974b; Sumner, 1971). As a result, about 185,000 status offenders were being detained annually in the mid-1970s, comprising almost 30 percent of all detainees (Poulin et al., 1980:28–29).

Those who sought the reasons for these detentions found that authorities were often responding to the demands of parents, teachers, and welfare workers who felt they needed help in disciplining children who were considered to be incorrigible.

[T]ruant officers appeal to the court to use its authority and its threatened sanctions to get truants to attend school; school officials to discipline and control in-school "behavior problems;" the Child Welfare Department to augment caseworker and group home to control over-troublesome youths; and parents to support efforts to deal with their recalcitrant children (Emerson, 1969:270).

c. Detention of girls. The use of detention for girls, in particular, seems to have reflected the sensitivity of the court to the requests of these influential people. They, as much as the police, have referred girls to the court, often for traditional female offenses—running away and being sexually promiscuous. As a result, a double standard of justice came into play. "Females who commit juvenile code offenses, regardless of race and prior court contacts, have a larger percentage of detention than males who commit such offenses" (Pawlack 1977:6). Indeed, some observers suggested that 75 percent of all females charged with status offenses were detained, as contrasted with only 25 percent of the male status offenders (Chesney-Lind, 1977:124; Sarri, 1974:18).

There are horror stories relative to these practices. Chesney-Lind noted, for example, that all girls brought before the courts in New York and Philadelphia were given vaginal smears to test for venereal disease, even if the charges against them were nonsexual (1977:124). Similarly, Wakin reported that, in one detention center, all girls were required to undergo a pelvic examination to determine if they were pregnant (1975:45). Describing the same sort of situation in Philadelphia, an official noted that girls did not have a choice in the matter:

> 'We do put a girl on the table in the stirrups and we do have a smear. . . . We do have a swab. You go in and get a smear.' When asked whether a girl who refused to undergo this pelvic exam would be placed in 'medical lockup'—a polite term for solitary

confinement—he responded, 'Yes, we may have to' (Chesney-Lind, 1977:125).

It is impossible to say how widespread such practices have been. But, in general, they have reflected the rather common assumption that, if a girl comes to the attention of authorities, she must be sexually promiscuous. By contrast, tests for venereal disease among boys have been almost unheard of. Thus, it appears that the powers of the court have subjected girls not only to a legal double standard, but also to degrading physical examinations as well.

d. Race and social class. Despite the traditional equation of poverty with crime in this country, the evidence is by no means clear that minority and poor youth have suffered higher rates of detention than white, middle-class youth. Most studies do indicate that minority and lower-class juveniles have experienced somewhat higher rates of detention, but differences between them and others have been surprisingly small (Cohen, 1975a; Pawlack, 1977; Sarri, 1974a; Sumner, 1971).

Two factors seem to have been at work. On the one hand, as we have seen, minority and poor youth have experienced higher rates of arrest and victimization for criminal offenses than have their more affluent peers. This may explain why slightly higher proportions of them have been detained. On the other hand, research indicates that officials have been inclined to discriminate against white, middle-class youths particularly white females, for the commission of status offenses. These groups have experienced the highest rates of confinement for status offenses (Cohen, 1975; Pawlack, 1977). Thus, as Cohen put it, "These findings do necessitate qualifying the widespread accusation of racial and class discrimination in all phases of juvenile processing" (1975a:43).

While the results of a few studies cannot be taken to represent court practices nationwide, they are contrary to expectation. They may reflect, in fact, a kind of reverse discrimination. The persistent tendency for officials to act paternalistically toward higher-status youths by confining them could mean that they have been more concerned about their morality than about the morality of lower-status youths. If so, that may help to explain why the detention rates of both groups have been almost equal. Detention has been viewed as a desirable way of disciplining those whom officials have considered worth saving.

e.   Confinement in jails.   Were these problems not sufficient, the National Council on Crime and Delinquency (1967:122) found, in the mid-1960s, that 93 percent of the nation's counties, serving 50 percent of the youth population, had no juvenile detention facilities. As mentioned earlier, juveniles in these counties have been detained in adult jails, police lockups, and drunk tanks, despite the fact that the laws in their states have prohibited this.

Indeed, this discrepancy between ideology and practice dates back to the first juvenile court in Illinois. After passing the laws which created the juvenile court and prohibited the use of jails for young people, Illinois refused to vote one penny to construct detention facilities (Schultz, 1974:245). Other states did likewise; most of them simply continued to put children in jail.

In the 1970s, about two thirds of the juveniles in jails nationwide were awaiting trial (LEAA, undated). Likewise, almost half of them were status offenders, the majority of whom were not segregated in quarters separate from adult criminals (Sarri, 1974:7–9; Children's Defense Fund, 1976:20). Some judges, in fact, reported that they "chose jails for juveniles to 'teach them a lesson'" (Sarri, 1974a:10). Meanwhile, others were being held in protective custody because they were abused or neglected children. "One child was in jail because her father was suspected of raping her.

Since the incest could not be proven, the adult was not held. The child, however, was put in jail for protective custody" (Children's Defense Fund, 1976:21).

Moreover, it has been estimated that more than 80 percent of the jails in which juveniles were confined were unsuitable for adults, let alone children (NCCD, 1967:121). And sometimes, the results have been deadly:

> In Iowa a girl is thrown into jail because she runs away to get married: she hangs herself. She is 16 years old.
>
> In Missouri, a 17-year-old is homosexually assaulted and kicked to death by jail cellmates.
>
> Another 17-year-old is murdered in a Miami jail (Goldfarb, 1976:307–308).

In numerous cases, children have suffered brutal treatment or death in jail at the hands of adult offenders. For example, three brothers—Billy, age 12; Brian, age 13; and Dan, age 14—were suspected of stealing some coins from a local store and placed in jail with adult prisoners:

> After the lights were out in the jail, the men ordered the boys to take off their clothes. When they refused, . . . the men tore off the boys' clothing and then, one by one, each of the men forcibly raped the three brothers. Pointing to a long electric cord hanging in the cell, one of the men warned the boys that if they uttered a sound . . . he would choke them to death. . . . The boys obeyed . . . and were silent (Children's Defense Fund, 1976:1).

Brutal treatment has sometimes been administered by authorities. Two 13-year-old boys, one white and one black, while confined in a state hospital, were caught having homosexual relations with each other:

> Officials at the hospital . . . bound them to their beds for a period of 77½ hours, and they tied their hands and feet to the bedposts, and spread-eagled them on the beds in such a position that the boys could only move their hands about three or four inches in each

direction. They were allowed up only to shower (Goldfarb, 1976:308).

A comment by Patricia Wald (1976:124–125) summed up the opinions of most critics regarding these practices—an opinion not much different from those expressed in 1899:

> There is no responsible evidence to indicate that we know how to predict dangerous or violent behavior in a juvenile any more than we do in an adult. Yet juvenile courts have operated on the premise that they are authorized to detain for possible future criminal behavior. . . .
>
> [Equally as bad], status offenders are also held for the longest periods in detention. It is ironically and bitterly true that most lawbreakers can go back home but those who offend against their parents usually cannot.

It appears that many juveniles have been confined while awaiting court action, and many have been confined in adult facilities contrary to law. Worse still, many have not been criminal offenders, but dependent and neglected children, or truants and insubordinate children. The evidence seems to indicate that the juvenile court had abused its power, and that society had not lived up to its professed ideals by providing shelters for the many children whose inadequate disrupted lives demanded them.

f. Results of intake procedures. Given the fact that approximately half of all court referrals were detained during the intake process, one might assume that virtually all of them were subjected to a formal court hearing and stern procedures following it. Ironically, however, the evidence suggests that some, perhaps many, were handled informally, since anywhere from 50 to 60 percent of all referrals were not given a formal hearing by a judge (Blumstein and Stafford, 1974; California Youth Authority, 1974; National Center for Juvenile Justice, 1977:14; Sarri and Hasenfeld, 1976).

In its study of several hundred juvenile

courts, for example, the Michigan research group reported that approximately 58 percent of all juveniles during the early 1970s were handled unofficially (Hasenfeld, 1976:70).

> The most typical pattern is either to dismiss the case, or to counsel, warn, and release the youth. Only a small fraction . . . are put on informal probation (16 percent) or referred to other social service agencies. In other words, most courts seem to cope with the inflow of juvenile cases through very minimal intervention which may, at most, produce a court record, but no significant action by court staff (Hasenfeld, 1976:69).

What is striking about these procedures, however, is the fact that officials have not always handled status offenders informally and criminal offenders formally. Indeed, the Michigan study found that status offenders were as likely to be tried officially as were property offenders, and that together they comprised more than 7 in 10 court hearings. Only juveniles charged with violent crimes were more likely to receive a court hearing (see Table 15–4).

In summary, then, this review of actual intake procedures has revealed a paradoxical set of findings. Despite the fact that until recently, society had never provided the juvenile court with the resources it needed to carry out its child-saving functions, the court has continued to implement the benevolent assumption that the moral and social condition

---

TABLE 15–4

Actions at intake by type of offense charged (in percentages)

Type of offense	Dismiss	Action taken	
		Informal handling	Formal handling
Status	26	36	38
Misdemeanor	33	34	33
Property	39	34	35
Person	16	32	51

Source: Creekmore, 1976:127.

of the child should take precedence over strict procedure and the protection of individual rights. When intake personnel have encountered children who were out of parental control, persistently truant, or who dependent and neglected, they have placed these children in detention centers and jails almost as often as they have placed young criminals in them,— thus taking action that was not governed by formal hearings and judicial oversight. As a consequence, this feature of the juvenile court offended child savers as much as it offended those who believed in the classical concept of justice.

Adjudication

Partly because of these practices, the juvenile court was subjected to a series of reviews by the United States Supreme Court in the late 1960s—reviews designed to alter the adjudicatory process, if nothing else (Gault, 1967; Kent, 1966; Winship, 1970). In contrast to the practices of Judges Baker, Mack, and Alexander, the Supreme Court concluded that juveniles should receive many of the same constitutional protections afforded to adults in criminal trials: a clear statement of charges, the employment of defense counsel, and the use of due process procedures. If these requirements were actually translated into practice, therefore, they should have been evident in the actions of the court, at least by the mid-1970s.

The national study by the Michigan group reveals, however, that such was not always the case. By 1975, virtually all courts had begun to give written notice to juvenile defendants of the specific charges made against them; no new charges could be sprung on them in court as Judge Baker had done. Likewise, 7 in 10 judges indicated that they tried to explain charges in simple as well as legal language, and agreed that juveniles had a right to legal counsel and that one would be appointed if necessary (Sosin and Sarri, 1976:195).

Despite these kinds of changes, the actual number of prosecutors and defense attorneys participating in formal proceedings for juveniles remained small. For example, juveniles had the theoretical right to a hearing, with legal counsel present, if detention was contemplated for them. However, quite often such hearings were not even held, and, in those states where they were held, they averaged less than three minutes long and lawyers were seldom present (Sarri, 1974b:7).

The same picture prevailed in the adjudication of a case. While, in a study of 234 courts, the judges said that prosecutors had a moderate influence in deciding whether a petition should be filed against a juvenile, they had little to do with formal proceedings in court (Creekmore, 1976:139). The same was true of defense attorneys. Only about half of the judges reported that attorneys always confronted prosecution witnesses; only 20 percent called their own witnesses; and few made legal motions for dismissal of cases (Sosin and Sarri, 1976:196). As a result, prosecutors in 25 percent of the courts, and defense attorneys in 33 percent, were reported by judges to have no influence whatsoever (Creekmore, 1976:138–39).

The type of offense with which a child was charged, however, did make a difference. Juveniles charged with serious crimes—assault, burglary, or robbery—were almost always defended in formal proceedings. Children charged with status offenses, by contrast, were rarely defended, despite the fact that these were the most ambiguous kinds of charges and were the most difficult to prove (Sosin and Sarri, 1976:196).

Another problem was that, even in serious cases, lawyers did not take an active role in formal proceedings, as they would in criminal court for adults:

For the most part, attorneys tended to prefer to plea bargain with the judge on small points rather than on the adjudication decision itself. For example, some lawyers would have their clients admit guilt on three of six counts if the other three would be dropped. Judges often agreed to this arrangement, and for good reasons: once a child is adjudicated delinquent, three rather than six counts make[s] no legal difference, as legally the judge need not fit the disposition to the number of charges (Sosin and Sarri, 1976:196).

Since it has only been in recent years that attorneys have participated in juvenile proceedings, they seemed to have been unsure of themselves and to have shared the traditional view that children should not be permitted to escape censure, even if their guilt has not been proven in court. Sanford Fox describes their feelings:

> Lawyers generally tend to share the view that misbehaving children ought not to be permitted to believe that they can get away with breaking society's rules. To the extent that a vigorous demand for legal rights would produce an acquittal on delinquency charges, there develops a conflict between this shared belief and the professional role as children's advocate (1970:161).

In short, this review of adjudication illustrates the extent to which the decisions of the Supreme Court have been tempered by traditions favoring the informal treatment of children. In a relatively small number of juvenile courts, those decisions were, in fact, incorporated into judicial proceedings; but in many, their effects were slow in coming. Indeed, it is likely that many juvenile courts today remain as much like the original juvenile court in their practices as the more formal court envisioned by the Supreme Court.

Disposition

The same is also true of dispositional hearings. By the mid-1970s, the majority of such hearings were still informal. As in earlier times, it was the judge and the probation officer, without much input from prosecutors and defense attorneys, who decided on the treatment (Creekmore, 1976:147–49). Before considering the results of their deliberations, however, it should be recalled that, because most juveniles were handled informally at intake, something less than half of them remained for disposition following the adjudicatory hearing. In the Michigan survey, for example, almost 6 in 10 juvenile cases were handled informally; only 42 percent remained for dispositional decisions. Of the latter group, 12 percent of the juveniles were dismissed without a finding of guilt; 22 percent were put on probation; 7 percent were committed to a correctional institution; and 1 percent were waived to adult court (Hasenfeld, 1976:70). While these proportions undoubtedly varied from court to court, the pattern prevailed—most adjudicated juveniles were put on probation rather than confined in training schools (Blumstein, 1974; California Youth Authority, 1974; Cohen, 1975b; Hasenfeld, 1976).

1. Long-term versus short-term confinement. Such practices raised a provocative question: Why, after a formal hearing by a judge, were so few juveniles sent to long-term facilities when, during the period prior to court action, so many had been locked up in detention centers and jails?

In 1974, for example, approximately 650,000 juveniles were detained in short-term detention facilities and jails awaiting intake, adjudicatory, or dispositional decisions. Yet, only about 112,782 were confined in long-term public facilities following the dispositional process—21,734 in reception and diagnostic centers and 91,048 in training schools, ranches, forestry camps, and halfway houses—a ratio of almost six to one (LEAA, undated:62).

The answer to our question seems all too clear. It was the informal decision making of police and probation officers, not the more formal procedures of the judge, that resulted in the early detention of most juveniles, even if only for short periods of time. As a consequence, the President's Crime Commission (1967c:23) concluded that detention was being utilized as a punishment device, although proof of guilt or the precise character of a child's problems had not been established. Based upon their broad discretionary powers, officers of the juvenile court were taking actions that, to say the least, were questionable.

2. Dispositions of minority offenders. Juveniles from minority groups were (and still are) more likely to be incarcerated following court action than are majority youths. Like the police, therefore, the court has been accused of being biased and discriminatory.

The evidence regarding this accusation, however, is not definitive, particularly since chronic offenders are more likely to be numbered among minority groups. While some investigators tended to believe that the accusation was true (Arnold, 1971; Lemert and Rosburg, 1948), others contended that dispositional decisions were more likely to reflect the delinquent histories and prior records of offenders than to reflect outright bigotry (Cohen, 1975b; Eaton and Polk, 1961; Terry, 1967). Furthermore, the evidence indicated that decisions varied widely from court to court, reflecting possible bias in some courts but not in others (Cohen, 1975b).

The question was further complicated by the fact that, along with prior record and seriousness of offense, social disadvantage, family neglect, truancy, and incorrigibility also played key roles in decision making. And since

minority, more than majority, juveniles were likely to come from deprived environments and to be school dropouts, they were more likely to be incarcerated (Axelrad, 1952; Scarpitti and Stephenson, 1971).

Finally, investigators found a link between intake and dispositional decisions. Cohen (1975b) reported, for example, that children who had been detained and had had formal petitions filed against them were the most likely to be committed to a training school, although the reasons for these actions varied widely from court to court. While the reasons in one court might be severity of offense and prior record, those in another might be idleness, referral by a community agency, and coming from a broken home. Thus, the procedures of juvenile justice did not follow a uniform pattern for minority and majority juveniles; rather, they varied from court to court, reflecting broad differences in community norms (Cohen, 1975b; Emerson, 1969).

3. Dispositions of males and females. Because of their greater involvement in deviant behavior, three times as many males as females have been sentenced to correctional institutions. But it was not only this fact that stirred dissension; two other factors provoked the greatest concern.

The first was the fact that anywhere from one quarter to one third of all juveniles in state correctional facilities were status offenders (Lerman, 1979). To be sure, those who had committed violent crimes were the most likely to be locked up. But what concerned many investigators was the finding that status offenders were about as likely as property offenders to be incarcerated.

Second, girls were the most likely to suffer this fate. In 1974, for example, fully one half of all female delinquents were in custody for status offenses, as contrasted with only 10 percent of all males (LEAA, undated:14). Furthermore, girls were often confined for longer periods of time than were boys (Gibbons and Griswold, 1957; Lerman, 1979). These practices, like many we have already discussed, led to increasingly strident criticisms of the juvenile court.

THE TARNISHED SUPERPARENT

When combined into more general categories, these criticisms can be summarized as follows: the wide net of the juvenile court; the lack of due process; assembly line justice; rising crime rates; and liberal ideology.

The wide net of the juvenile court

The first criticism had to do with the laws that granted to the juvenile court legal jurisdiction over the lives of status offenders. At its meeting in London in 1960, the Second United Nations Congress on the Prevention of Crime and the Treatment of Offenders recommended ". . . that the meaning of the term juvenile delinquency should be restricted as far as possible to violations of the criminal law" (United Nations, 1961:61). Such misbehaviors as running away, defying parents, or being truant should no longer be defined as delinquent. Moral standards with respect to children were changing, and people of other nations as well as America began to argue that the only clients of the juvenile court should be those who violate the criminal law.

The President's Commission on Law Enforcement and Administration of Justice agreed:

> The [legal] provisions on which intervention . . . is based are typically vague and all-encompassing: growing up in idleness and crime, engaging in immoral conduct in danger of leading an immoral life. They establish the judge as arbiter not only of the behavior but the morals of every child (and to a certain extent the parents of every child) appearing before him. The situation is ripe for over-reaching, for imposition of the judge's own code of youthful conduct. . . . One need not expound on the traditional American virtues of individuality and free expression to point out the wrong-headedness of so using the juvenile court . . . (1967b:25).

The commission recommended, therefore, that "serious consideration, at the least, should be given to complete elimination of the court's power over children for noncriminal conduct" (1967b:27). Its wide net should be made much smaller.

Lack of due process

The second criticism was based upon the lack of due process in the juvenile court. As we have already learned, the Supreme Court of the United States rendered several decisions in the 1960s and early 1970s which disavowed the idea that probation officers and judges should ignore constitutional protections for juveniles and concentrate on only their personal and moral problems.

In a now celebrated case, *Kent* v. *U.S.*, the justices of the court observed that, while there can be no doubt

> of the original laudable purpose of the juvenile courts, studies and critiques in recent years raise serious questions as to whether actual performance measures well enough against theoretical purpose to make tolerable the immunity of the process from the constitutional guarantees applicable to adults. . . . *There is evidence, in fact, that there may be grounds for concern that the child receives the worse of two possible worlds: that he gets neither the protections accorded to adults nor the solicitous care and regenerative treatment postulated for children* (383 U.S. 541, 1966, emphasis added).

In a second landmark case, the *Gault* case (387 U.S. 1), the Supreme Court held in 1967 that the code and practices of the state of Arizona deprived children of procedural safeguards guaranteed by the Fourteenth Amendment. Gerald Gault was a 15-year-old boy charged with making an obscene phone call to a neighbor. As a result of the juvenile court process, Gerald was incarcerated in a state institution where, according to law, he could have been held until the age of 21. By contrast, the maximum punishment he could have received, had he been an 18-year-old adult, would have been a fine of from $5 to $50 or imprisonment in jail for not more than two months.

Although the severity of this penalty alone was questionable, it was but one of a long list of dubious court practices that the Supreme Court noted in reversing the original decision: Gerald was arrested and held in detention without notification of his parents. A petition outlining the charges was not served on his parents prior to trial; in fact, the petition made no reference to any factual basis for taking court action. It recited only that "said minor is under the age of 18 years and in need of the protection of this Honorable Court [and that] said minor is a delinquent minor."

Although the police and court actions leading to the incarceration of Gerald were based on a verbal complaint by his neighbor, she never appeared in court to give sworn testimony. In fact, no one was sworn in at the hearing, nor were any transcripts or recordings kept, nor was Gerald represented by counsel. Gerald was alleged to have confessed to making the call, but his "confession" was never reduced to writing, was obtained without his parents present, without legal counsel, and without any advice of his right to remain silent. In short, due process, so carefully pursued in adult criminal proceedings, was totally disregarded in his case.

Expressing his opinion of the case, Mr. Justice Fortas wrote as follows:

> Under our constitution, the condition of being a boy does not justify a kangaroo court. The

traditional ideas of Juvenile Court procedure, indeed, contemplated that time would be available and care would be used to establish precisely what the juvenile did and why he did it—was it a prank of adolescence or a brutal act threatening serious consequences to himself or society unless corrected? Under traditional notions, one would assume that in a case like that of Gerald Gault, where the juvenile appears to have a home, a working mother and father, and an older brother, the Juvenile Judge would have made a careful inquiry and judgment as to the possibility that the boy could be disciplined and dealt with at home, despite his previous transgressions. . . . The essential difference between Gerald's case and a normal criminal case is that safeguards available to adults were discarded in Gerald's case. The summary procedure as well as the long commitment was possible because Gerald was 15 years of age instead of over 18 (*In re Gault*:28–29).

The Supreme Court also suggested that the failure to exercise adequate safeguards is a general one that characterized many jurisdictions, not just the Arizona court in question. The Supreme Court added that "juvenile court history has again demonstrated that unbridled discretion, however benevolently motivated, is frequently a poor substitute for principle and procedure." Most of the justices concluded that "due process of law is the primary and indispensable foundation of individual freedom."

The Supreme Court reaffirmed many of these ideas in 1970 in the *Winship* case (397 U.S. 358). Again, it broke new ground by noting that proof of guilt beyond a reasonable doubt is required in juvenile as well as adult cases. Wrote Mr. Justice Brennan: "The same considerations that demand extreme caution in fact-finding to protect the innocent adult apply as well to the innocent child" (*In re Winship*:365). Along with *Kent* and *Gault*, then, *Winship* set forth two important guidelines for the juvenile court: (1) procedures that insure fairness cannot be discarded merely because the juvenile court purports to be benevolent and rehabilitative; and (2) guarantees of due process need not interfere with the rehabilitative and other traditional goals of the juvenile court (Paulsen and Whitebread, 1974:20).

Assembly line justice

A third criticism suggested that the juvenile court was administering assembly line justice. As originally conceived, judges and probation officers were to be mature and wise individuals who had access to a rich array of resources for helping children. But there was considerable evidence that this objective was not being realized.

To begin with, the structure of the juvenile court had taken many different forms. In some states it was a unit of county government; in others, it was a statewide system. In some states, it was exclusively a family court; in others, it was part of a broad based, trial court system, on either the highest superior court level or the municipal court level, where lesser criminals were tried; in still others, it was a part of a probate court where civil as well as criminal matters were heard. In short, there was no uniform, nationwide system of juvenile justice (Rubin, 1976b:133–34).

To make matters worse, judges were not uniformly qualified. In 1963, one fifth of all judges had received no college education; almost half had not earned a college degree; and one fifth were not members of the bar. Rather than being selected for their expert knowledge of child psychology, three fourths of them had been elected to office—indeed, almost two thirds were probably continuing political careers, having previously held elected to other offices (President's Commission, 1967a:6–7).

A 1973 survey produced similar findings. Of 1,314 judges, only 12 percent devoted their full time to juvenile matters. By contrast, almost nine in ten said they spent half of their time or less and more than two thirds said they spent less than a quarter of their time on such matters (Smith, 1974:33).

These findings make it clear that the juvenile court had not attained much stature in the court system or the legal profession. Few law schools even had courses on juvenile court law and, in those jurisdictions where the juvenile court was a part of the superior or district court system, the feeling among judges was that assignment to the juvenile division was an assignment to Siberia (Rubin, 1976b:135).

Given these problems, it seemed likely that many courts were operating a kind of assembly line justice. For example, Cohen (1975b:13) discovered that, in one court, it took an average of 76 days for intake personnel to decide what should be done about a case; if it required judicial action, the average waiting period was doubled, to 130 days; and, if it was contested in court, the wait was 211 days. But when a court hearing finally did take place, it often lasted no longer than 10 or 15 minutes (President's Commission, 1967a:7).

These problems were sometimes compounded by interfering and intolerant communities. In one case, a judge who refused to transfer a murder case to adult court because he believed the youngster involved could be more thoroughly rehabilitated in the juvenile justice system was defeated for reelection for being too permissive. By contrast, another judge was very popular in his community because he believed that several nights in detention were good for any children apprehended by the police, even if their cases were later dismissed for insufficient evidence (Rubin, 1976b:146).

A related problem had to do with the fact that most communities had not provided concerned judges with the resources they needed to help juveniles. In Los Angeles, for example, the juvenile court handled 26,604 cases in 1972–73, or 83 more cases than the adult, superior court. Yet, it had only half the judicial personnel (*L.A. Times*, June 19, 1974).

Probation was also to be the cord upon which all the pearls of the juvenile court are strung. Yet, in 1965, one third of all fulltime judges reported that they had no probation officers to assist them and 83 percent said that they also had no psychiatric or psychological assistance (President's Commission, 1967a:6). Most states did make provision for probation services, and 74 percent of the nation's counties had some probation officers, but their caseloads were high and their pay was low (President's Commission, 1967a:6). As a result, the average probation officer had between 75 and 80 delinquents to supervise at any given time, in addition to the social studies they were supposed to make of new cases coming before the court.

Given these conditions, Justine Polier, an eminent judge from the family court in New York, maintained that the lack of resources was the juvenile court's greatest problem, more than its lack of effort or good intent:

> The lack of appropriate services and facilities for delinquent children and to a much greater extent for neglected children has contributed more than any other single factor to negating the purpose of the court.
>
> The values of diagnostic studies and recommendations is too often reduced to a paper recommendation. In shopping for placement, probation officers are forced to lower their sights from what they know a child needs to what they can secure. Their sense of professional responsibility is steadily eroded. The judge, in turn, becomes the ceremonial official who in many cases approves a disposition which he knows is only a dead end for the child (1964:30).

In short, Judge Polier believed that, if society had permitted the court to live up to its ideals, many of the charges levied against it would not have been forthcoming.

Rising crime rates

This belief in rising crime rates was significant in light of the fact that many citizens tended to blame the juvenile court for the rapid rise in crime rates during the 1960s and 1970s. During this turbulent period, civil rights protests, urban riots, campus rebellions, and opposition to the Vietnam war gave the appearance of a nation gone berserk, particularly in its young:

> American youth in increasing numbers have withstood tear gas and mace, billy clubs and bullets, insults and assaults, jail and prison in order to lie-down in front of troop trains, sit-in at a university administration building, love-in in public parks, wade-in at nonintegrated beaches, and lie-in within our legislative buildings. . . . They have also challenged socially oriented norms with "mod" dress and hair styles, language, rock music, and psychedelic colors, forms, and patterns. [The nation] has watched the development of the hippy and yippy, the youthful drug culture, black, yellow, brown, and red power advocates, and organizations such as the Third World Liberation Front, the Peace and Freedom Party, and Black Studies Departments on the campus. We have been exposed to violence, vandalism, assault, destruction, looting, disruption, and chaos on our streets. (Carter and Gitchoff, 1970:52).

Although it is obvious that the juvenile court alone could scarcely have been responsible for these events, many Americans began to agree with the police that the court was incapable of dealing with them. Its progressive philosophy, like progressivism in general, had contributed to anarchy, not order. As a result, in 1968 Richard Nixon promised, if elected president, to wage a war on crime, even if the nation's youth had to be numbered among the enemy. The pervasive feeling was that the country no longer faced losses of one kind or another—it was in danger of losing everything! The only solution, therefore, was to return to a more retributive concept of justice, favoring punishment rather than rehabilitation. "Put 'em in jail," said one prosecutor. "It is no longer possible for a judge to act like a father—a judge today has to act like a judge. If you want to get inside the minds of delinquents and find out what is good for them, fine; but do it in prison" (*Los Angeles Times,* Feb. 17, 1977).

Liberal ideology

Were these reactionary comments not sufficient, criticism of the juvenile court came from the opposite end of the ideological spectrum as well—from criminologists and their liberal allies. The rehabilitative ideology of the court was built upon assumptions derived primarily from control theory; namely, the idea that delinquent behavior is due to the defective socialization of children and that, in order to rehabilitate them, they must be personally treated and cared for.

But other bodies of theory emerged and became much more popular during this chaotic period in America. From the cultural deviance theory of Shaw and McKay to strain theory, each new body of scientific thought had supported the idea that delinquent behavior could not be prevented and controlled by tinkering with the mind and morality of the delinquent. To do so would be to treat symptoms, not causes. It is society that segregates people by age, class, and race, and so it is society that produces delinquent subcultures among children and defines rules as favoring the powerful and then labels and stigmatizes the powerless who break them. Furthermore, as we will soon see, new bodies of theory emerged at this time which stressed the idea, even more strongly, that it is society that is criminogenic, not individual families or their children.

If that was the case, it was a "brave idea" indeed which suggested that the juvenile court

alone could both prevent and remedy youth misbehavior (Lemert, 1967:93). Twentieth-century criminology had constructed an ideological superstructure which not only lent support to the critics of the juvenile court but also helped to erode this notion that such a court could both prevent and remedy delinquency. Except for serious offenders, therefore, juvenile criminals would be best dealt with by other than legal means—means that would reduce unemployment, enrich slum schools, combat racial and economic segregation, shrink the generation gap, and give young people a stake in conformity. In short, such ideas helped to tarnish the image of the juvenile court and furthermore, to cast a pall of doubt over the entire concept of juvenile justice.

SUMMARY AND CONCLUSIONS

Reflecting the growth of the modern concept of childhood, the juvenile court was supposed to fulfill a grand mission on behalf of the young. It was expected to:

1.   Guarantee nurturance rights for children: the rights to life, food, shelter, loving parents, an education, and protection from immorality and crime.

2.   Have jurisdiction over four types of young people: Delinquents, status offenders, neglected children, and those who were dependent and in need of care.

3.   Fulfill five major functions: enforce the modern concept of childhood, act as a surrogate for failing families and schools, prevent delinquency, decriminalize the conduct of children; and rehabilitate those who required special care.

In pursuit of these objectives, the juvenile court was granted almost unlimited power and discretion. Its procedures, consisting of three major steps—intake, adjudication and disposition—would operate without the constitutional constraints imposed upon the criminal court, since its goal was to save children, not to punish them.

Few serious challenges were levied against the juvenile court until well after mid-20th century. However, a review of its methods of operation between 1958 and 1975 revealed that:

1. *The rate at which juveniles were referred to the court during this period increased steadily.* Furthermore, a steadily larger proportion of those referred were female, constituting about one fourth of the total.

2. *The juvenile court continued to serve as a backup institution, designed to enforce the moral rules governing childhood* Indeed, status offenders were as likely to be referred to court as property offenders. Together, they comprised more than 7 in 10 referrals.

3. *Court personnel continued to exercise a great deal of discretion, particularly at the intake stage, reflecting a highly contradictory set of behaviors.* On the one hand, court personnel released at least half of all court referrals at the intake stage, using informal procedures much like those used by the police. On the other hand, these officials confined far more juveniles in detention centers and jails at this stage than they ultimately sentenced to correctional facilities following adjudication and disposition.

4. *Though only a small fraction of all juveniles referred to court were finally confined in correctional institutions, poor and minority children were overrepresented among them.* Furthermore, officials were as likely to sentence status offenders to these facilities as they were criminal property offenders. Indeed, only violent offenders were more likely to be locked up than status or property offenders.

Figure 15–2 provides a graphic portrayal of these procedures. Like Figure 14–1 regarding the police processing of juveniles, it utilizes

1974 data. But since it derives estimates from a variety of sources, it serves better as a general, rather than a precise, illustration of how juveniles have been handled in the courts.

Because of the large gap between its professed ideals and its actual practices, the juvenile court was subjected to increasingly strident criticisms:

1. *Reflecting changes in social values and the concept of childhood, the laws which permitted the juvenile court to have jurisdiction over status offenders were condemned as vague, discriminatory, and unworkable.*

2. *The Supreme Court disavowed the discretionary powers of the juvenile court and demanded that it provide young people with most of the constitutional protections afforded adults.*

3. *The practice of confining large numbers of children in jails, as well as youth detention centers, was attacked as cruel and inhumane.*

4. *The officers of the juvenile court were accused of administering assembly line justice.*

5. *Rising crime rates were cited as evidence that the court had failed.*

6. *Liberals and conservatives, citing the same presumed defects in the system, came to contrary conclusions—the court was too lenient, or it was too punitive.*

But given the fact that their negative critiques were often based on contrasting ideologies, critics were united more by their disillusionment with the juvenile court than by their agreement on any remedies for it. Hence, the court was confronted with a host of dilemmas: Should it be principally concerned with the nurturance rights of juveniles or with their constitutional rights? Should it be

FIGURE 15–2

The juvenile court filtering process

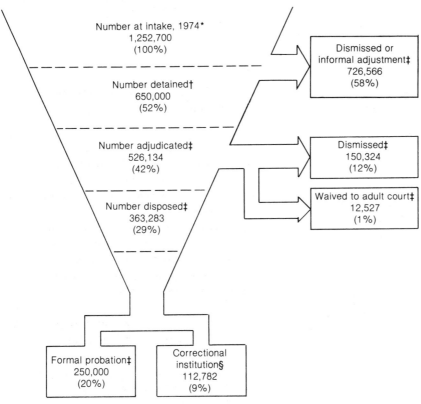

* National Center for Juvenile Justice. Juvenile Court Statistics, 1974. 1977:14.
† LEAA, undated:62 and 20; President's Crime Commission, 1967c:121; Sarri, 1974:5 and 7.
‡ Sarri and Hasenfeld, 1976:69–70.
§ LEAA, undated:62; Hasenfeld, 1976:69–70.

engaged in doing justice for young criminals or in trying to save truants, runaways, and neglected children as well? Should it risk censure for being too punitive by detaining and confining delinquents or too lenient by releasing them to the community? What principles should govern its operation? Should the concept of juvenile justice be discarded entirely?

In response to these dilemmas, today's reformers have been engaged in furious debate. In later chapters, we will examine those debates and determine how they have altered the concept of juvenile justice.

REFERENCES

Alexander, Paul W.
    1962   "Constitutional Rights in the Juvenile Court." Pp. 82–84 in Margaret K. Rosenheim, ed., *Justice for the Child*. Chicago: University of Chicago Press.

Arnold, William R.
  1971 "Race and Ethnicity Relative to Other Factors in Juvenile Court Dispositions." *American Journal of Sociology* 67 (September):211–227.

Axelrad, Sidney
  1952 "Negro and White Male Institutionalized Delinquents." *American Journal of Sociology* 57 (May):569–574.

Baker, Harvey H.
  1910 "Procedure for the Boston Juvenile Court." Pp. 318–327 in Hastings H. Hart, ed., *Preventive Treatment of Neglected Children*. New York: Charities Publication Committee.

Blumstein, Alfred, and Stafford, Richard A.
  1974 "Application of the Jussim Model to a Juvenile Justice System." *Proceedings of the National Council of Juvenile Court Judges,* December: 60–84.

California Youth Authority
  1974 *Juvenile Probation in California, 1973.* Sacramento: California Youth Authority.

Carter, Robert M., and Gitchoff, G. Thomas
  1970 "An Alternative to Youthful Mass Disorder." *The Police Chief* 37 (July):52–56.

Chesney-Lind, Meda
  1977 "Judicial Paternalism and the Female Status Offender." *Crime and Delinquency* 23 (April):121–130.

Children's Defense Fund
  1976 *Children in Adult Jails.* New York: Washington Research Project, Inc.

Cohen, Lawrence E.
  1975a *Pre-Adjudicatory Detention in Three Juvenile Courts.* Law Enforcement Assistance Administration. Washington, D.C.: U.S. Government Printing Office.
  1975b *Juvenile Dispositions: Social and Legal Factors Related to the Processing of Denver Delinquency Cases.* Law Enforcement Assistance Administration. Washington, D.C.: U.S. Government Printing Office.

Creekmore, Mark
  1976 "Case Processing: Intake, Adjudication; and Disposition" Pp. 119–151 in Rosemary Sarri and Yeheskel Hasenfeld, eds., *Brought to Justice? Juveniles, the Courts, and the Law*. National Assessment of Juvenile Corrections. Ann Arbor: University of Michigan Press.

Eaton, Joseph W., and Polk, Kenneth
  1961 *Measuring Delinquency.* Pittsburgh: University of Pittsburgh Press.

Emerson, Robert M.
  1969 *Judging Delinquents: Context and Process in Juvenile Court.* Chicago: Aldine.

Fox, Sanford
  1970 "Juvenile Justice Reform: An Historical Perspective." *Stanford Law Review* 22 (June):1187–1239.

Gibbons, Don C., and Griswold, Manzer J.
  1957 "Sex Differences Among Juvenile Court Referrals." *Sociology and Social Research* 42 (November–December):106–110.

Goldfarb, Ronald
  1976   *Jails: The Ultimate Ghetto.* New York: Anchor Books.

Harpur, W. R.
  1899   *The Report of the Educational Commission of the City of Chicago.* Chicago: Lakeside Press.

Hasenfeld, Yeheskel
  1976   "Youth in the Juvenile Court: Input and Output Patterns." Pp. 60–72 in Rosemary Sarri and Yeheskel Hasenfeld, eds., *Brought to Justice? Juveniles, the Courts, and the Law.* National Assessment of Juvenile Corrections. Ann Arbor: University of Michigan Press.

In re Gault
  1967   387 U.S. 1, 18L. Ed.2d 527, 87 S. Ct. 1428.

In re Winship
  1970   397 U.S. 358, 25L. Ed.2d 368, 90S.Ct. 1068.

Kent v. *U.S.*
  1966   383 U.S. 541, 16L. Ed.2d 84, 86 S.Ct. 1045.

Ketcham, Orman W.
  1962   "The Unfulfilled Promise of the American Juvenile Court." Pp. 22–43 in Margaret K. Rosenheim, ed., *Justice for the Child.* New York: Free Press.

Lathrop, Julia
  1916   "Introduction," Pp. 1–15 in Sophonisba P. Breckenridge and Edith Abbott, *The Delinquent Child and the Home.* New York: Survey Associates, Inc.

Law Enforcement Assistance Administration
  undated   *Children in Custody.* Washington, D.C.: U.S. Government Printing Office.

Lemert, Edwin M.
  1967   "The Juvenile Court—Quest and Realities." Pp. 91–106 in President's Commission on Law Enforcement and Administration of Justice, *Juvenile Delinquency and Youth Crime.* Washington, D.C.: U.S. Government Printing Office.

Lemert, Edwin M., and Rosberg, Judy
  1948   "The Administration of Justice to Minority Groups in Los Angeles County." University of California, Publications in Culture and Society, 2:1–28.

Lerman, Paul
  1979   "Order Offenses and Juvenile Delinquency." In LaMar T. Empey, ed., *Juvenile Justice: The Progressive Legacy and Current Reforms.* Charlottesville: University Press of Virginia.

Mack, Julian W.
  1910   "The Juvenile Court as a Legal Institution." Pp. 293–317 in Hastings H. Hart, ed., *Preventive Treatment of Neglected Children.* New York: Charities Publication Committee.

National Center for Juvenile Justice
  1977   *Juvenile Court Statistics, 1974.* Pittsburgh: National Council of Juvenile Court Judges.

National Council on Crime and Delinquency
  1961   *Standards and Guides for the Detention of Children and Youth.* 2d ed. New York: National Council on Crime and Delinquency.

1967   "Correction in the United States." Pp. 115–212 in President's Commission on Law Enforcement and Administration of Justice, *Task Force Report: Corrections.* Washington, D.C.: U.S. Government Printing Office.

National Probation and Parole Association
1957   *Guides for Juvenile Court Judges.* New York: National Probation and Parole Association.

Paulsen, Monrad G., and Whitebread, Charles H.
1974   *Juvenile Law and Procedure.* Reno: National Council of Juvenile Court Judges.

Pawlack, Edward J.
1977   "Differential Selection of Juveniles for Detention." *Journal of Research in Crime and Delinquency* 14 (July):1–12.

Platt, Anthony M.
1969   *The Child Savers.* Chicago: University of Chicago Press.

Polier, Justine W.
1964   *A View from the Bench: The Juvenile Court.* New York: National Council on Crime and Delinquency.

Poulin, John E.; Levitt, John L.; Young, Thomas M.; and Pappenfort, Donnell M.
1980   *Juveniles in Detention Centers and Jails: An Analysis of State Variations During the Mid-1970s.* Washington, D.C.: National Institute for Juvenile Justice and Delinquency Prevention.

President's Commission on Law Enforcement and Administration of Justice
1967a   *Juvenile Delinquency and Youth Crime.* Washington, D.C.: U.S. Government Printing Office.
1967b   *The Challenge of Crime in a Free Society.* Washington, D.C.: U.S. Government Printing Office.
1967c   *Task Force Report: Corrections.* Washington, D.C.: U.S. Government Printing Office.

Rothman, David J.
1978   "The Progressive Legacy: Development of American Attitudes Toward Juvenile Delinquency." Pp. 1–25 in LaMar T. Empey, ed., *Juvenile Justice: The Progressive Legacy and Current Reforms.* Charlottesville: University of Virginia Press.

Revised Statutes of Illinois.
1899 Sec. 21.

Rubin, H. Ted
1976   "The Eye of the Juvenile Court Judge: A One-step-up View of the Juvenile Justice System." Pp. 133–159 in Malcolm W. Klein, ed., *The Juvenile Justice System.* Beverly Hills, Calif.: Sage.

Sarri, Rosemary C.
1974a   *Under Lock and Key: Juveniles in Jails and Detention.* Ann Arbor: University of Michigan, National Assessment of Juvenile Corrections.
1974b   "The Detention of Youth in Jails and Detention Facilities." *Youth Reporter* April, 5–8.

Sarri, Rosemary, and Yeheskel Hasenfeld, eds.
1976   *Brought to Justice? Juveniles, the Courts and the Law.* National Assessment of Juvenile Corrections. Ann Arbor: University of Michigan Press.

Scarpitti, Frank R., and Stephenson, Richard M.
　　1971　"Juvenile Court Dispositions: Factors in the Decision Making Process."
　　　　　Crime and Delinquency 17 (April):142–151.

Schultz, J. Lawrence
　　1974　"The Cycle of Juvenile Court History." Pp. 239–58 in Sheldon Messinger
　　　　　et al., eds., *The Aldine Crime and Justice Annual.* Chicago: Aldine.

Smith, D. C.
　　1974　"A Profile of Juvenile Court Judges in the United States." *Juvenile Justice*
　　　　　25 (August):27–38.

Sosin, Michael, and Sarri, Rosemary
　　1976　"Due Process—Reality or Myth?" Pp. 176–206 in Rosemary Sarri and Ye-
　　　　　heskel Hasenfeld, eds., *Brought to Justice? Juveniles, the Courts, and the
　　　　　Law.* National Assessment of Juvenile Corrections. Ann Arbor: University
　　　　　of Michigan Press.

Sumner, Helen
　　1971　*Locking Them Up: A Study of Juvenile Detention Decisions in Selected
　　　　　California Counties.* New York: National Council on Crime and Delin-
　　　　　quency.

Terry, Robert M.
　　1967　"Discrimination in the Handling of Juvenile Offenders by Social Control
　　　　　Agencies." *Journal of Research in Crime and Delinquency* 4 (July):218–
　　　　　230.

United Nations
　　1961　*Report Prepared by the Secretariat.* New York: United Nations.

Wakin, Edward
　　1975　*Children without Justice.* New York: National Council of Jewish Women.

Wald, Patricia M.
　　1976　"Pretrial Detention for Juveniles." Pp. 119–137 in Margaret K. Rosenheim,
　　　　　ed. *Pursuing Justice for the Child.* Chicago: University of Chicago Press.

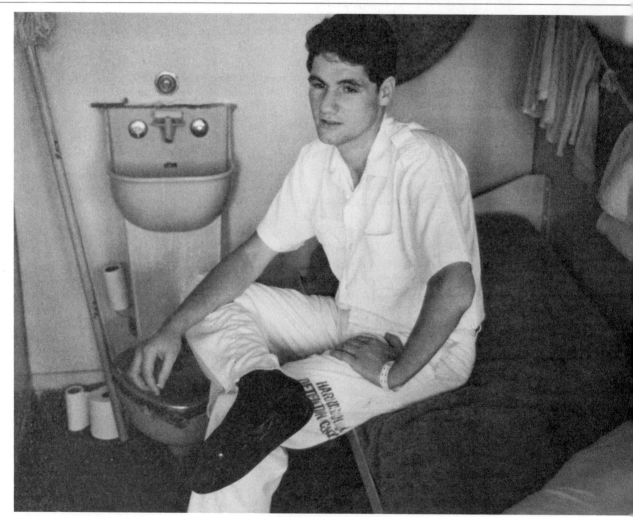

Because the treatment of juveniles has not lived up to the rehabilitative ideal, beliefs about its usefulness have turned from optimism to dismay.

REHABILITATING DELINQUENTS: FROM OPTIMISM TO DISMAY

In the previous chapter, we learned that, by the mid-1970s, it had become clear that the juvenile court had not lived up to the ideals expected of it. The same was true of society's efforts to prevent delinquency and rehabilitate offenders. Just as the concept of juvenile justice was viewed with disillusionment and cynicism, so was the concept of rehabilitation.

In order to discover how this came about, it is necessary for us to review the development of the rehabilitative philosophy and to explore the reasons why it was greeted with undeniable hope and optimism and why, ultimately, it was described as a bankrupt concept without redeeming value.

FORERUNNERS OF REHABILITATION

The philosophy of rehabilitation, like that of positive criminology, was a product of the late 19th and early 20th centuries. A short century earlier, however, delinquent children were still being treated with less than humane care.

Retribution

Despite the fact that the modern concept of childhood had grown rather pronounced by the last part of the 18th century, *retribution* was still the dominant response to young criminals, to the extent that they were sometimes put to death for property offenses:

> Nicholas Carter, about fourteen Years of Age, was condemned [hanged] for robbery. He said, That his Father imployed him in sewing and making of gloves: But he being Idle, and regardless of his Parents Good Admonitions, ran away from them, and joyned himself to bad Company. . . . [T]he Boy, desired all Young People to take timely warning by his so sudden a Death (Sanders, 1970:25).

Although a few children, like Nicholas, were hanged, most of them received clemency after being sentenced to die (Sanders, 1970:21). In 17th-century New England, for example, the laws of the colonies stated that children could be put to death for cursing or smiting their parents, treating the scriptures with blasphemy, being stubborn or rebellious, or committing other "notorious" crimes of this sort. In practice, however, punishments were usually less stringent. Consider the mercies of the court in the case of one Mistress How:

> The Court upon consideration of what is testified, ordered that for her swearing she pay ten shillings, and for her cursing speeches and rebellion to her mother, and profane speeches of the scriptures, tending to blasphemy, that she be corrected publicly by whipping, suitable to her years, and if this be not a warning but that she go on in these courses, it will come to higher censure (Bremner, 1970,I:38).

Besides whipping, other forms of corporal punishment were also common:

> William Carter a little Boy, about Ten Years of Age, was Indicted for stealing . . . two Gold rings . . . , a piece of Coined Gold, and Mony. . . . It was fully proved, so he was found Guilty [and sentenced to be burnt in the hand] (Sanders, 1970:25–26).

In North Carolina, a slave boy, Peter, confessed that he was present when his master was murdered by his brother:

> The Court haveing taken into consideration the youth of the said Peter and considering him under the Influence of his said older Brother Darby, have thought proper to pass his Sentence in the following words to wit.
>
> That the said Negro boy Peter be committed to Gaol and there to Remain under a Good Guard, till Tomorrow, and then between the Hours of one and four o'clock he be taken out thence and tied to a Post on the Court House lott and there to have one half of Each of his Ears cut off and be branded on Each Cheek with the letter M and Receive one hundred lashes well laid on his bare back and that the Sheriff See this order Executed (Sanders, 1970:324).

Finally, because disfigurement, death, and whipping were sometimes viewed as being too cruel or as ineffective deterrents to crime, English reformers suggested that two additional forms of punishment might be tried:

The methods now employed to dispose of delinquent children failing either to reform them or relieve society from their presence, it is certainly expedient a new experiment should be tried.

Now it appears to us that it would be real humanity towards these unfortunate creatures to subject them to compulsory and perpetual exile from England. . . . Abroad, in New South Wales [Australia], they often become prosperous and useful citizens; but, at home, they seem incapable of resisting the temptations presented by a luxurious and refined community (Sanders, 1970:137).

The new idea called "transportation" was quickly accepted and widely used in England and France. The following is an example of its application to a young English girl:

> Susannah Tyrell, a Girl about Ten Years Old, was Indicted for stealing two Gold Rings . . . and 14 shillings. . . . The evidence was that she confest, That one Elizabeth Sallowes (Now in Newgate) did give her a key to open the Door. . . . So that upon the whole, she was found guilty to the value of 9 shillings. She was ordered to be transported (Sanders, 1970:26).

Some notion of the extent to which transportation was used in England can be gleaned by reports that were made to the House of Commons. Between 1787 and 1797, 93 children and 5,765 men and women were transported to Australia. Between 1812 and 1817, 780 males and 136 females, all of them under the age of 21, were similarly transported. Five of these were "infants" of age 11, 7 were age 12, 17 were age 13, 32 were age 14, and 65 were age 15 (Sanders, 1970:69). Unlike the present, however, there were no program evaluators to determine how well the 11- and 12-year-olds enjoyed their trips abroad, but it is certain that they no longer committed crimes in England.

A somewhat similar method, which was even older than transportation, involved the removal of children to the "hulks"—abandoned, rotting ships, unfit for service, that were anchored off shore in rivers, bays, and inlets. Sometimes children served out their sentences along with adult convicts on these airless, vermin-infested ships, working as tailors, shoemakers, carpenters, and bookbinders. In other cases, they were confined on the hulks awaiting transportation to Australia. The following is one witness's description of the methods that were used to move children, bound in chains, from the various gaols of England to the hulks.

> After having pined and rotted in their respective county gaols . . . which varies from three months to as many years, . . . some [prisoners] are chained on tops of coaches; others, as from London, travel in an open caravan, exposed to the inclemency of the weather, to the gaze of the idle and the taunts and mockeries of the cruel. . . . Men and boys, children just emerging from infancy, as young in vice as in years, are fettered together, and . . . paraded through the kingdom. . . . [They are] ragged and sickly and carrying in their countenance proofs of the miseries they had undergone (Sanders, 1970:70).

The significant thing about the use of hulks, along with capital punishment, branding, whipping, disfigurement, and transportation, was that these methods, rather than treatment or imprisonment, were the primary forms of punishment prior to the 19th century. In virtually all Western countries, "prisons were uniformly considered to be merely places of safekeeping, that might serve a deterrent purpose but had no concern for the rehabilitation or reformation of those confined" (Sellin, 1964:xix). Gradually, however, the treatment of offenders was revolutionized.

Restraint

As Western societies moved from the 18th to the 19th century, efforts to control crime concentrated increasingly upon the notion that lawbreakers, young or old, could be reformed by *restraining* them in prison. Stimulated by the philosophy of the Enlightenment and the belief of classical criminologists that punishments should be decreased in severity and graded according to the seriousness of criminal acts, reformers began to construct prisons as alternatives to the barbaric punishments of the past.

The Pennsylvania system. Pennsylvania led the way. In 1790, the state passed a law which led to one of the most significant innovations in penal history: the construction of a prison in which convicts could be confined in solitary cells as a method of reforming them (McKelvey, 1968:6). Led by the Quakers, influential reform societies, and such individuals as Benjamin Franklin and William Braford, reformers assumed that by segregating offenders from all corrupting influences and denying them all but the physical necessities of life, they would recognize the errors of their ways and thus be deterred from further crime (Barnes, 1972:122).

This method was first tried in the old Walnut Street Jail in Philadelphia, but it soon failed due to excessive overcrowding. Not to be discouraged, however, reformers passed new legislation which permitted the construction of two entirely new prisons. The most famous was the Eastern State Penitentiary constructed at Cherry Hill, Pennsylvania, in 1829. Its design included a series of seven, massive stone corridors radiating like the spokes of a huge wheel from a central rotunda (Pettigrove, 1910). Each of the corridors contained a series of large cells, 8 by 15 feet, with 12-foot ceilings, into which offenders were placed in solitary confinement and left entirely by themselves for the duration of their sentences. These long cell blocks were only one story high so that each offender had access to his own small exercise yard, entirely walled off from other inmates. Eventually, some offenders planted small gardens and communed with nature, whatever nature they could create.

The ease with which discipline and control could be maintained under the Pennsylvania system roused the envy and interest of distraught reformers both in America and abroad. Indeed, Pennsylvania authorities were so pleased with what they had wrought that they often worked themselves into ecstasy in describing it:

> Shut out from the tumultuous world, [the criminal] can indulge his remorse unseen and find ample opportunity for reflection and reformation. His daily intercourse is with good men, who in administering to his necessities animate his crushed hopes and pour into his ear the oil of joy and consolation. He has abundance of light, air, and warmth; he has good and wholesome food; he has seasonable and comfortable clothing; he has the best of medical attendance; he has books to read, and ink and paper to communicate with his friends at stated periods; and weekly he enjoys the privilege of hearing God's holy word expounded by a faithful and zealous Christian minister (Barnes, 1972:130).

The Auburn (New York) system. Leaders in New York were dutifully impressed with Pennsylvania's theory of solitary confinement. Hence, in 1816, a law was passed permitting the construction of a prison at Auburn, New York, to be designed with individual cells. But where the cells at Eastern State in Pennsylvania were large and permitted access to the outside, those in the new Auburn prison were nothing more than cages, 3½ by 7 feet, with 7-foot ceilings and no outside access. The result was a disaster. Locked in their tiny cells, left in complete idleness, and lacking any means for exercise or human contact, many Auburn prisoners became ill or mad. It took only two years, from 1822 to 1823, for officials to conclude that the experiment had been a hopeless failure. The result was the development of an alternative system of prison discipline called the "Auburn" system (Barnes, 1972:133–36).

Although inmates in the new Auburn prison were locked up in their cages at night, they were permitted to work together during the day. But, in order to forestall disobedience and opposition, officials hit upon some new methods of social control. They required that prisoners keep complete silence at all times, march in lockstep, keep their eyes downcast, and never approach each other face to face (McKelvey, 1968:8; Barnes, 1972:136). Armed with these new means of maintaining order and the fact that working prisoners could help to pay for their own keep, Auburn officials, no less than those in Pennsylvania, waxed eloquent over their achievements:

> It is not possible to describe the pleasure which we feel in contemplating this noble institution. . . . We regard it as a model worthy of the world's imitation. . . .
>
> The whole establishment, from the gate to the sewer, is a specimen of neatness. The unremitted industry, the entire subordination and subdued feeling of the convict, has probably no parallel among an equal number of criminals. In their solitary cells they spend the night with no other books but the Bible, and at sunrise they proceed, . . . in solid columns, with the block march, to their workship; thence, in the same order at the hour of breakfast, to the Common Hall, where they partake of their wholesome and frugal meal in silence. Not even a whisper is heard; . . . When they are done eating, at the ringing of a little bell, . . . they rise from the table, from the solid columns, and return . . . to the workshops. . . . [I]t is the testimony of many witnesses that they have passed more than 300 convicts, without seeing one leave his work, or turn his head to gaze at them. . . . At the close of the day, . . . the work is all laid aside at once, and the convicts return, . . . to their solitary cells, where they partake of the frugal meal. . . . After supper, they can read scriptures undisturbed and then reflect in silence on the errors of their lives (Louis

Dwight, the foremost champion of the Auburn System, as quoted by Barnes, 1972:136–37).

Not mentioned in this glowing statement, however, was the fact that, in addition to silence, the lockstep, and downcast eyes, whipping was also used to encourage prisoners to maintain order and to reflect on the errors of their ways (Barnes, 1972:136).

Restraint for juveniles

Institutions designed exclusively for delinquents followed the construction of prisons by several years. Until then, and after, many juveniles were confined in the Auburn, Pennsylvania, and other prisons. Although asylums and houses of refuges, run largely by private groups had begun to appear about 1825, the first public reformatories and training schools were not built until almost 1850:

> The Lyman School for Boys opened in Westborough, Massachusetts, in 1846. Then came the New York State Agricultural and Industrial School in 1849 and the Maine Boys Training Center in 1853. By 1870, Connecticut, Indiana, Maryland, Nevada, New Hampshire, New Jersey, Ohio, and Vermont had also set up separate juvenile training facilities; by 1900, 36 states had done so (President's Commission, 1967a:141).

Just as the prison was viewed as a humane, forward-looking gesture, so was the development of these juvenile facilities. At the same time, the treatment of unruly and delinquent children did not suddenly partake of methods that we might consider enlightened or that were greatly different from the way adults were treated:

> Many of the juvenile reformatories were . . . , in reality, juvenile prisons, with prison bars, prison cells, prison garb, prison labor, prison punishments, and prison discipline. It was

recognized as a legitimate part of the purpose of the institution to inflict upon the child punishment for his wrongdoing (Hart, 1910:11).

As the 19th century wore on, however, there were signs of significant change. Perhaps the most profound was the increasing preoccupation of society with the developmental needs of children: "Every child allowed to grow up in ignorance and vice and to become a pauper or criminal is liable to become in turn the progenitor of criminals" (Platt, 1969:130). To many Americans it seemed that, if their worst fears were to be avoided, all poor, uneducated, and parentless children had to be treated as well as disciplined.

Paradoxically, these concerns over children percolated upward and were expressed as concerns over adults. The line between childhood and adulthood was becoming ever more blurred as the concept of adolescence began to develop and extend further and further into the adult years. Hence, as Rothman suggests, 19th century Americans eventually became so sensitive to childhood that "they stripped away the years from adults and made everyone into a child" (1971:76).

REHABILITATION

Following the wrenching traumas of the Civil War, these tendencies found direct expression in the recommendations of a remarkable gathering of America's leading penal reformers. Meeting at the Cincinnati Prison Congress of 1870, these reformers concluded that a great amount of good could be accomplished if criminals were made "the objects of generous parental care." Instead of suffering in prison, they should be "trained to virtue" (Henderson, 1910c:40). What they were implying, of course, was the concept of *rehabilitation.*

Declaration of principles

In a series of florid pronouncements, rarely exceeded for eloquence before or since, these reformers enunciated the first philosophy of rehabilitation and then embodied it in a formal Declaration of Principles. The following statement, attributed to Enoch Wines who also drafted the Principles, constitutes a kind of preamble to them:

> A prison governed by force and fear is a prison mismanaged, in which hope and love, the two great spiritual, uplifting, regenerating forces to which mankind must ever look for redemption, are asleep or dead.
>
> Why not try the effect of rewards upon the prisoner? Rewards, as truly as punishments, appeal to the inextinguishable principle of self-interest in his breast (Wines, 1910:12).

The difference between this preamble and the punishment philosophies of the past was striking, but Wines was not content to be an idealist philosopher. His Declaration of Principles not only spelled out rehabilitation in abstract terms, but outlined the specific methods by which it should be accomplished. The following are excerpts treating the more important terms (Henderson, 1910c:39–63):

1. Rehabilitation. Rehabilitation, not punishment, is the primary goal of penology:

> Whatever differences of opinion may exist among penologists on other questions . . . , there is one point on which there may be . . . almost perfect unanimity, namely, that the moral cure of criminals, adult as well as juvenile, . . . is the best means of attaining the repression of crime; hence . . . reformation is the primary object to be aimed at in the administration of penal justice (p. 17).

2. Treat criminals, not crimes. The Declaration of Principles directly opposed the premise of classical criminology that punishment and restraint should be allocated according to the seriousness of the criminal act.

Instead, rehabilitation should be administered according to the needs of the offender:

> The treatment of criminals by society is for the protection of society. But since such treatment is directed to the criminal rather than to the crime, its great object should be his moral regeneration. Hence the supreme aim of prison discipline is the reformation of criminals, not the infliction of vindictive suffering (p. 39).

3. The indeterminate sentence. The practice of giving offenders definite sentences, according to the seriousness of their criminal acts, should be replaced by sentences that are indefinite:

> Peremptory sentences ought to be replaced by those of indeterminate length. . . . Reformation is a work of time; and a benevolent regard to the good of the criminal himself, as well as to the protection of society, requires that his sentence be long enough for reformatory processes to take effect (pp. 40–41).

4. Classification. The practice of confining all prisoners together regardless of age, character, or sex should be eliminated. Prisons should be designed to meet the needs of different kinds of prisoners:

> Prisons, as well as prisoners, should be classified or graded so that there shall be prisons for the untried, for the incorrigible, and for other degrees of depraved character, as well as separate establishments for women and for criminals of the younger class (p. 41).

5. Education. Education is an indispensable element in rehabilitating offenders:

> Education is a vital force in the reformation of fallen men and women. Its tendency is to quicken the intellect, inspire self-respect, excite to higher aims, and afford a healthful substitute for low and vicious amusements (p. 40).

6. *Industrial training.* Occupational training is beneficial both for practical and personal reasons:

> Industrial training should have both a higher development and a greater breadth than has heretofore been, or is now, commonly given to it in our prisons. Work is no less an auxiliary to virtue than it is a means of support (p. 41).

7. *Rewards.* A reward is far more salient in producing change than is the fear engendered by punishment:

> Since hope is a more potent agent than fear, it should be made an ever-present force in the minds of prisoners, by a well-devised and skillfully applied system of rewards for good conduct, industry, and attention to learning. Rewards, more than punishments, are essential to every good prison system (p. 39).

8. *Self-respect.* Punishment only degrades; correctional practices should uplift:

> The prisoner's self-respect should be cultivated to the utmost, and every effort made to give back to him his manhood. There is no greater mistake in the whole compass of penal discipline than its studied imposition of degradation as a part of punishment. Such imposition destroys every better impulse and aspiration. It crushes the weak, irritates the strong, and indisposes all to submission and reform. It is trampling where we ought to raise and is therefore as unchristian in principle as it is unwise in policy (pp. 40–41).

9. *Parole.* Treatment in an institution completes only half the task; offenders require help when they return to the community:

> More systematic and comprehensive methods should be adopted to save discharged prisoners by providing them with work and encouraging them to redeem their character and regain their lost position in society. . . . And to this end it is desirable that state societies be formed, which shall cooperate with each other in this work (p. 42).

10. *Prevention.* Prevention is far more promising than is confinement after a crime has been committed:

> Preventive institutions, such as truant homes, industrial schools, etc., for the reception and treatment of children not yet criminal, but in danger of becoming so, constitute the true field of promise in which to labor for the repression of crime.
>
> It is our conviction that one of the most effective agencies in the repression of crime would be the enactment of laws by which the education of all the children of the state should be made obligatory. Better to force education upon the people than to force them to suffer for crimes (pp. 41–42;44).

Distinctive features

This remarkable declaration was characterized by three outstanding features. The first was *optimism.* In contrast to the pessimistic and retributive features of prior penal philosophies, the rehabilitative philosophy was conceived in the belief that men and women, as well as children, could be reclaimed from evil. To be sure, the task would require extensive conditioning and programming, but rehabilitation should appeal to the self-interest of the offender and of the state. Furthermore, this point of view became even more optimistic with the invention of the juvenile court. By calling all problem children *delinquents* rather than *criminals,* and by applying the principles of rehabilitation, the younger generation could be redeemed and future crime prevented.

The second feature of the rehabilitative philosophy was its singular *focus upon the individual* offender. It was the individual's morals which required regeneration; it was the individual's particular characteristics for which classification, separate institutions, and the indeterminate sentence were needed; it was the individual's educational deficiencies which demanded attention; and it was the individual's character from which society required protection. Indeed, nothing could be more democratic: delinquency could be prevented and crime controlled if, regardless of race or background, the individual was treated and given a helping hand.

The third outstanding feature of the declaration was its belief that the *institution* is the most effective means for treating children not yet criminal, as well as for rehabilitating those who are. Groups were organized throughout the 19th century that were opposed to institutional confinement for children, but they were in the minority. Thus, the idea prevailed that the best place for meeting the needs of deprived children was in self-sufficient correctional utopias which could provide everything an understanding family and well-organized community could provide, only better:

> In the ordinary family home the [delinquent] child is often at a great disadvantage. . . . The neighborhood may be thoroughly bad. The daily journey to and from school may lead past saloons. . . . The mother may be lazy, slatternly, and shiftless. The father may be drunken, vicious, improvident. . . . In the institution, however, we are able to control absolutely the child's environment. We can create ideal sanitary conditions. . . . We can select his school teacher and his Sunday School teacher. We can bring to bear upon him the most helpful and elevating influences. The [child] will never play truant, he will never be out with a gang, he will never be late to school. Under these circumstances, why should we not be able to produce satisfactory results? (Hart, 1910:62).

Overall, then, the rehabilitative ideology was both seductive in its optimism and revolutionary in its impact. Z. R. Brockway, who was the first correctional administrator to apply the principles of rehabilitation in a youth reformatory, immodestly declared that they

were "destined to change men's habits of thought concerning crime and the attitude of society toward criminals; to rewrite from end to end every penal code in Christendom; and to modify and ennoble the fundamental law of every state. It is a change from a plane where feeling sways to the loftier realm and reign of wisdom" (Brockway, 1910:93). Immodest or not, much of Brockway's prophecy came true.

CORRECTIONAL UTOPIAS

It is significant that the first place in which the principles of rehabilitation were applied was in a revolutionary new reformatory constructed for boys and young men, ages 16 to 30. The tendency for 19th-century Americans to "strip away the years" from adults was clearly evident here. Contrary to the idea that young children should be punished like adults, the exact reverse was suggested: young men were to be treated and disciplined like children.

The scientific reformatory

Once again the indefatigable Enoch Wines led the way. As leader of the New York Prison Association, he gained authorization in 1869 to plan for the new reformatory at Elmira, New York. The plant was completed about 1876, and Z. R. Brockway was chosen as its first superintendent (Brockway, 1910:88–107; Scott, 1910:95–98).

Brockway was profoundly impressed by the growth of positive science in the 19th century and viewed himself as an applicator of the scientific method. In 1877, as a result, he drafted and gained the passage of an "organic" law designed to implement fully the principles of the Cincinnati Prison Congress: the use of the indeterminate sentence; a system of classification; a program of treatment, education, physical discipline, and work; and the granting of parole governed by a parole board. The program and design of the new reformatory resembled a strict military school more than anything else. Although Brockway's conception of discipline was far stricter than that advocated by members of the helping professions today, his general approach has had lasting appeal: "To make a good boy out of his bundle of perversities, his entire being must be revolutionized. He must be taught self-control, industry, respect for himself and the rights of others" (Platt, 1969:52).

Reformatories for girls

The same was true for girls. According to Mrs. Frederick Wines, the daughter-in-law of Enoch Wines, female delinquents were characterized by the following list of problems, all requiring treatment and training:

> Neglect, brutality on the part of others; . . . disobedience, self-will, laziness, the love of dress, the want of education, poverty, animal appetites and passions cultivated; . . . curiosity to see life, social ambition, and the desire for a career; evil associations, the lack . . . of a good home, in general the want of training in the power of self-control (Barrows, 1910:147).

Given these problems, ideal reformatories for young females were said to operate like Brockway's for boys:

> There may be some difference in minor points, but in each one we find the graded system [classification], parole upon earning a certain degree of credit, industries that will be useful in the outer world, lighter employment as a means of recreation, physical drill in the gymnasium, with baths and scrupulous neatness of person and domicile, attention to music, . . . good academic schools, . . . outdoor work and recreation of all kinds. . . . Nowhere does the state do more than try to develop a religious and reverential atmosphere, and inculcate the belief that the noblest ideal of pure religion is to keep one's

self unspotted from the world (Barrows, 1910:139).

In theory, then, the new scientific reformatory, created by Wines and Brockway, became the prototype for progressive penology throughout the country.

Industrial and training schools

Just as reformatories were built for older youths so industrial and training schools were constructed for younger status offenders and delinquent children. New guidelines stressed the importance of locating both institutions in the country and reaffirmed the idea that they should emulate the character of the well-disciplined family. Hence, by the time the juvenile court was well established, they were widespread, except in the South which had not yet constructed special institutions for juveniles (Bremner, 1970, I:672; Platt, 1969:61–62). Furthermore, as child saving increased apace, it became steadily more difficult to distinguish among "industrial schools," "reformatories," and "training schools." Indeed, there were hints that all was not well in Camelot. As Hastings Hart put it,

> Juvenile reformatories were first known as house[s] of refuge; when that term became opprobrious, they were called reform schools; when that term in turn became obnoxious, the name industrial school was used; and when that name became offensive, they were called training schools (1910:70).

Likewise, it became increasingly difficult to distinguish among the types of children housed in these institutions. Since, according to juvenile court law, the purpose of rehabilitation was to treat children, not crimes, there was little need to distinguish among them—they all needed help. Furthermore, the growing influence of biological and psychodynamic theories added the ominous note that serious criminal acts were inevitable unless the hidden drives and unconscious motives of problem children were unlocked and treated. Schooling, recreating, and job training would do little good unless these obstructions were first eliminated.

TREND TOWARD THE COMMUNITY

Despite the construction of all these institutions, a growing number of reformers began to voice opposition to them in the early 20th century. The difficulty with locking children up, said Hastings Hart is "institutionalism":

> In a great institution like the New York House of Refuge, with 700 boys, or Girard College, with 1,700 boys, or the Catholic Protectory, with 2,700 children, the child is lost in the mass. He is one of a multitude. It is almost impossible to give him that personal attention which is essential to the normal development of a child. . . . The child lacks initiative; he lacks courage; he lacks power to act for himself. In the institution someone else is doing his thinking for him, someone else is planning his life for him; and when he goes into the world, he goes at a disadvantage (1910:62).

Hart was voicing a complaint that has since become common: children who have been raised by the state are incapable of free and independent judgment, accustomed to confinement as a way of life, and comfortable only in a setting where all decisions are made for them:

> However good an institution may be, however kindly its spirit, however genial its atmosphere, however homelike its cottages, however fatherly and motherly its officers, however admirable its training, it is now generally agreed . . . that institutional life is at the best artificial and unnatural, and that the child ought to be returned at the earliest practicable moment to the more natural environment of the family (1910:12).

It was this line of reasoning which led many of the first juvenile court judges to argue that probation, and not institutions, should be the cord upon which all the pearls of the juvenile court are hung. For more juveniles, treatment in the community was the preferable alternative:

> When we have exhausted the resources of the home, the church, and juvenile court, the probation office, then we turn to the juvenile reformatory and ask of it success in dealing with the problem in whose solution all other agencies have failed (Hart, 1910:11).

Probation

Actually, probation had roots far beyond the first juvenile courts (Diana, 1960). It was first used in Boston in 1841 when a shoemaker named John Augustus began to provide bail for minor adult offenders, women, and children, and to assist them following their court appearances. After Augustus died, the Boston Children's Aid Society and other volunteers continued his work. Massachusetts formalized these volunteer activities in 1869 by appointing a worker from the State Board of Charities, a private agency, to investigate children's cases, make recommendations to the criminal court, and receive children for placement. In 1878, an additional law was passed permitting the employment of paid probation officers in Boston (United Nations, 1951:29–42). A few other states, as well as Great Britain, legalized probation late in the 19th century, permitting first offenders, in particular, to be released on good conduct (Tappan, 1960:422). But it was the juvenile court movement which really legitimized probation and gave it its impetus. By 1925, all states except Wyoming had legalized it. Thus, as discussed in the last chapter, the practice today has become so widespread that far more delinquents are placed on probation or released informally without any court sanction than are confined in institutions.

Parole

Along with probation, another rehabilitative supplement which was gradually added to the array of rehabilitative techniques was parole (Carter and Wilkins, 1970:177–276). It will be recalled that parole was first suggested by the Cincinnati Prison Congress in 1870 and was first used at the Elmira Reformatory by Z. R. Brockway in about 1880.

Like probation, parole has a dual purpose: casework assistance for the offender and protection of the community. But unlike probation, parole is a community service that follows, rather than precedes, incarceration. The idea is that delinquents who have suffered "institutionalism" should not be suddenly released to the community without adult supervision and assistance. Instead, parole should be part of the indeterminate sentence. If delinquents are given help when they leave a training school, and can successfully adjust to the community, they will be permitted to remain there; but, if they seem unable to cope with the many demands of community life, they will be returned to the institution for further rehabilitation. Hence, following the pattern of the other elements of rehabilitative philosophy, parole was legalized in virtually every state as a part of the juvenile court movement.

JUSTICE REVOLUTIONIZED

All of these developments are evidence in support of Z. R. Brockway's prophecy that the principles of rehabilitation would modify the laws of every state. So great was their impact, in fact, that they revolutionized the administration of American justice. Prior to the application of the methods and principles set down in 1870, the fate of an offender, juvenile, or adult, was prescribed by law and decided by the judge once his or her guilt was established: imprisonment, hard labor, a fine,

or some other penalty. But, the rehabilitative revolution caused this power to be greatly diminished and transferred elsewhere. In the juvenile court, for example, new laws permitted the court to defer sentencing until the offender could be studied and recommendations made to the judge. Probation officers, psychiatric consultants, and others shared and influenced the judge's dispositional decisions. But this was only the beginning.

Once a dispositional decision was made, the court simply turned the offender over to probation or to institutional personnel for imprecisely defined treatment. Responsibility and power were divided, not only among people close to the court, but, eventually, throughout the whole correctional system. The adoption of the indeterminate sentence and the classification of offenders lodged new power and responsibility in probation departments and state departments of correction. The decisions handed down from these departments, in turn, led to the construction of diagnostic centers, specialized institutions, reformatories, industrial schools, farms, probation camps, and cottage programs. Hypothetically, these were designed to respond to different classes of offenders rather than classes of crimes—first offenders, neglected children, hard-core delinquents, as well as males and females.

This resulted in such specialized roles for correctional people as administration, care and feeding, custody supervision, casework, education, therapy, and vocational training. Then, following incarceration, the use of parole further divided power and responsibility and lodged them in parole boards and parole officers. They, rather than judges or correctional people, decided when offenders would finally receive their freedom.

In short, the concept of rehabilitation totally altered the classical system of justice. As a result, young delinquents were made to answer for their rehabilitation, not merely to a judge, but to a host of decision makers, all of whom were given a hand in deciding their fate and judging their performances. A crucial question, therefore, is: Did the grand and optimistic hopes of this revolution come true?

DISMAY OVER THE SYSTEM

For more than half of the 20th century, the belief that rehabilitation would work was not seriously challenged. The juvenile justice system operated in relative quietude with only occasional outcries from concerned legal or professional groups, the National Council on Crime and Delinquency, or academic criminologists (Tonry, 1976). But, during the past decade, dismay and cynicism have become the property of all Americans. The concept of rehabilitation is in a shambles.

Norman Carlson, director of the Federal Bureau of Prisons, described the situation in an address to the American Academy of Psychiatry and the Law in 1975. His first step was to disavow the most fundamental premise of rehabilitation; namely, that delinquency is a problem for which specific causes can be isolated and a successful treatment administered. "We cannot diagnose criminality, we cannot prescribe a precise treatment, and we certainly cannot guarantee a cure" (p. 1). But that was not all. Carlson also attacked the notion that by applying the principles of rehabilitation, the juvenile justice system could correct the worst consequences of such social ills as poverty, neglect, and racism and, thereby, save the younger generation from crime. "Neither you nor I," he told his audience, "can control unemployment, social inequity, racial discrimination, and poverty. Neither the psychiatrist nor the correctional officer can deal with broken families, poor neighborhoods, bad schools, and lack of opportunity" (p. 1). Such efforts are futile; if

better results are desired, other methods will have to be found.

One obvious reason for Carlson's disillusionment were the accelerating crime rates of the 1960s and 1970s. The desirable outcomes so confidently predicted by Enoch Wines, Z. R. Brockway, and the founders of the juvenile court had not come to pass. But beyond that, his cynicism was also generated by three factors: (1) the attacks on the concept of rehabilitation itself; (2) the lack of resources for fully implementing the methods of rehabilitation; and (3) the theories and findings of the scientific community.

Deficiencies in concept

Addressing a gathering of social scientists at Harvard in 1974, Rosemary Sarri, Robert Vinter, and Rhea Kish declared that the juvenile justice system represented "the failure of a nation." That system, they maintained, ". . . remains an anachronistic local-government vehicle, overwhelmed with the shortcomings of an entire society" (p. 1). Historically, the care and handling of children had been the responsibility of family, school, and community. Over the years, however, those tasks had been increasingly turned over to policemen, judges, and correctional authorities. The juvenile justice system, as a result, was inundated with clients. It was expected to solve problems which it could not possibly hope to address.

These critical remarks seemed to suggest that judges and probation officers, no less than delinquents, had been the unwilling victims of uncaring parents and communities. But while there was no denying that such had often been the case, history had shown that the dumping of unwanted children had often been invited by zealous officials. The reformers who wrote the Declaration of Principles in 1870, or who invented the juvenile court in 1899, argued that problem children *should* be turned over to the juvenile court, that treatment *should* be left to experts. Hence, because many judges and correctional people shared this belief, they were victims of their own philosophy as well as of an uncaring society. By assuming that rehabilitation would be a panacea, they had tacitly encouraged community irresponsibility.

As a reaction to this tendency, influential critics like Edwin Lemert (1967:96) called for a marked change in philosophy. Rather than assuming that the rehabilitative ideology is a cure-all, he suggested, judges and professionals within the system should leaven their arrogance with humility, and lower their expectations:

> [I]t would be well to delete entirely from [the laws of the land] pious injunctions that the care, custody and discipline of children under the control of the juvenile court shall approximate that which they would receive from their parents, which taken literally becomes meaningless either as ideal or reality. Neither the modern state nor an harassed juvenile court judge is a father; a halfway house is not a home; a reformatory cell is not a teenager's bedroom; a juvenile hall counselor is not a dutch uncle; and a cottage matron is not a mother (Lemert, 1967:92).

Lemert also suggested that, rather than the model of a physician, a more realistic model for those in the system would be that of a midwife. Judges, probation officers, psychiatrists, and counselors should recognize that, like midwives, they do not have the precise knowledge by which to diagnose ills and prescribe cures. At best, they could only assist the process of maturation and could not be expected to have much of an impact on its outcome. Hence, the only defensible philosophy for the juvenile justice system was one of "judicious nonintervention" (Lemert, 1967:96).

Lack of resources

In rebuttal to Lemert's critical remarks, many judges, correctional administrators, members of national commissions, and treatment personnel maintained that correctional problems were due more to a lack of resources than to flaws in the concept of rehabilitation. Indeed, this theme had been a persistent one since juvenile courts became widespread.

In the 1930s, two national commissions—the National Commission on Law Observance and Enforcement (1931) and the White House Conference on Child Health and Protection (1932)—noted the lack of support for rehabilitative facilities and programs: continued detention of juveniles in jails; poorly paid and unqualified judges; inadequate numbers of probation officers; few psychiatric services; inadequate foster homes and institutional care; and an ineffective parole system (White House Conference, 1932:21).

But, while these national commissions lamented the lack of rehabilitative tools, their faith in the ideology of individualized treatment remained unflagging. Thus, their recommendations continued to stress what Tonry (1976:287) describes as a "familiar litany": current problems would be solved if there were more rehabilitative programs and more, better-paid and better-qualified personnel.

Indeed, this theme persisted for nearly half a century. In 1967, the President's Commission on Law Enforcement and Administration of Justice continued to lament the lack of adequate resources. The average probation officer, for example, was expected to maintain a caseload of from 75 to 100 probationers, conduct presentence investigations, maintain extensive paper work, and carry out other functions as well. As a result, there was little time for dealing with the actual problems of juveniles:

A probation officer has arranged a meeting with a 16-year-old boy on probation for car theft. . . . The boy begins to open up and talk for the first time. He explains that he began to "slip into the wrong crowd" a year or so after his stepfather died. He says that it would help to talk about it. But there isn't time; the waiting room is full, and the boy is not scheduled to come back for another 15-minute conference until next month (President's Commission, 1967a:5).

Though the cost of probation was only about one tenth of the cost of housing delinquents in training schools, many states had simply failed to provide the juvenile court with sufficient probation personnel to meet the demands. No wonder that probation, heralded as the principal instrument of rehabilitation, was a failure.

The same was true of the nation's training schools. Too many of them were custodial institutions in which children were merely warehoused and thus isolated ". . . from the outside world in an overcrowded, under-staffed security institution with little education, little vocational training, little counseling or job placement, or other guidance or release" (President's Commission, 1967c:80).

When Sarri, Vinter, and Kish added up all these problems, therefore, they questioned whether society really *liked* its children: it offered them minimal protection of their constitutional rights and cast them aside, stigmatized but unaided; and it denied them other community services once they entered the juvenile justice system. "The expectation that [such a system] can offer effective remedial aid is as valid as an expectation that the highway department can resolve the energy crisis" (1974:3).

THE FINDINGS OF SCIENCE

Despite this catalogue of complaints, many of which were scarcely new, the theories and findings of science may have had an even more devastating impact. They questioned not only whether the concept of rehabilitation was effective, but also whether even desirable programs had a positive effect.

Effects of institutional programs

As a start, 20th-century criminologists added volumes to Hastings Hart's original complaint about institutionalism. Most of them questioned the effectiveness of institutional confinement, even under the most ideal of conditions.

Opposition to authority. There was some evidence that delinquents already had negative perceptions of authority when they entered an institution. Hence, the deprivation of liberty only heightened their resistances to change. Indeed, even among people who did not have a delinquent history—patients in mental hospitals, children in orphan asylums or soldiers in prisoner-or-war camps—captivity seemed to generate an inmate code whose function was resistance to authority rather than cooperation with it (Bartollas et al., 1976; Clemmer, 1940; Cressey, 1960; Schrag, 1954; Sykes, 1965; Sykes and Messinger, 1960).

Consider the statement of Jimmy Dunn, a young criminal who had already spent much of his life in juvenile institutions:

The easiest way to get a bad name [in an institution] is to talk to bulls. That's one of the rules: you don't talk to bulls, and bulls include anyone . . . who doesn't have a number. The best way to get along in the joint is to completely ignore the staff (Mannochio and Dunn, 1970:38).

The popular argument was that juvenile institutions were caste systems (Barker and Adams, 1959; Bartollas et al., 1976). Inmates and staff were divided into mutually exclusive groups. As a result, inmates like Jimmy Dunn played it cool and gave an outward appearance of good behavior without ever becoming involved with treatment staff or trying to change (Ohlin and Lawrence, 1959).

Rejection and fear. Investigators also argued that institutional life is characterized by personal isolation and fear (Bartollas et al., 1976; Clemmer, 1940; Glaser, 1964). Although inmates may stick together in resisting the efforts of staff members to change them, their own relationships are not sufficient to overcome the devastating effects of captivity. Even in cottage programs, to say nothing of training schools, inmate preys upon inmate, resulting in homosexual rape, exploitation of the weak, and assault (Polsky, 1962).

"Despite all the time I have spent in prison," Jimmy Dunn said, "it is a terrifying place to me; it is hopeless." Yet, he went on, prisons are "cakewalks" when compared to juvenile reform schools. "For the rest of my life I'll never have half the trouble I had in the years I spent there. Reform school kids' idea of a little friendly fun is a race riot!" (Manocchio and Dunn, 1970:158). Indeed, Dunn was nearly beaten to death when he originally entered reform school at age 13.

Among imprisoned girls, some qualitatively different patterns were found. The deprivation of normal relationships seemed to result in the artificial construction of all-female "families." These groups not only produced homosexual relationships of a physical nature, but also encouraged girls to adopt the roles of various family members in order to find functional substitutes for the normal relationships which confinement denied them. Ironically, in pursuit of satisfying, conventional life styles, they ended up playing roles that were deviant (Giallombardo, 1974).

Staff conflicts. Some investigators contended that staff members do not share a common belief in the importance of rehabilitative goals (Schrag, 1961). Treatment staff are at odds with custodial staff; counselors compete with cottage parents; work supervisors resent teachers (Bartollas et al.,

1976). Newly hired professionals and their techniques are often grafted on to existing programs without any heed to the problems they create (Ohlin, 1958; Weber, 1957). Too often, as a result, conflicts remain unresolved and staff members become more concerned with protecting their own interests than with insuring the overall welfare of inmates.

Overall, then, most critics concluded that even the most treatment-oriented of institutions were incapable of realizing desirable ends. They were so full of logical contradictions that, while they suppressed offenders, they could do little to rehabilitate them (Goffman, 1961). Indeed, some critics went much further. Bartollas et al. maintained that "the juvenile correctional institution, not unlike every other type of total institution, is or can be far more cruel and inhumane than most outsiders ever imagine" (1976:259).

Recidivism rates. Such devastating critiques appealed to common sense as well as scientific theory. For almost 200 years, there had been a swelling chorus of doubters who argued that, under conditions of captivity, people are not likely to change for the better. Yet, there were those who cautioned against excessive overgeneralization. Several studies suggested that group counseling, milieu therapy, and other techniques of this type, particularly in smaller institutions, were likely to improve institutional adjustment. The social distance between inmates and staff was decreased, and inmates were more manageable and cooperative (Lipton et al., 1975:299–322; Street, 1965).

If that was the case, it would be reasonable to assume that once these inmates were released from confinement, they would be more likely to stay out of trouble. Most studies, however, did not support that assumption; recidivism rates were not markedly reduced, if at all (Kassebaum et al., 1971; Lipton et al., 1975:528–29, Seckel, 1965). For example, the most defensible study on the subject revealed precisely this outcome. According to the best ideals of the rehabilitative model, Karl Jesness (1970) carefully diagnosed delinquents and classified them into different "maturity" types—categories that included both psychological and interactional dimensions. Then, he randomly selected among these types, dividing them into two groups. One group was assigned to an experimental program in which each received the type of treatment that was best suited to his or her particular needs; a second group was assigned to the regular institutional program.

After treatment was completed, Jesness found that, in accordance with his theory, the experimental group had shown greater psychological improvement. Yet, when these "improved" individuals were released to the community, their recidivism rates were not only high, but also identical to those of the control group who were not specially treated. Careful diagnosis, classification, and treatment, in short, had not produced lower rates of criminality.

Thus, when the results of this and similar studies were added up, they were far from encouraging. Instead, they seemed to suggest that no matter what form rehabilitation takes in institutions, it does not make a great deal of difference. The violation rates of inmates, whether in "enlightened" or "custodial" programs, remain about the same.

Effects of community treatment

Such findings helped to reinforce the arguments of early child savers, like Hastings Hart, that the principles of rehabilitation, if they are to work, must be applied in the community. In fact, this argument has been so persuasive that probation became the norm for convicted delinquents. By the mid-1960s, for example, five times more juveniles were placed on probation than were confined in institutions (President's Crime Commission, 1967a:133–43).

Spurred by psychodynamic theory, the Child Guidance Movement of the 1940s and 1950s also led to a number of clinical programs for "predelinquents"—unruly children who, in earlier times, might have been placed in houses of refuge or industrial schools. Finally, in the 1960s, some intensive community programs were created to treat serious delinquents who had already failed on probation—delinquents for whom incarceration would ordinarily have been the only choice. How successful, then, were these programs?

Probation.   We have already seen that probation usually consisted of little more than an occasional contact with an overworked probation officer. Yet, some evidence indicated that it was a useful tool. In a summary analysis of 15 probation studies, conducted in a variety of jurisdictions, Ralph England (1957) reported success rates varying between 60 and 90 percent. A second survey by Max Grunhut (1948), covering such states as Massachusetts, California, New York, and a number of foreign countries, provided similar results with the modal success rate at about 75 percent. Furthermore, Scarpitti and Stephenson (1968) found that probation was more effective for boys who were less delinquent and came from fairly stable backgrounds than for those who, ordinarily, would have been placed in training schools. Clearly, probation was not equally effective for everyone.

Surprisingly, however, such findings did not "prove" that probation rehabilitates, because most studies had not been designed to answer a crucial question: If the offenders placed on probation had been released without any supervision whatsoever, would they have been any more criminal?

One can answer such a question only after randomly comparing selected experimental and control groups regarding the effects of alternative programs on delinquents. The experimental group is treated—in this case, is assigned to probation—and the control group is not subjected to treatment or is treated in some other fashion.

Unfortunately, few probation studies followed this procedure. In fact, the most reliable studies of casework efforts began not with probation, but with parole. In 1953, the California Department of Corrections initiated a series of experiments to determine whether intensive supervision of adult parolees would reduce recidivism (Adams, 1970). Its goal, however, was not to determine whether parole was better than nothing, but whether the assumption was correct that more and better services would prove helpful. Thus, the department set up small, experimental caseloads ranging from 15 to 35 offenders, assigned them to selected parole officers, and, then, sought to determine whether their success rates would be superior to offenders who were placed in ordinary caseloads ranging from 72 to 90 persons. After 11 years of study, in which thousands of experimentally selected parolees were compared, few differences in outcome were observed. There was little evidence that lowered caseloads had produced lower recidivism rates (Adams, 1970:722–23).

Despite this disappointing result, these initial efforts stimulated further studies of both probation and parole by the California Youth Authority, the Los Angeles County Probation Department, and the Federal Department of Probation. Briefly, the results were these (Adams, 1970:724–25; Lipton et al., 1975).

After two years, the California Youth Authority discontinued the use of smaller caseloads because of an apparent lack of positive results. There was little evidence that caseloads of only 36 delinquents did any better after receiving intensive supervision than did caseloads of 72 persons.

The Los Angeles County Probation Department reported better results with juvenile probationers. Lowered caseloads and intensive supervision resulted in less time in detention, fewer court appearances, and fewer new arrests. This limited evidence was encouraging.

The Federal Department of Probation used three caseload sizes to test probation effectiveness: *regular* caseloads of 85 persons; *ideal* caseloads of 50 persons; and *intensive* caseloads of 25 persons. After two years of experimentation and random assignment, however, the outcome did not favor the use of lowered caseloads. Indeed, while the regular and the ideal caseloads had violation rates of 22 and 24 percent respectively, the intensive caseloads had a rate of 38 percent. Clearly, intensive supervision had resulted in higher rather than lower violation rates. The reason seems to have been that when probation officers on the intensive caseloads were able to monitor offenders more carefully, they noted more instances in which probationers did not live up to the conditions of their probation. Consequently, they were more inclined to define them as failures. Paradoxically, therefore, greater supervision during probation led not to greater success, but greater failure.

These findings produced two important outcomes. On the one hand, they tended to confirm nonexperimental studies of probation which indicate that about three quarters of all probationers do not become recidivists. On the other hand, they lent only partial support to the long-held assumption that, if probation officers could be given smaller caseloads, they could more successfully rehabilitate offenders. But, as important as these findings were, they still did not answer the fundamental question raised earlier: If the offenders placed on probation had been released without any supervision whatsoever, would they have been any more criminal?

In one of the few studies of the subject, McEachern and Taylor (1967) found that those offenders who were convicted and made wards of the court, but were not supervised by probation officers, had lower recidivism rates than those who were supervised. The same was true of delinquents who were treated informally and released at intake without actual conviction. Those who were not visited by probation officers did better than those who were.

Since this finding was contrary to traditional beliefs about the need for supervision, it must be treated with caution. Yet, additional evidence tends to support it, derived from several studies of prevention programs which, like probation, utilized casework methods as a means of preventing truants, emotionally disturbed, or unruly children from becoming serious lawbreakers.

Prevention for predelinquents. Perhaps the best-known study of a prevention effort for predelinquents was the Cambridge-Somerville Youth Study conducted between 1936 and 1945 (Powers and Witmer, 1951; McCord and McCord, 1959). In this study, 750 boys attending schools in Cambridge and Somerville, Massachusetts, were identified by teacher interviews, psychiatric evaluations, and psychological tests as troublemakers who were likely to become delinquent. Using random selection, 325 of the boys were then placed in an experimental group to receive services, while the remaining 325 were placed in a control group for which nothing was done.

The experimentals received all of the services which probationers were ideally supposed to receive: individual counseling, family guidance, tutoring, medical treatment, recreational services, and even occasional financial assistance. This rich array of services, which would have made the ordinary juvenile judge green with envy, was provided for an average of 5 years for each child. But, contrary to both theory and hope, repeated followup studies, made 5, 10, 25 and 30 years after treatment, revealed that, if anything, the experimental program had had a negative effect. Thirty years after treatment, experimentals had higher rates of crime, disease, and death, and lower rates of occupational success and status (McCord, 1978).

Following Cambridge-Somerville, prevention experiments used both similar and alternative methods: some identified first-graders as predelinquents and then sought to treat their emotional and familial difficulties (Craig and Furst, 1965). Some used nominations by teachers and principals to identify sixth-graders who were "headed for trouble" and then provided special role models and classes for them (Reckless and Dinitz, 1972). Some sought out "high risk" girls and boys in junior high schools, and then provided them with an array of individual and group services (Berleman and Steinburn, 1967; Meyer et al., 1965). Some used detached workers with delinquent gangs in an attempt to interest them in nondelinquent activities and, through agency coordination, recruit them into prosocial clubs (Miller, 1962; Klein, 1971).

Yet, in all these efforts there was virtually no evidence that the provision of casework and group services had made a difference (Berleman and Steinburn, 1969). Treatment programs that appeared to embody many of the ideals of rehabilitation proved to be no more effective in preventing and controlling crime than no program at all. By implication, therefore, the same may be true of probation.

Community alternatives to incarceration. Though the inconclusive findings of other studies might have deterred the development of still more community alternatives, such has not been the case. The desire to get away from institutions has seemed all-pervasive. Hence, the late 1950s and early

1960s were marked by the development of community programs for serious convicted delinquents—young people who, for the most part, had already failed in probation and seemed headed for incarceration in a training school.

One of the first of these programs was Highfields (McCorkle et al., 1958). Though it was not a community program in the full sense, High-fields was scarcely a traditional, institutional program. A group of no more than 20 boys, ages 16 and 17, were sent to live with a small staff without guards or detailed routines on the old Lindbergh estate in New Jersey.

During the day, the boys worked at a nearby mental hospital. In the evening, the total population was broken into two equal groups, each of which then had a meeting. Formal rules were scarce. Instead, control was exercised informally through the development of a group culture which presumably decreased distance between staff and offenders, and sponsored the offender in a more active, reformation role. The idea was that individuals are best helped when they become the helpers of others.

In order to test the effectiveness of Highfields, its graduates were compared to a group of boys who had been committed to the New Jersey State Reformatory at Annandale (Weeks, 1958). A lower percentage of Highfields than of Annandale boys recidivated (37 versus 53 percent). However, the results of the comparison were questionable because both groups were not randomly selected under experimental conditions. For example, the Annandale boys tended to be a little older, perhaps more experienced in delinquency, and from poorer social backgrounds than the Highfields boys. As a consequence, the most appropriate conclusion is that Highfields had proven neither less nor more successful than incarceration. In terms of recidivism, at least, it would be difficult to argue that one method was superior to the other.

Yet, the findings at Highfields were significant nonetheless, because they seemed to indicate that Highfields was able to do just as well as total incarceration, but at much less expense to the state and at much less personal cost to the delinquents involved. Delinquents stayed at Highfields only three or four months, as contrasted with many more months at Annandale. Still, they did just as well after release. Hence, a much cheaper form of community programming without the negative effects of confinement was just as successful as total incarceration.

A second, widely acclaimed project was the Community Treatment Program of the California Youth Authority, directed by Marguerite Q. Warren. Beginning in the early 1960s, this project utilized randomly selected experimental and control groups as a means of determining the effectiveness of programming in the open community as contrasted to total incarceration, or even "living-in" as in the Highfields program (Palmer, 1971; Warren, 1964; 1968).

The Community Treatment Program also followed much more closely the classical principles of rehabilitation than did Highfields. Each member of the experimental group was diagnosed and classified into one of several maturity types—types which indicated whether he or she was passive or aggressive, conformist or manipulative, neurotic or acting out. After classification, each delinquent was then assigned to a parole agent trained to treat the presumed needs of that particular individual.

The control group, by contrast, was assigned to one of the institutions of the California Youth Authority, from which, after confinement, its members were released on regular parole. While in the community, the caseloads in the experimental program were very small, from 9 to 10 offenders per agent, as compared to about 55 offenders per agent in the control program.

The findings of this experiment raised

considerable controversy. The overall success rates reported by the project staff favored the community program (Palmer, 1971:84). After two years, 58 percent of the experimental boys and 66 percent of the girls were defined as successes because their paroles had not been revoked. By contrast, the success rates for the control boys and girls were much lower: 46 and 52 percent respectively. Furthermore, there was evidence that some of the maturity subtypes had done much better than others because of the special treatment they received.

It has been pointed out, however, that these differential rates of success may have been more a function of the contrasting ways traditional parole agents and experimental staff handled their clients than the way clients actually behaved (Lerman, 1968; 1975: chap. 4). Warren and Palmer (1966), for example, noted that 68 percent of the failures among the control group were due to recommendations by their parole agents that parole be revoked, as contrasted with only 29 percent among the experimentals. Why did these great disparities occur?

The reason, apparently, is that regular parole agents were not as tolerant of new offenses among their parolees as were the experimental staff, particularly offenses that were of low and medium seriousness. Thus, they defined more of the control group parolees as failures even though their delinquent behaviors may not have been different from those of the experimentals. Indeed, the experimentals may have committed more offenses than controls. For example, the average number of new offenses per experimental boy was 2.8 versus only 1.6 per control boy—a highly significant difference (Lerman, 1968; Palmer and Warren, 1967:11–12). Consequently, most investigators have concluded that the evidence is not sufficient to warrant the claim of project staff that the Community Treatment Program was clearly superior to incarceration. Although it might have been more effective for some types

of offenders, it was not more effective overall.

In summary, then, an optimistic interpretation of available research could, at best, provide only two promising leads: (1) community programs might be cheaper than residential programs, with no increase in recidivism; and (2) some types of community programs might work better for selected types of offenders than others. Overall, however, the results were both baffling and disheartening.

Whether the object of study had been the variation of treatment within institutions, probation, parole, prevention or intensive community programming, it had been difficult to prove that one rehabilitative approach was consistently more effective for all offenders than any other (Robison and Smith, 1971). Moreover, these findings were ironic because they were produced by positive criminology— the same school of thought that had hoped, like the Cincinnati Prison Congress, to use science to save delinquents and eradicate crime. Nonetheless, such hopes did not die easily.

REVIEWING THE EVIDENCE

In 1966, the New York State Governor's Commission on Criminal Offenders financed a survey of correctional research to make sure that some promising leads had not been overlooked. Clearly, the commission hoped that, if isolated, some correctional programs might be redesigned and revitalized. Consequently, three criminologists—Douglas Lipton, Robert Martinson, and Judith Wilks— were commissioned to find them.

In pursuit of that task, they gathered and reviewed the results of 231 evaluation studies conducted in this country and elsewhere between 1945 and 1967. By 1970, they had completed their work and produced a report, which subsequently shocked the Governor's Commission. Rather than identifying successful programs, the report seemed to suggest that there were none. But because the commission was either disbelieving, defensive, or both, it decided to suppress the report. Indeed the report might still be unavailable for public scrutiny were it not for the fact that it was subpoenaed as evidence for a lawsuit by the Bronx Supreme Court. It was thus freed from the controls of the commission and published in a large volume entitled *The Effectiveness of Correctional Treatment* (Lipton et al., 1975).

Rehabilitation is dead

When this volume saw the light of day, particularly when it was publicly interpreted by one of its authors, Robert Martinson (1974), it was treated as though it was a coroner's report announcing the death of rehabilitation. "With few isolated exceptions," Martinson wrote, "the rehabilitative efforts that have been reported so far have had no appreciable effects on recidivism" (1974:25). In other words, *nothing works!*

In another era, when optimism rather than pessimism was the order of the day, this conclusion might have gone relatively unnoticed. But the 1970s were not such an era. Instead, reformers of every ideological stripe used it as a means for further condemning the juvenile justice system and, particularly, for suggesting that methods other than rehabilitation had to be found for controlling crime.

Retributive philosophy. Retributive philosophers contended that, in attempting to rehabilitate delinquents, the juvenile justice system had been excessively lenient, had denied the rights of victims, had eroded discipline and respect for authority, and now threatened to destroy a tenuous social order (Miller, 1973:454–55). Thus, the following reforms were advocated: (1) abolish the juvenile court (McCarthy, 1977); (2) lower the age of accountability for crime; and (3) punish and incapacitate offenders (van den Haag, 1975; Wilson, 1975).

Since the rehabilitative philosophy was a proven failure, it was futile for the justice system to attempt to control crime by trying to undo the effects of its causes (Wilson, 1975). Rather, its dual purpose should be to ensure that punishment is swift and certain and that chronic offenders are incapacitated for long periods of time, perhaps even until the age of 35 or 40, when the "impulse" to commit crimes drops sharply (van den Haag, 1975).

Liberal philosophy. Liberal reformers, by contrast, argued that growing rates of juvenile crime were due to the failures of the system itself. It had overcriminalized the young, labeled and stigmatized them unnecessarily, denied them their civil rights, and not only had failed to rehabilitate them, but also had been excessively punitive (President's Commission, 1967b; National Advisory Committee, 1973a; 1973b). The only defensible philosophy for the juvenile justice system, therefore, was one of "judicious nonintervention" (Lemert, 1967:96). "Leave kids alone wherever possible" (Schur, 1973:155).

Radical philosophy. Yet another philosophy was that of the radical left. These philosophers argued that the devotion of progressive child savers to the rehabilitative ideal had so dominated their thinking that they had failed to subject the practices of official agencies to serious criticism and research (Platt, 1974). But now that evidence proved the failure of rehabilitation, what was needed was a socialist system of government that placed the ownership and control by the means of production into the hands of the working class. Delinquency could not be controlled by tinkering further with a corrupt system. Instead, "when there is no longer the need for one class to dominate another, where there is no longer the need for a legal system to secure the interests of a capitalist ruling class, then there will no longer be the need for crime" (Quinney, 1974:25). Social revolution, not technocratic reform, was the answer.

Just deserts philosophy. Finally, there were the newer "just deserts" philosophers. Their philosophy suggests that, since nothing works, the only defensible policy is one which ensures that justice is uniformly administered and that guilty offenders are punished according to the gravity of their acts. They suggested that our treatment-oriented system of justice has "produced far too many instances of recorded abuse to think fairly that it is much more than simply a vehicle for abuse" (Fox, 1974:3).

Unlike retributive philosophers, however, just desserts proponents argued that we should not be deluded by the blind hope that the punishment of one person will deter the crime of others. Instead, the state should "scale down the length of sentences to the point where it satisfies our sense of equity, but no more than that: warnings for crimes low on the scale of seriousness, intermittent confinement (weekends or evenings) for more serious offenses, and . . . full-time incarceration only for the most serious crimes" (Gaylin and Rothman, 1976:xxv). In other words, social policy should be concerned "less with the administration of justice and more . . . with the *justice of administration*" (Fogel, 1979:xv).

Given this widespread search for alternatives, it was clear that many critics were convinced of the accuracy of the coroner's report announcing the death of rehabilitation. Nonetheless, some were ambivalent over the thought of burying it forever:

> We recognize that, in giving up the rehabilitative model, we abandon not just our innocence but perhaps more. [This model] was a scheme born to optimism, and faith, and humanism. It viewed the evils in man as essentially correctable, and only partially the responsibility of the individual (Gaylin and Rothman, 1976:xxvii, xxix).

But since "there is virtually no sound proof that, short of killing him, anyone knows how to stop another person from committing crimes" (Fox, 1974:3), other methods for dealing with delinquents needed to be found.

Death reports premature

The popularity of such conclusions notwithstanding, there were some who felt that the reported death of rehabilitation was premature. In 1977, a special panel of scientists from various disciplines—sociology, psychology, psychiatry, political science, economics, penology, and applied statistics— were convened by the prestigious National Academy of Sciences to examine the autopsy report. In light of the widespread belief that correctional treatment was certifiably dead, the conclusions of the panel were striking.

To begin with, the panel observed that, while "Lipton, Martinson, and Wilks were reasonably accurate and fair in their appraisal of the rehabilitation literature," they were "overly lenient" in their assessment of the quality of the research upon which their conclusion was based (Sechrest et al., 1979:5). Hence, the panel *did not* draw the same conclusion as that of the original researchers. Instead, it concluded that research on the effects of treatment programs was so weak that existing studies could not yield reliable knowledge about the effects of rehabilitation (Martin et al., 1981).

This did not mean, however, that the panel felt that the patient was alive and well, and that the utility of treatment had been demonstrated. Instead, its conclusions are best divided into two parts, as follows.

1. Death neither proven nor disproven. The panel noted that there may be limited evidence that "some treatments are effective for certain subgroups of offenders" (p. 6). Nonetheless, it argued that the safest and most objective conclusion would be that the utility of treatment methods had neither been proven nor disproven. Furthermore, if blame for the lamentable lack of knowledge was to be levied, the scientific community was responsible for some of it:

In general, techniques have been tested as isolated treatments rather than as complex combinations, which would seem more suited to the task. And even when techniques have been tested in good designs, insufficient attention has been paid to maintaining their integrity, so that often the treatment to be tested was delivered in a substantially weakened form. It is also not clear that all the theoretical power and the individual imagination that could be invoked in the planning of rehabilitative efforts have ever been capitalized on. Thus, the recommendation in this report that has the strongest support is that more and better thinking and research should be invested in efforts to devise programs for offender rehabilitation (Sechrest et al., 1979:3–4).

2. *A compelling ideal.* In addition, the panel concluded that society can ill afford to prematurely bury a humane ideal:

The promise of the rehabilitative ideal is so compelling a goal that the strongest possible efforts should be made to determine whether it can be realized and to seek ways to realize it before it is abandoned. Our society cannot avoid the perplexing and recurring problems of how to deal with criminal offenders and the consequences of its penal policy. It is crucial, therefore, that we avoid simplistic solutions and continue efforts to systematically develop, implement, test and evaluate a variety of intervention programs in the search for a more humane and effective correctional policy (Martin et al., 1981:10)

Coming from a panel of scientists supposedly known for their cold and dispassionate approach to emotional issues, this was a remarkable conclusion. But so convinced was the panel of the merits of the rehabilitative ideal that it met for an additional two years in an attempt to suggest ways by which research might be used more effectively to

determine whether rehabilitation is a viable goal (Martin et al., 1981). In later chapters, therefore, we will review the panel's final suggestions; but given the fact that so many others were already convinced that rehabilitation was dead, the suggestions may not be heeded.

SUMMARY AND CONCLUSIONS

Three important issues have been highlighted in this chapter:

History of correctional epochs

First, our review revealed that correctional history has been characterized by three revolutionary epochs:

Retribution. Prior to the 19th century, society's efforts to control crime were dominated by a philosophy of *retribution.* Punishments were cruel but were justified on the grounds that suffering is fair recompense for criminal acts. Little thought was given to the idea of redeeming offenders, young or old.

Restraint. In the first part of the 19th century, the retributive philosophy was gradually replaced by a philosophy of *restraint.* Stimulated by the principles of classical criminology, offenders were confined in prisons and reformatories, where the length of stay was now graded according to the seriousness of criminal acts. Reformers anticipated that both inmates and others would thus be deterred from further crime.

Rehabilitation. Throughout the 19th century, people became increasingly sensitive to childhood, not only softening their attitudes toward children but stripping the years away from adults. Toward the end of the century, therefore, these attitudes were crystallized into a complex philosophy of *rehabilitation.* By attending to the needs of the individual and by implementing scientific programs of diagnosis and treatment, offenders could be rehabilitated and crime among dependent and unruly children prevented.

Despite marked differences among these philosophies, each new one did not make a complete break from those preceding it. When prisons and reformatories were built, retributive punishments did not suddenly disappear—they just changed form. Transportation, burning, branding, and disfigurement were replaced by solitary confinement, silence, the lockstep, and milder forms of flogging. Though somewhat less severe, these were punishments nonetheless.

Equally obvious was the overlap of restraint and rehabilitation. Rather than suggesting that rehabilitation might be more successful in a different environment, the prophets of treatment merely argued that reformatories and training schools should not be eliminated, but made into correctional utopias. It was not until the 20th century that this idea became somewhat diluted.

Nevertheless, elements of all three philosophies remain in our belief structures today. And in times of stress, they reappear once again in the juvenile justice system.

From optimism to dismay

Each new revolutionary epoch has begun in a flurry of great optimism and ended in an outpouring of criticism and dismay. When retributive punishments became too difficult for humanists to tolerate, the invention of prisons was hailed as a gesture befitting the most noble inclinations of humankind. The same was true of the rehabilitative epoch. Indeed, the idea is still unthinkable that concerted efforts should not be made to reclaim children from evil—that somewhere, under some set of circumstances, dedicated correctional workers can change young offenders and return them to society as healthy and productive citizens.

Yet, in recent years, it has become increasingly unfashionable to think in such hopeful terms. Indeed, research on the effectiveness of correctional treatment has been interpreted as suggesting that the concept of rehabilitation is dead and should be buried. Consequently, recommendations for reform have ranged from the suggestion that children should be left entirely alone, to those that would see them confined in institutions and severely punished for their acts.

What these trends suggest, of course, is that history is repeating itself. Once again, we are in one of those transitional periods in which a philosophy that captured the imagination of the nation has ended in despair. But is this despair warranted? Is it based on fact or popular belief?

Separating fact from ideology

A review of the evidence by a scientific panel at the National Academy of Sciences suggests that the belief may be based more on ideology than on fact. There is no denying that an impossible burden has been laid upon the juvenile justice system; that, at times, it has been arbitrary and unfair; that it cannot, by itself, remedy the effects of poverty and discrimination; and that the resources with which it has had to work have often been inadequate. But the presence of these limitations does not mean that, under controlled conditions, delinquents cannot be rehabilitated. Instead, existing evidence neither proves nor disproves the hypothesis that delinquents can be changed.

But such a conclusion will not stem the tide of events. A new revolution is underway that will change forever the assumptions about and organization of the original system of juvenile justice. In the chapters that remain, therefore, we will examine the roots of that revolution and the direction in which it appears to be leading us.

REFERENCES

Adams, Stuart
    1970 "Correctional Caseload Research." Pp. 721–732 in Norman Johnston et al., eds., *The Sociology of Punishment and Correction.* 2d ed. New York: John Wiley & Sons.

Barker, Gordon H., and Adams, W. Thomas
    1959 The Social Structure of a Correctional Institution." *Journal of Criminal Law, Criminology and Police Science* 49 (January–February):417–422.

Barnes, Harry Elmer
    1972 *The Story of Punishment,* rev. ed. Montclair, N.J.: Patterson-Smith.

Barrows, Isabel C.
    1910 "Reformatory Treatment of Women in the United States. Pp. 129–167 in Charles R. Henderson, ed., *Penal and Reformatory Institutions.* New York: Charities Publication Committee.

Bartollas, Clemens; Miller, Stuart J.; and Dinitz, Simon
    1976 *Juvenile Victimization: The Institutional Paradox.* New York: John Wiley & Sons.

Berleman, William C., and Steinburn, Thomas W.
    1967 "The Execution and Evaluation of a Delinquency Prevention Program." *Social Problems* 14 (Spring):413–423.
    1969 "The Value and Validity of Delinquent Prevention Experiments." *Crime and Delinquency* 15 (October):471–478.

Bremner, Robert H. (Ed.)
    1970 *Children and Youth in America: A Documentary History.* 2 vols. Cambridge: Harvard University Press.

Brockway, Z. R.
    1910 "The American Reformatory Prison System." Pp. 88–107 in Charles R. Henderson, ed., *Prison Reform and Criminal Law.* New York: Charities Publication Committee.

Carlson, Norman
    1975 "Giving Up the Medical Model." *Behavior Today* 6 (November):1.

Carter, Robert M., and Wilkins, Leslie T.
    1970 *Probation and Parole.* New York: John Wiley & Sons.

Center on Administration of Criminal Justice
    1977 *An Evaluation of the California Probation Subsidy Program.* Vol. 4. Davis, Calif: University of California.

Clemmer, Donald R.
    1940 *The Prison Community.* New York: Rinehart.

Craig, Maude M., and Furst, Philip W.
    1965 "What Happens After Treatment? A study of potentially delinquent boys." *Social Service Review* (June):165–171.

Cressey, Donald R.
    1960 *The Prison.* New York: Holt, Rinehart & Winston.

Diana, Lewis
    1960 "What Is Probation?" *Journal of Criminal Law, Criminology, and Police Science* 51 (July–August):189–204.

England, Ralph
  1957 "What is Responsible for Satisfactory Probation and Postprobation Outcome?" *Journal of Criminal Law, Criminology, and Police Science* 47 (March–April):667–677.

Fogel, David
  1979 We Are the Living Proof: The Justice Model for Corrections. Cincinnati: Anderson.

Fox, Sanford J.
  1974 "The Reform of Juvenile Justice: the Child's Right to Punishment." *Juvenile Justice* 25:2–9.

Gaylin, Willard, and Rothman, David J.
  1976 "Introduction." Pp. xxi–xli in Andrew von Hirsch, *Doing Justice*. New York: Hill and Wang.

Giallombardo, Rose
  1974 *The Social World of Imprisoned Girls*. New York: John Wiley & Sons.

Glaser, Daniel
  1964 *The Effectiveness of a Prison and Parole System*. Indianapolis: Bobbs-Merrill.

Goffman, Erving R.
  1961 *Asylums*. New York: Doubleday.

Grunhut, Max
  1948 *Penal Reform*. New York: Clarendon Press.

Hart, Hastings
  1910 *Preventive Treatment of Neglected Children*. New York: Charities Publication Committee.

Henderson, Charles R. (ed.)
  1910 *Prison Reform and Criminal Law*. New York: Charities Publication Committee.

Jesness, Carl F.
  1970 "The Preston Typology Study." *Youth Authority Quarterly* 23 (Winter):26–38.

Kassebaum, Gene; Ward, David; and Wilner, Daniel
  1971 *Prison Treatment and Its Outcome*. New York: John Wiley & Sons.

Klein, Malcolm W.
  1971 *Street Gangs and Street Workers*. Englewood Cliffs, N.J.: Prentice-Hall.

Lemert, Edwin M.
  1967 "The Juvenile Court—Quest and Realities." Pp. 91–106 in the President's Commission on Law Enforcement and Administration of Justice, *Juvenile Delinquency and Youth Crime*. Washington, D.C.: U.S. Government Printing Office.

Lerman, Paul
  1968 "Evaluating Institutions for Delinquents." *Social Work* 13:55–64.
  1975 *Community Treatment and Social Control*. Chicago: University of Chicago Press.

Lipton, Douglas; Martinson, Robert; and Wilks, Judith
  1975 *The Effectiveness of Correctional Treatment*. New York: Praeger Publishers.

Manocchio, Anthony J., and Dunn, Jimmy
 1970 *The Time Game.* Beverly Hills, Calif: Sage.

Martin, Susan; Sechrest, Lee; and Redner, Robin, (eds.)
 1981 *Rehabilitation of Criminal Offenders: Directions for Research.* Washington, D.C.: National Academy of Sciences.

Martinson, Robert
 1974 "What Works? Questions and Answers About Prison Reform." *The Public Interest* 35 (Spring):22–54.

McCarthy, Francis B.
 1977 "Should Juvenile Delinquency be Abolished?" *Crime and Delinquency* 23:196–203.

McCord, Joan
 1978 "A Thirty-year Followup of Treatment Effects." *American Psychologist* 33 (March):284–289.

McCord, Joan, and McCord, William
 1959 "A Follow-up Report on the Cambridge-Somerville Youth Study." *Annals of the American Academy of Political and Social Science* 322 (March):89–98.

McCorkle, Lloyd W.; Bixby, Lovel F.; and Elias, Albert
 1958 *The Highfields Story.* New York: Henry Holt.

McEachern, Alexander W., and Taylor, Edward M.
 1967 *The Effects of Probation.* Probation Project Report No. 2, Youth Studies Center. Los Angeles: University of Southern California.

McKelvey, Blake
 1968 *American Prisons.* reprint ed. Montclair, N.J.: Patterson-Smith.

Meyer, Henry J.; Borgatta, Edgar F.; and Jones, Wyatt C.
 1965 *Girls at Vocational High.* New York: Russell Sage Foundation.

Miller, Walter B.
 1962 "The Impact of a 'Total-Community' Delinquency Control Project." *Social Problems* 10 (Fall):168–191.
 1973 "Ideology and Criminal Justice Policy: Some Current Issues." Pp. 453–473 in Sheldon L. Messinger et al., eds., *The Aldine Crime and Justice Annual.* Chicago: Aldine.

National Advisory Committee on Criminal Justice Standards and Goals
 1973a *A National Strategy to Reduce Crime.* Washington, D.C.: U.S. Government Printing Office.

National Advisory Committee on Criminal Justice Standards and Goals
 1973b *Report on Courts.* Washington, D.C: U.S. Government Printing Office.

National Commission on Law Observance and Enforcement
 1931 *The Child Offender in the Federal System of Justice.* Washington, D.C.: U.S. Government Printing Office.

Ohlin, Lloyd E.
 1958 "The Reduction of Role-conflict in Institutional Staff." *Children* 5 (March–April):65–69.

Ohlin, Lloyd E., and Lawrence, William C.
    1959   "Social Interaction Among Clients as a Treatment Problem." *Social Work*
            4 (April):3–13.

Palmer, Theodore B.
    1971   "California's Treatment Program for Delinquent Adolescents." *Journal of
            Research in Crime and Delinquency* 8 (January):74–92.

Palmer, Theodore B., and Warren, Marguerite Q.
    1967   *Community Treatment Project, CTP Research Report,* No. 8, Part 1. Sacra-
            mento: California Youth Authority.

Pettigrove, Frederick G.
    1910   "State Prisons of the United States Under Separate and Congregate Sys-
            tems." Pp. 27–67 in Charles R. Henderson, ed., *Penal and Reformatory
            Institutions.* New York: Charities Publication Committee.

Platt, Anthony M.
    1969   *The Child Savers: The Invention of Delinquency.* Chicago: University of
            Chicago Press.
    1974   "The Triumph of Benevolence: The Origins of the Juvenile Justice System
            in the United States." Pp. 356–389 in Richard Quinney, ed., *Criminal Justice
            in America.* Boston: Little, Brown.

Polsky, Howard W.
    1962   *Cottage Six.* New York: Russell Sage Foundation.

Powers, Edwin and Witmer, Helen
    1951   *An Experiment in the Prevention of Delinquency: The Cambridge-Somer-
            ville Youth Study.* New York: Columbia University Press.

President's Commission on Law Enforcement and Administration of Justice
    1967a   *Task Force Report: Corrections.* Washington, D.C.: U.S. Government Print-
            ing Office.
    1967b   *Task Force Report: Juvenile Delinquency and Youth Crime.* Washington,
            D.C.: U.S. Government Printing Office.
    1967c   *The Challenge of Crime in a Free Society.* Washington, D.C.: U.S. Govern-
            ment Printing Office.

Quinney, Richard
    1974   "A Critical Theory of Criminal Laws." Pp. 1–25 in Richard Quinney, ed.,
            Criminal Justice in America. Boston: Little, Brown.

Reckless, Walter C., and Dinitz, Simon
    1972   *The Prevention of Juvenile Delinquency: An Experiment.* Columbus: Ohio
            State University Press.

Robison, James, and Smith, Gerald
    1971   "The Effectiveness of Correctional Programs." *Crime and Delinquency* 17
            (January):67–80.

Rothman, David J.
    1971   *The Discovery of the Asylum.* Boston: Little, Brown.

Sanders, Wiley B.
    1970   *Juvenile Offenders for a Thousand Years.* Chapel Hill: University of North
            Carolina Press.

Sarri, Rosemary: Vinter, Robert D.; and Kish, Rhea
    1974 "Juvenile Justice: Failure of a Nation." Paper presented at the Annual Meeting of the Directors of Criminal Justice Research Centers. Unpublished. Cambridge: Harvard Law School.

Scarpitti, Frank R., and Stephenson, Richard M.
    1968 "A Study of Probation Effectiveness." *Journal of Criminal Law and Criminology* 59:361–369.

Schrag, Clarence
    1954 "Leadership Among Prison Inmates." *American Sociological Review* 19 (February):37–42.
    1961 "Some Foundations for a Theory of Correction." Pp. 309–57 in Donald R. Cressey, ed., *The Prison*. New York: Holt, Rinehart & Winston.

Schur, Edwin M.
    1973 *Radical Nonintervention: Rethinking the Delinquency Problem*. Englewood Cliffs: Prentice-Hall.

Scott, Joseph F.
    1910 "American Reformatories for Male Adults." Pp. 89–120 in Charles R. Henderson, ed., *Penal and Reformatory Institutions*. New York: Charities Publication Committee.

Sechrest, Lee; White, Susan O.; and Brown, Elizabeth, eds.
    1979 *The Rehabilitation of Criminal Offenders: Problems and Prospects*. Washington, D.C.: National Academy of Sciences.

Seckel, Joachim M.
    1965 *Experiments in Group Counseling at Two Youth Authority Institutions*. Research Report No. 46. Sacramento: California Youth Authority.

Sellin, Thorsten
    1964 "Introduction: Tocqueville and Beaumont and Prison Reform in France." Pp. xv–xl in Gustave de Beaumont and Alexis de Tocqueville, *On the Penitentiary System in the United States and its Application in France*. Carbondale: Southern Illinois University Press.

Street, David
    1965 "The Inmate Group in Custodial and Treatment Settings." *American Sociological Review*, February, 30:40–55.

Sykes, Gresham M.
    1965 *The Society of Captives*. New York: Atheneum Press.

Sykes, Gresham M., and Messinger, Sheldon
    1960 "The Inmate Social System." Pp. 5–19 in *Theoretical Studies in Social Organization of the Prison*. Social Science Research Council, Pamphlet No. 15.

Tappan, Paul W.
    1960 *Crime, Justice and Correction*. New York: McGraw-Hill.

Tonry, Michael H.
    1976 "Juvenile Justice and the National Crime Commissions." Pp. 281–298 in Margaret K. Rosenheim, ed., *Pursuing Justice for the Child*. Chicago: University of Chicago Press.

United Nations
  1951   *Probation and Related Measures.* New York: Department of Social Affairs.
van den Haag, Ernest
  1975   *Punishing Criminals.* New York: Basic Books.
Warren, Marguerite Q.
  1964   "An Experiment in Alternatives to Incarceration for Delinquent Youth: Recent Findings in the Community Treatment Project," in *Correction in the Community: Alternatives to Incarceration.* Sacramento: Board of Corrections Monograph No. 4 (June):39–50.
  1968   "The Case for Differential Treatment of Delinquents." Mimeographed. Sacramento: Center for Training in Differential Treatment.
Warren, Marguerite Qu., and Palmer, Theodore B.
  1966   *The Community Treatment Project after Five Years.* Sacramento: California Youth Authority.
Weber, George H.
  1957   "Conflicts Between Professional and Nonprofessional Personnel in Institutional Delinquency Treatment." *Journal of Criminal Law, Criminology, and Police Science* 48 (May–June):26–43.
Weeks, H. Ashley
  1958   *Youthful Offenders at Highfields.* Ann Arbor: University of Michigan Press.
White House Conference on Child Health and Protection
  1932   *The Delinquent Child.* New York: Century.
Wilson, James Q.
  1975   *Thinking About Crime.* New York: Basic Books.
Wines, Frederick H.
  1910   "Historical Introduction." Pp. 3–38 in Charles R. Henderson, ed., *Prison Reform and Criminal Law.* New York: Charities Publication Committee.

REVOLUTION IN JUVENILE JUSTICE

Introduction: Traumas and alternatives for reform

We are now in the early phases of a new revolution in juvenile justice. Like the earlier revolutions—the emergence of classical justice or the invention of the juvenile court—this one is the result of two factors: (1) traumatic social change and (2) new theories of delinquency and juvenile justice. It has taken the better part of two decades for these developments to be reflected in the legal and institutional fabrics of our society, for they originated in the tumultuous decade of the 1960s.

ROOTS OF REVOLUTION

The decade of the 1960s started on a bouyant note. John Kennedy had just been elected president and Americans responded warmly to his charismatic leadership. After a decade of little growth and limited vision, he suggested, it was time "to get the country moving again." Heroic undertakings were in order; America would continue to pursue its grand destiny.

No little part of that destiny, the new president maintained, lay with the nation's youth. The time had come for the burdens of inequality, racism, and delinquency to be lifted from the shoulders of the nation's poor and uneducated children. To help accomplish this task, therefore, Kennedy created the President's Committee on Juvenile Delinquency and Youth Crime and appointed his brother, Robert, the attorney general, as its chairperson. Furthermore, numbered among its members were several highly influential persons, including the secretary of Health, Education, and Welfare and the secretary of Labor. This was to be a serious effort.

Strain theory and reintegration

True to the spirit of the times, new perspectives on the delinquency problem provided the rationale for the work of the President's Committee. As we learned in prior chapters, the social programs of the Committee were guided by the arguments of strain and some other positive theorists which suggested that the nation's poor and minority youths were not being effectively assimilated into the country's opportunity structure. The gates to success were closed. As a result, inherently social children were being forced to resort to desperately deviant measures in order to get ahead. Ironically, they were delinquent, not because they rejected America's cardinal virtue—the success ethic—but because they believed so strongly in it. The solution was obvious: the nation had only to reopen the gates of opportunity in order to prevent crime and to redeem its prodigal children.

This arresting argument also seemed to indicate why the juvenile court had not successfully stemmed the tide of juvenile problems. It was not the court's intrepid efforts that were at fault, but its ideological and theoretical underpinnings. Rehabilitation was too narrow a guiding principle. Dependency, neglect, and lawbreaking were not due to intrafamily tensions and emotional disturbance, but to social inequality, disorganized neighborhoods, and the absence of legitimate opportunities. Indeed, the parents of delinquent children, as much as the children themselves, were the victims of social inequality.

Given this new definition of the problem, it was obvious that the nation's strategy should be changed. Rather than rehabilitation (or retribution), it should stress *reintegration*. Racial and economic discrimination should be eliminated, hope instilled in the members of lower-class families, education enriched for all, and legitimate work opportunities made available. If the underclass children of the country were reintegrated into the mainstream of American life, their motives for committing delinquent acts would be removed and the worst features of delinquency eliminated.

So persuasive were these ideas that they led to the creation of the Office of Youth Development and Delinquency Prevention in the Department of Health, Education, and Welfare; a modest federal program designed to assist local communities in concentrating more of their resources on the delinquency problem; and the creation of Mobilization for Youth program in New York City (chapter 11). But such efforts as these were far too modest for the implied goals of the reintegrative philosophy; it demanded steps that were far more heroic. That is why, in keeping with its logic, it eventually contributed to the creation of the War on Poverty and other Great Society programs of the late 1960s.

Destruction of morale

Yet, even as these unparalleled, remedial programs were being initiated, American morale began to hurtle down a psychic slide—and the grand aspirations of the early 1960s turned to ashes. President Kennedy was assassinated by Lee Harvey Oswald. Attempts to block integration were followed by civil disobedience, urban riots, and the burning of cities. Martin Luther King and Robert Kennedy, the two remaining symbols of hope were assassinated. Involvement in the Vietnam War continued to escalate, despite mounting opposition. More and more young people dropped out, turned to drugs, joined communes, ran away, marched on Washington, or found some other way to attack the establishment. As crime rates rose and violence begat violence, a decade which had begun with great buoyancy and great hope rapidly disintegrated into a period in American history sure to be remembered for its disillusionment, mutual distrust, and cynicism.

ALTERNATIVE PRESCRIPTIONS FOR REVOLUTION

In response to this state of affairs, President Lyndon Johnson appointed a Commission on Law Enforcement and the Administration of Justice in 1965 whose purpose was to take stock of declining morale and rising crime rates and to outline further reforms. In its report published in 1967, the commission continued to support the reintegrative philosophy of earlier years. But, besides stressing heroic measures, it added a second theme—a "hands-off policy"— which was to greatly change the original meaning of reintegration. First, however, let us consider the commission's continued stress on the need for heroic measures.

The heroic theme

The commission declared that it is inescapable that juvenile delinquency is directly related to conditions bred by poverty (1967:57). That is why reform should be reintegrative more than rehabilitative, and why it should be a community, not a court, function:

> The Commission doubts that even a vastly improved criminal justice system can substantially reduce crime if society fails to make it possible for each of its citizens to feel a personal stake in it—in the good life that it can provide and in the law and order that are prerequisite to such a good life (1967:58).

Pursuant to the good life, the commission recommended that steps be taken to provide a minimum family income for all Americans, reduce unemployment, foster activities that unite families, help slum children overcome inadequate preparation for school, raise the hopes and expectations of lower-class children for higher education, develop job placement in the schools, eliminate barriers to employment, and involve more young people in responsible community activities (President's Commission, 1967:66; 69; 74; 77).

In short, the commission's heroic theme was characterized by two distinguishing features. First, it was concerned with what strain and other positive theorists would call the "primary" sources of delinquent behavior: poverty, inequality, inadequate education, and lack of opportunity. Second, it was concerned far more with reforming the political, economic, and social structures of American society than with reforming the juvenile justice system. What was needed was a national youth policy designed to produce legitimate behavior rather than a juvenile justice policy designed to punish or reverse the effects of illegitimate behavior.

The hands-off theme

After so strongly stressing that poverty, discrimination, and lack of opportunity were the primary causes of the delinquency problem, the commission then suggested that an even greater culprit might be the juvenile justice system. Indeed, this part of its report reflected the nation's growing distrust of legal and other institutions and, instead of heroic measures, stressed a *hands-off policy* for the young.

Support for this theme was derived from two sources. The first was the presumed failure of the juvenile justice system, as outlined in preceding chapters—the continued detention of children in jails, assembly-line justice, the lack of due process, excessively large caseloads, crowded training schools, and the assumption that correctional programs, even under the best of circumstances, did not make a difference. The juvenile court and its allied programs had not lived up to expectations and clearly were not a panacea.

The second, and equally important, source was the growing popularity during the latter half of the 1960s of *labeling theory*. According to this theory, serious delinquent behavior is the product, not of primary causes like inadequate families, poverty, or lack of opportunity, but of society's reactions to youthful lawbreakers. It is these reactions which produce dangerous career behavior—what labeling theorists call "secondary" deviance. Thus, the failure of the juvenile court was used as evidence in support of the basic argument of labeling theory: the process of identifying, labeling, and stigmatizing children had only made their problems worse, not better. Indeed, if labeling theory was correct, high rates of juvenile crime were due less to the failure of social institutions than to the excessively zealous and moralistic interference of the juvenile court in the lives of children.

The President's Commission was obviously persuaded by these arguments because virtually all of its remaining recommendations were predicated on the assumption that the juvenile justice system was a major, if not *the* primary, source of increasing crime rates. As a result, the commission recommended a series of reforms designed to severely limit the power and jurisdiction of the court.

In taking this step, the commission did not acknowledge that its acceptance of these hands-off recommendations might, in any way, be in conflict with its *heroic* recommendations. Indeed, it apparently assumed that the two were complementary, since both exhibited greater faith in the capacity of community, rather than legal, institutions to solve youth problems. As it turns out, however, the two theories do possess some contradictory features:

1. While the commissions heroic theme was based on the assumption that serious crime is due to inequality, ignorance, poverty, and discrimination, its hands off theme suggested that crime is the result of the stigmatizing and oppressive effects of legal, and probably other child-saving, institutions. In a very real sense, therefore, the reasons for high rates of juvenile crime were defined by the commission in strikingly different ways.

2. The same was also true of the solutions that were recommended. While the heroic theme suggested that a national youth policy of massive proportions was needed to give all children a greater stake in conformity, the hands-off theme implied that children should be left alone whenever possible, that society should implement a policy of benign neglect in their behalf rather than one of massive intervention.

In short, the commission built ideological and theoretical schizophrenia into its suggestions—a disorder which proved, in the long run, to have some striking effects. Indeed, those effects were increasingly discernible in other bodies of theory and policy recommendations that began to appear following the work of the President's Commission.

The radical theme

As American society moved into the 1970s, the distrust of legal and bureaucratic systems, as implied in labeling theory, grew more pronounced. Indeed, the Vietnam war, as well as the burglaries, wiretaps, perjuries, and coverups of the Nixon administration spilled the crises of the 1960s into the 1970s. Not only were American streets filled with crime, but it had now penetrated the highest levels of American government. Even the presidency and the legal agencies subject to it—the FBI, the Justice Department, and the CIA— were charged with corruption. Thus, faith in the capacity of American institutions to insure tranquility and implement reforms had reached an all-time low.

Given these feelings, it was no accident that a group of theorists—known as *radical* theorists—picked up on the theme that virtually all of America's institutions were corrupt. Based on Marxist doctrines, radical theorists claimed that the problem did not lie in conventional crime and criminals but in the failures and inequities of the capitalist system. The current traumas were evidence of an awakening citizenry trying to throw off the political, economic, and legal bonds of an oppressive social order. It was clear, therefore, that society's problems could not be solved by working within the framework of the existing system. Even the heroic programs suggested by strain theory could not do that. Instead, the only solution lay in the enhancement of class consciousness, the overthrow of capitalism, and the creation of a socialist society dominated by the working class.

The neo-classical theme

As might have been expected, however, an alternative interpretation was supplied by *neo-classical* theorists from the opposite end of the ideological spectrum. They were far more inclined to view criminals, activists, and protesters, rather than the state itself, as the primary threat to social order. Therefore they resurrected classical theory and suggested that society should concentrate on doing justice, not on reclaiming offenders or changing the social order.

A century of experience had proven not only that rehabilitation was a failure, but also that the causes of crime as outlined by positive criminology, were so complex, that even if they were accurate, society could not hope to address and eliminate them. Consequently, the only justifiable policy was that of reconstructing the justice system and reinstituting the use of classical principles: see that offenders are caught, insure that they are given a fair trial; and insist that, when found guilty, they are punished according to the gravity of their acts. Indeed, some argued that the need to protect society had grown so pronounced that stern measures were required.

IMPLICATIONS

The implications of these alternative prescriptions for policy contrasted greatly. In order to understand them, therefore, we will first review the three new bodies of theory—labeling, radical, and neo-classical. Then, we will outline and assess their impact upon the legal processing and treatment of juveniles. Finally, we will attempt to draw some conclusions about the future—the future of childhood, scientific efforts to understand delinquency, the conduct of juvenile justice, and efforts to prevent and control youth crime.

When this is done, we will have discovered that we have, in fact, been witness to a new revolution in juvenile justice.

REFERENCES

President's Commission on Law Enforcement and Administration of Justice
1967   *The Challenge of Crime in a Free Society.* Washington, D.C.: U.S. Government Printing Office.

Many people agree with labeling theorists that juveniles should be left alone wherever possible.

LABELING THEORY

The positive theories of delinquency examined earlier were concerned primarily with one central issue: whether factors could be identified which would clearly distinguish law violators from conventional people. The causes for delinquent behavior were sought in the inherent characteristics of individuals, the ways communities are organized, and the groups with which delinquents associate.

In the 1960s and 1970s, however, there was a marked shift away from this central concern. Rather than devoting primary attention to the presumed causes of delinquent behavior, a new group of theorists—labeling theorists—became preoccupied with societal reactions to it.

Most labeling theorists are symbolic interactionists. Their assumptions about human nature and social order, therefore, are generally the same as those of interactionists, but with a special twist. Like symbolic interactionists, labeling theorists assume that human nature is relatively plastic and subject to change. Yet, they are far more concerned with the stigmatizing effects of arrest and trial on delinquents than with the processes of interaction that produce their illegal behavior in the first place. The reason is that labeling theorists are inclined to believe that delinquents are relatively normal people; hence, if they persist in delinquent behavior and become serious offenders, it is due less to evil tendencies on their parts than to the negative effects of police, judges, and correctional authorities upon them.

The assumptions of labeling theorists about social order reflect this same bias. Although they acknowledge that society is characterized by cultural conflict, they suggest that this conflict is usually resolved in favor of people in positions of power and influence. Thus, the definition and imposition of social rules will reflect their interests, not those of less powerful groups.

These assumptions about human nature and social order together suggest that delinquent characteristics are not an inherent property of individuals, but, rather, a property that is conferred upon them by others—by legal officials and those who have the power to

401

legislate their own brand of morality. Hence, children become delinquent, not because of their behavior or because a predisposition to crime, but because they are labeled as delinquent by someone in a position of power.

THE DRAMATIZATION OF EVIL

Frank Tannenbaum (1938), an historian, was probably the first person to set forth some of the principles of labeling theory. Tannenbaum argued that the final steps in the making of a serious delinquent occur, not when a child violates the law, but when he or she becomes enmeshed in the juvenile justice system. When this official step is taken, an insignificant problem turns into a serious one.

Many children break windows, push over garbage cans, skip school, shoplift, and annoy people. From their childish perspective, however, these acts are defined as "play, adventure, excitement, interest, mischief, fun" (p. 17). But the community has a different definition of them. They are seen as a nuisance, an evil, and delinquency. Hence, they often result in chastisement, court action, and punishment. Should these acts continue, and should this difference in the definition of the situation persist, two things will happen.

First, the attitude of the community will harden. Soon, its tendency to define specific acts as evil will be transformed into a tendency to define mischievous children as evil. "The individual who used to do bad and mischievous things [will] now become a bad and unredeemable human being" (p. 17).

Second, the community's view of "bad" children will leave a lasting and destructive effect on them. They will soon come to feel that they are different from other children. "The young delinquent becomes bad because he is defined as bad and because he is not believed if he is good" (p. 17). In short, these children will have acquired new and delinquent self-images produced by the negative reactions of the community to them.

Tannenbaum called this process the "dramatization of evil," and said that it sets up a self-fulfilling prophecy which tends to evoke and emphasize the very behavior that was complained about in the first place. As he put it, "The process of making the criminal . . . is a process of tagging, identifying, segregating, describing, emphasizing, making conscious and self-conscious; it becomes a way of stimulating, suggesting, emphasizing, and evoking the very traits that are complained of. . . . The person becomes the thing he is described as being" (p. 19).

The relatives of mischievous children, the police, the juvenile court, and correctional officials are often enthusiastic and well-intentioned in their efforts to reform them, but their very enthusiasm defeats their objective. "The harder they work to reform the evil, the greater the evil grows in their hands" (pp. 19–20). Left alone, mischievous children will not become serious delinquents or adult criminals. But, so long as they are defined as bad and thereby isolated from conventional groups and activities, their only recourse is to join other children like themselves—those who have also been defined as evil.

It is when this occurs that really serious problems begin to emerge. Delinquent gangs tend to develop which provide the only source of security for labeled children. Even worse, these gangs begin to generate their own delinquent norms—norms which now seriously overemphasize the conflict between gangs and the community. In other words, a whole new game is set up in which "innocent maladjustment" escalates into criminal behavior, and in which the delinquent gang becomes the child's major reference group.

Therefore, said Tannenbaum, the only way out is through a refusal to dramatize evil in the first place. "The less said about it the better" (p. 20). It is the community's action in labeling children as evil and then making them very aware of that label that is the major source of delinquent gangs and serious crime, not some evil inherent in the children themselves.

PRIMARY AND SECONDARY DEVIATION

In 1951, some 13 years after Tannenbaum made his pioneering analysis, Edwin M. Lemert, a professor at the University of California, added some new concepts to labeling theory. First of all, said Lemert, it is necessary to distinguish between two kinds of deviant behavior: *primary* deviance and *secondary* deviance (1951:75–76).

Primary deviance

Tannenbaum failed to mention the fact that many delinquent acts go undetected. This is *primary* deviance—deviance that is neither identified nor punished by anyone in authority. Such deviance is common, as self-report studies indicate, and can be due to any number of "original" causes. In fact, says Lemert (1951:75) there are an "embarrassingly" large number of theories designed to explain these original causes—control theories, cultural deviance theories, strain theories, and others which we have already discussed. Although most of these theories possess elements of truth and thus are important from a scientific standpoint, they are relatively unimportant in terms of actually explaining how official delinquents are created.

The reason is that, until primary deviance is detected, there are no delinquents. Hence, its impact on children will be minimal, and they will not develop a deviant identity. Rather, they will be inclined, as most people are, to use techniques of neutralization to disavow the implications of their deviant acts and to continue defining themselves as good. Since their reputations have not been destroyed by labeling, they will tend to retain a conformist self-concept and to avoid the negative consequences of being defined as evil persons.

If their primary deviance is discovered, however, the results may be like those described by Tannenbaum—the evil will be dramatized and the status of the offenders transformed. For example, labeled delinquents must not only deal with the stigma associated with their delinquent status, but also respond to a host of new clues regarding what is expected of them. The reactions of parents, teachers, and friends, as well as legal authorities, will tend to affirm their delinquent status. Hence, to the extent that labeled children are sensitive to the expectations of others, their behavior may mirror not their normal, conventional roles, but deviant ones. Even their clothes, their speech, or their mannerisms may be altered, reflecting the characteristics of the delinquent status now expected of them.

Lemert (1971:13) also suggests that once people are labeled, they are expected to adhere to an additional set of official rules that apply only to them. But, rather than helping to reduce their problems, these new requirements only increase them. When status offenders are placed on probation, for example, they are often forbidden to live with "unfit" parents or associate with their old friends; or, they may be expected to suddenly reverse their patterns of failure at school. Any slip in adhering to these special rules will, in itself, constitute a new act of deviance. In some states, in fact, such a failure can result in a status offender being redefined as a "criminal" offender. Hence, in attempting to treat delinquents, the juvenile justice system can actually escalate the number of rules whereby their future behavior may be termed delinquent—rules that do not apply to nondelinquents.

Secondary deviance

This increase in rules, coupled with the tendency for delinquents to behave in accordance with the expectations of their deviant status, may result in what Lemert defines as *secondary deviance.* This kind of deviance evolves from the adaptions that the labeled person makes to the problems created by official and conformist reactions to his primary deviance. "When a person begins to employ his deviant behavior as a role based upon it as a means of defense, attack, or adjustment to the overt and covert problems created by the consequent societal reactions to him, his deviation is secondary" (1951:76). Thus, even though unique personal or situational factors—"original" causes— contribute to a child's *primary* acts of deviance, the reactions of society to these acts are likely to escalate the chances that more serious *secondary* forms of deviance will be forthcoming. According to Lemert, these are the most important and "effective" causes of serious delinquent behavior. As Tannenbaum had suggested, "The person becomes the thing he is described as being." (1938:19).

Lemert (1951:77) does not suggest that secondary deviance will follow closely upon the heels of any single, even punitive, reaction to an individual. Rather, as Tannenbaum indicated, it is the product of a rather long process—primary deviance, social penalties, further deviance, more penalties, until eventually the individual accepts his deviant status and becomes a full-fledged delinquent. Inherent in the arguments of both men, then, are three basic ideas:

1. Some kind of deviant behavior—i.e., *primary* deviance—must occur as a means of initiating the labeling process. Though neither theorist thought that primary deviance by itself would cause a child to become a serious offender, neither would deny that official reactions do arise in response to initial misconduct.
2. Both men implied the existence of community norms which react against acts of primary as well as secondary deviance. Though they argue that overreaction on the parts of parents, teachers, and legal authorities inevitably makes the problem worse, they would not question the idea that these people do share a set of rules that define certain acts as deviant.
3. It is clear that both men are symbolic interactionists. But rather than suggesting that primary acts of deviance are, or could be, serious, and that they are learned and justified in intimate groups, as Sutherland and Cressey suggested, they hypothesize that *serious delinquent behavior (secondary deviance) is the product of labeling and stigma.*

When people react to juveniles as if they were deviant, even if those juveniles retain conformist self-images, they dramatize evil unnecessarily and are *themselves* the major cause of delinquent identities and lifestyles (Gove, 1980:27–28). In short, an interactional sequence is set up that could be diagrammed as shown in Figure 17–1.

FIGURE 17–1

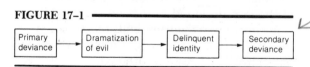

SOCIAL CREATION OF DELINQUENCY

The 1960s were characterized by a wave of excitement over this new way of constructing delinquency. Were it not for society's reactions to mischievous children, entangling them in a web of rigidity and self-fulfilling prophecy, there would be few career criminals.

To be sure, Tannenbaum and Lemert described the child as someone whose one behavior might contribute to the process by which he is labeled as delinquent—a fact that subsequent theorists acknowledged. Howard Becker, for example, said that ". . . whether a given act is deviant or not depends in part on the nature of the act (that is, whether or not it violates some rule) and in part on what other people do about it" (1963:14). But as increased attention was paid to this exciting conception of the problem, newer versions tended to concentrate less on acts of mischievous children, and more on society's role in making them delinquents.

As Schur (1971:19) describes it, labeling theory began to exhibit a high degree of ambivalence. On the one hand, early versions of labeling theory described delinquents as persons who had a hand in shaping their own fate by the commission of deviant acts. On the other hand, later versions described delinquents as being at the mercy of those who react to them. More and more, they were treated as passive social objects, helplessly transported, without much input on their parts, to the process by which they were labeled. In other words, the emphasis of the symbolic interactionists on the dynamics of the social process were downgraded in favor of a structural approach in which the organization of society became the center of attention (Finestone, 1976:208–211; Gove, 1980:9–32). A new kind of determinism was asserted that paid almost exclusive attention to three activities in society: the nature and construction of social rules, the selective enforcement of rules, and the social functions of deviance.

Social rules and moral crusaders

In a most significant series of statements, Howard S. Becker argued that it is not just the way the agents of control react to juveniles that determines whether they will be defined as deviant. The process of creating deviants occurs even earlier. It is rooted in the inclinations of all groups, particularly of "moral crusaders" to create rules:

> *social groups create deviance by making the rules whose infractions constitute deviance*

and by applying these rules to particular people and labeling them as outsiders. From this point of view, deviance is *not* a quality of the act a person commits, but rather a consequence of the application by others of rules and sanctions to the "offender." The deviant is one to whom that label has successfully been applied; deviant behavior is the behavior that people so label (1963:9).

Becker's statement requires some clarification. In one sense, there is little in it that is entirely new. Criminologists have long known that rules are of great importance because definitions of crime and delinquency vary considerably from society to society and are under constant change within each society. As Becker suggests, deviance is behavior that people so label; indeed, it cannot occur until there are rules by which the behavior can be defined as either good or evil. In the absence of rules, behavior is neither good nor evil; it is simply behavior. For example, a prehistoric man who took food from a weaker person did not really become a "thief" until the group of which he was a part decided that such an action was bad. Until a group consciousness evolved and shared expectations developed, there were no thieves, burglars, or cheaters. Likewise, there was little chance that a 13th-century child could be defined as a truant. Until schools were created centuries later and education was defined as important, truancy did not exist.

In short, it is not merely reactions to behavior that must be considered in understanding why people are labeled as deviant, but also the rules that serve to direct official attention to certain behaviors and not others.

But Becker (1963:147–163) was not interested in merely calling attention to an important and well-recognized fact. Instead, his concern was with directing attention to people in modern society whom he called "moral entrepreneurs"—people who become crusading reformers. They are the ones most likely to seek the new rules by which new forms of deviance are created. They are disturbed by some evil, and they will not be content until it is corrected. Typically, they believe their mission is a holy one. "They are . . . fervent and righteous, even self-righteous" (p. 148).

Moral crusaders, however, are not just busybodies. Often, they are like the ecologists of today or the child savers of past centuries who, in seeking to correct a set of problems, exhibit humanitarian concerns. They want new rules by which to address difficulties they consider important. Nonetheless, said Becker, moral crusades are typically dominated by people in positions of influence and power—people on the upper levels of society who want to change those beneath them. As a result, it is their vision of good and bad that is usually imposed upon society.

In their zeal, moral crusaders often fail to anticipate the consequences of doing good. For example, in order to correct some evil, it is not enough merely to pass a new set of rules. Rules must also be enforced, and this often requires the creation of a whole new set of agencies and officials. The crusade must be worked into the institutional fabric of society. Thus, a humanitarian drive that starts out to convince the world of the moral necessity of a new set of rules eventually becomes a bureaucracy devoted to their enforcement.

This bureaucratization can have all sorts of ramifications. Those people charged with enforcing the new rules are often less concerned with their content than with the fact that they are on the books. People are arrested, convicted, and punished because the rules say that they should be. Furthermore, it is in the self-interests of the rule enforcers to see that the rules are perpetuated. After all, rules now provide them with a job, a profession, a reason for being. Rule enforcers must justify their existence, therefore, by convincing others of the importance of the rules and by seeing that they are carefully safeguarded.

Sometimes the cure is worse than the disease:

In seeking to reduce sex crimes, laws have been passed which permit the indefinite confinement of "sexual psychopaths," although psychiatrists do not know for sure what a sexual psychopath is.

In seeking to prevent the reproduction of delinquent children, a eugenics movement was started and laws passed which permitted authorities to sterilize "hereditary criminals" and "moral degenerates." This was done despite the absence of scientific proof that crime is inherited or is the result of moral depravity.

In seeking to keep "giddy," "headstrong," and "restless" teenage girls away from temptation, some of them have been charged with status offenses and kept "safe" for a year or two in state-run industrial schools. It has been deemed more important that these girls should be institutionalized than that they should run the risk of violating the moral rules associated with childhood.

In short, deviance is a far larger enterprise than the commission of a particular act. Before any behavior can be viewed as deviant, moral crusaders must call attention to something about it that is undesirable and see that the necessary steps are taken to make rules that outlaw it. Once the rules are created, moreover, a new group of officials and agencies must be organized to enforce them—officials who have a vested interest in seeing that the rules are perpetuated. Only after all this is done are the necessary conditions set for creating deviants.

Selective enforcement of rules

Despite the intent of moral crusaders to establish rules that will be universally enforced, Becker suggests that, in fact, they are selectively applied (1963:156–61). Not everyone who is caught is labeled. Instead, the actual labeling of persons depends upon many factors that are extraneous to their behavior: who they are, of what class or race they are members, whether they show proper respect to officials, or whether the violated rule is high or low on an agency's list of rules to be enforced. The point is that rule enforcers use a great deal of discretion in deciding whom to label, if only because it is absolutely impossible for them to process all rule breakers. Hence, if they cannot tackle all violators at once, they must temporize with evil by selectively choosing individuals to label.

Other labeling theorists, writing during the same period, agreed with Becker. Universal definitions of good and bad, John I. Kitsuse (1964) argued, exist only in theory, not in fact. In a complex society like ours, it is virtually impossible to establish a set of moral rules that will be universally supported, moral crusaders notwithstanding. Consequently, "the socially significant differentiation of deviants from the nondeviant population is increasingly contingent upon circumstances of situation, place, social, and personal biography, and the bureaucratically organized activities of agencies of control" (p. 101). It is clear that factors other than actual behavior are of crucial importance in determining who will finally be labeled as deviant.

Reflecting similar thoughts, Kai T. Erikson argued that the most crucial factor is the "social audience:"

> Deviance is not a property *inherent* in certain forms of behavior; it is a property *conferred upon* these forms by the audiences which directly or indirectly witness them. The critical variable in the study of deviance, then, is the social audience rather than the individual actor, since it is the audience which eventually determines whether or not any episode of behavior or any class of episodes is labeled deviant (1964:11).

Even the most deviant of persons, Erikson noted, engages in delinquent acts only a fraction of the time. When the community decides to bring sanctions against him or her, therefore, "it is responding to a few deviant details in a vast array of entirely acceptable conduct. Thus it happens that a moment of deviation may become the measure of a person's position in society" (p. 11). Hence, the most pressing question is how it is that a community decides what forms of conduct should be singled out for attention.

The social functions of deviance

In seeking an answer to this question, Erikson did not concern himself with the characteristics of the deviant, as criminologists had historically done, but with the characteristics of society. Drawing upon the ideas of Durkheim (1952) and Mead (1918), he said that "it is gradually becoming more evident . . . that deviant behavior can play an important role in keeping the social order intact" (p. 12). Deviance serves important social functions.

Any social system requires boundaries. Some of these are geographical, but others are normative. In order to do business with one another, there must be rules, and people must have some assurance that those rules will be obeyed. Yet, the only material found in the system for marking its boundaries are the deviant behaviors of its members. In contrast to acts of conformity, deviant acts help to establish the outside limits of the kinds of behavior that can be tolerated. Should they become too extreme, the system will deteriorate. Therefore, said Erikson, "each time the group censures some act of deviation, . . . it sharpens the authority of the violated norm and declares again where the boundaries of the group are located" (p. 14):

> As a trespasser against the group norms, [the deviant] represents those forces which lie

outside the group's boundaries: He informs us what evil looks like, what shapes the devil can assume. And, in doing so, he shows us the difference between the inside of the group and the outside. It may well be that without this ongoing drama at the outer edges of group space, the community would have no inner sense of identity and cohesion, no sense of the contrasts which set it off as a special place in the larger world.

Thus deviance cannot be dismissed simply as behavior which *disrupts* stability in society, but may itself be, in controlled quantities, an important condition for *preserving* stability (p. 15).

According to Erikson, then, the selective labeling of persons by the agencies of control can be viewed as a boundary-maintaining activity. But, if such is the case, some delicate, possible frightening, questions are raised: Is it possible that society is organized to use labeled persons as a resource? Since the police, courts, and correctional agencies cannot catch everyone, it is possible that they selectively label some persons because they feel it is necessary to mark society's boundaries and to deter others?

Though final answers are not available, Erikson suggests that "the institutions devised by society for discouraging deviant behavior are often so poorly equipped for that task that we might well ask why this is considered their 'real' function at all" (p. 15). Victimization and self-report studies indicate that only a small fraction of all delinquents and criminals are apprehended. Yet, those who are caught are ushered into a deviant status by a dramatic ceremony—the court trial—a ritual that is clearly visible to everyone. Once that is completed, many deviants are then warehoused in institutions where, instead of being separated from deviant influences, they are tightly segregated into groups in which the opportunity to learn more criminal behavior is ever present. Furthermore, once having paid their debt to society, they are retired from their

deviant status with virtually no public notice. Nothing equivalent to the court trial is used as a rite-of-passage out of that status. Our agencies of control set up traffic patterns which concentrate on moving persons into a deviant status, not out of it and into a conventional one. So far as the public is concerned, therefore, these people are permanently labeled.

Hence, it could be that the major function of the agencies of control is not to act efficiently to suppress deviance, but to dramatize the deviance of the relative few they do process. By maintaining these people in an undesirable position, society can use them as permanent sign posts, indicating to others the outer limits of society.

If that is the case, the labeled person is a resource and is of greater worth to society as a deviant than as a nondeviant.

SUMMARY

In the course of its development, then, labeling theory moved further and further away from a consideration of the deviant acts that might bring an individual to the attention of authorities. Likewise, the reasons for these acts assumed less and less importance. As a consequence, the delinquency-generating sequence suggested by this lime of thought can be diagrammed as shown in Figure 17–2. This diagram implies that if children are lucky enough to avoid the labeling process, they will be the masters of their own fates and will grow up to be *insiders*—law-abiding persons. But if they acquire a deviant status, they will be known forever as an *outsider*—permanent pariahs whose only worth to society lies in defining its outer limits.

FIGURE 17–2

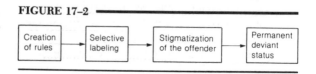

IMPLICATIONS AND IMPACT ON POLICY

These ideas had a profound impact on social policy. Indeed, labeling theory became a kind of legitimizing rationale for many of the criticisms of the juvenile justice system popular in the 1960s and 1970s. Writing for the President's Commission on Law Enforcement and Administration of Justice, Edwin Lemert stated its implications in classic form:

> The aims of preventing delinquency and the expectations of definitively treating a profusion of child and parental problems have laid an impossible burden upon the juvenile court, and they may be seriously considered to have no proper part in its philosophy. *If there is a defensible philosophy for the juvenile court, it is one of judicious nonintervention.* It is properly an agency of last resort for children, holding to a doctrine analogous to that of appeal courts which require that all other remedies be exhausted before a case will be considered. (1967:96 emphasis added).

Based upon such contentions, a series of reforms were proposed, all of which, coincidentally, started with the letter *D*, and which stressed the importance of keeping the hands of child savers off juveniles wherever possible. They were decriminalization, diversion, due process, and deinstitutionalization.

Decriminalization

The first suggested that status offenses—running away, defying parents, sexual promiscuity, or being truant—should be *decriminalized*. Indeed, a statement by the President's Commission noted earlier clearly reflected the contention of labeling theorists that moral crusades, like that which led to the invention of the juvenile court, are likely to produce rules and practices whose cures are worse than the disease they are supposed to correct:

> The provisions on which [legal] intervention . . . is based are typically vague and all-encompassing: growing up in idleness and crime, engaging in immoral conduct, in danger of leading an immoral life. They established the judge as arbiter not only of the behavior but the morals of every child (and to a certain extent the parents of every child) appearing before him. The situation is ripe for over-reaching, for imposition of the judge's own code of youthful conduct (1967:25).

In his role as consultant to the President's Commission, Lemert contended that since moral values have changed, these changes also required a reduction in the mandate of the court:

> The basic life process today is one of adaption to exigencies and pressures; individual morality has become functional rather than sacred or ethical in the older sense. To recognize this at the level of legislative and judicial policy is difficult because social action in America always has been heavily laden with moral purpose. However, if the juvenile court is to become effective, its function must be reduced to enforcement of the ethical minimum of youth conduct necessary to maintain social life in a high energy, pluralistic society (1967:97).

When these two arguments were combined, the conclusion was inescapable that children required protection from overly zealous officials. "It has become equally or more important to protect children from the unanticipated and unwanted consequences of organized movements, programs and services in their behalf than from the unorganized, adventitious 'evils' which gave birth to the juvenile court" (Lemert, 1967:97). Hence, according to the President's Commission, "Serious consideration . . . should be given to complete elimination of the court's power over children for noncriminal conduct" (1967:27). In other words, status offenses should be decriminalized.

Diversion

A second reform—*diversion*—was closely related to decriminalization. It too was based upon the premise that evils of children have been overly dramatized. Hence, in order to avoid labeling and stigma, potential arrestees or court cases should be diverted away from the juvenile justice system into other, less harmful, agencies—youth service bureaus, welfare agencies, or special schools.

Although this reform would represent a marked change, it still tended to compromise the intent of labeling theory. Both Tannenbaum and Lemert had implied that *nothing* should be done about the offenses of any but the most serious offenders. The less said about their acts, the better. Likewise, Edwin M. Schur suggested that children should be left alone wherever possible (1973:154–155). Our policy should be one of "radical nonintervention"—a policy that would "accommodate society to the widest possible diversity of behavior and attitudes, rather than forcing as many individuals as possible to 'adjust' to supposedly common societal standards" (Schur, 1973:154).

Policy makers, however, were not prepared to act quite so radically. Instead, the President's Commission (1967:82–84) recommended a more modest course in which petty offenders would be insured protection from the undeniably negative effects of the juvenile court, but would be guided and helped nonetheless. This, the commission suggested, could be accomplished in several ways.

There should be juvenile specialists at every police department whose function it would be to decide promptly which juveniles might be referred elsewhere rather than to court. Community agencies should be available to them to provide immediate counseling, and tutorial, occupational, or recreational services. Even better, every community or large neighborhood should have a Youth Service Bureau which could provide all of these

services in one setting for all children, delinquent or nondelinquent. Not only the police, but families, schools, and other agencies could refer children to such bureaus. In short, the President's Commission was not prepared to go all the way with labeling theory, but it was willing to go part of the way. If not radical nonintervention, society should at least be prepared to divert juveniles from the clutches of the juvenile justice system.

Due process

The third reform stressed the importance of *due process* in juvenile proceedings. It will be recalled that the Supreme Court of the United States had concluded in 1966, that when a child is referred to court, he "receives the worse of two possible worlds: that he gets neither the [constitutional] protections accorded to adults nor the solicitous care and regenerative treatment postulated for children" (Kent, 383, U.S. 541, 1966). Hence, in this and subsequent decisions, the court concluded that, except for jury trials, children should receive most of the protections that adults receive.

By no means was labeling theory totally responsible for these decisions. Instead, both were part of the growing distrust of governmental and other institutions in the 1960s. Nonetheless, one of the main themes of labeling theory was evident in the actions of the Supreme Court: the theme which stresses limiting the discretion of child savers and controlling their power over young people. Since all criminal acts by children could not be decriminalized, and some offenders would not be diverted, steps should be taken to insure that those who are referred to court are protected with constitutional procedures. In this sense, therefore, labeling theory did contribute to sentiments favoring greater due process for juveniles. If for no other reason, strict procedures would act to restrain the zealous interference of moralists in the lives of children.

Deinstitutionalization

The fourth reform to which labeling theory contributed was *deinstitutionalization*—the removal of children from detention centers, jails, and reformatories. Like programs of diversion, deinstitutionalization was to limit the destructive effects of legal processing and incarceration. It is also clear, however, that strain and other positive theories, as well as labeling theory, contributed to the reintegrative beliefs favoring this reform. They had long stressed the idea that, if delinquents are to be reformed, steps should be taken to improve attachments to home and school, increase academic skills, open up legitimate opportunities, and reduce identification with delinquent peers (see chapter 13 and Introduction to part 5). But, as the following comment indicates, the President's Commission (1967b:28) was also concerned with using deinstitutionalization to eliminate the harmful consequences of labeling:

> The correctional strategy that presently seems to hold the greatest promise, based on social science theory and limited research, is that of reintegrating the offender into the community. A key element in this strategy is to deal with problems in their social context, which means in the interaction of the offender and the community. It also means avoiding as much as possible the isolating and *labeling* effects of commitment to an institution. There is little doubt that the goals of reintegration are furthered much more readily working with an offender in the community than by incarcerating him (1967b:28 emphasis added).

In summary, labeling theory helped to legitimize four alternative and euphonious reforms: *decriminalization, diversion, due process* and *deinstitutionalization*. Although these reforms were due, in part, to other

constructions of the delinquency problem, they clearly reflected the major doctrine of labeling theory: hands off children wherever possible!

IMPACT ON CRIMINOLOGY

The impact of labeling theory on scientific criminology was as great as its impact on social policy. No longer, it suggested, could society and its reactions to delinquent behavior be taken for granted. All of the frustrations associated with 100 years of trying to explain delinquency now took on a new light.

In concentrating upon the characteristics of offenders—family backgrounds, failures in school, blocked opportunities, or subcultures and groups—positivistic science had been searching in the wrong places. It is society's reaction to delinquents, not delinquents themselves, that creates the problem. Indeed, the doctrines of labeling theory, when combined with the findings of self-report studies that indicated that most children had violated the law, led some people to draw conclusions that even labeling theorists might not have intended.

Crime does not exist

Expressing the new-found insights of labeling theory, Sue Titus Reid concluded, in her widely used textbook on criminology, that *crime does not exist.* "There is no basis," she maintained, "for assuming that there is a phenomenon called 'crime' that exists in reality . . . and that can be distinguished in its characteristics from 'noncrime'" (1976:239). As labeling theorists had pointed out, "The social meaning applied to the act or to the actor is the essential factor that determines crime," not a quality intrinsic to the behavior itself (Reid, 1976:239):

> What, then, is the conclusion? There is no theory of crime that meets the most

elementary demands of scientific theory. With the exception of labeling and conflict theory, all of the theories presume the existence of a phenomenon called "crime," which does not exist and which therefore cannot be distinguished from noncrime (Reid, 1976:240).

Criminals do not exist

The same is also true of criminals. *Criminals do not exist either.* Haven't self-report studies indicated that most people violate the law at some time or another? If that is the case, criminal behavior is normal human behavior (Reid, 1976:239). "It is perfectly natural for children to lie, cheat, steal, indulge in physical assault and behave indecently" (Morris and Hawkins, 1969:154). Once again, therefore, the "evidence" demonstrates the bankruptcy of all theories that attempt to explain law-violating behavior:

> If all people (or almost all people) engage in some acts that are defined by law as illegal, they are committing crimes and they are in one sense criminals. What sense does it make, therefore, to study "criminals" and attempt to distinguish them from "noncriminals"? Are we not spinning our wheels in a snipe hunt for something that does not exist (Reid, 1976:240)?

The implication, of course, is that criminology must find a new paradigm by which to guide its work.

The new paradigm

That paradigm is provided by labeling theory. *The one real thing that does exist, and that can be measured, is official reaction to crime* (Reid, 1976:240). Rather than hunting snipe, criminologists should be engaged in clarifying the processes by which society creates criminals. "Recent theoretical developments have emphasized that delinquency is an assembling production by

officials far more than it is a behavior pattern of young people . . ." (Goode, 1972:209). Consequently, the major way in which criminologists can be of use is to indicate "the differences between persons arrested but not brought to trial, tried but not convicted, convicted but not sentenced, convicted and sentenced and so on" (Reid, 1976:240).

In short, these interpretations of labeling theory are dramatic illustrations of some criminologists' hasty assumptions that there is nothing to be gained from studying primary deviance or seeking to determine why people break the law. Instead, the only justifiable role for science is that of determining how and why officials label and stigmatize some people, but not others.

RETHINKING LABELING THEORY

When the first flurry of excitement over these ideas died down, there was a general retreat from the extreme interpretations just described. On the one hand, labeling theory had successfully challenged the deterministic view of positive criminology. By questioning the idea that there are universal laws by which delinquency can be explained, it reaffirmed the relativity of culture. Delinquency is, in fact, a social construction that changes greatly from time to time and place to place. Certainly, our review of history supports this view.

Even more important, labeling theory clearly demonstrated the fact that, in attempting to understand delinquency, positive criminology had tended to ignore secondary deviance and the roles played by labeling and stigma in producing it. More than ever before, therefore, the importance of studying the effects of child savers on delinquents was indicated. No longer could the concepts of childhood and juvenile justice be taken for granted.

On the other hand, there was clearly a need

to avoid some of the rampant relativism suggested by intemperate interpretations which stated that crime and criminals do not exist. Indeed, some serious questions have been raised about such conclusions.

Crime does exist

In their concern with moral crusaders, labeling theorists tended to imply that virtually all rules are reflections of some elite group's special brand of morality, and that these rules work to the disadvantage of less powerful groups and are not shared by them. Among children, for example, such acts as truancy, premarital intercourse, drinking, or talking back to parents were defined as evil by 19th-century child savers and legally outlawed. But while these rules originally reflected a middle-class conception of childhood, they have become so common in all social classes today that it is difficult to separate deviants from conformists. But what about the rules that prohibit serious predatory crimes such as murder, unprovoked assault, robbery, or rape? Should they be viewed in the same way as those covering status offenses?

Wellford maintains that "all societies have found it functional to control certain kinds of behavior" and that this fact seriously questions the statement that no act is intrinsically criminal today (1975:335). Although labeling theorists were correct in suggesting that today's criminal acts did not constitute crimes until they were defined as such by some group, their predatory character has led virtually every civilization in history to establish laws prohibiting many of them. Were this not the case, there would be no norms by which labeling theorists could allude to "secret" deviance, or distinguish, as Lemert does, between primary (unsanctioned) and secondary (sanctioned) deviance. Some acts, in other words, can be readily identified by allusion to

widely shared norms, particularly in any one society.

Studies of American society, for example, indicate that, whether black or white, middle or lower class, educated or uneducated, people agree strongly on the kinds of acts that ought to be defined as crimes and thus condemned (Chilton and DeAmicis, 1975; Rossi et al., 1974). Hence, in considering the nature and function of social rules, there is need to recognize that there are various types of crimes and that not all of them can be attributed to the unique standards of some elite group of moral crusaders.

This point can be illustrated even more clearly when one closely examines Becker's famous statement that *"social groups create deviance by making the rules whose infractions constitute deviance"* (1963:9). Nettler warns that this statement is a "slippery" one which requires careful interpretation:

> It slides between the truth that social groups create the *definitions* of "crime" and the falsehood that the *injuries* condemned by these definitions would disappear (or would not have been "created") if the definition had not been formulated. To the layman, it sounds as though the labeling theorist believed that people would not wish to defend themselves against burglary or murder if they had not learned a rule defining these acts as crimes. It sounds, also, as though the labeling theorist believed that there would be less "burglary" if we did not use that term. The nonprofessional consumer of criminological explanations recognizes this for the semantic trick that it is—the trick of saying, "If a crime is a breach of a rule, you won't have the crime if you don't have the rule." The ordinary reaction to this semantic sleight of hand is to say, "A mugging by any other name hurts just as much" (1974:210).

In short, crime does exist; certain kinds of injurious acts have existed for a long time. It is not too surprising, therefore, that rules prohibiting them should have arisen and that those rules have had wide public support.

Criminals do exist

Problems are also associated with the contention that criminals do not exist. On the one hand, it is true that *official* delinquents do not exist until they are caught and labeled; until legal action is taken, they cannot be distinguished from *official* nondelinquents. It is also true that, since most young people report having violated the law at one time or another, the youth population cannot be cleanly divided into law-violating and law-abiding segments.

On the other hand, *chronic* law violators—those who have committed numerous injuries to others—can be distinguished from occasional, and usually petty, law violators. Self-report studies indicate that, at the most delinquent end of the juvenile continuum, there are a small group of young people whose law-violating behavior clearly distinguishes them from the preponderant majority (see chapter 6). Whether their acts have been detected or not, one could scarcely say that their criminal behavior is "normal," any more than one could say that people whose IQs are above 160 are "normal."

What is more, the results of longitudinal studies of official delinquents tend to support the findings of self-report studies. In chapter 5, for example, we learned that a group of chronic offenders, comprising only 6 percent of a total birth cohort in Philadelphia, were responsible for over 50 percent of all arrests. These offenders were a tiny proportion of the total cohort, but it would be foolish to suggest that their criminal behaviors could not be distinguished from its less delinquent members.

What is more, as discussed in chapter 13, when the differences among juveniles are taken into account, variables drawn from a variety of positive theories—attachment, achievement, commitment, and identification with delinquent peers—are able to predict *primary deviance* and identify those who have been the most delinquent. To be sure, these predictions have to be stated in probabilistic terms, but they isolate degrees of primary deviance nonetheless.

By contrast, labeling theory provides precious little insight into the sources of primary deviance. Gibbs, for example, has expressed concern over the inability of labeling theory to explain why the incidence of primary deviance varies so much from one population to another. "Are we to conclude," he asks, "that the incidence of a given act is in fact a constant in all populations and that the only difference is in the quality of reactions to the act?" (1966:12).

Obviously, the answer is no. Adults, for instance, are more likely than juveniles to commit murder or to engage in acts of embezzlement. Is this merely because the agents of control are more likely to label them? Such a conclusion is absurd (Gove, 1970; Wellford, 1975). Yet, it points to the excessive determinism of labeling theory.

Determinism of labeling theory

Extreme interpretations of labeling theory imply that labelers are the only creators of deviance (Akers, 1967; Mankoff, 1971):

> One sometimes gets the impression from reading this literature that people go about minding their business, and then—"wham"—bad society comes along with a stigmatized label. Then, forced into the role of deviant, the individual has little choice but to be deviant. This is an exaggeration of course, but such an image can be gained easily from an overemphasis on the impact of labelling (Akers, 1967:46).

Significantly, Lemert himself has objected to the "wham" conception of deviance, with its tendency to view the delinquent as a helpless "underdog."

Labeling unfortunately conveys an impression of interaction that is both sociologistic and unilateral; in the process deviants who are "successfully labeled" lose their individuality; they appear, as Bordua (1967) says, like "empty organisms" or, as Gouldner (1968) puts it, "like men on their backs" (Walton, 1973). The extreme subjectivism made explicit by the underdog perspective, reflecting sympathy for the victim and antipathy towards the establishment, also distorts by magnifying the exploitative and arbitrary features of the societal reaction. But more important, it leaves little or no place for human choice at either level of interaction (1974:459).

Lemert's comments do indeed raise some profound questions: What if labeling theory became the sole concern of criminology? What if no attention were paid to human choice, or to the idea that people are motivated by different forces? What if it was assumed that children do not begin to commit serious acts of delinquency until they are labeled?

Lemert suggests that such an approach would simply substitute one form of determinism for another:

> What began as some tentative and loosely linked ideas about deviance and societal reaction in my writings subsequently were replaced by the theoretical statement of Becker that social groups create deviance and that deviant behavior is that which is so labeled. This position got further elucidation in Erickson's functionalist-derived assertion that the social audience is the critical factor in deviance study. In retrospect these must be regarded as conceptual extrusions largely responsible for the indiscriminate application of "labeling theory" to a diversity of research and writing on deviance. Unfortunately, the impression of crude sociological determinism left by the Becker and Erickson statements has been amplified by the tendency of many deviance studies to be preoccupied with the work of official agencies of social control, accenting the arbitrariness of official action, stereotyped decision making in bureaucratic

contexts, bias in the administration of law, and the general preemptive nature of society's control over deviants (1972:16).

It is not that studies of official agencies are unimportant. Rather, an exclusive focus upon them would deny the possibility that the label of "delinquent" is ever earned, or that children differ from one another (Nettler, 1974:207). Such a denial would prove both misleading and inaccurate. Children do differ from one another, as we have seen, and the factors that contribute to these differences also contribute to the commission of delinquent acts. Thus, by denying the existence of these factors, intemperate interpretations of labeling theory also overlook individual variation and block efforts to do something about delinquency.

Finally, the concept of secondary deviance suggests that only after the delinquent behavior of juveniles has been labeled and dramatized are they likely to become career deviants. Were it not for the label, they would retain a conformist identity. Again, this is a deterministic oversimplification. Everyone does not respond uniformly to punishment and stigma. Upon being labeled, some young people feel so threatened that they refrain from further delinquent acts. They have such a stake in conformity—a loving family, a career, their entire future—that they choose not to endanger it by additional deviant behavior.

Conversely, there are some self-help groups—Alcoholics Anonymous, Synanon, or Weight Watchers Anonymous—which maintain that they cannot be successful with alcoholics, drug addicts, or overweight people until these individuals are willing to identify themselves as deviant. Ironically, these organizations have shown that until their clients are willing to acknowledge that they have a problem, little can be done to help them. In this instance, therefore, labeling acts as a device for motivating people to deal with their problems, not as a theory that states they do not exist.

In short, this implies that labeling theory has contributed to an increasing emphasis upon the arbitrary nature of social control, at the expense of careful investigation into the enormous complexities of law-violating behavior, the responses of society to it, and the constraints that are inevitable if society is to remain a functioning unit. Further, as Manning points out,

> A political and moral tone suffuses the work of labeling theorists which tends to cast us "good guys" in defense of politically weak groups against the "bad guys" lurking behind badges and guns, sinisterly wielding the establishment's power. . . . [T]he central drift has been toward the vulgarization and politicization of ideas, a failure to develop conceptual precision and to construct detailed analyses of the conditions (historical, cultural, social, social-psychological, biological) under which a given tenet of labeling theory might hold (1973:123).

RECONCILING LABELING AND OTHER THEORIES

Such criticisms have not been lost upon labeling theorists and the rest of the scientific community. In the first place, numerous observers have pointed out that the labeling perspective does not contain some of the elements of a sound substantive theory—for instance, a careful delineation and definition of concepts and a logically developed and integrated set of propositions (Gibbs, 1966; Goode, 1975; Schrag, 1974; Schur, 1971). Indeed, the most eminent labeling theorists maintain that they have been misinterpreted and that their statements were never intended as a full explanation of deviance. Hence, such statements do not warrant being called "theories" in any rigorous sense (Becker, 1974; Lemert, 1972; Rains and Kitsuse, 1973).

Becker also maintains that labeling theorists never intended to suggest that only after a

person has been labeled does that person begin to do deviant things. Such a notion, he indicates, is ridiculous:

> . . . [T]he act of labelling, as carried out by moral entrepreneurs, while important, cannot possibly be conceived as the sole explanation of what alleged deviants actually do. It would be foolish to propose that stick-up men stick people up simply because someone has labelled them stick-up men or that everything a homosexual does results from someone having called him a homosexual (1974:4–5).

There are reasons that people do these things quite apart from the way others react to them. Hence, the causes of delinquent behavior, no less than reactions to it, must be studied.

Given this need, both Lemert and Becker propose doing away with one-sided approaches and substituting an interactional model for studying delinquency. While we "can't go home again" to the old positivistic criminology, Lemert says, neither can we place total reliance upon the study of social reactions to deviance (1974:466–67). Becker agrees, and recommends that the term "labeling theory" be discarded and a new term adopted: "interactionist theory" (1974:6). In its simplest form, interactionist theory would be concerned with all the actors involved in any episode of deviance: rule creators, rule breakers, and rule enforcers. All three, not just one or the other, would be treated as raw material for scientific analysis (Gibbs and Erickson, 1975; Rains, 1975; Scheff, 1974).

These conclusions highlight a significant paradox. On the one hand, they represent a retreat by knowledgeable theorists from the more extreme versions of labeling theory, suggesting that we must be concerned with explaining and controlling law-violating behavior as well as with reactions to it. On the other hand, their retreat is ironic in light of the widespread popularity of labeling theory. Like the rare Broadway musical, it has become an instant success—lay people hum it familiar lines, and policy makers faithfully revise their roles according to it. Despite its many limitations as a comprehensive and well-articulated set of statements, therefore, labeling theory has had remarkable impact on cultural beliefs and practices.

SUMMARY AND CONCLUSIONS

Labeling theory has challenged the preoccupation of positivistic criminology with the presumed causes of delinquent behavior and has directed our attention to another part of the mosaic of which delinquency is comprised: the roles of rule makers and rule enforcers. It has made an exceedingly valuable contribution, markedly extending the range of behavioral phenomena with which both scientific and policy-making communities must be concerned.

1. Assumptions about human nature and social order. Given their recent reaffirmation of the interactionist position, labeling theorists tend to assume that human nature is plastic and subject to change. By humanizing the delinquent and normalizing his actions, they are inclined to believe that most children will be good if they are not pushed into adopting a delinquent self-image by the negative reactions of others to them. The assumptions of labeling theorists about social order reflect the same bias. Although society is characterized by conflicting definitions for behavior, it is the tendency of rule makers and rule enforcers to dramatize this conflict that exacerbates the delinquency problem and makes it worse.

2. Underlying content and logic of labeling theory. Early proponents of the labeling school stressed the notion that delinquents become bad because of the unnecessary dramatization of their primary acts of deviance. If this drama is repeated several times, offending children are likely to adopt a delinquent self-image and to engage in acts of secondary deviance. The process of

interaction implied by these theorists can be diagrammed as in Figure 17–3.

FIGURE 17–3

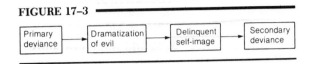

By contrast, more recent members of the labeling school have tended to treat the delinquent as a passive social object, helplessly transported from a normal to a delinquent status by society's legal apparatus: moral crusaders create unnecessary and arbitrary rules; rule enforcers selectively impose these rules; and the unlucky labelee is stigmatized and used as a symbol for maintaining social stability and marking society's boundaries. Hence, the process implied by this later version differs from that of the first (see Figure 17–4).

FIGURE 17–4

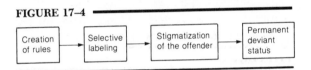

3. Policy implications. The more modest implication of these two bodies of theory is to use the juvenile court as an agency of last resort for only the most serious of offenders. The more radical implication is to do absolutely nothing—to refuse to dramatize evil.

Our society has tended to support the first implication. Consistent with the statements of labeling theory, some blatantly arbitrary and obviously discriminatory practices in the operation of the juvenile court have been documented. Consequently, four "reforms" are currently being pursued: *(a) decriminalization* narrowing the jurisdiction of the juvenile court, particularly over status offenders; *(b) diversion* turning juveniles away from the juvenile justice system and toward other social agencies for help; *(c) due process* requiring the juvenile court to become a court by insuring that alleged delinquents are provided with the constitutional protections afforded adults; and *(d) deinstitutionalization* removing delinquents from detention centers, jails, and reformatories.

Although these reforms are revolutionary in character, there is reason to remain skeptical about them. What proof is there, for example, that other social agencies are less likely to stigmatize diverted children than is the juvenile court? Since this is what the juvenile court set out to do in the first place, only the passage of time will tell whether our fervent reforms are more humane and helpful than were those of the 19th-century child savers.

4. Logical and empirical adequacy. In their extreme interpretations of labeling theory, some criminologists have contended that there are no crimes and no criminals, and that the only justifiable paradigm for criminology is one which focuses attention on social and legal reactions to crime. Along with others, however, most labeling theorists have discounted such intemperate interpretations of labeling theory: there are crimes, although societies create the definitions that define them as injurious; there are criminals, although societies distinguish their extreme behaviors from those of the majority. And social reactions to crime are not the only factors that produce law-violating behavior and deviant identities. In fact, interpretations of labeling theory which suggest that social reactions are sufficient to explain delinquency are unacceptably deterministic.

Reflecting this conclusion, recent statements by labeling theorists have suggested that we should return to an interactionist frame of reference in scientific study. While we cannot rely solely on the older models of positivistic criminology, neither can we adopt a one-sided approach stressing only social reaction. Instead, all the actors in the drama of creating delinquency—rule makers, rule breakers, and rule enforcers—must be taken into account in the thorough study of the phenomenon.

REFERENCES

Akers, Ronald L.
  1967 "Problems in the Sociology of Deviance: Social Definitions and Behavior." *Social Forces* 46:455–465.

Becker, Howard S.
  1963 *Outsiders: Studies in the Sociology of Deviance.* New York: Free Press.
  1974 "Labelling Theory Reconsidered." Pp. 3–32 in Sheldon Messinger et al., eds., *The Aldine Crime and Justice Annual.* Chicago: Aldine.

Bordua, David
  1967 "Recent Trends: Deviant Behavior and Social Control." *American Academy of Political and Social Science* 57:149–163.

Chilton, Roland, and DeAmicis, Jan
  1975 "Overcriminalization and the Measurement of Consensus." *Sociology and Social Research* 59 (July):318–329.

Durkheim, Emile
  1952 *The Division of Labor in Society.* Translated by George Simpson. New York: Free Press.

Erikson, Kai T.
  1964 "Notes on the Sociology of Deviance." Pp. 9–22 in Howard S. Becker, ed., *The Other Side: Perspectives on Deviance.* New York: Free Press.

Finestone, Harold
  1976   *Victims of Change: Juvenile Delinquents in American Society.* Westport: Greenwood Press.

Gibbs, Jack P.
  1966   "Conceptions of Deviant Behavior: the Old and the New."*Pacific Sociological Review* 9 (Spring):9–14.

Gibbs, Jack P., and Erickson, Maynard L.
  1975   "Major Developments in the Sociological Study of Deviance." *Annual Review of Sociology* 1:21–42.

Goode, Erich
  1972   Book Review: *"Observations of Deviance"*ed. by Jack D. Douglas and *"Juvenile Delinquency: A Reader."* ed. by James E. Teele. *Contemporary Sociology* 1 (May):207–209.

Goode, Erich
  1975   "On Behalf of Labeling Theory." *Social Problems* 22 (June):570–583.

Gouldner, Alvin
  1968   "The Sociologist as Partisan: Sociology and the Welfare State." *American Sociologist,* May:103–116.

Gove, Walter
  1970   "Societal Reaction as an Explanation of Mental Illness: an Evaluation."*American Sociological Review* 35 (October):873–884.
  1980   "The Labeling Perspective: an Overview." Pp. 9–32 in Walter R. Gove, ed., *The Labelling of Deviance.* 2d ed. Beverly Hills, Calif.: Sage.

Kent v. *United States*
  1966   383 U.S. 541, 16L. Ed. 2d 84, 86 S. Ct. 1045

Kitsuse, John I.
  1964   "Societal Reaction to Deviant Behavior: Problems of Theory and Method." Pp. 87–102 in Howard S. Becker, ed., *The Other Side: Perspectives on Deviance.* New York: Free Press.

Lemert, Edwin M.
  1951   *Social Pathology.* New York: McGraw-Hill.
  1967   "The Juvenile Court—Quest and Realities." Pp. 91–106 in the President's Commission on Law Enforcement and Administration of Justice, *Task Force Report: Juvenile Delinquency and Youth Crime.* Washington, D.C.: U.S. Government Printing Office.
  1971   *Instead of Court: Diversion in Juvenile Justice.* Public Health Service Publication No. 2127. Washington, D.C.: U.S. Government Printing Office.
  1972   *Human Deviance, Social Problems and Social Control.* 2d ed. Englewood Cliffs: Prentice-Hall.
  1974   "Beyond Mead: the Social Reaction to Deviance." *Social Problems* 21 (April):457–468.

Mankoff, Milton
  1971   "Societal Reaction and Career Deviance: a Critical Analysis."*Sociological Quarterly* 12 (May):204–218.

Manning, Peter
  1973   "Survey Essay on Deviance." *Contemporary Sociology* 2 (March):123–128.

Mead, George H.
  1918   "The Psychology of Punitive Justice." *American Journal of Sociology* 23:577–602.

Morris, Norval, and Hawkins, Gordon
  1969   *The Honest Politician's Guide to Crime Control.* Chicago: University of Chicago Press.

Nettler, Gwynn
  1974   *Explaining Crime.* New York: McGraw-Hill.

President's Commission on Law Enforcement and Administration of Justice
  1967   *The Challenge of Crime in a Free Society.* Washington, D.C.: U.S. Government Printing Office.

Rains, Prudence
  1975   "Imputations of Deviance: a Retrospective Essay on the Labeling Perspective." *Social Problems* 23 (October):1–11.

Rains, Prudence, and Kitsuse, John I.
  1973   "Comments on the Labeling Approach to Deviance." Unpublished manuscript.

Reid, Sue T.
  1976   *Crime and Criminology.* Hinsdale, Ill.: Dryden Press.

Rossi, Peter H., et al.
  1974   "The Seriousness of Crimes: Normative Structure and Individual Differences." *American Sociological Review* 39 (April):224–237.

Scheff, Thomas J.
  1974   "The Labelling Theory of Mental Illness." *American Sociological Review* 39 (June):444–452.

Schrag, Clarence
  1974   "Theoretical Foundations for a Social Science of Corrections." Pp. 705–743 in Daniel Glaser, ed., *Handbook in Criminology.* Chicago: Rand McNally.

Schur, Edwin M.
  1971   *Labeling Deviant Behavior.* New York: Harper and Row.
  1973   *Radical Nonintervention: Rethinking the Delinquency Problem.* Englewood Cliffs, N.J.: Prentice-Hall.

Tannenbaum, Frank
  1938   *Crime and the Community.* New York: Columbia University Press.

Walton, Paul
  1973   "The Case of the Weathermen: Social Reaction and Radical Commitment." In Ian Taylor and Laurie Taylor, eds., *Politics and Deviance.* London: Penguin.

Wellford, Charles
  1975   "Labelling Theory and Criminology: An Assessment." *Social Problems* 3 (February):332–345.

Radical theorists contend that capitalist societies perpetuate the poverty and discrimination that spawn delinquency.

RADICAL THEORY

Radical theory has also gained prominence in recent years. Like labeling theory, it represents the culmination of a line of social thought which has progressively led away from the notion that delinquent tendencies are inherent in individuals and toward the notion that such tendencies are inherent in the way society makes rules, enforces those rules, and selectively punishes some people and not others.

According to radical theory, delinquency is the product of a perpetual class struggle in which the ruling segments of capitalist society (1) define what delinquent behavior is, based on their particular self-interests; (2) create the social conditions which make delinquents out of the children of working-class people; and then (3) devise legal machinery by which to maintain control over these children. Therefore, the rules and practices that govern delinquency and the criminogenic conditions that produce it are products of the inequities and injustices of a capitalist social order.

In this view of the sources of delinquency, radical theorists strongly imply that human nature is inherently good. While children may be possessed of some selfish tendencies, they become really bad only if society defines or makes them that way. Hence, if they were liberated from the evils of the class struggle, the cooperative instincts of the young would become dominant and a humane, crime-free society would emerge.

ORIGINS

Radical beliefs of this type are not really new. Why, then, did they experience a revival in the last third of the 20th century? In part, they can be traced to the crises that arose in America during the 1960s and 1970s: the civil rights protests and urban riots, the Vietnam war, the Watergate coverup, and the evidence of corruption among America's political leaders (Krisberg and Austin, 1978:4). Furthermore, when the effects of events such as these were coupled with a growing sense of dismay over the decay of American cities, the Third World struggles against colonialism, the persistence of sexual inequality, the worldwide destruction of the environment, and the escalating arms race, and further frustrated by the seeming inability of the average citizen to do anything about these matters, faith in traditional values and the American system was gravely weakened. The nation experienced a crisis of legitimacy (Schaar, 1974).

This crisis not only undermined the principles and sources of authority upon which order and obedience are based but also contributed to widespread social despair. Pessimistic critics, many of them students, renounced their faith in the American system of justice, the capitalist division of labor, and the world of technology. They also made universities and academics the target of attack:

> Time is short; we cannot wait years for research to give us impregnable theses. America's academia fiddles while the fires are burning. Where are the studies of the new corporate power, of the Defense Department, of the military-industrial complex, of the new bureaucracies, of Vietnam? American academics are prisoners of liberal democratic ideology. Even as the chains rust, they do not move. A new current of reason and passion is arising in America—outside of its conventional institutions. The current of reason must flow faster to create an image of reality and hope for the future, for a ruling class in despair will soon reach for some other kind of ideology, and all that is left for the American establishment is "patriotism," that is fascism (quoted by Bendix, 1970:831).

In such a climate, it is not surprising that a new view of American justice should emerge. Responding to these feelings of despair, a new generation of criminologists began to search for political and legal alternatives. Radical theory is one result. It expresses dismay over the past, places blame on capitalist rulers for having created crime and injustice, and provides a different course of action for the future. In constructing this new view of delinquency and

justice, however, radical theorists did not create an entirely new body of theory. Rather, along with labeling theory, they borrowed heavily from two other bodies of theory: conflict theory and Marxian theory.

CONFLICT THEORY

In support of their belief that society is characterized by injustice and class conflict, radical theorists argue that greater attention should be paid to the nature of existing laws and the individuals served by those laws. They point out that it was not until early in this century that much attention was paid to these matters. At that time, however, a number of legal scholars were responsible for the development of a legal philosophy known as *sociological jurisprudence.* In order to understand the law, these scholars argued, one must examine its relationship to the social order: study its history in relation to the culture in which it developed and determine in what ways the law reflects the underlying values and morals of its people.

The social nature of law

Sociological jurisprudence emphasizes that the law is not merely a set of formal rules, immutable and unchangeable, but rather a dynamic body of norms heavily influenced by the society of which it is a part (Pound, 1942). It not only reflects this society, but also influences this society. As Quinney put it, the law is "both a social product and a social force" (1974:6). Like other cultural elements, it originally reflects the main course of a civilization and its people, and then, in a sense, takes on a life of its own—it helps to shape the course of a civilization as well as to be shaped by it.

A second point emphasized by sociological jurisprudence is that the law is a form of social engineering which will ultimately improve the social order. Roscoe Pound, who was perhaps the foremost proponent of this idea, believed that the law regulates social behavior and establishes the kind of social organization that will eventually, perhaps inevitably, improve society:

> I am content to see in legal history the record of a continually wider recognizing and satisfying of human wants or desires through social control; a more embracing and more effective securing of social interests; a continually more complete and effective elimination of waste and precluding of friction in human enjoyment of the goods of existence—in short, a continually more efficacious social engineering (1922:98–99).

Finally, sociological jurisprudence suggests that the law is an instrument for reconciling the many competing and different interests in society. It is a means of protecting the needs of the little people from the wishes of the powerful, seeing that justice is done for the lawbreaker, and mediating between the conflicting demands of many interests groups (Fuller, 1971; Selznick, 1968). The law, in short, represents society's attempt to accomplish the greatest good for the greatest number of people.

Few scholars today would take issue with the view that the law does have roots deep in our cultural history and is a force that strongly shapes the future. But radical criminologists sharply disagree with the notion that the law necessarily improves society or that it equitably serves the interests of all. Such a view, they suggest, represents a consensual view of social order: it assumes that there is general agreement among the members of society on basic goals and on the laws that should govern the pursuit of those goals.

This view, radicals argue, is a mythical contruction of reality designed to preserve order in an unjust society. Society is not organized by a widespread consensus, but by the exercise of undisguised power by a small ruling class (Quinney, 1974:*v*). "[T]hose who control the means of production also control the production of values in the society" (Chambliss, 1976:3). As a consequence, legal scholars have based their views of the nature and purpose of law upon a misguided, potentially sinister conception of the way social order is maintained. Perhaps even worse, the same is true of most social scientists. From Lombroso to Sutherland, from Freud to Cloward and Ohlin, they have developed theories of delinquency which not only provide misleading descriptions of its causes, but also furnish the ruling class with an ideology for maintaining its own self-serving brand of social control (Quinney, 1974:3–4).

In order to understand how this came about, say radical criminologists, it is necessary to contrast the *consensus* concept of social order, within which scientific positivists have conducted their analyses of delinquency, with the *conflict* framework, within which radical theorists have conducted their research.

The consensus framework

The consensus framework evolves from a long tradition in science which has stressed the importance of trying to understand any phenomenon in its entirety, whether it is the human body, the solar system, or society (Merton, 1968: chap. II). How do all parts of society contribute to its ongoing operation? Which of its parts and functions are necessary for it to survive? If some basic part is destroyed, how does society adapt? By attempting to answer such questions, scientists have sought to identify the key structural elements of any social system and to indicate how they function in its operation.

Advocates of the consensus model have assumed that while all the parts of society are never fully integrated, they do tend toward a condition of stability and equilibrium (Van den Berghe, 1963:695–97). While total stability is never fully achieved, it is toward stability that society moves. If change occurs, it is more likely to occur in gradual fashion rather than in a revolutionary or violent way. But, above all, societal integration and stability are made possible by the general agreement among its citizens on basic values and beliefs. In its most ideal form, therefore, the consensus model suggests that

> (1) society is a relatively persistent stable structure; (2) it is well integrated; (3) every element [in it] has a function; and (4) [it possesses] a functioning social structure . . . based on a consensus of values (Quinney, 1970:9 from Dahrendorf, 1959:161–163).

According to this model, then, there would be little disagreement in identifying the delinquent. By definition, a delinquent is anyone who rejects the community's basic values, violates the law, and threatens the stability of the whole. As the French sociologist Emile Durkheim put it, "The only common characteristic of crimes is that they consist . . . in acts *universally disapproved of* by members of each society" (1949:73 emphasis added).

People seek to control delinquency because they are uniformly against it. Furthermore, since the consensus model assumes that moral values are widely shared in society, it implies that anyone who becomes a delinquent is a person who has become somehow different from law-abiding people—a person who suffers from some psychological abnormality, is undersocialized, or has learned subcultural standards for behavior which run counter to those of the larger community. In some way, the delinquent is different. In seeking to control delinquency, therefore, efforts must be directed toward determining the causes for delinquent behavior and finding ways by which those causes can be remedied or prevented.

The conflict framework

In sharp contrast to this point of view, radical criminologists argue that the analysis of social order should be cast within the framework of a conflict model. Like the consensus framework, this model has a long and respected history in scientific study (Dahrendorf, 1959). But, unlike the consensus model, it attributes much less influence to shared traditions and mutual agreement as the sources of order. Instead, it stresses the importance of social change and the exercise of power by a limited few. It assumes that:

> (1) at every point society is subject to change; (2) it displays at every point dissension and conflict; (3) every element contributes to change; and (4) it is based on the coercion of some of its members by others (Quinney, 1970:9).

According to this point of view, then, society is held together, not by an overriding consensus on basic values and rules, but by force and constraint. Although certain values predominate, they are enforced more by dominant power groups than by the members of society as a whole (Chambliss, 1973; Dahrendorf, 1958; Turk, 1969). Hence, conflict theorists believe that while different ethnic groups or social classes may cling to their own unique values and customs, social order throughout society is maintained through the exercise of power by a ruling class. Acts are defined as delinquent because, and only because, it is in the interests of the ruling class to so define them.

If this is the case, the causes for delinquency are not to be understood by trying to explain the behavior of the delinquent. That is a fruitless task. Delinquency is merely a label attached to the youth whose behavior is contrary to the interests and morality of the ruling class. If we wish to understand it, therefore, we must concentrate on the distribution of power in society and the processes by which laws are written and labels attached to some individuals and not others.

MARXIAN THEORY

The interest of radical criminologists in the history of class conflicts and social order also springs from a second theoretical source: Marxian theory. Karl Marx was a German philosopher (1818–83) whose writings reflect the economic and social ferment that accompanied the growth of Western industrial capitalism in the early and middle 19th century. Like radicals today, Marx was a conflict theorist who adopted a dialectical theory of human progress: he viewed history as a reflection of a perpetual struggle between the economic classes.

Marx obtained the seeds for his dialectical theory from Georg Friedrich Hegel, another German philosopher (1770–1831). Along with others, Hegel had been bothered by the fact that philosophers had never been able to develop an explanatory system for the world because it was constantly changing (Taylor, 1967:8). In order to deal with this condition, he constructed a dialectical theory of change.

Webster's dictionary defines the term *dialectic* as the "practice of weighing and reconciling . . . contradictory arguments for the purpose of arriving at truth, especially through discussion and debate." Hegel suggested that whenever some basic idea prevails in society—he called it the "thesis"—that idea is eventually challenged by an opposing idea—the "antithesis." A conflict between the two ideas usually ensues, but rarely is there a clearcut victory for either side. Rather, a new "synthesis" of the two ideas emerges. In time, this synthesis is accepted and becomes the prevailing thesis. But, true to the march of history, the new thesis is challenged in turn by a new antithesis. Once again a new synthesis emerges, and thus mankind rolls forward and upward. This was Hegel's way of accounting for human progress and social change.

While he made use of Hegel's idea, Marx suggested that change is due, not to the conflict of contrasting ideas, but to the conflict of competing economic systems. History is a succession of economic arrangements in which the weak must forever struggle against exploitation by the powerful. The inevitable consequence of this struggle, however, is a succession of ever-improving economic orders. Time after time, the powerful are eventually overthrown by angry workers who rise up against their oppressors and install a more just order.

Marx's theory, therefore, became a theory of "dialectical materialism." Human progress, he suggested, is due to the rise and fall of contrasting economic systems rather than to the rise and fall of contrasting ideas.

Nature of economic history

Forcing history into this mold, Marx argued that humankind has gone through three major economic and social epochs: ancient slave society, feudal society of the Middle Ages, and capitalism (Meyer, 1968). Each has represented a step forward in the inevitable progress of humanity, but each has also included the seeds of its own destruction. Capitalism, for example, represents the peak of social development thus far. It has overthrown the stagnating influence of feudalism, provided abundant material goods, and instituted constitutional government. But capitalism—today's prevailing economic thesis—also possesses weaknesses that will lead to a new synthesis.

The ruling class under capitalism—the bourgeosie—has made the accumulation of wealth and property its goal rather than continuing to pursue fundamental human rights or using its wealth to eliminate human misery and chaos. The result has been the movement of larger and larger masses of people—the proletariat—into dehumanizing positions in society. Although people are inherently social and inclined to pursue freedom, these virtues have been distorted and imprisoned by capitalist economic arrangements. Workers have been converted into a commodity whose labor, talents, and personalities are for sale on the free market. Like any other element of production, these precious qualities are bought and sold. Human dignity and the worth of the individual have been sacrificed to the prevailing interests of the bourgeosie in accumulating wealth (Taylor et al. 1973:219–20).

Although this development has acted to dehumanize the masses, it has served one valuable purpose: it has helped to create the conditions that will lead to a liberated civilization. "Society as a whole is more and more splitting into two great hostile camps, . . . bourgeosie and proletariat" (Marx and Engels, 1955:10). Eventually, this split will lead to a new and final synthesis—an epoch of socialism, a dictatorship by the proletariat—in which all vestiges of capitalism will be liquidated, the class struggle will cease, and the historical dialectic will come to an end.

"In place of the old bourgeois society, with its classes and class antagonism, we shall have an association in which the free development of each is the condition for the free development of all" (Marx and Engels, 1955:32). The proletariat will become the liberators of society, rising above all narrow interests and ideologies to liberate humankind from the curses of property and class. The Millennium will have been reached.

Propositions of radical theory

Radical theory is a direct reflection of these historical antecedents. Following are six propositions by Richard Quinney (1974:24) which represent a contemporary expression of them.

1. "American society is based on an advanced capitalist economy."   The term *capitalism* is generally used to refer to an economic system in which "the greater proportion of economic life, particularly ownership of an investment in production goods, is carried on under private (i.e., nongovernmental) auspices through the process of economic competition and the avowed incentive of profit." (Cole, 1964:70). Those who favor such a system argue that if left free from governmental interference, capitalism maximizes production and results in the most equitable distribution of scarce resources.

Radical theorists maintain, however, that capitalism denotes a system in which the private owners of the means of production extract a profit by paying laborers less than the full value of their labor, thus exploiting them. This is particularly true in an advanced capitalist economy like ours where control has passed into hands of fewer and fewer financiers, bankers, and corporate investors who, though they are divorced from the day-to-day management of industrial enterprises, extract huge profits from them.

2. "The state is organized to serve the interests of the dominant economic class, the capitalist ruling class."   The few people who dominate the huge corporations and financial institutions are those who constitute the ruling class in American society. It is "that class which owns and controls the means of production and which is able, by virtue of the economic power thus conferred upon it, to use the state as its instrument for the domination of society" (Miliband, 1969:23).

This domination is not limited to the oppression of workingclass people; it overlaps with, and includes, other groups as well:

Youths. "Young people form a subservient

class, alienated, powerless, and prone to economic manipulation" (Krisberg and Austin, 1978:1).

Women. "Capitalism and sexism are intimately related. . . . Sexism is not merely the prejudice of individuals; it is embedded in the very economic, legal, and social framework of life in the United States" (Rafter and Natalizia, 1981:81).

Racial minorities. America is a racist country in which capitalism has not only resulted in the systematic oppression of black people, but the oppression of red, yellow, and brown people as well (Burns, 1974; Takagi, 1981).

For the sake of economic profit, in short, capitalism has systematically exploited and oppressed all of these people.

3. *"Criminal law is an instrument of the state and ruling class to maintain and perpetuate the existing social and economic order."* Law is "the ultimate means by which the state secures the interests of the ruling class. Laws institutionalize and legitimize the existing property relations" (Quinney, 1974:23). Even our delinquency laws are designed to accomplish this purpose. They were written by a group of elitist child savers who

> were concerned not with championing the rights of the poor against exploitation by the ruling classes but rather with integrating the poor into the established social order and protecting "respectable" citizens from the "dangerous classes." Given this perspective, it is not surprising that the child savers sought curbs on immigration, staunchly defended the unequal distribution of wealth, and discussed ways of imposing birth control on the lower classes. The child savers regarded the children of the urban poor with a mixture of paternalism and contempt (Platt, 1971:*ix*).

The only concern of the child savers was with keeping such children under control, thus securing their selfish economic interests.

4. *"Crime control in capitalist society is accomplished through a variety of institutions and agencies established and administered by a governmental elite, representing ruling class interests, for the purpose of establishing domestic order."* In the simple, undeveloped societies of earlier centuries, the modern state with its governing elite of armed policemen, judges, prison wardens, and other officials was unknown. Rather, order was maintained by democratic means in a communal social system. But, with the rise of capitalism, new methods of control were required. The emergence of a new ruling class required that the state be invented "as a means for coercing the rest of the population into economic and political submission" (Engels, 1942):

> It is through the legal system, then, that the state explicitly and forcefully protects the interests of the capitalist ruling class. Crime control becomes the coercive means of checking threats to the existing social and economic arrangements. The state defines its welfare in terms of the general well-being of the capitalist economy (Quinney, 1974:23–24).

5. *"The contradictions of advanced capitalism—the disjunction between existence and essence—require that the subordinate classes remain oppressed by whatever means necessary, especially through the coercion and violence of the legal system."* Capitalist society dehumanizes and alienates people because of the contradictions inherent in it (Edwards et al., 1974:430–34):

> Though it has created a wealth of consumer goods, it has failed to provide for "creative and socially useful work, meaningful community, and liberating education for

individual development" (Edwards et al., 1974:431).

It has been predicated on the pursuit of profit by creating obsolescent consumer goods and military waste, a pursuit that undermines the legitimacy of the irrational system that produced it.

It makes promises it cannot deliver. There is no hope, for example, that it will provide the means by which women, the poor, racial minorities, and the members of the Third World can be liberated.

It draws an ever larger share of the world's population into alienating wage and salary work, thereby creating an enormous expansion of exploited people.

By fostering education and worldwide communication so that its enterprises can be manned, it has created a sophisticated proletariat who grow increasingly dissatisfied with the present division of labor and unequal distribution of power. In short, capitalism has created a great gulf between humankind's present existence and its true essence.

Given this state of affairs, it is clear that the legal system must resort to whatever means necessary to maintain control over the exploited and dehumanized classes for several reasons:

The criminal law is obviously not the product of custom and consensus but "is a set of rules laid down by the state in the interests of the ruling class."

"[S]ome criminal behavior is no more than the 'rightful' behavior of persons exploited by extant economic relations—what makes their behavior criminal is the coercive power of the state to enforce the will of the ruling class."

"[C]riminal behavior results either from the struggle between classes wherein

individuals of the subservient classes express their alienation from established social relations or from competition for control of the means of production." (Chambliss, 1976:6).

Even the juvenile justice system was designed to advance the interests of the capitalist system and to insure an excess labor supply:

> The juvenile court system was part of a general movement directed towards developing a specialized labor market and industrial discipline under corporate capitalism by creating new programs of adjudication and control for "delinquent," "dependent," and "neglected" youth. This in turn was related to augmenting the family and enforcing compulsory education in order to guarantee the proper reproduction of the labor force (Platt, 1974:377).

Delinquents, in other words, are idle, obscene, dirty children who are in danger of producing not only crime but more children like themselves. Hence, it has been necessary to find legal means to discipline them; otherwise they would be unprepared to man the alienating system of capitalist work.

6. *"Only with the collapse of capitalist society and the creation of a new society, based on socialist principles, will there be a solution to the crime problem."*   Since capitalist rulers define any behavior as criminal that threatens the capitalist system, crime and delinquency can never be eliminated until that system is destroyed. The only alternative is a socialist system of government that places the ownership and control of the means of production into the hands of the community as a whole. "When there is no longer the need for one class to dominate another, where there is no longer the need for a legal system to secure the interests of a capital ruling class, then there will no longer be the need for crime" (Quinney,

1974:25). Once humankind is liberated from the curses of property and class, as Marx suggested, a crime-free, truly equalitarian society will emerge.

POLICY IMPLICATIONS

One cannot think in traditional terms when considering the policy implications of radical theory. Unlike other theories, it denies that the delinquency problem can be solved by working within the framework of capitalist society, tampering with its system of juvenile justice, or trying to rehabilitate juvenile offenders. Since crime in inherent in the alienating and oppressive character of the capitalist system, it is the classist, ageist, sexist, and racist rulers of that system who are the real criminals, not the ordinary street offenders who are their victims. Therefore, the only solution is socialist revolution.

Prescriptions for revolution

In the 19th century, Karl Marx and Frederich Engels (1967:120–21) argued that the only way any change could be made was by the violent overthrow of capitalist society. Radical criminologists, however, have not gone that far, at least not explicitly. Instead, they appear to believe that as criminologists, they should join others in promoting a self-conscious and self-educated political movement designed to promote radical change by peaceful means:

> Our task as students of crime is to consider the alternatives to the capitalist legal order. . . . At this advanced stage of capitalist development, law is a little more than a repressive instrument of manipulation and control. We must make others aware of the current meaning of crime and justice in America. The objective is to move beyond the existing order. And this means ultimately that we are engaged in socialist revolution (Quinney, 1974:25).

Two steps must be taken in order for by this revolution to become a reality. The leaders of such a political movement must:

1. *Understand the contradictions of capitalist society.* We must become better aware of the dialectical nature of history and the contradictions inherent in capitalism, as outlined earlier. The mere acknowledgement of these contradictions, however, is not enough, nor are individual rebellions, strikes, or campus protests. "The capitalist class is a privileged and exploiting class, and it is not about to give up its special place without resistance. It will . . . mystify discontent, offer sham concessions, co-opt leaders and causes, . . . and suppress movement organizations" (Edwards et al., 1974:432). Thus, a second developmental step is required.

2. *Create class consciousness.* "Fundamental social change will occur only if a self-conscious class emerges and engages in organized political struggle." This class "must articulate and struggle for a vision of a liberated society, in which all social relations are transformed and all hierarchical divisions of labor are abolished" (Edwards et al., 1974:432).

But what is the vision for which people should struggle? What are the goals of a liberated socialist society? How will it be organized?

The liberated society

The goals of the liberated society are clearly stated as follows: a society would be created in which all class and status differences, would end and nonalienating work, cooperation, and the use of production to meet human needs would begin; group differences and individual rights would be guaranteed; human greed and the historical tendency for people to disagree over religious, political, economic, or cultural differences would disappear; all racism, sexism, poverty, and crime would be eliminated (Edwards et al., 1974:433–434). Though the history of civilization has been characterized by value conflict and clashing interests, order in the new liberated society would apparently be maintained by an enlightened consensus.

Despite these impressive goals, the organizations of the liberated society is not clearly stated by radical theorists. They do suggest that private ownership of capital would be abolished and the wealth redistributed; all governmental bureaucracies and other social hierarchies would be destroyed; monolithic criminal law would be eliminated and replaced with local community laws (if such are necessary); and people would become self-governing and self-managing (Edwards et al., 1974:433–34; Quinney, 1972).

But, if all people are to be made equal and self-managing, without any differences in wealth or status and without the need for any governmental or industrial bureaucracies, an institutional redesign of the greatest magnitude is implied. Presumably the Constitution of the United States, its Bill of Rights, its system of government, and its legal, economic, and educational institutions would have to be drastically changed or eliminated. Hence, the need for a socialist blueprint of some kind is strongly implied, particularly since we are talking about the total alteration of an exceedingly complex, ethnically heterogeneous, highly technological society of more than 225 million people.

Indeed, in taking issue with the value-neutral stance of positivistic criminologists, Chambliss says that "the ultimate test of a theory's utility is not its logical structure or its 'fit' with empirical data, but its ability to create workable recipes for changing the existing set of social conditions (both material conditions and the superstructure derived therefrom)" (1976:3). Astonishingly, however, radicals have either failed to provide "workable recipes" thus far or have disavowed the need to be specific. To do so, Edwards et al. suggest, would be to appear excessively "utopian:"

> We cannot present a blueprint or an exact specification of how a socialist "utopia" would work; nor should we attempt to do so, since constructing imaginary utopias bears little relation to the actual task of building a decent society. Any *real* alternatives to capitalism will be historically linked to the forces and movements generated by the contradictions of capitalist society itself. *New institutions which liberate rather than oppress can only be created by real people confronting concrete problems in their lives and developing new means to overcome oppression.* The political movements arising from capitalism's contradictions therefore constitute the only means for society to move from its present condition to a new and more decent form, and only out of these movements will human as well as practical new institutions be generated (1974:433. emphasis added.)

In other words, radical doctrine should be accepted on faith. Having experienced a generation of social despair over the contradictions of capitalism, America should join its radicals in pursuing the socialist vision of tomorrow, even if it is somewhat clouded.

IMPACT ON POLICY

This philosophy has great implications. It helps us to focus on economic factors which other theories overlook or underplay. Cultural deviance theory, for example, stresses the ambiguous position of youths in American society: they are neither child nor adult; they do not have a responsible and productive role to play in society; left in a structural vacuum, their delinquent acts may be due to the development of deviant norms among them. Radical theory, however, helps to explain why these conditions have occurred. Capitalism and the Industrial Revolution have created an affluent machine-intensive society in which less and less human power is needed. Many young people, particularly those who are poor, are on a transmission belt that goes nowhere. There are no permanent jobs for them, and there will be none when they are adults.

Radical theory also enriches our sense of human possibility. Since the search for justice is based on hope, the values of radical theory, to those who despair, have a widespread appeal. Indeed, the period of social unrest from which radical theory grew, and probably the theory itself, resulted in the emergence of two activities which radicals feel must be present before revolution can occur: (1) the emergence of social movements that further highlighted the contradictions of capitalism, and (2) the creation of self-conscious groups as a result of these movements, that are still engaged in the struggle for economic and political power.

Civil rights.   During the 1960s, the franchise was extended to larger numbers of minority people: their consciousness was raised regarding the importance of organized political action and protest; the Civil Rights Act of 1964 prohibited discrimination in schools and places of employment, as well as in the voting booth; and the economic position of the black middle-class, if not others, was improved (See Geshwender, 1980a, 1980b; Glazer, 1980; Grimshaw, 1980; Williams, 1977; Wilson, 1980).

Poverty.   Efforts were made to reduce some of the more extreme effects of poverty through the Great Society programs—job training, preschool programs, Medicare and Medicaide, community action programs for the poor, legal services for the poor, and increased welfare benefits. And while questions remain regarding the degree to which these programs were successful (Cloward and Piven, 1974; Marris and Rein, 1973), the ideas which gave birth to them, at least for many Americans, were radical.

Women's rights.   The same was true of the women's rights movement (Friedan, 1963;

Millet, 1970). The Civil Rights Act of 1964 prohibited discrimination based on sex and today more women are entering the labor force than ever before. Hence, while women have not yet achieved political and economic equality, affirmative action on their behalf has produced a marked change in their favor in virtually every societal institution.

Children's rights.   Finally, efforts to eliminate oppression have been extended to children. "We are on the threshold of a new consciousness of children's rights," says Richard Farson, "a dramatically new concept of childhood itself. The fundamental change will be a recognition of the child's right to live with the same guarantee of freedom that adults enjoy, the basic right being that of self-determination" (*Los Angeles Times*, January 28, 1975).

This would be accomplished by writing into the Constitution a Bill of Rights for children analogous to the Equal Rights Amendment for women. In addition to bringing about reforms in juvenile justice, these rights would permit youngsters of all ages to (1) decide whether they wished to live with their parents, with someone else, or in state-run child care centers; (2) choose and design their own educational programs, including the option of no school attendance at all; (3) use alcohol or drugs and experience sex with no more restrictions placed upon them than those placed upon adults; (4) obtain employment; (5) manage their own money; (6) own credit cards; (7) enter binding contracts; (8) vote; and (9) share completely in the political process (Farson, 1974; Holt, 1974).

To be sure, these movements did not begin to give full expression to the implications of radical theory. Few of them, for example, were designed to eliminate capitalist ownership and place it in the hands of the workers. Furthermore, a conservative counterrevolution has developed in the 1980s which seeks to undo any changes that had been introduced.

Nonetheless, social movements that would have been radical a few years ago did emerge and did produce significant changes.

RADICAL INDICTMENT OF POSITIVE CRIMINOLOGY

Radical theory also had a marked impact on positive criminology because of its stinging indictment of positivists.

Positivists reinforce capitalist values

Radicals contend that positivists have been the enemies of freedom because they have helped to perpetuate the criminogenic values of capitalism—war, sexism, racism, and ageism. Because they do nothing about these values, criminologists ". . . systematically ignore moral questions about the legal order" (Quinney, 1974:13). What criminologists should be doing instead is redefining crime so that they become the guardians of human rights rather than defenders of a bankrupt and inhumane system (Schwendinger and Schwendinger, 1975).

Positivists falsify reality

Positivists have constructed a stereotyped of the delinquent "designed to convince us that [he] is different from the 'normal child' . . ." (Krisberg and Austin, 1978:118). Consequently, positive theories "must be exposed in terms of [their] racial, sexual, and class biases. . . ." (Krisberg and Austin, 1978:119). Rather than being viewed as representing reality, they "should be viewed as myths that can be used by oppressors to preserve the structure of domination" (Krisberg and Austin, 1978:120).

Positivists are technocratic servants of capitalism

Criminologists have provided the "brain trust" and the "technical skills" for the operation of the capitalist system of social control (Platt, 1974:356). Their research generates the ideas that "reproduce the hegemony of the existing relations of property, race, and sexual privilege" (Krisberg and Austin, 1978:119). Worse still, they do this" to regain prestige, to build research empires, or because they truly believe in the ideas of those in positions of power" (Krisberg and Austin, 1978:119). Consequently, "criminologists today are furnishing the information and knowledge necessary for the manipulation and control of those who threaten the social system" (Quinney, 1974:15).

Positivists propose false reforms

All of the foregoing criticisms taken together do not necessarily mean that positivists have failed to advocate reform. They had been critical of inefficiency, mismanagement, corruption, and brutality. They have urged reform in several ways: "reform of criminals, reform of the criminal justice system, and even reform of society. . . " (Platt, 1974:357). But in believing that such "technocratic solutions" as Mobilization for Youth, or decriminalization, diversion, due process, and deinstitutionalization would provide the answers, their efforts have been marked by a singular failure: they "are invariably formulated within the framework of corporate capitalism and designed to shape new adjustments to existing political and economic conditions" (Platt, 1974:357).

According to radicals, in short, positivists may be among the worst of criminals. "In the name of developing knowledge about crime, most criminologists support current institutions at the expense of human freedoms and social revolution" (Quinney, 1974:13). Indeed, given the gravity of the charges brought against criminology, as well as against capitalism, a most careful assessment of radical theory is warranted. If it does point the way to an equitable and crime-free society, that fact should be known.

ASSESSMENT OF RADICAL THEORY

Three major issues merit careful scrutiny in assessing radical theory: (1) its use of history to "demystify" law and legal practice; (2) its explanation for the existence of delinquency; and (3) its contention that crime would be eliminated if the means of production were placed in the hands of the working class.

Demystification of law and legal practice

Like labeling theory, radical theory has performed an extremely valuable service in directing our attention to the sources and effects of law and legal practice. Indeed, this book borrows heavily from some of the insights of labeling and radical theories.

1. Meaning of delinquency. We have seen that delinquency was legally invented in the 19th century as a result of historical changes that had been taking place for centuries. But this invention occurred, not because the behavior of children had changed, but because society had reorganized its methods for controlling children and had redefined the meaning of their behavior. Hence, it is clear that our analysis has helped to demystify this segment of our cultural history and to suggest that, in order to understand delinquency, we must look at the creation of law and systems of control as well as at the behavior of children.

2. Understanding creation of law. Radical theory has also been correct in suggesting that vagrancy and other laws have been written as a means of controlling members of the adult labor force and insuring that members of the working class do not disrupt the prevailing system of production (Chambliss, 1973; Krisberg and Austin, 1978: 7–11; Nelson, 1974). Yet, research does not support the view that poor and minority people are always subjected to harsher penalties than are higher status people (Chiricos and Waldo, 1975; Terry, 1967; Thornberry, 1973). Furthermore, Hagan and Leon (1977) found that the creation of the juvenile court did not result in a greater frequency of incarceration for working-class children, as radicals have contended:

> Although this legislation substantially changed the operations of the juvenile and criminal courts, probably with consequences both good and bad, intended and unintended, the overall effect was not to intensify a formal and explicit system of coercion, but rather to reinforce and increasingly intervene in informal systems of social control, particularly the family (Hagan and Leon, 1977:597).

Thus, while the greater use of historical analysis has helped to demystify the juvenile court, it has not always supported the radical belief that political and economic discrimination is the only reason for its existence. Other factors seem to have been at work.

3. Social science as oppressor. Radicals have also contended that the scientific study of delinquency has but one purpose: the legitimization of the existing social order. This contention, while possessing some truth, is grossly overstated.

One of the greatest achievements of social science is that it has played a leading role in altering the mythical view that any one legal or social system is inevitably superior: anthropologists have helped to demolish the belief of Western peoples that their values and institutions are always preeminent; the findings of social scientists have been instrumental in legal proceedings, for instance, in the 1954 Supreme Court decision which led to the desegregation of the public schools; sociologists and psychologists have helped to discount the notion that delinquency is solely the result of biological or genetic weaknesses by documenting the influence of cultural and structural factors; the conduct of self-report and victimization studies has served to document the existence of error and bias in arrest and court statistics; and, throughout this century, criminologists have called attention to society's protection of white-collar and other powerful criminals.

In short, the process of demystifying law and legal practice is not a new one and is not due just to the resurgence of radical theory (Meier, 1976). Yet, with all its limitations, radical theory does hold out the promise of a better understanding of law and justice, informed by a greater sense of history. It directs our attention to persistent discrimination and to collusion between governmental and ruling-class interests—matters to which criminologists have not paid enough attention. It correctly notes the persistence of exploitation, sexism, and racism. And it reminds us, as the 19th-century child savers needed reminding, that delinquency is not merely an expression of pathological individuals or depraved immigrant groups colliding with an eternally equitable and just legal system. Rather, that system, and its underlying values, must be taken into account and its contribution to creation of delinquents assessed. It is this lesson, therefore, that may constitute the greatest contribution of radical theory toward the demystification of the law.

Explaining delinquency

The contribution of radical theory to the explanation of delinquency is much less certain. Radical theorists assert that little is to be gained by trying to understand the causes of delinquent behavior. The only reason crime exists is because capitalism produces demoralization and because capitalist rulers create laws designed to discriminate against, and thereby control, the working class. Were the capitalism system eliminated, therefore, delinquent conduct would disappear.

1. Crime exists in every society. There is no doubt that poverty and discrimination are found in capitalist societies and that they are associated with delinquent behavior. But in asserting that these problems are peculiar to capitalism and would disappear in a socialist system, radicals fall prey to two of the same problems to which labeling theorists have had.

The first is the assumption that, if capitalists were not present to create the rules that define crime, there would be none of the *injuries*, the murders, the thefts, or the burglaries which those rules condemn. Clearly, such a contention is questionable, if not totally false. All societies—whether capitalist or socialist, developed or undeveloped—experience these injuries, and all have seen fit to condemn them. Hence, injuries are likely to exist, no matter who makes the rules that define them as crimes.

The second problem is that, like labeling theorists, radicals view the traditional criminal as an underdog. But while this perspective is badly needed, it can also lead to excesses, such as the suggestion that, because criminals are courageous opponents of an oppressive system, none of them merit being defined as criminal; indeed, each is a victim. Yet, for the same reasons that labeling theory was excessive, this perspective is excessive. Few criminals see their crimes as political crimes in which their main concern is with overthrowing oppression. Whether in capitalist or noncapitalist societies, there have always been predators who break rules for personal gain.

2. Causes for crime. Although crime exists in virtually every known society, radicals condemn other criminologists for seeking to explain it, asserting that their theories are nothing more than sophisticated rationalizations designed to justify oppression of poor people, minorities, women, and children. In light of this assertion, several issues should be considered.

First, Karl Marx's view of criminals was

unlike that of contemporary radicals. Marx was vitriolic in his condemnation of them. Such people, he maintained, are members of the *lumpenproletariat*—a "dangerous class," a "social scum," a "passively rotting mass thrown off by the lower layers of society" (Marx and Engels, 1967:92). Such people cannot be relied upon for any constructive actions. They are "a parasitic class living off productive labor by theft, extortion, and beggary, or by providing 'services' such as prostitution and gambling . . ." (Hirst, 1975:216).

Hence, in contrast to the notion that criminals are normal people, Marx clearly implied that they are different, and that some insight might be gained by trying to understand why this is so. Why do the lumpenproletariat, but not respectable members of the working class, succumb to the problems and pressures of capitalist society?

Second, the whole superstructure of radical theory rests upon the assumption that, since capitalist societies oppress the lower and working classes, class membership should be the best predictor of official delinquency and probably law-violating behavior. While it is true that poor and minority people are overrepresented in the juvenile justice system, the assumption that class membership is the best predictor of official delinquency is false.

Crime is related much more closely to age and sex than to social class. Whether in capitalist or noncapitalist societies, the highest crime-producing years usually occur during adolescence and young adulthood, and involve males far more than females. To be sure, radicals have suggested that youths are an oppressed group, and that this may account for the higher crime rates attributed to them. But even if that suggestion were accepted, what about the differences between males and females? Since females are supposed to be the more oppressed of the two, one should even expect higher crime rates among them. But

since this is clearly not the case, oppression alone cannot explain crime. Instead, there are other factors at work that require explanation.

Third, the findings of positive research are often contrary to radical theory. Radicals state that poverty and discrimination alone are responsible for delinquent behavior, and particularly arrest and trial; but positive research shows that poor attachment to home and school, a lack of commitment to conventional means for success, poor achievement, and identification with delinquent peers predict these outcomes among youths from all social classes, not just among those of the working or lower class.

Indeed, what about the crimes of advantaged youth? Why do they vandalize property, steal autos, use drugs, commit rape, and burglarize for the hell of it? Why have official crime rates increased more rapidly in affluent suburbs, in recent years, than in our urban centers? Not only do the crimes of bourgeosie youth require explanation, but also the evidence indicates that the agents of juvenile justice have not ignored them in favor of punishing only the poor.

In summary, then, this short review suggests that (1) crime and criminals are likely to exist in any society, not just capitalist societies; (2) chronic offenders may possess characteristics that distinguish them from more normal youths; (3) age and sex are far better predictors of delinquency that is class membership; (4) oppression alone will not explain differences in rates of delinquency among various segments of the population; and (5) positive theories have been useful in identifying factors that predict delinquency in all social classes, not just the lower class.

Why, then, do radical theorists disavow a concern with such matters? The answer lies in their preoccupation with capitalist rules and practices. Like labeling theorists, radicals are not much concerned with primary deviance, individual differences, or reasons for crime. Since it is political and economic oppression that determine the course of human events, the inclinations and motivations of individuals are unimportant. Indeed, if capitalism were destroyed, and people were left free to construct a socialist system, we would not need to worry about motives for crime or about ageism, sexism, classism, or racism. All would disappear. But how sound is this argument? In the remaining pages of this chapter, we will consider that question.

Elimination of crime

If taken at face value, radical theory implies a perspective for solving crime much different from the perspective dominating American thought thus far:

> Characteristically, Americans are individualists. If some good is achieved in the social order, Americans assume that some individuals deserve credit and reward for the accomplishment. On the other hand, existence of a social problem is assumed to imply that some persons must be individually to blame. If unemployment is too high, it must be the President's fault. If use of heroin proliferates, some organized crime boss must be responsible. If crime in general proliferates, it must be the doing of some perverse group of offenders. Curing or eliminating social problems is regarded as synonymous with curing or eliminating individual culprits. Identify the culprits, bring them to justice (or perhaps help them to overcome personal deficiencies), and the problem will be solved (Pepinsky, 1980:307).

By contrast, a truly radical perspective "assumes the dynamics of a social structure to be the source of crime and its control" (Pepinsky, 1980:308). Far more important than individuals are the ways that crime and criminality are affected by industrialization, technology, the division of labor, bureaucratic growth, and social stratification. These

elements of the social structure organize social relations, govern the passage of law, and produce crime and criminality. If crime is to be controlled, therefore, "it is unnecessary and even counterproductive to identify criminals or potential criminals as a prelude to implementing crime control measures" (Pepinsky, 1980:309). Rather, attention should be devoted to changing those elements of the social structure that produce crime.

For example, the invention of the juvenile court resulted in the creation of a large bureaucracy designed not only to control destructive acts like burglary and theft but also to enforce the modern concept of childhood. The court, in fact, was but one part of a much larger effort to insure the perpetuation of an age-segregated social system. As a result, many delinquents were produced, not merely because they committed predatory acts, but because society insisted on keeping them in school, penalizing them if they ran away from home, and preventing them from taking adult positions in the labor force. If one wanted to reduce delinquency rates, therefore, one might be more successful in doing so by reducing age-segregation, rewriting the laws, and reducing the power of the juvenile court—not by identifying and punishing status offenders.

The idea of structural change, however, is not new. It was suggested by labeling theorists, for example, when they recommended a policy of radical nonintervention in the lives of juveniles. By decriminalizing status offenses and diverting petty criminals, delinquency rates might be reduced without any change in the behavior of individual children. Nonetheless, the idea is a challenging one. In place of identifying and blaming individuals for crime, much might be accomplished by changing the structure and organization of societal institutions. But because they have failed to outline a strategy for doing this, radicals have been the object of serious criticism:

1. Eschewing reforms. David Downes suggests that "by equating specifiable and documented proposals for change with 'mere' reformism, by—indeed—dismissing the idea of gradual and therefore reversible change as contemptible (1979:11), radicals leave us without any clue as to what should be done. Thus, because they make a virtue out of obfuscation, they should not be too surprised when others view their proposals with caution.

Harold Pepinsky (1980), himself a radical, is more caustic. He contends that, by suggesting that the only real criminals are rich capitalists, Marxists do no better than liberal criminologists. Instead of outlining ways for changing the social structure, they simply blame the rich and would resocialize or even liquidate them (p. 300). Even more important, they provide no assurance that, if members of the working class were to assume power, they would somehow be more humane, more wise, and more just than those whom they were replacing.

> Even Marx (1963, originally published in 1843) himself conceded that political revolution alone was insufficient to rid a social system of class oppression and its byproduct, crime. Incapacitation of the rich and powerful cannot succeed in ending class oppression unless the revolutionaries themselves are disinclined to achieve wealth and power for themselves. Incapacitation of the rich and powerful itself implies a lust by some to gain power over others. It presages the rise to power of a "new class" (Djilas, 1957) of offenders, not an end to criminality (Pepinsky, 1980:307).

It is no wonder, then, that criminologists have been slow to entertain the notion that the only solution to the crime problem is a proletarian revolution. There is little in the experience of humankind that suggests such a solution would be viable.

2. Logical deficiencies. Radical theory also possesses some logical deficiencies which make it virtually impossible to confirm or deny. The most serious of these deficiencies is its circularity. That is, repression is inferred from capitalist society while capitalist society is explained by repression. Values which produce sexism, racism, poverty and crime are, at one and the same time, both the cause and the consequence of capitalism. But circularity is not the only problem of radical theory.

In relying upon the dialectical-conflict theory of social order, radical theory maintains that history has been characterized by a succession of economic orders in which the law inevitably reflects the interests of the powerful. "The problem with this position is that it can never specify the conditions under which law would not simply be an instrument of a currently powerful interest" (Taylor et al., 1973:266).

Every society allocates power and status according to some set of criteria. Indeed, social stratification is not unique to capitalism: the Egyptians made slaves of Jews, as did the Romans and the Babylonians; the status of women in most societies has been subservient to that of men; and children are treated differently from adults in most societies. Yet, "Critical criminologists too often write as if imperialism was monopolized by capitalist societies, as if the tanks had never rolled into Prague or Budapest, as if people in capitalist societies were utterly dehumanized (except where they are struggling heroically against the bosses)" (Downes, 1979:9).

This does not mean that exploitation and discrimination are to be considered inevitable. Nor does it mean that radicals have failed to ask important questions about capitalism. Rather, it is that they have allowed their questions to *stop* at capitalism, as if oppression and corruption were confined to its boundaries (Downes, 1979:9). China and Cuba are often cited as socialist societies whose streets are relatively safe from delinquents and criminals. But the same is also true of Norway, Finland, or Sweden, all of which are capitalist welfare states. Why is this? Conversely, countries such as China and Cuba are scarcely democratic countries in which there is freedom of choice, speech, and movement. Yet, because of their preoccupation with the weaknesses of capitalism, radicals have paid little attention to these matters. As a result, there is no alternative body of knowledge supplied by radicals by which their assertions can be confirmed or denied (Bottomore, 1972:4–5; Shichor, 1980).

3. Alternatives for viewing radical theory. Given these problems, there are two alternatives for interpreting radical theory. The first is to ignore its inconsistencies and accept it as a doctrine that is not to be confused with theories in the scientific tradition. This is an attractive alternative because mankind has always aspired to create a civilized utopia in which intolerance, exploitation, and crime no longer exist. Once the repressive rules of modern society were eliminated, love, brotherhood, and freedom would prevail.

The second alternative is to construct and test new theories in which the insights of radical theory would be combined with those of other theories. Cultural deviance, strain, and even interactionist theories, for example, might contribute much to the concern of radical theory with the dynamics of social structure and the need for altering this structure in the interest of reducing crime.

Likewise, several theorists have suggested that neither a conflict nor a consensus model, alone is adequate for explaining the origins and maintenance of order, but both having something to offer (Dahrendorf, 1959; Greenberg, 1976; Hills, 1971; Hopkins, 1975). Many of our laws, for example, do seem to reflect a high degree of *consensus*—laws that prohibit murder, assault, fraud, embezzlement, or rape. The interest of most people, not just the powerful, are served by them. Other laws produce *conflict* and are expressions of special interests—laws that prohibit marijuana use, gambling, vagrancy, or laws that encourage opportunities for women and minority groups. More attention could be devoted to the historical origins of both types of laws, the ways they are imbedded in the social structure, and ways by which that social structure might be altered in the interest of reducing crime.

If this alternative were chosen, however, it would not lend itself to the optimistic outlook inherent in radical theory. Radicals are correct in suggesting that criminologists are skeptical about the notion that delinquency and other forms of deviant behavior can ever be eliminated. Most scholars believe that we must be leery of utopian schemes because crime, like disease, is a normal aspect of human life (Durkheim, 1938:chap. 3). It is virtually impossible to conceive of a society in which all passion, all innovation, all inclinations to rebel would be so effectively managed that deviant behavior would be nonexistent, or that its elimination would even be desirable. To accomplish this, one would have to purchase harmony at the cost of creating a totalitarian state. Hence, the idea that either crime or disease can be ultimately vanquished involves "a particularly trivial kind of utopian dreaming. Out of control, malfunction and crime could possibly overcome life, but control could never succeed in more than keeping them to a level appropriate to the prevailing form of human life" (Bittner, 1970:49).

Paradoxically, some scholars make this argument not just because they assume that people remain unalterably bad, but because their standards of morality are constantly changing. Consider Durkeim's (1938:68) well-known allegory:

> Imagine a society of saints, a perfect cloister of exemplary individuals. Crimes, properly so called, will there be unknown; but faults which appear venial to the layman will create the same scandal that the ordinary offense does

in ordinary consciousness. If, then, this society has the power to judge and punish, it will treat them as such.

What Durkheim meant was that

> if all those acts we know as crime were extinguished, small differences in behaviour that have no moral significance [at present] would take on new and larger meaning [in the future]. Small improprieties and breaches of manners and good taste would become crimes of a lesser degree, and so on. In short, there *cannot* be a society of saints because a process of social redefinition operates continuously to insure that all the positions on the scale from wickedness to virtue will always be filled and that some will always be holier than others (Cohen, 1973:5).

In other words, there is a law in social relations which suggests that the solution to a current set of problems inevitably produces its own set of new problems. We mortals seem to have a chronic tendency to redefine misery, injustice, delinquency, or poverty in such a way that regardless of what we do about them, they are always with us (Cohen, 1973:5). There can be little doubt, for example, that actual rates of malnutrition, infant mortality, and disease during the Middle ages were higher than they are today. But we are no less concerned about them. Indeed, radical theory, itself, suggests that we are more concerned, since capitalism represents an improvement in morality over feudalism, and socialism will be an improvement over capitalism. Our standards are getting higher. But, if this is the case, why will morality stop improving in socialist society if it does not do so among the saints in heaven? Even if life is improved according to today's standards, it will be marked by serious problems according to tomorrow's standards, and some people will be defined as deviant for violating those standards.

Thus, while it is difficult to take issue with the impressive values and the humane society which radicals pursue, serious questions can be raised about their contention that only capitalist societies are criminogenic and that, if they were eliminated, crime would be eliminated.

SUMMARY AND CONCLUSIONS

Radical theory cannot be viewed as theories in the positivistic tradition are viewed. Instead, it is built upon an entirely different set of philosophical principles.

The cornerstone of the positivistic philosophy is based upon the Enlightenment notion that the application of scientific study to human affairs would lead to a better world. Although knowledge can be gained only by patience, skepticism, and considerable tolerance for uncertainty, scholarly investigation will contribute ultimately to humankind's long search for a more just and humane society.

Radical theorists argue that this faith not only reflects a particular set of questionable values, but that it is naive with respect to the way the world operates. By clinging to a positivistic philosophy, scientists not only fail to eliminate oppression and injustice, but give tacit approval to those who would perpetuate them. Radical theorists, as a consequence, suggest that criminologists should be guided by values which oppose the status quo. Since delinquency is the product of capitalist oppression, criminologists should be engaged in documenting this oppression, making the public aware of it, and joining in socialist revolution.

In brief, then, the radical school of criminology stresses research and action toward predetermined socialist goals while the positive school stresses tentativity and scholarly detachment in the pursuit of goals that are not always predetermined. Since ultimate truth is not known, scientists must keep an open mind while pursuing it. More than theories in the positivistic tradition, therefore, radical theory is doctrinal in character: it expresses beliefs that are laid down as true and beyond serious dispute. What, then, are these beliefs?

1. Assumptions about human nature and social order. Radical theory assumes that human nature is good. Were people not enslaved by the historical struggle between the classes, their humane inclinations would produce an enlightened and liberated civilization. The social order, by contrast, is characterized by conflict and coercion and maintained through the oppression of the masses by society's rulers.

2. Underlying content and logic of radical theory. The history of civilization has been characterized by a succession of economic arrangements in which the powerful have always exploited the weak. The period of advanced capitalism now existing in America is the latest development in this series of arrangements. A modern society like ours, its laws, and its legal system are organized to serve the capitalist ruling class. Delinquency, therefore, is any behavior that threatens the vested interests of this class.

3. Policy implications. Delinquency cannot be eliminated by working within the framework of a capitalist society or by attempting to reform its system of juvenile justice. The only solution lies in the formation of class consciousness, the overthrow of capitalism, and the creation of a socialist society.

4. Assessment of radical theory. Radical theorists have extended the boundaries of knowledge in several important ways. They have questioned the limitations of positivistic philosophy, analyzed social conflict and its role in maintaining social order, stressed a better understanding of law and legal practice, and pointed out the persistence of sexism, racism, and exploitation in modern society.

At the same time, radical theory is marked by serious contradictions and omissions:

It presents a circular argument that is virtually impervious to confirmation or falsification.

By insisting that social order has always been characterized by conflict, it cannot specify the conditions under which law would not be an instrument of some powerful group. Yet, it concludes that socialist society will be characterized by cooperation, brotherhood, and equality.

In relying solely upon the notion that delinquency and crime are artifacts of political and economic oppression, it tends to deny that the delinquent label is ever earned by offenders or that their personal motivations, however induced, are important in explaining their acts.

It holds that crime will disappear in the liberated society, but it also maintains that capitalists are criminals. How will these enemies of socialism be treated? Will they not be defined as criminals?

It denies the possibility that cultural forces other than those which are political and economic have been instrumental in the creation of childhood and the invention of delinquency.

In concentrating upon class conflict, it ignores the fact that age and sex are more closely related to the commission of delinquent acts than is the class structure.

Given these problems, several questions might be raised. The first is concerned with the nature of radical philosophy. Radicals are correct in suggesting that traditional criminologists have tended to confine their research to the context provided by existing values and laws and that this practice sometimes gives tacit approval to injustice. But what about the radical approach to research?

What if investigators insisted on conducting research in which only their values provided the context for analysis? Would this not be like the anthropologist who goes to a foreign country and, without trying to understand the values which give rise to behavior there, judges that society as inferior because it does not conform to his values?

In some ways, that is what radical theorists have done. Like Marx, they have been more intent on using research to justify conclusions they have already reached than to weigh carefully both the pros and cons of their arguments. This approach to research is an old one, but it is closer to the version used by lawyers and debaters than that used by scientists. The object of science is not to win a debate or a legal case, but to weigh evidence on both sides of the question.

It must be pointed out, however, that positivists also have not been free of this problem. For a century now, the changing construction of delinquency has sometimes been as much the result of new values and beliefs as it has been the result of confirmed scientific evidence. Earlier groups of social scientists did not reject biological explanations, Freudian theory, or the mental testing movement for scientific reasons only. Their objections instead were often as value-laden and political as the radical movement today.

Hence, the differences between radicals and positivists are not absolute but rather a matter of degree. While positivists remain relatively more skeptical about the ultimate truth of their theories and proposed reforms, their personal values are apparent in their work nonetheless.

For these reasons, the ultimate tests of the radical school of criminology will remain much the same as it has for the positivist school. Its acceptance as a philosophy and as a method for studying and responding to delinquency will depend, in part, on its doctrinal character and, in part, on the evidence that can be found to support it. Thus far, the doctrine is much stronger than the evidence.

REFERENCES

Bendix, Reinhard
  1970   "Sociology and the Distrust of Reason." *American Sociological Review* 35 (October):831–843.

Bittner, Egon
  1970   *The Functions of the Police in Modern Society.* Washington, D.C.:U.S. Government Printing Office.

Bottomore, T. B.
  1972   *Varieties of Political Expression in Sociology.* Chicago: University of Chicago Press.

Burns, Haywood
  1974   "Racism and the American Law." Pp. 263–274 in Richard Quinney, ed., *Criminal Justice in America.* Boston: Little Brown.

Chambliss, William J.
  1973   *Functional and Conflict Theories of Crime.* New York: MSS Modular Publications.
  1976   "Functional and Conflict Theories of Crime: The Heritage of Emile Durkheim and Karl Marx." Pp. 1–30 in William J. Chambliss and Milton Mankoff Eds., *Whose Law? What Order?* New York: John Wiley & Sons.

Chiricos, Theodore G., and Waldo, Gordon P.
  1975   "Socioeconomic Status and Criminal Sentencing: An Empirical Assessment of a Conflict Proposition." *American Sociological Review* 40 (December): 753–772.

Cloward, Richard A., and Piven, Frances Fox
  1974   *The Politics of Turmoil.* New York: Pantheon Books.

Cohen, Albert K.
  1973   *The Elasticity of Evil: Changes in the Social Definition of Deviance.* Occasional Paper No. 7. Oxford: Oxford University Penal Research Unit.

Cole, G. D. H.
  1964   "Capitalism." Pp. 70–72 in Julius Gould and William L. Kolb, eds., *A Dictionary of the Social Sciences.* New York: Free Press.

Dahrendorf, Rolf
  1958   "Out of Utopia: Toward a Reorientation of Sociological Analysis." *American Journal of Sociology* 67 (September):115–127.
  1959   *Class and Class Conflict in Industrial Society.* Palo Alto: Stanford University Press.

Djilas, M.
  1957   *The New Class: An Analysis of the Communist System.* New York: Praeger Publishers.

Downes, David
  1970   "Praxis makes perfect: a critique of critical criminology." Pp. 1–16 in David Downes and Paul Rock, eds., *Deviant Interpretations.* New York: Barnes and Noble.

Durkheim, Emile
  1938   *The Rules of Sociological Method (1895).* Chicago: University of Chicago Press.
  1949   *The Division of Labor in Society.* New York: Free Press.

Edwards, Richard C; Reich, Michael; and Weisskopf, Thomas E.
  1974   "Toward a Socialist Alternative." Pp. 429–34 in Richard Quinney, ed., *Criminal Justice in America.* Boston: Little, Brown.

Engels, Friedrich
  1942   *The Origins of the Family, Private Property and the State.* New York: International Publishers.

Farson, Richard
  1974   *Birthrights: A Bill of Rights for Children.* New York: Macmillan.

Friedan, Betty
  1962   *The Feminine Mystique.* New York: Dell.

Fuller, Lon L.
  1971   "Human Interaction and the Law." Pp. 171–217 in Robert P. Wolff, ed., *The Rule of Law.* New York: Simon & Shuster.

Geshwender, James A.
  1980a   "On Analyzing Race Relations Without Theory." *Contemporary Sociology* 9 (March):215–218.
  1980b   "Response to Grimshaw and Glazer." *Contemporary Sociology* 9 (September):601–603.

Glazer, Nathan
  1980   "Comment on a Review Which Denies Black Progress." *Contemporary Sociology* 9 (September):599–600.

Greenberg, David F.
  1976   "On One-dimensional Marxist Criminology." *Theory and Society* 3:610–621.

Grimshaw, Allen D.
  1980   "A Different Perspective in Mutual Accommodation." *Contemporary Sociology* 9 (September):600–601.

Hagan, John, and Leon, Jeffrey
  1977   "Rediscovering Delinquency: Social History, Political Ideology and the Sociology of Law." *American Sociological Review* 42 (August):587–598.

Hills, S. L.
  1971   *Crime, Power, and Morality*. Scranton: Chandler.

Hirst, Paul Q.
  1975   "Marx and Engels on Law, Crime, and Morality." Pp. 203–232 in Ian Taylor, Paul Walton, and Jock Young, eds., *Critical Criminology*. Boston: Routledge and Kegan Paul.

Holt, John
  1974   *Escape from Childhood*. New York: Dutton.

Hopkins, Andrew
  1975   "On the Sociology of Criminal Law." *Social Problems* 22 (June):608–619.

Krisberg, Barry, and Austin, James
  1978   *The Children of Ishmael: Critical Perspectives on Juvenile Justice*. Palo Alto, Calif: Mayfield.

Marris, Peter, and Rein, Martin
  1973   *Dilemmas of Social Reform*. 2d ed. Chicago: Aldine.

Marx, Karl
  1963   *Karl Marx: Early Writings*. Translated and edited by T. B. Bottomore. New York: McGraw-Hill.

Marx, Karl, and Engels, Friedrich
  1955   *The Communist Manifesto (1848)*. S. H. Beer, ed.. New York: Appleton-Century-Crofts.
  1967   *The Communist Manifesto*. Baltimore: Penguin Books.

Meier, Robert F.
  1976   "The New Criminology: Continuity in Criminological Theory." *Journal of Criminal Law and Criminology* 67:461–469.

Merton, Robert K.
  1968   *Social Theory and Social Structure*. 3d ed. New York: Free Press.

Meyer, Alfred G.
  1968   "Marxism." Pp. 40–44 in David Sills, ed., *International Encyclopedia of the Social Sciences*. Vol. 10. New York: Macmillan.

Miliband, Ralph
  1969   *The State in Capitalist Society*. New York: Basic Books.

Millett, Kate
  1970   *Sexual Politics*. New York: Doubleday.

Nelson, William E.
   1974   "Emerging Notions of Modern Criminal Law in the Revolutionary Era: An Historical Perspective." Pp. 100–126 in Richard Quinney, ed., *Criminal Justice in America*. Boston: Little Brown.
Pepinsky, Harold E.
   1980   "A Radical Alternative to 'Radical' Criminology." Pp. 299–315 in James A. Inciardi, ed., *Radical Criminology: The Coming Crises*. Beverly Hills, Calif: Sage.
Platt, Anthony M.
   1971   "Introduction to the Reprint Edition." Pp. v–xvi in *National Conference of Charities and Correction, History of Child Saving in the United States*. Montclair, N.J.: Patterson-Smith.
   1974   "The Triumph of Benevolence: The Origins of the Juvenile Justice System in the United States." Pp. 356–389 in Richard Quinney, ed., *Criminal Justice in America*. Boston: Little, Brown.
Pound, Roscoe
   1922   *An Introduction to the Philosophy of Law*. New Haven: Yale University Press.
   1942   *Social Control through Law*. New Haven: Yale University Press.
Quinney, Richard
   1970   *The Social Reality of Crime*. Boston: Little, Brown.
   1972   "The Ideology of Law: Notes for a Radical Alternative to Legal Repression." *Issues in Criminology* 7 (Winter):1–35.
   1974   *Criminal Justice in America*. Boston: Little, Brown.
Rafter, Nicole Hahn, and Natalizia, Elena M.
   1981   "Marxist Feminism: Implications for Criminal Justice." *Crime and Delinquency* 27 (January):81–98.
Schaar, John H.
   1974   "Legitimacy in the Modern State." Pp. 62–92 in Richard Quinney, ed., *Criminal Justice in America*. Boston: Little, Brown.
Schwendinger, Herman, and Schwendinger, Julia
   1975   "Defenders of Order or Guardians of Human Rights?" Pp. 113–138 in Ian Taylor et al., eds., *Criticial Criminology*. Boston: Routledge and Kegan Paul.
Selznick, Philip
   1968   "The Sociology of Law." Pp. 50–59 in David L. Sills, ed., *International Encyclopedia of the Social Sciences*. Vol. 9. New York: Macmillan.
Shichor, David
   1980   "The New Criminology: Some Critical Issues." *British Journal of Criminology* 1 (January):1–19.
Takagi, Paul
   1981   "Race, Crime, and Social Policy: A Minority Perspective." *Crime and Delinquency* 25 (January):48–63.
Taylor, A. J. P.
   1967   "Introduction." Pp. 7–47 in Karl Marx and Friedrich Engels, *The Communist Manifesto*. Baltimore: Penguin Books.
Taylor, Ian; Walton, Paul; and Young, Jock
   1973   *The New Criminology*. New York: Harper & Row.

Terry, R. M.   "Discrimination in the Handling of Juvenile Offenders by Social Control
       Agencies." *Journal of Research in Crime and Delinquency* 4:218–230.

Thornberry, T. P.
    1973   "Race, Socioeconomic Status and Sentencing in the Juvenile Justice System."
       The Journal of Criminal Law and Criminology 64 (March):90–98.

Turk, Austin T.
    1969   *Criminality and the Legal Order.* Chicago: Rand McNally.

Van den Berghe, Pierre L.
    1963   "Dialectic and Functionalism: Toward a Synthesis. *American Sociological
       Review* 28 (October):695–705.

Williams, Robin W., Jr.
    1977   *Mutual Accommodation: Ethnic Conflict and Cooperation.* Minneapolis:
       University of Minnesota Press.

Wilson, William J.
    1980   *The Declining Significance of Race.* Chicago: The University of Chicago
       Press.

Neoclassical philosophers believe that we should return to the practice of punishing juveniles for their crimes.

NEOCLASSICAL THEORY

In this chapter, we turn to the final body of theory that sought to make sense out of the crime and turbulence of the 1960s. But in contrast to labeling and radical theories, which question whether any system of justice can be fair, this body of theory stresses the idea that the legal system should concentrate on *doing justice.*

Those who advocate this point of view are called *neoclassical* theorists. Convinced that the rehabilitative system of justice is without any redeeming value, they support a revival of the principles of classical criminology and a return to the practice of responding to crimes, not criminals. But while they agree on these points, they differ significantly on others.

Utilitarian philosophers believe that punishment serves two vitally important functions: (1) deterring potential offenders from committing crime, and (2) protecting society from those whose acts threaten the very existence of social order. *Just-deserts* philosophers, in contrast to utilitarians, question the utility of punishment as a means of deterring crime, and advocate its use only

because those who commit crime deserve to be punished. Since the rehabilitative system of justice has been nothing more than a vehicle for abuse, the only alternative is to restrict its power and replace it with a system based on classical principles.

In order to determine the grounds upon which these divergent constructions of reality are based, and to assess their implications for the future of juvenile justice, each will be analyzed separately.

UTILITARIAN PHILOSOPHY

Two persons—Ernest van den Haag (1975) and James Q. Wilson (1975)—have been primarily responsible for a sophisticated articulation of utilitarian philosophy. Their statements have been of immense importance during the past decade. Whereas positive theories and rehabilitation appeal to our compassionate sentiments, utilitarian theory and punishment appeal to the punitive feelings within us.

449

Assumptions about human nature

Van den Haag (1975:263–264) says that, for the past 200 years, theorists from Rousseau to Marx to Mao have argued that crime should be blamed on society's institutions because naturally good people are corrupted by them. Like Freud, however, he argues that just the reverse is true: "For the most part, offenders are not sick. They are like us. Worse, we are like them. Potentially, we could all be . . . criminals" (p. 118). Thus, it is humankind, not society, that is corrupt.

"If man were good by nature, no morality would be needed; he would always do what he should" (p. 23). But since people are naturally evil, the threats of law and punishment are imperative:

> If it became known that there are no conductors on trains anymore, the habit of paying would soon disappear. Driven only by their internalized moral sense, unsupported by conductors or policemen, fewer and fewer passengers would buy tickets. Cheating might be accepted enough to lose its disrepute. Ultimately, those who pay might be as few as those who now cheat (p. 23).

Wilson (1975) is somewhat more cautious on this matter. On the one hand, he is inclined, like most social scientists, to assume that people are neither good nor bad at birth, but are the product of socialization in a particular environment (pp. 57, 62). On the other hand, he clearly indicates that, for whatever reasons, wicked people do exist (p. 235). Hence, like van den Haag, he suggests that, were it not for the threat of law, many people would quickly take advantage of others. They are calculating, pondering society's reactions to wickedness and, if punishment is not forthcoming, they will engage in wicked acts themselves (p. 236). In short, both theorists suggest that most people would commit crimes if they dared.

Assumptions about social order

Like classical criminologists, van den Haag also assumes that society is held together by an implied social contract: "Human beings cannot exist but in society, and society is inconceivable without some order—we all owe society some allegiance in exchange" (p. 16). But since that allegiance is constantly threatened, people must be taught that conduct prohibited by law is wrong, regardless of the law. "Acts are forbidden either because [they are] regarded as inherently wicked (murder) or because, although not intrinsically wicked (e.g. driving on the wrong side of the street), they interfere with securing some good. Once forbidden, acts become offenses because they are unlawful, *whatever their moral quality* (p. 9, emphasis added).

Wilson is inclined to agree with van den Haag. Indeed, there is considerable consensus on the nature of acts that are inherently wicked:

> The most serious offenses are crimes not simply because society finds them inconvenient, but because it regards them with moral horror. To steal, to rape, to rob, to assault—these acts are destructive of the very possibility of society and [are] affronts to the humanity of their victims (1975:228–29).

In summary, then, utilitarian philosophers assume that, since most people will commit crime if given the chance, society is held together by a tenuous social contract. Were it not for the constraining influences of a shared morality and the threat of law, crime would be rampant and the preservation society would be impossible.

Bankruptcy of positive criminology

Given their assumptions about human nature and social order, both van den Haag and Wilson also contend that positive criminology is bankrupt.

1. Irrelevance of theory. First, positive criminologists have concentrated on trying to explain crime and discover its ultimate causes. But while this effort might help to make crime somewhat more intelligible for academic purposes, it is irrelevant for the conduct of social policy (van den Haag, 1975:77–78; Wilson, 1975:53):

> [U]ltimate causes cannot be the object of policy efforts precisely because, being ultimate, they cannot be changed. For example, criminologists have shown beyond doubt that men commit more crimes than women and younger men more (of certain kinds) than older ones. It is a theoretically important and scientifically correct observation. Yet it means little for policy makers concerned with crime prevention, since men cannot be changed into women or made to skip over the adolescent years (Wilson, 1975:55).

Second, van den Haag, if not Wilson, contends that because all people are inherently inclined to commit crimes, "the line between the offender and the nonoffender is as blurred as is the line between ordinary and extraordinary temptation" (1975:82). In other words, causes do not spell the difference between offenders and nonoffenders, but the degree to which each is subjected to temptation; the greater the temptation, the greater the criminality.

Finally, Wilson's (1975:67–70) experience with the President's Crime Commission between 1966 and 1968 convinced him that the policy recommendations of positivists are based on personal belief rather than scholarly knowledge. In recommending the War on Poverty, improvements in the quality of family life, or the enrichment of slum schools, positivists go beyond the implications of their data. Since they have never been able to prove that such efforts would reduce crime, they use liberal ideology, rather than scholarship, to justify their recommendations.

2. Futility of rehabilitation. By the same token, if positive theories are irrelevant, then the practice of rehabilitation, which is based upon them, is futile:

> If a child is delinquent because his family made him so or his friends encourage him to be so, it is hard to conceive what society might do about his attitudes. No one knows how a government might restore affection, stability, and fair discipline to a family that rejects these characteristics; still less can one imagine how even a family once restored could affect a child who has passed the formative years and in any event has developed an aversion to one or both of his parents (Wilson, 1975:54).

But even if these desirable goals could be accomplished, they are to be spurned. In seeking to control crime, it is far more important to do justice—to establish a direct link between crime and punishment—than it is to rehabilitate offenders (van den Haag, 1975:187). Consequently, we must adopt a more sober, less utopian, view of reality:

> I believe that our society has not done as well as it could have in controlling crime because of erroneous but persistent views about the nature of man and the capacities of his institutions. . . . I argue for a sober view of man and his institutions that would permit reasonable things to be accomplished, foolish things abandoned, and utopian things forgotten (Wilson, 1975:222–223).

Utilitarian principles

The sober view suggested by utilitarian philosophers is predicated upon two fundamental principles: (1) punishment deters crime; and (2) punishment vindicates the social order.

1. Punishment deters crime. Historically, positivists have rejected the classical argument that punishment deters crime because it assumes that people are rational—that, in pursuit of their own self-interest, they consciously decide to be criminal after having carefully balanced the gains against the losses. In some ways, both Wilson and van den Haag agree with positivists: people are not entirely rational. Yet, this does not mean that they are undeterrable:

> Prospective offenders need to be no more rational than rats are when taught by means of rewards and punishments to run a maze. . . . Legal threats are effective if those subjected to them are capable of responding to threats (whether or not capable of grasping them intellectually), of learning from each other, and of forming habits. Deterrence depends on the likelihood and on the regularity of human responses to danger, and not on rationality (van den Haag, 1975:113).

Most important of all, it should be remembered that punishment has not been devised with just the criminal in mind:

> It is a message addressed to the public at large. The punishment of the offender deters others by telling them: "This will happen to you if you violate the law." Deterrence protects the social order by restraining not the actual offender, who, *eo ipso,* has not been deterred, but other members of society, potential offenders, who still can be deterred. As an English judge succinctly remarked: "Men are not hanged for stealing horses, but that horses may not be stolen" (van den Haag, 1975:60–61).

2. *Punishment vindicates the social order.* Besides deterring potential offenders, punishment is also indispensable for the maintenance of social order. But in contrast to the usual tendency to view it as a form of social vengeance, it should be seen as *retribution*— fair payment, exacted by society, for the commission of crime. This fair payment, in turn, serves three functions.

First, it vindicates the legal order. "Prescribed by the law broken, and proportioned to the gravity of the offense committed, retribution is not inflicted to gratify or compensate anyone who suffered a loss or was harmed by crime—even if it does so—but to enforce the law and to vindicate the legal order" (van den Haag, 1975:2).

Second, retribution demonstrates society's willingness to pay its debts. "Laws threaten, or promise, punishments for crimes. Society has obligated itself by threatening. It owes the carrying out of its threats. Society pays it debt by punishing the offender, however unwilling he is to accept payment" (van den Haag, 1975:15).

Third, retribution reinforces those social sentiments which oppose crime. "[A] great part of the general detestation of crime . . . arises from the fact that the commission of offenses is associated . . . with the solemn and deliberate infliction of punishment wherever crime is proved" (Stephens, 1973:70–81, as quoted by Wilson, 1975:29). By contrast, if criminals were not punished, people who did resist temptation would feel cheated. If the threat of punishment were to prove altogether empty, "those who did not break the law would have been deceived" (van den Haag, 1975:21). Consequently, "the purpose of the criminal justice system is not to expose would-be criminals to a lottery in which they either win or lose, but to expose them . . . to the solemn condemnation of the community should they yield to temptation" (Wilson, 1975:230).

Implications for social policy

Both van den Haag and Wilson have spelled out the implications of their philosophy in considerable detail.

1. *Decriminalize status offenses.* Like other theories, utilitarian philosophy stresses the importance of decriminalizing status offenses. The purpose of any court is to catch and punish criminals, not to serve as a conduit for social services for wayward children (van den Haag, 1975:175–76).

2. *Lower the age of accountability for crime.* "[Young] children should not be held responsible for their conduct to the extent that adults are" (van den Haag, 1975:173). But juveniles over the age of 13 are another matter: "The victim of a fifteen-year-old mugger is as much mugged as the victim of a twenty-year-old mugger, the victim of a fourteen-year-old murderer or rapist is as dead or as raped as the victim of an older one" (van den Haag, 1975:173, 201). Hence, "there is little reason left for not holding juveniles responsible under the same laws that apply to adults" (van den Haag, 1975:174).

3. *Abolish the juvenile court.* Given their emphasis upon treating adults and juveniles alike, both van den Haag and Wilson imply that the juvenile court should be abolished (see also McCarthy, 1977). It is a diseased organ that no longer performs a useful function. Neglected children, and perhaps young criminals under the age of 13, would be handled entirely by family courts, while those over the age of 13 would be tried in criminal courts. Not only would their rights be better protected, but they would also gain a greater sense of the meaning of justice and of the gravity of their acts.

4. *Determinate sentences.* The sentencing of all offenders should also be governed by strict procedures. "In theory, the function of the courts is to determine the guilt or innocence of the accused. . . . But most of the time, . . . the important decision concerns the sentence, not conviction or acquittal" (Wilson, 1975:182). Since between 80 and 90 percent of all cases are decided by guilty pleas, the most important decision concerns the offender's sentence.

In the past, this decision has been guided by the utopian view that judges and correctional authorities are capable of reforming offenders. But since that view has now been discredited, all sentences should be predetermined by law and governed by procedures that insure uniformity in sentencing (Wilson, 1975:182–202).

5. *Graded punishments.* Since most people would commit crime if they dared, society must increase the costs of crime so that they exceed the benefits realized from it (van den Haag, 1975:251). A calculus is needed by which punishments can be graded according to both an offender's current offense and his or her prior record.

For first offenders, "every conviction for a nontrivial offense would entail a penalty that involved a deprivation of liberty, even if brief. . . . Only the most serious offenses would result in long penalties" (Wilson, 1975:202). "Unless they are dangerous, these convicts should be kept in prison only as long as is needed to stigmatize their offenses" (van den Haag, 1975:241). This does not mean, however, that efforts should be made to rehabilitate them:

> [While] the gravity of the offense must be appropriately impressed on the first offender, [any] effort to devise ways of reeducating or uplifting him in order to insure that he does not steal again is likely to be wasted—both because we do not know how to reeducate or uplift and because most young delinquents seem to reeducate themselves no matter what society does (Wilson, 1975:223).

As a result, such rehabilitative measures as probation or community correctional programs should be abolished (Wilson, 1975:202).

Meanwhile, sentences for recidivists would be far more severe, since they pose the greater problems. "What we do with first offenders is probably far less important than what we do with habitual offenders" (Wilson, 1975:223). Consequently, "conviction for a subsequent offense would inevitably result in an increased deprivation of liberty. If the second offense were minor, the increase would be small; if grave, the increase would be substantial" (Wilson, 1975:202). The length of a sentence might be doubled for a second offense or tripled for a third.

6. Use preventive incapacitation.

Increased sentences for repeaters would pose some difficulties for the concept of equal justice, since they would be much longer than those given to first offenders. But since repeaters pose the greater danger to society, "preventive incapacitation" should be used until they are no longer a threat to others (van den Haag, 1975:241–51).

In order to insure that this incapacitation is both regularized and humane, three steps would be taken. First, chronic offenders would serve their regular term in prison, based upon the last crimes they committed. Then, once these sentences were completed—once they were punished—special supervisory courts would be employed to determine the length of their post-prison incapacitation. And since "few offenders are dangerious after age 40, hardly any after age 60," these might be the best ages to which to hold them (van den Haag, 1975:421).

Finally, in order to make this incapacitation humane, new alternatives would be sought. Rather than confinement in prison, repeaters would be *banished* from "certain areas" (their homes and communities?), *exiled* to some "small and distant place" (a deserted island?), or *confined* in some "secure" but "nonpunitive" setting where their families could join them and where they might receive visitors (perhaps a detention center like those used for the Japanese during World War II?). But since these extraordinary measures are more in the interest of protecting society than in doing justice, offenders would be treated decently, so long as they did not attempt to escape. But if they did so, they would be returned to prison (van den Haag, 1975: 254–257).

7. Use capital punishment.

In making these recommendations, van den Haag and Wilson were not in complete agreement regarding the treatment of murderers or whether capital punishment should be employed. Wilson (1975:205–21) notes that research on the deterrent capacity of the death sentence is equivocal; that is, it does not indicate whether the practice does or does not decrease the murder rate. However, the tendency for people to fall back on scientific studies of the matter is really an attempt to avoid the most crucial issue—that of doing justice. "[T]he point is not whether capital punishment prevents future crimes, but whether it is a proper and fitting penalty for crimes that have occurred. [Since] such a question forces us to weigh the value we attach to human life against the horror in which we hold a heinous crime," this is the issue toward which we should be directing our attention (p. 221).

Van den Haag (1975:205–28) is more prescriptive. Although acknowledging the many arguments, pro and con, he says they boil down to one major issue: the symbolic importance of the death sentence:

> No matter what can be said for abolition of the death penalty, it will be perceived symbolically as a loss of nerve: social authority no longer is willing to pass an irrevocable judgment on anyone. Murder is no longer thought grave enough to take the murderer's life . . . Life becomes cheaper as we become kinder to those who wantonly take it. . . . Yet if life is to be valued and secured, it must be known that anyone who takes the life of another forfeits his own (p. 213).

In summary, utilitarian philosophers believe that the legal system should concentrate on catching and punishing delinquents, not on trying to rehabilitate them. Hence, they would lower the age of accountability for crime to age 13, abolish the juvenile court, require judges to give sentences set by law, deprive every first offender of some liberty, incapacitate chronic offenders until they are middle-aged or older, and probably approve of killing murderers.

Assessment of utilitarian philosophy

Perhaps the most striking feature of utilitarian philosophy is the extent to which it would further erode the responsibility of the community for dealing with young criminals. Since the advent of the Industrial Revolution, society has looked increasingly to remote and formal institutions—like the police, courts, and training schools—to exercise the kinds of social control that were formerly exercised by families, schools, churches, and employers.

Obviously, the effort has not worked. Rising crime rates alone testify to the inability of ever larger legal and bureaucratic systems to provide the kinds of personal relationships and opportunities for legitimate identities which, in more simple societies, make social control effective. Consequently, any endeavor to evaluate utilitarian philosophy should be done with this in mind. To what degree can the policies it implies be expected to redress the increasing loss of social control by community institutions?

1. The threat of punishment. Because utilitarian philosophers assume that all people are animals who would violate the law if they dared, they suggest that the only way crime can be controlled is if potential offenders are sufficiently threatened by punishments administered by a rigid and implacable legal system. This idea is called *general deterrence,* and applies to the use of the death penalty as well as to lesser punishments.

Because of its increasing popularity in recent years, a large number of scientific studies have been undertaken to determine whether general deterrence works. And because these studies have differed over its usefulness, a special panel was set up by the most prestigious scientific body in the United States—the National Academy of Sciences—to examine the evidence and report its findings (Blumstein et al., 1978).

With respect to the death penalty, the panel concluded that "the available studies provide no useful evidence on the deterrent effects of capital punishment" (p. 9). If the death penalty is to be used, therefore, it will have to be justified on other than scientific grounds, since the crude estimates used thus far simply cannot be considered sufficient to make a definitive conclusion.

The deterrent effects of other kinds of punishment, however, may be somewhat more detectable. "Certainly, most people will agree that increasing sanctions will deter crime somewhat, but the critical question is, By how much? There is still considerable uncertainty over whether that effect is trivial (even if statistically detectable) or profound" (Nagin, 1978:135–136; Blumstein et al., 1978:6–7)

The panel went on to say that its "reluctance to draw a stronger conclusion does not imply support for a position that deterrence does not exist, since the evidence certainly favors a proposition supporting deterrence more than it favors one asserting that deterrence is absent" (Blumstein et al., 1978:7). But until research on the subject is improved, any unequivocal policy with regard to punishment is unwarranted.

The reason for this caution is that factors other than deterrence may help to reduce crime—factors that often get confused with it.

For example, suppose that the legislature decided to incapacitate chronic offenders for long periods of time, as utilitarian philosophers recommend. Suppose that during the same period, crime rates went down. To what shall we attribute the decrease? Was it due to the fact that potential offenders were deterred when they saw what happened to chronic offenders? Or was it due to the fact that the repeaters could no longer commit crimes while locked up? Or was it due to both factors? Until we could answer these questions with certainty, we could not know how much of the decrease should be attributed to deterrence and how much to incapacitation.

2. *Knowledge of punishment.* But difficulty in evaluating is not the only issue. Erickson et al. (1977) points out that the deterrence doctrine is really based upon a psychological theory which states that if the fear of punishment is to be successful in deterring potential offenders, they must be correctly informed about it. Indeed, legislators, like utilitarian philosophers, are fond of believing that, if they get tough with criminals, other people will be aware of this fact and will be deterred by it. But how accurate is this assumption? Are people well informed about the penalties associated with crime?

In order to answer this question, the Assembly Committee on Criminal Procedure (ACCP, 1968) of the California legislature obtained responses from a sample of several subgroups in California—high school students in areas of both low and high delinquency, college students, members of the general adult population, and convicted delinquents and criminals who were confined in California institutions. The answers they gave were startling.

High school students—potentially the most criminal population—along with the general public, were extremely ignorant of the specific penalties associated with 11 serious felonies. By contrast, the most informed groups were the delinquents and criminals who had already been imprisoned (ACCP, 1968:13). Hence, said the committee,

> it appears that knowledge of penalties comes *after* the crime—that is, penalties cannot act as a deterrent since these are unknown until after a person has committed a crime or become a prisoner. [Furthermore], since approximately one third of all persons who are imprisoned once, continue to engage in crime after their release, it would appear that even

when they have knowledge about penalties, it does not act as a strong deterrent to their continuation of criminal activity (ACCP, 1968:13).

Likewise, both students and adults were almost totally ignorant of the fact that in the previous year, the California Legislature had increased penalties for several offenses, including a minimum of *15 years* for rape, robbery, and burglary, where great bodily injury was involved. Again, however, it was not the nondelinquent respondents who were best informed, but incarcerated adult criminals. Indeed, imprisoned delinquents were no better informed about these increases than were high school students (ACCP, 1968: 13–14; 17).

Finally, concerning the question of serious crime and its possible solutions. Two thirds of all delinquents and criminals agreed with the general public that the crime rate was too high. But the two groups differed sharply over "what would bother them most if they were convicted of a crime." The most likely potential offenders—conventional adults, high school and college students—were most concerned over the loss of their reputations, personal feelings of guilt, and the shame that would be brought upon their families. By contrast, the incarcerated felons—those for whom general deterrence was no longer an issue—were most concerned about legal matters and the possibility that they might be returned to prison (ACCP, 1968:16).

In short, there was little in these findings to support the idea that an awareness of severe penalties deters potential offenders from committing crimes. Indeed, said the Committee on Criminal Procedures these findings are paradoxical: *"If a knowledge of penalties is an essential ingredient for deterrence, then how is it that criminals have the most knowledge and are seemingly the least deterred?"* (1968:15, emphasis added).

Yet, this was not the only paradox. Even though conventional students and adults were ignorant of the penalties associated with criminal offenses, they did anticipate shame and loss of status if they were convicted of a crime. As a consequence, the possibility that punishment plays a role in controlling crime cannot be ruled out.

3. *Symbolic importance of punishment.*
In an endeavor to discover what role punishment might play, Gibbs (1975) and Erickson et al. (1977; 1978) have come up with some provocative findings. On the one hand, they discovered, like other investigators, that there is an inverse relationship between the certainty of actual arrest and punishment and the official crime rate—the greater the certainty, the lower the rate. Although this relationship was not particularly strong, it did lend some support to the deterrence doctrine (Erickson et al., 1978).

On the other hand, they discovered, as did the Criminal Procedures Committee in California, that people—particularly juveniles—are ignorant of the penalties associated with crimes and of the fact that most reported crimes are never solved and offenders are thus never punished. Indeed, most people grossly overestimated the efficiency of the legal system. How, then, could it be said that they were capable of weighing the costs of punishment, if they did not know how the system operates? Again, the evidence seemed to suggest that punishment might be serving some function other than that of threatening people.

In an effort to identify what that function might be, Erickson et al. (1977) first asked people to rank a series of offenses in terms of seriousness, and then asked them to indicate the likelihood that offenders would be arrested and punished for them. The researchers discovered a strong, almost one-to-one, relationship between the two concepts—the higher the perceived seriousness of an offense, the more certain people were that offenders would be punished for it.

Following that, Erickson et al. (1977) asked the same people to indicate how many times they had violated each of the offenses they had previously ranked. They discovered that the more serious an offense was perceived to be, the less likely people were to report having violated it. As a consequence, the findings seemed to indicate that the public perception of the certainty and severity of punishment was associated, not with a reasonable understanding of how the legal system actually operates, but with the way people felt it *ought* to operate. If an offense was viewed as serious, people were not only less inclined to report having violated it, but also more certain that it should be punished.

Given such findings, Erickson et al. concluded that the primary function of punishment is not general deterrence but the maintenance of social norms. "Surely," they said, "there is some significance in the difference between (1) an individual refraining from a criminal or delinquent act out of fear of legal punishment and (2) an individual refraining from or not even contemplating such an act because he or she condemns it" (1977:315–316). Indeed, if society had to count on the efficiency of the legal system to control crime, lawbreaking would be even more rampant than it is today. For example, the proportion of all reported crimes that are cleared by arrest in only about 20 percent, and the proportion for which the offender is found guilty after trial is only about 5 percent (FBI, 1971:115; FBI, 1980:179).

Nonetheless, even if many conventional people refrain from serious crime because they think it is wrong, they also fear the shame and loss of status that would be associated with a conviction. Consequently, it would appear that both factors contribute to the deterrence of crime.

4. *Stake in conformity.* If that is so, what about the tendency of utilitarian philosophers to discard as impractical those findings which suggest that the best way to promote the belief that crime is wrong and shameful is to give young people a stake in conformity? Is nothing to be gained by strengthening their attachments to home and school, designing educational programs that give them access to legitimate opportunities, and providing them with the sense that they can affect their own destinies through conventional means of success? Even though punishment may have some deterrent effect, these findings imply that at the very least, other policies may have to be combined with it if crime is to be controlled.

At issue, of course, is our society's concept of justice. Should it be defined in narrow utilitarian terms? Or should it take into account the relationship between crime and the malfunction of social institutions such as the family, the school, and political and economic systems? Relative to these questions, let us reconsider several points that we have discussed concerning delinquency:

Throughout the history of this country, the highest incidence of self-reported, as well as official, delinquency has been located in areas characterized by physical deterioration, ethnic segregation, poverty, and high rates of disease, infant mortality, and mental illness.

Rates of juvenile unemployment in these areas may run as high as 50 percent.

High rates of illegitimacy and single parenthood among ghetto teenage girls are becoming less a symbol of disgrace than a means of survival, through the subsequent collection of welfare.

Adolescents suffer from rates of violent crime that are eight times greater than those suffered by the elderly.

Juvenile gang wars in our urban barrios and ghettos have become as deadly as the wars between the Palestinians and the Israelis, or between Ireland's Catholics and Protestants.

Hirschi contends that, when utilitarian philosophers argue that nothing can or should be done about these problems, their confusion over the logic of positive theories is "absolute" (1979:209). For example, is it reasonable to assume that, so long as these problems continue, increases in the threat of punishment alone will successfully reduce crime to manageable proportions? Are we to assume that social and legal justice will be served by greater punishment?

Consider the comments of a 15-year-old Brooklyn boy concerning these matters:

In Brooklyn you fall into one of two categories when you start growing up. The names for the categories may be different in other cities, but the categories are the same. First, there's the minority of the minority, the "ducks," or suckers. These are the kids who go to school every day. They even want to go to college. Imagine that! School after high school! . . . They're wasting their lives waiting for a dream that won't come true.

The ducks are usually the ones getting beat up by the majority group—the "hard rocks." If you're a real hard rock you have no worries, no cares. Getting high is as easy as breathing. You just rip off some duck. You don't bother going to school; it's not necessary. You just live with your mom until you get a job—that should be any time a job comes looking for you. Why should you bother to go look for it? Even your parents can't find work.

I guess the barrier between the ducks and the hard rocks is the barrier of despair. The ducks still have hope, while the hard rocks are frustrated. They're caught in the deadly, dead-end environment and can't see a way out. Life becomes the fast life—or incredibly boring— and death becomes the death that you see and get used to every day. They don't want to hear any more promises. They believe that's just the white man's way of keeping them under control (Hunter, 1980:14–15).

There is nothing in this description to suggest that the police and courts are unnecessary in helping to protect society. But honest cops and judges are among the first to point out that, unless social justice for both "hard rocks" and "ducks" is considered and unless they are given a greater stake in conformity, policemen and courts will be relatively helpless.

Furthermore, let us recall the findings of self-report studies which indicate that only 10 cases in 100 receive any official attention and that, of this number, less than 1 (5 percent of all reported crimes) result in a conviction. How realistic is it, then, to assume that the threat of punishment by distant officials can serve as the primary mechanism for preventing or controlling crime? Our young friend from Brooklyn says that

> Hard rocks do what they want to do when they want to do it. When a hard rock goes to prison it builds up his reputation. He develops a bravado that's like a long, sad joke. But it's all lies and excuses. It's a hustle to keep ahead of the fact that he's going nowhere (Hunter, 1980:15).

By all counts, therefore, the findings suggest that, unless policies are directed toward helping families, schools, employers, and communities to control crime, we cannot expect punishment alone to control crime.

5. *Incapacitation.* This possibility notwithstanding, utilitarian philosophers argue that the incapacitation of violent and chronic offenders may prove to be the answer. Society will be protected by longer prison terms, exile, banishment, and preventive detention. How accurate is this contention?

In order to examine it, three major questions must be addressed: (1) By how much would crime rates be reduced if violent or chronic offenders were locked up for longer periods of time? (2) How many of those locked up would not have committed additional serious offenses had they remained free in the community? and (3) Would society be willing to bear the costs that are entailed when larger numbers of offenders are confined?

a. Reduction of crime rates. Estimations vary considerably concerning the reduction of crime rates that would result if offenders were incarcerated for longer periods of time. Greenberg (1975) and Erlich (1974) conclude that a one-year increase in sentences would reduce the commission of all index offenses by only 1 to 5 percent, and violent offenses by only about 2.5 percent. By contrast, Shinnar and Shinnar (1975) suggest that the effect might be considerably larger, particularly if specific offenses, such as robbery, were analyzed separately. After examining these studies, however, the panel at the National Academy of Sciences recommended caution in interpreting the findings. The task of estimating the effects of incapacitation is so difficult, using general arrest and confinement rates, that the validity of existing estimates must be questioned; more research is badly needed (Blumstein et al., 1978; Cohen, 1978).

In a later attempt to improve that research, Van Dine et al., (1979) chose another approach. First, they identified a population of 342 adult recidivists in Franklin County, Ohio, who were charged with violent offenses in 1973. Then they sought to determine how much the rate of violent crime would have been reduced had these offenders been kept in prison, based on their convictions for crimes committed some time during the previous five years.

The findings were striking. If all 342 recidivists had been kept in prison, only 111 of 2,892 violent crimes, or 3.8 percent, would have been prevented in 1973. But since some of those who were charged with a new crime were found not guilty, when tried, the number of violent offenses prevented by their incarceration might have dropped to 48 of 2,892 cases, or only 1.7 percent. In short, like several of the studies mentioned above, this one suggests that the preventive effects of incapacitation would have been very slight.

b. False positives. Furthermore, these findings imply that most of the 342 persons would have been kept in prison unnecessarily had preventive incapacitation been enforced.

They would have become *false positives*—people who do not continue to violate the law, although they are assumed to do so by others.

In order to determine how large the number of false positives might be if incapacitation became public policy, the panel from the National Academy of Sciences carefully reviewed the research literature on the subject (Blumstein et al., 1978:75–78; Monahan, 1978). Again, the findings were startling: *predictions of future criminality were wrong between 50 to 99 percent of the time!* Whether prior records, personal characteristics, or clinical diagnoses were used to make these estimates, they were wrong more often than they were right.

This was a disappointing finding, in one sense, considering the undeniable existence of chronic offenders from whom society needs protection. But in advocating the use of preventive incapacitation for them, utilitarian philosophers did not reckon with the extreme difficulty of identifying these offenders *before*, rather than after, they engage in a continued series of offenses. Said the National Academy of Sciences panel: "[E]ven good prediction procedures suffer very high false positive rates" (Blumstein et al., 1978:77; Petersilia et al., 1977:XIV).

There are some good reasons why these rates are high: some offenders continue to violate the law, but evade detection; offenders' offense patterns and their arrest records do not always correlate; offense behavior begins to decline as juveniles grow older; offense patterns, even among adults, are rarely specialized; and many criminals, both juvenile and adult, commit violent offenses only once in their lives (Hamparian et al., 1978; Petersilia et al., 1977). Thus, if incapacitation is used as a method for controlling crime, it may prove to be a perilous enterprise in which many offenders may be denied freedom although they may not have committed crimes had they been free.

Not only might false positives suffer incalculable personal costs from being exiled, banished, or otherwise confined, but also there is precious little proof that many would avoid being made more criminal while imprisoned, particularly since utilitarian philosophers would do away with attempts to rehabilitate them. "If . . . prisons have a criminogenic effect, increasing an individual's propensity to commit crimes or extending the duration of criminal careers, the benefits in reduced crime from incapacitation may be offset by the additional crimes a criminal commits once released" (Blumstein et al., 1978:66). Rather than being better protected, society might be even more vulnerable with increased confinements.

c. Costs. Let us consider the social and economic costs of incapacitation. The economic burdens associated with housing, feeding, and guarding ever-increasing numbers of offenders might be more than society would be willing to bear. Consider but one example. Van Dine et al. (1979) estimate that, if Ohio were to adopt a strict incapacitative policy, the number of inmates in its prisons would rise from 9,000 to 42,000 within five years. Thus, if the annual costs for confining each inmate for one year were $15,000, annual expenditures would increase from $135 to $630 million. This figure includes neither the capital costs of constructing the new prisons, nor the increases in welfare required to care for inmates' families, nor the possible diversion of funds from the very educational and social programs that are crucial to giving potential offenders a stake in conformity. In short, incredible expenditures would be entailed by such a policy, although there is no evidence that society would experience a substantial decrease in crime rates.

SUMMARY

In summary, this assessment of utilitarian philosophy has indicated that

1. The threat of punishment by the legal system does have some deterrent effect, but it is difficult to estimate how great that effect may be.

2. Many people appear to refrain from serious crimes, not because they are well informed about their chances for being punished, but because they believe that such crimes are wrong, and would be shamed by a conviction.

3. The possibility that a distant and inefficient legal system can control crime would seem to be slight, unless its practices are supplemented by the efforts of community institutions to promote social justice by giving juveniles a greater stake in conformity.

4. It is unlikely that preventive incapacitation would result in large reductions in crime rates, although it would be incredibly expensive and would incarcerate many people who would not have committed crimes had they been left free in the community.

JUST DESERTS PHILOSOPHY

Just deserts philosophy is similar to utilitarian philosophy in the sense that it would have us concentrate on doing justice rather than redeeming offenders. But that is about the only similarity between the two.

Basic assumptions

While utilitarian philosophers stress the need to protect the state from the wickedness of its citizens, just deserts philosophers seek to protect citizens from the wickedness of the state. They would revive the use of classical principles, not because they believe the state requires more power to arrest and punish, but because they believe its use of this power has been oppressive. Indeed, under all conditions, the rights of the individual should take precedence over the welfare of society.

Such ideas are derived from several sources:

a committee of scholars set up to analyze the weaknesses of prisons and recommend improvements (Gaylin and Rothman, 1976; Von Hirsch, 1976); a practicing correctional administrator and former executive director of the Illinois Law Enforcement Commission (Fogel, 1979); and a legal scholar seeking to reform the juvenile justice system (Fox, 1974). From a variety of perspectives, therefore, these philosophers have joined in condemning not only the rehabilitative concept of justice, but also the utilitarian concept. Indeed, their negative critiques of both philosophies represent a remarkable expression of the despair and pessimism that characterize currently popular views of American justice.

Despair over rehabilitation. "We recognize that, in giving up the rehabilitative model, we abandon not just our innocence but perhaps more. [The concept of rehabilitation] was a scheme born to optimism, and faith, and humanism. It viewed the evils in man as essentially correctable, and only partially the responsibility of the individual" (Gaylin and Rothman, 1976: xxvii, xxix). But since "there is virtually no sound proof that, short of killing him, anyone knows how to stop another person from committing crimes" (Fox, 1974:3), the time has come to discard our maudlin beliefs.

Mechanized justice. "We are recommending a greater mechanization of justice because we have not achieved either the individual love and understanding or the social distribution of power and property that is essential if discretion is to serve justice" (Gaylin and Rothman, 1976: xli). Our treatment-oriented system of justice has "produced far too many instances of recorded abuse to think fairly that it is much more than simply a vehicle for abuse" (Fox, 1974:3).

Utilitarianism threatens the individual. The rights of the individual are paramount. Therefore, these rights may not be sacrificed for the good of others. The utilitarian theory of deterrence, for example, "could lead to punishing the offender more severely than he deserves . . ." (Von Hirsch, 1976:70). Hence, utilitarianism cannot be used as a cornerstone for the construction of a just social policy.

Discretion is evil. The rehabilitative concept of justice sought to do good by allowing officials to exercise discretion in adapting individual treatment to individual needs. Such discretion, however, has proven to be an unmitigated evil:

> The Committee insists that the potential benefit done to any one offender under a system of massive discretion is more than offset by the harms done to the vast majority of persons through such a normless scheme, and hence advocates the abolition of the indeterminate sentence and the adoption of sentencing standards that limit judicial discretion (Gaylin and Rothman, 1976:xxxv).

Indeed "abuse and discretion are two sides of the same coin" (Fox, 1974:7).

In summary, just deserts philosophers are irredeemable skeptics. "If Progressive reformers [those who invented the juvenile court] shared a basic trust in the state, more eager to involve its power in the society than to limit it, we as a group shared a basic mistrust of the power of the state" (Gaylin and Rothman, 1976:xxxii). Benevolent motives should not be allowed to cloak legal authorities in the mantle of unbridled power.

Just deserts principles

If the just deserts philosophy is to be built upon a foundation of profound skepticism, what are its guiding principles?

Avoid doing harm. First, we must avoid doing further harm:

> Both in tone and in content, the recommendations of the Committee represent a departure from tradition. Permeating this report is a determination to do less rather than more—an insistence on not doing harm. The quality of heady optimism and confidence of

reformers in the past, and their belief that they could solve the problem of crime . . . will not be found in this document. Instead, we have here a crucial shift in perspective from a commitment to do good to a commitment to do as little mischief as possible (Gaylin and Rothman, 1976:xxxiv).

Sentence delinquency, not the delinquent. In order to avoid "mischief," the decision concerning offenders' sentences should be based, not upon their needs, but upon the penalties that they deserve for their acts (Von Hirsch, 1976:98). We should sentence delinquency, not the delinquent (Fox, 1974:6).

Punishment as a "desert." Punishment for a crime should not be viewed as retribution—a fair payment for a deviant act—but as a just desert—a punishment that an offender deserves. Furthermore, punishment is not justified because it serves the utilitarian function of deterring others. Rather, it is justified only because the offender deserves it (Von Hirsch, 1976:45–54).

Interfere parsimoniously. Since the rights of the individual are paramount, and since the only justification for punishment is a just desert, the state is obligated to observe strict parsimony in interfering in the lives of convicted offenders. Not only should it have to justify the use of severe penalties for them, but it should have to justify *any* intrusion into their lives (Von Hirsch, 1976:5)

Restrain efforts to prevent crime. The pursuit of justice must override every other consideration. Therefore, it requires that we restrain efforts to prevent crime, by incapacitating chronic offenders or trying to rehabilitate them (Von Hirsch, 1976:5). In short,

> the concept of just deserts is intellectual and moralistic; in its devotion to principle, it turns back on such compromising considerations as generosity and charity, compassion and love.

It emphasizes justice, not mercy, and while it need not rule out tempering justice with mercy, by shifting the emphasis from concern for the individual to devotion to the moral right, it could lead to an abandonment of the former altogether (Gaylin and Rothman, 1976:xxxiv).

In other words, social policy should be concerned "less with the administration of justice and more . . . with the *justice of administration*" (Fogel, 1979:xv).

Implications for social policy

Although based on different principles, many of the policy implications of just deserts philosophy are similar to those implied by utilitarian philosophy. Just deserts philosophy implies that society should:

Decriminalize status offenses, not only because justice requires it but because attention to noncriminal offenses encourages legal oppression in the name of benevolence.

Lower the age of accountability for crime, since justice demands attention to crimes, not criminals.

Abolish the juvenile court, in the interest of both eliminating its unbridled powers and protecting the rights of juveniles.

Use determinate sentences as a means of eliminating official discretion.

Punish rather than treat offenders.

Grade punishments along two dimensions: "(1) the seriousness of the crime for which the offender currently stands convicted, and (2) the seriousness of his prior record" (Von Hirsch, 1976:133). The greater the seriousness and the longer the history of crime, the greater the punishment.

Despite these similarities, there is also one important difference between utilitarian and just deserts philosophers. Whereas the former would make punishments more severe, and would exile, banish, or incapacitate chronic offenders, just deserts proponents would not only discard the death penalty but also "scale down the length of sentences to the point where it satisfies our sense of equity, but no more than that: 'warnings' for crimes low on the scale of seriousness [fines based on ability to pay], intermittent confinement (weekends or evenings) for more serious offenses, and . . . full time incarceration only for the most serious crimes" (Gaylin and Rothman, 1976:xxv; Von Hirsch, 1976:119–23). Rather than severity, therefore, the principle that should govern the choice of punishments, according to just deserts philosophers, is the *least restrictive alternative* commensurate with the gravity of the criminal act.

In fact, the only reason that these reformers would continue to use incarceration at all is because they cannot think of a better alternative (Von Hirsch, 1976:111). But since it is a necessary evil, "the preference should be for open facilities, without bars or restraining walls. There should also be strict limits on the size of institutions, to reduce the need for regimentation" (Von Hirsch, 1976:115). And even then, "it bears repeating: incarceration, even with shorter sentences, should only be invoked against offenders whose crimes are serious" (Von Hirsch, 1976:114).

Assessment of just deserts philosophy

Two major issues must be considered in assessing the implications of the just deserts philosophy. On the one hand, it emphasizes doing justice—protecting the rights of the accused, seeing that legal procedures are fair, respecting the worth of the offender, and mitigating, where possible, the destructive impact of punishment. Such ideas are basic to the precepts of Enlightenment philosophy and must form the cornerstone of any continuing effort to promote justice. Their importance cannot be denied.

On the other hand, just deserts philosophers advance a depressingly pessimistic, if not nihilistic, argument in their attempts to discredit any effort to promote social or legal justice. Because legal bureaucracies have not always been successful in doing so in the past, the humane sentiments that gave rise to them must be discarded. Rather than seeking new social inventions by which to combine justice with mercy, we must become even more legalistic and resort to a system that is based upon "despair, not hope," upon "a determination to do less, rather than more." It is as though we no longer have the will or the inventiveness by which to incorporate compassion, love, and charity in our dealings with the young. In light of this argument, therefore, consider but a few of the problems that are left unattended by the just deserts philosophy:

Just deserts in an unjust society. Von Hirsch points out that some serious moral problems are associated with sentencing and punishing offenders in an unjust society. "Consider the impoverished and alienated ghetto dweller who turns to crime in the absence of lawful opportunities for making a decent living: what, if any are his deserts?" (1976:143–49).

But while the inventors of the juvenile court considered it their responsibility to do something about these matters (to say nothing of the implications of positive or radical theories), Von Hirsch concludes that, in their mechanized system of justice, "It may not be feasible to treat social deprivation as a mitigating factor" (1976:147). Indeed, he is correct: the system will be morally flawed.

The just deserts philosophy is no more capable of promoting social justice than is the utilitarian philosophy. Because its proposals for reform are based on despair and an uncompromising mistrust of the state, no attempt would be made to remedy the discrimination, inequality, or powerlessness that are so often associated with delinquency. Hence, the concept of just deserts is a despairing concept indeed.

Ruling out discretion. The individualized concept of justice requires that considerable discretion—the ability to exercise judgment and make decisions—be granted to judges and correctional authorities. But because discretion has been misused in the past, deserts philosophers would like to see it eliminated. On the surface, the rationale is a sound one: in a discretionary system, a rich man's son may be given probation for smoking marijuana while a white hippie or a black youth may be sent to prison. "In a nondiscretionary system, everyone—or no one—must go to prison" (Greenberg and Humphries, 1980:209).

However, discretion is often used to avoid injustice as well as to promote it. For example, similar offenses are not necessarily committed by similar persons: a 16-year-old joy rider is not like, nor is he motivated by the same interests as, a professional auto thief; and a 12-year-old numbers-runner, who is deserted by his parents, is not like the racketeer who grows rich on the numbers game. Rather than always discriminating against the powerless, therefore, judges often do the reverse: they seek ways to soften the severity of statutory penalties in an effort to avoid imposing pain unnecessarily or unfairly (Cressey, 1977:24).

Equally significant is the fact that policemen and prosecutors also know that justice demands discretion and will find ways to exercise it, if judges and probation officers cannot. Indeed, as we learned in our review of police behavior, police officers probably exercise more discretion than any other legal authority. Consequently, as Fox points out, deserts philosophers have "taken no account . . . of the waterbed principle of justice which decrees that when you push down on a problem over here, you should expect a bulge to appear over there. The 'over there' bulge is, of course, the sticky matter of police and prosecutorial discretion" (1974:9). If judges and correctional authorities cannot exercise discretion, other will. Hence, profound questions of two types are raised.

The first asks whether policemen and prosecutors are somehow better equipped than judges and correctional personnel to exercise discretion. Are they better prepared to take into account family relations, gender, race, poverty, or youthful naivete in deciding whether to arrest or prosecute young people, or in deciding on actions to be taken to insure that their crimes are not repeated? There is no evidence that they are thus equipped.

The second question is even more disturbing. It asks whether police, in particular, since they have been known for their own brand of "street justice," have a greater reputation for fairness than that of judges. It should be noted that, when police and prosecutors exercise discretion, their actions on the streets or behind closed doors are even less subject to oversight by higher authority and to judicial appeal than are those of judges and correctional personnel. By whom would an offender rather be judged?

In short, the issue is not whether discretion will be exercised. It will. Rather, the issue is whether discretion can be circumscribed in such a way that it is both sensible and fair. On the one hand, we must insure that the young and the poor are not punished more severely than the rich and powerful. On the other hand, we must insure that, in our zeal to punish equally, discretion is used in such a way that the ends of justice are served. Special tribunals, courts of appeal, and other groups can be used to reduce glaring inconsistencies in sentencing practices, but their decision making must not be so circumscribed by rigid rules that they lose complete sight of the differences among individuals.

The right to punishment.   In their desire to overcome the evils of individualized justice, deserts philosophers have also stressed juveniles' rights to punishment. Rather than focusing upon the factors that may have caused their crimes or may lead to future crimes, justice requires that the focus be upon their past offenses and the punishment they deserve for them.

The quandries posed by this argument are horrendous. Suppose, for example, that a 15-year-old girl is arrested for shoplifting. Suppose further that, upon investigation, the court discovers that she has a rather common problem: she is a runaway who stole in order to survive, and who left home because her stepmother refused to protect her from the sexual abuses of her father.

If the deserts philosophy were followed to the letter, the court would be required to punish the girl for shoplifting but would be precluded from taking action based upon her home condition or her sexual abuse. To be sure, authorities could seek to have her father prosecuted. But unless her stepmother were willing to testify against her father—and in many cases she is not—it is unlikely that any charges could be sustained. Thus, short of convicting the father, the court would have no recourse for protecting the daughter.

The same sorts of problems might be encountered in places of confinement for more serious, male delinquents. Says Von Hirsch: "We favor minimum interference with confined offenders. The sanction should consist only of the deprivation of the freedom to leave" (1976:115). If delinquents wished, they might participate in vocational training, traditional schooling, or counseling, but any such participation would have to be strictly voluntary.

What, it might be asked, would inmates be doing if they did not participate in such activities? Would they be left in complete idleness? Is it to be assumed that, in the absence of any rules for behavior beyond prohibitions against running away, a safe and humane environment could be anticipated?

The failure of deserts philosophers to address such questions is mind boggling, especially when those to be held in captivity are adolescents, many of whom have already failed in schools and places of work, and who are now looking to the standards of the delinquent subculture for guidance. Should we believe that, without experience in constructive self-government, this group of alienated and peer-conscious adolescents would be inclined to choose schooling over weightlifting, counseling over rapping with peers, or shop work over smoking smuggled dope? Deserts proponents imply, of course, that such would be the case. But in making this assumption, they overlook two rather obvious points.

First, if most of those in capitivity were committed to conventional means for success, they would not have been confined in the first place; they would be pursuing their careers. Second, those prosocial inmates who are concerned with such matters—and there are some—could safely indulge their interests only if they were protected from the demands of inmate leaders or rival groups whose goal is to establish control over all inmates. Hence, unless those in charge were permitted the discretion to work with inmates toward the creation of a culture in which constructive behavior was rewarded and deviant conduct punished, the standards of the most delinquent groups would prevail (see Fogel, 1979, who addresses these problems). Indeed, if such a culture were not built, homosexual rape, rackets, exploitation, and brutality, not education and counseling, would be the rule.

Perhaps that is why Fox suggests that "maybe some indeterminacy should be allowed back in the form of 'time off for good behavior' laws, simply as a recognition of the fact that institutions' administrators need some method of imposing control over the children in their charge" (1974:9).

Perhaps that is why Gaylin and Rothman (1976:xl–lxi) also express ambivalence over a concept of justice which, on the one hand, holds that the rights of delinquents to be left alone are paramount, but which, on the other hand, would discard the individualized concept of justice precisely because of its concern with the individual. They should be ambivalent; one cannot have it both ways. The practices of exploitation and oppression in places of captivity are not confined to authorities: if given the chance, many inmates will exploit and oppress each other as well. Therefore, unless attempts are made to create a social system that honors individual differences and seeks to eliminate oppression from both sides, tyranny will continue. Yet, because of their despair, deserts philosophers would no longer have us concern ourselves with such matters:

> We recognize that by retreating from a concept of individualized justice, discretion in sentencing, we are giving up an important aspiration. . . .
>
> We are not so naive as not to recognize that we will pay a price. Each retreat from individualism in one field will extend to others, ultimately diminishing the position of every individual. It matters little whether the field is criminal justice or the practice of medicine. More and more, in the push for space, food, and pleasures, we are progressively being reduced and regimented, homogenized and dehumanized. In abandoning individualism here, we make it progressively easier to abandon it elsewhere (Gaylin and Rothman, 1976:xli).

Indeed, like utilitarian philosophy, deserts philosophy symbolizes the end of an optimistic era—a period in American history that was based on hope and dedicated to the proposition that delinquency and crime, like other social problems, could be addressed by compassion and mercy, by knowledge and imagination. Now, however, it appears that none of these are of use to anyone.

SUMMARY AND CONCLUSIONS

Convinced that the rehabilitative concept of justice has failed and that scientific criminology is bankrupt, two groups of neoclassical philosophers would have us return to the practice of treating delinquency, not delinquents. One group—the utilitarian school—stresses the use of punishment to deter others and protect society. The second group—the just deserts school—objects to the use of punishment as a deterrent, and advocate its application only as a means of doing justice.

Assumptions

Utilitarian philosophers assume that people are inherently wicked. Hence, the threat of punishment is the only means of protecting the state and maintaining social order. Deserts philosophers, by contrast, assume that the state is the wicked party and that its citizens require protection.

Based upon these contrasting assumptions, each group has different reasons for rejecting individualized justice. Utilitarians would reject it because it is utopian, it is optimistic, and it assumes that the wicked inclinations of young people can be changed. Meanwhile, deserts philosophers would reject it, not because it is utopian and benevolent, but because the state cannot be trusted to be utopian and benevolent.

Principles

Utilitarian philosophy is based upon two fundamental principles: (1) punishment deters potential offenders; and (2) punishment is indispensable for the maintenance of social order. Hence, the only way to control crime is to submit offenders to the solemn and severe condemnation of the community.

Deserts philosophy, by contrast, is built upon principles of despair. It supports (1) mechanizing justice in order to avoid doing harm; (2) sentencing delinquency, not the delinquent; (3) viewing punishment as a just desert; and (4) restraining efforts to prevent crime or rehabilitate offenders. In short, deserts proponents would shift the emphasis from a concern with the individual to a higher morality of uniform punishment.

Implications for policy

The two philosophies have many common issues with regard to policy. Both support (1) decriminalizing status offenses; (2) lowering the age of accountability for crime; (3) abolishing the juvenile court; (4) using determinate sentences; and (5) grading punishments to fit current and past offenses.

Within these general policies, however, are some significant differences. Whereas utilitarians would use the death penalty, would punish criminals more severely, and would incapacitate chronic offenders for long periods of time, deserts philosophers would eliminate the death penalty, lessen the severity of penalties, and use incarceration only as a last resort.

Assessment

With regard to utilitarian philosophy, research indicates that (1) the threat of punishment does have some deterrent effect, but it is difficult to estimate how great that effect is; (2) many people appear to refrain from serious crimes because they believe they are wrong, not because they are well informed about punishments for them; (3) the possibility that the legal system can control crime is slight, unless efforts are made by other social institutions to provide young people with a stake in conformity; and (4) despite incredible costs in human and monetary terms, preventive incapacitation is not likely to result in large reductions in crime rates.

Because of its commitment to minimizing harm, meanwhile, just deserts philosophy (1) would not attempt to provide juveniles with a stake in conformity; (2) would shift the use of discretion by judges and correctional personnel to police and prosecutors, despite the fact that their conduct is less subject to judicial oversight; and (3) like utilitarian philosophy, would discard any concern with individual differences and needs.

Perhaps we should not be too surprised by the limitations of these neoclassical philosophies. The reason that efforts were made to improve classical principles and practices in the 19th century was because the legal system alone could not be expected to insure justice and control crime. After all, its role in socializing the young is more negative than positive—better designed to indicate what young people should not be and do than what they should be and do.

Thus, society must depend upon other institutions to accomplish these tasks. Indeed, if it is serious about wanting to reduce crime, it must pursue policies which, in addition to improving the legal system, are designed to (1) identify those institutions—the family, the school, the work place, or the church—that are most likely to provide desirable models for conduct and legitimate avenues for success; (2) strengthen these institutions or to invent new ones so that these desirable goals are enhanced; and (3) discard those institutions that now tend to foster criminal behaviors and identities.

To be sure, neoclassical philosophers are correct in suggesting that such a task is profoundly complex. Yet, if nothing else, we should have learned by now that delinquency is an historic phenomenon that does not lend itself to easy solutions.

REFERENCES

Assembly Committee on Criminal Procedure
    1968   *Deterrent Effects of Criminal Sanctions.* Sacramento: Assembly of the State of California.

Blumstein, Alfred; Cohen, Jacqueline; and Nagin, Daniel, eds.
    1978   *Deterrence and Incapacitation: Estimating the Effects of Criminal Sanctions on Crime Rates.* Washington, D.C.: National Academy of Sciences.

Cohen, Jacqueline
    1978   "The Incapacitative Effect of Imprisonment: A Critical Review of the Literature." Pp. 187–243 in Alfred Blumstein, Jacqueline Cohen and Daniel Nagin, eds., *Deterrence and Incapacitation: Estimating the Effects of Criminal Sanctions on Crime Rates.* Washington, D.C.: National Academy of Sciences.

Cressey, Donald R.
    1977   "Doing Justice." *The Center Magazine* 10 (January:21–28.
    1978   "Criminological Theory, Social Science, and the Repression of Crime." *Criminology* 16 (August):171–191.

Erickson, Maynard L.; Gibbs, Jack P.; Jensen, Gary F.
    1977   "The Deterrence Doctrine and the Perceived Certainty of Legal Punishments." *American Sociological Review* 42 (April):305–17.

Erickson, Maynard L., and Gibbs, Jack P.
    1978   "Objective and Perceptual Properties of Legal Punishment and the Deterrence Doctrine." *Social Problems* 25:253–264.

Erlich, Issac
  1974 "Participation in Illegitimate Activities: An Economic Analysis." In G. S.
        Becker and W. M. Landes, eds., *Essays in the Economics of Crime and
        Punishment.* New York: Columbia University Press.

Federal Bureau of Investigation
  1971 *Crime in the United States: Uniform Crime Reports—1970.* Washington,
        D.C.: U.S. Government Printing Office.
  1980 *Crime in the United States: Uniform Crime Reports—1979.* Washington,
        D.C.: U.S. Government Printing Office.

Fogel, David
  1979 *We Are the Living Proof: The Justice Model for Corrections.* Cincinnati:
        Anderson.

Fox, Sanford J.
  1974 "The Reform of Juvenile Justice: The Child's Right to Punishment." *Juvenile
        Justice* 25 (August):2–9.

Gaylin, Willard, and Rothman, David J.
  1976 "Introduction." Pp. xxi–xli in Andrew Von Hirsch, *Doing Justice: The Choice
        of Punishments.* New York: Hill and Wang.

Gibbs, Jack P.
  1975 *Crime, Punishment and Deterrence.* New York: Elsevier.

Greenberg, David
  1975 "The Incapacitative Effect of Imprisonment: Some Estimates." *Law and
        Society Review* 9 (Summer):541–580.

Greenberg, David F., and Humphries, Drew
  1980 "The Cooptation of Fixed Sentencing Reform." *Crime and Delinquency*
        26 (April):206–225.

Hamparian, Donna M.; Schuster, Richard; Dinitz, Simon; and Conrad, John
  1978 *The Violent Few: A Study of Dangerous Juvenile Offenders.* Lexington:
        D. C. Heath.

Hirschi, Travis
  1979 "Reconstructing Delinquency: Evolution and Implications of Twentieth-
        century Theory." Pp. 183–212 in LaMar T. Empey, ed., *Juvenile Justice:
        The Progressive Legacy and Current Reforms.* Charlottesville: University
        Press of Virginia.

Hunter, Deairich
  1980 "Ducks vs. Hard Rocks." *Newsweek* 18 (August):14–15.

McCarthy, Francis B.
  1977 "Should Juvenile Delinquency be Abolished?" *Crime and Delinquency,*
        23:196–203.

Monahan, John
  1978 "The Prediction of Violent Criminal Behavior: A Methodological Critique
        and Prospectus." Pp. 244–269 in Alfred Blumstein et al., eds.; *Deterrence
        and Incapacitation: Estimating the Effects of Criminal Sanctions on Crime
        Rates.* Washington, D.C.: National Academy of Sciences.

Nagin, Daniel
  1978 "General Deterrence: A Review of the Empirical Evidence." Pp. 95–139
        in Alfred Blumstein et al., eds., *Deterrence and Incapacitation: Estimating*

the Effects of Criminal Sanctions on Crime Rates. Washington, D.C.: National Academy of Sciences.

Petersilia, Joan; Greenwood, Peter W.; Lavin, Marvin
    1977   *Criminal Careers of Habitual Felons.* Santa Monica, Calif.: Rand.

Shinnar, Shlomo, and Shinnar, Reuel
    1975   "The Effects of the Criminal Justice System on the Control of Crime: A Quantitative Approach." *Law and Society Review* 9 (Summer):581–611.

Stephens, James F.
    1973   *A History of the Criminal Law of England.* First published in 1883. New York: Burt Franklin.

van den Haag, Ernest
    1975   *Punishing Criminals: Concerning a Very Old and Painful Question.* New York: Basic Books.

Van Dine, Stephen; Conrad, John P.; and Dinitz, Simon
    1979   *Restraining the Wicked: The Incapacitation of the Dangerous Criminal.* Lexington: D. C. Heath.

Von Hirsch, Andrew
    1976   *Doing Justice: The Choice of Punishments.* New York: Hill and Wang.

Wilson, James Q.
    1975   *Thinking About Crime.* New York: Vintage Books.

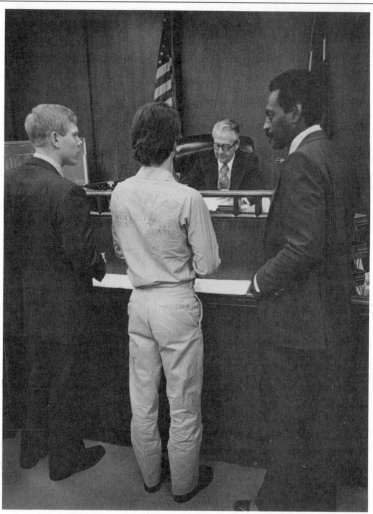

Under the new concept of juvenile justice, juveniles will be treated more like adults.

SCHIZOID REVOLUTION: COMPETING MODELS FOR JUVENILE JUSTICE

Preceding chapters have revealed that, in response to an almost universal condemnation of our traditional system of juvenile justice, a bewildering array of prescriptions for reform have been advanced:

Strain and other positive theorists have recommended heroic measures designed to give juveniles a greater stake in conformity.

Labeling theorists have urged a hands-off policy, stressing decriminalization, diversion, and deinstitutionalization.

Radical theorists have advocated social revolution.

Utilitarian philosophers have stressed the importance of increasing the certainty and severity of punishment.

Just deserts philosophers have advocated a reduction in the power of the legal system and a concentration upon doing justice.

Given these contrasting prescriptions for reform, policymakers, legislators, and the agents of juvenile justice have been confronted with a host of dilemmas:

Should they continue to use legal means in an attempt to protect the *nurturance* rights of children—the right to a home, loving parents, an education, and training in moral principles—or should they concentrate on granting them all of the *constitutional* rights afforded adults?

Should they *decriminalize* the acts of status offenders, or should they continue to act *paternalistically* toward them?

Should they continue to permit policemen, probation officers, judges, and correctional authorities to exercise a great deal of *discretion* in deciding what should be done with delinquents, or should their decision making be severely constrained by *carefully defined procedures?*

Should they seek *to prevent* delinquency and *to rehabilitate* offenders, or should they increase the *certainty* and *severity* of *punishment?*

Should they *deinstitutionalize* correctional programs, or should they make greater use of *incarceration?*

473

The basic question, in short, is whether deviant children should be viewed as immature people who are in need of special supervision and help, or as accountable and self-directed lawbreakers for whom strict procedures, determinant sentences, and punishment are the only answer.

In an attempt to resolve this question, two new but different, models for juvenile justice have been constructed—a *family court model* and a *just deserts model*. But since neither model has yet achieved the universal acceptance enjoyed by the traditional model for over half a century, current legal procedures for juveniles are characterized by a split personality. In this chapter, therefore, we will carefully examine both models because one of them, or some uneasy compromise between the two, is likely to dominate the legal treatment of young people in the future.

FAMILY COURT MODEL

The family court model was constructed by a Task Force on Juvenile Justice and Delinquency Prevention that was organized by the Law Enforcement Assistance Administration in 1975 (see National Advisory Committee, 1976). Made up of eminent and experienced professionals and social scientists, this task force was charged with setting standards for federal policy and for the passage of federal legislation.

Guiding philosophy

The guiding philosophy of the family court model incorporates three major ideas:

1.   Need for nurturance.   First, it stresses the traditional idea that juveniles are different from adults and that the juvenile justice system should take their unique needs into account:

> [T]he consensus among those who have studied the problem is that recognition must be given to the fact that juveniles commit delinquent

acts—not crimes; they are taken into custody—not arrested; and they are subjected to disposition—not sentenced. In short, we have come to know that the disposition of the juvenile delinquent from the inception of his involvement with delinquency must be in a specialized atmosphere that takes particular cognizance of age and of the fact that when dealing with youngsters, certain kinds of behavior are particularly indigenous to them (Byrne, 1976).

2.   The family.   Secondly, the family model stresses the central importance of the family:

> Adoption of the family court structure would . . . provide for an integrated family court that would minimize duplication of efforts and provide for a comprehensive treatment of family problems. The family court structure better enables the court to view juvenile behavior as part of a much broader framework and focus on the family as a whole (National Advisory Committee, 1976:16).

3.   Constitutional rights.   Finally, even though the family model would pay special attention to individual and family needs, it would honor the constitutional rights of both. Due process would govern the conduct of all formal procedures.

Clientele

The clientele of the family court model would be much the same as that of the traditional juvenile court:

1.   Delinquents.   It would include as delinquents any young people, between the ages of 10 and 18, who violate any law that, if committed by adults, would constitute a violation of federal, state or local criminal law (NAC, 1976:293).

2.   Families with service needs.   The family court would discard references to status offenders, or to any of the stigmatizing labels by which they have been known in the past.

Instead, the focus would be upon "families with service needs"—needs that could be identified by problems of five kinds: truancy, misuse of or disregard for, parental authority, repeated running away, repeated use of intoxicating beverages, and delinquents acts committed by children under the age of 10 (NAC, 1976:312).

3. Endangered children. The family model would also discard the concept of dependent and neglected children in favor of calling them "endangered children"—children who have no parent or guardian, who have suffered or are in danger of suffering severe bodily harm, who are suffering serious emotional damage, who have been sexually abused, who require medical treatment of a serious disorder, and who commit delinquent acts as a result of parental pressure (NAC, 1976:335–336). But while the clientele of the court would remain much the same as before, its methods of intervention would be governed by standards that are far different from those of the traditional juvenile court.

Standards for intake

The standards governing intake would make room both for the exercise of considerable discretion as well as for procedural fairness:

1. Discretion. "Intake personnel should have clearly defined authority to either refer the case to the family court prosecutor for court action or to refer the juvenile and/or his family for noncourt services" (NAC, 1976:651). Based on their assessment of needs and backgrounds, they should "protect those juveniles who do not require formal judicial proceedings from the negative consequences of being labeled delinquent, as well as from the harmful effects of associating with more sophisticated delinquents" (p. 651).

The same is also true of cases involving families with service needs or endangered children. Before a petition could be filed, intake personnel would have to demonstrate:

a. That one or more defined behaviors took place.
b. That all available and appropriate outside services had been exhausted.
c. That the behavior or behaviors require court intervention to provide services (p. 314).

2. Procedural fairness. If a petition must be filed, fairness at the intake stage is essential. It should include the right to counsel, "the right to fair and full notice of the allegations of the petition; . . . the right to the assistance of a bilingual interpreter; and the right to have one's parent present at court proceedings" (p. 374).

3. Detention. Since the abuse of detention constitutes "a significant national problem," it should also be carefully circumscribed. No child should be detained unless his or her bodily safety is threatened or unless he or she threatens bodily harm to others. Secondly, he or she should be kept in the least restrictive setting possible—in shelter rather than locked facilities. Furthermore, the law should provide for a judicial review of the need for detention within 48 hours, and if the need is not demonstrated, the child should be released (p. 374).

4. Waiver to adult court. Family court standards would also reject the automatic waiver of some delinquents to adult court, either by legislative mandate or by a decision of the prosecutor. "Even though they have committed serious offenses, some juveniles are far more in need of special services than deterrence or punishment" (p. 304). Therefore, any waiver would not be permitted unless the juvenile were at least 16 and unless the family court determined, in a formal hearing, that there was actual need for the waiver.

Adjudication

Once the intake procedure had demonstrated the need for the Family Court to exercise its jurisdiction, several standards would apply:

1. Plea bargaining. "Plea bargaining in all forms would be eliminated from the delinquency adjudication process. Under no circumstances should the parties engage in discussions for the purpose of agreeing to exchange concessions by the prosecutor for the juvenile's admission to the petition" (p. 409).

2. Admission of guilt. Even though a defendant—a parent or a child—admits guilt, the court would still be required "to undertake a thorough inquiry to insure that the admission is competently, knowingly, and voluntarily made" (p. 407).

3. Contested adjudications. If any alleged delinquent denies guilt, he or she should have all the rights given to a criminal defendant, except the right to trial by jury. Meanwhile, proceedings for endangered children or for families with service needs should be governed by rules covering the trial of civil matters, since they are meant to be nonpunitive. The requirement in this case would be clear and convincing evidence, not proof beyond a reasonable doubt (pp. 336;407–408).

4. Right to appeal. Finally, judgments made by the family court should be subject to appeal; first, to eliminate any errors made by the court and, second, to insure uniform application of the law and to avoid great disparity in sentencing (p. 408).

Disposition

Once responsibility for a delinquent act or for a family problem had been established, the disposition of any case could take one of two forms:

1. Community supervision. The most common alternative would involve *mandatory* participation in a deinstitutionalized community program. "This approach avoids the sometimes unfortunate effects of

institutionalization and is consistent with the philosophy of employing the least coercive dispositional alternative appropriate to a particular case" (p. 673).

The use of community programming is also particularly relevant to families with service needs. "The family court will have a direct jurisdictional tie to any person, school system, treatment facility, or service associated with the child's behavioral problem" (p. 313):

> One example would be the child who repeatedly runs away from home because the parent's behavior has made the home situation intolerable. The family court could order the child returned to the home. But at the same time, it could order the parents to modify their behavior to make the home life more acceptable. Another example would be the child who is truant from school because an inability to read at his or her grade level makes classroom work impossible. The family court could make complementary orders that the child attend school and that the school provide some kind of remedial reading service to make his or her school attendance profitable (p. 313).

In other words, the family court might use its legal powers to *"command the assistance and cooperation of institutions serving children and families"* (p. 313, emphasis added). In addition, several other steps would also be taken in the interest of treatment:

The creation of a statewide network of services.

A treatment plan that would "not interfere with the juvenile's schooling, regular employment, or other activities necessary for normal growth and development."

The opportunity for juveniles and their parents to participate in the formulation of a treatment plan.

It is also significant that, even if these clients did not adhere to the treatment plan, community court workers could not escalate the use of coercive controls without first obtaining a new petition and returning them to court for a new hearing (pp. 673–674).

2. *Residential placement.* In the event that community supervision and in-home services did not suffice, the family court could order out-of-home placement. Any such placement, however, would be different for delinquents than for the children of families with service needs, or for endangered children.

For *delinquents,* a statewide network of public and private residential facilities should be organized in lieu of large training schools, none of which would include more than 100 children. Indeed, most should be camps, ranches, or small group homes which do not contain more than 20 beds, and they should be located in or near communities.

Professionals in these small units should then make an educational assessment of each delinquent, provide educational and vocational programs, make use of community schools wherever possible, and provide opportunities for work or educational furloughs (pp. 697–698).

Status offenders from families with service needs, by contrast, could not be confined in any residential setting where delinquents are placed. Furthermore, while such children would be provided with a complete range of services, their residential placement could not make use of locked doors or fences, since they are not criminal offenders. Indeed, if the court found that they were sufficiently mature and were capable of independent self-support, they might be permitted to live on their own, free from parental control (pp. 313–314).

Finally, standards for endangered (dependent and neglected) children would guard against the indiscriminate use of foster care and out-of-home placements. Because parental autonomy is to be honored wherever possible, any out-of-home placement must be reviewed every six months by the court. If after 6 to 12 months it is determined that an endangered child, cannot be returned home,

"parental rights should be terminated so that the child may attain another permanet family placement" (p. 336).

Summary

In summary, the new family court would attempt to do two things. On the one hand, it would heed the demands of the Supreme Court that juveniles and their families be provided with procedural safeguards whenever formal court action is anticipated. On the other hand, it would continue to exercise wide powers on behalf of children, both before and after legal processing:

1. It would involve the agents of juvenile justice in efforts to prevent delinquency.
2. It would continue to act paternalistically on behalf of status offenders.
3. It would permit officers of the court to exercise a great deal of discretion in deciding whether to divert juveniles from legal processing or to use formal procedures on their behalf.
4. It would use its powers to coerce other institutions to improve their services for children and their families.
5. It would require both children and their families to participate in reintegrative programs, in lieu of seeking to control crime by punishment and deterrence.
6. It would virtually preclude the use of secure incarceration in favor of community programs and small residential units.

In short, the family court model strongly reflects the imprint of both positive and labeling theories. While positive theories point to the myriad of community institutions and social forces that cause delinquent behavior, labeling theory stresses the way society defines, labels, and reacts to it. Taken together, therefore, these theories suggest that efforts to control delinquency should involve families, teachers, and employers as well as policemen, judges, and correctional workers. Since social as well as legal change is required, the goal of juvenile justice should be to destigmatize problem youths, to reintegrate them into the opportunity structures of the community, and to normalize their conduct.

JUST DESERTS MODEL

The just deserts is the second model for which there are many advocates. No less than the family model, it is based upon a detailed and comprehensive set of new standards— standards that fill no fewer than 23 volumes. Developed over a period of several years, these standards were written by the Joint Commission on Juvenile Justice Standards—a commission that was organized by the Institute for Judicial Administration of New York University and the prestigious American Bar Association. Like the task force that constructed the family court model, moreover, this commission was made up of eminent professionals, lawyers, judges, administrators, and social scientists, and even included some of the same people (See Flicker, 1977).

Guiding philosopy

Far more than the family model, the guiding philosophy of the just deserts model reflects the rising sense of despair that has characterized responses to the juvenile court during the past two decades. Indeed, said the IJA–ABA Commission, its basic philosophy is "genuinely shattering" with regard to the traditional functions of the juvenile court.

1.   Rejection of treatment. "Heretofore the court's intervention was assumed to be in the best interests of the child, designed to help the child to overcome difficulties in conforming to society's expectations because of his or her deficient home environment or psychological problems" (Flicker, 1977:23). But rather than providing this help,

closed hearings and unregulated procedures have resulted in arbitrary decision making and unjustifiable disparity in outcomes. Cultural biases, discrimination because of race or sex, subjective attitudes, and excessive moral or religious zeal frequently influenced decisions that fell within the wide range of official discretion (Flicker, 1977:23–24).

Given these unjust outcomes, therefore, the major decision of the commission *"was to reject the medical or rehabilitative model of the juvenile court. . . . The prescribing of treatment or services by the court is not inherently beneficial to the juvenile . . . and should be restrained"* (Flicker, 1977:23, emphasis added).

2.   Doing justice.   In lieu of past practices, the juvenile court should concentrate on doing justice:

> The commission adopted the view that the best way to protect juveniles was to ensure fair proceedings through procedural safeguards, representation by counsel, fixed criteria to guide official action, written decisions subject to judicial review, and full participation by juveniles in consultations with counsel and their parents if the parents' interests are not adverse to the juveniles (Flicker, 1977:24).

Attempts by a legal body to exercise love, benevolence, and charity, in other words, are misplaced. The juvenile court should be a court of law and nothing more.

Yet despite its sharply different philosophy, the actual standards outlined by the deserts model are often strikingly similar to those of the family model. These standards specify, for example, that the juvenile court should be a family court, organized not as a minor civil court but as a division of the highest court of trial jurisdiction in every state. Thus, the greatest differences between the two models have to do with the extent to which the deserts model would restrain legal authorities in their efforts to solve youth problems, would employ determinate sentencing for those convicted of crimes, and would sentence delinquency not the delinquent.

Clientele

Reflecting these differences, the deserts model would no longer permit status offenders to fall under the jurisdiction of the juvenile court. Indeed, except for their use of narcotics, juveniles who commit victimless crimes—drinking, gambling, or prostitution—would not be subject to legal constraints either. Since juvenile court intervention in these areas has tended to make criminals out of unruly children, parents and their offspring would have to look to voluntary community services for help—to crash-pads for runaways, to the school system for truancy, or to counseling centers for family problems (Flicker, 1977:22). The deserts court would have no part in organizing these programs or commanding a use of them. Thus, the clientele of the juvenile court would include only two groups—*delinquents* between the ages of 10 and 18 who have committed criminal acts and *abused and neglected* children whose bodily or emotional well-being is endangered by their parents.

Standards for intake

The intake standards for these two groups would be virtually identical with those of the family model. Except for serious or chronic offenders, they would allow policemen, prosecutors, and probation officers to exercise broad *discretion* in *diverting* juveniles from a formal hearing; they would ensure *fairness in procedure,* if formal adjudication were contemplated; they would severely restrict the use of *secure detention;* and they would reject the automatic *waiver* of serious delinquents to adult court (Flicker, 1977).

But where the family court might require the participation of juveniles or their families in a diversion program and might "command"

community resources in their behalf, the deserts court would command restraint. Every action that might limit the freedom of youth would have to make use of the "least restrictive alternative" and would have to be justified in writing. Indeed, involuntary treatment in lieu of legal processing could not be ordered. Instead, any participation would have to be voluntary, "unhampered by the implied threat that nonparticipation [would] result in a complaint being filed" (Flicker, 1977:76). In short, constraints on delinquents who did not go beyond the intake stage would be severely restricted.

Adjudication

Most adjudication procedures in the deserts court would also be like those in the family court: the *juvenile prosecutor* (not the probation officer) would determine whether the juvenile is a proper subject for juvenile court jurisdiction; *admissions of guilt* would still require a thorough investigation by the court to insure that they were competently made; *contested adjudications* would grant juveniles all the rights granted to criminal defendants; and the *right of appeal* would be insured (Flicker, 1977). However, there would be two notable exceptions:

1.   Plea bargaining.   Like the adult criminal court, the deserts model would permit plea bargaining, where the family model would not. Efforts by defense counsel could be made to alter the charges against a juvenile in exchange for a guilty plea to a lesser charge.

2.   Child rights.   In contrast to the idea that the rights of parents or of families are paramount, the desert model suggests that *"family autonomy frequently must yield to the rights of minors"* (Flicker, 1977:78. Emphasis added.). Indeed, its standards strongly reflect the impact of the child rights movement, suggesting that, under specified conditions, children have a right to sue their parents, to have their own attorneys, to establish a residence separate from their parents, and to manage their own financial affairs (Flicker, 1977:79–80).

Disposition

This emphasis upon the rights of juveniles notwithstanding, it is with respect to disposition that the deserts model differs most from the family model. Whereas the latter would assess the juvenile's needs, would develop a treatment plan to meet those needs, and would base sentencing on this plan, the sentence in the deserts court would be based upon the crimes he committed. This sentence, in turn, would be dictated by three criteria:

1.   Proportionality.   Length and type of sentence would be proportional to the seriousness of the juvenile's offense and his or her prior record. It might include a suspended sentence, restitution, a fine, community service, supervision in the community, or confinement in an institution (Flicker, 1977:200–202).

2.   Determinate sentencing.   The deserts model would not permit the use of indeterminate sentences, nor would it allow correctional personnel to decide when a juvenile is rehabilitated and should be released. Instead, "the nature and duration of all coercive dispositions should be determined by the court at the time of sentencing, within the limitations established by the legislature" (Flicker, 1977:196). These limitations would depend upon two things: (1) the delinquent's current offense and (2) his prior record. For example, if the juvenile had no prior record and had committed a burglary, punishment might be confinement for 6 months or conditional freedom for 18 months. But if the offender did have a prior record, the punishment would be increased.

3.   Least restrictive alternative.   Faced with the choice between upper and lower

limits, the judge should normally select the lower limit—the least restrictive alternative. But should he choose the upper limit, "he must state in writing the reasons for finding the less drastic remedies inappropriate or inadequate. . . ." (Flicker, 1977:22).

Clearly, then, the goal of the disposition is punishment not rehabilitation. Indeed, great care should be taken to distinguish between the two, so that punishment is not tainted either by correctional discretion or by attempts to change the juvenile. For example, while a delinquent might be required to attend school as a condition of punishment, his or her presence is all that is required. "Compliance is defined in terms of attendance . . . , not in terms of performance" (Flicker, 1977:203).

> Those who are delinquent enough to be sent to institutions also have the right to refuse counseling and therapy; they cannot be punished for not cooperating, and since their terms are established beforehand, they cannot be denied release (Serrill, 1979:50).

What all of this means is that, while wide discretion is granted to policemen and intake officers prior to ajudication, it is almost completely denied to correctional authorities following it. Although they must insure the presence of a humane and safe environment, they cannot mandate the use of any services—education, counseling, work, or recreation—unless they are so directed by a court order (Flicker, 1977:207–213).

> The principle of determinate sentences . . . eliminates the discretion of the correctional agency to determine the nature or duration of dispositions, restricting its role to selection of the program in which to place the juvenile within the category ordered by the court. Finally, juveniles are not subject to parole or to aftercare supervision . . . , unless community supervision has been part of the court's dispositional order (Flicker, 1977:207–208).

Summary

In summary, the standards set by the IJA–ABA Commission remain remarkably faithful to the just deserts philosophy and to those proponents of labeling theory who, except for serious crimes, recommend radical nonintervention into the lives of juveniles. In taking refuge in legal rules and bureaucratic procedure, those who constructed the deserts model would go much further than the family court in their commitment to doing as little mischief as possible.

In using diversion, they would reject the use of involuntary treatment in the interest of prevention and would concentrate on the use of the least restrictive alternative.

In stressing the legal rights of juveniles, they would lessen the rights of parents and perhaps even those of the community.

In order to avoid doing harm, they would sentence delinquency not the delinquent.

In punishing delinquency, they would concentrate neither on deterrence nor on rehabilitation but on just deserts.

In stressing justice, in short, they would rule out attempts to alter either the juvenile or the community.

THE PROGRESS OF REFORM

Except for the state of Washington which has adopted the deserts model, few states have adopted either model in its entirety. Nonetheless, several reforms, implied by either or both of them, have been tried. In the pages that follow, therefore, their implications for the future of juvenile justice will be assessed.

Decriminalization versus paternalism for status offenders

America remains divided over appropriate policies for the status offender. On the one hand, such divergent groups as the International Chiefs of Police, the National Council on Crime and Delinquency, and the framers of the model act for family courts have supported just deserts standards by recommending that the jurisdiction of the court over status offenders be eliminated (National Task Force, 1977:3). As of this writing, however, only a few states have taken that step. In Washington, for example, status offenders are now the responsibility of the Department of Social and Health Services, rather than the juvenile court (*Revised Criminal Code of Washington*, 1977). And since any treatment is supposed to be voluntary, the new law makes it very difficult for status offenders to be held in detention or, along with their families, to be required to submit to any form of intervention (Schneider and Schram, 1979).

On the other hand, most states, along with the National Advisory Commission on Corrections and the framers of the Uniform Juvenile Court Act, have joined in supporting the notion of the family court that, while status offenders should not be called "delinquents," they should remain under the jurisdiction of the juvenile court. Indeed, the movement in this direction began in California as early as 1961, when a new legal code defined status offenders as 601s, while criminal offenders were called 602s (Lemert, 1970). The following year, the state of New York created a somewhat similar category by calling the status offender a person in need of supervision (PINS). Then, the movement really gained steam, with different states creating new acronyms for the status offender: minor in need of supervision (MINS), child in need of supervision (CHINS); or unruly child (UC) (Rubin, 1974:607). By 1973, 25 states had created a separate category for the status offender, with most remaining states to follow.

These early changes notwithstanding, it was not until more recent years that widespread attempts were made to adopt other features of the family court model: to divert more status offenders from legal processing, to mobilize more community programs in their behalf, and to eliminate their confinement in detention centers and training schools. But rather than discussing these changes here, we will turn to them in the following sections. For now, it is enough to know that most states have permitted the juvenile court to retain jurisdiction over status offenders.

Discretion and diversion

Despite their philosophical differences, both the family and the deserts models stress the importance of encouraging police and intake personnel to exercise wide discretion in deciding whether to divert both delinquents and status offenders from official processing. What, then, have been the consequences of these efforts?

1. Diversion. Diversion has become the most popular of all innovations in recent years. Legislatively sanctified and spurred by federal and state funds, literally thousands of new diversion programs were set up during the 1970s, supposedly for minor criminals as well as for status offenders. Indeed, a whole new child-saving bureaucracy was created (Carter and Klein, 1976; Rutherford and McDermott, 1976).

Some of the new programs were conceived and run by private agencies. But contrary to the standards of both the family and the deserts models, the majority have either been connected with, or run by, justice personnel (Austin and Krisberg, 1981; Baron et al., 1973; Klein and Teilmann, 1976; Klein, 1979; Lemert, 1981). Rather than referring juveniles to nonlegal agencies, rather than attempting to alter the way schools deal with marginal children, rather than suggesting better work-study programs or mobilizing support for a better integration of family roles, legal authorities have either sponsored or organized their own inhouse programs. Hence, nothing could have been further from the intent of the standards of either court model. Indeed, it has become apparent to juveniles that diversion does not mean escape from the justice system (Klein et al., 1976:113).

But this is not the only paradox. Other outcomes were also paradoxical and unintended. First, diversion was supposed to turn the flow of juveniles away from the juvenile justice system and back toward the community. But rather than doing that, several studies reveal that as many as half of all referrals have come, not from police and intake officers, but from schools, welfare agencies, and parents—the very people and institutions that were supposed to be mobilized to serve youth in lieu of legal processing (Humphreys and Carrier, 1976; McAleenan et al., 1977; Palmer et al., 1978; Statsky, 1974).

Second, many juveniles were assigned to diversion programs, not on a voluntary basis, as the just deserts model suggests, but on an involuntary basis. That is, they were told that if they cooperated and performed well in their programs, no further legal action would be taken against them. But if they were uncooperative, they could be petitioned to court and treated as delinquents (Lieberg, 1971; Klein et al., 1976:112–114).

Finally, given the extent to which many diversion programs were dominated by law enforcement personnel, it is obvious that assignment to them was not necessarily less stigmatizing, particularly since referrals often came from, rather than to, families, schools, and other community agencies. Consequently, says Lemert (1981:43), "the cooptation of the diversion movement by law enforcement leaves the rather sour conclusion that not only have the purposes of diversion been perverted but, moreover, police power has been extended over youths and types of behavior not previously subjected to control." "Placed under the control of the criminal justice system, diversion programs have been transformed into a means for extending the net [of legal control], making it stronger, and creating new nets" (Austin and Krisberg, 1981:170).

If these conclusions are at all accurate, it is surprising that just deserts proponents have not raised any legal challenges against the discretionary authority that makes diversion possible. Although diversion was instituted under the guise of improving the network of community services and of insuring that intervention was less intrusive, it appears that the constitutional rights of divertees may have been less well protected than those who have actually been subjected to a formal court hearing.

2. *Prevention.* In light of all these unanticipated consequences, a key question is whether diversion has helped to prevent delinquency. As yet, however, conclusive evidence is unavailable. In their examination of nine of the "better evaluated" programs, Gibbons and Blake (1976) found that, while juveniles assigned to some projects had lower recidivism rates than those who were inserted into the system, the same was not true of others.

In one instance, Klein (1975) found that juveniles who had simply been counseled and released had lower *official arrest* records than those who had either been assigned to a diversion program or had been referred to court. Yet when he interviewed juveniles in these groups, he found their *self-reported* rates of delinquency did not differ; all were equally delinquent. He concluded, therefore, that divertees had not actually been more delinquent. Rather, they had higher arrest records because the delinquent acts they did commit were simply more visible to law enforcement personnel.

These sorts of inconclusive results have also been confirmed by studies of other, more general efforts to prevent delinquency. In his review of the 10 best scientific studies on the subject, Berleman (1980) found that none

appeared to produce more desirable results than merely leaving juveniles alone. Overall, therefore, the results of efforts to utilize official discretion and diversion have been discouraging. But in contrast to the notion that the fault lies with the intent of such efforts, one prominent investigator has concluded that it lies, instead, in the pervasive unwillingness of law enforcement personnel to relinquish control over *minor offenders* and to their failure to allow, let alone support, the kinds of community programs that were intended by the family and deserts models (Klein, 1979). As Dunford (1977) puts it:

> [W]e have good reason to be concerned that diversion as conceived by its creators and proponents . . . will never receive a fair test. It is evident that the practice of diversion may be rejected, not because it could not fulfill its promise, but because it was never given a chance to do so.

Due process

Even though the use of discretion and diversion has not conformed to that envisioned by today's reformers, their stress upon the need for due process in pre-adjudicatory and adjudicatory hearings has been heeded. Investigations have shown that conformity to the requirements of the various Supreme Court decisions is growing; that lawyers are being seen more frequently in court; and that many court personnel themselves support the introduction of due process standards (Franklin and Gibbons, 1973; Reasons, 1970; Rubin, 1976). But lest we assume that formality is not without its problems, consider but two brief examples:

1. *Overcoming assembly-line justice.* The traditional juvenile court has been attacked for dispensing assembly-line justice, of expending too little time and attention on each case. But such problems are no less true of the model the juvenile court is

supposed to follow; namely, the adult criminal court. The reason is that due process procedures take more time, more personnel, and more resources than do informal procedures. As a result, many criminal courts are characterized by a massive backlog of cases that take months, sometimes years, to resolve.

Constitutional safeguards also depend heavily upon a family's capacity to hire expensive lawyers and other legal assistance. Poor parents and their children, however, usually must depend upon overworked and underprepared public defenders. Consequently, just because more people now pay lip service to the need for due process, there are few grounds for assuming that standards favoring it will be implemented—that juvenile courts will be raised to superior court levels and that the numbers and skills of prosecutors, defense attorneys, and judges will be increased. Indeed, there is reason to believe these resources will be in short supply. Because of increasing distrust of our justice system, taxpayer revolts and political conservatism, we have now entered a period, of uncertain duration, in which public funds for these purposes have become increasingly difficult to obtain. Hence, if there is danger, it is that the very parents and children who can least afford capable counsel, but who often need it the most, will not have the means by which to guarantee that evidence in their behalf is capably presented and fairly judged.

2. *Due process and status offenders.*
Since most states have retained jurisdiction over status offenders, due process in their behalf still presents problems. On the one hand, the statutes of many states still prohibit such acts as "growing up in idleness or delinquency," being "beyond the lawful control of parents," or "deportment endangering the morals, health, or general welfare of a child." As a result, some appeals courts have declared such laws unconstitutional. In *Gonzalez* v. *Maillard*

(1971), a three-judge panel in California ruled that the phrase "in danger of leading an idle, dissolute, lewd, or immoral life" was too vague. "If the statute under which a juvenile is charged is so uncertain and all-encompassing that the state need prove no specific crime," said the court, "defense counsel has little idea of what he must defend against." Due process cannot be insured.

On the other hand, most higher courts *have not* seen fit to sustain the contention of deserts proponents that status offenses should be decriminalized, even though they have ruled that vague laws must be made more specific (Paulsen and Whitebread, 1974). In a New York case, for example, an appeals court made the following ruling regarding a 13-year-old boy who would not go to school and who habitually stayed out until 2 or 3 A.M. against his parents' wishes.

> While the doctrine of *parens patriae* does not permit any unfairness in judicial procedure toward juveniles . . . [it is] this court's opinion . . . that the state has the power to perform the parental role of insuring the child's education and training, when the parent is unable to control him sufficiently to perform it. . . . Enforcement against the child of the compulsory school law appears still to be constitutional (Paulsen and Whitebread, 1974:46).

In short, the matter of deciding what to do in cases like this does not readily lend itself either to formal procedure or to inaction. So long as children are viewed as immature and in need of special supervision, attempts to solve their developmental problems will be difficult. However, there is a third alternative: new laws can be used in an attempt to define such problems out of existence by granting children the same rights as adults.

In the state of Washington, which has adopted the just deserts model, the first great step in this direction has been taken. Not only have status offenses been decriminalized, but the law now permits juveniles to reject any attempts by parents and legal authorities to use coercive means in an effort to solve their problems:

> If [children] run away from home . . . , they can refuse to go back home. . . . If the problem is not resolved within 72 hours, the case will be taken to court. But the judge cannot order the child to go back home . . . , as judges in other states still can. If the child refuses to cooperate, he cannot be declared "ungovernable" and sent to an institution. Parents, judges, and community workers can . . . recommend counseling . . . but the youngsters have the right to refuse it (Serrill, 1979:49–50).

In short, like adults, children cannot be subjected to coercive legal controls unless they have committed a criminal offense.

Most states have apparently rejected this solution because of their belief that the total decriminalization of status offenses will only mask, not do away with, a host of slippery problems; namely that an elimination of the rules against status offenses would not eliminate the behaviors the rules were designed to control. There would still be children who reject the need for schooling, who become homeless street people, or who seriously jeopardize their futures in some other ways. Thus, if society chose to ignore these children, it would be engaging in a legislative sleight-of-hand in which only the rules, not the problems, were changed.

The Department of Social and Health Services in Washington has been given the responsibility for dealing with status offenders, but in the absence of legal means by which to require children and parents to engage in a search for solutions, it is encountering a bewildering set of new problems (Schneider and Schram, 1979). Hence, this new experiment will be watched with great interest.

Deinstitutionalization

As we have seen, both the family and the deserts models have stressed the importance of deinstitutionalizing correctional programs for the clientele of the juvenile court and of using the least restrictive alternative in disposing of their cases. But while the reasons for encouraging this reform have differed—the family model for reintegrating juveniles into normal child-serving community settings and the deserts model for minimizing involuntary intrusions into their lives—the results have been the same. Speaking on behalf of legislation to encourage deinstitutionalization, Senator Birch Bayh (1971) summed up the sentiments of the early and middle 1970s:

> Today, too many young people are thrown into custodial institutions who should be handled in the community. We want to find ways to establish meaningful alternatives to incarceration. . . . Punishment, isolation, neglect, and abuse seem to be the hallmarks of institutional life. This includes harassment, affront to human dignity, and the gross denial of human rights.

These sentiments were then translated into legislation. The Juvenile Justice and Delinquency Prevention Act of 1974, and subsequent revisions of it, have made federal funds available to the states in order to encourage deinstitutionalization, and then required those who receive them to remove all status, if not delinquent, offenders from secure places of precourt detention and postadjudication incarceration (Senate and House of Representatives, 1974). What have been the consequences of these efforts?

1. Deinstitutionalization of status offenders. Even before the passage of the federal legislation, seven states had passed laws prohibiting the secure confinement of status offenders following a court appearance. Spurred by the federal legislation, however, the number of such states grew markedly. By 1978, 17 had prohibited postadjudication institutionalization, and 22 had barred *both* precourt detention *and* postadjudication confinement (Klein, 1979:179). But appearances may not always be what they seem. Instead, efforts to deinstitutionalize correctional programs have encountered some of the problems that diversion programs encountered.

One sizable group of investigators, for example, contends that authorities have used two methods to subvert the intent of the deinstitutionalization movement. First, if status offenders cannot be detained or institutionalized, other ways may be found for "encapsulating" them in group homes or in foster care in the community—in what Spergel (1976) calls "community incarceration." Thus, instead of having 'institution kids' we now have a new group of 'agency kids' "—kids who are now under the control of mental health, welfare, or social service systems, if not the legal system (Coates et al, 1978:173; Klein, 1975:109).

Second, legal authorities may *relabel* status offenders in order to maintain their control over them. This is done either by calling them dependent and neglected children or by calling them delinquents (Klein, 1979:183). In other words, by relabeling them, ways can be found to continue the use of out-of-home placements.

Sometimes the reasons for relabeling may be necessary. Paulsen and Whitebread (1974:67) cite the example of a 15-year-old girl in Ohio. Technically, she was a status offender, unresponsive to her parents and out of their control. But she was also unmarried and had just given birth to a baby. Furthermore, the court psychologist argued that the girl presented "a poor prognosis for successful self-management and an even poorer prognosis for success as a mother."

What should be done in a case like this? How should the girl be labeled, if at all? Should the court place her in a special program for unwed mothers, since she was beyond the control of her parents? Or should it simply define the new baby as neglected, separate it from the mother, and ignore the latter? Or should it define both mother and child as dependent and then attempt to place or to otherwise supervise them as a new family unit? Or should the court have no jurisdiction at all in either case? And, if it has no jurisdiction, should the two children be ignored or should some other agency make the necessary decisions—an agency from which there might be no legal appeal if the mother or her parents did not like its decision? In cases like this, the stakes are often high. Hence, someone has to assume responsibility, if worse problems are not to ensue.

Miller (1979:98) contends, however, that the more common reasons for relabeling status offenders and keeping them under control are self-serving and bureaucratic. Besides the *manifest* function of serving youth, he says, institutions and other programs for juveniles serve many *latent* functions as well—"employment in remote areas, political patronage, contracts with vendors of services, arrangements between specific institutions and particular courts, or the self-interests of professional and custodial groups. Much of the juvenile justice system remains geared to these considerations, not to its manifest functions."

Given these obstructions, evidence with regard to deinstitutionalization for status offenders is mixed. On the one hand, the data indicate that their confinement in secure settings has declined (Handler and Zatz, 1981). In their study of nine different sites across the country, Kobrin and Klein (1980) found that the use of detention had decreased by 24 percent and assignment to a training school by 51 percent. And while these figures were much less than the 75 percent mandated by Congress, a decrease did occur.

On the other hand, the data are unclear as to what is likely to happen in the future to those who are deinstitutionalized. During the mid-1970s when federal support for the deinstitutionalization movement was at its highest, it appears that many status offenders were simply transferred from the direct controls of the legal system and encapsulated in programs run by the mental health, welfare, and private agency systems. Rather than successfully altering the normal network of families, schools, and neighborhoods, misbehaving juveniles were simply placed under the control of alternative bureaucracies.

In more recent years, however, there is reason to believe that the number of status offenders who are being ignored is increasing, that nothing is being done for, or to, them (Handler and Zatz, 1981). Not only are many legislators as well as citizens increasingly persuaded by deserts doctrines favoring total decriminalization, but they have grown increasingly hostile to those juveniles who commit criminal acts. Hence, it is the latter, not status offenders, on whom they want legal controls focused.

Second, as the law prohibiting the detention of status offenders take increasing effect, many authorities seem less inclined to take any action whatsoever. With no secure place to hold runaways or drunken juveniles while remedial steps are taken, the police in particular turn their attention to other matters, often with relief because they would rather be fighting crime than dealing with mixed-up kids (Schneider and Schram, 1979).

Finally, taxpayer revolts and declining federal funds have resulted in a situation in which resources for shelter homes and other services are declining. Indeed, many states have not appropriated funds for these purposes, even though they have passed laws prohibiting detention and incarceration. Consequently, other agencies are increasingly disinclined to accept status offenders.

Taken as a whole, these changing problems indicate that, like diversion, the

deinstitutionalization movement has not been entirely successful. Even when funds were available, the net of bureaucratic control was not decreased, only shifted from legal to other networks. But now that funds are declining, the laws that prohibit incarceration may be subverted in two ways. Authorities can either relabel status offenders and thus continue to confine them, or they can treat them with a policy of benign neglect. While other alternatives are possible—alternatives that would pay greater attention to the families, neighborhoods, and schools—we have either lacked the knowledge or the will to address them successfully.

2. Deinstitutionalization for criminal offenders. With all these difficulties, efforts have also been made to deinstitutionalize correctional programs for serious delinquents. The most dramatic example occurred in Massachusetts. In 1972, after two years of "constant crisis, confrontation, and confusion," during which he tried to reform the state's training schools, Jerome Miller the director of Youth Services, decided to shut them down entirely (Ohlin et al., 1977:4–12). This was a radical step because Massachusetts had been the first state in the nation to open training schools—one for boys at Westboro in 1846 and one for girls at Lancaster in 1854. But after Dr. Miller's drastic step, all correctional programs in Massachusetts were transferred to the community.

This drastic step was not taken, however, without some knowledge of its possible consequences. During the 1960s, some well-known experiments were conducted in which deliberate efforts were made to utilize community programs in lieu of incarceration for serious criminal offenders. One was the Community Treatment Program of the California Youth Authority which was discussed in Chapter 16. But while this experiment was based upon psychological theory, two others—the Provo Experiment (Empey and Erickson,

1972) and the Silverlake Experiment (Empey and Lubeck, 1971)—were derived from strain and symbolic interactionist theories and stressed the importance of reintegration.

Both experiments assumed that (1) because official delinquents tend to be the children of lower-class parents, their lives are characterized by learning situations which limit their access to success goals and (2) in response to this lack of opportunity, the greater part of delinquent behavior is a group phenomenon— a shared deviation which is the product of a differential group experience in a delinquent subculture. Consequently, in an effort to address these problems, three major steps were taken: (1) delinquents were permitted to live at home (Provo) or in a small group home in a middle-class neighborhood (Silverlake): (2) a daily group meeting was held in which the delinquent group itself became both the medium and the target of change; and (3) efforts were made to open up conventional opportunities by reintegrating offenders into the local schools and by finding employment for them. These programs, in short, sought to replace the coercive controls and methods of the institution with the social controls and opportunities of the local community.

The deinstitutionalization movement for criminal offenders, of which these and the Massachusetts experiment were symbols, did receive increased support during the late 1960s and 1970s. California, for example, passed a probation subsidy bill in which local counties received state subsidy for keeping offenders out of state institutions. As a consequence, the rate at which delinquents were committed to the California Youth Authority declined from a rate of 178 per 100,000 in 1960 to 49 per 100,000, in 1974 (California Youth Authority, 1980:14). Yet there was also evidence which indicated that, as more community programs were created, they did not result in a widespread emptying of training schools across the country (National Criminal Justice Information Service,

1979; 1980). Instead, such programs were used for petty offenders, many of whom would have been placed on probation under ordinary circumstances. Hence, some of the same unintended consequences were associated with this reform as with other reforms; namely, rather than greatly reducing the net of official control, they maintained or expanded it (Vinter et al., 1975:45–52; Klein, 1979).

Given this outcome, an important question is whether deinstitutionalized community programs are more effective than places of incarceration and whether greater use should have been made of them for serious offenders. In order to answer these questions, therefore, two issues must be examined: (1) whether such programs are a danger to the community while young criminals are participating in them and (2) whether they reduce recidivism rates once offenders are released from them.

The first issue was carefully studied in the Provo Experiment (Empey and Erickson, 1972:73–94). But contrary to public fears, the evidence clearly indicated that boys in the community program were significantly less delinquent while they were under supervision than were the members of a randomly selected group who had been placed on regular probation. Even more important, the experimental boys not only had low rates of arrest while under supervision, but they also were no more delinquent than a matched group who were incarcerated in a state training school. Even though the latter were supposedly securely confined, they committed as much crime when they went home on short furloughs or when they escaped as did the experimental group while they remained free in the community. Moreover, the same general conclusion seems to have been true in Massachusetts (Coates et al., 1978).

By contrast, an analysis of *postprogram* recidivism rates revealed few differences between experimental and control groups; community programs, in other words, did not seem to be consistently superior to the use of incarceration. Instead, the best that could be said was that they do at least as well as training schools (Coates et al., 1978; Empey and Erickson, 1972; Empey and Lubeck, 1971).

But this was not the only issue. Rather than merely asking whether one program was superior to another, those who conducted the Provo and Silverlake Experiments also asked whether the crime rate had been reduced by them. This was accomplished by comparing the preprogram arrest rates for each group with its postprogram rates. And when completed, the results were striking. Whether boys were incarcerated or left in the community, their arrest rates were reduced anywhere from 25 percent for those who were incarcerated to 70 percent for those who remained free in the community (Empey and Erickson, 1972).

Although this finding seemed to suggest that all correctional programs might be having far more impact than most people believed, it had to be treated with caution. Rather than the result of treatment, these large reductions might have been due to maturational reform— the possibility that as delinquents grow older, they commit less crime—or that their violation rates had reached a peak just before they were assigned to a program and had now declined to a more normal level. Hence, relatively little was made of them.

In recent years, however, a large study by Murray and Cox (1979) produced the same striking outcome. In this instance, though, somewhat larger reductions in crime rates occurred among delinquents who had been incarcerated, rather than among those who had remained in the community. But because they too could have been due to maturational reform or to selection biases, these findings became the subject of national debate (McCleary et al., 1978; 1979). Those who favor incarceration hailed them as proof of the need for punishment, while those who favor deinstitutionalization attacked them as being

inhumane, if not scientifically inaccurate and misleading (See Empey, 1979). Hence, even though the evidence regarding the effectiveness of deinstitutionalization is by no means entirely negative, it is subject to competing interpretations. While the optimist is likely to view the evidence as suggesting that the glass of reform is half full—that is, that deinstitutionalization is not only more humane but is at least as successful as incarceration— the pessimist is likely to view the glass as half empty, as indicating that deinstitutionalization for criminal offenders is a failure and ought to be discarded.

Punishment versus reintegration

In light of these competing interpretations, our final issue becomes all the more relevant; that is, whether delinquents should be rehabilitated and reintegrated as the family model suggests or whether they ought to be punished as the deserts model indicates.

Our review of the reforms of the past decade has not been particularly supportive of the family model. Rather than mobilizing family, educational, and employment services for delinquents, they appear to have enlarged the net of legal control; rather than fostering reintegration, they have encouraged parents, schools, and welfare agencies to refer even more children to the juvenile justice system; and rather than demonstrating that diversion and deinstitutionalization have successfully reduced crime, they have produced equivocal results. Consequently, any casual observer is likely to conclude that the despair of deserts philosophy is warranted. Optimism, benevolence, and charity have not stemmed the rising tide of youth crime.

Should that be the conclusion, the result is likely to be filled with irony. Just deserts philosophy advocates the use of punishment only because efforts to promote benevolence have often been discriminatory, unfair, and oppressive. Punishment should be chosen, therefore, not because it appeals to our higher sentiments but because it is the lesser of two evils. In order to avoid compounding evil, the punishment of young people should not be long and harsh but should be used simply to symbolize the fact that justice has been done—indeed, to avoid doing them further harm.

But is that the interpretation that political leaders and the public are likely to make of classical philosophy? In response to fear and despair, are they likely to favor reducing the severity of punishment? There is evidence that such is not the case, that instead, they are more likely to adopt *utilitarian* solutions—to believe that the punishment of young criminals should be harsh, that it can be used to deter others, and that it should be employed to protect society.

In 1976, the state of New York enacted a series of bills that provided for mandatory and greatly extended periods of incarceration for juveniles who commit certain "designated felony acts." Then in 1978, it extended this "special treatment" to 13-year-olds; indeed, if they commit murder, they can be sentenced to terms as long as life (Paulsen, 1979:223). Likewise, California has a new law that makes certain offenders, 16 years and older, automatically subject to prosecution in adult court and, therefore, subject to adult sanctions (*California Welfare and Institutions Code,* 1976: Chapter 1071:1–24). Finally, contrary to both family and deserts standards, a dozen states have now amended their laws so that juveniles can be prosecuted as adults for certain crimes and sentenced to long terms (Serrill, 1979:48).

Even the new code in Washington State, hailed as a model for the nation, reflects the impact of utilitarian philosophy. Not only does its list of priorities pay almost no attention to treatment (ranked fifth along with custody), but it lists community protection as its first priority:

1. Protect the citizenry from criminal behavior.
2. Provide for determining whether accused juveniles have committed offenses.
3. Make the juvenile offender accountable for his or her criminal behavior.
4. Provide for punishment commensurate with the age, crime, and criminal history of the juvenile offender.
5. Provide due process for juveniles alleged to have committed an offense.
6. Provide necessary treatment, supervision, and custody for juvenile offenders.
7. Provide for the handling of juvenile offenders by communities whenever consistent with public safety.
8. Provide for restitution to victims of crime (*Revised Code of Washington,* 1977:80).

What is more, the adoption of determinate sentencing in Washington has extended, not reduced, the length of incarceration:

> Under the current guidelines, . . . chronic burglars and other property offenders are being sentenced to terms of from 8 to 12 months, depending upon their age and prior record, while those convicted of violent offenses are receiving terms ranging from 20 to 40 months.
>
> Many critics of institutions would be appalled at the length of these terms, which are three and four times the average time served by delinquents in many other states (Serrill, 1979:52).

Indeed, if determinate sentencing for juveniles follows the pattern set by that for adults, increases in the number and length of institutional confinements can be anticipated. Contrary to the intent of deserts philosophies, punishment has increased in severity, not decreased (See Austin and Krisberg, 1981:181–182). As a result, overcrowded prisons have now become smoldering volcanoes waiting to erupt.

What all of this suggests, in short, is that our

schizoid reaction to delinquents during the past two decades is now beginning to shift. Rather than the family court model, recent legislative changes reflect the imprint, not merely of deserts, but of utilitarian philosophy. In response to the mixed results of decriminalization, diversion, and deinstitutionalization, society is tending to agree with neoclassical philosophers that rehabilitation and reintegration should be discarded in favor of due process, determinate sentencing, punishment, and deterrence. Even if still immature, individuals, not society, should be held responsible for delinquent acts. Since efforts to nurture and to help children have not worked, they should be held accountable for their crimes and punished.

SUMMARY AND CONCLUSIONS

This chapter has shown that, in response to a bewildering array of prescriptions for reform, two models for juvenile justice have been constructed:

Family court model

The *family court model* is the more traditional of the two. While it incorporates standards that make due process imperative, it also stresses the importance of continuing to act paternalistically toward status offenders, of mobilizing community services on behalf of youth, and of seeking to control crime by reintegrating delinquents into the opportunity structures of society. Prevention and social services, as well as due process, are basic to its philosophy.

Just deserts model

The *just deserts model,* by contrast, is committed to minimizing harm by doing justice. Rather than attempting to alter either the delinquent or the community, it would decriminalize status offenders, would concentrate on due process, would sentence delinquency, would punish those who commit delinquent acts, and would make treatment voluntary. The mechanization of justice, and a withdrawal from benevolent pursuits by the court, are central to this philosophy.

Effects of reform

Despite philosophical differences, both models stress certain reforms: *discretion* at intake, *diversion, due process,* and *deinstitutionalization.* But while the family model would use these reforms as a means of rehabilitating and reintegrating offenders, the deserts model would divert them in order to minimize the uses and effects of legal processing. Since a benevolent concern with the individual does not work, legal intervention should concentrate on the protection of constitutional rights and on the use of punishment.

Our review of these reforms revealed that, aside from increased efforts to ensure due process, most have had unanticipated and unintended consequences. Rather than reducing legal intervention or mobilizing family, educational, and employment services for juveniles, they appear to have enlarged the net of legal control. Rather than reversing the flow of juveniles toward the juvenile justice system, or of reintegrating them in normal youth institutions, they have encouraged parents, schools, and welfare agencies to refer even more not fewer children to the system; and rather than demonstrating that diversion and deinstitutionalization have successfully reduced crime, they have produced equivocal results.

What many people fail to recognize, however, is that as long as diversion and deinstitutionalization are dominated by the agents of juvenile justice, they are likely to have the paradoxical consequence of increasing, not decreasing, the *official* crime rate. A self-fulfilling prophecy is created in which greater surveillance in the community inevitably increases the detection of delinquent acts, even though the actual incidence of those acts may not have increased.

Conclusions

Given these outcomes, the increasing fears of a despondent public are likely to resolve our schizophrenic policies of the past two decades in favor of a deserts model for juvenile justice. Ironically, however, the gradual adoption of this model also reflects the imprint of a more retributive utilitarian philosophy. In its stress upon due process, determinate sentencing, and punishment, the deserts model has given inadvertent but understandable support to reforms favoring incapacitation and deterrence as well. Since efforts to nurture and to rehabilitate children have not worked and since society requires protection, less attention should be paid to status offenders and more to holding young criminals accountable for their acts by punishing them.

If this conclusion is at all accurate and if current trends continue they portend remarkable changes in our concept of childhood, in our concern with understanding the sources of delinquent conduct, and in our efforts to control it. In the concluding chapter, therefore, we will turn our attention to these changes and to their implications.

REFERENCES

Austin, James, and Krisberg, Barry
    1981   "Wider, Stronger and Different Nets: The Dialectics of Criminal Justice Reform." *Journal of Research in Crime and Delinquency* 18 (January):165–196.

Baron, Robert; Feeney, Floyd; and Thornton, Warren
    1973   "Preventing Delinquency Through Diversion: The Sacramento Court 601 Diversion Project." *Federal Probation* 37 (March):13–18.

Bayh, Birch
    1971   Statement to U.S. Senate Committee on the Judiciary, Subcommittee to Investigate Juvenile Delinquency, 92nd Congress, First Session, May 3–18.

Berleman, William C.
    1980   *Juvenile Delinquency Prevention Experiments: A Review and Analysis.* Washington, D.C.: National Institute of Juvenile Justice and Delinquency Prevention.

Byrne, Brendan T.
    1976   "Foreword." In *National Advisory Committee on Criminal Justice Standards and Goals.* Juvenile Justice and Delinquency Prevention. Washington, D.C.: Law Enforcement Assistance Administration.

California Youth Authority
    1980   *Annual Report:1979.* Sacramento: California Youth Authority.

Carter, Robert M., and Klein, Malcolm W.
    1976   *Back on the Street: The Diversion of Juvenile Offenders.* Englewood Cliffs: Prentice-Hall.

Coates, Robert B.; Miller, Alden D.; and Ohlin, Lloyd E.
1978   *Diversity in a Youth Correctional System: Handling Delinquents in Massachusetts.* Cambridge: Ballinger.

Dunford, Franklyn W.
1977   "Police diversion: an illusion?" *Criminology* 15 (November):335–352.

Empey, LaMar T., and Lubeck, Steven G.
1971   *The Silverlake Experiment: Testing Delinquency Theory and Community Intervention.* Chicago: Aldine.

Empey, LaMar T., and Erickson, Maynard L.
1972   *The Provo Experiment: Evaluating Community Control of Delinquency.* Lexington, Mass.: D. C. Heath.

Empey, LaMar T.
1979   "Foreword." Pp. 9–26 in Charles A. Murray and Louis A. Cox, Jr., *Beyond Probation: Juvenile Corrections and the Chronic Delinquent.* Beverly Hills, Calif.: Sage.

Flicker, Barbara D.
1977   *Standards for Juvenile Justice: A Summary and Analysis.* Cambridge, Mass.: Ballinger.

Franklin, Jerry, and Gibbons, Don C.
1973   "New Directions for Juvenile Courts—Probation Officers' Views." *Crime and Delinquency* 19 (October):508–518.

Gibbons, Don, and Blake, Gerald F.
1976   "Evaluating the Impact of Juvenile Diversion Programs." Paper presented at the Annual Meetings of the Pacific Sociological Association, San Diego.

Gonzalez, v. *Mailliard*
1971   Civ. No. 50424, N.D. Cal., 2/9/71. Appeal docketed, U.S. No. 70–120, 4/9/71.

Handler, Joel F., and Zatz, Julie, eds.
1981   *Neither Angels or Thieves: Studies in Deinstitutionalization of Status Offenders.* Washington, D.C.: National Academy of Sciences.

Humphreys, Laud, and Carrier, Joseph M.
1976   *Second Annual Evaluation Report: Pomona Valley Juvenile Diversion Project.* Clarement, Calif.: Pitzer College.

Klein, Malcolm W.
1975   *Alternative Dispositions for Juvenile Offenders: An Assessment of the Juvenile Referral and Resource Development Program.* Los Angeles: Social Science Research Institute, University of Southern California.
1979   "Deinstitutionalization and Diversion of Juvenile Offenders: a Litany of Impediments." Pp. 145–200 in Norval Morris and Michael Tonry, eds., *Crime and Justice,* Vol. I. Chicago: University of Chicago Press.

Klein, Malcolm W., et al.
1976   "The Explosion in Police Diversion Programs." Pp. 101–120 in Malcolm W. Klein, ed., *The Juvenile Justice System.* Beverly Hills, Calif.: Sage.

Klein, Malcolm W., and Teilmann, Kathie S.
1976   *Pivotal Ingredients of Police Diversion Programs.* Washington, D.C.: National Institute for Juvenile Justice and Delinquency Prevention.

Kobrin, Solomon, and Klein, Malcolm W.
  1980   *National Evaluation of the Deinstitutionalization of Status Offender Programs: Final Report.* Los Angeles: Social Science Research Institute, University of Southern California.

Lemert, Edwin M.
  1970   *Social Action and Legal Change: Revolution Within the Juvenile Court.* Chicago: Aldine.
  1981   "Diversion in Juvenile Justice: What Hath Been Wrought." *Journal of Research in Crime and Delinquency* 18 (January):35–46.

Lieberg, Leon
  1971   *Project Crossroads: Final Report to the Manpower Administration, U.S. Department of Labor.* Washington, D.C.: U.S. National Committee for Children and Youth.

McAleenan, Michael, et al.
  1977   *Final Evaluation Report: The West San Gabriel Valley Juvenile Diversion Project.* Los Angeles: Occidental College.

McCleary, R., McDowall, Gordon D. and Maltz, M.D.
  1978   *A Reanalysis of UDIS: Deinstitutionalizing the Chronic Juvenile Offender.* Chicago: Illinois Dept. of Corrections.
  1979   "How a regression artifact can make any delinquency program look effective." In Lee Sechrest and Associates (eds.), *Evaluation Studies Review Annual* (Vol. 4). Beverly Hills, Ca: Sage.

Miller, Jerome G.
  1979   "The Revolution in Juvenile Justice: From Rhetoric to Rhetoric" Pp. 66–111 in LaMar T. Empey, ed., *The Future of Childhood and Juvenile Justice.* Charlottesville: University Press of Virginia.

Murray, Charles A., and Cox, Louis A.
  1979   *Beyond Probation: Juvenile Corrections and the Chronic Delinquent.* Beverly Hills, Calif.: Sage.

National Advisory Committee on Criminal Justice Standards and Goals
  1976   *Juvenile Justice and Delinquency Prevention.* Washington, D.C.: Law Enforcement Assistance Administration.

National Criminal Justice Information and Statistics Service
  1979   *Children in Custody.* Washington, D.C.: U.S. Government Printing Office.
  1980   *Children in Custody: 1979 Advance Report.* Washington, D.C.: Office of Juvenile Justice and Delinquency Prevention.

National Task Force to Develop Standards and Goals for Juvenile Justice and Delinquency Prevention
  1977   *Jurisdiction—Status Offenses.* Washington, D.C.: National Institute for Juvenile Justice and Delinquency Prevention.

Ohlin, Lloyd E.; Miller, Alden D.; and Coates, Robert B.
  1977   *Juvenile Correctional Reform in Massachusetts.* Washington, D.C.: U.S. Government Printing Office.

Palmer, Ted; Bohnstedt, M.; and Lewis, R.
  1978   *The Evaluation of Juvenile Diversion Projects: Final Report.* Sacramento: California Youth Authority.

Paulsen, Monrad
   1979 "Current Reforms and the Legal Status of Children." Pp. 211–233 in LaMar T. Empey, ed., *The Future of Childhood and Juvenile Justice.* Charlottesville: University Press of Virginia.

Paulsen, Monrad, and Whitebread, Charles H.
   1974 *Juvenile Law and Procedure.* Reno, Nev.: National Council of Juvenile Court Judges.

Reasons, Charles E.
   1970 "Gault: Procedural Change and Substantive Effect." *Crime and Delinquency* 17(April):160–167.

Revised Criminal Code of Washington
   1977 *Title 13. Juvenile Courts and Juvenile Delinquents:* 66–90.

Rubin, H. Ted
   1974 "Transferring Responsibility for Juvenile Noncriminal Misconduct from Juvenile Courts to Non-authoritarian Community Agencies." Phoenix: Arizona Conference of Delinquency Intervention Mimeographed.
   1976 *The Courts: Fulcrum of the Justice System.* Pacific Palisades, Calif.: Goodyear.

Rutherford, Andrew, and McDermott, Robert
   1976 *Juvenile Diversion: Phase I Summary Report.* Washington, D.C.: National Institute of Law Enforcement and Criminal Justice.

Schneider, Anne L., and Schram, Donna D.
   1979 "A Proposal to Assess the Consequences and Significance of a Major Innovation in Juvenile Justice: House Bill 371 in the State of Washington." Eugene, Oreg.: Institute of Policy Analysis (unpublished).

Senate and House of Representatives
   1974 Juvenile Justice and Delinquency Prevention Act of 1974. Public Law 93–415, 93rd Congress, S. 821, September 7.

Serrill, Michael
   1979 "Police Write a New Law on Juvenile Crime." *Police Magazine* 2 (September):47–52.

Spergel, Irving A.
   1976 "Interactions between Community Structure, Delinquency, and Social Policy in the Inner City." Pp. 55–100 in Malcolm W. Klein, ed., *The Juvenile Justice System.* Beverly Hills: Sage.

Statsky, William P.
   1974 "Community Courts: Decentralizing Juvenile Jurisprudence." *Capital University Law Review,* 3:1–31.

Vinter, Robert D.; Downs, George; and Hall, John
   1975 *Juvenile Corrections in the States: Residential Programs and Deinstitutionalization: A Preliminary Report.* Ann Arbor: University of Michigan.

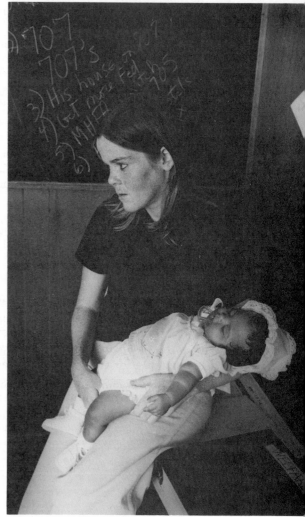

Under the new concepts of childhood and juvenile justice, less attention will be paid to status offenses.

CONCLUSIONS: CHILDHOOD, DELINQUENCY, AND THE FUTURE

Our review of the history of delinquency suggests that the current revolution in juvenile justice is part of a larger transitional phase in American life. Faith in prior beliefs and social institutions has declined, and new alternatives are being sought. In response to these trends, two new models for juvenile justice have been constructed.

While the family model reflects some of our traditional preoccupation with nurturing and protecting children, the just deserts model pays much greater attention to their constitutional rights and to the belief that children should be held accountable for their delinquent acts. But because efforts to resolve the differences between these models have mirrored our growing sense of despair and pessimism, we now seem more inclined to follow the standards of the just deserts than of the family model—more inclined to reduce the age of accountability for crime and to mechanize justice for juveniles than to stress their immaturity and their need for benevolence and charity.

These tendencies should give us pause. As David Rothman (1971:xiv–xv) has so cogently pointed out, there is a prevailing tendency to regard major societal innovations as "reforms"—as improvements over that which existed before. The reformatory, for example, was regarded as a humane improvement over prior methods of punishment and the juvenile court as an improvement over older methods of dealing with the problems of juveniles. Yet it would be difficult to maintain, in the light of history, that either innovation was a pure and unmistakable step in the progress of humanity. To do so, Rothman suggests, would not only be bad logic but bad history.

If that is the case, how should today's revolution be regarded? Is it a progressive step in the treatment of the young? Will the new system of juvenile justice reduce delinquency? Let me paraphrase Rothman's answer (1971:xv): If we are to describe it as a "reform," we will be taking for granted precisely what should be the focus of investigation. Our new model for juvenile justice should be carefully scrutinized rather than accepted outright. Otherwise, we will fall into the same trap as most of the reformers who have preceded us; namely, the tendency to equate change with effectiveness and to assume that our reforms are somehow superior to those of earlier generations.

There is no fool-proof way to avoid this trap, but we may be able to gain some useful insights by recalling that delinquency and juvenile justice are social constructions and that, in order to understand them, we must review the elements of which they are now comprised: (1) our rapidly changing concept of childhood, (2) what we have learned about the extent and nature of delinquent behavior, (3) the current state of delinquency theory and its relation to juvenile justice, and (4) the evidence that bears upon the likely effects of current reforms. By reviewing each of these, our conclusions about current trends may be better informed.

OUR CHANGING CONCEPT OF CHILDHOOD

As we began our study of childhood and delinquency, we discovered that in premodern times children were treated with indifference and were often exploited. With the discovery of childhood, however, Western civilization became increasingly preoccupied with youth. During the past century in particular, major bodies of knowledge and social institutions have been modified and new ones erected to take into account the assumption that children are qualitatively different from adults and must be carefully safeguarded. As a result, children have become both the most indulged and most constrained segment of our society (Coleman, 1974:29). The invention of delinquency, the creation of the juvenile court, the drafting of child labor laws, legal requirements regulating the school-leaving age, pediatricians, child psychiatrists, and elementary and secondary school teachers are all a reflection of our modern construction of childhood. But, just as we are now changing our beliefs and practices

with regard to juvenile justice, so we are changing our beliefs and practices with regard to the treatment of children.

Children's rights

At the cutting edge of this change is a small group of new, moralist reformers whom we discussed in Chapter 18. Two of the most prominent, Richard Farson (1974) and John Holt (1974), would do away with childhood as we know it. "We are on the threshold of a new consciousness of children's rights," says Farson, "a dramatically new concept of childhood itself. The fundamental change will be a recognition of the child's right to live with the same guarantee of freedom that adults enjoy, the basic right being that of self-determination" (Farson, 1975:5).

In order to liberate children, they should be empowered against their parents and adult oppressors. The only way to really protect them is to grant them all the constitutional rights afforded adults. Anything that is legally permissible for grown-ups should be permissible for children.

As one might guess, Farson's conclusion has been greeted with disbelief and no little derision. "Can you imagine," asked James Dobson (1975:5) a professor of pediatrics, "a six-year-old girl driving her own car to an escrow office, where she and her preschool male friend would discuss the purchase of a new home over a martini or two?" Given our present beliefs, such an event would strain the imagination. Yet, changes have occurred during recent decades which would have strained the imaginations of our founding fathers or the childsavers who invented the juvenile court.

1. Political suffrage. Until 1920, adult women did not enjoy the right to vote, to say nothing of property-less, dependent children. But in 1944, Georgia lowered the voting age from 21 to 18. In 1955, President Eisenhower urged that Congress and the states pass a constitutional amendment establishing 18 as the voting age for the entire country. In 1960, the White House Conference on Children and Youth urged greater participation of the young in political affairs. Finally, in 1971, the 26th Amendment to the Constitution was ratified by the states granting full suffrage to young people 18 and older (Coleman, 1974:42).

2. *Free speech.* Children have customarily been denied the right to free speech because of their subordinate status and the belief that parents and principals know what is best for them. During the 1960s, however, a variety of higher court decisions supported their rights to freedom of speech.

In one case, where high school students were protesting the Vietnam War by wearing armbands, the Supreme Court held that children were "persons" under the Constitution, not mere chattel. Thus, their rights to express their opinions should not be constrained, except where those opinions might severely disrupt classwork or interfere with the rights of others (*Tinker* v. *Des Moines Independent School District*, 1969).

3. *The right to work.* Child labor legislation was originally written to protect children from exploitation in the sweatshops, the mines, and the factories of the 19th century. During the 20th century, even more restrictive legislation has had the effect of confining adolescents to low-paying, part-time, or dead-end jobs without any career potential. In 1970, however, delegates to the White House Conference on Youth (1971) asserted that "earlier laws and conventions designed to 'protect' the weak (women and children) are increasingly viewed as constraints that must be cast aside." Other opponents to child labor legislation have voiced similar sentiments, suggesting that "protection from responsibility (in the guise of exclusions from the world of work and too-long exposure to the artificial atmosphere of the classroom) constitutes a

deprivation of [children's] rights to participate in 'meaningful activity' " (Coleman, 1974:43).

Reacting to these criticisms, several states have relaxed the enforcement of mandatory schooling or have lowered the school-leaving age to 16. In the state of California, for example, 16-year-olds may leave high school by passing an "equivalency" test—an examination which, besides including a modest amount of academic material, tests their ability to acquire a driver's license, to fill out a job application, to complete tax forms, and other practical tasks of this type. The assumption is that, if teenagers can read and write at a minimal level, they should be liberated from public schooling, presumably to enter the job market.

4. *Sexual freedom.* Well into this century, children were expected to remain chaste and were warned about the sinful character of sexual license and the dangers of "masturbation insanity" (Skolnick, 1973:175). "The sexual secretions," it was said, "must be conserved, lest character and intellect be weakened or destroyed" (Hale, 1971:465). Today, by contrast, young people are besieged by the media with pictures, stories, and plays about the joys of sex and the rights of all people—young or old—to enjoy it without restraint. Indeed, as we have seen, the just deserts model for juvenile justice would, among other status offenses, decriminalize sexual promiscuity and prostitution.

This point of view is reinforced by the fact that today's youth reach physical maturity at a far earlier age than in generations past. For example, in 1900 boys did not reach their full growth until about age 23; now, they are fully mature at 17 and are capable of reproducing far earlier than that (Gillis, 1974:188). The same is true of girls. Formerly, they did not begin to menstruate until their late teens; now they do so at a much younger age. Hence, ideological demands for greater sexual freedoms are reinforced by changing biological drives.

Finally, the Supreme Court has held that,

as a matter of constitutional right, an unmarried, pregnant teenager has the option to decide whether to bear the child or to have it aborted. Neither parents nor boyfriend can veto her choice (*Los Angeles Times,* July 5, 1976). Such an option for a "child" would have been unthinkable a generation or two ago.

5.   *Freedom without responsibility.*   The protected, and increasingly affluent, status of middle- and upper-class youth has permitted them to enjoy an increasing number of freedoms which would have been unavailable to adults a few generations ago.

> Grand tours of foreign countries were once the exclusive prerogative of sons of noblemen; now a broad segment of middle-class youth enjoys foreign travel along with the ability to gratify its tastes in clothes, music, and a multitude of forms of entertainment. . . . Young people today are far more cosmopolitan in outlook than their predecessors (Coleman et al., 1974:128).

But this is not all. Freedoms previously associated with university-age youth have been rapidly appropriated by adolescents in high school: "passion pits" on wheels, skiing vacations for unmarried couples, or trips to Florida during Easter vacation. Furthermore, because of the anonymity of urban civilization, young people have not had to account to their elders for their behavior. It is impossible to quarantine them from "evil" when both biological and social conditions render older methods of control obsolete.

In summary, then, the children's rights movement means that we are in a transitional phase in our beliefs about childhood in which reforms in juvenile justice are but the tip of the iceberg. How, then, shall that movement be interpreted? Although it has introduced changes that prior generations of reformers would have found unthinkable, it has also posed a host of dilemmas: whether children are capable of unfettered self-determination, whether the nuclear family can survive the

onslaught of the movement, whether the institutional and demographic structures of society are designed to facilitate equality for children, or whether current reforms in juvenile justice really correct the presumed failures of the traditional juvenile court.

Child development

As an advocate of child liberation, Farson (1979) joins radical and neoclassical theorists in attacking the theories of social science. Traditional social scientists, he contends, are incapable of recognizing the capacities of the young for mature behavior because they are the captives of their own developmental theories—theories which suggest that, while children go through the various stages of development, they are not capable of responsible, informed behavior. Farson contends, however, that this is not true.

In her review of the literature, Skolnick (1979) gives some qualified support to Farson. Developmental psychologists, she says, "have tended to describe all young people in terms of their inadequacies rather than their competencies" (p. 144). Yet, when asked to deal with problems that are relevant to the world in which they live, children are capable of rather advanced reasoning. But, adds Skolnick (1979:146), this does not mean that there are no differences between young children and adolescents, or between adolescents and adults. While young children are much less inept than previously thought, they "still do not do well at tasks involving sophisticated forms of abstract reasoning, and the use of their capacities is erratic and fragile." Hence, the evidence with respect to child liberation is mixed.

On the one hand, it suggests that civil rights might be extended further down the ladder of age. Indeed, the American Psychological Association joined other child advocates in supporting a class action suit which contended that children, aged 12 and over, should be accorded the same due process protections in legal proceedings as adults.

On the other hand, if one analyzes the social and economic structures of American society, the literature does not suggest that children could function as adults right now.

> If the roles and statuses of children are determined to a greater or lesser degree by social structure, they will be difficult to change unless the social structure also changes. For example, if adolescence was "invented," at least in part, because the economy no longer needed the labor of young people, it is likely to remain a part of the life cycle until the economy changes enough to absorb adolescents into the labor force. In a society which cannot provide full employment for adults, the prospects for young people becoming workers seems quite dim (Skolnick, 1979:167).

Equally important, there are serious reasons to question whether justice for juveniles should be mechanized and steps taken to sentence delinquency rather than the delinquent.

> Here again, it is one thing to say that children and adolescents are capable of knowing right from wrong and of realizing the consequences of their acts, and quite another to leap to the conclusion that they should be treated by the criminal justice system as fully responsible adults. . . . What is needed is a system of justice which recognizes varying degrees of cognitive and emotional maturity and which, therefore, is more capable of judging moral and legal responsibility (Skolnick, 1979:169).

Franklin Zimring (1979:324–325), a legal scholar, agrees. Just as it would be absurd "to pick any birthday as the only qualification for becoming an engineer, a doctor, or a lawyer," Zimring says, so it would be absurd to assume that a certain birthday equally qualifies all children as being responsible for delinquent acts. Instead, he suggests that we continue to utilize a "learning permit" theory of

adolescence where we recognize that there is a period of transitional learning, during which young people may be ready to *learn* to exercise responsibility—such as driving a car—but during which we do not hold them entirely responsible if they have an accident. The extension of privilege is a gamble that society must take in order to nurture and to train children for adulthood.

Child liberation and population structure

The emphasis of these two scholars upon structural impediments to child liberation and upon the need for a learning permit theory of adolescence can be further illustrated by considering the profound, unparalleled changes that are now occurring in the demographic and population structures of modern society. In the late 17th century, the average expectancy at birth was 32 years in England and about 27.5 years in Germany (Gillis, 1974:10). This meant that the ratio of young to old people was extremely high:

> It has been estimated that, in the English village of Stoke-on-Trent in 1701, 49 percent of the population was under 20 years of age. In Sweden in 1750 the ratio of those persons age 15–29 years to every 100 persons aged 30 years and over was 63 percent. In France in 1776 the ratio was 65 percent; and as late as 1840 it was approximately 77 percent in England (Gillis, 1974:11).

More to the point, Davis (1979) points out that, while 15- to 19-year-olds made up 10.5 percent of the American population in 1890, they make up only 9.8 percent today and will constitute only 7.8 percent in the year 2000.

The reasons for these changes are twofold: (1) a decline in the birth rate and (2) an increase in life expectancy. Since 1957, the fertility rate has dropped from a peak of 3.76 children per woman to a record low of 1.75 in 1976. The United States may well be on its way to the goal of zero population growth. Meanwhile, average life expectancy at birth has increased to about 70 years for men and 78 years for women (Metropolitan Life Insurance Company, 1980:13).

The obvious consequence of both of these trends is a striking change in the age structure of society. Whereas it used to be exceedingly heavy with young people at the bottom, it is now growing heavier at the top with older people. For example, the growth in population from 1950 to 1970 was lowest for people under 45 (30.5 percent). By contrast, the population of people over 65 increased by 63 percent. Even more striking was the growth in the number of people over 75, 97 percent—from 3.9 million in 1950 to 7.6 million in 1970 (U.S. Department of Commerce, 1971). What, then, are some of the implications of these remarkable trends?

1.   The rights of the elderly.   One obvious implication has to do with the character of a society whose population is growing progressively older. Current trends may hasten a decline in our protective stance toward the young and focus it instead on older populations (Davis and van den Oever, 1981). "By the year 2020 there will be almost twice as many people over 65 (43 million) as there are today, exerting immense new pressures on the social security, pension, and medicare systems" (*Time,* February 28, 1977). Sociologist Amitai Etzioni says that "this means a less innovative society in which fewer people will have to attend, care, feed, house, and pay for a larger number" (*Time,* February 28, 1977). Children may enjoy the right to work, to enjoy sex, and to vote at younger ages, but they may also be saddled with a great many responsibilities. Rather than being the major recipients of society's largesse, they may have to be the providers of it.

In the short run, the changes will be less dramatic but nonetheless serious. For children to be liberated, they must have jobs. Yet because of the growing numbers of older people, the young are in direct competition with the elderly for employment. Fourteen states have already passed laws limiting the right of employers to force employees to retire at age 65. In 1978, the Congress of the United States passed a similar law to cover the entire country. But while these laws will block the employment or the occupational advancement of some teenagers, the elderly are not the only source of competition. Adult women have become an even more potent source.

2.   The rights of women.   Davis (1979) points out that, between 1951 and 1976, the proportion of males over 65 who were employed declined from 44.9 percent to 19.4 percent. But paradoxically, this decrease was not accompanied by a compensatory increase in the employment of the young, male or female. Instead, virtually all of the increase has been among mature women, particularly among married women (Carter and Glick, 1976:424). Thus, while the number of working women was less than one half the number of working men in 1960, it was nearly two thirds as great in 1974, and is larger still today.

The rise in employment among adult women, like the potential rise among the elderly, is obviously a serious obstacle to the fulfillment of the right to work for children. In 1933, when unemployment was high, a spokesman for the National Child Labor Committee declared that the employment of children had become an economic menace. "Children should be in school, and adults should have whatever worthwhile jobs there are" (Coleman et al., 1974:35). Child advocates notwithstanding, the same sentiment tends to prevail today. In a highly competitive job market, the preference is for supplying adults with jobs, not children.

As a result, almost half of the nation's unemployed in 1976 were youths aged 16 to 24—3.5 million of them (National League of Cities, 1977:1). Economists are concerned that 17.5 percent of America's high school and college graduates cannot find a job (*Time,* October 10, 1977). But if unemployment is a problem for this group, consider the problems of the lesser educated school dropout or early school-leaver. Estimated unemployment rates for adolescents in general run anywhere from 20 to 40 percent, but for minority teenagers in urban areas they may be as high as 60 percent (Calvin, 1981; National League of Cities, 1977). "A generation of young people is moving into its 20s—the family forming years—without knowing how to work, since many have never held jobs" (*Time*, August 29, 1977).

What all of this means is that the movement to grant greater freedoms to children is not yet matched by a set of institutional arrangements by which their so-called rights can become a reality. Indeed, that is what Skolnick meant when she said that, unless economic and political structures change, the roles and statuses of the young cannot change either. The notion that children's rights should be equal with those of adults is relatively empty unless it is congruent with the means to become self-sufficient.

But this is not the only bind. It was mentioned earlier that, since the advent of the Industrial Revolution, young people have been the principal beneficiaries of society's largesse. Because they were not needed in the labor force, they were subsidized by their families and by society. Now, however, they are not only in direct competition with others for jobs, but they are in competition with an increasingly older population for educational, economic, and social services. And since the numbers of older people will continue to grow proportionately larger, it is virtually certain that their share of society's resources will increase, while that of the young will decrease: money for education, medical care, scholarships, and certainly for luxuries. The young, in short, are in a double bind.

Alterations in family life

This double bind is directly reflected in marked alterations in the meaning and character of family life. To begin with, the cost of raising children grows increasingly onerous. Inflation has already made the cost of rearing a large family almost prohibitive, particularly when that cost must compete with the desires of husband and wife to travel, to own their own automobile, or to purchase a home. As the world's basic resources grow smaller, the cost of these things grows larger.

Secondly, children now interfere not only with the professional aspirations of the father but also with those of the mother. As demographer Judith Blake Davis puts it, "you won't find those sacrificial mothers any more" (*Time*, February 28, 1977). Women, as well as men want to forge their own destinies, and children can be distinct hindrances to doing so. Indeed, that is one major reason the birth rate has declined so precipitously and why abortion, to say nothing of contraception, has become as commonplace as infanticide and abandonment in the Middle Ages.

Ironically, the child rights movement has contributed to these trends. In 1972, for example, a 15-year-old girl in Minnesota brought court action against her parents because they wanted to take her on a trip around the world and she did not want to go. What her actions reflected was the increasing tendency for children, as well as for adults, to resort to complex legal procedures to solve family squabbles. As a result, Harvard law professor Frank Sanders was led to conclude that, "We're going to make being a parent tougher and tougher. We're going to have to explain our actions to the courts. The ultimate, absurdity would be if my son, who gets mad at going to bed at 10:30, goes to court and asks for a later bedtime. This is a trend one needs to worry about" (Goodman, 1976). Indeed, in addition to all the other pressures to which the family is now subjected, the increasing legal rights of children are threatening the traditional rewards enjoyed by parents—children who are economic assets, who respect their parents wishes, and who provide economic and emotional sustenance when they grow old.

But if the rewards for parents are declining, what about the impact on children of the changing character of family life? In his analysis of the subject, Davis (1979) highlights the dramatic finding that, because of high divorce rates and the current trend toward single parenthood, the likelihood that an American child will remain with both parents throughout childhood has been reduced to about the same level as it was in the preindustrial era, when it was high death rates, not divorce and single parenthood, that separated families. Not only has the divorce rate tripled since 1933, but the ratio of illegitimate births has gone up 314 percent. "In 1940, only 1 child in 30 was born to unmarried parents. By 1960, the rate had increased to 1 in 20. In 1970, it was 1 baby in 10." But by 1977, *it had reached one in six* (Nye and Lamberts, 1981; U.S. Center for Health Statistics, 1978). Furthermore, there is no sign that the trend is leveling out (Carter and Glick, 1976: 392–394; Timmick, 1979).

National surveys reveal that between 1957 and 1976, the tendency for people to evaluate marriage positively dropped dramatically, particularly among women (Douvan, 1979). Although 70 percent of the men, versus 56 percent of the women, felt that marriage had more advantages than single life, 80 percent of the total sample approved of divorce. "Today, marriage and parenthood rarely are viewed as necessary, and people who do not choose those roles are no longer considered social deviants" (Douvan, 1979:4).

Such surveys are often limited, however, because they tend to reflect majority views, particularly those of the white middle and upper classes. Yet, it is among underprivileged Americans, particularly among blacks, that fatherless households are the most common. Moreover, as we learned in a previous chapter, it is among blacks that the rate of single parenthood has increased most dramatically in recent years.

In 1959, 18 percent of all black families were headed by females; in 1969, the proportion had risen to 27 percent; and by 1977, it had reached 41 percent (Bronfenbrenner, 1974; Monahan, 1957; Davis, 1979). Thus, if present trends continue, well over half of all black families will be headed by unmarried women by 1985, versus 19 percent for whites (Davis, 1979). Indeed, conditions are such that many black as well as white girls regard pregnancy as a way to welfare and welfare as a gateway to independence (Nye and Lamberts, 1981).

The implications of such trends are profound. Although the birth rate, in general, has been declining, it is still much higher among the poor and minorities than among the white and the nonpoor.

> In 1976, only 24.1 percent of American males were below the age of 14. Among the population officially classified as poor, on the other hand, 39.7 percent were under 14 years of age; and among poor black males, no fewer than 48.3 percent were in that age group. (The proportions were even higher among poor Puerto Ricans and Mexican-Americans.) In short, . . . the most rapid growth of all will occur in urban slums and ghettos, where criminal violence has been concentrated (Silberman, 1978:35–36).

These trends, while often unfamiliar to whites, are not lost on the leaders of minority groups. As the founder of PUSH (People United to Save Humanity), the Reverend Jesse Jackson has toured the country, speaking to children and seeking to acquaint them with other alternatives (Krier, 1979). Jackson dramatizes the issues by pointing out that he, too, is the child of unmarried adolescents: his mother was 17 when he was born, and his grandmother was 14 when she gave birth to her first child. Furthermore, neither his mother nor his grandmother ever married. But, says Jackson, it need not be this way. Instead, like so many other people from backgrounds of poverty and discrimination, he is a conservative when it comes to the virtues of the monogamous family.

Rather than espousing a new set of values, he seems bent on reasserting the importance of traditional standards for children: self-discipline, hard work, respect for authority, and deferred gratification—virtues first enunciated by the child savers of the 18th and 19th centuries, not those advocated by today's reformers. As a consequence, it seems quite clear that, when the child rights movement is viewed from below, it takes on quite a different cast than when viewed from above. Jackson seems to be saying that freedom and license are not the same thing. Therefore, until lower class children receive the nurturance rights so long taken for granted by the middle class, they cannot realize their full potential.

But lower class youth are not the only people experiencing difficulties. According to periodic national surveys, many young people have reflected a growing sense of disorientation and anxiety during the past 25 years:

> Compared to the 1957 sample, the 1976 sample found their social integration to be a problem and their social roles and their interpersonal relationships to be a source of distress. The advantage of traditional social roles which were more prevalent in the 50s was that they facilitated automatic coping with life problems. In our less rigidly defined society, people are forced to cope with their own very personal integrations of experience. The price is increased worry and anxiety (Veroff, 1979:4–5).

Single parenthood, divorce, and changing family mores, in other words, have had a large impact on the young.

The schools

Worry and anxiety are also associated with changes in the school. For the better part of three centuries, Western countries have placed increasing emphasis on the school as a vital institution for socializing the young (second only to the family in importance). Education has been described as the means by which our cultural life might be shaped into a new, more moral pattern. But as Short (1979) points out, the belief is steadily gaining strength that schools should no longer play an *in loco parentis* role. Not only is it argued that children be allowed to assert their independence from familial controls, but from school constraints as well. As a consequence, we should not be surprised that many of our schools have become unstable sources of training for the young, marked by defiance and violence as well as by a decrease in educational effectiveness.

Citing a series of recent studies, Short (1979) points out that educational authorities have responded to this state of affairs by absolving themselves of responsibility for high levels of turbulence in the schools. Current difficulties, they argue, are rooted in society as a whole. Given the emphasis upon child liberation and the autonomy of the individual, "the traditional reliance on the school as the primary medium for resolving social problems is no longer tenable" (Ianni, 1978:34). Indeed, for every change we pay a price.

At the very time that minority leaders like Jesse Jackson are stressing the importance of discipline, respect for authority, and deferred gratification, the power of the schools to promote those characteristics has been reduced. To be sure, this decrease in power has its positive side. Corporal punishment, for example, has been constrained. Yet, the loss of authority by the school goes well beyond its loss of power to punish.

The new IJA–ABA standards for juvenile justice symbolize the change. They specify that the duty of students to attend school should not be coerced, that all rules for behavior should be published in writing, that no students should be permanently excluded from school, and that students threatened with disciplinary action should have the right to notice in writing, receipt of all evidence to be used against them, a private hearing, representation by counsel, and the right of judicial review if such is necessary (Flicker, 1977:119–132).

Because of our growing distrust of institutional authority, we are not only taking refuge in legal rules and formal procedure in court proceedings, but in the school as well. And while this refuge protects against the excessive use of authority, it also contributes to an increasing tendency on the parts of teachers, principals, and students to look to formal rather than informal methods for resolving interpersonal, social, and educational problems. Paradoxically we seek to remedy our declining sense of community in modern society by resorting, not to institutional arrangements that promote mutual interdependence and informal methods of social control, but to controls that are legalistic, impersonal, and bureaucratic.

Summary

It is no wonder that our efforts to liberate children and to increase their personal autonomy are beset with difficulty as well as with virtue. This review has revealed that, while the child rights movement has indeed altered the status of children, that movement has also been associated with a host of dilemmas:

The child development literature continues to stress the idea that the treatment of young people by families, schools, and juvenile courts should pay heed to their varying degrees of cognitive and emotional maturity and should take these into account in organizing their lives and holding them responsible for their behavior.

An analysis of the changing demographic structures of society reveals that efforts to grant greater freedoms to children have not been matched by new institutional arrangements by which their rights can become a reality. They are in direct competition with the elderly, as well as with working men and women, both for jobs and for the largesse of the society—a competition that may decrease, not increase, their relative power.

There are marked alterations in the meaning and character of family life: peoples' desire for children is decreasing; single parenthood has reached unprecedented proportions, particularly among the poorest and youngest segments of society; and, in response, young people reveal an increasing sense of disorientation and anxiety.

This disorientation is then exacerbated by the declining influence of the school as a means for socializing the young. In short, efforts to use legal and bureaucratic efforts to enhance the rights of children have been accompanied by uncertainty, an increasing sense of social isolation, and a diminution in the quality of interpersonal relationships.

DELINQUENT BEHAVIOR TODAY

Given this state of affairs, there is merit in reviewing the implications of that which we have learned about delinquent behavior. The facts are fraught with irony.

Although, on the one hand, delinquent behavior has always been prevalent throughout the youth population, delinquency rates rose precipitously during the very years that cultural instability in American society was at its greatest—conflicts over civil rights, urban riots, youth protest, and the assassinations of American leaders. Seeming to reflect the turbulence about them, young people not only continued to commit a disproportionate amount of all property crimes, but they also became relatively more violent. Acts that heretofore had been confined largely to adults moved down the ladder of age and out into the streets and into the schools. And while rates of youth violence and crime have now begun to level out, they have not retreated to earlier, more modest levels. Hence, serious problems remain: juveniles continue to be more precocious in a criminal sense, and research reveals that the most chronic and violent offenders are concentrated more heavily in the poorer and minority segments of society than in other segments.

On the other hand, research also reveals that the victims of crime are not evenly distributed throughout society. Instead, juveniles are more likely to victimize people of their own age, race, and social class than they are to victimize people of different ages, races, and social classes. Thus, the fact that chronic offenders are concentrated more heavily in the male, the minority, and the poorer segments of society means that males are more vulnerable to crime that females; blacks and Hispanics are more vulnerable than whites; the poor are more vulnerable than the affluent, and ghetto-dwellers are more vulnerable than suburbanites. Indeed, murder is the leading cause of death among young, black males. Although blacks comprise only about 11 percent of the population, they comprise about half of all murder victims.

In short, those segments of society most likely to suffer from or to commit violence are precisely those for whom many of the problems we described earlier are the greatest—divided families, increasingly ineffective schools, poverty, and uncertainty about jobs. Consequently, this picture of the delinquency problem literally cries out for explanation and understanding. What, then, is the current state of delinquency theory? With what issues are todays criminologists most concerned?

DELINQUENCY THEORY AND CRIMINOLOGY

In order to answer these questions, let us review briefly the history of both delinquency theory and of criminology. Their parallel developments, particularly in recent years, reveal some striking outcomes.

Positive criminology

Until about a century ago, there were few theoretical alternatives to the classical perspective. "[P]oliticians and philosophers . . . routinely assumed that criminals simply choose to be bad and will choose to change their ways if they are punished severely enough" (Cressey, 1978:181–182). Then, along with the growth of science in general, positive criminology developed. Just as scientists in other fields were seeking to establish cause-and-effect relationships in biology, chemistry, and physics, so criminologists began to ask: "What causes delinquent conduct?" "Why do some juveniles, but not others, commit serious crimes?"

Such questions were based on an ancient and honorable principle; namely, that the control of any problem—whether it be a disease, a natural disaster, or a crime—is gained by first achieving an understanding of its causes and then using that knowledge to modify or to eliminate those causes (Cressey, 1978:177). Indeed, because classical justice had failed to address these issues, early theories, with all their limitations, "were at the base of many significant criminal justice innovations . . . , including the juvenile court, the probation system, the parole system, changes in the insanity defense, and changes in the conditions of imprisonment" (Cressey, 1978:173–174).

Over time, theories of many different types were constructed—control, cultural deviance, symbolic interactionist, and strain theories. And while many of these theories were inadequate by themselves, they did contribute collectively to the identification of several causes that do predict delinquent behavior. More than other young people, chronic delinquents appear to lack a stake in conformity: their attachments to the basic child-rearing institutions—the home and the school—are weak or disrupted, their academic achievement is low, they are not committed to the conventional means for success, and they are inclined to defy authority by identifying with delinquent peers. Consequently, several principles for intervention are implied: to reestablish and reinforce attachments to home and school, to provide delinquents with renewed opportunities for education, to seek their commitments to conventional pursuits, and to assimilate them into groups that emphasize law-abiding behavior. Indeed, given the picture of delinquency we have just reviewed, such principles would still appear to be relevant today.

Labeling criminology

But when efforts to implement these principles were halting at best, or were unsuccessful, an alternative perspective—labeling theory—emerged. Rather than stressing the effects of cultural conflict, unstable families and schools, blocked opportunities, and delinquent subculture, this perspective suggested that the real cause of serious crime is the dramatization of evil. Society and the legal system are at fault. Were it not for discriminatory rules and the effects of labeling and stigma, there would be no serious criminals.

In a strictly scientific sense, indeed even to the major labeling theorists themselves, this perspective was meant to refocus attention upon rule makers and rule enforcers, as well as upon rule breakers. The basic concerns of positive criminology, first suggested by Edwin H. Sutherland in 1934, were simply being reasserted; namely, that criminology should be devoted to constructing theories designed to explain the processes of making and enforcing laws, as well as of breaking laws, and of explaining the interrelationships among these processes (Cressey, 1978:175).

But to a new breed of criminologists, the implications of labeling theory meant something quite different. To them it meant that, short of legal processing, there is no crime and there are no criminals. Since the legal system is the source of *secondary* deviance (serious crime), efforts to understand *primary* deviance (the reasons misbehaving children break the law in the first place) are wasted. Instead, the only role for science, if there is one, is to study the processes by which some people, but not others, are labeled as criminals and subjected to destructive legal controls. Furthermore, social policy should be directed, not to measures designed to alter families, schools, and communities, or to enhance economic opportunities, but to reforms designed to leave children alone wherever possible—*to a policy of benign neglect.* If status and victimless offenses are decriminalized, and if young criminals are diverted from legal processing, delinquency will take care of itself.

Radical criminology

To radical theorists, this was nonsense. As representatives of yet another offshoot of criminology, they not only attacked the philosophy of benign neglect implied by labeling theory, but they also attacked the underlying assumptions of positive criminology. According to radicals, delinquency is endemic to capitalist society—a product of a perpetual class struggle in which capitalist rulers create the social conditions that spawn delinquency and then turn around and prosecute those who are oppressed and exploited by the capitalist system.

In seeking to justify these contentions, radicals did not endear themselves to most other criminologists because of their stinging indictment of positivism. Rather than joining with others in the pursuit of freedom and equality, radicals contended, positivists are the technocratic servants of capitalism—an intellectual elite who, like good capitalists everywhere, bastardize the pursuit of truth in their own self-interest.

Stated in this way, the effects of radical theory have been paradoxical. On the one hand, the theory has been justifiably criticized as a better statement of ideology than of theory. It is concerned more with promoting social revolution than with formulating and testing propositions designed to explain the effects of recent changes in advanced capitalist societies—some of the very changes described above. It has also failed to explain why age and sex continue to be better predictors of crime than social class. And it has failed to indicate why, contrary to all of the lessons of history, sociology, and anthropology, delinquency can be expected to disappear in a truly socialist society—why such a society could be expected to avoid the disorienting, often crime-producing, conditions that all advanced societies—capitalist *and* noncapitalist—are now experiencing. In terms of traditional scientific standards, at least, the theory has been deficient.

On the other hand, the halting efforts of American society to prevent delinquency, to say nothing of the subversion of many legal reforms by the agents of juvenile justice, have lent indirect support to radical arguments. Instead of mobilizing the political will, the economic resources, and the innovative ideas necessary to promote adequate familial, educational, and employment opportunities for juveniles, our capitalist society has grown increasingly pessimistic, is cutting back on its support for such programs, and now threatens to resort once again to more punitive measures for controlling the young. Ironically, therefore, radical theory comes closer to positive theories than to any other in suggesting why recent reforms have not been effective. Hence, one might argue that, rather than continuing to savagely disparage one another, radicals and positivists should make up and wed.

If positivists would only concentrate more on the relationship of political and economic institutions to crime, and if radicals would only acknowledge that culture includes some institutions besides those that are political and economic, the two might become partners. Indeed, that is not a bad idea. The greatest limitations of both kinds of theory have to do with their inability to comprehend and to articulate recent changes in developed societies—changing age and demographic structures, the unprecedented effects of the child and women's rights movements, and the consequences of placing children in vigorous competition with other segments of society for scarce resources.

In the near future, however, such a wedding is not likely. In their vulgar squabbles with each other, these potential lovers have been upstaged in criminology by neoclassical philosophers—by the proponents of just deserts, mechanized justice, punishment, and deterrence.

Neoclassical criminology

As in the past, the activities and interests of these proponents are a remarkable example of the extent to which the intellectual concerns of criminologists are a reflection of changing cultural beliefs. Whereas positive criminology was born in a time of optimism and was sustained by the belief that humankind could be perfected through the pursuit of knowledge, contemporary criminology is a reflection of a belief in the imperfectibility of humans and of their social institutions.

Neoclassical philosophy is the prime example of these despairing beliefs. While its proponents differ somewhat over the solutions they propose, they do agree on one thing: *we must discard the esoteric search for knowledge and concentrate on being practical.* Their justifications for practicality, however, are not only varied but also inconsistent.

On the one hand, utilitarian philosophers contend that positive theories are impractical because the causes they identify cannot be addressed by social policy: child-rearing practices cannot be improved, schools cannot be made more effective, identification with delinquent peers cannot be altered, and the pockets of poverty and demoralization produced by capitalist society cannot be remedied. Yet, after having discredited the relevance of these "causes," these philosophers identify other causes which they contend are amenable to policy.

Utilitarians believe that people commit crime either because they are inherently wicked or because they are hedonistic calculators who ponder society's reaction to crime and, if punishment is not forthcoming, will engage in it themselves. In short, their reasons for rejecting the theories of science are not merely because they consider them impractical but because they have alternative explanations for crime. They are adherents of the hedonistic school of psychology first enunciated by the classical philosophers of the 18th century. Hence, if delinquency is to be controlled, the certainty and severity of punishment must be increased.

Just deserts philosophers, by contrast, have a different reason for stressing the need to be practical. It is not that positive theories are necessarily wrong. Instead, it is because judges, probation officers, and social workers cannot be trusted to exercise the benevolence, love, and charity that are necessary to see that the causes of delinquency are addressed. Like labeling theorists, but for different reasons, deserts philosophers view authorities as oppressors, not benefactors. In the interest of minimizing harm, therefore, we must do two things.

First, we must divide juveniles into two groups (a) the misbehaving, but still deserving, kids—kids who commit status, victimless and petty crimes, and (b) the criminal, but essentially nondeserving, kids who commit serious crimes or are chronic offenders. Then, we must adopt separate policies for each: decriminalizing the acts of the deserving kids, while doing justice for the undeserving—eliminating discretionary concern for individual differences among them, concentrating on protecting their rights, and submitting them to standardized punishments if they are found guilty of crime.

When the new IJA–ABA model for juvenile justice was constructed, it remained remarkably faithful to just deserts principles. But those who constructed the model did not reckon with society's despairing mood, nor with the extent to which the logic of the child rights movement would be combined with the retributive logic of utilitarian philosophy; namely, that if children have the right to live with the same guarantees of freedom and privilege that adults enjoy, particularly if their status offenses are decriminalized, they should expect the same severe punishments when they commit criminal acts. Consequently, if new legislation in several states becomes the norm, two goals will dominate the conduct of social policy: (1) protection of society, rather than rehabilitation for convicted delinquents, and (2) benign neglect, if not total decriminalization for status offenders.

But these new policies may not be the most astonishing result of the resurrection of classical philosophy. Instead, it may be the impact of that philosophy on criminology (Bayer, 1981). "Until about a decade ago, . . . most criminologists were arguing that repression is neither scientifically nor democratically sound and that therefore the effort to understand the conditions spawning crime and criminals should be enlarged" (Cressey, 1978:181). Now, by contrast, "criminologists, like politicians, are saying that our efforts to change criminals and the society that produces them have been ineffective and that we must therefore retain punishment and abandon the effort to understand criminals and society . . ." (Cressey, 1978:180).

Part of this change is due to new membership in the discipline. Until about 10 or 15 years ago, most criminologists were ivory-tower, research-oriented social scientists. Now, however, its constituency includes many lawyers, professionals, and even policemen whose primary concern is with "doing something" about crime (Cressey, 1978). But this does not change the fact that many ivory-tower types have also joined the movement. More than ever before, therefore, there is merit in the contention of radicals that criminologists have joined politicians in seeking to repress criminals, even if they are young. What, then, are the implications of these profound changes in criminological as well as political thought?

POLICY DILEMMAS

There are four issues for which recent changes are highly important—those having to do with delinquency prevention, due process for juveniles, the increasing tendency to treat status offenders with benign neglect, and the growing popularity of punishment.

Prevention

When we reviewed the implications of positive theories in Chapter 13, we found that they implied certain principles for the prevention of delinquency:

1. The primary focus of efforts to prevent delinquency should be upon the establishment among young people of a stake in conformity.
2. A stake in conformity is most likely to occur if children are effectively socialized: attached to concerned families and schools, committed to conventional pursuits, provided with opportunities for the assumption of legitimate adult roles, and identified with conventional peers and adults.
3. Effective socialization is a product of

institutional design and process—a result of the way homes, schools, employment structures, and communities are organized.

In short, programs designed to prevent delinquency should be a part of the ongoing, relatively normal, processes of the community.

But while these principles have always been attractive in a theoretical sense, they have rarely been tried in a systematic way. Even in recent years, when federal leadership and support were at their greatest, welfare programs did more to promote dependency and single parenthood than to provide a better integration of family roles and self-sufficiency. Rather than altering the ways schools dealt with marginal children, the use of diversion increased their flow toward programs controlled by justice or mental health personnel. And because educational and vocational programs did not link the world of the adolescent with the adult world of work, their effects were marginal at best. Consequently, it cannot honestly be said that the implications of either positive or radical theories were fairly tested.

Even more important, the increasing competition of the young for scarce jobs and resources, combined with the newfound faith in a classical model of juvenile justice, suggest that the practice of prevention may be rejected, not because it is without promise, but because it will not be given a chance to fulfill that promise. To be sure, successful prevention programs would demand herculean effort, political will, and a renewed interest in attempting to implement and to test theory, but in the present social, economic, and ideological context, such efforts are not likely.

Due process

The invention of the juvenile court was predicated on the following assumptions: (1) that children are qualitatively different from adults; (2) that legal intervention in their lives is justified because of their dependent and protected status; and (3) that the goal of intervention is rehabilitation, not punishment. As a result, children's rights were defined in terms of protecting them from parental neglect, physical abuse, immorality, and excessive and dangerous work and insuring that they attended school in order to prepare themselves for adulthood.

In our extended review of court practices, however, we found that the agents of juvenile justice often abused the tremendous powers granted to them: status as well as delinquent offenders were detained, tried, and deprived of liberty without the benefit of written and specific charges against them, without the benefit of legal counsel, without the right to confront witnesses, and, until about 15 years ago, without the benefit of appeal to higher courts.

Coupled with these indignities is the fact that our assumptions about children have also changed: (1) that children are not qualitatively different from adults, at least not so much as we thought; (2) that their right to self-determination should prevent legal interference into their lives for behavior which, if exhibited by adults, would not be considered illegal; and (3) that they should be granted greater rights, not merely in legal proceedings, but also in their dealings with their parents, with the schools, and with the political system. Thus, it is not surprising that the advocates of virtually every philosophy have joined in demanding the implementation of due process in all legal proceedings.

But while the need for due process goes without saying, constant vigilance with regard to its use must be exercised. Constitutional safeguards depend heavily upon the capacities of parents to find and to employ competent legal counsel; the juvenile court in many states has not been raised to the stature of the adult criminal court; and the increased resources and personnel necessary to implement formal procedures have not been forthcoming.

Even more important, the formalities of due process—written charges, plea bargaining, codified procedures, and the presence of prosecutors and defense attorneys—are not designed to solve youth problems. Instead, they are designed to insure fairness and to protect the innocent. Thus, to the degree that punishment replaces rehabilitation as the primary goal of juvenile justice, there is always the chance that the mitigating circumstances associated with the commission of a crime will be ignored.

All juveniles are not the same, and their reasons for committing crime differ. That is why, in the Gault case (1967:21), the Supreme Court said that "the observance of due process standards intelligently and not ruthlessly administered will not compel the States to abandon or displace any of the substantive benefits of the juvenile process . . ." Yet, the growth of faith in the rules of evidence, determinate sentencing, punishment, and deterrence threatens to eliminate our concern with individual differences. Somehow, many of today's reformers seem to feel that, rather than needing to complement social with legal justice, the two are one and the same—that if crimes are fairly proven, justice is done. Hence, to the degree that this belief becomes transcendent, we will simply substitute one form of injustice (the failure to insure due process) with another (the failure to address individual differences). Indeed, this is such a crucial issue that we will discuss it further in our consideration of punishment.

Status offenders and benign neglect

One of the most telling criticisms of the traditional juvenile court has been the fact that the one type of offender most often referred to it has been the status offender and that this offender has been as likely as the criminal property offender to be sentenced to a correctional institution. Such outcomes might not have offended the sensibilities of reformers had court referral and the confinement of status offenders proved to be of clear benefit to them, but such has not always been the case. Instead, the evidence suggests that confinement in particular has not successfully changed young people and has not returned them to society as healthy and productive citizens. Thus, in the interests of justice, if not rehabilitation, decriminalization has been hailed as a constructive reform.

Like other outcomes of the child rights movement, however, decriminalization has done more to highlight undesirable practices than to promote desirable alternatives. We have already seen that, as the socializing influences of family and school have declined, that decline has not been matched by compensatory changes in other social institutions. Thus, it is significant that decriminalization represents more of the same. While few would disagree with the assertion that children should be protected from official abuse, it is quite another thing to suggest that they require no controls. What will happen if the juvenile court, along with other child-oriented institutions, loses its capacity to place limits on any behaviors except those that are clearly criminal?

Critics from both ends of the ideological spectrum have voiced cries of alarm. Herman and Julia Schwendinger (1979), who are radical theorists, argue that while decriminalization may reduce the harassment of working-class children by the police, it might also do them lasting harm. Working-class families already have a difficult time controlling their children in the face of meager family resources, poor public schools, and the attraction of unfettered gang and street life. Hence, if decriminalization is combined with all the other freedoms advocated by the child rights movement, it would simply result in another instance of benign neglect, justified by high-flown but class-biased principles. While well-to-do

parents may have sufficient resources to make recourse to legal controls unnecessary, the parents of the inner city need the juvenile court as a backup institution. Otherwise, their children will continue to suffer from ignorance, poverty, and high rates of illegitimacy and crime.

Writing as a traditional advocate of the juvenile court, former Family Court Justice Justine Wise Polier (1979) says much the same thing. In so doing, she cites a problem with which every police officer, judge, and correctional worker is familiar, namely, that such terms as *incorrigibility, lewd conduct,* or *truancy* may cover a multitude of problems, as well as "sins." Desperate parents often come to officials asking for help, not only because their children are truant, stay out late, and get drunk but also because they are drug users, gang members, prostitutes, or thieves. But because these children have been referred to officials by their parents, they have usually been defined legally as status offenders, since the officials have had no firsthand knowledge of any crimes having been committed. If, however, all status offenders are decriminalized, officials could not take action, parental wishes notwithstanding. Lacking proof of criminal behavior, they would have to ignore any pleas for help.

By way of example, a judge of the Family Court in Manhattan recently dismissed charges against a 14-year-old girl for prostitution on the grounds that "sex for a fee" is a "recreational" not a criminal act. Reflecting contemporary libertarian views, the judge said that "however offensive it may be, recreational commercial sex threatens no harm to the public health, safety, or welfare, and therefore may not be proscribed" (Goodman, 1978:7).

For some people, however, this action pushed the outrage button. "It's absolutely bizarre," opined one columnist, "to have to prove that a young girl committed a crime, in order to help her. . . . The one thing on which everyone agrees is that a 14-year-old girl selling sex in Times Square needs and deserves help" (Goodman, 1978:7). Nonetheless, to the degree that status offenses are decriminalized and are not otherwise addressed, help may not be forthcoming.

The same sorts of dilemmas are associated with the runaway problem:

> The dramatic revelation that some three quarters of a million adolescents leave home each year without parental permission, coupled with the fact that some of them are murdered, become prostitutes, or become drug addicts, has caught the attention of Americans as has few other happenings in this century. Yet most lay people and many professionals know little more about runaways than what they have read in the Sunday supplements (Nye, 1980:1).

Given this lack of information, it is noteworthy that the prototypical runaway closely fits the prototypical portrait of the problem child painted by positive and radical theories: almost half of all runaways are 15 years old or younger; they are more likely to come from low-income, single-parent, large families; their relationships with their parent(s) are hostile; they have failed in school; and they run around with delinquent peers (Nye, 1980). The parallels between delinquents and this group of status offenders are stunning.

Since that is the case, some serious questions are raised about the assumptions upon which decriminalization and benign neglect for status offenders are based. As we saw above, today's reformers assume that there are qualitative differences between status and criminal offenders and, as a result, offenders should be divided into two groups: (1) misbehaving, but deserving, kids whose only sin is that of violating outmoded moral standards; and (2) criminal, but nondeserving, kids who commit criminal acts.

As a result of their research, however, both Maynard Erickson (1979) and Joseph Weis (1980) provide empirical findings that seriously question these assumptions. Whether based on official or self-report offense data, they find that the presumed differences between status and delinquent offenders is a *myth*. The overwhelming majority of all juveniles have committed both types of offenses and in no particular order. As a result, only a small fraction of all offenders would not merit prosecution if status offenses were decriminalized.

Extensive research also provides little support for the contention of labeling theorists that serious criminal behavior is the consequence of official processing. The commission of delinquent acts occurs before, as well as after, processing and does not normally follow an escalating pattern from minor to major (Erickson, 1979; Hindelang, Hirschi and Weis, 1981). Instead, throughout their careers, juveniles commit a garden variety of delinquent acts—some status offenses and some criminal offenses. Consequently, if one were to justify decriminalization as a social policy, one would be advised to rely less on the assumptions that status and criminal offenders are qualitatively different and more on a strictly classical concept of justice; namely, that authorities should respond strictly to acts not to people.

In so doing, of course, one would have to pay the price of ignoring the problems of runaways or other status offenders until, or unless, they were apprehended for criminal offenses. But even then, there is question as to whether their personal problems would ever be addressed. Because, on the one hand, runaways have no place to live, they are often exploited, and they frequently turn to crime and prostitution in order to survive. Consequently, concerned parents often implore officials for assistance in locating and controlling these children. But to the degree that runaway behavior is decriminalized, officials lose their power to sustain parental requests, at least by coercive means. Since, in many states, it has now become illegal to detain runaways in secure facilities, the police and other officials are less and less inclined to bother with them. Reflecting the new parity argument, they seem to feel that, if children are to be treated like adults, they should be free to do all the harm to themselves they want so long as they do not injure others.

On the other hand, if they do injure someone, there is no guarantee that a new classical system of justice, with its emphasis upon determinate sentencing and punishment, would insure that the causes of their crimes were addressed. To the extent that deterrence and community protection take precedence over rehabilitation, such efforts will inevitably be diminished. Even if such offenders were sentenced to pay a fine or restitution or to render some community service, the kinds of involuntary intervention needed to mobilize conflicted families, to demand better performance in school, or to find a job might be lacking.

Punishment

This possibility leads us to our final topic—punishment. In order to weigh the dilemmas it poses, several issues must be considered.

1. Child rights and punishment. The first has to do with the new "parity" argument for juveniles (Zimring, 1979); namely, the idea that if children are to have the same freedoms as adults, they should also expect the same punishments. Throughout this review, whether considering delinquents or status offenders, we have found that they tend to share a common set of antecedent problems: poverty, disrupted families, poor schooling, and participation in a delinquent subculture. It seems likely, therefore, that the perception of the child rights movement by such juveniles might be perverted, causing them to confuse license with

freedom and to believe that no one—not parents, not teachers, not employers, not even probation officers—has any right to infringe on their momentary impulses and passing interests. As a consequence, a preoccupation with granting such children greater autonomy is vacuous unless steps are also taken to insure their rights to a decent home, to self-discipline, to effective schooling, and to a responsible job.

Because they have viewed these problems from "below," rather than from the privileged vantage of the middle and upper classes, many minority leaders have continued to preach self-discipline, self-respect, and deferred gratification. And in the face of pressures to the contrary, they have also stressed compliance with the traditional requirements of childhood, graduating from school, marrying, finding employment, and seeing that one's own children follow the same pattern.

> Countless employers, black as well as white, will tell you depressing stories of youngsters who, while eager for jobs, come to the personnel offices scarcely able to read and write, with few basic marketable skills or even marketable attitudes. . . .
> Maybe blacks can't do much about the general economy or about shaping federal policies. But we can do quite a lot more than we are doing to work with the schools that are turning out illiterates, to help the youngsters develop the attitudes that make them more attractive to employers, to help them learn skills and find and keep jobs (Raspberry, 1980:7).

Paradoxically, then, the message from those who have suffered most from discrimination is that, unless nurturance and discipline are somehow reconciled with the drive for greater autonomy for children, the results of the child rights movement will have an effect that is the opposite of that intended, at least for those who are at the bottom of the heap. Without some traditional restraints, the capacities of these young people to cope with an increasingly complex society and to act responsibly in their own self-interest might never have a chance to develop.

If that is true, what about the growing movement to hold juveniles fully accountable for crime, without attention to their backgrounds or developmental histories? What about the idea that we should sentence delinquency and not the delinquent? What about the belief that punishment and incapacitation will deter crime?

If a juvenile has experienced a decent home life, has attended school and might be able to find a job, then, ironically, accountability and punishment may make sense. In this case, the offender is better prepared to benefit from the experience and to make an informed choice among realistic alternatives. But if he or she is illiterate and without the aid of external support systems, then punishment makes less sense, since he or she is incapable of informed and reasonable choices. Indeed, that is why, for the most criminal population—those juveniles whose backgrounds are characterized by deprivation, ignorance, and abuse—an exclusive emphasis on the letter of the law, mechanized justice, and punishment is bizarre.

Lacking any stake in conformity, such juveniles have much less to lose by committing crime. Since crime may be about the only alternative to continued deprivation and self-degradation, the infliction of punishment only helps to widen the gap between the offender and society. Consequently, if accountability is emphasized at the expense of social justice, the most vulnerable juveniles will become the victims of a cruel hoax which, at best, will subject them to a policy of benign neglect, if their crimes are not particularly serious, or which, at worst, will extract punishments from them, if they are serious—punishments that have no positive meaning. One cannot expect responsibility and autonomy from those who have never experienced them and who do not know what they mean.

2. **Brutal pessimism.**   In light of these considerations, why not reject the concept of punishment and concentrate upon rehabilitating or reintegrating offenders? The answers are threefold:

First, as we learned in prior chapters, society has been besieged with reports that nothing works. Since, at best, the available evidence indicates that rehabilitation or reintegration are no more successful in reducing recidivism than is incarceration, we should concentrate on protecting society.

Secondly, experience tends to support the contention of deserts philosophers that the actual treatment afforded juveniles has never approached the goals envisaged for it. Correctional bureaucracies have become self-perpetuating organizations which use professionals and professionalism to justify their existence. Under the guise of scientific diagnosis and treatment, these bureaucracies have been little more than isolated repositories for society's undeserving children. For over a hundred years, diagnostic labels and treatment procedures have changed markedly; yet the process of extrusion, exclusion, and isolation remain the same (Miller, 1979).

Finally, the past 20 years has been characterized by a growing and brutal sense of pessimism. The belief that nothing works is but a small symbol of a much wider sense of disillusionment with all of our social institutions. Thus, it is not merely that we lack evidence that rehabilitation can reduce crime but that we are losing faith in the belief that benevolently motivated intervention will work, even with children (Bayer, 1981).

3. **Limitations of punishment.**   What is remarkable about this sense of pessimism is the extent to which it permits today's reformers to forget the limitations of punishment. When we reviewed the deterrence literature, we discovered that its ability to deter crime is limited and that, if incapacitation were

employed in the hope that it would protect society, it would be at the expense of many young people who would not have committed serious crimes had they been left free in the community and not incarcerated.

Erickson (1979) also points out that if deterrence is to work, it depends far more upon the *certainty* than upon the *severity* of punishment. Yet because the likelihood of apprehension for any offense is extremely low and because most delinquent acts are committed in groups, the chances that any single offender will escape punishment are astronomical. Since the odds are all on the side of the chronic offender, in particular, the chances that the certainty of punishment will deter him are small. Hence, there is no little irony in the fact that after 200 years of seeking an alternative, we are reverting once again to more severe punishments in the hope that they will be successful.

The only serious counterargument comes from those unlikely bedfellows—radical and positive criminologists. While a small band of radicals continues to push for socialist solutions, a declining band of positivists insists that the compelling ideal implied by rehabilitation has never really been tried (Glaser, 1979; Sechrest et al., 1979; Martin et al., 1981). We do not know whether or not it works because the intervention principles implied by scientific theory have never been systematically implemented and evaluated. Their application has been primitive; promising approaches have been undermined by methods that are substantively weak and without integrity; sound experimental designs have been rare; and the resources needed to sustain a search for solutions—like that associated with research on cancer or heart disease—have not been available. Instead, today's "reforms," no less than those in the past, have been guided by a kind of "intuitive opportunism," *a strategy of activity*.

Rather than identifying specific target groups, using theory and research to isolate their unique problems, and then devising appropriate programs for them, we employ such "reforms" as decriminalization, diversion, and deinstitutionalization in indiscriminate ways to indiscriminate populations. One can only imagine the disasters that might have occurred had such a strategy been used in an attempt to cure polio or to put a man on the moon.

By contrast, a more promising strategy might be a *strategy of search*—a strategy that would commit resources and set target dates that are more consistent with the difficult problems involved. With regard to rehabilitation, for example, such a strategy would hope to impose the rigors of scientific investigation in a way that was analagous to the efforts that were made a generation ago to learn more about space, when the talents of theorists, scientists, and engineers were united in a common endeavor. But rather than more technology, communication satellites, and a space industry, the goal in this case would be the invention of new social arrangements and methods by which the socialization of young people, and their introduction to the world of adulthood, might be more equitable, less characterized by serious deviant behavior, and more satisfying to all.

Relative to these tasks, Glaser (1979) points out that it is not *rehabilitation*—restoration to some prior state—that most marginal youngsters need most, but *habilitation*—the opportunity to live in a warm and supportive environment and to be prepared for, and to experience, legitimate adult roles for the first time. In other words, the rehabilitation task has too often been approached negatively. Rather than conceiving of correctional programs as devices by which structural as well as individual change is facilitated, we have concentrated on ways by which to control and to undo the criminogenic influences that are presumed to inhabit only the individual. It is no wonder, then, that success has been so limited.

STRATEGY OF SEARCH: SOME EXAMPLES

While it is impossible to state in advance the kinds of new social arrangements that might be successful in reducing youth crime, it is possible to provide some examples of new approaches on which a strategy of search might be concentrated. Whether any advanced society is capitalist or socialist, such inventions will be required.

Child care

An increasing number of Americans are unwilling to agree on the virtues of monogamous marriage and the nuclear family as the nursery for the next generation. Recognizing that trend, we might avoid the worst features of child abuse, neglect, and crime by pledging ourselves to the welfare of children directly, providing day care and communal child-rearing arrangements for children from any class or race whose parents are unable or unwilling to maintain a nurturing environment. By no means would this include the majority of children, but it may help those whose futures are the most endangered.

By way of example, a movement started by Dr. Hermann Gmeiner, an Austrian, has resulted in the creation of children's villages, involving more than 10,000 children in 48 countries (Bourne, 1974). Unwanted or homeless youngsters are placed in family-size units with carefully selected "mothers"— women who are not only screened and carefully trained but many of whom have already raised children of their own. They are assisted in this task by a lesser number of resident males in the villages who help to supply a father image.

While these children are growing up, they participate in local community schools and other normal activities. When they reach the age of employment, they are then required to get jobs, to pay for their keep, and to put half of their money into bank accounts. Then, when they are ready to move out, they are assisted in finding apartments, which they often share with each other. Moreover, a similar, but less comprehensive, approach to creating substitute families has been tried in this country (Fixen et al., 1979).

Schooling

The one institution in society that is supposed to resolve all class, ethnic, and other differences and to provide a uniform socialization for all children is the school. People expect it to provide equal opportunity for every child, and since it is the one major link between childhood and adulthood, any failure on its part has serious consequences. Yet these expectations notwithstanding, the overall structure of the educational system, especially in our urban centers, is often ill-adapted to the different localities and subcultural groups to which it must relate. Its local branches, the neighborhood schools, usually operate on centralized policies set up and administered by people whose view of the world is often vastly different from those of the children and parents whom it is supposed to serve. This often results in lack of communication, conflict, and delinquent behavior.

If the school could do things like the following, its capacity to give the young a greater stake in conformity might be enhanced:

1. It could do more to analyze the peculiar characteristics of any neighborhood in which it is located. Its curriculum, its organization, and its activities could then be tailored to better fit the needs of the clientele it is trying to serve.

2. By facilitating its linkage with other

legitimate institutions in the community, other school functions could also be performed more capably. For example, in an endeavor to upgrade the level of academic achievement in its schools, the Oakland School District recently took the following steps: It created a council of teachers and parents charged with establishing standards of achievement and with enforcing the pursuit of those standards; it tested students periodically to determine their progress; and it established a three-party learning contract to which parents, teachers, and pupils were signatories:

> Under this agreement, *the student* obligates himself to do homework in a quiet place for two hours each night, unaccompanied by television. *The parent,* in turn, agrees to provide an environment suitable for concentration to enforce the no-TV clause. *The teacher,* meanwhile, promises to insist on the daily completion of homework assignments, and vows to help each student reach the newly designated scholastic standards (*Los Angeles Times,* October 22, 1977).

The virtues of this approach lie not merely in its assistance to the educational process, but to the establishment of a network of social control comprised, not of law enforcement personnel, but of parents, teachers, and youth. What the Oakland School District is helping to do is to reestablish a coherent network of social relations and expectations that has been progressively lost in our increasingly anonymous, urban civilization. We have no modern equivalent of the tight-knit network of family, school, church, and community which characterized the small, New England towns of 18th century America. In that day, professional police forces were unknown because they were not needed. The program of the Oakland School District represents an effort to reestablish such a network. In seeking to improve education, however, it is also having

the effect of defining and reinforcing appropriate roles for juveniles.

3. This network of relationships, and its bridging of the gap between the generations, could be expanded evern further. Traditionally, the school has failed to provide children with the kinds of experiences that give adults a sense of usefulness and competence. Yet, there are any number of constructive roles which students do not now play but which could be sponsored by the school: *(a)* in conjunction with teacher-parent councils, analyses could be made of the school's tracking, stratification, and discipline systems to see if, in some way, these could be changed to enhance involvement rather than alienation; *(b)* tutorial programs could be organized so that students at all levels help others; *(c)* drug education programs, or programs designed to reduce racial conflict or conflict with the police, could be organized, and students given the chance to educate adults as well as the reverse; *(d)* the school could act as an advocate in behalf of its students so that it could contribute a youth perspective to the policy decisions made by many community groups and agencies; and *(e)* the school could make it possible for students to participate in constructive community programs—cleaning the environment, registering voters, participating in crisis-intervention and delinquency prevention programs, and so on.

Obviously the schools could not perform these functions without a significant enlargement of its mandate, a change in educational philosophy, and greatly increased resources. These are not forthcoming ordinarily because neither citizens nor the school see the role of the school as that of preventing delinquency. But this is because prevention has been defined in terms of controlling deviance rather than enhancing legitimacy. By reversing the definition, however, many of the foregoing could be justified. Citizens and policymakers need to recognize the social-psychological as well as the educational side of educational programs.

Linking school and work

Perhaps the most glaring omission in the socialization of youth has been the lack of a coherent link between the educational experience and the world of work. Rather than working alongside, and being socialized by, successful adults, peer groups and street gangs have filled the void.

By contrast, work-study programs have been tried on a sporadic basis; they seek to discourage the formation of deviant groups by providing economic incentives for remaining in school. Students receive remedial and occupational education in the morning and are employed in related jobs in the afternoon. In Baltimore, for example, an alternative school curriculum has employed the following steps.

First, Baltimore's labor market projections were studied to identify current skill shortages and future occupational needs. Then, special curricula were created which offered courses in the kinds of occupations for which workers were needed—occupations in business, health, communications, and community services. Students in health studies, for example, took courses in medical history, laboratory techniques, and math during which time they were also employed in health-related occupations. Hence, they received both academic credit and wages for their work. Indeed, the traditional structures of both the schools and employers were enlarged and changed.

4. Job creation. Work-study programs cannot become widespread, however, unless these kinds of structural changes are greatly expanded. Hence, in addition to research the most difficult policy decision of all is whether government should be the employer of last resort for unemployed youth when jobs are unavailable in the private sector. Not only is job creation by government often inflationary, but vested interests—labor unions as well as employers—often block legislation designed to provide jobs.

There are examples, however, of cases in which government and private funds have been used to support encouraging projects. One is the Maverick Corporation which runs a tire-recapping operation in Hartford, Connecticut (*Time*, August 29, 1977). Its purpose is to provide both work experience and an income until employees can be placed in better positions. Among its 350 employees, Maverick has employed many adolescents. Typically, these workers are offered the minimum wage but are told that if they show up to work on time, they will receive a bonus. By contrast, if they are so much as one minute late, they lose their bonus for the entire week. Overall, morale has been high, and many workers have moved on to other, higher paying jobs.

In short, like the Oakland School District, this program is designed to establish a network of social control that defines appropriate roles and provides rewards for constructive behavior rather than merely punishing young workers for deviant behavior. Whether any young person is lower, middle or upper class, such forms of social control are both useful and productive.

By contrast, what is often overlooked when jobs are not available is the incredible cost—socially as well as economically—of keeping youth in idleness. For example, the cost of incarcerating a delinquent today runs anywhere from $14,000 to $20,000 a year, while placement in a psychiatric hospital may exceed $30,000. Consequently, more than humane considerations are involved when it is suggested that a disciplined strategy of search might be useful in seeking new alternatives. Its principal virtue would be its capacity to produce a cumulative record, to permit us to learn from failure as well as from success. And since one or more young people could be sent to an expensive university or employed for a year for the price it takes to confine, to feed, and to guard a delinquent, there is much to be said for such a search.

CONCLUSIONS

We have seen in this chapter that there are many reasons to regard current reforms in juvenile justice as something less than a panacea. While they are a part of a larger social movement designed to grant greater rights to children, their concentration upon avoiding the negative effects of legal processing and incarceration has led to many unanticipated consequences, all of which are not desirable in a democratic society. They have done little to rectify the ambiguous position of children in society, to remedy some of the worst features of neglect, poverty, and ignorance, and they have helped to foster a counterrevolution that favors a punitive reaction to juvenile criminals. And, while current reforms have helped to undo some of the worst features of the juvenile court, they have failed to address adequately the most significant feature of the delinquency problem, namely, the heavy concentration of criminal activities during the adolescent and early adult years. It would appear, therefore, that until ways are found to reorganize that crucial phase in the life cycle we call "childhood," and to give young people a greater stake in conformity, society will continue to bear the exhorbitant costs of crime.

REFERENCES

Bayer, Ronald
    1981   "Crime, Punishment, and the Decline of Liberal Optimism." *Crime and Delinquency* 27 (April):169–190.

Bourne, Eric
    1974   "Forging New Families for Homeless Children." *Christian Science Monitor,* June 6, p. F–1.

Bronfenbrenner, Urie
    1974   "The Origins of Alienation." *Scientific American,* 231 (August):48–59.

Calvin, Allen D.
    1981   "Unemployment Among Black Youths, Demographics and Crime." *Crime and Delinquency* 27 (April):234–244.

Carter, Hugh, and Glick, Paul C.
    1976   *Marriage and Divorce: A Social and Economic Study.* Rev. ed. Cambridge: Harvard University Press.

Coleman, James S., et al.
    1974   *Youth: Transition to Adulthood.* Chicago: University of Chicago Press.

Cressey, Donald R.
    1978   "Criminological Theory, Social Science, and the Repression of Crime." *Criminology* 16 (August):171–191.

Davis, Kingsley
    1979   "Demographic Changes and the Future of Childhood." Pp. 113–137 in LaMar T. Empey, ed., *The Future of Childhood and Juvenile Justice.* Charlottesville: University Press of Virginia.

Davis, Kingsley, and van den Oever, Pietronella
    1981   "Age Relations and Public Policy in Industrial Societies." *Population and Development Review* 7 (March):1–18.

Dobson, James
    1975   "Self-Determination for Kids? Nonsense." *Los Angeles Times*, October 19, p. IV:5.

Douvan, Elizabeth
    1979   "Twenty-Year Comparison: Family Roles." *ISR Newsletter*, Winter, p. 4–5.

Erickson, Maynard L.
    1979   "Some Empirical Questions Concerning the Current Revolution in Juvenile Justice." Pp 277–311 in LaMar T. Empey, ed., *The Future of Childhood and Juvenile Justice.* Charlottesville: University Press of Virginia.

Farson, Richard
    1974   *Birthrights: A Bill of Rights for Children.* New York: Macmillan.
    1975   "Here Comes 'a New Liberation Movement.' " *Los Angeles Times*, October 19, IV:5.
    1979   "The Children's Rights Movement." Pp. 35–65 in LaMar T. Empey, ed., *The Future of Childhood and Juvenile Justice.* Charlottesville: University Press of Virginia.

Fixen, D. L.; Phillips, E. L.; and Wolf, M. M.
    1978   "Mission-Oriented Behavior Research: The Teaching Family Model." In A. C. Catania and T. A. Brigham, eds., *Handbook of Applied Behavior Analysis.* New York: Halstead Press.

Flicker, Barbara D.
    1977   *Standards for Juvenile Justice: A Summary and Analysis.* Cambridge, Mass.: Ballinger.

Gault, In re
    1967   387 U.S. 1, 18L, Ed. 2nd 527, 87 S.Ct. 1428.

Gillis, John R.
    1974   *Youth and History.* New York: Academic Press.

Glaser, Daniel
    1979   "Disillusion with Rehabilitation: Theoretical and Empirical Questions." Pp. 234–276 in LaMar T. Empey, ed., *The Future of Childhood and Juvenile Justice.* Charlottesville: University Press of Virginia.

Goodman, Ellen
    1978   "Children's Rights." *Los Angeles Times*, November 10, Part II:7.

Hale, N.
    1971   *Freud and the Americans.* New York: Oxford University Press.

Hindelang, Michael J.; Hirschi, Travis; and Weis, Joseph
    1981   *Measuring Delinquency.* Beverly Hills, Calif.: Sage.

Holt, John
    1974   *Escape from Childhood.* New York: Dutton.

Ianni, Francis A. J.
    1978   "The Social Organization of the High School: School Specific Aspects of School Crime. In Ernst Wenk and Nora Harlow, eds., *School Crime and Disruption.* Davis, Calif.: Responsible Action.

Krier, Beth Ann
  1979 "Carrying Charisma to Teen-Agers." *Los Angeles Times,* March 16, IV:1.

Martin, Susan; Sechrest, Lee; and Redner, Robin, eds.
  1981 *Rehabilitation of Criminal Offenders: Directions for Research.* Washington,
        D.C.: National Academy of Sciences.

Metropolitan Life Insurance Company
  1980 "Expectation of Life in the United States at New High. *Statistical Bulletin*
        61 (October–December): 13–15.

Miller, Jerome G.
  1979 "The Revolution in Juvenile Justice: From Rhetoric to Rhetoric." Pp. 66–
        111 in LaMar T. Empey, ed., *The Future of Childhood and Juvenile Justice.*
        Charlottesville: University Press of Virginia.

Monahan, Thomas P.
  1957 "Family Status and the Delinquent Child: A Reappraisal and Some New
        Findings." *Social Forces* 35 (March):250–258.

National League of Cities
  1977 *CETA and Youth: Programs for Cities.* Washington, D.C.: National League
        of Cities and U.S. Conference of Mayors.

Nye, F. Ivan
  1980 *Runaways: Some Critical Issues for Professionals and Society.* Extension
        Bulletin 0744. Pullman: Washington State University.

Nye, F. Ivan and Lamberts, Martha B.
  1981 *School-Age Parenthood.* Extension Bulletin 0667. Pullman: Washington State
        University.

Polier, Justine Wise
  1978 "Prescriptions for Reform—Doing What We Set Out To Do?" in LaMar
        T. Empey, ed., *Juvenile Justice: The Progressive Legacy and Current Re-
        forms.* Charlottesville: University Press of Virginia.

Raspberry, William
  1980 "A Fuse is Burning: Joblessness Among America's Black Youth." *Los Angeles
        Times,* May 29, Part II:7.

Rothman, David J.
  1971 *The Discovery of the Asylum.* Boston: Little, Brown.

Schwendinger, Herman, and Schwendinger, Julia
  1978 "Delinquency and Social Reform: A Radical Perspective." Pp. 245–290 in
        LaMar T. Empey, ed., *Juvenile Justice: The Progressive Legacy and Current
        Reforms.* Charlottesville: University Press of Virginia.

Sechrest, Lee; White, Susan O.; and Brown, Elizabeth, eds.
  1979 *The Rehabilitation of Criminal Offenders: Problems and Prospects.* Wash-
        ington, D.C.: National Academy of Sciences.

Short, James F., Jr.
  1979 "Social Contexts of Child Rights and Delinquency." Pp. 175–210 in LaMar
        T. Empey, ed., *The Future of Childhood and Juvenile Justice.* Charlottesville:
        University Press of Virginia.

Silberman, Charles E.
  1978 *Criminal Violence, Criminal Justice.* New York: Random House.

Skolnick, Arlene
  1973 *The Intimate Environment: Exploring Marriage and The Family.* Boston: Little, Brown.
  1979 "Children's Rights, Children's Development." Pp. 138–174 in LaMar T. Empey, ed., *The Future of Childhood and Juvenile Justice.* Charlottesville: University Press of Virginia.

Time Magazine
  1977 "Looking to the ZPGeneration." Vol. 110 (February 28):71.
  1977 "The American Underclass." Vol. 110 (August 29):14–27.

Timmick, Lois
  1979 "Single Women Opt for Motherhood in Growing Numbers." *Los Angeles Times,* January 17, Part I 29.

Tinker v. *Des Moines Independent School District*
  1969 393 U.S. 503.

U.S. Center for Health Statistics
  1978 *Vital Statistics of the United States.* Washington, D.C.: U.S. Government Printing Office.

U.S. Department of Commerce
  1971 *Bureau of Census Reports, 1950–1970.* Washington, D.C.: U.S. Govenment Printing Office.

U.S. Senate Subcommittee on Delinquency
  1977 *Challenge for the Third Century: Education in a Safe Environment.* Washington, D.C.: U.S. Government Printing Office.

Veroff, Joseph
  1979 "Twenty-Year Comparison: Feelings of Well-Being." *IRS Newsletter.* Winter:4–5.

Weis, Joseph G.
  1980 *Jurisdiction and the Elusive Status Offender: A Comparison of Involvement in Delinquent Behavior and Status Offenses.* Washington, D.C.: U.S. Government Printing Office.

White House Conference on Youth
  1971 "Preamble." *Recommendations and Resolutions.* Washington, D.C.: U.S. Government Printing Office.

Zimring, Franklin E.
  1979 "Privilege, Maturity and Responsibility: Notes on the Evolving Jurisprudence of Adolescence." Pp. 312–335 in LaMar T. Empey, ed., *The Future of Childhood and Juvenile Justice.* Charlottesville: University Press of Virginia.

AUTHOR INDEX

SUBJECT INDEX

This book has been set CAP in 10 and 9 point Gael, leaded 2 points. Chapter and part numbers are 12/15 Gael bold; chapter titles are 16/18 Gael and part titles are 16/18 Gael bold. The size of the text area is 37½ by 47½ picas.